Child and Adolescent Therapy

Child and Adolescent Therapy

Science and Art

Second Edition

Jeremy P. Shapiro

WILEY

Published by John Wiley & Sons, Inc., Hoboken, New Jersey.
Published simultaneously in Canada.

For general information on our other products and services please contact our Customer Care Department within the United States at (800) 762-2974, outside the United States at (317) 572-3993 or fax (317) 572-4002.

Wiley publishes in a variety of print and electronic formats and by print-on-demand. Some material included with standard print versions of this book may not be included in e-books or in print-on-demand. If this book refers to media such as a CD or DVD that is not included in the version you purchased, you may download this material at http://booksupport.wiley.com. For more information about Wiley products, visit www.wiley.com.

Library of Congress Cataloging-in-Publication Data:

Shapiro, Jeremy P.
  Child and adolescent therapy : science and art / Jeremy P. Shapiro. – Second edition.
     pages cm
  Includes bibliographical references and index.
  ISBN 978-1-118-72211-4 (hardback: acid-free paper) – ISBN 978-1-118-72218-3 (epdf) –
ISBN 978-1-118-72207-7 (epub) 1. Child psychotherapy. 2. Adolescent psychotherapy. I. Title.
  RJ504.S516 2015
  616.89'140835–dc23
                                                                        2015008313

Cover image: ©tomchat/Getty Images
Cover design: Wiley

This book is printed on acid-free paper. ∞

Printed in the United States of America

10 9 8 7 6 5 4 3

Contents

PART II

THE NEEDS OF CLIENTS

Preface

The Therapist's Challenge

The purpose of this book is to equip readers with the knowledge and skills they need to provide effective psychotherapy to children and adolescents. I aim to provide an understanding of the major theoretical approaches, knowledge about the findings of outcome research, training in a variety of therapeutic techniques, and lots of good words to say to young people and their parents. This is an academic text and a how-to book in which intellectual rigor and practical application are viewed as equally important and complementary objectives. The goal is to articulate the knowledge base and thought processes of skilled therapists making scientifically and clinically well-informed decisions about what to do when. Thus, the book is about theory, etiology, change agents, technique, meta-analysis—and what to say to the kid.

Weisz (2004, p. 5) defined psychotherapy as "an array of nonmedical interventions designed to relieve psychological distress, reduce maladaptive behavior, or enhance adaptive functioning through counseling, structured or unstructured interactions, training programs, or specific environmental changes." The common element linking these activities is this: Psychotherapy relies on *talking* as a method of resolving problems. Therapy is not alone in its purposeful use of conversation, and people have sought help by talking to trusted relatives, friends, and clergy for far longer than counseling has existed. But therapy is also a professional service and, to justify the remuneration we receive, counselors should be able to provide forms of help that laypeople cannot reliably offer. There needs to be something different about our talk.

Psychotherapy fulfills a distinctive and rather remarkable function in our society. When something goes wrong with our cars, we go to automobile mechanics to fix them. When something goes wrong with our bodies, we go to physicians for treatment. When something goes wrong with our emotions or behavior, society recognizes psychotherapists as the people to call for help with these central aspects of self.

Given the deeply personal nature of the problems for which therapy is sought, clients and parents are in a position involving considerable vulnerability and trust. They are generally willing, just moments after meeting a stranger, to describe important, painful, and, perhaps, embarrassing aspects of their lives. Therapy is about issues that people do not usually discuss with full openness, such as love, rejection, anger, sex, hopes, fears, despair, guilt, and so forth. Clients and parents are often willing to disclose information and feelings they have never told anyone before, just because the stranger sitting in front of them has a license indicating her commitment and ability to respond helpfully to this type of disclosure.

The trust that parents demonstrate by bringing their children to therapists imposes an important responsibility on us. It is an honor and a privilege to work with people on the deepest, most personal aspects of their lives, and, in order to be worthy of this trust, we must do our best not to let our clients down.

Language is the main tool of the therapy trade. Although play and artistic activities sometimes supplement verbal communication with children, and our talk often refers to actions, for the most part the work of therapy consists of a search for good words. Physicians have their laboratory tests, radiological devices, medicines, and surgical instruments—we have our words. At first, this might be an intimidating thought, because we are up against a lot. The causes of mental health problems include genetic abnormalities, poverty, family dysfunction, child maltreatment, trauma, irrational thoughts, maladaptive learning histories, and so forth. By the time a child becomes a therapy client, factors like these may have operated in his life day after day, month after month, for years. Confronted with forces like these, words might not seem like much.

When I was a graduate student in my first clinical placement, a client with severe problems resisted my invitation to therapy on the grounds that "I don't see how talking about it will help." I did not have an adequate response. In fact, I was frightened that the young man might be right, and talking about his unhappy life would do nothing to make it better.

I panicked prematurely. As discussed in the outcome research sections of the chapters to follow, psychotherapy is generally an effective means of treating emotional and behavioral problems. During the past 100 years or so, clinicians and researchers have developed a number of methods that, for most clients, are at least moderately helpful. In a sense, this book represents a long, detailed response to the fear that therapy (i.e., mere talk) might be overmatched by the causes of mental health problems and might lack the power to create significant changes in damaged, troubled lives. The therapist's challenge is a daunting one, but most of the time it can be met. Talking about problems—in certain, specific ways—really can help.

The chapters that follow describe these ways. Part I presents the major theoretical orientations and the therapeutic techniques associated with them. These theoretically based approaches are the tools of the therapist's trade, the primary colors of our palette, and the main options from which clinicians select the strategies they will use with each client. Part II, which is organized by categories of diagnoses, applies these strategies to the mental health problems that are common in children and adolescents.

The website associated with this book includes a number of forms and handouts that therapists can use with clients. The forms can be printed out as they are, or you can modify the documents to customize them for particular clients. The web address is http://www.wiley.com/college/shapiro.

Acknowledgments

A number of people made important contributions to this book. My coauthors for the first edition, Robert Friedberg and Karen Bardenstein, provided a great deal of fine material that remains in the revised edition, and I greatly appreciate their clinical knowledge and acumen. I would like to thank Shira Wiesen, Nora Feeny, Rebekah Dorman, Karen Tucker, Tim Gesing, Sarah Dickman, and Rebecca Lord for specific suggestions that I incorporated into the text. I am particularly indebted to Amy Murrell, who spent hours on the phone with me explaining the fine points of doing acceptance and commitment therapy with children. My editor and assistant editor at John Wiley & Sons, Patricia Rossi and Kara Boberly, provided valuable help with the writing process. My post editor, Elisha Benjamin, was masterful at spotting and fixing every little flaw in the writing. Christina Verigan was dogged and wonderfully good-natured about handling my mistakes as she set up the Power-Points and website that accompany this book. I also thank Nicolle Simonovic for her precise, meticulous work in helping me prepare the manuscript.

On a more personal level, I want to express deep gratitude and appreciation to my wife, Nancy Winkelman, who not only provided endless patience and support during the long process of writing but also edited every chapter of the book. I also want to thank my parents, Felicia and Jack, who are the source of the energy for learning and thinking that culminated in this text.

PART I

THE TOOLS OF THE THERAPIST

1

Therapy Fundamentals

OBJECTIVES

This chapter explains:

- *The orientation toward clients at the foundation of therapy.*
- *Therapeutic language, including some specific words and phrases to use with young people.*
- *What to do in the first meeting with children and parents.*
- *What can and cannot be kept confidential from the youth's parents.*
- *Reflection of feeling and reflection of meaning.*
- *Therapy goals that motivate and organize clients' efforts for improvement.*
- *How to use play and art in child therapy.*
- *Motivational interviewing, a strategy for overcoming resistance.*
- *Simple, directive therapeutic interventions.*
- *Therapy termination.*

Case Study
Simplicity

Brent, a 5-year-old African American boy, was having trouble in kindergarten. The teacher reported that his academic skills and peer relationships were age-appropriate, but there had been repeated incidents of disobedience toward the teacher, accompanied by tantrums. Brent was not physically aggressive, but he screamed and cried, and it sometimes took 10 to 15 minutes to bring him under control. His behavior was generally pleasant and appropriate in between these outbursts, which had occurred two or three times per week during the several months since school began.

Brent lived with his mother, an older sister, and his maternal grandparents, who provided much day-to-day childcare. The caregivers reported that Brent saw his father once a month or so and seemed sad at the end of the visits. The caregivers said there were no problems with Brent's behavior at home, and they described him as a happy, energetic, cooperative child.

The therapist's impression of Brent was consistent with his caregivers' description. In both play and conversation, his behavior was organized and compliant. His play with puppets depicted exciting activities and interactions, with no unusual themes of distress or defiance. Because Brent had exhibited no problems prior to starting school, the counselor made a diagnosis of Adjustment Disorder with Mixed Disturbance of Emotions and Conduct.

While most of the chapters in this book are organized around specific theories of psychotherapy or categories of disturbance, in this chapter we begin with basic therapeutic principles and procedures that crosscut theoretical orientations and apply to most diagnoses. Research has produced a great deal of evidence that such shared or common factors of therapy are central to its effectiveness (Baskin, Tierney, Minami, & Wampold, 2003; Imel & Wampold, 2008; Wampold, 2010).

The Therapeutic Orientation Toward Clients

While the activity of psychotherapy is based largely on theory and technique, there is a certain attitude that lies at the foundation of our endeavor. This attitude orients us to our job, organizes our efforts, and governs the interpersonal tone of our behavior with children and families. The idea behind the therapeutic orientation is so simple that it might sound like a cliché, but its ramifications are important to consider. The moment-to-moment behavior of therapists should convey that they are there to help the client with her problems and her life. This is the role of therapists as established by professional ethics and licensing regulations.

Although this point seems obvious, it is worth making because parents and children sometimes fear their therapists are *not* there to help. Youth sometimes think that being brought to counseling is a serious form of getting in trouble (an impression that is not always inaccurate). Children and parents sometimes think that therapists are there to evaluate and judge them—to identify and point out their failures and inadequacies. This fear seems particularly common in low-income and ethnic minority families who feel intimidated by encounters with "the system" (Sue & Sue, 2013). Therapists should be alert to the possibility of these concerns in clients so they can counteract them either with explicit explanations of their role or by making sure to convey a help-focused agenda in their way of interacting with families. If families seem more concerned about your approval or disapproval than about benefiting from counseling, it may be useful to say something like, "Remember—you don't work for me, I work for you."

When the therapeutic attitude is translated into behavior, the therapist models an attitude toward life that is adaptive and constructive. She does not hesitate to discuss any issue or experience, no matter how awkward or upsetting. The counselor's stance toward the client does not change whether the child reveals things about himself he considers wonderful or things he considers shameful; the therapist's unvarying desire is to understand and help.

The issue of counselors making judgments about clients has two aspects. The therapeutic attitude is based on unconditional acceptance, respect, and caring about the client *as a person*. However, this attitude does not include unconditional approval of all client *behaviors*. On the contrary, in many cases our efforts to assist clients necessarily involve helping them change maladaptive behaviors. This two-part attitude can be explained to children using words like the following:

> "I like *you*; I just don't like what you did. In fact, I like you too much to want you to go on doing what you did."

The idea of unconditional respect for clients generally makes sense to therapists when they read about it in a book, but in the midst of real clinical work with difficult clients, maintaining this attitude is not always easy. Our commitment to a humanistic, forgiving view of people is sometimes tested by contact with child and parent behaviors that are obnoxious, mean-spirited, and cruel. No one knows how to increase the resilience of the therapeutic attitude, but I will try to provide some guidance by offering personal, experience-based reflections.

The therapeutic attitude seems based on an awareness of certain fundamental truths about human life. People, especially children, usually do not choose the situations in which they find themselves. They do not choose the family environments, neighborhoods, and schools that influence their development. People also do not choose the genetic endowments, physical constitutions, and neurophysiologically based temperaments that, operating from within, strongly influence their experience and behavior. Within these constraints, people try to do the best they can for themselves, seeking happiness where opportunities present themselves and avoiding pain when dangers occur. People become therapy clients when their efforts to adapt are disrupted by neurophysiological dysregulation, environments that are harmful or poorly matched to their needs, unrealistic thinking, and painful emotions. As a result, clients often stumble, grope, and flail in their efforts to be happy, sometimes leaving painful experiences for other people in their wake. But clients do not wake up in the morning and decide to spend the day making themselves and others miserable—these are unchosen outcomes. Even when people do poorly, they are generally doing the best they can in a world perceived as confusing and painful.

Therapists' initial, natural response to obnoxious or purposely hurtful behavior is often emotional distancing, perhaps even revulsion. However, I have found that the most effective response to this therapeutic challenge is not distancing but attending *more* closely to the parent or child, because increased awareness of the other person's experience usually counteracts anger and disrespect. Looking closely into a person's face, feeling the rhythm of her speech and movements, and sensing the emotions behind her behavior strengthen our appreciation of that person's humanity. When your therapeutic attitude toward a client is threatened, I would suggest trying to imagine what his life feels like to him, moment to moment, as he wakes up in the morning, goes about his day, and encounters you in this strange context called therapy. If you do this, I predict your respect and concern will be rescued, not by abstract humanistic principles, but by the little things people do and say that express something intimately human and reveal their struggle and suffering.

The Therapist's Interpersonal Style

The theoretical orientations described in the chapters to follow differ somewhat in their recommendations for the counselor's style of interacting with clients. Nonetheless, there are some basic principles that crosscut the different therapeutic approaches, and we will begin with these.

One of the most robust findings in psychotherapy research is that the quality of the therapist-client alliance predicts continuation in therapy (versus dropout) and improvement in client functioning (Horvath, Del Re, Fluckiger, & Symonds, 2011; Marcus, Kashy, & Baldwin, 2009; Norcross, 2010; and see McLeod, 2011 for a meta-analytic review focusing on child and adolescent therapy). This association, which is generally of modest but significant strength, has been found across a variety of theoretical orientations and diagnostic groups.

Research indicates that therapists should try to combine the behavioral qualities of professional expertise and empathic warmth—science and heart—in their interpersonal style with clients.

The next question is: What can therapists do to engender positive relationships with clients? Therapist *empathy* seems to be the single most important factor in the development of the treatment alliance (Bohart, Elliott, Greenberg, & Watson, 2002). Most clients respond best to counselors who come across as friendly, kind, and warm (Najavits & Strupp, 1994). A review of studies by Orlinsky, Grave, and Parks (1994) identified client perceptions of therapist credibility and professional skill as important to the therapeutic relationship. Thus, research indicates that therapists should try to combine the qualities of professional expertise and empathic warmth—science and heart—in their interpersonal style with clients.

Social psychology research has found that people like others more when the person mirrors their nonverbal behavior and interacts with a similar tone of voice, energy level, and rhythm (Chartrand & van Baaren, 2009). When two people interact in an engaged, harmonious way, their styles tend to converge and become more similar over time. This phenomenon occurs in psychotherapy: Therapists whose moment-to-moment fluctuations in physiological arousal mirror those of their clients are rated as more empathic by those clients (Marci, Ham, Moran, & Orr, 2007). We can capitalize on this phenomenon by tuning into our clients' styles and allowing ourselves to fall into their rhythms. We cannot be chameleons—and it is counterproductive to try, because imitating others in a contrived way backfires and reduces liking (Chartrand & van Baaren, 2009)—but we can adjust our style to somewhere in between our baseline and the client's style, which enables us to connect while remaining anchored in our usual way of interacting. This would mean being soft and gentle with a shy, anxious child and being rougher, jauntier, and more casual with a rebellious adolescent.

Although the early influence of psychoanalysis once popularized a neutral, observant style for therapists, research indicates that most clients do not connect well with reserved, distant counselors. Instead, treatment alliances are strongest when the client perceives the therapist as a real person who is fully engaged, present, and authentic in the relationship (Geller, Greenberg, & Watson, 2011; Klein, Golden, Michels, & Chisholm-Stockard, 2002), and when the client believes the therapist likes and cares about him (Farber & Lane, 2002). I have heard young clients complain about past therapists who "sat there and waited for me to say something," and who "stared at me and didn't talk." Counselors seem to be most effective when they allow themselves to be natural and emotionally present in the context of a professional but genuine person-to-person relationship.

The traditional, analytic style excluded therapist self-disclosure, but there are problems with this exclusion. Clients sometimes ask us questions. Himelstein (2013) noted that many youth are put off by the analytic response of asking why the client desires this information; this type of answer might seem evasive. In my experience, it is better to answer the questions I feel comfortable answering (most of them) and to respond to questions that seem too personal by saying I do not want to answer for this reason. If the question seems to have emotional meaning to the client, it is more effective to inquire about this *after* giving an answer.

As an empirical matter, research generally supports the value of therapist self-disclosure. In studies of adults, counselor self-disclosure is associated with positive client outcomes (Barrett & Berman, 2001; Hill & Knox, 2002). Self-disclosure can help clients feel comfortable by showing that therapists have feelings too and are not ashamed to share their emotions, which can strengthen the therapeutic relationship by adding an element of mutuality (Tsai et al., 2009). Modeling emotional self-expression provides a direct form of training in talking about feelings (Goldfried, Burckell, & Eubanks-Carter, 2003). Of course, therapists should self-disclose only to achieve some therapeutic benefit for the client, not to fulfill any personal need of their own (Hill & Knox, 2002).

The therapist-client alliance seems to develop best when a certain balance is achieved, and the therapist's manner is warm and caring but without an emotional intensity that would change the relationship from a professional to a personal one. Therapists should be cheerleaders for their clients, rooting for them to make progress against their problems. Our faces should light up when we hear reports of progress and should express concern when setbacks occur. However, there should be boundaries on our expression of reactions, which should never be so intense that clients come to worry about upsetting us or letting us down.

Empathy is much more important than sympathy in psychotherapy, but when people express genuine suffering, there is a place for both. If these words convey your feelings, there is no reason not to say, "I am so sorry that happened to you," or "I am sorry you are hurting so badly."

Therapy Language

Therapists' talk should consist of ordinary language and speaking styles. I would caution against adopting a stereotypically therapeutic manner because this might come across as inauthentic and affected to clients. Counselors should avoid technical jargon, intellectualized language, and an overtly "touchy-feely" style. Youth generally like therapists who talk like regular people, not "shrinks."

The phrases "It sounds like …" and "It seems like …" are convenient and useful as long as they are not overused. Statements beginning with the pronoun "I"—such as "I think that …," and "I wonder if …"—have a straightforward quality—for example:

- "I think you would like to do well in school, but you don't know how to go about doing that."
- "I can see you're mad at yourself for losing your temper with him."

Much therapy talk involves words for feelings. Most preschool children know basic emotion words like "sad," "mad," "scared," "fun," and "happy." The word "yucky" describes a certain type of discomfort or disgust. Most elementary school children can verbally label more complicated emotions like "nervous," "disappointed," "excited," "frustrated," "upset," and "bored." Adolescents can usually talk about still subtler varieties of emotion.

Discussion of emotional issues need not consist entirely of words for feelings. Talking about motives, goals, meanings, and reactions also builds self-awareness and clarifies issues.

Clinicians talk about what clients want and do not want, what they hope for and fear, and what they like, love, dislike, and hate. As other examples:

- "You love the teddy bear your aunt brought you, and it was horrible when Debbie spilled grape juice on it."
- "You really had your hopes up, and it was awful when she said no."

Ambivalence can be described as "mixed feelings" or "having two different feelings about the same thing at the same time." Motivational conflict can be discussed by referring to "parts of you" that want different things. Counselors can also portray the co-occurrence of conflicting emotions by using the word "and" and connecting the two feelings with a tone of voice implying that their co-occurrence is perfectly plausible—for instance:

- "You're scared to go, and you're excited to go."
- "You want to tell me what happened, and you don't want to tell me what happened."

Several words and expressions come in handy for conveying certain important concepts to clients. The word "work" is a good description of therapy-related efforts (e.g., "I'm glad you're ready to start working on your behavior"). The best single term to describe your job with clients is "help." Because children think in terms of "good" and "bad," it is usually unnecessary to replace these words with the fancier alternatives of "positive" and "negative." The word "choice" is useful when discussing client actions because it highlights their capacity for control and responsibility. Thus, it is often useful to talk about good choices and bad choices. The word "mistake" is a useful term for maladaptive behavior. Therapists sometimes distinguish between the persona the client presents to the world and what goes on inside.

When working with children, therapists face the challenge of discussing complex issues in language that young people can understand. Finding words to use with children requires us to leave behind the familiar complexities of technical terminology and distill our messages into stark, basic terms. Albert Einstein said that if you really understand something, you can explain it to a 5-year-old. I have no idea how this applies to the theory of relativity, but it does apply to the issues of concern in therapy—for example:

- "You want to be good, but sometimes it's fun to be bad."
- "You feel like it's wrong to be mad at someone you love."
- "You think the bad things that happened to you must mean you're a bad person."

Getting Started

Most child clinicians begin treatment by meeting with the parent(s) alone for one session to obtain a description of the youngster's problems and the parent's goals for therapy. This practice is consistent with the legal structure of child treatment, which occurs at the behest of parents or guardians and is directed largely by their agenda (Weisz, Ng, Rutt, Lau, & Masland, 2013). Therapists usually meet the youngster at the second session.

Meeting the Parents

The purpose of the first meeting is to establish a treatment contract with the parents. This "contract" is not a written, legalistic document but a shared understanding of the goals and nature of what will occur.

First sessions consist mostly of clinician questions and parent answers about the child's presenting problems, development, general functioning, and history. It is usually best to start off with a simple, open-ended question, such as, "What brings you to our clinic?" or "What are your concerns about your son?" Specific questions depart from the parent's answer to this first question.

After the therapist has inquired about the child and family, he should invite the parents to ask any questions they have about him, particularly his credentials, education, experience, and methods of working with children. This part of the meeting is like a job interview for the therapist in the sense that the parents, as consumers, are entitled to inquire about the services they are thinking about purchasing. In my experience, however, while parents appreciate the invitation to inquire, they rarely have any questions about professional qualifications. Most of what they need to know they have already learned in the process of talking to the counselor—namely, whether he seems like a nice person who knows what he is doing and is genuinely concerned about their child.

First meetings should produce a decision about whether the therapist is the right person for the job of treating the child. The clinician is responsible for being ethical about her part of the decision, which depends on the fit between her areas of expertise and the child's problems. If the clinician's self-assessment suggests she does not have expertise in the child's specific difficulties, she should make an appropriate referral.

Parents generally want to know whether therapy is likely to help their child. I would suggest addressing this question with a combination of scientific information and human response. As is generally indicated by the outcome research sections of the chapters to follow, psychotherapy typically produces improvement in approximately 70%–85% of clients, with some variation as a function of diagnosis and history. However, this type of information is the beginning, not the end, of what parents want to know. Guarantees should never be given, but most parents appreciate sincere statements of determination and realistic optimism about the new endeavor they are embarking upon. Probabilistic statements based on research with large samples of clients are usually less meaningful to parents than statements like the following:

- "I believe I can help your son."
- "Therapy can certainly help children with problems like Lloyd's."
- "I'm going to do my best to help Alison. I see what caring parents you are, and your description shows that Alison brings important strengths to therapy. We've got a lot going for us here, and if we work as a team, I think things are going to get a lot better for your daughter."

Parents sometimes ask how long therapy will take. Although this is a reasonable question, the state of our science is such that we cannot give precise answers with confidence. Successful therapy typically involves about 5 to 12 sessions, but there are lots of exceptions on both ends of this range. Clients whose general development is proceeding well and who have mild, circumscribed problems tend to need less therapy than clients with serious, pervasive dysfunction. Brent was an example of the first type of client, so his clinician predicted that therapy would be brief.

First meetings usually conclude with talk about scheduling. Child therapy typically occurs on a weekly or biweekly basis. Weekly sessions seem to work best at the beginning, so children can establish a sense of continuity and interventions can get underway. After this launching phase, biweekly sessions might be more efficient because they provide time between sessions to assess the effects of interventions. The family's practical needs and preferences are also important considerations in scheduling.

Meeting the Child

At the next session, the child will be there, waiting to meet his new therapist. Except with some older adolescents, I generally begin by inviting the child and parent into my office together. This gives the child some time to transition from being with the parent to being with me, and it allows the three of us to make sure we are on the same page concerning the purpose of therapy. I ask the child what the parent has explained and proceed from there.

Providing children with an explanation of therapy might seem like a daunting task, but usually it is not. For some reason, most children seem to have an intuitive grasp of therapy, so a few sentences of explanation are all they need. When Freud first proposed that talking about emotional problems could lead to their resolution, the scientific establishment of his time rejected this proposal as ridiculous, but the idea seems to make sense to children.

With young children, you can start off by saying:

> "I'm a therapist. Do you know what a therapist is?"

Clinicians with doctoral degrees have access to a word that is handy for explaining therapy, because children understand that doctors help people with physical problems. The terms "talking doctor" and "feelings doctor," along with a statement that, "I don't give shots," convey the idea of counseling. Regardless of the clinician's degree, words like the following can be used to explain therapy:

> "Therapists help kids with problems. These problems have to do with feelings, behavior, and getting along with people. Like, if a kid was real sad, or mad, or she got in a lot of trouble at school, a therapist could help with that. In therapy, we talk about what's wrong, and we find ways to make things better."

With older children and adolescents, it is useful to ask, "Have you ever done anything like this before?" Even if you know the answer from the parent, asking this question often sets the stage for useful conversation. If the youth has had therapy before, it is important to learn about his experience. If the experience was negative, you can find out why and say you will try hard to do better than the previous therapist. If the youth has not had counseling before, you can empathize with the unfamiliarity of the experience and ask whether she has an impression of therapy from movies or TV. Most young people do. After asking about these impressions, you can say something like, "Well, by the time we're done today, you'll know whether TV and movies get it right, because you'll find out what therapy is actually like."

After a general introduction, discussion should move to the specifics of the youth's situation—for instance:

> "Your mom and dad thought it would be a good idea for us to talk because you seem sad a lot of the time. They said you don't go out and have fun the way you used to, and when things go wrong, like with homework, you get upset, put yourself down, and say you can't do it. Your parents don't think this is okay because they want you to be happy, so they brought you to see me because this is the kind of thing I help kids with."

If the youth understands the reasons for therapy but seems unhappy or ashamed about needing help, you could say something like:

> "Look, people are sometimes unhappy about starting therapy because it means there are problems in their life. Still, if you give it a chance, I think you'll find it's interesting, and good things can come from therapy. There's nothing like it."

The comfort level of young children is less a function of their abstract understanding of therapy than their visceral sense of what it is like to be with the therapist as a person. Counselors should not only be friendly and warm but should also allow shy children some space and time to warm up. Inviting children to explore our offices and toys provides a way to be together without the pressure of structured conversation.

Questions about favorite things help us enter the child's world, and giving our own answers helps clients get to know us. It may be pleasant and useful to talk about favorite foods, colors, animals, games, sports, books, TV programs, music, websites, and so forth. We need not be all business, and there is value in talking about interests, hobbies, and activities.

Research on the placebo effect indicates that, whether the target of intervention is physical or psychological, expectations of improvement tend to be self-fulfilling, so that optimism promotes healing (Duncan & Miller, 2000; Snyder, Michael, & Cheavens, 1999). Clients who expect therapy to work achieve better outcomes, compared to clients with less optimistic expectations (Joyce & Piper, 1998). Therefore, it is therapeutically useful for clients to depart from their first session with feelings of hope. Counselor statements about the likelihood of change will not be credible if they are unrealistic, but counselors can acknowledge difficulties while expressing determination and realistic optimism.

Research on the placebo effect indicates that expectations of improvement tend to be self-fulfilling, so that optimism promotes healing.

> "Next week, when you come back, we'll roll up our sleeves and get started. We'll put our heads together and think of different strategies. If one thing doesn't work, we'll try something else, and we won't stop until things get better for you."

One good line with which to conclude is, "I'm glad you came to see me." If said with the right tone of voice, this statement refers both to the seriousness of the problems and to the therapist's optimism about helping, while also communicating warmth and a sense of enjoyment about the process.

Confidentiality

The ethical and clinical issues involved in confidentiality for child clients are potentially complex, and laws vary slightly from state to state. This chapter does not address these complexities but offers guidelines that should suffice in the vast majority of cases. If needed, therapists can do additional reading (e.g., Ascherman & Rubin, 2008; Koocher, 2003) and/or consult with colleagues. If a difficult question arises, it is useful to request guidance from one's state professional board because, in the event of an allegation of misconduct, compliance with these authoritative opinions provides an effective defense.

In work with adults, therapists cannot divulge any information about the client without consent unless there is a danger of harm to self or others or a court order. The situation for children is different. Clients under age 18 have no legal right to confidentiality or privacy from their guardians. In fact, parents have a legal right to all information about their child's therapy—if they insist on it.

This description of the law might make it sound as though therapy must involve difficult conflicts between children's needs for privacy and parents' right to information. Fortunately, in practice, things usually work out quite easily. Most parents understand that, if therapy is to be effective, clients need some privacy in which to speak openly. Clinicians should present both sides of this issue to parents so they understand both their legal right to information and the clinical value of privacy for the child.

There are two types of information that parents should always receive even if they are willing to honor their child's desire for privacy. First, clinicians must inform parents about any danger of harm to the client or another person. Therapists must tell parents about client statements related to abuse, neglect, and violations of the law. Information about abuse and neglect must also be reported immediately to the state child protection agency. Client disclosures about nondangerous sexual behavior and circumventions of family rules are in a gray area; decisions about sharing this type of information should depend on possibilities of harm and the overall therapeutic situation. The second form of information parents should always receive is a general description of the overall direction of their child's treatment. This means describing what the child is working on, the treatment strategies being used, and the child's progress or lack thereof.

Therapist decisions about whether to report details of the client's thoughts, feelings, opinions, and experiences should usually depend on what the youngster wants. If the client wants this material held in confidence, the therapist should honor the request as long as this is acceptable to the parents. Often, however, youth *want* therapy material conveyed to their caregivers, either to help the parents understand them or for use in problem solving.

Children's desire for privacy from their parents generally increases with age. Adolescents usually need substantial privacy to feel comfortable in therapy.

Therapists should be honest with clients about limits to confidentiality. At the beginning of therapy, counselors should tell clients what can and cannot be kept private, so there will be no surprises.

When sensitive material must be disclosed to parents, counselors should approach this as a therapeutic opportunity, not a matter of the youth being "busted." Counselors can invite clients to participate in these meetings, so they know exactly what is said. If the youth is willing, it might be useful for her to report the information, with the therapist in a position to ensure that nothing important is left out (Santisteban, Muir, Mena, & Mitrani, 2003). This procedure allows the youth to preserve some control over the disclosure of sensitive material.

Basic Child Therapy Skills

The chapters that follow present detailed recommendations based on theoretical orientation and diagnostic category. This chapter offers some general guidelines that apply across theories and diagnoses.

Assessment

Although research has produced a number of structured interview protocols that produce detailed diagnostic information, the old-fashioned clinical interview and behavioral observation are the main methods of assessing clients and planning therapy in most clinical settings. Freedheim and Shapiro (1999) present guidelines for general assessments of child functioning; Form 1.1 on the website for this book presents their list of diagnostic interview questions.

Regardless of the therapist's theoretical orientation and the client's diagnosis, assessment should address the concrete specifics of the presenting problems, when they get better and when they get worse, the history of the problem's origination, variables associated with fluctuations in problem severity, the parent's and child's thoughts about causes of the problems, past efforts to address them, and the results of those efforts. Assessment research demonstrates that different informants often report different perceptions of the same child, making it important to obtain information from more than one perspective (De Los Reyes & Kazdin, 2005).

To be useful clinically, assessments should aim not simply to assign a diagnosis but also to illuminate the **etiology** of the client's problems. This word was originally defined as the cause of a disease (e.g., a pathogenic virus). In this book, the word "etiology" is used in a broad sense to include all the factors that cause, maintain, or contribute to a client's mental health problem (e.g., poverty, trauma, family dysfunction, irrational beliefs). This word originated in medicine, but my use of it is not meant to invoke the medical model of mental health problems.

Questions for the child should focus on the thoughts, feelings, and behaviors associated with the difficulties. This aspect of the assessment aims to achieve an empathic understanding of what the disturbance feels like to the client. Simple, basic questions are important here, with mainstays including, "How did you feel when _____?," "What was that like for you?," and "How did that feel to you?"

"Why questions"—questions about causality—are often more difficult for children, and they might not be able to answer them. Identifying the causes of difficulties is more the therapist's job than the child's, but it is often informative to ask for her thoughts about reasons for the problems.

Questions for clients are usually most effective when framed from their perspective, which means inquiring about what the behavior feels like to the child, not what it looks like to adults. For example, instead of asking, "Do you stay in your seat in school?" one could ask, "Do you ever get bored and antsy in school, so you feel like you have to get up and move around?" Therapists can encourage open, informative responses by acknowledging the pressures underlying negative behaviors, because this enables clients to disclose their difficulties without portraying themselves as bad kids.

One of the nitty-gritty problems in child therapy is that some youngsters do not talk much, especially about emotional issues, not because they are resistant but because they are unaccustomed to this type of conversation and are not skilled at translating experiences into words. This obstacle to communication occurs more frequently in males (Jansz, 2000; Kring & Gordon, 1998). Counselors can help by doing some of the work of verbalization for the client, but without making undue assumptions. One technique for doing this is the multiple-choice question. Generally, counselors should begin with open-ended questions, but if the client does not respond with informative answers, providing some plausible options gives him a way to convey information without floundering in words. Perhaps the most common example is when the client says he feels "bad" about something; the follow-up question could ask whether he feels mad, sad, or scared. Here is a more complicated example of a multiple-choice question from therapy with a child who worried when her father, recently divorced from her mother, travelled out of town:

"Are you worried about him flying in an airplane, or are you scared something bad might happen to him while he's away, or is it more that you think he might decide not to come home and then you won't see him anymore?"

One formula for framing empathic questions makes use of the words "easy" and "hard" to provide options from which the client can choose. These questions acknowledge the possibility of an unchosen quality in the problems—for instance:

- "Is it easy for you to pay attention in school, or is it hard?"
- "Is it easy to feel cheerful most of the time, or does life sometimes seem crummy, so you can't help feeling depressed?"

Questions that use the words "trouble" or "problems" to refer to negative behaviors also provide a palatable way to admit difficulties—for example:

- "Do you sometimes have trouble following your parents' rules?"
- "Do you have any problems with fighting?"

Assessment does not cease after the first session but is an ongoing element of therapy. Counselors monitor the child's presentation on multiple channels by attending to their words, physical behavior, tones of voice, facial expressions, and body language. They appraise, conceptualize, and integrate different forms of information, including the client's in-session functioning, reports from parents and teachers, and the child's history.

In the process of assessment, one useful question to ask ourselves is, "Why *would* a youngster feel and behave this way?"—for example:

- "Why would a child be so afraid of a father who seems so nice?"
- "Why would a 10-year-old spend so much time alone in her room?"
- "Why would an adolescent run away from home?"

Clinicians tend to focus on problems, because this is why clients come to see us, but assessment should also include attention to positive aspects of the child's life. Focusing exclusively on problems produces an incomplete, distorted picture of the youngster.

Treatment should make use of the client's strengths, and this cannot be done unless the therapist knows what these resources are. Important examples of client strengths include awareness of the problems, ability to form relationships, openness, determination in pursuit of goals, artistic talents, sense of humor, and so forth.

The most important part of Brent's assessment was the clinician's phone conversation with his teacher, who noticed a simple pattern: In practically all the incidents of concern, Brent had been enthusiastically focused on some toy or play activity when the teacher interrupted him with a directive to move on to something else. He was apparently unable to accept this external direction and shift his attention away from the activity in which he was immersed, and the teacher's efforts to get him to do so resulted in tantrums.

Session Structure and Activities

With children, early adolescents, and older adolescents in therapy for disruptive behavior problems, work with the parents is an essential part of treatment that should be part of practically every session. This is less so with older adolescents whose problems are primarily emotional, not behavioral. It is not generally necessary to speak with their parents at every session, and these clients can attend some sessions alone if they have their own transportation.

When parents are an integral part of the process, it is usually advisable to spend the first 10–15 minutes talking alone with them. This is the time to ask about recent life events, changes in the client's functioning, responses to therapy, and interventions conducted by the parent at home. Then, when the parent leaves and the child comes in, the clinician has an external view of the behaviors in question, and she needs to hear the child's view—for example:

> THERAPIST: How have things been going?
>
> CLIENT: Pretty good.
>
> THERAPIST: That's not what your mom said.

Much child treatment involves going back and forth between the parent and client while trying to integrate their two perspectives in a way that does justice to both—for instance:

- "Your mom said you were really mad the other night. What was going on?"
- "Your dad told me about the soccer game. What happened?"

In work with youth, conversation does not stay focused on therapy issues all the time, and there is also some talk about other topics, including the client's interests and activities. This is especially true with young children, who often spend some session time on play activities with no obvious connection to their treatment goals. Therapists need to find a balance in which there is a focus on therapeutic work but the client also has some freedom to pursue topics and activities of his own choosing. One way to strike this balance is to follow the child's lead while being alert for signs of his issues in play or conversation. When these signs appear, we can respond by addressing the issues in a context that is meaningful to the child. As examples, therapists could respond to talk about peers in school by teaching a social skill, and clinicians could respond to self-denigrating talk during play by addressing self-evaluation and self-esteem issues.

Therapists who follow the child's lead will sometimes find themselves playing ball, watching dramas enacted by puppets, and talking about TV programs, hobbies, parties, and so forth. One technique for building rapport is to ask clients to bring in and share favorite things from their everyday life, such as toys, hobby materials, photographs of friends, favorite music, or their prom dress. Video games are so important to some clients that spending time watching them show us how these games are played is a worthwhile investment in relationship building. Clinicians with a strong work ethic might feel uncomfortable having fun with clients, and there might be thoughts like, "Uh oh—am I working? Is this therapy?"

The answer to both questions is probably yes, because the therapist-client relationship is the launching pad of counseling—you won't get far without it. Therapists join with young people on their terms by sampling their interests and experiencing what they enjoy. Spending some time following the client's lead establishes a connection that makes it more likely she will be willing to follow yours. It is like click-and-drag: First we go to clients and then, hopefully, they will come with us.

When therapy produces important insights, ideas, and plans, we want these advances to take root in clients' minds, so they do not slip away. Counselors can galvanize the memory process by being emphatic and earnest in stating important points. Therapists should not be afraid of sounding simplistic or corny, because children need simple, strong messages to hold onto. Counselors can facilitate the client's comprehension and memory of therapeutic material by providing occasional reviews and by asking the client to summarize what he has learned in therapy—for example:

> **THERAPIST:** What should you do if you get mad?
>
> **CLIENT:** Take a deep breath and use my words instead of my fists.

Putting ideas and strategies in writing is an effective way to summarize and preserve therapeutic insights and plans, so the client can take therapy home.

One common problem is that clients sometimes understand and affirm positive plans in sessions but then forget or lose touch with these plans when they need them in the everyday environment. Putting ideas and strategies in writing is an important way to summarize and preserve therapeutic insights and plans, so the client can take therapy home (J. S. Beck, 2011). The activity of completing worksheets, lists, and diagrams provides structure for conversation, facilitates comprehension, and provides documents that support the child's memory. Pictures can serve the same function for children who do not read. Older clients can keep notebooks in which they record material learned in sessions, homework assignments, and their thoughts about therapy-related issues.

When counselors and clients put insights and plans into writing, a ritual can evolve in which, at the end of the meeting, they take the paper to the office copy machine and reproduce it, so there is one for the client and one for the chart. In addition to being an efficient means of documenting interventions, this is a nice way to end sessions, because many children enjoy operating grownup machines and because the child creates a physical object that transports therapy to her everyday environment. Thus, when things go well, the child leaves with a written plan for handling the problem that the parent described at the beginning of the session. It is our version of a prescription.

Table 1.1 Eric's Therapy Prescription

Why is it bad to yell at Mom?

1. It hurts the relationship.
2. It makes Mom feel bad and sad.
3. It is disrespectful.

The solution is for me to be in control of my emotions.
How can I be in control of my emotions?

1. Think before I act.
2. Take deep, slow breaths.
3. Remember my values: Nothing is as important as my family.

(End with the therapist's and client's signatures, with dates.)

(See Table 1.1 for an example.) Clients should review the written material at home until they remember it well.

Maintaining Discipline

The issue of discipline during sessions rarely comes up in child therapy. Even youth who are defiant or aggressive in everyday life usually behave appropriately in the controlled environment of counseling sessions. Clients seem to view therapy offices as our turf, where they are visitors and we are in charge.

On the rare occasions when disruptive or aggressive behavior occurs, therapists must respond. The priorities, in descending order, are protection of people and property, the maintenance of order, and the provision of therapeutic experiences. In practice, there are no significant conflicts between these priorities. I describe a progression of therapist responses to child misbehaviors ahead.

The first response should usually be a brief, simple statement of the expectation for the child, such as "Please don't do that," "I want you to sit down now," or, "Felicia, give that to me." If the child persists in a minor negative behavior, the best response is usually to ignore him and, when he stops, to reinforce the change of behavior. (See Chapter 10 on disruptive behavior.) Occasionally it is necessary to wait for a while, in which case I do paperwork, partly to make efficient use of the time and mostly because this makes my ignoring more convincing to the client.

If the misbehavior involves physical aggression, counselors should make assertive statements that portray the therapy setting as a safe place where rules have been established to ensure appropriate behavior—for instance:

- "Don't throw that toy. There's a rule here against breaking things."
- "There's no hitting here. I don't hit you and you don't hit me."

If the misbehavior continues or escalates, the next step is to state a negative consequence that will occur if the child does not comply. These consequences could include time-out or the loss of toys or activities. The next response could be to get the parent from the waiting room and obtain her assistance. Finally, there is the option of ejecting the client from the session. This action might be combined with a request that the parent impose an additional consequence at home.

Empathic Reflection

Research by Greenberg and colleagues (2002; Greenberg & Pascual-Leone, 2006; Greenberg & Malcolm, 2002) has shown that adult clients who express emotions openly and extensively in therapy usually achieve more progress than those who do not. Neuroscience research indicates that emotional expression, in and of itself, can help people feel better. Specifically, the act of naming feelings as they are experienced reduces activity in the amygdala, a brain structure centrally involved in fear and anger (Hariri, Bookheimer, & Mazziotta, 2000). Also, the process of translating emotions into words seems to increase clients' ability to think about, understand, and gain control over their feelings.

The fundamental skills for encouraging expression and elaboration of feelings were first described by Carl Rogers (1951, 1957) and applied to children by Virginia Axline (1947). These methods were originally identified with **client-centered therapy**, but the techniques have spread far beyond the theoretical orientation in which they originated and are now part of the general therapeutic repertoire (Gaylin, 1999).

According to client-centered theory, counselors can engender self-expression, self-awareness, and growth by conveying **empathy** to clients (Cooper, O'Hara, Schmid, & Bohard, 2013; Prouty, 1994). Empathy means that the counselor adopts the client's perspective, views situations through her eyes, and vicariously experiences the client's emotions. Empathy has a neurological basis in mirror neurons, with which we can partially reproduce other people's patterns of neural activity in our own brains (Cozolino, 2006; Iacoboni, 2009). Empathy demonstrates to clients that another person can register and comprehend their experiences. Interpersonally, empathy provides a sense of being heard, understood, and accepted—a good feeling.

Empathy is an act of guided imagination. The way to empathize with someone is to listen closely to his words and tone of voice, observe his facial expressions and body language, use your preexisting knowledge of the person to provide context, consider how the events and situations he encounters would feel to you, and weave this information together to imagine what he is experiencing.

Empathy is therapeutic only if it is communicated to clients. The technique for doing so is called **reflection**. In this technique, the therapist distills the essence of what the client has said and echoes it back to her—for example:

> **CLIENT:** My mom and dad have been arguing a lot. They keep yelling at each other, and sometimes my dad says, "I've *had* it."
>
> **THERAPIST:** Their yelling upsets you, especially that thing your dad says.

Sometimes, reflections simply rephrase or summarize what the client has said. In more complex versions of the technique, the therapist clarifies and amplifies what the client has only implied. By drawing out feelings and thoughts that had been expressed only vaguely or partially, therapists articulate clients' experiences more fully than the clients did themselves. By making connections that clients implied but did not state, counselors help youth face and make sense of their experiences. It is a matter of reading between the lines—for instance:

> CLIENT: My mom and dad have been arguing a lot. They keep yelling at each other, and sometimes my dad says, "I've *had* it."
>
> THERAPIST: You're scared they might get divorced.

Therapists sometimes reflect the meanings contained in client statements without using emotion words. Here is an example of a **reflection of meaning**, as opposed to a **reflection of feeling**:

> CLIENT: Katie and Jessica were playing Barbies by the swings, and I went over and said, "Hey, can I play?" but they said they didn't have enough dolls for three people.
>
> THERAPIST: But maybe it seemed like, if they wanted to be friends, there would have been enough Barbies.

Especially early in therapy, when clients begin describing a new issue, they sometimes feel intimidated by the communication challenge, and they say things like, "I can't explain it." At these times, the clinician's task is to create a sense of confidence about the shared endeavor by conveying that he is there to supply whatever is needed for the client to get his message across.

> THERAPIST: Are you afraid you won't be able to think of the right words?
>
> CLIENT: Yeah.
>
> THERAPIST: Oh, you don't have to worry about that, because in therapy kids don't have to use the right words; I'll work with you to figure out what you mean. Just say whatever words you think of, and we'll go back and forth until you feel I've got it.

Sometimes clients are hesitant to speak, not because of a word-finding problem, but because they feel guilty or ashamed about what they have to say. This is an important therapeutic opportunity. The key is to respond, not from an external, judgmental perspective, but from an empathic sense of the client's experience. The first emotions to address are the guilt or shame themselves:

- "I can see you feel really bad about doing that."
- "Feeling ashamed hurts. Ouch."
- "Feeling guilty is painful."
- "Embarrassment is such an uncomfortable feeling."

Some reflections provide clients with feedback about emotions they have not verbalized at all. For instance, if a child stalked into the therapist's office with a scowl on her face, sat down without saying a word, and began scribbling hard with a crayon, the counselor might say, "You seem mad at me today." Counselors identify and verbalize clients' feelings to teach them how to do so themselves.

Reflections of feeling can usually be reduced to the formula, "It sounds like you're (e.g., upset)." However, I would caution against overusing this phrase, because doing so makes us sound like stereotypical shrinks. In videotapes of Carl Rogers doing client-centered therapy, he almost never says, "It sounds like you're ..."

Reflections can be put in the form of questions as well as statements—for example, by asking, "Are you angry about this?" It makes sense to phrase reflections as questions when you are unsure of their accuracy. Similarly, you can check out the accuracy of your impressions by summarizing what the client has said and then asking, "Have I got that right?" This type of question sends the respectful message that clients are the experts on their own experiences.

Clinicians can fall back on the reliable technique of empathic reflection at difficult times in therapy when they are confused by what the client presents and are not sure what to do next. Empathic reflection is usually the best thing to do when clients are highly upset. Empathy is also an effective response to clients who do not want to be in therapy and are required to attend by their parents (e.g., "You hate being forced to come here"). When in doubt, empathize.

Goal Setting and Self-Monitoring

In a variety of contexts, including athletic training and dieting as well as therapy, it has been found that merely setting a goal and monitoring progress toward it, by themselves, often produces gains (Latham & Locke, 2002; Locke & Latham, 2006). Goal setting and self-monitoring seem to focus attention and galvanize effort. Therapy clients who monitor their problem behaviors often show improvement before any other technique is applied (Pope & Jones, 1996).

Clients often begin therapy with an array of vague desires and dissatisfactions, and therapists can help by organizing these feelings into clear goals.

Clients often begin therapy with an array of vague complaints and dissatisfactions. Therapists can help by organizing these feelings into clear goals. Youth can then measure their progress and root for the numbers to go in the desired direction, which gives therapy a game-like quality of striving for victory.

In several ways, effective goals strike a balance between opposite qualities (Burton & Naylor, 2002; Burton & Weiss, 2008; Weinberg, 2014). Goals should be moderately ambitious—neither so high that they cannot be achieved nor so low that they elicit little effort and leave serious problems intact. Specific goals are more motivating than general good intentions, but when goals are defined too narrowly, important sources of value might be missed. Short-term goals are more motivating than long-term goals, but the most effective goal orientation links a coordinated set of short-term objectives to a long-term purpose.

Goals are different from wishes. The difference is a matter of controllability. Counselors should help clients distill feasible, specific goals from their wishes so they can focus their efforts in a constructive manner.

Usually, psychotherapy can help only with the psychological aspect of achieving goals. We can do nothing about a mean teacher; all we can do is coach the client in dealing with her as effectively as possible. We cannot bring a deceased loved one back to life; all we can do is help with grief-work. As other examples:

- "You have to go to school; there's no way out. But I think we could change the way you *feel* about school, so you don't hate it so much. Do you want to make that a goal for therapy?"
- "I know your dad's girlfriend rubs you the wrong way, but I still think things would improve if you figured out a better way to deal with her. Do you want to work on that?"

Table 1.2 presents additional examples of goals for therapy.

Research on goal striving has found that stated goals and actual behavior show surprisingly weak relationships, with verbal statements typically accounting for only 20%–30% of the variance in behavior (Latham & Locke, 2002; Locke & Latham, 2006). People frequently verbalize good intentions but fail to act on them. Gollwitzer (1999; Gollwitzer & Brandstaetter, 1997) discovered a self-regulatory strategy that helps people translate their intentions into behavior with more consistency. **Implementation intentions** are if-then statements that operationally define goals in terms of where, when, and how their constituent behaviors will be performed. While goal intentions are abstract and general, implementation intentions are concrete and procedural, and they specify the situations or cues that will prompt the desired behavior. When people carefully compose and rehearse implementation intentions, the planned stimulus-response sequence becomes a solid mental representation that, when activated by a cue, produces the planned behavior with little thought or effort. In this proactive strategy, people make plans when they are calm and thinking clearly; then, in stressful situations, they only need to implement their plan. For example, in work on aggression, a general intention not to fight is less effective than clear specification of the client's anger triggers and a written plan for what to do in response to each one. Therapists should help clients make plans that are concrete and situation-specific, and they should review these plans until the client knows them by heart.

Envisioning is a technique that takes implementation intentions one step further. In addition to clear if-then statements, the client envisions the desired behaviors in a detailed, sensory way. Sports psychologists make extensive use of this technique with athletes (Gould, Voelker, Damarjian, & Greenleaf, 2014; Martin, Moritz, & Hall, 1999). Just as a baseball pitcher might repeatedly imagine the precise muscle movements

Table 1.2 Examples of Therapy Goals

- Feel okay, not sad, most of the time.
- Follow school rules almost all the time.
- Have a friend over, or go to their house, at least once a week.
- Talk respectfully to my father even when I'm mad at him.
- Manage my anxiety about talking in class enough to do it at least twice a day.
- Don't let my brother get me to hit him.
- Defend my happiness against mean people, so they can't ruin my life.

involved in throwing a curveball over the lower right corner of the plate, a client could picture himself complying with a directive he dislikes, resisting the temptation to bite his nails by performing an alternative behavior, or flirting with an attractive peer despite feeling anxious.

Envisioning works best when it is practiced in situations that are similar to those in which the new behaviors will be performed (Smith, Wright, Allsopp, & Westhead, 2007). At minimum, this means the client should picture the locations, individuals, events, and emotions that have been problematic in the past and then imagine performing the goal behaviors in these contexts. Optimally, the client would practice her imagery under these actual conditions. For example, a girl who has been physically aggressive with her brother could sit next to him while imagining both his provocations and her successful self-control.

Envisioning is a learning strategy that works in basically the same way for sensory-motor skills and psychosocial skills. In both cases, repetition is key, and clients should practice their step-by-step procedures between sessions.

In therapy, Brent learned to close his eyes and imagine, in a moment-to-moment way, the action of relinquishing an enjoyable activity in order to listen to the teacher's voice and follow her directions. The counselor asked his mother to prompt this envisioning several times per day at home.

Using Play in Therapy

Because play involves physical as well as verbal means of expression, and it draws on imagination as well as reason, play engages processes that are well-developed in young children, making it a developmentally appropriate window into their internal lives (Erickson, 1963; Gardner, 1993; Russ, 2004). Young children have limited language abilities, but they are remarkably able to express emotions, act out concerns, and work through problems using the metaphors of play. Once children reach the age of 6 or so, they become progressively more able to sit and talk, but until this occurs, unstructured play is an important means of conducting therapy with children.

Child therapy offices should be stocked with human and animal figures, blocks, and drawing materials. I get a remarkable amount of use from soft foam balls that are safe for indoor use and versatile, lending themselves to all sorts of games, including ones in which the balls are bounced off walls. Many clients find this type of play remarkably enjoyable.

In imaginative play, children act out wishes, fears, and beliefs, and their inner life is translated into a public form that counselors can see.

Structured games, such as checkers and card games, reveal how the child thinks strategically, competes, and responds to success and failure. However, these activities usually provide less fertile ground for the exploration of emotional issues than does **pretend play**, which involves human or animal figures, imagination, and stories with themes and meanings (Russ, Fiorelli, & Spannagel, 2011). Children realize the dolls and puppets are just toys but, at the same time, they experience them as animated by human emotions, needs, and goals. In imaginative play, children act out wishes, fears, and beliefs, and their inner life is translated into a form that counselors can see (Chethik, 2000; Landreth, 2012).

Therapists ask clients questions about their symbolic play. Children typically answer as if the play figures have a life of their own, which the child observes rather than controls (e.g., "What are the monkeys having for dinner?" "Pizza."). Here are some examples of questions that bring out themes in play:

- "Where are they going? Who are they looking for? Why are they in such a hurry? What happens next?"
- "Why did the father doll leave? Is he going to come back? Did he get into an argument with the mother doll? Do the children miss him? Do they wish there was something they could do to bring him back?"

The technique of reflection is just as applicable to play as to talk (Axline, 1947)—for instance:

- "You're setting up the doll house slowly and carefully."
- "Look at those bears fight! They sure seem mad at each other."
- "The little dinosaur is looking everywhere for his mother; he must be scared he won't find her."

This combination of talk and play creates a connection between the imaginative, magical experiences of young children and the controlled, logical thought processes of adults. The therapist is the bridge between the two. To perform this function, let yourself be drawn into the child's world of play, vicariously experience what it is like to be there, and then cross the bridge back by asking yourself what the play themes might indicate about your client's real life.

Interpreting pretend play is difficult because imaginative dramas and logical analyses can be related in a number of different ways. Sometimes play figures represent different aspects of the child's self (e.g., her scared and confident sides). Sometimes play figures represent other people in the child's life. An angry monster might depict the client's aggression, or it might represent her fear of powerful, scary adults. Therapists must make educated guesses about which play figures represent aspects of self and which represent other people. Children often identify with the small, child-like figures in their dramas, and the large figures often represent adults or older children, but this is not a rule.

Another source of interpretive ambiguity is that imaginative play can reflect different types of mental processes. Children's play depicts experiences that they: (a) *expect to* happen, (b) *fear might* happen, (c) *wish would* happen, and (d) *have* actually *had*. For example, the departure of a mother figure might reflect a real experience, a fear, or a wish that Dad would get rid of his new wife. The emotions accompanying play often illuminate its meanings, but sometimes these emotions are transformed or disguised. Because of these interpretive ambiguities, therapists should not draw conclusions from small units of play but should gradually build an understanding of the child by noting patterns that emerge over time and integrating these observations with other information about the child.

Children's symbolic play depicts their problems and also their strivings for resolution and gratification. Play is an opportunity to try out and practice a variety of verbal, emotional, and behavioral options. Children often set up the situations that distress them in an (unconscious) attempt to master these situations by experimenting with different responses until they find something that, on a symbolic level, works for them

(Erikson, 1963; Gardner, 1993). Sometimes children are able to translate these symbolic discoveries into behavior in real life (Harris, 2000).

However, the play of children with mental health problems often has a quality of being "stuck"—the children portray the same distressing themes over and over, but they do not find solutions to the problems depicted in the play. This is where the counselor comes in. Research on play training has found that when adults facilitate children's play by providing reflections, questions, modeling, and praise, the play becomes more imaginative and emotionally rich, which may lead to improved coping (Lang et al., 2009; Moore & Russ, 2008).

By translating the actions of play into words, therapists help clients cognitively process and organize the emotional issues they express, so these issues seem more finite and manageable. By summarizing play themes and sequences with coherent narratives that identify cause and effect, therapists help clients transform confused, swirling feelings into an understanding of important issues (Russ, 2004). These understandings can then provide a basis for problem solving.

In psychodynamic work, therapists use play to learn about the child's unconscious conflicts and help her work out resolutions of these conflicts (Chethik, 2000; Winnicott, 1971). Clinicians can enter the game to enact a symbolic solution that helps the child resolve the problem depicted in the play. If the proposed resolution clicks for the child on a symbolic level, it might produce change in the everyday environment—for instance:

> "Every time the big bear builds something with the blocks, the little bear sneaks up and knocks it down. Maybe she feels jealous that she can't build things as well as the big bear. I wonder what would happen if the little bear asked to help. Maybe then they could build something together and the little bear would learn how."

Cognitive-behavioral therapists make use of the "fantasy rehearsal" function of play: The clinician uses toys and pretend activities to model adaptive thoughts and behaviors, and the client practices these skills in the context of play (Knell, 1993; Knell & Meena, 2011; Strayhorn, 2002). Brent's therapist used dolls and puppets to enact school scenes and teach him the skills he needed to learn. Knell recommends using role reversals to create a variety of modeling and practice opportunities. Accordingly, Brent sometimes played the teacher while the therapist operated the student-puppet and modeled the skill by thinking out loud (e.g., "This game is *fun*—but the teacher is talking now, so I'd better stop and listen to what she says"). Sometimes Brent operated the student-puppet and practiced this skill while the therapist played the teacher, and sometimes Brent took the role of a peer who coached a distressed student-puppet in self-control.

Using Art in Therapy

Art is related to play: Both are imagination-based activities that lend themselves to nonverbal expression of feelings and meanings and to experimentation with possibilities (Graves-Alcorn & Green, 2013; Lombardi, 2013). Art is frequently a useful medium of communication in therapy with children, and some adolescents are comfortable expressing themselves in art.

Artistic activities sometimes get the therapy process going with clients who have trouble expressing themselves in words. Clients' pictures of themselves may provide information about self-concept. Drawings of the client's family may reveal information about these relationships. Purely spontaneous drawings are often useful, too. Books by Case and Dalley (2014), Malchiodi (2006, 2011), and Buchalter (2009) provide a wide variety of art therapy activities and techniques.

Questions about the client's pictures bring out the meanings they express. Counselors might ask why a person who looks angry is mad, or what happened to a tree that looks broken, or why no one wants to play with the little boy shown alone on a playground.

Therapists can ask clients to draw a picture of their problem. These drawings may provide either concrete or abstract depictions of the issues. Concrete depictions sometimes produce information of practical value. For instance, when a boy experiencing academic problems drew a picture of himself in school, he drew the student sitting next to him as a bully who harassed him while he tried to work. Abstract depictions of problems illuminate the client's internal, subjective experience of the difficulties. For example, anxious clients might depict their fears as terrible, vicious monsters, and depressed children might draw their sadness as a dark, dreary landscape.

Clients can also draw solutions to their problems. An example of a concrete depiction of a solution would be a socially isolated child drawing herself initiating a conversation with a peer. Abstract or metaphoric solutions might include an anxious client drawing a picture of a kitten making friends with the monster she had feared, or a depressed child drawing sunbeams and fruit trees into his landscape. Such drawings might not lead directly to real-world solutions, but this artistic type of envisioning often galvanizes the process of change.

Overcoming Obstacles to Client Engagement

Ordinary Hesitancy

At the beginning of therapy, it is common for children to be hesitant about engaging in the process. Counseling might seem like an intimidating, uncomfortable activity in which they will be alone with a stranger who will inquire about their problems and inadequacies. Some youth are afraid they will not understand what is expected of them and will not know what to do and say.

Sometimes children feel awkward because they are unfamiliar with conversations about emotions and behavior, and they do not understand what the clinician is trying to accomplish with his questions. Phrases that convey our agenda include "Help me understand," "Take me into your mind," and "Explain what it's like for you."

If the client seems worried about performing adequately in therapy, the counselor should reassure her that therapy is not a performance situation. For example, if the client seems embarrassed about responding to a question with, "I don't know," the therapist could say:

- "That's a good, honest answer—much better than making something up. I just want to know how things look to you as we start our therapy together."

- "It seems like you're confused about this. Well, confusion is a useful feeling, because it means you know there's something you don't understand. We can work on that."

Guardedness is not an unreasonable reaction to a first encounter with a stranger in an unusual situation. Clinicians can empathize with a wary, cautious reaction by saying something like:

"This is a new situation for you. You don't know me, and maybe you don't see why you should trust me—so it makes sense that you're not ready to talk openly about things."

Reinforcing clients for producing therapeutically useful material makes it more likely that they will do so again in the future. To let the client know exactly what she did that you found useful, say something like:

"Ah, now I get it: (summarize what the client said). Good, that helps me understand."

Positive reinforcement is especially important when clients disclose material that is difficult, embarrassing, or painful for them. Useful comments for this type of situation include:

- "I'm glad you brought that up, because it's important for us to talk about. You really get the idea of what's good to work on in therapy."
- "I can see that was hard to get out, and I really respect the courage it took for you to tell me that."

Addressing Reasons for Resistance

If the client remains highly guarded, it is time to inquire about reasons for resistance beyond ordinary caution and shyness. Clinicians can inquire about these reasons by asking the client why he believes he has been brought for therapy, whether he agrees or disagrees, what he thinks counseling involves, whom he believes it is for, what he thinks might be bad about therapy, what he thinks might be good, and whether there is something the therapist does not know but needs to understand about how he feels about coming to counseling.

Sometimes clients do not understand why counselors want to talk about negative experiences and painful emotions, particularly when the immediate effect is to make them feel worse. Therapists should offer clients a reasonable answer to the reasonable question of why we want to talk about bad things—for example:

"I know it hurts to talk about this stuff, and I don't want to bring you down. But there are reasons why people talk about painful things in therapy. Sometimes it helps to get things off your chest and share them with another person. Sometimes we can figure things out, so you understand your situation and your feelings better. Sometimes we can think of strategies, ways for you to do better or feel better. But we can't do any of these things without talking about what's wrong."

Therapists can gently ease clients toward discussion of sensitive issues by talking about these problems in regard to *other* people, rather than the client herself. This is an occasion for using your general knowledge about the issue the client is dealing with (e.g., depression, puberty, bullying). Intellectually inclined clients are often interested in research about the issues they face. Placing problems in a general context normalizes them, provides some distance, makes it easy to offer relevant information, and often makes problems easier to discuss. The implication is that the youth's struggles are shared by many people. Portraying the human condition as fraught with difficulties reduces clients' sense of deviancy and reassures them that, even when they struggle with problems, they remain part of the human community (Medini & Rosenberg, 1976).

When the focus turns to the client personally, movement can still be gradual. It is sometimes effective to begin by discussing concrete, surface manifestations of difficult issues and then move gradually toward more abstract, emotional aspects of the problem. For example, discussion of a client's adjustment to his new blended family might begin by focusing on practical concerns, such as changed routines and sharing his room. This conversation might lead to more emotional issues, such as the client's feeling that his original family relationships have been disrupted.

Resistance in Externalizing Clients

Factor analytic studies have revealed two large, basic categories of psychopathology (Achenbach & Rescorla, 2000, 2001). **Internalizing** dysfunction involves symptoms of emotional distress, such as depression, anxiety, low self-esteem, somatization, and withdrawal. **Externalizing** dysfunction consists of overt, disruptive behavior problems, such as noncompliance, aggression, and delinquency. In internalizing, the problem is with how the youngster *feels*. In externalizing, the problem is with what the child *does*. Many youth have both forms of dysfunction, but there is a tendency for one or the other to predominate (Angold, Costello, & Erkanli, 1999). These two types of disturbance are often associated with different attitudes toward therapy. Because internalizing dysfunction involves distress, these children are usually willing to participate in counseling once they become acclimated, and they typically share their parents' goals for treatment.

Externalizing clients often resist therapy for reasons extending much beyond initial shyness (Clarkin & Levy, 2004). Typically, these youth see nothing wrong with their behavior and blame their problems on other people. Given this view, there is no reason why the client *would* want to participate in therapy. For example, if her definition of the problem is, "My parents are always nagging me about school," and she believes homework is for nerds, her goal would be for her parents to accept her underachievement, not for her to improve her performance.

Therapists need to work hard to achieve buy-in from externalizing clients, and they need to realize that a little bit of buy-in is better than none at all. The task is to think of changes in the youth's life that would be desirable, or at least acceptable, to both him and his parents. One strategy for accomplishing this is to portray the parents' expectations as unalterable facts and then invite the youth to join you in a search for ways to improve his life *within* this constraint. Looking at the problem from the client's perspective sometimes makes it possible to reframe therapy in a way the youth finds acceptable—for example:

- "We need to find a way to get your parents off your back. But I'm talking about something that will work, not just wishing they'll let you flunk out of school."
- "Your parents aren't going to stop having rules. Given that fact, how can I be helpful to you? How could we make things more livable in your family?"

Because internalizing and externalizing are correlated (Achenbach & Rescorla, 2000, 2001; Angold et al., 1999), externalizing youth are not usually happy, and therapists can sometimes channel this unhappiness into the development of treatment motivation. Although externalizing clients are not usually brought to treatment for this reason, including their dysphoric emotions in the targets of therapy sends the message that counseling could accomplish changes desired by the youth as well as the parents.

One key to overcoming resistance is inducing clients to verbalize the reasons why they do not want to participate in therapy. Salespeople encourage potential customers to express all their objections to buying the product because objections cannot be overcome unless they are put on the table. Similarly, therapists marketing their services to resistant youth need to convey that they genuinely want to know what the client distrusts or dislikes about the idea of counseling so they can address those concerns in an effective fashion. Sometimes this inquiry reveals objections that are not based on fact, such as that counselors function purely as agents of the parents, with no interest in the youth's point of view. This objection can be overcome by basic information.

Therapists need to form alliances with both parties. It is difficult but not impossible for the counselor to position himself between the client and parents in such a way that both perceive him as an ally. As one important example, counselors can convey both commitment to the parent's standards for appropriate behavior *and* keen interest in the youth's perspective on the situation, including possible complaints about the parents, insights into the causes of problems, and ideas for improving life in the family.

One useful technique is to use the word "we" to convey that you share the client's and parent's goals—for example:

- (To adolescent) "If we can figure out a way to get your grades up, I'll be able to help on the clothes problem with your parents. If we work together on this, I think we'll get somewhere."
- (To parent) "We've got to stop her from hanging out with kids who use drugs after school. Nothing much can be accomplished if she's high half the time."

Despite the therapist's best efforts, young clients are sometimes involuntary participants in therapy. This is undesirable but not the end of the world. Parents sometimes ask whether there is any point in forcing youth to receive counseling against their will. Generally, the answer is yes. Externalizing clients *usually* begin therapy involuntarily, but the outcome research reviewed in Chapters 10–12 indicates that positive outcomes are possible, nevertheless. If the parent is unsure whether she can get the youth to the first appointment, one strategy is to offer a trial period of three sessions, after which the youth can decide whether to continue. Usually they end up saying yes. However, parents should offer this choice only if they can accept either decision the youth might make.

Motivational Interviewing

Motivational interviewing (MI; Miller & Rollnick, 2012; Miller & Rose, 2009; Rosengren, 2009) is a counseling method with one main purpose: engendering client motivation to change maladaptive behaviors. It is most relevant to clients who are not motivated to change and who, therefore, resist engaging in therapy. Typically, clients are most resistant when their problem behaviors are pleasurable or reinforcing for them (e.g., substance use, truancy), and/or when achieving treatment goals requires effortful, uncomfortable self-control (e.g., inhibiting impulses to overeat or explode aggressively). MI is more relevant to youth with externalizing than internalizing dysfunction.

Theory. MI is closely associated with the transtheoretical model of stages of change (Prochaska, DiClemente, & Norcross, 1992; Prochaska, & Norcross, 2010). This model describes stages of readiness for change and emphasizes the importance of therapeutic conversations being congruent with the client's current stage. In MI, therapists do not attempt to achieve quick changes by debating, urging, or imploring clients to stop their maladaptive behaviors. Instead, they create conversations that nurture an evolution of the client's own thinking and motivation in the direction of positive change.

These conversations typically occur in a certain sequence, although some back-and-forth movement is common. Here is the typical sequence:

1. The client verbalizes attraction to the problem behavior and resistance to treatment goals. The therapist responds with *reflective listening* to convey interest in the client's thinking and empathy with her experiences.
2. The counselor attempts to *develop discrepancy* between the client's attachment to the target behavior and her other goals and values. However, when clients express opposition to recommended changes, counselors "roll with the resistance," rather than arguing.
3. When clients begin to explore the possibility of change, therapists *support self-efficacy*, perhaps by teaching techniques or suggesting resources, so clients believe they have the ability to achieve treatment goals, if they decide to pursue them.

MI is nonjudgmental, nonconfrontational, and nonadversarial. This does not mean the therapist has no opinion about whether the client should choose harmful behaviors; it is a matter of therapeutic technique. MI is based on the idea that it is more effective to pursue change through reflective listening and skillful discussion than through authoritative provision of information, reasoning, or debate. Clients generally assume their therapists do not support maladaptive behaviors, and MI counselors do not contradict this assumption, but they keep their opinions to themselves except at certain points in the process.

MI is based on the idea that it is more effective to pursue change through reflective listening and skillful discussion than through authoritative provision of information, reasoning, or debate.

MI seeks to nurture whatever motivation to change the client has at the beginning of therapy. There is an assumption that most clients feel at least some ambivalence about their behavior, with some desire for change coexisting with attachment to the status quo. MI aims to explore both sides of the conflict, to nurture ambivalence, and eventually to resolve it by embracing positive change. The expectation is that the client's own thought process, supported and facilitated by conversation with the therapist, will eventually reveal disadvantages of the problem behavior and benefits that could be achieved by changing.

Therapists use several techniques to develop clients' sense of discrepancy between the target behavior and other of their desires and goals. Counselors ask clients to articulate their values, and they bring clients' attention to conflicts between these values and maladaptive choices (Hanson & Gutheil, 2004). Therapists ask clients to envision a better future and to think of realistic steps they could take to move toward that future; then they point out ways in which the problem behavior would interfere with successful completion of the steps.

Outcome Research. The Society of Clinical Psychology of the American Psychological Association (APA) conducts systematic reviews of outcome research on an ongoing basis. These reviews evaluate the empirical support for interventions based on well-defined criteria. Their website (http://www.div12.org/PsychologicalTreatments/treatments.html) maintains current summaries of these reviews. APA rates MI for alcoholism and substance abuse in adults as having *Strong Research Support*, their highest designation. There is also extensive evidence for MI as a means of increasing health-promoting behaviors and adherence to medical regimens in adults (Lundahl et al., 2013).

In research with young people, MI has produced positive results in a number of studies with adolescents who abuse substances (e.g., Barnett, Sussman, Smith, Rohrbach, & Spruijt-Metz, 2012; Jensen et al., 2011), and who have difficulties with medical compliance and dietary control (Erickson, Gerstle, & Feldstein, 2005). MI is more effective with adolescents than younger children, probably because it requires abstract thinking (Lundahl, Kunz, Brownell, Tollefson, & Burke, 2010; Strait, McQuillin, Smith, & Englund, 2012).

Outcome studies of MI have typically obtained effects that are statistically significant but small in magnitude. This might be because MI interventions are brief, usually involving one to four sessions. MI can be a stand-alone therapy, but it is more often used as an adjunctive or preparatory intervention that motivates clients to engage in more extensive therapeutic work using other strategies that address the client's particular problem behaviors.

Techniques. MI is built on a foundation of client-centered therapy (Rogers, 1951, 1957). This means the typical therapist action is a reflection of feeling or meaning. Because the focus is on motivation, many of these reflections refer to what the client wants and does not want, likes and dislikes, hopes and fears.

MI adds some techniques to its client-centered therapy base. Many of these techniques consist of questions, not statements. Here are some basic MI questions:

- "Are you completely satisfied with the way you're doing things now, so there's nothing you want to change, or might you be interested in doing some things differently?"
- "Are you completely satisfied with your life right now, or could your life be better in some ways?" "How would you like things to be different?"
- "Do you have any goals for the next month? For the next year? What do you want to do to move toward those goals?
- "What are your values?" "What do you think is most important in life?" "What kinds of people do you respect the most?" "What kind of person do you want to be?"
- "How does _____ (the problem behavior) get in the way of achieving your goals or doing the things you want to do?" "How does it interfere with putting your values into action?"
- "If you could change _____ (the problem behavior) without it being too hard, how would that change your life?"

The transtheoretical model (Prochaska et al., 1992; Prochaska & Norcross, 2010) posits a normative sequence of stages through which people progress on their way toward change.

In MI, clinicians connect with clients at the stage where they are in the present, rather than urging them to move on to the next stage. Here are examples of therapist statements appropriate to each of the model's stages of change:

1. *Precontemplation*: "You are not ready to change this behavior now—you haven't really thought about it, but when you do, all you can think of is reasons not to change. You believe that what you're doing now is fine, and you don't see what would be gained by changing."

2. *Contemplation*: "You are thinking about whether you want to change _____ (the problem behavior). It seems like there's a part of you that would like to change this behavior, but another part is like, 'Whoa, I'm not sure—there could be big disadvantages to changing.'"

3. *Preparation*: "It seems like you are getting ready to change. You're not happy with the way things are, and you want to make them better. You're getting psyched up, you've told some people about the changes you want to make, and you've done some things to prepare."

4. *Action*: "It's on. You have started to make some of the changes you planned, which is exciting, but it's hard, too, which is no surprise. Now is a time to be determined and tough, because it's easy to slip back into the old way of doing things. It's also important to be smart, so let's take a look at how you're going about this."

5. *Maintenance*: "You have succeeded at changing the behavior you wanted to change. That's a big accomplishment, and I hope you feel really good about this. To make sure you keep it going, it's important to stay careful and keep an eye out for situations that have messed you up in the past, so you can handle them more effectively this time."

When clients argue against change, MI calls upon therapists to inhibit argumentative responses and to "roll with the resistance." This means exploring the client's reasons for holding onto the behavior, discussing what he feels he gains from it, and learning why he feels he cannot or should not give up the behavior. The therapist conveys that she wants to examine the target behavior from the client's point of view. As the client describes its perceived benefits, the clinician responds not with refutations but with reflections and empathy.

Order matters. Once the perceived benefits of the target behavior have been described, it is time to consider the costs. One technique for working with ambivalence is the **double-sided reflection**, which articulates both sides of an issue in a single statement—for example:

- "You really like that feeling of being high—all your troubles melt away, and the laughing is so much fun—but it's nerve-wracking to think about the trouble you could get into, and you don't like the way your grades go downhill when you smoke a lot of weed."
- "Sitting there doing homework gets really boring, and it's frustrating to think about the fun you could be having, but you also care about your future—homework affects grades, and grades affect college. The future versus the present—that's the dilemma."

Another strategy for organizing, processing, and resolving ambivalence is to guide the client through a systematic weighing of the pros and cons of two alternative courses of action (Fishbein & Izjen, 2009)—in this case, continuing the problem behavior versus working on change. To do this in writing, divide a page down the middle and then divide the two halves down their middles, so the costs and benefits of the status quo versus change can be clearly seen. For a simpler version, divide the page in half and combine the advantages of the target behavior with the disadvantages of change in one column, and combine the advantages of change with the disadvantages of the status quo in the other column.

MI makes much use of scales from 0 to 10. By answering questions with a quantitative rating rather than a simple yes or no, clients become more aware of the two-sided nature of the issues they face.

Therapists ask clients: (a) how certain they are that they want to continue the target behavior, and (b) how extensively they want to engage in this behavior in the future. Clients usually do not give a rating of 10 to both questions, and it is significant when they do not. Any response below 10 indicates the presence of some ambivalence, and the distance from 10 indicates its degree. The next questions for the client are why they are not certain they want to continue the target behavior and why they do not want to engage in it to the maximum extent possible. Answering these questions requires clients to articulate the costs of the problem behavior and the potential benefits of change. In this way, the client's own responses fuel his treatment motivation.

If the client cites no disadvantages of the problem behavior, MI is not so accommodating that it lets the conversation end there. Still, MI requires us to tread lightly. Before giving input, ask the client whether she would like to know more about the issue, say you have some important information or thoughts about it, and ask whether she would like to hear this. If she says no, move on; perhaps her curiosity will be stimulated, and she will ask for your input at another time. If she says yes, offer your information, concerns, and reasoning. Then, ask the client what she thinks about what you have said. I often close not by asking whether she agrees with my points or will follow my recommendations but whether she is willing to give what I said some thought.

MI addresses clients' self-perceived ability to make changes, or **self-efficacy**, which often affects their willingness to try. Therapists ask clients to rate how confident they are that they *could* achieve treatment goals, if they were to attempt them. If the response is greater than zero, the counselor notes that the client has some belief in his ability to change. If the client gives a low or moderate number, the therapist asks what would need to happen to move the number up. This question can elicit useful information about perceived obstacles to change and what the client believes he needs in order to overcome these obstacles.

MI encourages clients to verbalize their resistance, but sometimes this does not happen. Some clients say the right things in therapy but come back week after week without making the efforts they said they would. Their resistance is real, but unexpressed resistance cannot be engaged therapeutically. Therefore, the objective is to get the client to verbalize her resistance.

Clinicians can broach this issue by noting that "Your words say you want to _____ (e.g., look for a job), but your actions say you don't." If the client does not respond in a substantive way, we can dig a little harder:

"Listen, you don't seem like a kid who does things for no reason, so I know that if you're not _____, there are reasons; you must see problems or disadvantages with _____. I'd like to know what those disadvantages are, because maybe I'm not getting something about this."

Sometimes clients are not able to disclose their reasons for resistance, either because they cannot put their reasons into words or because they are not consciously aware of them. If so, therapists can help clients identify and communicate their objections to change by offering educated guesses in a multiple choice format. It is important to present the options in a face-saving way, as understandable responses to her situation (e.g., "dieting is *hard*, because sometimes you're just dying for something sweet").

Finally, I would offer a cautionary note. MI involves an unusually egalitarian way for adults to talk to young people about harmful behaviors, in that it requires us to nod with interest as clients describe the appeal of, for example, gang involvement and noncompliance with medical directives. The positive outcomes achieved by MI certainly attest to the value of this type of conversation, but this value might have limits, and other types of conversations might have different forms of value. One important proviso is that MI is less effective with younger children than adolescents (Lundahl et al., 2010; Strait et al., 2012). One reason for this difference might be that children are more amenable to influence by straightforward, authoritative reasoning and values statements from adults, since these are basic means of socialization in the natural environment. Therapists who are flexible in their use of MI can combine it with other ways of nurturing treatment motivation.

Simple Therapeutic Interventions

Therapy is generally quite complicated, as the next 14 chapters will make clear. However, sometimes there are simple things therapists can do that are quite helpful to clients, and we should not look past these in our search for more sophisticated interventions.

Making Sense of Problems

One of the first services therapists can provide is helping parents and children make sense of their difficulties. Explanations of problems span a wide range of complexity and depth. At the beginning of therapy, clinicians can offer families a basic sense of understanding by positing a few factors that help to explain the problems. For example, a therapist might attribute a child's aggression partly to witnessing domestic violence, or she might explain a client's anxiety as resulting partly from unrealistically fearful thoughts. Even simpler formulations that merely name, describe, and organize the problematic experiences can provide the beginning of a sense of coherence. Here is an example for parents:

"It seems like life is just too much for Aaron right now. The challenges of school and peers feel overwhelming because, even though you might know he can do it, he doesn't. He's scared, so he's retreated into a shell."

Here is an example for clients:

"Sometimes life seems so crummy it's like a sad feeling in your heart that takes over your whole body. That feeling is called depression."

These statements are not real explanations, but they organize distress and confusion in a coherent way that makes problems seem finite and manageable. Clear descriptions of the client's situation articulate the obvious in a useful fashion, cutting through the flux and murk of moment-to-moment experience to identify the basic outlines of problems—for instance:

> "Sometimes things happen that you don't like. Then the question is, what should you do? Having tantrums doesn't help. Would you like to talk about other possibilities?"

Sometimes a description of a dilemma, with balanced attention to both sides, clarifies the challenge facing the client:

> "You want to have fun with your friends when they stay out late, but you also want to get along with your parents. I guess the dilemma is that, so far, you haven't found a way to do both things at the same time."

Planning Simple Solutions to Problems

In this section, I describe very simple, brief therapeutic interventions. This type of strategy is not a comprehensive treatment but may be helpful for some clients and for a few provides all the help that is needed. Rudimentary flaws in simple psychological processes sometimes cause serious trouble for children, in which case therapists who discern the obvious can often help in a quick, efficient way. Simple problems can sometimes be solved by simple strategies, without ever addressing complicated, deep-seated issues.

Perhaps the simplest therapeutic intervention is providing some factual information that the child does not have but needs. Children sometimes lack very basic information about how the world works, and the misunderstandings that result can be upsetting. For instance, in the aftermath of 9/11, when videotapes of planes crashing into buildings were shown repeatedly on television, some children did not realize these were replays of the same events, and they thought planes were continuing to destroy buildings and kill people in great numbers. Another example of this type of etiology is self-blame based on immature, egocentric thinking, which is sometimes compounded by misinformation from caregivers. For instance, children sometimes believe they caused their parents' divorce, their own abuse or foster placement, or other misfortunes they could not possibly have caused. In another type of misunderstanding, children sometimes fear that contact with a loved one who is ill might cause them to catch a disease that is not contagious, such as cancer.

In this type of situation, the key skill for therapists is an assessment one: identifying the misunderstanding responsible for the client's distress. Usually, the challenge is not that the missing information is complicated but that it is so obvious it is difficult to see.

In somewhat more complicated work, the counselor and child sit down with a piece of paper and make a plan to solve a problem. At the top of the paper, the therapist writes a title describing their shared mission—for example:

- How to Cope With Stress
- What to Do if My Brother Teases Me
- What to Do if I Have a Scary Thought

Then, the therapist and client discuss the problems that have occurred and brainstorm ways to prevent or manage them in the future. Counselors can ask themselves two questions to organize their thinking about these plans. The first one is: What is the psychological process or function that the client needs to perform in order to master the problematic situation? In other words, what does the child need to do that she is not doing now? The second question is: How can that function be distilled into a simple formula that the child can understand, remember, and use when needed?

Being directive in this way is not a matter of "telling the client what to do." I usually conclude my recommendations by asking, "Are you willing to give this a try?" If the answer is no, more work is needed.

For example, one boy got into trouble because he responded to situations too quickly, without taking a moment to think about what to do. The therapist and child drew several red stop signs, which the boy placed in his school desk, book bag, and several rooms at home. The client learned to catch himself at the beginning of his reactions; then he took out a stop sign and asked himself the question written underneath it: "What should I do?" That was it—and most of the time it worked. Simple strategies like this are effective when they bring the right plan to the right situation at the right time. Table 1.3 presents another example.

The activity of list making sometimes helps clients organize their resources. For example, therapy for low self-esteem might include making a list of "Good Things About Me," or "Reasons Why I Am Not a Failure." Therapy for antisocial behavior might include making a list of the disadvantages of lying or stealing. Children who feel their lives will be turned upside down by an imminent change, such as a geographical relocation, might benefit from listing aspects of their lives that will remain the same after the change occurs.

As another example, one child's anxiety symptoms turned out to be the result of rumination about his family's financial situation. The therapist figured out that he misinterpreted his mother's ordinary complaining about bills as an indication that the family was running out of money. The clinician relayed this information to the mother, who provided her son with an age-appropriate, realistic account of the family's finances that laid his fears to rest.

How is it possible that something so simple could work? The reason is that children sometimes develop upsetting misunderstandings that could easily be reassured except that they keep their fears to themselves. Children sometimes tell their counselors worries that they withhold from their parents, sometimes because they do not want to upset their mother or father, and sometimes just because they do not know how to verbalize their fear without prompting. In these situations, therapists can help by reassuring the child about the parent's ability to handle his concern and assisting him in articulating the worry.

Much therapy seems to involve the following sequence of events, which is summarized in Figure 1.1. First, there is an airing of the child's problems, and the client comes to believe

Table 1.3   A Simple Therapeutic Plan

How to Get Rid of Tantrums

Mom or Dad can:
1. Give me some food.
2. Give me a hug.

I can:
1. Pet my dog.
2. Go away from the problem and think about something good.

No more tantrums. Do what needs to be done and *be happy*!
   (End with signatures of client, mother (or father), and therapist.)

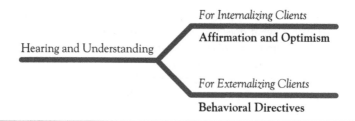

Figure 1.1   Common therapeutic sequences.

that the therapist understands him, as a result of which the therapist attains *credibility*. Then, there is a fork in the road corresponding to the two basic types of child psychopathology. Internalizing clients make progress when they believe their therapist understands the upsetting, disappointing, or shameful things they have disclosed but thinks well of them anyway. Externalizing clients make progress when they believe their counselor understands why they misbehave, including the appeal of misbehavior, but continues to state that they can and should change their behavior nevertheless.

Some simple therapeutic directives include no information or reasoning but simply *depict* an adaptive behavior that the client could try. These therapist statements do not address reasons for the problem, and they do not offer justifications for the option being recommended. The power of these statements lies simply in the compelling way they portray the path they recommend; the appeal of the option is either self-evident or not there at all—for example:

- "When you lose a game, the thing to do is be a *good sport*. Do you know what that is? Here is what a good sport does when she loses …"
- "When Mom tells you to do something that you don't want to do, you can argue back and make yourself and her miserable, or you can just do it and get it over with. Maybe that's the answer: Just do it."
- "I know it doesn't sound like fun, but why don't you give it a chance?"

Therapist actions like these are not a matter of technique but of sincere statements in the context of a relationship. The only technique is to say it like you mean it. Many children are open to taking advice from adults they like and trust.

Brent's tantrums in kindergarten did not seem to be the result of complex factors, so there was little to analyze or plan. The first couple sessions combined talk about pleasant topics, brief discussions of the problem with reflective listening (e.g., "It's *fun* to play with dinosaurs, so you don't want to stop for the teacher"), and an active game somewhat related to baseball, which resulted in lots of laughter and the development of a positive relationship. Then, the therapist looked Brent in the eye and said something like this:

"To do well in school, you have to listen to the teacher. You might be having fun with something else, but when the teacher starts talking, you need to have a little bell go off in your mind and then a voice that says, 'Hey! It's time to listen to the teacher!' If you hear what the teacher has to say, and you do what she says, you won't get in trouble, and you'll do fine in school."

Then, the counselor and Brent drew a series of cartoon-like pictures depicting a five-part sequence of events: (1) Brent was playing a fun game. (2) The teacher began talking to the class. (3) A bell rang in Brent's mind. (4) Words (drawn as little lines) travelled from the teacher's mouth into Brent's ears. (5) Brent left his activity and walked toward the teacher. This series of pictures helped Brent envision the behavioral sequence he needed to perform in school.

Therapeutic Collaborations

Young people's lives are nested in social environments and are greatly affected by the individuals and organizations constituting these environments. As a result, collaboration with parents and child-serving systems offers therapists important opportunities to channel assistance into the client's environment.

Work With Parents

Child treatment should always include work with parents or guardians. Parents are generally the most important people in their children's lives and the core of the formative environments that shape children's development. If the parents' everyday practices, behaviors, or messages are harmful to the client, hour-long therapy sessions have limited capability to undo the negative effects. More commonly, work with parents provides an efficient way to bring large quantities of therapeutic benefit to the client in small amounts of session time. Therapists can spend 15 minutes giving a suggestion or teaching a child management technique that will then be there to help the client every day for the foreseeable future. This is the way to plant a source of help for the child in her home environment.

Parents usually understand their importance in child treatment, but sometimes they do not. Parenting a child with behavioral or emotional problems can be exhausting, and parents sometimes wish they could give responsibility for solving the child's problems to the clinician. However, child therapy will generally not be effective if the parent drops the client off at the office and returns an hour later to pick him up.

One source of parental resistance to therapy participation is anxiety about being blamed for the child's difficulties (Barkley, 2013). This fear seems based on an old, obsolete view that children's mental health problems are always the result of deficient parenting. However, research in developmental psychopathology indicates that child mental health is a complex outcome influenced by genetic factors, neurophysiology, socioeconomic variables, life events, peer influences, and parent-child fit, as well as parenting effectiveness (Cicchetti & Walker, 2003; Harris, 2009; Pinker, 2002). Therapists should explain that children are not simply products of the upbringing they receive; they are separate individuals who bring their own temperaments and qualities into families. As a result, many loving and competent parents have children with mental health problems. (See Chapter 8 for guidance in discussing genetic factors with parents.) Counselors can usually recruit parents' active involvement by explaining that their participation is important not because they caused the problems but because they can contribute to solutions. The message is, "I need your help to help your child."

There are five main categories of work with parents. These treatment activities are described in detail in the chapters to follow, and brief descriptions are presented in Table 1.4.

Table 1.4   Types of Work With Parents

1. *Assessment and monitoring of change:* The clinician utilizes the parent's observations of the child for the initial assessment and for monitoring change over time.

2. *Helping parents understand their child:* The therapist identifies reasons for the child's feelings and behavior and then conveys this understanding to the parents.

3. *Parent training:* The counselor teaches the caregiver skills and techniques for managing the child's behavior and addressing the child's problems.

4. *Parent guidance:* The therapist offers suggestions and recommendations that are smaller and more specific than what is involved in skills training (e.g., reducing screen time, finding a quiet place for homework).

5. *Parent counseling:* The therapist works with the caregiver on her feelings and beliefs about the child and any personal issues that affect her functioning as a parent.

Basic Parenting Principles

One principle of effective child management is to replace negative statements about the child as a person with more specific criticisms of the child's behavior.

The distinction between criticism of behavior and criticism of personal characteristics, discussed earlier in this chapter, is just as important for parents as therapists. One principle of effective child management is to replace negative statements about the child as a person (e.g., "You're so stubborn") with more specific criticisms of the child's behavior (e.g., "I don't like it when you disobey me"). Criticisms of personality are counterproductive because they insult the child and do not provide clear information about what he should do differently the next time. Criticisms of behavior have a legitimate role in both therapy and child management. Thus, parental anger does not need to be eliminated but to be directed against the child's negative behavior.

Many parents worry that their child's mental health problem has dire implications for the future. Therapists can help restore optimism by saying that, whatever the reasons for the problem's origination, parents can guide children onto positive developmental tracks by responding effectively to problems in the present. This view enables parents to view difficult incidents as opportunities to provide the child with the learning experiences he needs—for instance:

> "Children are not born knowing how to behave; they learn this, gradually, as their parents teach them how. And one of the most important opportunities is when kids misbehave. When Celia acts up, I'd like you to ask yourself what you want to teach her by your response to her misbehavior."

For parents, thinking about child development within a long time frame may help to maintain a calm, constructive attitude. Parents all face upsetting moments in the course of their child's growing up; there are times when the child seems terribly distressed, irrational, or dysfunctional in some way. If parents extrapolate from such moments, they may panic at their vision of the future, but linear extrapolation is not realistic because, given time and effective help, most youth with problems traverse the twists and turns of development and emerge, eventually, as successful adults. Counselors can say:

> "Kids make thousands of mistakes as they grow up; in a way, that's their job. The parent's job is to respond to those mistakes in a helpful, corrective way—day after day, for about 18 years. When the whole thing is over, you'll have a competent adult. So take a breath, because there's plenty of time to work on this."

Brent's therapist asked his mother and grandparents to give him opportunities to practice activity switching at home. The procedure was to interrupt his play, give him a directive, coach him in making the transition, praise his success, and remind him that this was the skill he needed to use in school.

Collaborating With Other Child-Serving Systems

Children with relatively mild, circumscribed problems usually do not need services beyond psychotherapy. Clients with more complicated problems may also need services from the special education, medical, child welfare, and juvenile justice systems. Therapists should collaborate with the professionals in these systems who work with their clients (Henggeler, Cunningham, et al., 2009; Stroul, Blau, Broderick, & Lourie, 2008).

When clinicians have a narrow definition of their work that is bounded by the 1-hour session, their ability to help clients is reduced. There is a practical factor contributing to this limited job definition: Insurance companies typically are willing to pay only for direct contact with clients, so the consultative work needed for intersystem collaboration usually cannot be billed. Nonetheless, if we understand our job as doing whatever we can to help clients with their mental health problems, we will do this work.

In effective intersystem collaboration, information flows in all directions, and the collaborating organizations enhance each other's work. Teachers, caseworkers, youth workers, and probation officers often have knowledge that therapists need about their clients' functioning in settings outside the office. Therapists' understanding of their clients and their general knowledge about mental health enables them to offer insights and recommendations to other professionals for implementation in other systems. For example, therapy might provide information about why a foster child is exhibiting behavior problems in his placement and how the child would be likely to respond to reunification with his biological parent. As another example, a therapist might tell a teacher about an anger management technique the client has learned so the teacher can coach her in use of the technique when she becomes angry in class. This type of work can be highly efficient in that one phone call might result in major benefit to the client.

In effective intersystem collaboration, information flows in all directions, and the collaborating organizations enhance each other's work.

Termination

One aspect of treatment planning is determining when therapy is finished. In general, there are two types of situations that make termination appropriate. Sometimes therapy does not seem to be helping the child. When this occurs, therapists and parents should consider a change of plan, whether use of a new treatment strategy by the same counselor or referral to a new service provider. More frequently, termination becomes appropriate when the client's functioning has shown sufficient improvement. Termination is sometimes justified by a combination of these two situations: The client has shown some improvement, with significant problems remaining, but progress has stopped, and the client seems to be on a plateau in which additional work is not producing much benefit.

For treatment goals to be realistic, therapists and parents need to think about the problem levels that typify real children. All youngsters sometimes feel depressed, behave disobediently, and so forth. Termination should occur when the child's difficulties no longer constitute a mental health problem but are a matter of the imperfect nature of the human condition; counseling is not a cure for life. Therapy should end when the parent and client have the skills necessary to cope with remaining difficulties on their own.

In practice, parents play a more important role than therapists in decision making about termination; we provide recommendations, but parents decide what to do. Termination is considered "premature" and is construed as "dropout"—from the perspective of the clinician—in about 50% of child therapy cases (Harpaz-Rotem, Leslie, & Rosenheck, 2004; Nock & Ferriter, 2005; Shuman & Shapiro, 2002). However, in many of these cases, the parents probably believed enough therapy had been provided.

There is a classic view of termination in which therapy should be needed only once because the client's problems should be permanently resolved. The hope is that no "relapse" will occur, so the client will never need counseling again. This type of termination involves a final good-bye for the therapist and client. Terminations sometimes occur this way.

In practice, however, termination is usually less dramatic. Unless the counselor retires or relocates, it is common for parents and children to return to therapy at intervals through the years, when they believe the clinician could help with a problem that has arisen. Many parents and children appreciate having a relationship with someone they can call if a mental health problem occurs, just as they call their pediatrician if a medical need arises. I usually say that I am not going anywhere and will be available any time I am needed, whether this is the day after our supposedly last appointment or in ensuing years. One of the rewards of practicing in the same community for a long time is working with children at different stages in their development and watching them grow up.

When therapists think the time for termination is approaching, they should discuss the issue with the parent and child. If there are no objections, a plan should be designed to make the ending comfortable and therapeutic for the client. The usual procedure is to wind down by increasing the time interval between sessions, so the client can prepare and process the transition with the counselor. If the treatment episode was brief, this might require only one or two sessions. For long-term therapy, there should be a more gradual winding down.

The possibility of return notwithstanding, termination is an ending. Clients who have achieved a positive outcome generally experience a combination of positive and negative feelings, because they are happy about reaching their goals but sad about losing a good relationship. Therapists should help clients understand and work through this combination of feelings—for example:

> "Your mom brought you here to see me because you were having trouble doing what she said. Now that you have gotten good at listening, we have reached our goal, and you don't need therapy anymore. That is something to be happy about because your mom and I are really proud of you, we hope you are proud of yourself, and things are happier in your house. At the same time, you might feel sad about finishing therapy, because we had a good time together, and it's sad to say good-bye to someone you like."

One purpose of termination sessions is **relapse prevention**—that is, maintenance of the gains that have been achieved. There should be a review of past learning to prepare for the future. There are two main questions for the client:

- "What did you learn in counseling?"
- "How will you use what you learned in the future?"

Summary

This chapter describes basic features of child and adolescent therapy that characterize most theoretical orientations and apply to most client problems. Generally, therapists can build strong treatment alliances with children and parents by conveying warmth, empathy, expertise, and a commitment to help. Counselors can most effectively engage clients by means of a professional but natural interpersonal style and clear, age-appropriate language.

In their first meeting with parents, counselors should obtain a description of the child's difficulties and encourage realistic hopes for a positive therapeutic outcome. In their first meeting with children, therapists should provide honest, age-appropriate explanations of the nature of therapy and the parent's purpose in obtaining this service for the child. When youth resist participating in therapy, counselors can encourage buy-in by asking the client about aspects of his life he would like to improve and by identifying ways that therapy could help with this.

Reflections of feeling and reflections of meaning convey empathy and facilitate self-expression by bringing out the implications of the client's statements. Clarifying the nature of problems, setting clear and attainable objectives, monitoring progress toward the objectives, and envisioning desired outcomes all help the client organize her efforts toward therapeutic goals.

Motivational interviewing is a package of techniques designed to nurture the development of motivation to change in clients. The strategy is not to debate or oppose the resistance but to facilitate its full expression while also eliciting the expression of values and goals whose pursuit is blocked by the problem behaviors. The therapist then tactfully offers input to help clients resolve their ambivalence by embracing positive change.

Although problem etiologies and therapeutic strategies are often complex, simple interventions sometimes help clients in direct, immediate ways. Some therapy sessions involve a sequence in which, first, the parent identifies a problem to the counselor and, then, the counselor and youth develop a plan to resolve the problem. When practical, a summary of these problem-solving efforts should be preserved in writing to support the client's memory of the plan.

Sometimes a more indirect approach is needed to uncover and address the emotions and misunderstandings responsible for the client's disturbance. Especially with young children, play and art may supplement language as a medium of thought, communication, processing emotions, and solving problems.

Child therapy generally involves work with parents, and counselors also collaborate with other professionals to coordinate care for clients involved in multiple systems. If they share insights and strategies, professionals in the mental health, medical, education, child protection, and juvenile justice systems can enhance each other's work.

Therapy should be terminated when the goals have been basically achieved or progress is no longer being made. Traditionally, termination has been viewed as a final conclusion, but many parents and children value having a familiar resource to whom they can turn when emotional or behavioral problems occur. Termination should include work on relapse prevention, but therapists can also leave the door open for any additional help the parent and child might desire in the future.

Case Study

The simple, directive intervention provided by Brent's therapist proved to be what this child needed to solve his problem. The episodes of noncompliance and tantrums in school came to an end.

Brent sometimes expressed sadness and confusion about his infrequent contact with his father. However, because this concern did not seem to affect his overall functioning, it did not seem necessary to make a therapeutic issue of it.

As a result of his previous misbehavior, Brent had to contend with some teasing from classmates who predicted that he would get in trouble just as he had in the past. The teacher once overheard his retort: "Dr. Shapiro said if I listen to the teacher I'll do *fine* in school."

2

Behavior Therapy

OBJECTIVES

This chapter explains:

- *How behavior therapy developed from experimental research on learning.*
- *How parents sometimes unintentionally reinforce maladaptive child behaviors.*
- *Behavior therapy's view of personality-related behaviors as learnable skills.*
- *Behavior assessment's focus on the antecedents and consequences of behaviors.*
- *The technique of exposure, which desensitizes clients to previously anxiety-producing stimuli.*
- *Contingency contracting, which uses operant conditioning to treat behavior problems.*
- *Relaxation training based on deep breathing and progressive muscle relaxation.*
- *Social skills training, which teaches children how to make and keep friends.*

Case Example
Attention

Barry, a 6-year-old European American boy, was brought to therapy by his mother because of his noncompliance and annoying, pestering behavior, constant seeking of attention, and difficulty playing independently. The mother complained that Barry was constantly getting into things and making a mess. She said that if she took her eyes off him for more than 10 minutes, there was liable to be trouble. She reported a number of everyday tasks that elicited defiance in Barry, including getting dressed in the morning, performing age-appropriate chores like putting toys away, and ending play activities when told to do so. The mother also described Barry as an imaginative, fun-loving child who behaved well as long as he was provided with entertaining activities and demands were not placed on him. The therapist made a diagnosis of oppositional-defiant disorder.

Barry was the youngest of three children. His mother said he usually got along well with his siblings, although they sometimes complained about him pestering them. The client's parents had been divorced for 2 years. Barry spent every other weekend and some holidays with his father. His mother noted bitterly that her ex-husband claimed to have no problems managing his son's behavior, but she attributed this to the father making few demands and providing Barry with lots of toys and activities: "He's a typical Disneyland Dad."

Barry was in first grade in school. His report card indicated satisfactory academic functioning and a level of self-control and compliance that seemed below average but not clinically significant. His behavior was better controlled in school than at home.

Learning Theory

Unlike most other therapeutic approaches, behavior therapy originated in the research laboratory, not the mental health clinic. Behavioral treatment was developed by applying scientific knowledge to the design of interventions for mental health problems. Just as biochemistry research has led to the development of medicines, basic research on the psychology of learning has led to the design of therapeutic techniques.

This scientific tradition has implications for behavior therapy as an approach to clinical work. Counselors can be confident that the psychological processes utilized by behavioral techniques do exist and do operate in the ways presumed by the techniques. Also, research has produced a more definitive understanding of learning principles than, for example, the workings of the unconscious. Behavioral techniques are generally subjected to rigorous outcome research as soon as they are developed, and they are discarded, modified, or retained on the basis of the results they produce with clients.

Behavior therapists emphasize careful **operational definitions**; they describe behavior in objective, observable, measurable terms. When behaviorists criticize the more abstract therapeutic approaches (e.g., psychoanalysis), they say things like: "What does *superego* actually mean? What do people *do* when they have a harsh superego?"

Learning is defined as any lasting change in behavior that results from experience.

Behavior therapy is based on the area of psychological research called **learning theory**. The technical definition of learning is quite broad: Learning is defined as any lasting change in behavior that results from experience. Learning occurs whenever a person has an experience that changes his future behavior.

The Core Idea: Both Adaptive and Maladaptive Behaviors Are Learned

The central idea in behavior therapy is that problems are learned and, therefore, they can be unlearned (Follete & Darrow, 2014; Guinther & Dougher, 2013; Skinner, 1953; Spiegler, 2013). Learning processes are equally capable of producing adaptive or maladaptive behavior, depending on the environmental stimuli and consequences experienced by the learner. As a result, when maladaptive behaviors are acquired, therapists can use the same learning mechanisms that were responsible for problem etiology to treat the difficulties, so problems leave by the same door they entered.

Behavior theory also acknowledges genetic influences on behavior and behavior problems. But even when the root causes of dysfunction include genetic factors, learning processes generally maintain the specific, behavioral manifestations of the dysfunction, and this means that therapeutically engineered learning experiences can make a positive difference (Kazdin, 2012; Spiegler & Guevremont, 2010).

Behavior therapy is based on three types of learning: **classical conditioning**, **operant conditioning**, and **observational learning**. Although other, more complex forms of learning also exist, there is no doubt that these three types of learning are fundamental processes by which human beings change as a result of their experiences. Behavior therapy may miss out on some of the mysterious, esoteric features of human life, but it focuses effectively on core, basic processes.

Classical Conditioning

In classical conditioning, people learn *associations between stimuli* (Gottlieb & Begej, 2014; Lattal, 2013; Pavlov, 1927; Watson, 1924). This type of learning is about which stimuli occur in association with, or predict the occurrence of, which other stimuli. Classical conditioning does not involve learning new behaviors; it involves learning new stimuli for old behaviors. In other words, following classical conditioning, the learner does not do any behaviors she did not do before, but she does these behaviors at different times—she produces behaviors in response to stimuli that did not formerly elicit them.

Ivan Pavlov (1927) discovered classical conditioning in his famous experiments with dogs. Pavlov repeatedly paired food with a light or tone. In time, the dogs learned to salivate in response to the signal, before the food was given. Dogs do not naturally salivate in response to a light or a tone but, through classical conditioning, they learned to do so. Thus, the dogs learned to do an old behavior (salivation) in response to a new stimulus (a light or tone).

Classical conditioning explains how neutral stimuli can come to elicit emotional, even physiological responses: What is necessary is a repeated *pairing* of the neutral or **conditioned stimulus** with an **unconditioned stimulus** that, prior to learning, elicits an innate response. Pairing produces learning most efficiently if the conditioned stimulus slightly precedes the unconditioned stimulus in time.

Once learning has occurred, the conditioned stimulus activates a memory trace representing the unconditioned stimulus (e.g., food or pain), and this activated memory then produces the conditioned response (Gottlieb & Begej, 2014; Jacobs & Blackburn, 1995; Lattal, 2013). The conditioned and unconditioned stimuli are different from and possibly not even related to each other. The conditioned and unconditioned responses, as behaviors, are similar to each other, but they occur in response to different stimuli.

In the 1920s, John Watson (1924) demonstrated classical conditioning of emotion in an early application of learning research to a clinical issue—namely, the development of phobia. In a single subject experiment that could not be performed today for ethical reasons, Watson presented a 10-month-old infant ("Little Albert") with a white bunny. At first, Little Albert played happily with the rabbit. Then, Watson paired presentation of the rabbit with a loud, unpleasant noise, which elicited crying from the child. After a few pairings of bunny and noise, Little Albert cried at the appearance of the white rabbit, even when no noise followed. He had learned to transfer his noise reaction to the bunny; he reacted to the rabbit *as if* it were the noise, because he had learned this association.

In addition, this Pavlovian learning **generalized** to other stimuli that were similar in some way to the rabbit but that had never before been associated with an aversive stimulus in Little Albert's experience. The child not only developed a phobia of white rabbits but also cried in response to anything white and fluffy, such as a ball of cotton and a man with a white beard. He had learned that white, fluffy stimuli signal or predict the arrival of painful stimuli.

What do these laboratory experiments have to do with the development of emotional problems in the real world? A great deal. The classical conditioning paradigm explains how people learn new reactions to stimuli. These learned associations can be pleasant and positive: A child whose father cuddles her while reading bedtime stories may develop warm, happy associations with books—and with men. Classically conditioned associations can also be painful and maladaptive: A child who is sometimes nurtured and sometimes abused by her father may learn to associate closeness to men with both gratification and pain, and these conflicting associations may distort her future relationships.

Classical conditioning is of particular importance to our understanding of post-traumatic stress disorder (PTSD; De Young, Kenardy, & van Eys, 2014; Ford & Cloitre, 2009). Trauma victims sometimes experience surges of anxiety in response to stimuli that just happened to be present when they were hurt, even if those stimuli had no causal relationship to what happened. For instance, sexual abuse victims sometimes re-experience their trauma in response to a smell that happened to be in the room during their molestation.

Classical conditioning is an emotional and experiential process, not a rational one, occurring primarily in subcortical, primitive areas of the brain (Damasio, 1994; LeDoux, 1998). As a result, conscious, reality-oriented thinking usually does not undo the raw, gut feelings that are conditioned into memory by the Pavlovian mechanism.

Classical conditioning is a mechanism of treatment as well as etiology, because Pavlovian learning also runs in reverse, and acquired associations can be unlearned or, at least, suppressed and negated (Pavlov, 1927; Jacobs & Blackburn, 1995; Vurbic & Bouton, 2014). In the process called **extinction**, stimuli that had been associated are repeatedly *un*paired—that is, the conditioned stimulus is presented but is not followed by the unconditioned stimulus. For Pavlov's dogs, there was a light or tone but then no food. For the abuse victims mentioned earlier, there would be the smells but then no molestation. When this unpairing occurs, the learned response is suppressed, so it weakens and eventually disappears. The learning mechanism of extinction is the basis of the therapeutic technique of exposure.

Operant Conditioning

In operant learning, there are four ways that consequences influence behavior—in other words, there are four contingent relationships between behavior and consequences (Grace & Hucks, 2013; Miltenberger, 2015; Skinner, 1938), as presented in Table 2.1. A **contingency** is a causal relationship between two events: If Event A (a behavior) occurs, then Event B (a consequence) follows. In operant conditioning, organisms learn to do the behaviors that lead to pleasant consequences and avoid the responses that lead to painful consequences. Operant learning is the process by which organisms learn what works and what does not.

There is a 2 × 2 organizational structure to these four types of consequences: There are two types of stimuli (pleasant and unpleasant), and each can be either presented or removed. People sometimes confuse negative reinforcement and punishment, perhaps because both involve unpleasant stimuli. The key to the distinction is that reinforcement, by definition, always increases the frequency of behavior; if it does so by presenting something pleasant, it is called reward, and if it does so by removing something painful, it is called negative reinforcement.

Table 2.1   Mechanisms Through Which Consequences Influence Behavior

1. In **positive reinforcement** or **reward**, the behavior is followed by something pleasant and, therefore, its frequency increases (e.g., praising a child for cleaning up).

2. In **negative reinforcement**, the behavior is followed by the removal of something unpleasant, and the frequency of the behavior, therefore, increases (e.g., a child stays in his room to avoid being teased by his sister).

3. In **punishment**, the behavior is followed by something unpleasant, and the frequency of the behavior decreases (e.g., scolding a child for aggressive behavior).

4. In **response cost**, the behavior is followed by the removal of something pleasant, and the frequency of the behavior decreases (e.g., taking away an adolescent's driving privileges because she stayed out after her curfew).

Operant **extinction** occurs when the contingency between a behavior and consequence ceases, and there is no longer a connection between the response and consequence (Grace & Hucks, 2013; Skinner, 1938; Vurbic & Bouton, 2014). Extinction means that nothing contingent happens. The result is an unlearning of connections between behaviors and consequences. For example, when therapists believe that disruptive child behaviors have been reinforced by parental attention, they may suggest that the parent ignore the misbehavior, in order to extinguish its contingent relationship with attention.

Operant conditioning can lead to the acquisition of new behaviors through a process called **shaping** or **successive approximation** (Follette & Darrow, 2014; Murphy & Lupfer, 2014; Skinner, 1938, 1953). For example, rats do not naturally press levers. If experimenters try to train rats to press levers simply by rewarding them when they do so, the experimenters will end up waiting a long time, because behaviors cannot be reinforced unless they occur. The strategy that works is to begin by rewarding the rat for any behavior that moves toward lever-pressing in some way—for instance, walking toward the lever, pressing on something else, sniffing the lever, and so forth. Soon, the rat is spending most of its time in the vicinity of the lever and, once this occurs, an actual lever press will eventually take place. Animal trainers use successive approximation all the time, and if you have ever taught a dog to perform a trick like shaking hands (paws), you are familiar with the procedure. **Chaining** is a related technique that teaches a sequence of behaviors by separately rewarding each individual step and then training the learner to put these steps together in the correct sequence.

The type of reinforcement schedule that is best for the *acquisition* of new behaviors is opposite to the type of schedule best for the long-term *maintenance* of behaviors (DeLeon, Bullock, & Catania, 2013; Miltenberger, 2015; Skinner, 1938; Spiegler & Guevremont, 2010). New behaviors are learned most quickly when reinforcement occurs immediately, frequently, and consistently. In contrast, behaviors resist extinction and persist for the longest time when reinforcement is **intermittent**—that is, when reinforcement occurs some but not all of the time. If a child expects to be rewarded every time he does a behavior, and reinforcement does not occur, the child will quickly recognize that the contingency has changed, and the behavior will extinguish. But if the child has learned that reward occurs only a fraction of the times he does the behavior, the nonoccurrence of reinforcement does not signal that the contingency has changed, and the child will continue the behavior in the expectation of eventual reinforcement. One classic example of an intermittent reinforcement schedule is gambling; some individuals persist in this costly behavior, without receiving much reward, because reinforcement occurs just often enough to keep the behavior going.

The gap between the continuous schedule of reinforcement best for response acquisition and the intermittent schedule best for response maintenance can be bridged by the technique called **fading** (Kazdin, 2012; Martin & Pear, 2014). Fading is gradual reduction in the frequency of reinforcement.

In summary, operant conditioning produces and maintains new behaviors most effectively when a three-phase sequence of reinforcement scheduling is used. The optimal order is: (1) continuous reinforcement, (2) fading, and (3) intermittent reinforcement.

Reinforcement contingencies are situation-specific; the same behavior that elicits reward in one situation might elicit punishment in another. (As examples, think of the behaviors appropriate to sporting events and religious services.) Some children's behavior problems are less a matter of doing the wrong thing than of doing the right thing at the wrong time. Competence requires the ability to read the situational cues or **discriminative stimuli** that signal which reinforcement contingency is in effect (McIlvane, 2013; Skinner, 1938, 1953). Traffic lights are discriminative stimuli that tell drivers whether they will be reinforced for stopping or going forward. Discrimination learning enables people to behave in situationally appropriate ways. Note that the word *discrimination* here does not imply prejudice but has the positive connotation of *telling the difference* between situations.

Operant conditioning is the basis of a number of therapeutic techniques, including token economies, contingency contracting, and any systematic use of reinforcement. Also, principles of operant conditioning are key to assessing the effects of intended and unintended consequences of rewards and punishments on children's behavior.

Observational Learning

Social learning theory (Bandura, 1977, 1986) originated in the recognition that people often learn and change their behavior without directly experiencing any stimuli, by means of observational learning. For instance, a child who sees his sister burn her hand on a hot stove might learn to avoid this consequence without ever experiencing it. Social learning theory forms a bridge between behavioral and cognitive theory.

Observational learning greatly expands people's ability to acquire new behaviors. In operant and classical conditioning, the only information available to the learner is the data of her own direct experience. Observational learning makes the data of *other people's* experiences available to the learner. Observing is a more efficient way to learn than trying different behaviors to see what is reinforced.

Modeling is a direct way of providing an observational learning opportunity: The model does what the learner wants to do. Children's natural tendency to imitate the behavior they see enables them to learn readily from models. In behavior therapy, counselors often model the behaviors their clients are trying to learn.

Observational learning can utilize symbolic models as well as live ones (Friedberg & McClure, 2002, 2014). The printed word makes possible a quantum leap in the possibilities for observational learning, enabling readers to learn from the stimuli, responses, and consequences experienced by people living long ago and far away. Multimedia and computer programs mix different media to further expand possibilities for observational learning.

What Causes Mental Health Problems?

There is an element of paradox in learning-based explanations of psychopathology: Learning is an adaptive, reality-oriented process, and yet it sometimes results in disturbed behavior and emotion. All three types of learning involve some form of information-based adaptation to the environment. How could such learning produce maladaptive functioning?

This question has two main answers. First, learning can produce dysfunctional behavior when the formative environment's stimulus associations, reinforcement contingencies, and modeled behaviors differ from those typical of the rest of the world. When this is the case, information acquired in the formative environment is a misleading guide for behavior in other settings. If a child's family operates by different rules than most people do, the behaviors needed to adapt to this family will be out of kilter and maladaptive in most other settings. By learning to adapt to her family, the child develops behaviors that do *not* work in the rest of the world. For instance, in some families, aggressive behavior is operantly reinforced with respect and access to tangible rewards. Children who adapt to such reinforcement contingencies get in trouble when they go to school, where aggressive behavior is generally punished.

Similarly, classical conditioning of stimulus associations that are uncommon outside the learning setting results in reactions that are inappropriate in most environments. For example, children abused by a man might learn to experience anxiety in response to all adult males, even though this association was realistic with only one, unrepresentative person.

There seems to be no etiology of mental health problems more fundamental than overgeneralization of learning. Although behavior theory has focused more systematically on this mechanism than have other therapeutic approaches, it is transtheoretical in its implications and is also emphasized, albeit with different terminology, by cognitive theory (Chapter 3) and psychodynamic, especially object relations, theory (Chapter 5). In overgeneralization, learning that was valid and adaptive in one setting is transferred to other settings where it is not valid and does not apply. Conveying both halves of this understanding to clients acknowledges the validity of what they learned from their experiences and identifies the boundaries to valid application of these lessons. In such cases, therapeutic intervention should involve discrimination learning, with the objective of helping the client *sequester* or limit the application of his learning to situations in which these lessons genuinely apply (Dollard & Miller, 1950; Wachtel, 1977). This is the process by which the future can be unchained from the past.

> *In overgeneralization, learning that was valid and adaptive in one setting is transferred to other settings where it is not valid and does not apply.*

The second reason why learning sometimes produces maladaptive behavior is that, because of the subtlety and complexity of the processes involved, learners sometimes extract inaccurate information from their experiences. In classical conditioning, stimulus generalization causes people to feel afraid of stimuli that have never hurt them, as Little Albert did with balls of cotton and white beards. In operant conditioning, parents sometimes administer consequences, such as negative attention, that they think are punishments but are actually experienced as rewards by the child. Failures of discrimination learning cause people to engage in behaviors that worked in one situation but do not work in others. Intermittent reinforcement results in the maintenance of behaviors that are ineffective most of the time but persist because they are occasionally followed by a reward.

One common mistake made by parents of children with behavior problems is failing to reward the minor examples of improved behavior that occur, at times, in all children (Barkley, 2013; Kazdin, 2005; McMahon & Forehand, 2005; Patterson, 1982). The caregiver's reason for not rewarding these behaviors is generally that they are not considered good enough—the behaviors do not meet the parent's standards of acceptable child functioning. Although this stance is not illogical, it will not work, because the parent's criterion for reward is so far above the child's current level of behavior that she will never receive reinforcement—and learning depends on reinforcement.

Reinforcement is a function of the experiences of the learner, not the intentions of the trainer.

There is a paradox at the heart of behavioral parent training: Why would parents need therapists to help them reinforce the behaviors they desire in their children when, presumably, parents would naturally do so on their own? The answer seems to be that, because of the subtle complexities of operant conditioning, translating *intended* reinforcement contingencies into *actual* contingencies is no easy task. Reinforcement is a function of the experiences of the learner, not the intentions of the trainer. When the consequences intended by parents differ from the consequences experienced by the child, parents reinforce behaviors they do not want. Behavioral assessments sometimes reveal this irony, resulting in an "Aha experience" for the parent. This occurred for Barry's mother when she realized that she generally ignored Barry's quiet, appropriate play but gave him lots of attention when she heard a crash in the living room.

Reinforcement is not a mechanical process but a subjective, individual one. An experience that would be a reward for one person might be a punishment for another. Reinforcement is also a comparative phenomenon, in that people seek out the most positive experiences available to them, in comparison to the alternatives.

The subjective, comparative nature of reinforcement explains why **negative attention** is rewarding for some children. Almost all children have a profound need for adult attention. When this need is satisfied by pleasant interactions, the child has no need for negative attention, and reprimands are experienced as punishments, just as the adults intend. However, when children do not receive enough pleasant interaction from adults to satisfy their need for attention, reprimands may help to meet this need (Barkley, 2013; Kazdin, 2005; McMahon & Forehand, 2005; Patterson, 1982). Under these conditions, being yelled at may be (subtly) reinforcing. Poor-quality food that disgusts well-fed people will be eaten eagerly by people who are starving, and the same holds true for human interactions. This formulation is captured by the saying, "Beggars can't be choosers." This etiological process is discussed further in Chapter 10, on disruptive behavior.

Assessment and Case Formulation

Kazdin (2012), Spiegler and Guevrement (2010), Follette and Darrow (2014), and Antony and Roemer (2011) provide detailed explanations of behavioral assessment procedures. Clinical interview and behavioral observation are the most important methods of conducting these evaluations. Because behavior theory emphasizes the situation-specificity of children's responses, these clinicians try to obtain information about the client's functioning in multiple settings, perhaps by interviewing teachers as well as parents.

Standardized, validated instruments also provide valuable information. The most widely used set of instruments for measuring the spectrum of child problems was developed by

Achenbach and Rescorla (2000, 2001, 2007, 2010). These instruments were developed through decades of research, and they are based on a vast amount of normative data based on age, gender, and ethnic group. The instruments include a parent-report measure called the *Child Behavior Checklist*, a self-report instrument for youngsters 11 years and older called the *Youth Self-Report*, and a measure of school behavior called the *Teacher Report Form*. These three measures have similar content—most of the questions inquire about the same behaviors. Nonetheless, when used to assess the same client, the versions often produce different scores, because they depend on the perspective of the reporter, and informants often have different perceptions of the child's functioning (De Los Reyes & Kazdin, 2005). The most complete picture comes from considering all the available perspectives.

Behavioral assessment is defined by careful scrutiny of the sequences of antecedents, responses, and consequences involved in the client's difficulties (Follette & Darrow, 2014; Guinther & Dougher, 2013; McMahon & Forehand, 2005). There is little emphasis on meanings, abstractions, or speculations. Instead, there is a focus on specifying exactly what happens when the problem behaviors occur and do not occur.

Often, parents come in with vague, global complaints about their child: "He's impossible"; "She's disobedient"; "He has low self-esteem." This type of impressionistic description is insufficient for the behavioral assessor, and her initial work consists of obtaining clearer and more detailed information. The behaviorist wants to find out what she would see if she were there when the problems occurred. For example, if a parent said his child was "depressed," the clinician would ask about the behaviors the parent believes indicate depression, such as crying, verbal reports of sadness, slumped posture, and so forth.

The behaviorist concern for precision, like most good things, can go too far and become counterproductive. We do not want to burden parents with demands for exact, quantitative tabulations that are beyond their capability. The goal of assessment is clarity, not obsessive detail, so a moderate degree of precision is sufficient. Assessment questions should be laced with words such as "about," "approximately," and "give me an idea of how often." We do not need answers like "12 times a day" or "45% of the time." Instead, we need to find out whether problem behaviors happen "several times a day," "some of the time," or "most of the time when he's with his sister."

Because behaviorists generally emphasize the power of situations to influence behavior, they try to learn as much as possible about the situations in which problem behaviors occur. For example, does the child usually tantrum first thing in the morning, last thing at night, when with her grandmother or babysitter, when her big sister is absent or her little brother is present, or when she hears her mother berate her father? Classically conditioned stimuli signal the imminent occurrence of a significant event and cause the child to begin responding based on that expectation. For example, if a child's anxiety symptoms are generally preceded by his mother's drinking, this might be because her drinking signals the imminent occurrence of disturbing behavior. Antecedents involved in operant conditioning include the discriminative stimuli or cues that signal which reinforcement contingency is in effect. For instance, if a child refuses to do her homework only when her father is tired, that might be because this is the only situation in which refusal is reinforced by successful avoidance of homework.

Clinicians investigate vicarious learning processes by asking about reinforcement contingencies that the client has observed rather than experienced directly (Bandura, 1977, 1986). The client's observation of siblings is sometimes important here. For example, if a client sees an older brother reinforced for demanding, inconsiderate behavior, the client might engage in such behavior even if she has not received direct reinforcement for doing so.

Questions to Ask

In behavioral assessment, clinicians ask parents to walk them through typical instances of the problem behavior in a careful, step-by-step fashion. Details are important, because features of these sequences that seem trivial to the parent might turn out to be part of a learning process that is maintaining the problem. Behavior therapists focus like a laser on three questions:

1. Exactly what do the child's problems consist of, *behaviorally*?
2. What typically happens *before* the problem behavior occurs?
3. What typically happens *after* the behavior occurs?

Behavioral clinicians help caregivers operationally define their child's problems by replacing large, abstract, trait descriptions like "mean" and "selfish" with identification of specific behaviors that can be observed. These clinicians respond to abstract descriptions by saying things like:

> "Let's slow down and be more specific. Take me through some typical examples, step by step. If I were in the room when your child was misbehaving, what would I see and hear?"

A parent who described her child as "impossible" might hear the following questions:

- "What does your child do when she is being impossible?"
- "About how often does the impossible behavior happen? Twice a day? Once every 5 minutes?"
- "Does she ever do what you say? How much of the time? About half? Once in a while?"
- "What type of direction is she more likely to follow? What type is she more likely to defy?"

The process of slow, careful description often stimulates parents to produce information they did not know they had. As caregivers walk through several examples of problem behaviors, they often find themselves saying things like, "I thought I was real firm with him but, now that I think about it, sometimes he wears me down with his arguing and I let him get away with things." Such statements signal the discovery of real consequences in the midst of intended consequences.

Behavior therapists emphasize the importance of direct observation, especially of parent-child interaction (Barkley, 2013; McMahon & Forehand, 2005; Patterson, 1982). It is useful to conduct two types of observation: one in which the child takes the lead in playing and the parent follows along, and one in which the parent directs the child's behavior by giving her instructions. You can ask the parent to show you both types of interaction as part of the assessment process. While people might be on their best behavior in therapists' offices, their habitual behaviors usually come through. Parents might be embarrassed when their child acts up, but this is a time to say, "It's good that I'm getting a chance to see what happens at home, because we will make use of this information."

Patterns to Look For

Behavior therapists search for patterns in clinical data that match the processes described by learning theory. When you see these patterns emerge from the messy, idiosyncratic details of clinical presentation, you will perceive the workings of classical, operant, and observational learning in real life.

Behavior therapists are open to the possibility that seemingly irrational, maladaptive behaviors are based on learning from past experiences that has been overgeneralized or misapplied to current situations. Therefore, one strategy for developing hypotheses about etiology is to work backwards: Ask yourself what learning experiences *would* produce the client's problematic behaviors as operantly conditioned responses. The question is, in what type of environment would the client's dysfunctional behaviors work better than the alternatives?

Behavior therapists assess seemingly irrational emotional responses to stimuli and situations by inquiring into the experiences that have been paired with those stimuli and situations in the past (Guinther & Dougher, 2013; Lattal, 2013; Spiegler & Guevremont, 2010). For example, if a girl's father frequently used drugs while watching TV, she might become upset when he turns on the set. Classical conditioning is about stimulus associations in the child's history.

Because behavior theory assumes that persistent responses must be receiving some type of reinforcement or they would not continue, these therapists scrutinize clinical data in search of unintended reinforcement for the presenting problems. One pattern to look for is a combination of low parental attention when the child behaves appropriately and high attention when the client's behavior is negative (Harvey & Metcalf, 2012; Pardini, Fite, & Burke, 2008; Patterson & Chamberlain, 1994). The resulting parent-child presentation looks unpleasant, with a lot of anger and yelling going back and forth, and such interactions might appear to be the opposite of reinforcing—but such appearances can be deceiving. Similarly, if a child finds that his busy, preoccupied parents suddenly pay attention to him when he complains of stomach pain, this attention might reinforce his somatic complaints. In these situations, an assessment informed by knowledge of learning principles might reveal that, underneath the apparent unpleasantness, a subtle form of reinforcement is occurring.

Another common glitch in the operant conditioning process occurs when parents have inappropriately high standards for their child's behavior, which results in a low rate of approval and reward (Barkley, 2013; Kazdin, 2005; McMahon & Forehand, 2005; Patterson, 1982). What determines whether a standard is too high? The criterion is this: If the child is never or rarely rewarded, the parent's standards must be considered too stringent, because the child's behavior will not improve if her movement in a positive direction is not shaped by reinforcement. Parental standards must be individualized to the child's existing competencies if they are to promote learning.

Clinically, this pattern presents as a parent who is displeased by nearly everything the child does and a child who has given up on pleasing his parent. It is as if the parent's standards and the child's existing level of compliance are so far apart that no contact ever occurs. The parent sees the child as undeserving of reward (e.g., "disobedient"), and the child sees the parent as unrewarding (e.g., "mean"). Sometimes these clients say their parents hate them. When Barry's therapist asked his mother whether she ever reinforced him for playing quietly by himself, her reply was, "I'd love to—but it never happens." As a result, the brief periods of independent play he did sometimes achieve were essentially ignored.

While our discussion thus far has emphasized parents as a source of reinforcement for children, obviously they are not the only source. As children mature, peers become an increasingly important source of rewards and punishments. Therapists have no ability to change the way peers respond to a client—except by changing the client's interpersonal behavior with peers. If the child's social skills are weak, treatment should include training in these skills. Unlike parent-based interventions, social skills training leaves environmental reinforcement contingencies unchanged, relying instead on increased client skills to elicit more rewards from the same environment.

Change Processes

Behavior therapy utilizes as change agents the same processes believed to be responsible for the development of problems, so that difficulties are resolved by the same processes that created them: classical conditioning, operant learning, and observational learning. Behavior therapists seek to reverse the reinforcement contingencies and stimulus associations that produced the client's problems, so that new contingencies and associations will produce adaptive behavior.

However, to make this picture fully accurate, we must make it a little less neat. Although the correspondence between etiology and treatment is clear on a theoretical level, in practice behavior therapists are not highly concerned about how client problems originated. These counselors have confidence in the ability of learning processes to change behavior even if treatment does not simply reverse the learning processes involved in etiology. For instance, most phobias do not seem to originate with a pairing of some traumatic event and a phobic object but, nonetheless, repeated presentation of this object without an ensuing painful stimulus does extinguish phobic anxiety in the substantial majority of cases (Grills-Taquechel & Ollendick, 2013; Head & Gross, 2009; Storch, 2014). Similarly, disruptive child behavior may sometimes originate as the result of emotional factors rather than operant learning but, nevertheless, a therapeutic restructuring of reinforcement contingencies usually ameliorates the problem.

Behavior therapy based on operant conditioning generally involves training parents to change the reinforcement contingencies experienced by the child, in a technique called **contingency contracting** (Barkley, 2013; Kazdin, 2005; McMahon & Forehand, 2005; Patterson, 1982). The assumption is that, if the child is consistently reinforced for behaving positively, these behaviors will be learned and maintained. Rather than focusing on internal processes, this type of intervention changes the child's environment in order to improve her behavior. Also, in such interventions, the parents are the direct providers of therapeutic experiences for the child, and the therapist's role is to train the parents how to do this most effectively.

Behavioral interventions are all about *information*. The strategy of behavioral parent training is to provide the child with more accurate, clear, and detailed information about what behaviors her caregivers desire from her. Therapeutically engineered information is different from the comparatively ambiguous, incomplete, and sometimes self-contradictory feedback contained in the informal, unstated reinforcement contingencies that evolve naturally and without much thought. Caregivers might say they have already given the child clear information (e.g., "I *told* him to be good"), but such vague, general statements do not contain nearly as much information as the consequences contained in their moment-to-moment interactions with the child in everyday life. Telling is less informative than showing.

Behavioral interventions also address the child's motivation to engage in positive behavior. Praise is the most important type of reward used in behavior therapy, but tangible rewards, such as treats, toys, and privileges, as well as symbolic reinforcers, such as stickers and poker chips, often add an important increment of power to interventions.

If the assessment indicates that negative parental attention is driving the behavior problems, the intervention should change both halves of this pattern: The parents should reduce the amount of attention they pay to negative behavior and increase their attention to positive behavior. For example, if one reason why a client resists chores is that her resistance results in emotional battles with a father who otherwise ignores her, then reversing the overall reinforcement contingency would involve both (a) asking the father to ignore her when she refuses to comply and (b) asking him to pay attention to the child when she does her chores. If parents reinforce adaptive behaviors in the same way they had (unintentionally) reinforced maladaptive ones, the reinforcers that gave rise to the problem should be just as effective at producing the opposite, positive behavior.

When parental standards are so far above the child's current level of competency that reinforcement rarely occurs, the solution is to (temporarily) lower the parent's criteria for reward down to the level at which they make contact with the child's behavior. Then, successive approximation can begin to shape the child's behavior in a more competent, compliant direction. For Barry, who had much difficulty playing quietly by himself, this principle meant that his mother began reinforcing him for very brief periods of independent, appropriate play. Parents can be reassured that, as the child's behavior improves, the criteria for reward will be raised. It is like clicking and dragging with a mouse; the idea is to make contact with the learner where he is and then pull him in the desired direction.

Behavior therapists see skills where other clinicians see personality traits or internal issues, and these therapists believe that skills can be taught (Antony & Roemer, 2011; Miltenberger, 2015; Skinner, 1974). People often think of calmness and friendliness as internal qualities but, to behaviorists, these are learnable skills. Behavioral treatment involves breaking these abstractions down into their concrete components and then training clients in these behaviors.

Behavior therapists see skills where other clinicians see personality traits or internal issues, and these therapists believe that skills can be taught.

This chapter describes two types of behavioral skills training. **Relaxation training** is a treatment for anxiety, depression, and anger. This type of therapy consists of training in deep breathing and progressive muscle relaxation. **Social skills training** is a treatment for peer rejection and social isolation. This therapy teaches behaviors for making friends and resolving interpersonal problems.

Outcome Research

It is necessary to know the basics of research methodology to make good use of the outcome research sections of the chapters to follow. You will also want to remember three abbreviations introduced in this section, because they will be used throughout the book.

Research Methodology

The most important method used in treatment outcome research is the **randomized controlled trial** (RCT). An RCT is a scientific experiment designed to assess the efficacy of an intervention. RCTs involve the same basic design whether they are used to evaluate medicines or psychotherapies.

In RCTs, clients are randomly assigned to two or more groups. Because assignment is random, the two groups of clients are considered equivalent at the beginning of the study. Pretests are administered to measure client functioning in the dependent variables of interest, which generally include the symptoms for which the clients need therapy. Then the intervention(s) is conducted. At termination, the measures are administered again. If the groups produced similar scores at pretest and significantly different scores at posttest, the divergence can be attributed to different effects of the experimental conditions.

The control groups used in RCTs are of great importance in interpreting the results of these studies. A control group is like the bar that the experimental treatment must jump over to receive support from the study, and different types of control groups are like bars of different heights. The simplest experimental control is no treatment. This usually consists of clients who are on a waiting list while the intervention group receives the experimental therapy. A higher bar is provided by control groups that receive a placebo therapy, which consists of a "generic" form of counseling in which the clinician provides attention, listening, and support but no active, bona fide interventions. Generally, clients who receive a placebo therapy improve more than clients in wait-list control groups. A more stringent control condition is provided by **treatment as usual** (TAU). TAU consists of whatever therapies the counselors at participating clinics provide when they are not participating in a study. Unlike clients in wait-list or placebo control groups, clients in TAU groups are receiving therapy that is genuinely intended to help them. Finally, the most rigorous type of comparison involves a therapy that previous research has found to be effective; such interventions are sometimes called **evidence-based psychotherapies** (EBPs). Clients receiving EBPs make up what is usually called a comparison group, not a control group. EBPs provide the highest bar for the treatment of interest to jump over.

In summary, all statistically significant differences are not equal, and their different meanings are not only a function of the numbers involved. The strength of support for an intervention indicated by a significant result depends largely on the stringency of the control or comparison conditions used in the study, with the order as follows: Waiting list < Placebo < TAU < EBP.

Research on psychotherapy outcomes frequently makes use of a statistical technique called **meta-analysis**, which combines the results of individual studies into one large data analysis, thus summarizing an area of research. Meta-analysis transforms the diverse forms of data found in individual studies into one equivalent form, so the results of studies using different methods and measures can be combined and compared. Meta-analyses produce a summary statistic called an **effect size**, which is an index, in standard deviation units, of the difference between two groups (typically a treatment group and a control group). According to Cohen (1988), effect sizes of approximately .20 represent small differences between groups; effect sizes around .50 can be characterized as medium in magnitude; and effect sizes of .80 or greater should be considered large.

Behavior Therapy Results

Therapy outcome research provides more extensive support for behavioral interventions than for any other single type of therapy.

Therapy outcome research provides more extensive support for behavioral interventions than for any other single type of therapy. However, the main reason there are more studies supporting behavior therapy is that more outcome research has been performed on it than any other type of therapy, not that behavior therapy has consistently outperformed other treatments in direct comparisons, although this has sometimes occurred. Overall, the outcome research justifies a high degree of confidence in the effectiveness of behavioral interventions for most clients.

Contingency management—that is, the systematic use of positive and negative consequences—is probably the single most empirically well-supported strategy for changing behavior in the mental health field. Contingency management is the core of behavioral interventions for disruptive behavior disorders (Anastopoulos, Shelton, DuPaul, & Guevremont, 1993; Chacko et al., 2009; Curtis, 2010; Gerdes, Haack, & Schneider, 2012; Nixon, Sweeney, Erickson, & Touyz, 2004; Rejani, Oommen, Srinath, & Kapur, 2012; Thomas & Zimmer-Gembeck, 2007), and application of operant learning principles and techniques play roles in behavioral interventions for other disturbances as well. Because there has been so much outcome research on contingency management, description of this research is distributed among the chapters about the disturbances to which it has been applied, rather than concentrated in this chapter.

The behavioral technique called **exposure**—which extinguishes classically conditioned fear and desensitizes clients to previously frightening stimuli—is the single most empirically well-supported technique for treatment of anxiety (Storch, 2014; Zalta & Foa, 2012) and PTSD (Foa, Hembree, & Rothbaum, 2007; Ford & Cloitre, 2009). Chapter 13 includes a review of outcome research on exposure-based therapy for anxiety (Barrett, Dadds, & Rapee, 1996; Kendall, 1994; Kendall, Hudson, Gosch, Flannery-Schroeder, & Suveg, 2008; Nauta, Scholing, Emmelkamp, & Minderaa, 2003; Reynolds, Wilson, Austin, & Hooper, 2012; Walkup et al., 2008). Chapter 15 includes a review of research on exposure-based therapy for PTSD (Cary & McMillen, 2012; de Arellano et al., 2014; Deblinger, Mannarino, Cohen, Runyon, & Steer, 2011; Jensen et al., 2014; Webb, Hayes, Grasso, Laurenceau, & Deblinger, 2014).

APA's Society of Clinical Psychology rates relaxation training for Panic Disorder in adults as having *Modest Research Support*. This is the second-highest rating in their system.

Carlson and Hoyle (1993) performed a meta-analytic review of 29 RCTs examining relaxation training based on progressive muscle relaxation with a variety of adult behavioral medicine and mental health populations. They obtained a large effect size of .91, indicating that relaxation is an efficacious treatment for conditions as diverse as headache, cancer chemotherapy side effects, anxiety, and depression. Bernstein and Carlson (1993) obtained similar results in their meta-analysis of 30 RCTS and again, 24 years later, in their meta-analysis of 24 RCTs published in the interim (Bernstein, Carlson, & Schmidt, 2007).

Outcome research on children has also produced support for relaxation training. In a study with a nonclinical sample of children, Lohaus and Klein-Hessling (2003) found that progressive muscle relaxation was an effective means of reducing tension, producing effects on both physiological indices of anxiety, such as heart rate and skin conductance, and self-report measures of mood and well-being. In a study of adolescent depression, Reynolds and Coats (1986) compared progressive muscle relaxation to a wait-list control and found that the intervention produced large reductions in depressive symptoms. Improvements in anxiety were also documented. In a study of aggression in male adolescents with high levels of stress, Nickel et al. (2005) found that progressive muscle relaxation produced improvement in several measures of anger, social functioning, and mental health, compared to a no-treatment control group.

In a study conducted in Germany, 6- to 15-year-old outpatients with diverse diagnoses who received relaxation training achieved more reduction in parent-reported behavioral and emotional problems, compared to children in a wait-list control group (Goldbeck & Schmid, 2003). The magnitude of change was in the small/medium range, with effect sizes of .49 for the CBCL and .36 for a measure of somatic complaints. Kahn, Kehle, Jenson, and Clarke (1990) found that children who received relaxation training achieved more reduction in depression than children in a wait-list control group.

Beelmann, Pfingston, and Losel (1994) conducted a meta-analysis of 13 studies of the effects of behaviorally oriented social skills training on directly observed social interaction skills; they obtained a medium-sized effect of .61. They also meta-analyzed 11 studies that assessed the effects of social skills training on measures of social adjustment and obtained a small/medium effect size of .35. Their sample of studies included both children with mental health problems and children in regular school classrooms.

Meta-analyses of research on social skills training for clinical samples of children have produced weaker results. Quinn, Kavale, Mathur, Rutherford, and Forness (1999) found an effect size of .20, representing a small difference between treated and untreated groups. They found slightly stronger effects for studies targeting specific social skills (e.g., cooperation), compared to studies measuring more global outcomes, such as social competence. In a meta-analysis examining studies of social skills training for students with learning disabilities, Kavale and Forness (1996) obtained a small effect size of .21.

Turning to individual studies, in research on treatment for 8–10-year-old children with attention-deficit/hyperactivity disorder (ADHD), Pfiffner and McBurnett (1997) delivered a group social skills program that taught good sportsmanship, taking turns, saying nice things, identifying feelings in self and others, and assertiveness. Compared to a no-treatment control group, participants achieved more improvement in parent-reported social interactions and behavior problems at home. Group differences decreased, but remained significant, at the follow-up assessment conducted 3 to 4 months after conclusion of treatment. In another study of children with ADHD (ages 8 to 12 years), Antshel and Remer (2003) found that, in comparison to a no-treatment control condition, social skills training resulted in greater improvement in assertiveness skills, as measured by both parent-report and child self-report, but did not produce change in the other domains of social competence assessed in this study. In a school setting, DeRosier (2004) identified third-grade children with peer relationship problems and randomly assigned some to a social skills training group and some to a no-treatment control group. Following intervention, the group receiving social skills training self-reported better peer relationships, higher self-esteem, and reduced social anxiety. The magnitude of change was small, with effect sizes in the .20 to .25 range.

As demonstrated by the small effect sizes reported in these studies, it has proven difficult to help clinical populations achieve large gains in social skills. This might be why few studies or meta-analyses of social skills training have appeared recently in the literature. However, this does not mean this type of intervention is without value. Spence (2003) noted a general consensus that social skills training does not provide an adequate stand-alone treatment for most clients but should be viewed as a useful component of therapy for some youth. Many packages of cognitive-behavioral techniques include social skills training as a component.

The Therapist's Style

Behavior therapy is highly structured (Antony & Roemer, 2011; Miltenberger, 2015; Spiegler, 2013). These clinicians do not hang back and listen quietly, encouraging clients to talk about whatever comes to mind. Their style is active, informative, and directive. Behavior therapists function as coaches for parents and children, providing them with the training they need to ameliorate their problems.

Behavioral intervention does not involve exploring clients' thoughts and emotions, nor does the theory emphasize therapist empathy as a change agent. Nonetheless, behavioral clinicians are just as warm, kind, and supportive as counselors utilizing other approaches.

A positive therapeutic relationship facilitates client learning and use of the skills and techniques that behavioral clinicians teach.

Behavior therapy is an *action-oriented* form of treatment (Kazdin, 2012; Martin & Pear, 2014). The focus is on the concrete details of behavior rather than abstract, theoretical conceptualizing. Sessions have a specific agenda with defined goals, careful note taking, and frequent use of handouts and worksheets. Much session time is spent explaining, modeling, and practicing the new skills to be learned. Homework is often assigned and reviewed.

Exposure

Classical conditioning can cause people to become anxious in response to stimuli that, in themselves, are not threats. The technique of exposure runs classical conditioning in reverse to extinguish associations between conditioned stimuli and fear. The presentation ahead draws on recommendations by Kendall and Hedtke (2006a), Cohen, Mannarino, and Deblinger (2006), Grills-Taquechel and Ollendick (2013), and Davis, Whiting, and May (2012). Exposure procedures for treating anxiety and PTSD are described in Chapters 13 and 15, respectively.

The technique of exposure runs classical conditioning in reverse to extinguish associations between conditioned stimuli and experiences of fear.

Exposure is a simple intervention. It means putting clients in the situations they fear and helping them tolerate and remain in those situations long enough to discover that, other than anxiety, nothing terrible is going to happen. Repeated exposure produces desensitization to stimuli that previously elicited fear. Exposure can be combined with coping techniques such as relaxation to reduce clients' discomfort, but this is not an important component of the procedure. The key is simply for the client to learn that he can sustain contact with the feared situation and survive. Even when the procedure is painful, exposure is effective at reducing anxiety and trauma symptoms.

Exposure was originally developed as a treatment for phobias of concrete objects and situations, and it is a straightforward intervention for this type of problem. Clients who are afraid of elevators need to get in and ride; those who are phobic of insects need to touch a bug, and so forth. Exposure procedures can also be adapted to treat sources of fear that are more complex and more internal than concrete phobic objects.

Whenever possible, exposure should occur in vivo (Beidel & Alfano, 2011; Kendall, 2011). If this cannot happen in the office, therapists should train clients and parents to conduct exercises in settings where direct, live exposure is possible.

In **imaginal exposure**, the client imagines anxiety-producing stimuli or situations in as much vivid, realistic detail as possible. Therapists can conduct imaginal exposure by verbally presenting these stimuli to clients. The goal is the same as for in vivo exposure: desensitization to previously frightening stimuli. Imaginal exposure is the best option when in vivo exposure is not possible (e.g., for fear of flying in an airplane). Imaginal exposure is the only option when the anxiety-provoking stimuli do not originate externally but come from the client's own mind in the form of thoughts and feelings, as is the case with generalized anxiety disorder and panic disorder (see Chapter 13). Imaginal exposure is also useful as a facilitative strategy that paves the way to live exposure.

Exposure is a stressful procedure and, initially, some children are afraid to do it. The therapist should explore the child's concerns, explain the technique's rationale, and assure her that she will control the pace of the procedure. Clients can stop their exposure procedure any time they want to.

Exposure is much less stressful when it is accomplished in a gradual fashion. The first step is construction of an **anxiety hierarchy**: a rank ordering of anxiety-producing stimuli or situations arranged from least to most frightening. Kendall and Hedtke (2006a, 2006b) call this type of hierarchy a "fear ladder" and, with clients, they draw it in this way. For example, a hierarchy for an adolescent with social anxiety might begin with saying hello to a passing acquaintance and progress to chatting at a football game, mixing at a party, and asking someone out on a date. As another example, a hierarchy for someone with fear of heights might begin with looking out a second-story window and progress to being in a car driving up a mountain, standing on a balcony, and walking on an elevated bridge. Exposure therapy is complete when the client makes it to the top of her ladder.

Contingency Contracting

Contingencies are like rules governing if-then relationships between behaviors and consequences, and contracts are tools for defining these rules in a clear form, usually in writing. Contingency contracting applies principles of operant learning to the behavior problems of clients. These contracts are the central component of behavioral treatment for noncompliant, oppositional behavior in children and conduct disturbances in adolescents. This form of behavior therapy has accumulated extensive, strong empirical support (Anastopoulos et al., 1993; Chacko et al., 2009; Curtis, 2010; Gerdes et al., 2012; Nixon et al., 2004; Rejani et al., 2012; Thomas & Zimmer-Gembeck, 2007).

When therapists introduce the idea of a reinforcement system, parents sometimes sigh and say they have already tried a "behavior chart." Therapists can respond by saying that the parent's system might not have been set up in an effective way, in which case it was doomed to failure. Having a "chart" in itself does not mean anything; everything depends on the way the system is set up.

My description of contingency contracting is based on Barkley (2013), McMahon and Forehand (2005), Kazdin (2005), and Forgatch and Patterson (2010). Contingency contracts for children are usually put in the form of charts, as illustrated in Figure 2.1. These

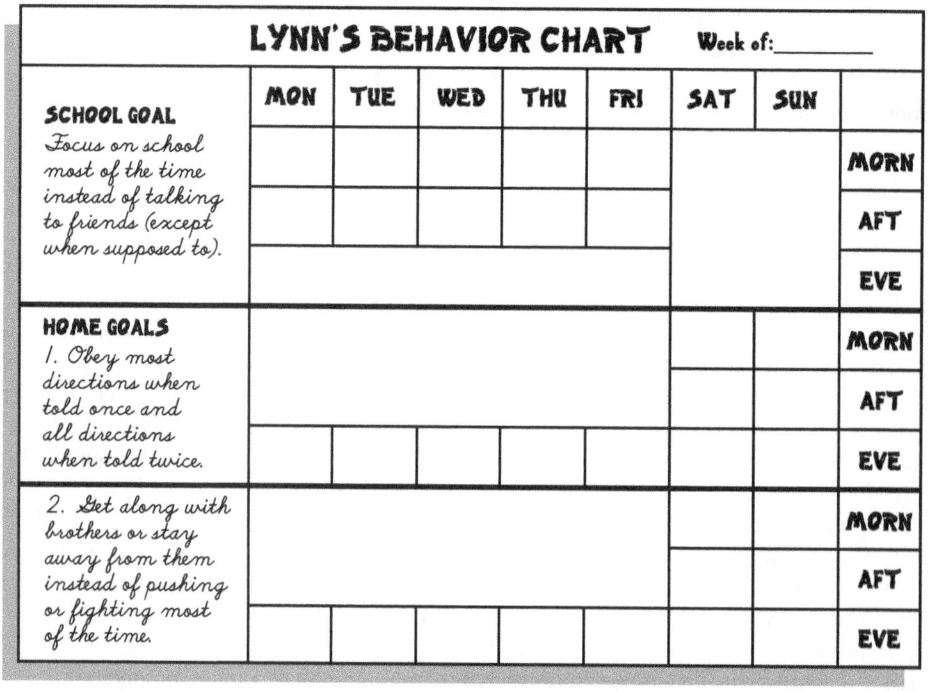

Figure 2.1   Example of a behavior chart.

charts are set up like calendars because they document the child's behavior through time. The charts are structured as grids. The columns are labeled with the days of the week. The rows are labeled with briefly stated, specific behavioral goals. With grids consisting of one column for each day of the week, usually subdivided into morning, afternoon, and evening, and one row for each behavioral goal, one piece of paper can usually contain 1 week of charting.

Setting Goals

Developing behavioral goals requires a clear understanding of learning theory, client functioning, and connections between the two. Goals should accord with what the child can realistically be expected to achieve. Because learning cannot occur without reinforcement, and reinforcement cannot occur without success, goals should be set a small distance above the client's present, typical level of functioning, in the top part of his current range of behavior (Antony & Roemer, 2011; Martin & Pear, 2014; Murphy & Lupfer, 2014). For example, Barry could sometimes play by himself for about 10 minutes before needing attention. For him, 10 minutes of independent play was a good criterion for reinforcement.

Because learning cannot occur without reinforcement, and reinforcement cannot occur without success, goals should be set a small distance above the client's present, typical level of functioning.

To be specific, therapists should set behavioral goals that the client can achieve *approximately two thirds of the time*, because this level of task difficulty seems to produce the most efficient learning. Once the contingency contract is in place, this proportion should be used as a guideline for mid-course correction. If the client is achieving the behavioral criterion less than half the time, the target should be lowered. If the child is earning rewards almost all the time, the standard should be raised.

Sometimes parents feel that the goals suggested by therapists are too low. Understandably, these parents want to see age-appropriate behavior in their children as soon as possible and, also, they might feel the child does not "deserve" to receive rewards for a level of behavioral control that is below average for her age. Counselors can respond by saying that the important question is not what the child "deserves," because therapy is not about justice. Behavior therapy is a learning technology, and goals should be set to produce learning in the most efficient way possible. Also, counselors should emphasize that goal setting is an incremental process and, once the initial goals are attained, it will be appropriate to raise the bar and expect higher levels of positive behavior.

The level of the goals affects the setup of the chart, because these levels determine the length of time that behavioral control must be maintained for rewards to be earned. If a client is capable of behaving in accordance with a goal for a full day, then days should be the basic unit of time shown on the chart. However, younger children and those with limited self-control skills will rarely be able to maintain appropriate behavior for this length of time. Their behavioral targets need to involve smaller units of time, such as parts of the day (morning, afternoon, and evening). Still smaller units of time, such as hours or even minutes, can be charted, and this is sometimes done in day treatment settings with high staff-to-client ratios. Such detailed charting, however, exceeds the inclinations of most parents and teachers. These caregivers should be asked to consider a part of the day successful if the client achieves some improvement in terms of the behavioral objective, compared to his previous level of performance. Barry received a sticker for independent play during each part of a day in which he produced at least three 10-minute periods of this behavior, with his accomplishment of each period marked by verbal reinforcement from his mother.

The number of goals, like the ambitiousness of goals, should be determined by the child's capabilities. Young children with cognitive limitations will not be able to understand and consciously strive for more than one or two goals at a time. Barry's therapy involved only two basic goals: compliance with caregiver directives, and appropriate, independent play. Most adolescents can pursue five to seven goals simultaneously.

When possible, goals should be described in positive rather than negative terms. This is not a rule, however, and when the prevention of negative behavior is a treatment priority, these behaviors should be stated in their negative form. Examples of behavioral goals include: "No fighting," "Complete most or all homework assignments," "Share toys while playing with my brother about half the time," "Do what Mom and Dad say after being told no more than twice," and "Get along with my sister without yelling most of the time."

Choosing which goals to start on immediately and which to put on hold is a judgment call that involves weighing two competing considerations: We want to start working on the most serious problems, but it is vital that the child experience some success as the system is launched. It is often useful to choose one easy goal and one more difficult goal, so the child can achieve some success quickly and the system will also target a behavior of serious concern to the parent.

Types of Reinforcers

Behavioral interventions based on operant learning generally involve three types of reinforcers: social, symbolic, and tangible (Bell & McDevitt, 2014; DeLeon et al., 2013; Grace & Hucks, 2013). Social reinforcement consists of positive attention, praise, and affection. Praise for positive behavior is a crucial aspect of behavioral intervention that is not replaced by the other types of reinforcement involved in the system.

Symbolic reinforcement involves whatever visible means of keeping track of the child's performance is used in the intervention. If charting is used, successful performance can be documented with colorful stickers. Poker chips, perhaps with different values for the different colors, also make good symbolic reinforcers that children can hold in their hands and accumulate in glass jars. One good way for parents to begin a contingency contract system is to go to a store and have the child pick out the stickers or chips to be used. These objects provide concrete symbols of the child's accomplishments, and they bridge the time gap between performance of positive behaviors and receipt of tangible rewards, so they accumulate reinforcing qualities of their own (Bell & McDevitt, 2014). Children can put a poker chip in their pocket when they go to school to remind them of the consequences in place for positive and negative behavior. For adolescents, a written ledger involving check marks and numbers is usually more age-appropriate.

Tangible reinforcers are rewards that are intrinsically valued and enjoyed by the child. These rewards are also called **backup reinforcers**, because they are provided after a predetermined quantity of symbolic reinforcement is earned, and because these reinforcers are administered less frequently than symbolic and social reinforcement. Backup reinforcers include dessert, toys, material possessions, activities, outings, and privileges, such as later bedtimes and screen time. For adolescents, money makes a simple and effective tangible reinforcer. The best way to determine backup rewards is simple: Ask the child what he likes. Barry wanted to earn video games, action figures, and restaurant meals with his mother.

Setting Up a Contract

Setting up a contingency contract usually takes about two sessions of work with parents and children. Implementation of the system should be carefully monitored in ensuing sessions, because adjustments may be necessary. The procedure for designing a system involves three steps, in the following order:

1. The parents and therapist determine the behavioral goals.
2. The child provides the list of tangible reinforcers, or the "reward menu."
3. The parents and therapist determine the exchange rate, assigning different numbers of points to different backup reinforcers.

Children are often suspicious of contingency contracts, especially when they are used to treat noncompliance. The child's initial understanding is typically that her parents have brought her to therapy because they are fed up with her misbehavior and are bringing in the big guns to force compliance no matter what it takes. Then, the child spends what feels like a long time in the waiting room, while the counselor and parents discuss her negative behaviors and what to do about them. Finally, the child is brought in to hear the results of these discussions. As she grits her teeth and prepares for the worst, she hears the following from her new therapist:

> "Your parents and I have been talking about your behavior, and we've decided the problem is that you haven't been earning enough rewards. There's been too much arguing and criticizing, and not enough praise and rewards like treats, movies, going to restaurants you pick, trips to amusement parks, and toys. So we're going to start a new system that will tell you exactly what you need to do to earn these rewards. Want to hear more about it?"

Contingency contracting is not a free ride. For these systems to be effective, the child's appetite for privileges and products cannot be satisfied in a noncontingent manner. Just as animals will not learn to run a maze for food if they are not hungry, contingency contracting will not work if the child receives the items on the reward menu regardless of his behavior. Therefore, the therapist and parents usually need to reduce the amount of noncontingent treats, TV time, purchases of toys, and so forth. When clients hear this news, they sometimes react negatively. However, the good news is that they should be able to earn *more* privileges and material goods than they received prior to the introduction of the contract. Also, most children are pleased by the predictable, controllable process of earning symbolic and material rewards, and they are encouraged by hearing that the therapist and parents will coach them in how to achieve higher rates of positive behavior so they can earn more and more rewards. Although youngsters might perceive contingency contracts as a threat, they should also perceive these systems as an opportunity.

One happy moment occurs when the time comes to construct the reward menu, and the therapist, with a serious air, takes out a legal pad and pen, says, "Now, what do you want your rewards to be?" and then carefully writes down what the child says. Although unrealistic desires could conceivably be a problem, in my experience this rarely occurs—clients generally want ordinary things that their parents are able to provide.

Once the behavioral goals have been identified by the parent and the reward menu has been developed by the child, the task is to define a crosswalk connecting behaviors and rewards. This is the most complicated part of the procedure. Contingency contracts explicitly define the relationship between symbolic and tangible reinforcers; it is like an exchange rate. The question is, how much positive behavior should the child need to produce to earn a given reward?

As a realistic example, suppose a child has two behavior goals for school, with separate assessment of morning and afternoon, and two behavior goals for home, assessed on evenings and weekends (with weekend days containing three periods). This child would have the opportunity to earn 6 stickers and/or poker chips per day, which results in 42 for the week. Given an optimally effective two-thirds success rate, the child would be expected to earn about 4 chips per day, or 28 per week. That is her income. Now, what are her expenses?

The system should require the child to spend about two thirds of her earnings (i.e., two or three chips) on daily rewards that most children receive noncontingently (e.g., desert, screen time) *and* have a chip or two left over each day to bank toward the purchase of a larger reward. Medium-sized rewards (e.g., a sleepover or game of miniature golf) should cost about a week's worth of surplus earnings—here, about 10 chips. Large rewards (e.g., an expensive toy or a trip to an amusement park) should cost about a month's worth of surplus earnings—here, about 50 chips. There could also be reinforcers with sizes and prices in between. If the child's expected rate of positive behavior would not produce enough points to earn substantial rewards, the exchange rate is too stringent and should be made more generous, so the child does not become discouraged. If the child could earn large rewards with only small improvements in behavior, the exchange rate should be made more stringent, so she will be motivated to strive for major improvement.

It is important to emphasize that contingency contracting does *not* depend on precision. It is necessary only to attain a roughly appropriate relationship between positive behavior and tangible rewards. Therapists and parents should not obsess about these exchange rates; the important thing is to make sure that small rewards cost a small number of chips while large purchases cost many, and to make sure that earning tangible reinforcers requires some effort from the child but is within his capabilities. As Alan Greenspan, past chairman of the Federal Reserve, said, "It is better to be roughly right than exactly wrong."

It is up to the child how she spends her chips. For most youngsters, this decision making is an enjoyable, empowering part of the process. If a child spends all her chips on one reward, that is okay, because she will have opportunities to earn the chips necessary for the next day's routine privileges on the next day.

It is important to "keep the system dynamic," which means changing the target behaviors, goal levels, and rewards as time goes by, so the experience does not become stale for the child. Youngsters become bored if they work on the same behaviors and receive the same rewards month after month. Clients maintain interest and energy for the system when they work on different types of behavioral competence and strive to earn different rewards.

In a variation of this system that is occasionally useful, we can challenge clients to achieve a *streak*: success each day, for a certain consecutive number of days, at one behavioral goal. Streaks create a distinctive type of excitement in sports, and sometimes they do for clients, too. Once the goal has been achieved and commemorated with a reward, a longer streak can be attempted. Streaks sometimes generate their own momentum when clients feel stimulated by the idea of achieving as many days in a row as they can, and they hate the idea of failing once, ending their streak, and starting over at zero. This characteristic of streaks makes them an effective means of reducing the frequency of seriously negative behaviors down to zero.

Contingency contracts do not need to stay in place, in their formal fashion, for the client's whole childhood. As competence and self-control increase, reinforcement fading should occur: Behavior should be monitored in a less detailed fashion, and rewards should be administered in a smaller number of larger units. If the child's behavior improves to an age-appropriate level, parents should make fairly high levels of reward almost a matter of routine, contingent on the child's ongoing maintenance of positive behavior. Some special incentives for extra chores and so forth can remain in place, but the charts, chips, and ledgers will become unnecessary once the client has assimilated the information they contained into his habitual way of behaving. Contingency contracting fulfills the function of training wheels on a bicycle: This extra help for the child is necessary while he is learning, but once his competency is established, the support can be withdrawn, as he goes forward on his own.

Coordination With Teachers

The biggest obstacle to use of reinforcement-based systems with schools is that, unless the child is in a special program, teachers must attend to a large number of students, and they have limited time for using behavior management systems with individual children. The solution to this problem is for the therapist and parent to do as much of the work as they can for the teacher, and to leave her responsible only for that last small contribution that only she can make. In the system described next, the teacher provides the information, and the parent administers the consequences, which is an effective division of labor. These "daily report cards" are an effective means of improving children's behavior in school (Fabiano et al., 2010; Jurbergs, Palcic, & Kelley, 2010).

The first step is for the therapist and parent to write a simple behavior chart that applies to a single day. This chart should have two columns: one for morning and one for afternoon. There should be a row for each target behavior, described in a few words. Two target behaviors are usually about right. Thus, the piece of paper is divided into four parts; there are four cells in this design.

The piece of paper has a simple scoring system written right on it, so there is nothing for the teacher to remember. A three-level system is usually optimal. A drawing of a smiling face can be used to indicate success; a frowning face can indicate behavior problems; and a face with a straight line for a mouth can indicate an in-between level of behavior. Alternately, the system can use check marks, X's, and dashes. The therapist and parent copy a stack of these minicharts, which usually fit on a half-sheet of paper. Then, the teacher is asked only to make four marks per day on the form. Once the system is learned, the teacher's effort involves less than 60 seconds per day. When you make things this easy, most teachers are willing to cooperate. Figure 2.2 presents an example of a daily report card for a child who has one teacher for the whole school day. More complex versions of the procedure are appropriate for older youth who have different teachers for each class period; just add more rows to the form.

It is the child's responsibility to bring the daily report card home each day. Of course, when the report is negative, children sometimes throw it away and say they lost it. Therefore, parents should treat the absence of a report card as equivalent to a negative report and administer consequences accordingly. Most youngsters learn to bring the report home.

Seth's Chart

	Morning	Afternoon
Is considerate of classmates (no teasing, pushing, or fighting).		
Pays attention to the teacher.		
$\sqrt{}$ = Most of the time — = Some of the time X = Not very much of the time		

Figure 2.2   Example of a daily behavior chart for teachers.

Contingency Contracts With Siblings

One problem that sometimes arises is that siblings resent the extra attention and rewards the client receives in association with her reinforcement system. If left unchecked, this resentment can impel brothers and sisters to sabotage the client's success by provoking her to misbehave. The best way to handle this situation is to create a chart for the siblings, too. Parents' main objection is that this requires the expenditure of some time. Therapists can respond by saying that child behavior problems take much more time from parents than reinforcement systems do.

The siblings should not have the same reinforcement system as the client unless they have the same capabilities, which is unlikely. The purpose of the systems—to improve the children's behavior—is the same and, as explained earlier, this purpose is most likely to be accomplished when children achieve their behavioral objectives approximately two thirds of the time. If, initially, siblings behave more appropriately than the client, they will need to achieve higher goals to receive rewards. Brothers and sisters might complain that this is not fair. Parents can respond by saying that fairness does not mean treating everyone the same; fairness means giving everyone what they need.

If the problem is conflict between siblings—that is, arguing and fighting—the contingency contract should be applied to *interactions between* the children, rather than to the individual behavior of either one. If the siblings get along acceptably well, they both receive rewards. If they fight, they both receive negative consequences. This strategy makes sense because determining individual responsibility for fights is often impossible, and the sibling interaction is the more meaningful unit of analysis. Yoking the siblings to each other in this way, so they either both win or both lose, removes parents from the difficult position of trying to figure out "who started it." Also, social psychology research has found that placing previously antagonistic individuals in the position of teammates who have a shared goal improves their relationship (Brewer, 1996; Sherif, 1966). If the incentives are sufficiently potent, most brothers and sisters will figure out how to get along with each other well enough to earn the rewards they desire.

The Meaning of Contingency Contracting

Some nonbehaviorists believe that contingency contracting is a mechanical, manipulative method of changing behavior. This is a false charge, for several reasons. First, reinforcement systems should be completely transparent and understood by both the parent and child, with nothing hidden about either the procedure or its rationale. The essence of

contingency contracting, and the reason for its effectiveness, is its
replacement of vague, unstated reinforcement contingencies with clear,
detailed information about what the child can expect as consequences for
different behaviors. This knowledge gives children the power to earn the
rewards they want while developing the competencies and self-control
they need.

The essence of contingency contracting is its replacement of vague, unstated reinforcement contingencies with clear, detailed information about the consequences of different behaviors.

Furthermore, the question of who controls whom is a matter of perspective. There is an old cartoon showing two rats in a Skinner box being
reinforced for pressing a lever by an experimental psychologist in a lab
coat. One rat says to the other, "Boy, have I got this guy conditioned:
Every time I press this lever, he drops in a piece of cheese!" Accordingly,
therapists should present contingency contracting to the child as a means
by which he can obtain the praise and backup reinforcements he desires from his parents.
Contingency contracts are a way for children to increase their control over their parents'
behavior, as well as the other way around, because if the child performs his goal behaviors,
he must be rewarded. The parents have no discretion; their administration of consequences
should be unaffected by their mood or feelings about the child so that, within the structure
of the system, the youngster's behavior completely governs the consequences he receives.

Control is not a zero-sum affair in which parents gain control by taking it away from
their children. When contingency contracting works, parents and children both feel they
have increased their control over their own behavior *and* the other's behavior.

A complete description of the network of reinforcement that operates in behavioral
child treatment would include the following components. First, because new child management techniques usually take some time to produce results, it is important for the therapist
to reinforce the parent for using the techniques, to keep her going until her efforts bear fruit.
In time, the child's behavior usually improves, which reinforces the parent for using the
new strategies. Finally, the parent's satisfaction with the counselor's services reinforces the
clinician for providing effective behavior therapy. It is a nice circle in which the reinforcers
flow as follows:

$$\text{Therapist} \rightarrow \text{Parent} \rightarrow \text{Child} \rightarrow \text{Parent} \rightarrow \text{Therapist}$$

Relaxation Training

Behavior therapists recognize that, when people are anxious or upset, they generate all
sorts of thoughts and feelings that feed back into their distress. However, these counselors
also believe that, to a significant extent, the physical process of relaxation can cut through
cognitive-emotional complexities and reduce stress without resolving issues. Therefore,
when treating clients suffering from anxiety, depression, or violent anger, behavior therapists provide training in relaxation techniques (Grills-Taquechel & Ollendick, 2013;
Hazlett-Stevens & Bernstein, 2012; Head & Gross, 2009; Martin & Pear, 2014).

Relaxation training is a *psychophysiological* intervention: It involves
both the mind and the body. In fact, the emphasis is on relaxing the body
and, by doing so, calming the mind. Relaxation training is a mirror image
of the physical arousal it seeks to reduce. Arousal involves rapid heartbeat, high blood pressure, rapid breathing, tightened muscles, and release
of adrenaline and cortisol into the bloodstream. Relaxation training aims

Relaxation training is a psychophysiological intervention: It involves both the mind and the body.

to reverse these physiological processes (Bernstein, Carlson, & Schmidt, 2007; McGuigan & Lehrer, 2007; Smith, 2007).

Relaxation training begins with an explanation of the procedure and the rationale for its use. This explanation consists essentially of the previous points translated into child language. ("Fear happens in our bodies as well as in our minds ...") To convey the idea of learning a new skill, and to prepare the client for some initial feelings of unfamiliarity and awkwardness, you can use the analogy of learning to ride a bicycle: At first, you have to pay careful attention to every little thing you do but, after some practice, it starts to come naturally.

Relaxation training should be conducted in a quiet room, with the child seated in a comfortable chair. Counselors can ask the youngster to turn her chair away so she does not feel observed. While conducting the procedure, the therapist's tone of voice should be calm, slow, and soft. Relaxation training has a lot in common with hypnosis—the spirit and feeling are similar—and a calming, hypnotic quality should flow from the therapist's voice into the child's experience. Guided imagery, described in Chapter 15 on stress and trauma, can be added to the physiological techniques described here.

The first component of relaxation training is deep, diaphragmatic breathing (Dixhoorn, 2007; Hazlett-Stevens & Craske, 2009). Deep breathing increases oxygen and decreases carbon dioxide levels in the bloodstream. The brain has sensors that monitor these levels, and when they are optimal, the brain lowers the body's arousal level, and a sense of well-being results. Some clients find this information interesting to know.

The second component of relaxation training is progressive muscle relaxation (Hazlett-Stevens & Bernstein, 2012; Smith, 2007). The muscle training involves a two-part sequence of tensing and relaxing, which is repeated for each muscle group. The contrast between tension and relaxation helps the child perceive the difference so he can gain control over these physical changes. First, the client tenses a designated muscle group for 5 to 10 seconds. Then, the child relaxes that body part and remains relaxed, taking a couple of deep, slow breaths, for another 20 seconds or so. The website associated with this book includes a relaxation training script that therapists can use with young people (Form 2.1).

Here is a tip for how to use the deep breathing part of the procedure to develop harmony between yourself and the client. At frequent intervals, in between the tensing/relaxing sequence for each body area, pause and say, "Breathe in ... breathe out ...," and *synchronize* these words with the client's breathing, so you say "breathe in" when she inhales, and you say "breathe out" when she exhales. In other words, while supposedly you are giving directions and the client is following them, in reality you are watching the client's breathing and timing your directives to fit *her* rhythm. By following the client in this way, you can build a sense of effortless synchrony and coordination for her. It is another example of therapeutic click-and-drag: We go to them, so they will come with us.

Messages conveying growth in self-control should be intermixed in skill training procedures to support development of the client's sense of mastery. For instance, in treating an anxious client, you could say something like, "With each breath in and each breath out, you are becoming more in charge of your anxiety."

Therapists should tailor relaxation procedures to the youngster's developmental level. Because of children's shorter attention spans, these procedures should be briefer for them than for adults, with a maximum duration of about 20 minutes. Whistles and bubble blowing can be used as aids to help children acquire and practice controlled breathing skills (Cabe, 2001).

All skill acquisition depends on practice, and the more, the better. Relaxation training always involves homework. Different techniques can be used to transport the relaxation procedure from the therapist's office to the child's environment. With younger children, parents can implement the relaxation script. Recordings of the counselor talking through the procedure can be effective. After a while, most clients memorize the directions.

Once the full relaxation procedure is learned and practiced, it can be abbreviated to make it convenient for use in the midst of everyday life. Although a quiet, comfortable setting is necessary for skill acquisition, our final goal is for relaxation skills to transfer into ordinary situations. Therefore, relaxation training concludes by helping the child make his new skills more flexible and portable. The client should practice achieving the state of relaxation in a shorter period of time by doing the tension/relaxation sequence with a smaller number of larger muscle groups. With sufficient practice, a brief, self-administered cue such as "so calm" or "chill out," combined with a few deep breaths, becomes capable of producing a relaxed state. The client should practice using this abbreviated technique whenever he wants to relax. The full procedure should continue to be used intermittently to support the abbreviated technique. When a few deep breaths can calm the client in an anxious or angry situation, he will appreciate this new form of self-control.

Social Skills Training

No human quality seems more subtle and undefinable than "being good with people"—but behavior therapists propose to teach exactly that. Social skills training is based on the behaviorist belief that personality-related behaviors can be analyzed into their components and taught as skills, without working through emotional issues or past experiences (Antony & Roemer, 2011; Miltenberger, 2015; Skinner, 1974).

Social skills training is not distinctively associated with any one category of diagnosis but is a component of cognitive-behavioral treatment packages for many types of disturbances. The reason is that social skills are such a fundamental, multifaceted human competency that weaknesses in these skills lead to many different types of problems. This book introduces social skills training here and then describes several specific subtypes in later chapters on the disturbances most associated with deficiencies in these skills. Training in social problem solving is presented in Chapter 10 on disruptive behavior. Training in social perception, communication, assertiveness, and conflict management are presented in Chapter 12 on aggression. This chapter focuses on the most basic social skill of all: talking to people in ways that get them to like us, or, to use the more technical term, **friendship initiation and maintenance**.

Behavioral skills training generally proceeds through the four stages shown in Table 2.2. This type of therapy focuses on the nitty-gritty aspect of behavior. Nothing is considered too simple or mundane to be discussed and taught. *Nothing* is left to "come naturally"—everything is spelled out explicitly. Skills training should be conducted in a step-by-step manner that presents the behavioral components one at a time and allows the client to practice each step before the next is introduced (Kinnaman & Bellack, 2012; Krumholz, Ugueto, Santucci, & Weisz, 2014). This approach allows clients to distill the concrete behaviors comprising interpersonal skills, so they can learn competencies they had not been able to develop on their own.

The modeling component of social skills training is based on principles of social learning theory and observational learning (Bandura, 1977, 1986). Modeling can be conducted

Table 2.2   Four Stages of Behavioral Skills Training

1. *Explaining* the rationale of training, which includes identifying the child's skill deficits, explaining why they produce negative outcomes, and explaining the new, more effective behaviors.

2. *Modeling* the skills by demonstrating the new behaviors for the client.

3. *Skill practice* by the child, which means rehearsing the new behaviors, usually in role-played interactions with the therapist.

4. *Feedback* from the counselor, which means constructive comments about what the child did well and which skill components need to be strengthened.

using live, videotaped, symbolic, and covert modeling. Live modeling by the therapist is usually the most important type. This clinical activity may feel odd at first, but counselors are capable of role-playing peers in interactive practice sessions with child clients. Your goal is not to make the scene seem real or to capture nuances of behavior but to provide the client with an approximation of the social stimuli he will encounter with peers so he can practice the new behaviors he is learning.

Especially for younger children, **symbolic modeling** can help to make the training process engaging (Drewes & Bratton, 2014; Friedberg & McClure, 2002, 2014; Knell & Meena, 2011). Puppets and action figures can be used to model and practice social skills. Stories in books can be used if the characters and situations demonstrate the behaviors that need to be learned. If there are no published materials that suit this purpose, therapists and clients can make up stories to model the competencies being developed.

In **covert modeling**, the person imagines herself or someone else performing the new skill successfully. It is often useful for the client to be her own imagined model of the desired behavior. As discussed in Chapter 1, the techniques of implementation intention and envisioning prepare clients to perform desired behaviors on the right occasions and in efficient, almost automatic ways.

Cultural factors often need to be considered in social skills training, because interpersonal behaviors that are effective in one group might not work in another social context (Sue & Sue, 2013; and see Chapter 9). As one example, direct eye contact generally indicates respectful attention in Western culture, but it is considered disrespectful and/or challenging in a number of non-Western societies (Cartledge & Milburn, 1996; Hays, 2008). Counselors should investigate clients' cultural norms enough to make sure we do not train them in behaviors that will not work in their families, schools, and neighborhoods.

Social skills training can teach a variety of behaviors, depending on the client's needs. Barry's counselor taught him to recognize when he wanted his mother's attention and to pursue that goal using words (e.g., "Mommy, would you play with me?") rather than getting into mischief.

The basic strategy of learning a behavior under controlled, easy conditions so it can then be implemented under natural, more difficult conditions is applicable to all sorts of problems, large and small. As examples, parents can set up practice trials for child behaviors such as getting out of bed and dressed in the morning, managing teasing from a sibling in a nonviolent fashion, and terminating a play activity before being finished with it. Behaviors are generally easier to perform when they have been practiced several times before.

Friendship Initiation

There is probably no quality of social behavior more sought after by American youth than that of being "cool." The generally modest effect sizes for social skills training described in this chapter's outcome research section suggests that this type of training usually cannot change rejected, awkward youth into popular paragons of cool, but it can help them achieve more normal social functioning and integration into peer groups. In other words, we do not know how to teach charisma, but we can teach a developmentally appropriate version of cocktail party conversation. The skill of friendship initiation includes several trainable components related to facial expression, body language, showing interest, asking questions, and making comments. The presentation ahead is based largely on recommendations by Krumholz et al. (2014), Rapee et al. (2006), Beidel et al. (2000), and Rutherford, Quinn, and Mathur (1996).

Training in friendship initiation is a component of cognitive-behavioral treatment packages for anxiety (Rapee et al., 2006), especially social anxiety (Beidel, Turner, & Morris, 2000), and depression (Curry et al., 2003; Stark et al., 2006). The fears of socially anxious youth are not only the result of unrealistic cognitions; these youth often do have weak social skills and, as a result, are rejected by peers (Greco & Morris, 2005; Spence, Donovan, & Brechman-Toussaint, 1999). Similarly, depressed youth have social skills deficits that result in unpopularity and loneliness (Prinstein, Borelli, Cheah, Simon, & Aikins, 2005; Shih, Abela, & Starrs, 2009). When interpersonal problems are mostly a matter of distorted interpretations and self-perceptions, cognitive intervention is likely to help, but when these problems are based on the reality of weak social skills, behavior therapy can change that reality.

It may be useful to give clients the homework assignment of observing their peers' social interactions and noticing their language, nonverbal behaviors, and topics of conversation. This safe way of beginning the study of social behavior provides opportunities for clients to learn from their peers.

Initiating a conversation is most likely to be successful when it is attempted at the right time and with the right person. Clients can look around their social worlds and assess who might be interested in making friends with them. The most popular kids in class might feel they already have enough friends and do not need more. Also, timing counts. It is hard to initiate a conversation when the other person is busy, hurried, or talking to someone else. It is easier to start talking when the other person has a free moment or is doing something that can be accompanied by conversation.

Behavior therapists model greetings—that is, how to say, "Hi" or "What's up?"—with good eye contact and a tone of voice that is friendly but not needy. Then the client practices these greetings, and the counselor provides feedback. The client should practice greeting peers several times per day as homework.

One effective approach to generating topics of conversation is to look for things we have in common with the other person. The easiest place to start is with the surface of everyday life. For youth, this could mean what is going on in class, a recent event at school, and common interests, such as sports, video games, TV, and music. Conversations can be maintained by open-ended questions (e.g., "What are you doing this summer?") and by expanding on a point the other person seemed to find interesting.

Joining group activities and conversations often feels awkward to socially isolated children. Observational research indicates that, contrary to adult expectations, the most effective way to join a group is not to make a formal request, such as, "Can I play?" but rather to join the game or conversation as it is going on, in a seamless fashion (Putallaz & Wasserman, 1990). Socially competent youth slide smoothly into groups without drawing attention to themselves or disrupting the flow of activity. When entering a group, the first comment should not be about joining but should refer to the activity at hand, so the comment blends into the ongoing conversation.

Body language, physical positioning, and gestures are most socially effective when they strike a balance between clinging and avoidance. Clients should generally stand about three feet away from the person with whom they are speaking. Similarly, an occasional touch can be engaging, but hanging on the other person will not work.

Showing interest in what the other person says is accomplished through both verbal and nonverbal communication. In most Western cultures, people show interest by making eye contact and nodding their heads. Conversational responses should stay on the topic. If the peer reports something striking or remarkable, the client should convey that he is impressed (e.g., "Wow!" or "No kidding!"). If the peer describes an activity or interest she and the client have in common, that should be noted, and the client should describe her experience with the activity. Making friends is about getting to know the other person and letting them get to know you.

Asking questions conveys interest in what the other person has said, keeps the conversation going, and expands the interaction. Counselors and clients can develop a list of generically appropriate questions that can be used in many situations—for example, "What did you do last weekend?," "What was the homework assignment in math class?," and "Did you see the game last night?" Any time the client and her peer have shared some experience, there is a question available to be asked—for instance, "What did you think of that _____ (assembly, video, test, etc.)?"

Questions that lead to expanded responses develop conversations and build friendships. As a strategy for thinking of these questions, the client can imagine himself having the experience the peer is describing, notice the gaps in his picture as the description proceeds, and then ask questions to fill in those gaps. The same strategy provides a basis for thinking of empathic statements. Youth can generate such verbalizations by putting themselves in the other person's shoes and imagining what the experience would be like for them. They can learn to make inferences from reported occurrences to emotions by asking themselves the question, "How would I feel if that happened to me?" (Of course this type of self-inquiry is not a foolproof means of inferring another person's experiences, but it is a good place to start.)

Experientially, the process of social skills training might feel contrived and artificial at first, for both therapists and clients. People typically think of social skills (aka "charm") as something that should come naturally, and there is nothing natural about breaking a skill down into its component parts and teaching them. However, the results of outcome research indicate that this training does help youngsters interact more successfully with their peers, regardless of whether the training initially feels awkward. The behaviorist insight is that a feeling of artificiality is not a problem as long as clients learn to perform important, skilled behaviors.

Therapists can even turn the contrived nature of social skills work into an advantage by acknowledging and sharing this aspect of the experience with clients in an open, humorous manner. One particularly fertile source of humor is provided by Krumholz et al. (2014), who suggest that counselors model and clients enact *ineffective* social behaviors, to contrast them with effective ones. Just as alternating between muscle tension and relaxation helps clients gain control over this dimension of behavior, clients can learn the difference between effective and ineffective social behavior by, for example, experiencing the contrast between frowning and looking away on one hand and attentive listening with eye contact on the other hand. It is useful for clients to both enact and receive these two types of behavior. Weisz, Thurber, Sweeney, Proffitt, and LeGagnoux (1997) suggest videotaping clients performing positive and negative examples and then reviewing the tapes to help them understand the differences. Playing with these behaviors is an opportunity to be goofy and have fun. Humor frequently decreases anxiety, reduces inhibition, and provides distance, all of which are advantages in work on the potentially sensitive issue of likeability and popularity.

Some forms of therapy seek to work through emotional issues in the expectation that this will lead to positive behavior change. But if social skills training improves the reality of the client's peer relationships, there may be no feelings of loneliness or rejection to work through. Sometimes behavior advances first, and emotions follow.

Sometimes behavior advances first, and emotions follow.

Summary

Behavior therapy is a clinical application of experimental research on learning, particularly research on operant conditioning, classical conditioning, and observational learning. Behavior therapy emphasizes concrete definition of problems and interventions, step-by-step instruction in skills, and empirical validation of therapeutic techniques. This approach has received strong support from outcome research.

Behavior theory views mental health problems as the result of learned behaviors and inadequately developed psychosocial skills, rather than emotional conflicts or personality traits. Behavioral assessment involves detailed examination of the antecedents and consequences that precede and follow the problem behaviors. The strategy of treatment is to provide experiences that sever old connections between stimuli, reinforce more adaptive behaviors, and train clients in the skills they need. There is no etiological mechanism more fundamental than the overgeneralization or misapplication of valid learning to new situations in which the old lessons do not apply, and there is no change mechanism more important than limiting or sequestering the old learning to its legitimate domain, so new situations can be approached in a fresh way.

The technique of exposure runs classical conditioning in reverse to extinguish associations between conditioned stimuli and past painful experiences. Clients confront the situations they fear and tolerate remaining in them long enough to discover that, other than anxiety, nothing terrible will happen.

Contingency contracting, a clinical application of operant learning principles, is used to treat child noncompliance, disruptive behavior, and a variety of other problem behaviors. Rather than administering contingency contracts themselves, therapists train caregivers to implement these interventions in the client's everyday environment. Behavioral targets are set within the child's reach so that reinforcement and, therefore, learning can occur; as the child's behavior improves, the targets should be raised. Explicit systems of reinforcement are used to help parents translate their intentions into the actual consequences experienced by the child. Symbolic reinforcers, such as charts, stickers, and poker chips, are used to increase the quantity and quality of information contained in the feedback received by the client. Backup, tangible reinforcers are determined by the child's preferences, within the constraints of feasibility.

Behavior therapists treat disturbances involving stress, anxiety, and overarousal by teaching the skill of relaxation. This psychophysiological intervention relaxes the mind by relaxing the body. The core components of relaxation training are deep breathing and progressive muscle relaxation.

Social skills training in friendship initiation addresses the problem of peer rejection by improving real relationships in the client's life. This training distills the specific behaviors necessary for making friends and teaches these behaviors to clients by means of modeling, guided practice, and feedback. Therapists demonstrate and role-play skills such as greeting peers, initiating conversations, asking questions, and expanding conversations.

Case Study

Barry's therapy did not achieve one of its goals for his busy, single mother; treatment did not reduce the amount of time she spent attending to her son, although Barry eventually became capable of about one-half hour of independent play. However, therapy did change the emotional quality of these interactions because Barry's behavior improved and, from his perspective, so did his mother's; she did less scolding and more praising. She learned to ignore Barry's minor negative behavior and attend selectively to his positive behavior (e.g., "I'll explain this when you're ready to listen; if you whine, I won't be able to show you how to do it"). Barry's therapy was relatively simple, straightforward, and brief.

The attention-seeking, pestering quality of Barry's behavior became more prominent during his time with his father, who was unable to keep up with the boy's increasing demands. One weakness of reinforcement-based interventions is that they are situation-specific; their effects do not reliably transfer to other settings. Barry's father was not willing to take part in the therapy described here, so services ended with an open-ended invitation to the father to participate in his son's behavior therapy at any future time of his choosing.

3

Cognitive Therapy

OBJECTIVES

This chapter explains:

- *Interrelationships among situations, thoughts, feelings, and behaviors.*
- *How to help clients change their feelings by changing their thoughts.*
- *Self-monitoring with daily thought records.*
- *Scripted self-instructions that guide clients through difficult situations.*
- *How self-reinforcement provides people with independence from environmental consequences.*
- *How Socratic questioning helps clients come to adaptive conclusions on their own.*
- *A procedure for helping clients evaluate the evidence for and against their beliefs.*
- *How clients can test their beliefs by conducting personal experiments.*
- *How to use 10-point scales as visual tools to treat problems based on dichotomous thinking, including perfectionism.*

Case Study
Nothing Without Her

Vance was a 16-year-old European American male whose parents brought him to therapy because of depression, low self-esteem, and expressions of hopelessness about his life. There was a clear precipitating event: His girlfriend of the previous 6 months had recently broken up with him. He seemed crushed by this loss and very sad. He made negative statements about himself and was apathetic about activities he had formerly enjoyed. The therapist made a diagnosis of adjustment disorder with depressed mood.

Vance described his life prior to meeting his girlfriend, Kelsey, as "nothing awful, but nothing special either; I was just existing." Objectively, Vance did well in many areas of his life. He was a responsible adolescent who got along well with his parents, younger brother, and friends. He earned mostly Bs in school and was on the junior varsity basketball team. However, he took no pride in these accomplishments, saying that anyone can get Bs and, because he was not in the starting lineup, his basketball skills were nothing to be proud of.

His first serious romantic relationship had a dramatic impact on Vance. Kelsey made life seem special, and his everyday experiences became important because he talked about them with her. When she ended the relationship, he felt that nothing of value remained in his life.

Cognitive Theory

The Latin root of the word *cognition* means *to know*. Cognition includes all of the psychological processes with which people attempt to know the world and the self. These processes include sensation, perception, learning, memory, interpretation, reasoning, and belief. Cognitive therapy focuses on people's thinking and the effects of their thoughts on their emotions and behavior.

Cognitive therapy was originated by clinicians who were trained in psychoanalysis but rebelled against it, with Albert Ellis (1962, 1973) and Aaron Beck (1967, 1976) as the most important pioneers. In the course of their work with clients, these therapists came to believe that the elaborate mental structures and hidden processes postulated by psychoanalysis were less important to treatment than the thoughts occurring in their clients' minds.

Historically, behavior therapy and cognitive therapy originated quite independently, and for a while there was considerable debate between adherents of these two theoretical orientations. In time, however, the two approaches converged to a point approaching merger—hence the term *cognitive-behavioral therapy*, or CBT. Most therapists who use one approach also practice the other. There are meaningful differences between focusing on overt, observable behaviors and focusing on private thoughts, but the rapprochement was made possible by cognitive researchers and clinicians who found ways to make thoughts observable by operationally defining them with standardized instruments and identifiable structures of words. With these methodological advances, cognitions could be measured, the scientific standards of behaviorists were met, and the synthesis took place.

There is a general consensus that the differences between behavioral and cognitive techniques are complementary, not incompatible. Most EBPs are combinations of cognitive and behavioral techniques packaged in one treatment manual.

The Core Idea: Thoughts Affect Feelings

Cognitive therapy began when Ellis (1962, 1973) noted that people's emotional reactions to events were determined less by the objective nature of what happened than by the person's beliefs about the meaning of the event. Ellis found that if therapy produced change in clients' thinking about their situations, their emotions and behavior would usually change, too.

People are made happy and sad not by the objective nature of events but by the meanings they perceive in events.

Cognitive therapy has ancient roots. Ellis identified a philosophical foundation for his understanding of the relationships among events, thoughts, and emotions in the ancient Roman philosophy of **Stoicism**, which stated that people are made happy and sad not by the objective nature of events but by the meanings they perceive in events.

Ellis's theory can be summarized—for clients as well as professionals—by the principle he called **the ABCs of emotion**, as diagrammed in Figure 3.1.

Figure 3.1   The ABCs of emotion.

This diagram presents two ideas. The solid line depicts what Ellis considered to be the truth about the origin of emotion: Antecedent events occur first, they stimulate thoughts and beliefs, and then the beliefs cause emotional consequences. In other words, the relationship between events and emotions is **mediated** by beliefs: Beliefs provide the causal bridge that determines how antecedent events cause emotional consequences. The dotted line in the diagram depicts what Ellis considered the most common misconception about emotions—namely, the idea that events, by themselves, cause emotional responses.

Ellis believed that learning the truth about the ABCs of emotion helps people overcome mental health problems and live more successfully. His therapeutic approach, called **rational emotive therapy** (RET), is based on the idea that psychological disturbances are caused by *irrational thinking* and, therefore, treatment that strengthens the rationality of clients' thinking will lead to the resolution of their disturbances. When Ellis joined the cognitive-behavioral convergence, he changed the name of his therapy to **rational emotive behavior therapy** (REBT; Ellis, 2001; Ellis & MacLaren, 2005), and a new emphasis on behavior was added to the original emphasis on rational thinking.

Cognitive therapy is based on the idea that human life is largely *interpretive*: Events have different emotional effects on different people, depending on how they interpret the events. Now, the plausible interpretations of an event or situation typically do not range from good to bad; cognitions usually cannot reverse the emotional valence of events. However, thoughts can modify the intensity of people's reactions by changing the degree of good or bad perceived in an event or situation, and such modifications have important effects on mental health. For example, the difference between nondepressed and depressed people often lies in whether they interpret negative events as unfortunate or disastrous. Therapy is not a cure for the disappointments, failures, and losses that are an inevitable part of life, but counseling can help people cope with the negative events that occur. Typically, the objective of cognitive therapy is to change the client's understanding of her situation from extremely, completely, and hopelessly bad to mildly, partially, manageably, and temporarily bad.

In the years since Ellis's and Beck's original formulations, cognitive therapists have gained a greater appreciation of the complex processes linking thoughts and feelings, and this relationship is no longer viewed as unidirectional. The **content specificity hypothesis** states that there are specific associations between emotions and cognitions—for example, people generally do not have depressed feelings and happy thoughts at the same time—but the hypothesis is open regarding the direction of causality (Beck & Alford, 2009; Lamberton & Oei, 2008; Schniering & Rapee, 2004). Current formulations of cognitive theory and therapy (Beck & Haigh, 2014; Dobson, 2014; Hofmann, Asmundson, & Beck, 2013) describe multidirectional influences among the physiological, emotional, cognitive, and behavioral dimensions of functioning. All four dimensions are viewed as capable of influencing all the others. Feelings can affect thoughts as well as the other way around, and behavior can influence physiology, physiology can affect thinking, and so forth. As a result, treatment-induced change in any of the levels can lead to improved functioning in the other three.

The Structure of Cognition

According to cognitive theory, cognitions are structured in hierarchical levels (Beck, 2008; Dobson & Dobson, 2009; Hofmann et al., 2013; Padesky, 1994), as arranged in Figure 3.2. Starting at the surface of experience and working our way down, there are three levels of cognition, as follows:

1. **Self-talk** or **automatic thoughts** are the running commentary that goes through our minds from moment to moment in a habitual, unexamined way. Automatic thoughts can involve visual images as well as words. Vance often had the automatic thought, "I just can't be happy without Kelsey."
2. **Intermediate beliefs** are the general rules, attitudes, and assumptions that structure our responses to events. We articulate these when asked about our beliefs. Vance had the intermediate belief, "I don't think I'll ever have another girlfriend as good as Kelsey."
3. **Schemas** or **core beliefs** are deep-level cognitions concerning our most basic sense of ourselves and other people. Schemas cannot be articulated without reflection and effort because they seem self-evidently "the way things are." After some time in therapy, Vance articulated a core belief that he was a mediocre person, so no wonderful girl would want to be with him.

When events occur, we are generally aware only of our automatic thoughts, but schemas operate on a deeper level to structure the patterns of our self-talk, so related situations tend to elicit similar automatic thoughts. Schemas simplify people's interpretations of their experiences by fitting them into preexisting patterns and categories, in a process called **assimilation**. Schemas are like molds of certain shapes, and assimilation squeezes the data of experience into these molds, even if the data have to be reshaped to make them fit. Assimilation helps people manage the complexity of life, but at the expense of losing some information when interpreting new experiences.

There are important individual differences in the process of assimilation. If people's schemas are fairly accurate models of reality, new experiences require little shaping to fit into them, and experiences are perceived in a realistic fashion. If core beliefs are inaccurate

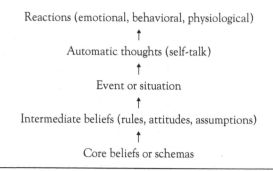

Figure 3.2   Hierarchical structure of cognitions in reaction to events.

representations of reality, experiences must be distorted in order to fit, and the person's interpretations of personal events and situations are more a function of her schemas than of what actually happens.

Automatic thoughts are conscious or preconscious; people are aware of them, or they can become aware of them just by paying some attention. It takes a little more self-reflection to verbalize intermediate beliefs, but it is not difficult to do so. Under typical conditions, schemas are unconscious, and people do not articulate them. Thus, conscious self-talk derives from unconscious schemas. However, the division between conscious and unconscious cognition is not absolute. Concerted introspection can make schemas accessible to the conscious mind, and cognitive therapy aims to achieve this. (The concept of the unconscious in cognitive therapy is partly similar and partly different from the concept of the unconscious in psychodynamic therapy, which is explained in Chapter 5.)

Moderation as a Balance Between Extremes

In ancient times, several major philosophers and religious leaders, living in separate cultures and with no knowledge of each other, developed the idea that optimal human functioning generally involves a moderate balance between two opposite extremes. In ancient Greece, Aristotle coined the term **Golden Mean** to summarize this idea; in India, Buddha used the term **Middle Way**; and in China, Confucius espoused his **Doctrine of the Mean**. These are different terms for the same idea: Adaptive functioning is generally moderate and balanced, and maladaptive behavior typically involves extremes, including opposite extremes.

This principle has appeared in the psychotherapy field in several forms, including the concept of assertiveness as a midpoint between passivity and aggression, described in Chapter 12. The cognitive therapy literature includes the related idea that black-and-white thinking is dysfunctional and adaptive cognition attends to shades of gray (J. S. Beck, 2011; Burns & Beck, 1980; Egan, Pieka, Dyck, & Rees, 2007; Oshio, 2009). Dialectical behavior therapy, described in the next chapter, includes the idea of integrating opposite extremes into a balanced synthesis. I think the moderation principle has a great deal of additional potential as a conceptual and therapeutic tool, as explained further on. My analysis and recommendations build on the foregoing sources, but my formulation is based largely on clinical experience, so it awaits empirical investigation.

Aristotle taught that moderation is the key to virtue. In his Nicomachean Ethics (translated by Sachs, 2002), he analyzed virtue and vice by identifying quantitative (ordinal) relationships among words used to describe opposite extremes and midpoints on dimensions of behavior. For instance, he conceptualized courage as the adaptive midpoint between the two maladaptive extremes of cowardice and recklessness. As another example, miserliness is a negative quality, and so is its opposite, wastefulness, while the quality lying in between, thrift, is positive.

The principle of adaptive moderation applies to a wide variety of psychological characteristics but not to all of them. This principle does not pertain to aptitudes, capabilities, and talents, or to characteristics that are positive by definition, such as health and well-being. These qualities are desirable in a simple, linear way—the more, the better—while the moderation principle posits a curvilinear (inverted U-shaped) relationship between adaptive value and the dimension in question (e.g., risk taking, spending vs. saving). The principle applies to *styles* of cognition, personality, and behavior that have subjective valences. People have different stylistic preferences—but their preferences are not all equally adaptive.

Scaling Dimensions of Functioning. Opposite extremes and moderate middles can be represented as points on a scale that depicts a personality-related dimension of functioning. Cognitive-behavioral therapists have used a technique called **scaling the problem** to help clients decatastrophize negative events by thinking of them in quantitative terms (Spirito & Esposito, 2008; Spirito, Esposito-Smythers, Wolff, & Uhl, 2011); this technique is described in Chapter 13 on anxiety. In the strategy described here, 10-point scales are used in a different way. The issue is not how bad something is; instead, the scales are used to depict styles of functioning. Also, the scales are used as visual tools, on paper or screens. This technique supplements verbal reasoning with a diagrammatic way of presenting material, which is helpful for many young clients (Stallard, 2002). Here are three examples of personality-related dimensions diagrammed on scales.

Many mental health problems can be conceptualized as points close to the poles of scales like these. Many adaptive cognitive and behavioral styles can be represented as midpoints on these spectra.

These 10-point scales help clients think about their difficulties in a constructive way by locating their personal style within the range of possible styles on the dimension in question. As elaborated later, these scales equip counselors to provide several forms of help, including:

- Replacing dichotomous choice with quantitative calibration and the possibility of synthesis
- Acknowledging the benefits of the client's existing style while pointing out its costs
- Pointing out the benefits of the rejected style while acknowledging its costs
- Portraying recommended changes as relatively small and feasible

This type of visual tool is well suited to assessing and treating black-and-white thinking. The diagrams, by their design, help clients see how they could replace dichotomous choices with the possibility of optimal balances or syntheses.

What Causes Mental Health Problems?

From a cognitive perspective, mental health problems are caused by maladaptive automatic thoughts, rules, attitudes, assumptions, and, at the deepest level, maladaptive schemas, which result in misinterpretations of events, irrational beliefs, and failures to see the world and the self in a realistic, adaptive fashion (Beck & Emery, 2005; Dobson & Dobson, 2009; Ellis, 2001; Kuyken, Padesky, & Dudley, 2009; Padesky & Greenberger, 1995). Psychopathology is associated with cognitive **biases**. Depressed people are biased toward self-blame and pessimism; anxious people are biased toward the perception of threat; aggressive individuals are biased toward seeing others as hostile, and so forth.

Maladaptive schemas are assumed to originate during childhood and to result from early, emotionally potent experiences (Beck, 2008; Padesky, 1994; Young, Klosko, & Weishaar, 2003). It is also considered likely that genetic factors play a role in the formation of schemas. Like behavior therapists, cognitive clinicians are not very interested in figuring out the origins of mental health problems, first because it is usually not possible and second because it is generally not necessary—problems can be solved by effectively addressing the factors maintaining them in the present.

When core beliefs are unrealistic, perceptions of ongoing events and situations will frequently be distorted, because information that does not fit a schema cannot be assimilated. The person's perceptions are so dominated by the effects of her past experiences that she cannot see new events and situations for what they are. This is the cognitive version of the behavioral principle introduced in the previous chapter: When old learning is applied to situations different from the ones in which it originated, the resulting mismatch between internal model and external reality is likely to produce maladaptive functioning.

The moderation principle implies that extreme forms of functioning are likely to be maladaptive, and there is evidence for this idea in findings that black-and-white thinking is associated with maladjustment (J. S. Beck, 2011; Burns & Beck, 1980; Egan et al., 2007; Oshio, 2009). Clinical observation and reasoning provide more support. When personality-related styles are conceptualized on continua, both sides involve advantages, both involve disadvantages, and optimally adaptive syntheses are located in the middle of the spectrum.

Given that youth are more likely than adults to think in a black-and-white fashion (Spritz & Sandberg, 2010) and that this form of thinking is associated with maladjustment, dichotomous thinking is probably an issue for many child and adolescent therapy clients. These young people often simplify continua into dichotomies and see their desired or valued style (not necessarily their self-perceived one) as located in one half. Therapists can understand clients' cognitive distortions on a deep level by figuring out how their dichotomies map onto the relevant continua. The question is: Where does the client dichotomize the spectrum? It is not usually at the midpoint, as explained next.

Here is a spectrum concerning an issue of importance for many young people: the trade-off between schoolwork and recreation.

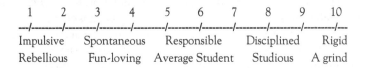

For people whose styles are located at an extreme, the perceived dividing line between the dichotomy's valued and disvalued halves is not usually at the midpoint as perceived by well-adjusted people who function in the middle of the spectrum. Instead, their cut-point is usually close to the pole where their desired style is located. Thus, clients divide these dimensions into two unequal halves—a small one, skewed to their desired side, which is viewed positively, and a large one, making up most of the continuum, which is viewed negatively. For example, impulsive, rebellious youth might perceive points 1–3 as representing cool kids and points 4–10 as representing goody-goodies, while rigidly disciplined youth might see points 8–10 as corresponding to good students and points 1–7 as representing lazy kids. A youngster in the middle of the spectrum might be perceived as a nerd by school-rejecting peers and a slacker by perfectionistic ones.

Clients seem biased toward perceiving behaviors on the other side of their cut-point as more extreme than they really are—as, in a sense, pushed toward the pole opposite the one they desire. Thus, clients at the 9-position would tend to perceive behaviors in the 1–5 range as skewed toward 1, and clients at the 2-position would tend to perceive behaviors in the 6–10 range as skewed toward 10. This may be one reason why clients often resist adults' suggestions for more moderate behaviors. For example, if a therapist suggested to a school-rejecting youth that he could do 40 minutes of homework a day and still have lots of time for fun, he might respond as if the clinician suggested he become a boring grind. As an example concerning a different dimension, an emotionally guarded youth might experience even mild expression of feelings as embarrassing, while a flamboyantly emotional youth might view any degree of reserve as inhibited and standoffish. (This phenomenon is striking in the political arena, where conservatives tend to see liberals as extremely liberal or "socialist," and liberals tend to see conservatives as extremely conservative or "reactionary," which often results in both sides distorting the other's views into caricatured extremes that imply malevolent intentions [Shapiro, 2011].)

Dichotomizing continua in this asymmetric way has a serious ramification: The moderate middle, where adaptive functioning is located, falls into the half of the client's dichotomy that he wants to avoid. In this type of cognitive distortion, regardless of whether the adaptive middle is viewed from the extreme left or the extreme right, it looks unappealing and is likely to be rejected.

In addition to producing extreme styles of functioning, dichotomous thinking leads to distorted interpretations of events. One important example occurs in perfectionism—a personality trait with two semi-independent factors. Perfectionist *striving* is a motivational phenomenon that involves efforts to achieve excellence and is not associated with psychopathology, while perfectionistic *concern* is a cognitive phenomenon that involves unrealistically high standards for self-evaluation and is associated with maladjustment, especially internalizing problems (Rice, Ashby, & Gilman, 2011; Stoeber & Childs, 2010). Clinical discussions of perfectionism generally refer to the cognitive, maladaptive type, which is characterized by dichotomous thinking that recognizes only two categories of performance: perfect and inadequate (Egan et al., 2007). The dichotomy's cut-point is so close to the end of the spectrum that almost all performances are categorized as failures.

As the example of perfectionism illustrates, this formulation is not only about the way clients see themselves; it is also about the way they want to be. It is clients' desired or valued styles of functioning, not necessarily their self-perceived styles, that are located close to the poles of continua. Sometimes desired and self-perceived styles are similar—this is often the case in conduct disturbance—and sometimes they are dissimilar—this is often the case in low self-esteem. In both cases, pursuing an unbalanced style of functioning is likely to result in maladjustment.

Assessment and Case Formulation

Assessment in cognitive therapy is a two-step process. First, there needs to be a general, descriptive assessment of the child's mental health problems and functioning. Then, clinicians can investigate the client's thinking in search of cognitive factors playing a role in his disturbance.

The *Beck Youth Inventories of Emotional and Social Impairment* (BYI; J. S. Beck, Beck, & Jolly, 2001) are grounded in cognitive theory and DSM criteria. These measures have well-established reliability, validity, and normative information for youth from 7 to 18 years of age. There are inventories for depression, anxiety, anger, disruptive behavior, and self-concept.

Questions to Ask

A note on wording: Cognitive therapists sometimes refer to "thoughts" with clients, but because this word has an intellectual or objective quality, these counselors usually prefer the phrase "going through your mind" as a more inclusive way to refer to mental activity. Thus, questions like, "What did you think when she said that?" tend to pull for conceptualization, while questions like, "What went through your mind when she said that?" elicit a broader range of responses that includes analysis but also includes simpler, gut-level reactions (Beck & Alford, 2009; J. S. Beck, 2011; Leahy, Holland, & McGinn, 2011). Thus, in cognitive assessment, the staple question for clients is:

"What goes through your mind when _____ (the presenting problem) happens?"

Or:

"What goes through your mind when you feel _____ (e.g., depressed)?"

This question should be applied to a number of instances of the problematic emotions or behaviors. There should be questions about cognitions occurring before, during, and after the problems. These sequences sometimes suggest patterns that contribute to the client's disturbance.

It is important to investigate the events and situations that elicit dysfunctional thoughts and feelings. For example, Vance experienced feelings of shame and hopelessness when he saw Kelsey at school. These emotions were accompanied by cognitions like, "There must be something wrong with me to be rejected by someone so nice," and "The other girls around here don't compare to Kelsey."

The next step is to investigate cognitive processes by asking follow-up questions. These questions should address the structure and content of the client's cognitions—that is, their logical form, degree of realism, biases, and assumptions. The goal is to discover how the child evaluates himself, explains past events, and forms expectations of the future. Table 3.1 presents a number of questions that are useful in cognitive assessment.

More specific lines of follow-up questioning will depend on the client's presenting problems. Because depression is characterized by a negative bias toward the self (Beck, 1967, 1976; O'Connor, Berry, & Weiss, 1999; Tilghman-Osborne, Cole, & Felton, 2012), its assessment should focus on how the client processes self-evaluative information—for example, scores on tests, performances in athletic contests, and peer reactions to the client. The question is whether the client is *fair* to herself in the way she translates concrete facts into evaluative judgments. For example, is a B- a good grade or a bad grade? Is one hit in four at-bats an adequate or inadequate performance in baseball? Another question is whether the child selectively focuses on her strengths or weaknesses. Depressed children may talk at length about tests on which they did poorly but forget

Table 3.1   Questions for Assessing Client Cognitions

"What do you make of this? What does it mean about you?"

"Why do you think _____ happens?" "How do you explain it?"

"What are your reasons for believing this?" "What is the evidence for this belief about yourself? What is the evidence against this belief?"

"Do you think this is the only way to look at what happened?" "Would everyone look at it this way?" "What is another way someone could look at this?"

"Where did you learn this belief? When did you learn it?" "Who taught you this way of looking at things?"

"How does this belief make you feel?" "How could another way of looking at this situation make you feel?"

"What are the advantages (or good things, pluses) of looking at things this way? What are the disadvantages (or bad things, minuses)?"

to mention the As and Bs they achieved. Obtaining a view of the client's performance from an external observer, such as a parent or teacher, may reveal biases in her self-evaluations.

Aggressive youngsters tend to exhibit the opposite cognitive bias: While depressed clients are unfair to themselves, the thinking of aggressive youth is often unfair to other people (de Castro, Veerman, Koops, Bosch, & Monshouwer, 2002; Dodge & Coie, 1987; Lochman & Wells, 2002). Assessment of aggression should focus on how the client thinks about conflicts between himself and others, with one question being whether he perceives others in an unbiased fashion or misinterprets information about people in a way that justifies aggression toward them. It is useful to ask the client about his overall view of peers and people in general. Describing others as inferior, exploitative, or hostile is of concern, because these views justify treating others disrespectfully and aggressively.

Anxiety is a future-oriented emotion: Anxious clients are worried about what *might* happen. The cognitions underlying anxiety can be assessed by questions about the perceived likelihood and magnitude of negative events, with inquiry into the evidence that justifies these expectations (Beck & Emery, 2005; Cannon & Weems, 2010; Taghavi, Moradi, Neshat-Doost, Yule, & Dalgleish, 2000). Therapists should ask the client about her sources of information, including past experiences, observation, and input from other people.

Counselors can use the hierarchical model of cognitions to organize their assessment efforts. This model implies a sequence of inquiry, with movement from the surface to the core of the client's cognitions. In other words, we can begin by sifting through the raw data of the client's automatic thoughts and responses to everyday situations. The search should be for recurring patterns and unifying themes that point toward intermediate beliefs. As therapy proceeds, and we continue to organize the concrete and particular into the abstract and general, we should eventually be able to identify the small number of core schemas that structure the child's interpretations of events.

Clinicians can use diagrams of 10-point scales to investigate client cognitions. A technical note: The scale's left pole should be designated with a 1, not a zero. Zero indicates the absence of a quality, while the purpose of these scales is to represent *opposite* qualities, not more or less of a single one.

The first step in using these continua is conceptual: Therapists need to identify the dimension most relevant to the client's disturbance. Dimensions are defined by their poles—that is, by the opposite extremes that are their endpoints. When this conceptual task is done, you can sketch a 10-point scale (or use a copy), label the 1-point and 10-point, present it to the client with an explanation, and begin a discussion. One question is, what is the midpoint? It is also useful to flesh out the two intermediate regions between the midpoint and the poles.

Then, ask the client to mark where he sees himself on the scale. If the youth pauses to decide between two adjacent scale-points, suggest he mark a spot in between and use a fraction or decimal to place himself on the spectrum.

Patterns to Look For

Cognitive therapists search for patterns and connections among events, thoughts, emotions, and behavior (Ellis, 2001; Hofmann et al., 2013; Kuyken et al., 2009; Leahy et al., 2011). The clinician's job is to conceptualize these patterns—that is, to translate the child's experiences into the theoretical terms of cognitive therapy. The question for case conceptualization is: What are the thoughts underlying the client's presenting problems?

This formulation suggests an aspect of what it means to "understand" someone: It means to identify the internal picture of self and situation in response to which the person's feelings and actions make sense. If you find yourself confused by a client's emotions or behavior, it may be useful to ask yourself what perceptions and beliefs would generate such feelings and actions.

If you find yourself confused by a client's emotions or behavior, it may be useful to ask yourself what perceptions and beliefs would generate such feelings and actions.

If a client's thoughts and feelings seem incongruent with each other, one possibility is that he is mislabeling his emotions—for instance, feeling sad but calling that feeling "mad." Another possibility is that the child might not have disclosed the most emotionally potent thought occurring in reaction to the event in question. For example, one 13-year-old girl who seemed quite sad after a school dance explained her feeling by saying, "It wasn't any fun." The counselor assumed that more negative thoughts must have occurred or the girl would not be so downhearted, and the inquiry continued, eventually revealing the thought below the sadness. ("No one danced with me, so I must be ugly.")

The schemas underlying and structuring automatic thoughts are of central concern to cognitive assessment. Schemas can usually be verbalized as simple, powerful statements about the self and world (e.g., "I will be loved only if I hide my anger," and "People will push you around if you don't push them around first"). When core beliefs are distilled from the raw data of the client's automatic thoughts and reactions, the direction of therapy usually becomes clear.

Cognitive distortions occur in many variations, but these errors tend to take a relatively small number of basic forms. Table 3.2 presents some of these forms, based on descriptions by J. S. Beck (2011).

As suggested by its number one position in the foregoing list, dichotomous thinking seems to be a particularly important characteristic of much maladaptive cognition (J. S. Beck, 2011; Burns & Beck, 1980; Egan et al., 2007; Oshio, 2009).

Table 3.2   Examples of Common Cognitive Distortions

1. *All-or-nothing thinking* (also called black-and-white, polarized, and dichotomous thinking): The person thinks in terms of only two, opposite categories, rather than a continuum.

   Example: "If I'm not a total success, I'm a failure."

2. *Catastrophizing*: The person expects disastrous events to occur in the future, without considering other, more likely outcomes.

   Example: "The kids in my new school will all hate me."

3. *Disqualifying or discounting the positive*: The person tells himself that positive incidents, actions, and qualities do not count.

   Example: "I did that project well, but it doesn't mean I'm competent; I just got lucky."

4. *Mental filter* (or selective abstraction): The person focuses on one negative detail instead of the whole picture.

   Example: "Because I got one bad grade, I'm a lousy student."

5. *Overgeneralization*: The person makes a sweeping negative conclusion that goes far beyond the current facts.

   Example: "Because I felt uncomfortable at the party, I don't have what it takes to make friends."

6. *Tunnel vision*: The person sees only the negative aspects of a situation.

   Example: "My teacher is horrible. He's mean and he doesn't know what he's doing."

Source: Adapted from *Cognitive Therapy: Basics and Beyond* (2nd ed.), by J. S. Beck, 2011, New York, NY: Guilford Press.

Dichotomous thinking often causes extreme reactions, because the moderate, nuanced middle is missing from the person's interpretations of events.

Sometimes, clients' maladaptive cognitions can be understood in terms of one or two key dichotomies. Vance thought of personal success—in academics, basketball, romance, and so forth—in all-or-none terms. As a result, he viewed getting Bs, being second-string on the team, and getting rejected by one girl as moving him from the success category into the failure category.

Change Processes

The primary strategy of cognitive therapy is to test the accuracy, validity, and utility of the client's beliefs (Beck & Alford, 2009; J. S. Beck, 2011; Dobson & Dobson, 2009; Ellis & MacLaren, 2005; Leahy et al., 2011). There are many different techniques, but cognitive therapy involves a single, fundamental change agent: modifying the cognitions underlying the client's emotional and/or behavioral problems.

Although it misses some of the complexities of cognitive science, Ellis's (1962, 1973) A-B-C paradigm provides a simple framework that captures the heart of the matter and can be used with young clients. Even if antecedent events and external situations remain the same, interventions that create positive change in client beliefs usually result in improved emotion and behavior. Cognitive therapy focuses on the B segment of Ellis's model and attempts to change the thoughts occurring in between events and emotional consequences.

Cognitive processes include both conceptual thinking and specific, concrete thoughts, and there are different interventions for these two types of cognition. In **scripted** interventions, the therapist and client develop set formulae of words or visual images, and the child memorizes these self-statements (or "mantras") so she can say them to herself in problematic situations (Kendall & Hedtke, 2006a, 2006b; Loades, Clark, & Reynolds, 2014). For example, anxious clients might learn a self-statement like, "Stay calm and you'll get through this," and aggressive children might employ a self-statement like, "Use your words, not your fists." In **conceptual** work, the therapist teaches the client more complex, general strategies for analyzing situations, interpreting evidence, and drawing conclusions (Bernard & Joyce, 1984; Gregory, 2011; Young et al., 2003). Conceptual skills include evaluating the evidence for and against a belief, seeking out information beyond what is immediately available, thinking of possible alternative explanations for the event in question, and testing hypotheses by conducting little experiments in the natural environment.

Thus, scripted techniques change the content of thought, and conceptual techniques change the form of thought. Scripted work can be viewed as a top-down approach in that it intervenes on the surface of cognition, with the expectation that changing the client's everyday self-talk will lead to modification of his underlying schemas. Conceptual work can be viewed as a bottom-up approach, with the expectation that evaluation of the evidence bearing on a core belief can change that schema, which then will change the internal commentary in the client's moment-to-moment experience of everyday life.

Typically, scripted interventions are more appropriate for younger children whose thinking is relatively concrete, while conceptual techniques are more appropriate for older clients who think abstractly. Often, client needs are best met by a combination of the two types of intervention.

The spectrum method combines abstract and concrete features. Conceptualizing problems as extremes and solutions as balanced syntheses is an exercise in abstract thinking, but the method also provides visual cues and behavioral examples to concretize the model for clients. These diagrams combine words, numbers, and a spatial analogy in a multimodal strategy for building comprehension of the shades of gray that lie between black and white.

If psychopathology is a matter of extremes, different clients need to move in different directions, depending on which end of the spectrum was their starting point. Thus, clinicians try to help rigid youngsters loosen up and relax, and they try to help impulsive clients become more controlled and disciplined. To approach the Golden Mean, internalizing youngsters need to become easier on themselves, and externalizing youth need to become stricter with themselves.

An affirming implication of this formulation, and one stated explicitly by Aristotle, is that maladaptive functioning can be framed as too much of a good thing. Therapists can often portray the client's problems as an excess of a quality that, in moderation, is positive. Weaknesses emerge as strengths that have gone too far.

Outcome Research

Overall, cognitive therapy has received substantial support from outcome research. The APA Society of Clinical Psychology rated cognitive therapy as having *Strong Research Support* (the highest rating) as a treatment for depression in adults. APA rated REBT as having *Modest Research Support* (the second highest rating) for this population.

However, any presentation of outcome research on cognitive therapy is complicated by its convergence with behavior therapy in CBT. In outcome studies, cognitive techniques are not generally provided alone but are combined with behavioral strategies in packages of techniques, which makes it difficult to isolate the effects of the cognitive techniques. Even when interventions are labeled as cognitive therapy, they usually include behavioral components. For instance, in APA's description of the "cognitive therapy" rated as strongly supported by research, there is a statement that this intervention includes behavioral techniques such as activity scheduling. Such interventions would be more accurately labeled as CBT (and they usually are).

As a result of this entanglement, researchers generally have been able to assess the effects of cognitive techniques only by using complex, indirect methods. Research with adult clients has provided some support for the theory on which cognitive therapy is based, although the results have not been consistent. Tang and DeRubeis (1999) observed that the "sudden gains" clients sometimes make in therapy are often preceded by cognitive changes, as if clients grasp the role of negative thinking in their depression and then quickly feel better. Hofmann et al. (2007) found that improvement in panic disorder was partly mediated by reduced catastrophic cognitions, especially thoughts about physical symptoms, in clients who received CBT but not clients treated with medication. In another study of panic disorder, Clark et al. (1994) found that the clients who had the fewest catastrophic cognitions at the end of therapy were least likely to relapse. Strunk, DeRubeis, Chiu, and Alvarez (2007) found that depressed clients who achieved competence in the cognitive skills taught in therapy were less likely to relapse following termination, compared to clients who did not learn these skills well. Crits-Christoph, Gibbons, and Mukhefjee (2013) reviewed a complicated set of results from research on cognitive therapy for depression in adults and identified evidence that treatment works by changing depressive cognitions, but they also noted that some studies failed to find this effect. Also, dismantling studies and components analyses have not generally found that cognitive techniques added significant benefit to what was achieved by behavioral strategies, such as behavioral activation or exposure, alone (Hayes, 2004; Longmore & Worrell, 2007).

Research on the mediation of treatment effects in young clients has suggested that cognitive therapy produced changes in beliefs, automatic thoughts, and cognitive coping skills, and that these changes were associated with symptom reduction, although again there have been some inconsistent results. A mediation analysis by Hogendoorn et al. (2014) found that decreases in young people's anxiety symptoms were preceded by changes in five cognitive processes taught by therapists: problem solving, cognitive restructuring, seeking distraction, perceiving control, and positive thoughts. Several studies have found that decreases in anxious self-statements mediate reductions in anxiety symptoms (Kendall & Treadwell, 2007; Lau et al., 2010; Treadwell & Kendall, 1996). Two studies found that reductions in depressive symptoms were associated with the adaptive changes in attribution patterns predicted by cognitive theory (Jaycox, Reivich, Gilham, & Seligman, 1994; Yu & Seligman, 2002). Studies of nonattributional negative beliefs as mediators of change in young people's depression have obtained some predicted results but a number of inconsistent findings (Ackerson, Scogin, McKendree-Smith, & Lyman, 1998; Kaufman et al., 2005; Stice et al., 2010). In research on CBT for aggression, a mediation analysis by Lochman and Wells (2002) indicated that cognitive processes played a role in the intervention's effects: Reduction in aggression was partly mediated by decreases in hostile attributions and reduced belief in the instrumental utility of violence. Studies by Guerra and Slaby (1990) and Larson and Gerber (1987) showed that the positive effects of CBT on aggressive behavior in adolescents were partly mediated by improved problem-solving skills.

There is one important exception to the typical combining of cognitive techniques with behavioral strategies in outcome studies. *Problem-solving skills training* (PSST; Kazdin, 2003, 2010; Shure, 1996) is a cognitive intervention that is often implemented alone. PSST is not an intervention like Beck's or Ellis's—it does not focus on self-talk or evaluation of beliefs—but it is cognitive in nature: PSST teaches children simple, practical formulas for thinking through problems, generating response options, anticipating consequences, and choosing what to do in challenging situations. PSST is typically used as a therapy for disruptive behavior problems and aggression in young people, and the outcome research on this intervention is reviewed in Chapters 10 and 12. In brief, PSST has received considerable empirical support as a therapy for these problems, as indicated, for example, by Sukhodolsky, Kassinove, and Gorman's (2004) meta-analysis, which obtained a medium/large effect size of .67. Overall, evidence for the independent effects of problem-solving work (without behavioral components) on externalizing problems is more consistent than evidence for the independent effects of general cognitive therapy on internalizing problems.

Among the general public, there is a view that although therapeutic conversations may be helpful to clients, psychotropic medications are a more serious, powerful treatment for the biological disturbances in brain functioning that are sometimes the root cause of mental health problems. This view is incorrect. Neurobiological research using fMRI, PET scan, and other brain imaging technologies has produced abundant evidence that cognitive-behavioral therapies change brain structures that mediate affective regulation, problem solving, and self-referential cognition (Hofmann et al., 2013). CBT for anxiety changed functioning in prefrontal, anterior cingulate, and insular areas of the cortex that mediate responses to threat; the changes suggested increased cortical control over limbic system activity, resulting in decreased emotional reactivity and improved problem solving (Hofmann, Ellard, & Siegle, 2012; Ochsner & Gross, 2008). Frewen, Dozois, and Lanius (2008) showed that CBT changed left dorsolateral prefrontal cortex functioning in ways that are associated with improved problem solving in stressful situations. Ochsner and Gross (2005) found that CBT resulted in changes in the anterior cingulate cortex and other cortical areas involved in the regulation of emotions. Northoff et al. (2006) showed that CBT changed the functioning of cortical midline structures that mediate self-referential thinking. Our words change clients' brains.

> *Cognitive-behavioral therapies change brain structures that mediate affective regulation, problem solving, and self-referential cognition.*

Most outcome research on CBT is disorder-specific. This research is reviewed in the diagnosis-based chapters making up the second half of this book.

The Therapist's Style

Cognitive therapists vary a great deal in how directive their styles are. Ellis (1962, 1973, 2001) used a direct, argumentative style, confronting the client's logical errors and debating his maladaptive beliefs using reason and evidence. Clinicians using this style sometimes sound more like lawyers arguing a case than typical therapists, although their intention is to defend the client against her own negative thoughts. On the other hand, Overholser (1993, 2010, 2013) argues that Socratic questioning (described later), a nondirective method, is the most effective way to engender new thinking in clients. Clinicians following Beck's model (1967, 1976; A. T. Beck & Alford, 2009; A. T. Beck & Emery, 2005) have a gentler style than Ellis's. They focus on reason and evidence, but, rather than engaging in debate, they use the Socratic method, gather information, and think along with their clients. These therapists try to stimulate the client's own thinking while steering him in adaptive directions, make tentative suggestions for new cognitions and ask clients to assess their usefulness, and propose behavioral experiments for the client to perform, with the results of these experiments furnishing the basis for new cognitions. Currently, Beck's style seems to be much more widely used than Ellis's.

Beck's approach is based on **collaborative empiricism**: The client and therapist, in a cooperative working relationship, evaluate the validity and utility of beliefs by comparing them to observations and evidence from everyday life. Beliefs are viewed as hypotheses to be tested against data. Proposed changes are set up as experiments: If a strategy works, it is supported, and if not, it is discarded.

Beck's model describes the process of assessing beliefs as **guided discovery**. The *discovery* half of this term means that the youth does her own thinking and draws her own conclusions. The *guided* half means that the therapist coaches the client in her voyage of self-discovery because, although the clinician does not know what the child will find, he does know how to voyage effectively.

Therapists can adjust their level of directiveness to fit the client's needs. If a nondirective series of questions enables the youth to come to adaptive conclusions on his own, stronger therapist input is unnecessary. However, if the client does not develop more realistic beliefs in response to Socratic questioning, clear statements of realistic thinking by the counselor might exert a therapeutic influence. Authoritative statements by adults sometimes have credibility with clients, especially younger children and compliant clients with low self-esteem, many of whom are reassured by strong therapist statements to the effect that they are not unintelligent, bad, or losers. A strategy of gradual, contingent increase in therapist input enables us to take advantage of the strengths of both nondirective and directive styles. By individualizing our level of input to each youth, we can encourage clients to think for themselves as much as they can while supplying whatever input they need to arrive at adaptive conclusions.

This chapter emphasizes counseling techniques that are distinctive to cognitive treatment, but cognitive therapy also includes general counseling techniques that are used across theoretical orientations (see Chapter 1). Cognitive therapy sessions should include time for exploration of the client's emotions, so his feelings are expressed and the therapist has an opportunity to express empathy and support. If clinicians move too quickly into cognitive techniques, the work may become intellectualized and dry (Friedberg & McClure, 2002, 2014). Also, expression of clear, strong emotions facilitates the process of identifying the cognitions underlying those emotions (Greenberg, 2002; Greenberg & Pascual-Leone, 2006).

Traditionally, use of cognitive techniques with children under the age of 8 has been controversial, because these techniques require significant verbal and thinking ability. However, it appears that younger children can benefit from cognitive interventions when the therapeutic activities are modified in developmentally appropriate ways (Doherr, Reynolds, Wetherly, & Evans, 2005; Grave & Blissett, 2004). These modifications include simplification of the techniques and explanations, extensive use of concrete examples, increased parent participation in sessions, and packaging treatment techniques in game-like activities. CBT for anxiety, modified in these ways, has produced positive outcomes for young children (Hirshfeld-Becker et al., 2010; Monga, Young, & Owens, 2009). Knell and Meena (2011) and Drewes and Bratton (2014) provide useful suggestions for play therapy activities in CBT for young children.

Self-Monitoring

In **self-monitoring**, clients use structured formats to notice, organize, and record their everyday experiences as they occur in the natural environment (Clarke, DeBar, & Lewinsohn, 2003; Rohde, Lewinsohn, Clarke, Hops, & Seeley, 2005; Stark et al., 2006). Self-monitoring begins as an assessment procedure for collecting information about the client's cognitive-emotional patterns, and then it becomes part of the process of treating those patterns.

Daily thought records are structured formats for organizing information about relationships between events, cognitions, and emotions. For each unit of experience, there is a column for the external event, a column for the thought following the event, and a column for the feeling resulting from the thought. With older children, there should also be a column for a numerical rating of the intensity of the emotion. Completion of daily thought records is a common homework assignment in cognitive therapy. Recording this sequence of event-thought-feeling for a number of experiences provides structured data that makes patterns apparent to both client and therapist. The website for this book includes a daily thought record that therapists can print, copy, and provide to clients. Form 3.1 is appropriate for children ages 10 years and older.

Therapists should carefully explain how to complete daily thought records because the distinctions between the sections are not as obvious as they might seem. The event column is for an objective description of what happened, externally. It is important to prevent interpretations and automatic thoughts from infiltrating the event column. For instance, one client reported an event as "My mother hates me." However, inquiry revealed that this was an interpretation, and the factual event consisted of a reprimand for misbehavior.

The distinction between thoughts and feelings is often more clear in theory than in practice, and clients sometimes confuse the two. In a sense, feelings are simpler than thoughts; emotion words are *descriptions* of how a person feels, while thoughts are *explanations* of why things are a certain way. If someone reports an emotion, he could conceivably be lying but he cannot be wrong. In contrast, it takes some work to evaluate whether a thought is a valid interpretation of an event. One tip for teaching this distinction is that feelings can usually be identified by a single word, while thoughts generally take a number of words to convey (Friedberg & McClure, 2002, 2014).

Because of this interweaving of emotion and cognition, the experience of strong feelings, especially *changes* in emotion, is a signal that an important thought has occurred (J. S. Beck, 2011). Informing clients about this clue helps them become more skilled at noticing and identifying their automatic thoughts.

When the assessment period is over and therapy proper begins, counselors usually add two more columns to the thought record. The first is for realistic thoughts designed to *counter* the client's maladaptive, automatic cognitions (see the next section on self-instruction). In the final column, the child rerates the intensity of her feelings. Form 3.2 on our website provides a daily thought record that can be used to track treatment progress. Table 3.3 shows an example from Vance's work.

Entries in daily thought records should be made when the youth has a distressing experience or an experience related to the reasons for treatment. The best time for completing these records is when thoughts and emotions are occurring or soon afterwards. Used as homework, this tool provides an effective means of transporting cognitive therapy into the client's everyday life.

Table 3.3 Vance's Daily Thought Record

Event	Thoughts Going Through My Mind	Feelings	Ratings	Realistic Thoughts	Reratings
A friend asked if I wanted to go out with a group of boys and girls on Saturday night.	Everyone knows Kelsey dumped me; they will view me as pathetic.	Embarrassed Ashamed	9 7	People know that everyone gets rejected sometimes, and it doesn't mean you're pathetic.	6 4
	The other girls don't compare to Kelsey; I'll just be reminded of how much worse off I am now.	Depression Loss	8 10	As I go through my grief process, I'll start noticing the good things about other girls.	7 10
	I won't have any fun the whole night.	Hopeless	9	I might have fun if I'm open to it.	8
	I'll have to act like I'm okay even though I'll be miserable.	Tense Self-conscious	6 8	My friends will accept me being down; they wouldn't want me to put on an act.	4 5
In the junior varsity basketball game, I got only 10 minutes of playing time, and I made only 1 of the 4 shots I took.	I stunk.	Like a failure	8	Going 1 for 4 isn't that unusual, and I did get a rebound and an assist.	7
	I made a fool of myself.	Humiliated	8	The crowd was focused on the game as a whole, not on me.	5
	The team depends on the starters; what we second stringers do doesn't make any difference.	Useless	6	An effective bench can make a big difference in a team's performance.	4
	I've got no natural ability at basketball.	Depressed Hopeless	8 7	I'm comparing myself to the best players; I'm better than most guys; if I practice more, I'll improve.	7 7

Self-Instruction

Self-instructions are purposeful statements that people say to themselves to manage their emotions and direct their behavior. Athletes commonly use self-instruction to guide their performance of complex physical tasks. Cognitive therapists teach clients self-instructional techniques for steering themselves through stressful situations (Kendall & Hedtke, 2006a, 2006b; Meichenbaum, 1985; Velting, Setzer, & Albano, 2004).

When clients have a maladaptive automatic thought, they need to respond with an adaptive **counterthought**. Counterthoughts are a fundamental tool of cognitive therapy, and helping clients develop them is a basic part of this work. Effective counterthoughts are not wishful thinking. Self-statements that deny problems or are positive in an excessive, contrived way do not have credibility and are not effective for clients (Loades et al., 2014; Wood, Perunovic, & Lee, 2009). Counterthoughts need to combine optimism and realism in a balance that acknowledges the negative situation but portrays it as manageable.

By grasping this principle, clients can develop the skill of composing counterthoughts for each new situation that arises. Also, clients can identify counterthoughts that apply to multiple situations and are reliably effective. Such counterthoughts can be written on index cards or in a file in the client's phone, so he has access to them as reminders in everyday life. Used in this way, counterthoughts become a simple, direct strategy in which the client memorizes a few set formulae for use in difficult situations. This scripted technique should be a mainstay of therapy for younger or less intellectually inclined children who will not benefit from more conceptual interventions.

Self-instructions of this type are usually brief, declarative sentences that do not involve logical analysis but simply assert a thought that is comforting and/or adaptive. Examples include:

- "Be cool." "Stay calm." "Chill out."
- "I'll get through this; it's not the end of the world."
- "This is just something that's happening right now; it doesn't mean anything about me."
- "Stop and think before doing anything."
- "Handle this in a way you'll feel good about afterwards."

Clients and counselors should brainstorm ideas for self-statements. The child should supply as many of these as she can, and the therapist should fill in gaps when necessary.

The inclusion of positive self-descriptors or identity components sometimes increases the power of self-instructions. One client whose anger had felt terribly "hot" developed the following self-instructions for anger management:

- "I am the Ice Man; I can freeze my anger."
- "When I am the Ice Man, I am in control."
- "The Ice Man has tactics: I can take a deep breath, say something assertive, or laugh it off."

Sometimes automatic thoughts take the form of sensory or visual images, not words. J. S. Beck (2011) suggests two techniques that can help with distressing automatic thoughts that take this form. One problem is that clients often stop the painful "movie" before its completion, thus avoiding the ending they fear. This response is perfectly understandable, but it is counterproductive, because it results in the loss of exposure experiences that could, over time, desensitize the client to the frightening imagery. Beck suggests that counselors explain this to the client and then guide her through the sequence of feared imagery until its conclusion, helping her power through the junctures where, in the past, she usually escaped. If the youth repeats this procedure enough times, in sessions and as homework, she will master the imagery and no longer be intimidated by it.

The second technique is to develop a new ending for the sequence of imagery. The added imagery must have emotional plausibility, which means it cannot be unrealistically wishful. For example, it probably would not help a sexual abuse victim to imagine himself fighting off his abuser if this was not what happened. Instead, the effective strategy is to add content to the sequence and extend the ending forward in time, so elements both optimistic and realistic can be included. It is like adding a panel or two to a comic strip, so the old ending is not denied but is followed and superseded by a new ending with different meanings. For instance, an abuse victim could mentally take his story to its conclusion of disclosure, receiving support, possibly reporting the perpetrator, working on recovery, and looking forward to a better future. The meaning of this story would be that the victim overcame the abuse and did not allow it to defeat him.

After new thoughts have been developed, the client must learn to use them in the situations where they are needed. This is sometimes the most difficult part of self-instruction as a therapeutic technique. As discussed in Chapter 1's sections on implementation intentions (Gollwitzer, 1999; Gollwitzer & Brandstaetter, 1997) and envisioning (Gould, Voelker, Damarjian, & Greenleaf, 2014; Martin, Moritz, & Hall, 1999), it is important for clients to formulate and rehearse concrete if-then plans, to create detailed, situation-specific mental images of their new responses, and to practice these in role-plays with their therapist and in the natural environment. It is a general finding in psychotherapy research, demonstrated in a meta-analysis by Kazantzis, Whittington, and Datillio (2010), that clients who do more homework achieve better outcomes. Once sufficiently prepared, when clients encounter the type of situation that has been problematic for them, they usually think of their self-instructions almost automatically.

Self-Reinforcement

Self-reinforcement is similar in many respects to externally supplied reinforcement, and the same principles of operant conditioning, as described in the previous chapter, apply. The difference is that, instead of being reinforced by someone else, the client reinforces herself for behaviors she views as positive (Bandura, 1986). Therapists change maladaptive self-reinforcement patterns by training clients to reward themselves when they perform positive behaviors, especially in situations that were difficult for them in the past (Clarke et al., 2003; Rohde et al., 2005; Stark et al., 2006).

Some cognitive therapy techniques are simply internalized versions of behavior therapy techniques. Self-monitoring, self-instruction, and self-reinforcement are analogous to the charts, prompts, and rewards that behavior therapists train parents to use, with the difference being whether the procedures are implemented by a person in the child's environment or by the child himself.

Procedurally, self-reinforcement follows self-monitoring and self-instruction as the youth first observes herself, then instructs herself, and, finally, if warranted, rewards herself. Youth can self-reward by buying themselves something they like, engaging in an enjoyable activity, and praising themselves in their thoughts. Self-reward can be explained to children using words like "treating yourself to something you like," "patting yourself on the back," "telling yourself you did a good job," and "feeling proud of yourself."

Self-reinforcement is a more specific procedure than trying to cheer oneself up with positive thoughts. Just as in other forms of operant learning, self-reinforcement is effective when it is contingent on behavior and provides clear informational feedback. Self-affirmations that are not contingent on specific responses are not self-reinforcement.

Self-punishment does not play a role in cognitive therapy. Counselors train clients to respond to their negative behaviors by withholding self-reward, identifying what they did wrong, and making a plan for doing better in the future.

Self-reinforcement expands people's capacity for self-direction because it provides independence from external feedback. This type of self-direction becomes important when contingent relationships between behavior and external reinforcement are imperfect, so that connections between behavior and reinforcement are not apparent in the short term. Games involving combinations of skill and luck provide an analogy for this type of situation, which is common in life. Therapists can explain to intellectually inclined clients that most of life is not like chess, which is 100% skill, or like the lottery, which is 100% luck, but is like poker, which is a combination of both, and in a specific way. In games like poker, short-term success depends mostly on the cards one is dealt, and skillful play only slightly increases the odds of winning with any individual hand. However, in the long run, luck evens out, and the more skillful players always win, while the less competent ones always lose. Self-instruction and self-reinforcement are the processes that maintain persistence of skillful play during the long stretches in which the player does the right things but negative outcomes occur anyway.

Self-reinforcement expands people's capacity for self-direction because it provides independence from external feedback.

Self-reinforcement is an important process for resisting negative peer pressure because it provides something to offset the rewards for negative behavior and punishments for positive behavior that youth sometimes receive from their peers. Therapists treating clients in situations of this type can help by making statements like the following:

"In your situation, there is a difference between doing the right thing and doing what will pay off immediately. Deep inside, you know who you are, and you know what you want to be, but the people around you keep pulling you in other directions. You need someone patting you on the back when you do the right thing—and for a while, that someone is going to have to be you and, while I'm around, me. Because when you do things right, you have a right to feel proud."

In clinical work with children, our hope is always that the external environment either is or can become favorable to positive development. However, if no one in the home or neighborhood will reward the client for positive behavior, it becomes vital that he learn to do this for himself. Reinforcement by the therapist can provide a bridge between external reinforcement and self-reinforcement if the client internalizes the clinician and learns to say to herself what the clinician would say to her.

Self-instruction and self-reinforcement make it possible to account for outcomes that are not otherwise easily explained. In addition to the resilience of children who develop positively in the midst of dysfunctional social environments, self-instruction and self-reinforcement may explain the altruism and heroism that occur in extraordinary individuals who do the right thing in the face of pain and even death, when no one is watching and there is no externally supplied reinforcement for their self-sacrifice.

Socratic Questioning

Socrates conducted his philosophical inquiries by asking people questions, in well-organized sequences, until they arrived at meaningful conclusions. In cognitive therapy, Socratic questioning is a basic technique of guided discovery that leads clients toward more adaptive, realistic understandings of self and life (Overholser, 1993, 2010, 2013; Rutter & Friedberg, 1999). Most children age 8 and older can benefit from this technique.

In Socratic dialogue, the therapist and client collaborate and share control over the process. The clinician does not tell the client what to think but asks questions to help him come to his own conclusions. However, the therapist's stance is not totally open-ended; she wants to lead the client's thinking in more adaptive directions, although the specific cognitive steps are determined by the client. The desired conclusions differ from the client's maladaptive cognitions. As examples, the objectives might be more positive self-evaluations in depressed clients, less frightening perceptions of threat in anxious clients, and less angry interpretations of other people's behavior in aggressive clients.

To guide Socratic inquiry, therapists need to ask questions of themselves, such as:

- What cognitive distortions are operating?
- What evidence is the child overlooking?
- What evidence is the child magnifying or exaggerating?
- Are there alternative explanations for the facts?

Once the counselor has located inaccuracies in the client's thinking, **thought testing** can begin. One way to introduce this process is to make an empathic statement that links events, thoughts, feelings, and behaviors (Friedberg & McClure, 2002, 2014)— for instance:

"I understand that when you believe you are nothing without Kelsey, you feel miserable and hopeless; how else could you feel with that view of your situation? Let's take a look at the thinking that says you're nothing without her and figure out whether it's realistic. Are you willing to check this out?"

Sometimes clients resist the process of evaluating their beliefs. If this happens, Socratic dialogue can be used to examine their resistance. This process often leads to insights into the client's thinking. Useful questions include:

- "What makes you feel like you don't want to examine this?"
- "What are the pros and cons of examining your thinking about this?" "What could happen that would be bad? That would be good?"

Socratic questioning is based on the idea that people usually possess the knowledge necessary for developing more adaptive understandings, but they need help organizing and applying this knowledge. The therapeutic effects of Socratic questioning probably go beyond helping clients come to particular adaptive conclusions; this technique may also train clients *how* to think in an organized, realistic fashion. Table 3.4 presents questions for Socratic inquiry drawn from J. S. Beck (2011), DiGuiseppe (1999), and Rutter and Friedberg (1999).

Socratic questioning often unearths a variety of observations, impressions, and possibilities. The resulting complexity sometimes leaves youngsters feeling confused, which might be a good thing, because a confused appreciation of mixed evidence is an advance from simplistic, erroneous certainty. Socrates said that an awareness of one's ignorance is the beginning of knowledge. To help clients move toward the next stage, which is the formulation of new beliefs, cognitive therapists ask clients to organize and summarize the new thinking they have generated—for example:

- "So what do you make of all this? What does it add up to?"
- "What is your conclusion from all these different points and possibilities? How would you put it all together?"
- "What does this information tell you about the belief we set out to test? What does it tell you about yourself?"

Table 3.4   Socratic Questions

"In thinking about this situation, are there any facts or possibilities that might be relevant but you haven't fully considered them?"

"Has anything ever happened that does not go with this belief?" "Has anything ever happened that makes you think this belief might not be completely true?"

"What do you do that a total _____ (loser, geek, failure) would not do?" "What do total _____ do that you do not?" "Is there anything about you that does not fit the picture of a total _____?"

"Is it possible there was another reason why this happened?"

"What are the advantages of looking at this the way you've been?" "What are the disadvantages?" "What would be the advantages of looking at it a different way?" "What would be the disadvantages?"

Adaptive conclusions are usually more complex and nuanced than cognitive distortions, because they include a larger amount of information. There might not be any firm conclusions, or the conclusion might be to keep an open mind. Simplicity and certainty are not goals—the purpose of Socratic dialogue is to facilitate the development of the youth's thinking in realistic, adaptive directions.

Cognitive Restructuring

Cognitive restructuring, a core strategy of cognitive therapy, seeks to change clients' unrealistic beliefs and maladaptive interpretations of events (A. T. Beck & Alford, 2009; Bernard & Joyce, 1984; Dobson & Dobson, 2009; Hofmann, 2011). Ellis's original A-B-C model provides a simple, practical tool that helps clients think about the effects of thoughts on feelings. In Ellis's later work, he added a D (for disputation) and an E (for more effective thoughts) to his acronym (Ellis, 2001; Ellis & MacLaren, 2005).

Because this model is visual, it can be drawn for clients, with arrows indicating the causal relationships between events (or "what happened"), thoughts, and feelings (see Figure 3.1). Clients should practice organizing their experiences in terms of this model. For example, Alexandra, a 9-year-old girl who berated herself for minor failures in school, produced the following:

> EVENT: I got a D on the spelling test, and the teacher said she knew I could do better.
>
> THOUGHTS: My mistakes were stupid; no smart kid would have made so many mistakes; I must really be stupid; my teacher used to like me, but not anymore.
>
> FEELINGS: I hate myself for being a failure; I feel ashamed and miserable.

For Vance, the following thoughts connected the event of being rejected by Kelsey and his feelings of worthlessness and depression:

> • "Kelsey was like a miracle—no one has ever made me feel that way before, and I'll never find anyone like her again."
> • "Kelsey knew me better than anyone ever has, and she rejected me, so there must be something bad about me."
> • "Compared to the times I had with Kelsey, everything else I do is dull and pointless; without her, I don't live, I just exist."

According to Ellis, most clients begin therapy mistakenly believing that their feelings are caused by events. Initially, Vance believed that the reason he was depressed was simply that Kelsey broke up with him. Thus, the Beliefs step was missing from his understanding of his experience. Cognitive therapy seeks to change the client's sense of an automatic connection between events and emotions; treatment should create an understanding that, despite the sometimes unalterable nature of events, new cognitions are possible, and they will make a difference to emotional experience. One way to approach this point is to ask the client whether everyone she knows would have the same reaction to the event in question. J. S. Beck (2011) provides a list of questions with which clients can critically evaluate the validity and utility of their thoughts. Table 3.5 presents these questions with slight rewordings for young clients.

Once the client realizes that other thoughts and emotional reactions are possible, the question becomes what new cognitions he would *like* to apply to events that, in the past, have led to distress and dysfunction. The challenge is to find thoughts that acknowledge the negative reality of the event but limit its awful implications and facilitate the client's coping. To initiate a search for such cognitions, therapists can ask something like:

"If _____ (the antecedent event) happens, what are some things that *could* go through your mind to help you feel okay and deal with it?"

The next step is to write a new version of the A-B-C diagram or Form 3.2 that leaves the antecedent as it was but changes the thoughts in an adaptive direction and, therefore, alters the emotional consequences. Alexandra developed the following thoughts about getting disappointing grades on tests:

- "This is just one test; I have gotten good grades before, and I will get good grades again."
- "I'm not a robot, so I can't do well at everything all the time."
- "Some of the smartest and most successful people in the world had trouble with school at times (e.g., Albert Einstein)."
- "There are things I can do about the bad grade: I can make sure I understand what I did wrong, and I can study harder or smarter for the next test."

A diagram of a fork in a road provides a visual metaphor for the way that a given event can give rise to different thoughts that, in turn, lead to different emotional consequences. Drawing the adaptive path on top and the maladaptive one on the bottom of the page provides a visual clue indicating which is preferable. Therapists can use Form 3.3 from our website as a template for cognitive restructuring by filling it in with descriptions of the

Table 3.5 Questions for Assessing Client Cognitions

"What is the evidence that your thought is true? What is the evidence that your thought might not be true?"

"Is there another way of looking at this situation?"

"What is the worst thing that could happen? What would you do if it did?"

"What is the best thing that could happen?"

"What is the most likely thing to happen?"

"How does believing this thought make you feel? How does it affect your behavior? How might it affect you to believe a different thought?"

"If a friend of yours was in this situation and had the same thought, what would you say to him or her?"

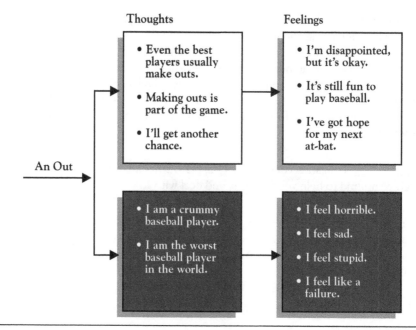

Figure 3.3   Example of a diagram used in cognitive restructuring.

events and possible cognitive-affective sequences pertaining to their clients. Figure 3.3 shows an example from therapy with an 8-year-old boy who got so upset when he made an out in his Little League games that he wanted to give up baseball.

Sometimes it is useful for clients to realize not only that their thinking is unrealistic but also *how* it is inaccurate—this purpose can be accomplished by teaching clients how to recognize and label their cognitive errors. J. S. Beck's (2011) list of common cognitive distortions, presented in Table 3.2, provides a basis for this optional technique that is sometimes useful with older, intellectually inclined clients.

Recognizing patterns sometimes helps clients correct them. For example, a youth's examination of her thought process might yield an insight like, "Uh oh—that's tunnel vision; when I do that, it means I'm missing something in the situation." As another example, Vance caught himself minimizing the importance of positive information about himself so frequently that he learned to view feelings of worthlessness as a signal that he was probably engaging in this thinking error.

Tests of Evidence

Tests of evidence call upon clients to think in the fashion of scientists and judges, who examine data to evaluate the validity of a hypothesis or assertion.

In tests of evidence, the therapist helps the client evaluate the evidence for and against his beliefs and, if appropriate, revise those beliefs based on the evidence (Beck & Alford, 2009; Padesky & Greenberger, 1995; Hofmann, 2011; Leahy et al., 2011). Tests of evidence call upon clients to think in the fashion of scientists and judges, who examine data to assess the validity of a hypothesis or assertion.

One way to evaluate a large, general belief is to break it down into its component parts and then test the elements of the belief, individually.

If the youth describes himself with a broad negative concept, this concept should be analyzed to assess the extent to which it applies to the youth. The client should ascertain which of the elements of the negative concept fit him and which do not, and he should decide which of his personal characteristics fit the negative concept and which do not.

The first step is to define the belief to be tested. This step involves sifting through a variety of negative self-statements to distill the schema underlying them. These beliefs usually take forms like, "I am a _____" (negative noun), "I am _____" (negative adjective), or "People are _____" (negative characterization). Then, write the belief at the top of a piece of paper.

Next, the negative descriptions that the youth applied to herself should be defined in terms of the behaviors and characteristics making up the concept. For example, a child who describes himself as a "failure" or "reject" should say exactly what such an individual does and does not do. These behaviors and characteristics should be written on the left side of the paper.

At the top of the right side of the paper, the counselor or youth should write a heading such as *True for Me?* Then, the client should go through the list of negative components and make one of three ratings: (1) Completely true of me (indicated by an X), (2) Partly or sometimes true of me (indicated by a "−"), and (3) Not true of me (indicated by a check mark). I suggest using Xs for the presence of a characteristic and check marks for their absence when the characteristics are negative, because then an X indicates a bad thing and a check means a good thing, which are the usual associations children have to these marks, from school.

Next, the client should list his personal characteristics and behaviors that do *not* fit the negative descriptor. For example, Vance acknowledged a number of activities that do not fit the concept of "a nothing," such as playing varsity basketball, helping his younger sister with her homework, and having friends. Counselors should push clients to think of everything applicable and not leave anything out. As a homework assignment, clients can monitor their behavior through the day and write down everything they do that does not fit the negative belief about themselves.

At the end of this exercise, most clients will see a piece of paper listing a number of negative characteristics that they possess to varying extents—with a mix of Xs, dashes, and checks—and a number of positive behaviors that do not fit the negative self-definition they had believed was true of them. Usually, the test produces *mixed evidence* concerning the belief. Such data do not transform a negative self-concept into a positive one, but the evidence usually produces a more differentiated, balanced self-evaluation, and such self-concepts are generally more realistic and adaptive than the one with which the client began. The client might point to the Xs and say, "See, I *am* a loser in some ways," but the counselor can reply, "Everyone is a loser in *some* ways, and this test shows there are many things about you that do not fit the definition of a loser. Let's build on those." Table 3.6 presents an example from a 15-year-old girl with a history of delinquent behavior.

One optional step in this exercise is to guide the youth in making downward comparisons that have self-enhancing implications. These comparisons can be either to individuals who approximate the negative exemplar or to the client herself at times in the past when she was doing worse. The purpose of these comparisons is to provide the youth with a more accurate and negative picture of how bad things could be, so she becomes more aware of her distance from that low point.

The last step is to ask the client to construct a belief that fits all the evidence. It usually takes more words to express the new, more complicated belief than the old, simplistic

Table 3.6   Example of a Test of Evidence

Belief: I am a bad kid.	
Characteristics of a Bad Kid	*True for Me?*
Fights a lot	X
Steals	X
Gets arrested	X
Takes drugs	—
Has a lot of sex	X
Does badly in school	—
Parents think she's awful	X
Hates her parents	—
Believes in crime	√

Things about me that don't go with being a bad kid.

Visit my grandmother to cheer her up.

Do well in art classes at school.

Don't like to see kids get picked on.

Like to dress in nice clothes.

one. For example, "I am a loser" might be replaced with "I have some strengths and some weaknesses, and I want to do better in the future." It might also be useful to ask the youth how completely he used to believe the original belief and how much he does now, in percentage terms.

It is not necessary for cognitive work to definitively refute clients' self-derogating or pessimistic beliefs in order to reduce the power of those beliefs over their lives. Some freeing effect is achieved when the client *gains distance* from the beliefs—that is, when he views them as ideas, not facts, understands that they describe some aspects of reality but not others, and realizes that one can believe these ideas, not believe them, or partially believe them (J. S. Beck, 2011; DiGiuseppe, Doyle, Dryden, & Backx, 2014). This approach to distressing cognitions is elaborated further in the next chapter's description of acceptance and commitment therapy.

Tests of evidence are an effective technique for treating dichotomous thinking. Clients, particularly depressed ones, often feel that possessing one feature of a negative trait means they possess the trait in its entirety. This exercise in analyzing complex personal data, with different facts fitting different traits to varying degrees, paints pictures in shades of gray. Once clients become aware of their proclivity toward black-and-white thinking, you can remind them of the antidote with brief statements, such as "Gray, Vance, gray is the color."

Tests of evidence can be used to treat maladaptive beliefs about the world and other people as well as irrational beliefs about the self. Therapist inquiries should guide a search for inconsistencies and exceptions that call into question the client's rigid views. For example, one 17-year-old girl believed that "Only good-looking, thin, popular girls have boyfriends." Her therapist gave her the homework assignment of listing every couple among her peers and indicating which of the girls were, in fact, good-looking, thin, and popular. The finding was that some of them were and some were not. Since the client's belief allowed for no exceptions, this empirical inquiry disconfirmed the maladaptive belief.

Sometimes clients cite evidence they believe supports their view but that actually has a more plausible alternative explanation. Vance believed that being rejected by Kelsey meant he did not have the type of personality that attractive girls want in a boyfriend. There was no denying the fact of the rejection, but there were alternative explanations that were less depressing in their implications. Vance's homework assignment was to interview several older friends and relatives about their romantic histories and to tabulate their relationships that did and did not work out. These data confirmed the view that "It's tough out there," because all his informants reported experiencing rejection—and yet these individuals did not seem like losers to Vance. This finding disconfirmed Vance's impression of attractiveness as a unidimensional characteristic and increased his appreciation of the subjective, individual, and sometimes quirky nature of romantic compatibility. The resulting sense of unpredictability increased his hope for a good future in the romantic arena.

Personal Experiments

When the data needed to test a belief do not exist, an experiment can be performed to collect these data. In personal experiments, the client uses the basic strategy of science: setting up a procedure to collect data that will test a hypothesis.

Therapeutic experiments take two forms: making systematic observations and trying out new behaviors. In both cases, the results are compared to the youth's expectations (A. T. Beck & Emery, 2005; DiGiuseppe et al., 2014; Gregory, 2011; Hofmann, 2011). Instead of speculating about what might happen, the client and therapist find out what does happen, in the real world.

Because an experiment would not be an experiment if the results were known in advance, this therapeutic technique is risky: The client's experience might support his gloomy predictions and self-deprecating beliefs. Therapists should design personal experiments to minimize this risk. Realistic definitions of success are crucial to the effectiveness of this technique. It is important not to aim too high and not to define success too narrowly. Optimal definitions of success are realistic and broad enough to include all the likely outcomes. Clients might object that they want levels of success higher than the initial aim of the exercise. Clinicians should respond by stating that *any* progress from the client's starting point is movement in the right direction because, if this movement continues, the youth will end up where she wants to be.

The task of developing realistic definitions of success is sometimes aided by the tendency of many clients to be pessimistic, because any positive outcome exceeds their expectations and can be considered a relative success. For instance, an adolescent with a long history of school failure believed that it was pointless to study because he would fail no matter how hard he tried. His personal experiment was to pick one subject and commit to doing one-half hour of work on it per night. The goal was to earn a C in the class. The therapist was willing to take a calculated risk that the planned amount of effort would produce this outcome.

Personal experiments are common components of treatment for shy individuals who avoid social interactions because they are certain that failure will result. For instance, Nancy was a shy 16-year-old who avoided parties because she was sure no one would talk to her. Her therapist proposed putting this belief to a test. Nancy's assignment was to drive herself to a party, stay for 45 minutes, and then leave. Success was defined as having one conversation, of any length and any type, at the party. Nancy objected that one brief conversation was not a successful social outcome. The clinician replied that she had to start somewhere, and she could use one conversation, no matter the length or quality, as a stepping stone toward her eventual goal of having a good time at a party. The therapist supplemented this intervention with social skills training (see Chapter 2, Behavior Therapy) to increase the likelihood of a positive outcome.

One way to develop attainable standards of success is to emphasize the client's internal experience rather than his objective performance. To continue with the preceding topic, shy individuals often expect that if they are not successful in a social situation, they will feel anguish and misery. Self-instruction and self-reinforcement can be used to change sitting alone at a party from a humiliating disaster to an uncomfortable but tolerable experience. This outcome can even be defined as a success, as long as the client tolerates the discomfort, avoids a panic reaction, and thus increases his ability to cope with a situation he wants to learn how to master.

Perhaps the most reliable strategy for developing attainable definitions of success is to emphasize the value of the client's efforts, rather than the external outcome that results (Ellis, 1962, 1973). The idea is that as long as the client practices the skill she wants to develop, the immediate external outcomes do not matter, because practice will lead to success in the long run. As a young man, Ellis overcame his own shyness with women by forcing himself to initiate as many conversations as he could on a daily basis. The results included an enormous amount of rejection, with which he learned to cope, the development of stronger social skills, and, eventually, positive romantic relationships.

Cognitive therapists sometimes take this line of reasoning to its ultimate conclusion by redefining failures *as* successes. For instance, dating is impossible if one is unwilling to risk rejection. For clients who find this possibility devastating, a useful assignment might be to ask someone out, receive a "no" in return, and cope with the disappointment. The counselor can add some irony by noting that if the person says yes, the assignment will be ruined.

When the client's goal is to develop personal capabilities, rather than to achieve immediate outcomes, definitions of success and failure become abstract and even paradoxical. Definitions of success based on the client's efforts provide outcomes over which she has control. Clients who achieve some independence from short-term environmental contingencies gain a space within which to overcome fears, explore new behaviors, and develop skills. In the long run, these new capabilities will lead to positive outcomes in the external world.

Using Spectra to Develop Moderation

Just as cognitive-behavioral therapists have long used continua as conceptual tools to help clients move beyond dichotomous thinking about outcomes, we can use 10-point scales as visual tools to help clients move beyond dichotomies in choosing their styles of cognition and behavior. The strategy begins with the following steps:

- Identify the dimension on which the youth's habitual or desired style of functioning is extreme. This is the most important step; everything follows from here.
- Operationally define the end of the continuum where the client's habitual or desired style is located and identify its advantages and disadvantages.

- Define the other end of the continuum, which describes the style of functioning the youth wants to avoid, and identify its costs and benefits.
- Describe the adaptive mid-range of the scale, which involves a balanced combination of qualities from both poles. Intermediate regions may also be described.
- Ask the client to indicate where she currently is on the spectrum.

These steps should be accompanied by discussion, including Socratic questioning and, when appropriate, your own input. It is important to validate the client's currently chosen end of the spectrum:

"I see why you're here—I get what you like about it. The things the adults want you to do seem so boring, and you get sick of it. After school, you want to have some fun, and homework is such a grind. Plus you feel like the school has no right to take away your freedom when you're not even there. You don't like those nerdy teacher's pets who always do what the grownups want. That's not who you want to be."

Then, point out what the client is missing: the advantages of the other side of the spectrum.

"But I also want to take a look at what you're losing by being so far over here to the left; there are disadvantages to it. School is hard work, but there can be good things about it, like learning, getting better at things, succeeding, and building a better future. I think the problem is that, up till now, you haven't found a way to do this that feels comfortable. But what if you could?"

Having articulated both sides of the dilemma, therapists are in a position to sketch a resolution.

(Pointing to the diagram) "Now this is an important point: You don't have to go from one end of this scale to the other. Your parents and I aren't trying to get you to move from a 2 to a 9; we don't want you to become a grade-grubber who spends all your time doing homework. There's a better option: moving toward the middle. Of course, you'd have to give something up—you'd have less time for video games and hanging out—but you could still do plenty of that and have some time for homework too. You would get a lot in return, because the middle of the spectrum has most of the good things from *both* ends."

The next step is to flesh out the middle so the client has a clear, concrete sense of what is involved. Therapists can explain that balanced moderation is inherently more versatile and flexible than one-sided development. Then, we can present the recommended changes as an expansion of the youth's capabilities that will enable her to experience more types of success and enjoyment. For example, an averagely responsible high school student might study for an hour or so per night and several hours during the weekend while preserving lots of time for relaxation and recreation. Therapists can explain that "It's not about giving up what you've been doing—it's about adding something more."

Adaptive functioning does not come in only one form. There are many ways to function successfully, so there are ranges of effective styles in each dimension. These ranges occur around the midpoints of continua, but they include more area—more diversity—than the midpoints alone. In terms of our scales, this means that effective functioning is not limited to a tight band between 5 and 6 but extends outward to a broader range such as 4 to 7 or even 3 to 8.

The spectrum technique provides a way to construct individualized therapy goals that are realistic, comfortable, and relatively attractive for clients. Youth can function more effectively while maintaining their basic style as long as some degree of moderation and balance is achieved. Clients need to move toward the mid-range of the spectrum, but they do not need to arrive at the midpoint; they can stay on their preferred side and develop an adaptive style that is compatible with their preferences. Therapists can say:

> "You don't need to become a different kind of person to _____ (achieve therapy goal). You don't have to go from a 2 to a 9—you don't even have to go from a 2 to a 5. If you moved from a 2 to like a 4, you would still be a kid who likes to hang out and have fun, and you wouldn't be a real serious student, but you'd balance things out—do some work to stay in the game, get decent grades, develop some skills."

At this point, counselors can ask clients to mark the scale at the place where they would like to be. Usually, this is only about two scale-points away from where they placed their current functioning—and the therapy goals have been cut down to size. There may be a sense of relief that the goals did not turn out to be very daunting once the issues were discussed and understood. In regard to personal identity, clients are often relieved that they do not need to become a different type of person to achieve therapy goals.

These scales provide a way of presenting the issues underlying client problems as two-sided, not simple matters of good versus bad. Because advantages have been identified on both sides of the spectrum, counselors can acknowledge the legitimacy of the client's present style while identifying needed revisions at the same time. The counselor's message is that the client already has one side of the issue down pat, and now he needs to complete his capabilities by adding the other half. This procedure provides a face-saving way for clients to pursue therapy goals, because they do not have to repudiate their past self to strive for needed changes.

Application to Perfectionism

Therapists can use the spectrum technique to help perfectionistic clients rethink and moderate their personal standards of quality. Here is the spectrum relevant to perfectionism.

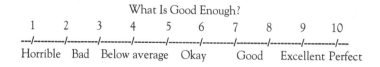

Perfectionistic clients dichotomize this continuum between 9 and 10. To demonstrate the unfair and unworkable consequences of doing so, draw an arc over each side of the dichotomy, label the large one "failure," and label the small one "success." This diagram depicts the skewed, onerous nature of the standards by which perfectionistic people evaluate themselves. Counselors can say:

"It doesn't seem fair: If you define everything below perfect as a failure, of course you're going to fail most of the time. It's like saying everyone who isn't six feet tall is short. Also, you ignore the differences between very good, average, and bad, and those differences are important. This is a very hard way to live."

Perfectionism itself can be conceptualized as an extreme on a spectrum of evaluative standards varying in rigor and stringency.

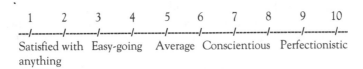

Some clients cling to perfectionism because, in their dichotomous view, the alternative is low standards for performance, and they emphatically do not want that, so they seek safety from the feared end of the continuum by going to the opposite extreme. The remedy for this problem is moderation, which can be developed by using the procedure just presented. When perfectionistic clients understand the range of possibilities on the dimension of concern to them, they usually see that a small adjustment from a 9 or 10 to a 7 or 8 would preserve their rigorous style while adding enough flexibility to allow some ease and satisfaction in the achievement realm. Once clients agree to this in principle, the next step is to operationally define the newly chosen scale-point with the thoughts, emotions, and behaviors to which it corresponds.

The practical problem with perfectionism is that time and energy are limited resources, life has many facets, and being perfectionistic about some of them necessarily leads to short-changing the others. Perfectionism is not compatible with living a well-rounded life. Counselors can say:

"Being such a perfectionist about your schoolwork is making the rest of your life very imperfect, because you don't have time for anything else. If you want to be a perfectionist about your life, you'll have to give up being a perfectionist about your homework."

Perfectionism is viewed as an important cause of mental health problems by many cognitive therapists, and they try hard to help perfectionistic clients come to terms with being human (Bernard & Joyce, 1984; DiGiuseppe et al., 2014; Ellis & MacLaren, 2005). Conceptually, this work involves extending clients' conceptions of successful, admirable people to include some mistakes, faults, and failures. To provide experiences that loosen the hold of perfectionism, these therapists sometimes suggest, as homework assignments, that clients purposely do a messy or incomplete job with some task. J. S. Beck (2011) suggests clients turn in sloppy, half-finished therapy worksheets, to see what imperfection is like and how easily it can be survived. In CBT, practice is viewed as the key to skill development, including the skill of being comfortably imperfect.

Summary

Cognitive therapy focuses on the thought processes with which people interpret their experiences. The strategy of treatment is to test the validity and utility of clients' beliefs and to help them develop more realistic and adaptive cognitions.

The theory posits a hierarchical model of cognition in which automatic thoughts derive from rules, attitudes, and assumptions that, in turn, are based on deep-level schemas. Therapy works from the top down, first identifying and modifying misinterpretations and distortions in clients' conscious self-talk and, progressively, identifying and modifying the cognitive structures from which internal commentary arises.

Cognitive assessment focuses on the client's characteristic patterns of thinking. Clinicians inquire about interpretations and explanations of emotionally potent events, beliefs about the self and other people, and evidence for and against these beliefs. Daily thought records are first used as a method of assessing connections between events, thoughts, and feelings, and then are used to track progress in counseling. Therapists and researchers have identified a number of specific cognitive distortions that commonly occur in people with mental health problems. Older clients can learn to identify and label their thinking errors, which helps to correct them.

Cognitive interventions, typically in combination with behavioral techniques, have received extensive support from outcome studies. However, it has proven somewhat difficult to isolate the effects of cognitive techniques from the behavioral strategies that accompany them in CBT packages.

Self-monitoring, self-instruction, and self-reinforcement are internal analogues of the charts, prompts, and rewards that, in behavior therapy, are supplied by parents or other figures in the child's environment. Therapists and clients compose adaptive counterthoughts as responses to the habitual, automatic thoughts that have impaired the client's mood and/or functioning. Self-instruction can be a scripted technique in which the therapist and client compose a few brief self-statements that reliably help the child cope with difficult situations. Self-reinforcement is often more reliable than external reinforcement, so it provides youth with a measure of independence from the environment and supports persistent adaptive behavior when this is not reliably rewarded by other people.

Cognitive therapists and their clients collaborate in a scientific spirit that emphasizes observation, reasoning, and experiment as criteria of truth. Therapists use Socratic questioning to encourage clients to reason toward their own conclusions while also providing input when needed. In tests of evidence, counselors help clients evaluate the data bearing on important beliefs by providing a structure for arraying and assessing evidence for and against those beliefs. When additional data is needed, counselors help clients conduct personal experiments in the natural environment.

Counselors can use written scales from 1 to 10 as a visual tool to treat dichotomous thinking, including perfectionism. A procedure based on this tool can help clients see the gradations between extreme styles of functioning and help them appreciate the value of a moderate balance between extremes. Clients generally need to move toward the mid-ranges of these dimensions to function more successfully, but they do not need to arrive at the midpoints; they can maintain their basic style as long as they moderate it. This strategy can be used to construct therapy goals that seem comfortable and feasible to clients. Then, the client's newly chosen scale-point needs to be operationally defined by the cognitions, emotions, and behaviors to which it corresponds.

Cognitive therapy does not typically reverse clients' thinking to the point that events or personal characteristics that were formerly viewed as negative are seen as positive. However, by guiding clients in a more unbiased, fair assessment of personally relevant information, cognitive therapy frequently changes rigidly self-derogating, pessimistic, and/or catastrophizing beliefs into a more balanced appreciation of the mixtures of strengths and weaknesses, successes and failures, that make up most people's lives, including the client's. Cognitive therapy helps youth understand and accept the mixed realities of being human.

Case Study

Vance's treatment emphasized work on two cognitive distortions: his belief that Kelsey was the only girl who could make him happy, and his idea that being rejected by someone who knew him well meant there was something inadequate about him. Therapy involved systematic testing of these beliefs against evidence, some from Vance's own life and most from the lives of older individuals who had romantic histories longer than his. These inquiries changed Vance's specific beliefs about losing Kelsey and also his more general understanding of romantic relationships.

Vance discovered that mistakes in his thinking had deprived him of deserved satisfaction with his life in areas besides dating. These mistakes caused him to undervalue his academic and athletic performance and to discount the worth of any activity at which he did not excel, even if he enjoyed the activity. His therapist asked Vance to consider the implications of defining success in such a way that only a tiny number of people can attain it, with everyone else considered a failure.

These interventions helped Vance get through the acute phase of his loss. However, the teen retained a quality of angst and melancholy, with a nagging feeling of emptiness that therapy did not eliminate. There were conflicts in his relationship with his mother that were not a focus of treatment because these difficulties did not seem central to his presenting problems. Counseling helped Vance develop a view that his life was a mixture of positive and negative elements and that working toward more happiness would be an ongoing endeavor for which he was now better equipped.

4

Mindfulness-Based Cognitive-Behavioral Therapies

OBJECTIVES

This chapter explains:

- *The definition of mindfulness as focusing attention in a certain way: on purpose, in the present moment, and nonjudgmentally.*
- *How mindfulness practice changes the brain and strengthens self-regulation of attention.*
- *Mindfulness exercises that therapists can do with clients and clients can do on their own.*
- *Dialectical behavior therapy principles and strategies, including:*
  - *—Integrating opposing truths into adaptive syntheses.*
  - *—Validating client emotions without reinforcing maladaptive thoughts and behaviors.*
  - *—Distress tolerance techniques: Behaviors that create positive emotions in the midst of distressing situations.*
- *Acceptance and commitment therapy principles and strategies, including:*
  - *—Helping clients give up futile efforts to avoid painful thoughts and feelings so they accept all their experiences.*
  - *—Weakening the hold of thoughts and feelings on choices and behaviors.*
  - *—Strengthening the hold of values and goals on choices and behaviors.*

Case Study
Intensity

Cheyenne was a 17-year-old girl who lived with an emotional intensity beyond what is normal for adolescents, and her emotions were predominantly dysphoric. Her mother was Hispanic and her father European American, and the family spoke English at home. Both parents grew up in difficult family situations that included financial stress, medical illness, and divorce. The family they created had none of these difficulties but, nonetheless, Cheyenne had been "a malcontent" from an early age. Her mother observed that "Everything bothers her, and she freaks out over little problems that really wouldn't have bothered me growing up."

Cheyenne was bright, and she did fairly well in school despite inconsistent attendance and study habits. Most of her energy and emotion went into her stormy relationships with parents, peers, and especially her boyfriend, Cody. These relationships were filled with drama, much of which took place on the various forms of social media that occupied Cheyenne for hours every day.

Cody was her first real boyfriend. Cheyenne felt surges of hope for a truly fulfilling, long-term relationship—but when problems occurred, her distress was even more intense than her hope. Problems happened frequently because Cheyenne was prone to feeling unappreciated, neglected, and jealous. She reacted with hurt and anger to Cody's interactions with female peers, even though these involved nothing romantic, and she became upset when he spent significant time with male friends or family. She misinterpreted ordinary fluctuations in Cody's attention as indications that he had lost interest in her, which threw her into panic and ignited feelings of inadequacy and self-hatred.

Cheyenne's emotions and behavior spiraled out of control at these times. She refused to do homework, spent long periods of time in her room, and alternated between refusing to talk to her parents and screaming at them about an array of grievances. She listened to "emo" music constantly, and doodled images of darkness, rage, and despair. Several times, these escalations of dysfunction ended with scratches and cuts appearing on Cheyenne's forearms, which alarmed the parents enough to overcome her objections to counseling. The therapist made a diagnosis of persistent depressive disorder and noted the presence of borderline features.

Mindfulness and Psychotherapy

This chapter describes "hybrid" therapies that bring together three major intellectual traditions as sources of insight into human problems and change. Behavior therapy is based on laboratory discoveries about mechanisms of learning; cognitive therapy traces its origins to the ancient Roman philosophy of Stoicism; and this chapter focuses on a third source whose insights and techniques have been blended with the other two: Eastern spiritual traditions, especially Zen Buddhism. Our field draws on diverse resources, including science, philosophy, and spiritual practice, with science, in the form of outcome research, as the final common pathway that must be traversed to evaluate the effectiveness of therapeutic techniques, wherever they originated.

The role of Buddhism in hybrid cognitive-behavioral therapies is not religious. These treatments involve no religious doctrine or ceremony, and there is no emphasis on the person called the Buddha. There is nothing in these therapies that conflicts in any way with clients' existing religious beliefs or practices. Buddhism's contribution to the hybrid therapies is psychological and technical in nature.

This chapter describes three related types of interventions: general mindfulness work and two treatment packages, dialectical behavior therapy (DBT) and acceptance and commitment therapy (ACT). By "general mindfulness work," I refer to a body of writing and technique based on Buddhist practice and adapted for Western participants, with the psychologist Jon Kabat-Zinn and the Zen Buddhist monk Thich Nhat Hanh, who sometimes work together, as two prominent authors in this area.

Mindfulness exercises are not therapeutic interventions in and of themselves. Most people who do mindfulness exercises are not in therapy, and their interest is in personal development and enhanced life experience, not treating psychopathology. Nonetheless, mindfulness exercises have found their way into the psychotherapeutic repertoire, and they have proved effective as tools in cognitive-behavioral treatment packages, with DBT and ACT as the most prominent examples. DBT and ACT are complete treatments that include mindfulness exercises along with other cognitive-behavioral strategies.

DBT is an intensive and expensive form of therapy that combines group skills training, individual and (for young clients) family therapy, telephone consultation with clients, and peer consultation for therapists, the sum total of which can involve well over a hundred hours. There are official courses of training and certification that therapists should complete before labeling their work as DBT. (I have not completed this training.) Thus, in its pure form, DBT is not feasible in most clinical settings, and few readers of this book will conduct DBT in its official sense. However, both DBT and ACT include important, insightful ideas and empirically well-supported techniques that can be drawn from the packages and used effectively either by themselves or in combination with other strategies. This is how I use these two therapies myself, and this is why our book includes instruction in DBT and ACT.

The Core Idea: Mindfulness

Buddhism's contribution to psychotherapy consists of the concept of *mindfulness* and techniques for achieving this state of being. During the past 2,500 years, Buddhist practitioners have developed meditation techniques for developing mindfulness. During the past 25 years, psychologists and neuroscientists have documented the benefits of these techniques, and therapists have imported them into mental health interventions.

Jon Kabat-Zinn defines mindfulness as "paying attention in a certain way: on purpose, in the present moment, and non-judgmentally."

Jon Kabat-Zinn (1994, 2012, 2013), a psychologist and meditation teacher who played a major role in bringing these fields together, defines mindfulness as "paying attention in a certain way: on purpose, in the present moment, and non-judgmentally" (1994, p. 4). In a way, mindfulness is a simple mental activity and, in another way, it is subtle, elusive, and profound in its implications. Let's examine Kabat-Zinn's definition.

To be mindful means to be fully aware of what is happening in the present moment, whatever that might be. This can be done while sitting quietly, and it can be done while engaged in an activity; it does not matter, because mindfulness is not about what we do but how we do it. Mindfulness can involve focusing internally on physical sensations and emotions, and it can involve focusing externally on the immediate environment (sounds, smells, etc.). To the degree that we *notice* what is going on in the moment, we are mindful.

Focusing on the present seems like a simple thing to do, but most people find it surprisingly unfamiliar and difficult at first. Because we tend to live our lives in relation to the past and future, when we pause for a moment, the thoughts that bubble up usually concern memories and anticipations, leaving little room for what is happening in the moment. The mental act of gently redirecting attention from the past or future back to the present is central to mindfulness practice.

The term "nonjudgmental" in Kabat-Zinn's definition has two main elements: self-acceptance and acceptance of experiences. Acceptance of self means that, during the moments in question, we engage in no self-evaluation of any kind. Because self-praise is just as judgmental as self-criticism, we let go of the mental habit of assessing whether we are doing well or poorly and simply allow ourselves to be as we are. This nonjudgmental stance applies to mindfulness practice itself: If we have the thought that we are doing poorly at the exercise, rather than criticizing ourselves for criticizing ourselves, we respond simply by noticing (e.g., "I am judging my practice negatively right now").

People cannot fail at mindfulness practice because success consists of going through the process. Mind-wandering and self-evaluation are not failures or setbacks; they are the reasons why we need the practice in the first place. The mental activity of encountering and responding to these inevitable obstacles, over and over again, is precisely what strengthens our capacity for mindfulness.

Being nonjudgmental of experience, a less familiar and perhaps more radical concept, means we accept all aspects of our experience without evaluating them as good or bad, worthy or unworthy, desirable or undesirable. Although we notice that some experiences are pleasant and others are painful, we accept both as parts of the reality of life. This means we do not try to weaken or intensify, shorten or prolong, pull in or push away experiences depending on whether they are pleasant or painful. In this counterintuitive stance, we do not prefer some experiences to others. The goal is not pleasant experience but clear, full experience, whether pleasant or not.

The opposite of mindfulness occurs when we lose awareness of the present moment. This might involve being in a numb or dazed state, being preoccupied with the past or future, being immersed in analyses or judgments, or suppressing feelings because they are painful. These types of mental operations are not inherently dysfunctional, and there are situations in which it is not useful to be mindful, but research to be reviewed later demonstrates that cultivating mindfulness reduces mental health problems, increases cognitive efficiency, and enhances well-being.

Dialectical Behavior Therapy

DBT was originally developed by one person, Marsha Linehan, a psychologist. In an interview with the *New York Times* (Carey, 2011), Dr. Linehan revealed that, as an adolescent and young adult, she suffered from borderline personality disorder (BPD), with the suicide attempts, self-injury, and severe emotion dysregulation characterizing this diagnosis. Dr. Linehan conceived the project that was to be her life's work during the years she spent in the agony of BPD. She had no specific content at that time, but she had a mission, as expressed in the interview: "I was in hell. And I made a vow: When I get out, I'm going to come back and get others out of here." She has fulfilled her vow.

DBT includes a great deal of material, with many more techniques and procedures than most types of therapy. There are four main sources of ideas and strategies. First, DBT is a cognitive-behavioral therapy, and it includes most of the principles and techniques presented in our two preceding chapters and the CBT sections of the diagnosis-based chapters to follow. Linehan added a number of ideas and strategies to this CBT foundation. She found in dialectical philosophy a framework for encompassing the contradictions in her clients' lives (explained ahead). She imported mindfulness practices into psychotherapy and combined these exercises with CBT. Finally, Linehan developed a number of innovative techniques for her intervention. This chapter focuses on the distinctive components of DBT, and readers should understand that these elements are combined with a general cognitive-behavioral approach to therapy.

Client Populations. DBT was first developed and validated as a treatment for adults with BPD (Linehan, 1987, 1993a). Since its beginning, DBT has greatly expanded its reach both diagnostically and developmentally. Outcome studies have provided strong support for DBT as a treatment for almost every basic category of psychopathology except psychosis (e.g., mood disorders, trauma disorders, conduct disturbances, eating disorders, and substance abuse).

Miller, Rathus, and Linehan (2007; Rathus & Miller, 2014) developed a version of DBT for adolescents. Their treatment manual is mostly similar to Linehan's original (1993b) manual, with the main modification being inclusion of parents in the work.

In its original form, DBT is not practical with children under 12 because it involves abstract thinking and complex skill development. Callahan (2008) presents DBT-related activities for children and adolescents that can be used in both individual and group settings. In their book for parents, Harvey and Penzo (2009) applied DBT to the challenge of raising children who have trouble with emotion regulation. While these resources may be valuable, they do not currently have empirical support from outcome research.

The Concept of Dialectic. For Linehan (1987, 1993a), dialectical philosophy's essential insight is that opposite truths can coexist. This means that opposite beliefs can both be true, opposite values can both be valid, and opposite emotions can both be felt at the same time. Furthermore, opposites can be embraced and reconciled in syntheses that combine the best aspects of both. The formula *thesis→antithesis→synthesis* summarizes the idea of a dialectical process. This is a philosophical idea with important psychological implications, and Fruzzetti and Fruzzetti (2008) discuss both.

> Dialectical philosophy's essential insight is that opposite truths can coexist.

Internal conflicts can be painful, and there is often an impulse to resolve conflict by choosing one side over the other, but facing and exploring the tension between opposing thoughts and emotions are more likely to engender a process of learning, healing, and growth (Rizvi, Steffel, & Carson-Wong, 2012). Often, both extremes of the continuum contain partial truths that people need to balance and integrate in order to progress, as per the moderation principle introduced in the previous chapter.

Linehan (1993a, 1997, 2014) states that the dialectic between acceptance and change is at the heart of DBT. People resist change when they view it as an admission of being unacceptable in the present, and current self-acceptance makes people more capable of striving for change in the future (Holmes, Georgescu, & Liles, 2005). Clients become more open to change when they feel accepted by their therapists, and children become more open to change when they feel accepted by their parents (Harvey & Penzo, 2009).

Acceptance and Commitment Therapy

ACT (Eifert & Forsyth, 2005; Hayes, Pistorello, & Levin, 2012; Hayes, Strosahl, & Wilson, 2011) is a distinctive and somewhat radical approach to psychotherapy that developed within the cognitive-behavioral tradition but departs from that tradition in important ways. The goal of ACT is not to help clients feel better. In fact, this approach characterizes direct efforts to reduce painful thoughts and emotions as ineffective, counterproductive, and "hopeless." Instead, ACT includes two components: (1) helping clients accept all their experiences, both pleasant and painful, and (2) helping clients identify their values, commit to acting on these values, and overcome obstacles to these commitments. The link between the two components is this: Acceptance training enables people to tolerate the distress that often accompanies pursuit of the activities and goals to which they are committed.

Acceptance training enables people to tolerate the distress that often accompanies pursuit of the activities and goals to which they are committed.

ACT makes extensive use of one behavioral principle: Avoidance reduces distress in the short term but increases it in the long term, and the way to manage distress is to sustain *exposure* to feared stimuli until they are tolerated. (Exposure was introduced in Chapter 2, Behavior Therapy, and is discussed more fully in Chapter 13, Anxiety.) ACT links the behavioral concept of exposure to the Buddhist concept of acceptance (Baer & Krietemeyer, 2006).

Like mindfulness practices in general, ACT does not purport to help clients feel better but to feel more *fully*, without attempts to avoid, escape, or numb emotions. Because direct efforts to avoid or reduce emotional pain are generally counterproductive (Biglan, Hayes, & Pistorello, 2008; Hayes, 2004), giving up these efforts often results in a reduction of distress; clients feel better because they stop doing something that makes them feel worse. ACT views this reduction in distress as a desirable byproduct but not the goal of therapy (Hayes et al., 2011). The goal, instead, is to decrease the constricting *effects* of emotional pain on clients' lives, so they can engage in activities they value, regardless of whether dysphoric feelings happen to accompany these activities (Ciarrochi & Bailey, 2008; Wilson & Murrell, 2004).

The word "values" sounds abstract and high-minded, but ACT emphasizes translating values into specific, behavioral terms (Bach & Moran, 2008; Wilson & DuFrene, 2009). The questions are, what would the client like to *do*, and what *would* she do if she were not avoiding painful feelings? Most young clients value goals like getting along with their families, having close friendships, doing well in school, developing nonacademic skills, participating in organized groups and clubs, helping others, practicing religion and spirituality, and engaging in sports, games, arts, and other hobbies. This is what ACT means by "values" in the context of child and adolescent therapy.

What Causes Mental Health Problems?

Difficulty with self-regulation of emotion plays an important role in a wide range of psychopathology, especially internalizing problems (Aldao, Nolen-Hoeksema, & Schweizer, 2010). BPD involves an extreme level of emotion dysregulation, but this issue is of general importance in psychopathology, and therapists need to know how to treat emotion dysregulation regardless of whether they see clients with BPD.

The mindfulness-based theories of psychotherapy all share the idea that nonacceptance of internal experience is a basic cause of maladjustment and dissatisfaction with life.

The mindfulness-based theories of psychotherapy all share the idea that *nonacceptance of internal experience* is a basic cause of maladjustment and dissatisfaction with life. In mindfulness work without CBT components (e.g., Kabat-Zinn, 1994, 2012, 2013) and in ACT (Hayes et al., 2011), nonacceptance of experience is considered the root cause of mental health problems and is the one etiological agent that receives emphasis. DBT's view is more ... dialectical. This intervention certainly affirms the value of acceptance, but DBT addresses a number of etiological factors with a number of CBT techniques, including some designed to change internal experiences (Dijk, 2013; Koerner, 2012; Linehan, 1993a, 2014).

DBT's Biosocial Theory

The biosocial theory describes how genetics and environment interact to produce the symptoms of emotional dysregulation that are epitomized by BPD and occur in a wide range of disturbances (Crowell, Beauchaine, & Linehan, 2009; Linehan, 1993a; Lynch, Chapman, Rosenthal, Kuo, & Linehan, 2006). The theory postulates that genetically based neurophysiological over-reactivity produces emotional vulnerability in some children. This over-reactivity manifests itself in three ways: (1) a high degree of sensitivity to emotional stimuli, (2) intense arousal in response to stimuli, and (3) slow return to baseline. There is a disproportion between stimulus and neurophysiological response, so that mildly negative events elicit jolts of stress hormones, clutched muscles, red faces, and screams, as if the child's brain has gone into a spasm of distress. This is what Cheyenne's parents meant when they said their daughter had always over-reacted to minor negative events.

While neurophysiological vulnerability is an important risk factor, the biosocial theory places equal emphasis on the response of the child's caregivers to his expression of emotion. The theory focuses on whether parental responses are predominantly *validating* or *invalidating* (Linehan, 1997). Parents validate a child's feelings by acknowledging them as important and understandable reactions to events or situations. (This does not necessarily mean concurring with the feelings.)

Parents and families invalidate children's emotions by characterizing them as mistaken, inappropriate responses to the events in question, as if to say, "You shouldn't feel this way," or "That emotion is wrong." Invalidating messages are sent in a variety of ways, such as by ignoring, trivializing, mocking, disputing, or punishing the expression of emotion. Invalidating parents minimize the seriousness of the problems their children face, portray solutions as easy, and blame children for the distress they experience. In essence, the child tries to communicate that "I'm dealing with something difficult here," and the parent replies, "No, you're not."

Invalidation causes painful emotions and physiological overarousal (Shenk & Fruzzetti, 2011). Children in invalidating environments learn that the expression of emotion is punished, so they fear and try to suppress their own emotions. The mechanism of *self-invalidation* evolves as an attempt to cope with invalidation by others, in essence by internalizing it. There is a transition from the parent saying, "There is no reason for you to be upset," to the child saying, "There is no reason for me to be upset." The result of this process is the opposite of mindful acceptance: The child pushes away her own emotions and tries not to feel what she is feeling until she becomes cut off from her own internal experience.

Extreme suppression of emotion often leads to extreme emotional outbursts, in a pendulum-swing mechanism consistent with dialectical theory (Linehan, 1993a). When emotions become too intense to be suppressed, they often explode into behaviors like tantrums, aggression, self-injury, and suicide attempts. These dysfunctional behaviors may represent attempts to communicate distress intensely enough to break through others' indifference and get the message across. This type of escalation frequently works, in that caregivers are finally forced to acknowledge the child's distress—and the maladaptive behavior is reinforced (Harvey & Penzo, 2009; Miller et al., 2007; Rathus & Miller, 2014). Cheyenne acknowledged that she could have cut herself on a part of her body less visible than her forearms, and she realized that she "wanted to get something through their thick skulls."

There is a related pendulum-swing that occurs internally. People who succeed too well at emotional suppression sometimes hate the numbness that results, and they cut or burn themselves in a desperate attempt to break through this numbness and feel *something* (Strong, 1999).

ACT's Concept of Experiential Avoidance

ACT emphasizes one etiological agent in its account of maladjustment: **experiential avoidance** (Eifert & Forsyth, 2005; Boulanger, Hayes, & Pistorello, 2010). ACT's conception of avoidance is broader than what is usually designated by this term; experiential avoidance encompasses all efforts to prevent, reduce, or control experiences of distress. In addition to simple, physical avoidance of feared situations, experiential avoidance would include behaviors such as tantrums, sexual acting out, substance abuse, and self-injury *if* (and only if) the function of these behaviors is self-numbing or distraction from internal pain.

There is evidence indicating that experiential avoidance does not work, in that direct efforts to change thoughts and feelings are not only ineffective but counterproductive. It is a common observation that the directive "Don't think of an elephant" causes us to think of an elephant. In laboratory experiments, when people suppress a thought, they later show a rebound effect in which they think the thought more than people who did not suppress it (Clark, Ball, & Pape, 1991; Gold & Wegner, 1995; Wegner, Schneider, Carter, & White, 1987). Naturally occurring thought suppression is no more effective. People who suppress thoughts as a primary coping strategy have high levels of depression and obsessive symptoms (Wegner & Zanakos, 1994). People who are highly avoidant of anxiety end up having more of it, compared to people who are willing to feel anxiety (Hayes, 2004). Experiential avoidance is a major factor in adolescent self-injury (Howe-Martin, Murrell, & Guarnaccia, 2012). A review by Biglan et al. (2008) found that experiential avoidance correlates with a wide range of mental health problems, while the ability to persist with desired actions in the face of distressing thoughts and feelings predicts many different forms of successful functioning. These findings support the account of etiology on which ACT and other mindfulness approaches are based.

Assessment and Case Formulation

As cognitive-behavioral therapies, DBT and ACT can include any assessment procedure that is part of CBT. This chapter will not review these procedures but will focus on assessment issues and methods that play distinctive roles in the mindfulness-based therapies.

DBT therapists assess parental invalidation of the client's feelings by noting how respectful versus dismissive of their child's emotions the parents seem to be (Miller et al., 2007; Rathus & Miller, 2014). Self-invalidation is indicated when clients short-circuit their expression of feelings by interrupting themselves, questioning or derogating their emotions, and/or taking back their statements.

Cheyenne's therapist noticed that her parents faced a dilemma in dealing with her feelings. When Cheyenne over-reacted to minor occurrences, her parents often swung to the opposite extreme and emphatically assured her that the event in question was no problem and would work out okay. These reassurances never calmed Cheyenne; she responded either by exploding with frustration or withdrawing into silence. The parents genuinely wanted to comfort their daughter, but their attempts to do so invalidated Cheyenne's feelings, and invalidation does not help people manage their emotions.

Like traditional cognitive therapists, ACT clinicians investigate the thoughts associated with dysfunctional behaviors, but they do so for a different reason. ACT therapists do not believe that evaluating the validity of thoughts is a useful endeavor (Eifert & Forsyth, 2005; Hayes, Barnes-Holmes, & Roche, 2001; Hayes & Pankey, 2002). Instead, the focus is on the behavioral consequences of thoughts, especially for avoidance.

ACT assessment focuses on the avoidance of both external situations and internal experiences. ACT therapists, like others, inquire about client efforts to cope, control their thoughts and emotions, and feel better, but their perspective on this material is distinctive. These clinicians carefully assess the *costs* of the client's control efforts, noting the constriction of experience and avoidance of activities that result. It is also important to identify encouragement or reinforcement of avoidance by the social environment.

Questions to Ask

Therapists can inquire about emotion regulation with questions that refer to events that have been stressful for the client:

- "How do you usually react when _____ (e.g., 'your mom says you can't do something,' 'someone isn't friendly to you')?"
- "What do you do to try to feel better? Does it usually work?"
- "How long does it usually take for your feelings to go back to normal?"

DBT and ACT emphasize *functional analysis* of cognitions and emotions, which focuses on their behavioral implications, not their logic or realism (Dijk, 2013; Hayes et al., 2011; Linehan, 1993a). The assessment question is whether thoughts and feelings generate adaptive or maladaptive behavior. The question for clients is:

- "What does that thought (or feeling) tell you to do?"

ACT assessment focuses on experiential avoidance. Clinicians can ask:

- "Do you ever give up doing things you want to do because _____ (e.g., anxiety, anger, depression) comes with them?"
- "When painful feelings come into your mind, what do you do with them?" "Do you let the feelings be? Try to change them? Push them away?"

ACT assessment includes inquiry into the client's values (Hayes et al., 2011; Wilson & Murrell, 2004). Clinicians can inquire about values with questions about goals and with words like, "the things you care about," "what means the most or is most important to you," and "what makes life worth living." Some children have trouble thinking in such abstract terms; for them, the assessment goal is simply to identify the actions and activities they consider important and desirable. Murrell, Coyne, and Wilson (2004) suggest drawing a large outline of a heart and asking clients to write words or draw pictures of activities and involvements that are "close to your heart."

Finally, ACT therapists inquire about obstacles that have blocked the client from translating his values into action. Clinicians can ask:

- "If you didn't have any problems with _____ (painful emotions), how would that change what you do in your life? What activities would you do, and what goals would you go after, that you don't now, because of the _____?"
- "What are you missing out on while you're battling with the _____ (emotions)?"
- "How has trying to control your _____ (emotions) gotten in the way of _____ (valued activities and goals)?"

Patterns to Look For

ACT assessment focuses on one etiological pattern: experiential avoidance. ACT clinicians seek to identify and help clients understand the ways in which their efforts to prevent distressing emotions have blocked their engagement in valued activities.

DBT Chain Analysis. Chain analysis is central to assessment in DBT, both in the initial phase and throughout therapy (Linehan, 1993a, 1993b, 2014; Miller et al., 2007). Chain analysis is based on the stimulus-response-consequence sequence traditionally emphasized in behavioral theory, and there are three additional components. First, DBT chains begin at an earlier point than traditional behavioral sequences, with identification of *vulnerability factors* that existed prior to the first antecedent event. Vulnerability factors include physical illness, tiredness, intoxication, previous stressful events, and, especially, the emotional state the person was in when the initiating event occurred.

Second, DBT chains include not only overt behaviors but also thoughts and emotions. Finally, these chains do not end with the occurrence of a consequence unless this terminates the sequence involving the behavior of concern. Typically, the environment's response to the client's behavior is followed by the client's next response to the environment, and the chain analysis does not end until this back-and-forth interaction culminates in the behavior of concern, which might be a seriously maladaptive behavior, such as self-injury.

DBT therapists draw their chains with circular links. Therapists can also use arrows, which youth generally interpret as "one thing leading to another." Here is the general form of a chain analysis:

Vulnerability factor → Antecedent event → Thought → Feeling → Behavior → Consequence → Cognitive and emotional reactions to consequence → Behavioral reaction → Consequence → ...

Chain analyses can look complicated on a piece of paper, but they actually distill and organize real-life transactions that are much more complex. Clients often feel this technique brings order to chaos and helps them make sense of life events that had been confusing. Here is an example from Cheyenne's therapy:

Was lethargic and bored → Boyfriend didn't return text for hours → Thought: "He's tired of me" → Felt rejected and hurt → Texted him three times in 10 minutes → He texted, "Could you please chill?" → Thought: "He doesn't care about me anymore" → Felt lonely, then mad → Texted, "I'll chill with a new boyfriend" → He texted back, "Good" → Thought: "Now I've lost him too; no boy will ever love me once they get to know me" → Unbearable hurt, loneliness, and self-hatred → Thought: "I'll show him how much he's hurt me" → Cut myself and texted him a picture of my bleeding arm → He came rushing over and said he loves me and just wants me to be okay (immediate positive reinforcement), but I feel like a pathetic nutcase (continuing punishment).

When there are two or more people whose behavior affects the client, the diagram could include segments sketched like this:

Mom got mad at me

↓ ↓ ↓

→ I felt like I was going to explode →

↑ ↑ ↑

Dad got mad at Mom for getting mad at me

Working through chain analyses enables therapists and clients to identify recurring patterns that underlie the particulars of specific incidents. These analyses provide information about the types of experiences the client has trouble handling, skill deficits, and reinforcement contingencies maintaining maladaptive behaviors.

Dialectical Dilemmas. This is the DBT term for two-sided issues that people have trouble integrating into adaptive syntheses (Koerner, 2007; Rathus & Miller, 2000). While all sorts of dialectical dilemmas can occur, DBT has identified several that are fundamental and common. The most basic polarity consists of over- and underregulation of emotion.

Just as a pendulum swing to one extreme sets up the ensuing movement to the opposite extreme, undercontrol and overcontrol potentiate each other. Often, it is *because* the client explodes when he allows himself some emotional expression that he feels he must clamp down so severely on his self-expression, and often it is *because* his emotions are so rigidly overcontrolled that, when released, they explode in such extreme fashion. This pattern fits with the dialectical idea that extreme positions imply their opposites, an idea expressed graphically by the ancient yin/yang symbol.

Rathus and Miller (2000, 2014) described three dialectical dilemmas that often characterize the child-rearing practices of parents of emotionally dysregulated adolescents. These parents frequently vacillate between the extremes of:

- Excessive leniency versus authoritarian control
- Normalizing pathological behaviors versus pathologizing normal behaviors
- Forcing autonomy versus fostering dependence

Change Processes

Traditional CBT, DBT, and ACT deal with client cognitions in different ways. In traditional CBT, therapists use reason and evidence to increase the rationality and realism of client thoughts, but this is not a focus of the hybrid therapies. In DBT, the focus is on increasing the adaptive value of cognitions by facilitating the development of thoughts that lead to positive emotions and behaviors; this might but need not mean increasing the logic and realism of the cognitions (Koerner, 2012; Linehan, 1993a, 2014). In ACT, therapists help clients accept but *detach* from their thoughts as guides for action, especially when the cognitions block engagement in valued activities (Eifert & Forsyth, 2005; Hayes et al., 2011).

Traditional CBT, DBT, and ACT also deal with client emotions in different ways. Traditional CBT includes a number of strategies designed to reduce painful feelings. ACT excludes such strategies, and helps clients accept all the emotions they experience. DBT uses both approaches, and guides clients in moving flexibly between changing their emotions and accepting their feelings. In a number of ways, DBT can be conceptualized as standing in between traditional CBT and ACT.

Mindfulness Training

The term "mindfulness" refers both to exercises done at particular points in time and to a general mental state or way of being that can accompany any activity at any time (Hanh, 1991, 1999; Kabat-Zinn, 1994; Kabat-Zinn & Hanh, 1990). The purpose of the exercises is to increase our general capacity for mindfulness, so our quality of experience is enhanced during the vast majority of time when we are not doing the exercises.

According to Tolle (2004), mindfulness reduces suffering because most distress results from three types of mental activity that the practice diminishes: reviewing the past, anticipating the future, and making judgments. Present moments, in and of themselves, are generally okay (unless something intrinsically hurtful is occurring in the present instant, which is rare). Mindfulness works because it redirects attention away from sources of suffering—the past, future, and judgments—to a location of experience that is almost always okay: right now.

> *Mindfulness works because it redirects attention away from sources of suffering—the past, future, and judgments—to a location of experience that is almost always okay: right now.*

Mindfulness training has a range of positive effects on psychological and neurobiological functioning. On the level of cognitive skills, mindfulness practice enhances self-management of attention, concentration, and working memory (Baer, 2003; Jha, Stanley, Kiyonaga, Wong, & Gelfand, 2010).

Mindfulness training improves the accuracy with which people perceive visceral phenomena, such as heart rate, gastrointestinal functioning, and breathing, which are closely associated with emotion (Corcoran, Farb, Anderson, & Segal, 2009; Holzel et al., 2011). By becoming more aware of their bodies, practitioners become more aware of their minds.

The effects of mindfulness training have been conceptualized as strengthening **metacognition**—awareness and understanding of one's own thinking (Grabovac, Lau, & Willett, 2011; Teasdale et al., 2002). Mindfulness practitioners learn, in an experiential way, that mental contents are profoundly impermanent. Physical sensations, thoughts, feelings, and urges change ceaselessly, often lasting no longer than seconds. By monitoring their moment-to-moment experience, practitioners learn to step back from thoughts and feelings and to view them as mental events that come and go.

This sensory-attentional practice, repeated and accumulated over time, produces a new metacognitive self-understanding.

Viewing mental events as ceaselessly changing experiences rather than perceptions of fixed truths provides distance from thoughts and emotions and reduces their dominance over our lives (Kabat-Zinn, 1994, 2013; Grabovac et al., 2011; Tolle, 2004)). Mindfulness training enables people to moderate their emotional reactions, slow down and balance their thinking, and delay their expression of impulses. Thus, mindfulness training produces effects that are the opposite of BPD in particular and emotion dysregulation in general.

The effects of mindfulness training have been studied extensively by neuroscientists, who have scrutinized the brains of Buddhist monks, other meditation practitioners, and mindfulness trainees with PET scans, CAT scans, fMRI, and other neurobiological measures. This research has found that mindfulness practitioners show long-term changes in brain functioning and enhanced growth in both white matter (axons) and grey matter (dendrites; Kerr, Sacchet, Lazar, Moore, & Jones, 2013). These changes occur in prefrontal cortex regions involved in self-direction of attention (Davidson et al., 2003; Farb et al., 2007), as well as other brain areas. The ability to concentrate on a chosen target involves filtering and prioritizing the flow of information through the brain, in particular by screening out irrelevant inputs; self-directed alpha wave modulation seems to be the main neurophysiological mechanism for accomplishing this (Waldhauser, Johansson, & Hanslmayr, 2012).

Dialectical Behavior Therapy

According to Linehan's theory (1993a, 2014; Linehan et al., 1991), effective self-regulation involves a balance in which we utilize our emotions but are not overwhelmed by them. This occurs when there is an aspect of self that stands above the swirl of changing feelings and respects those feelings, considers the information they contain, and decides whether to act on the basis of the emotions. DBT refers to this aspect of self, located at the intersection of reason and emotion, as *Wise Mind*. DBT therapists use a Venn diagram with two overlapping circles to explain this concept to clients. One circle is labeled as Reasonable Mind and one as Emotion Mind; Wise Mind is their area of overlap.

Self-regulation of emotion requires two complementary capabilities: (1) the ability to accept, experience, express, and utilize emotion, and (2) the ability to change emotion, including the ability to avoid, distract from, and suppress feelings (Greenberg, 2002, 2010). This combination of abilities enables people to capitalize on the assets of emotion, which evolved because of their adaptive value, while minimizing the liabilities of emotion, which occur when feelings disrupt effective cognition and behavior. DBT helps clients develop both skill sets and achieve some control over which they use at different times.

Validation is a fundamentally positive human experience that produces immediate calming effects, reduces physiological arousal, and prompts adaptive self-regulatory processes that modulate emotion (Shenk & Fruzzetti, 2011). Thus, validation is an interpersonal process that directly promotes emotion self-regulation.

DBT capitalizes on another psychological principle: Behaviors can generate emotions (just as emotions can generate behaviors). Social psychology experiments have demonstrated that people who follow directions to adopt confident physical postures then feel more confident and show physiological changes associated with confidence, including increased testosterone and decreased cortisol (Carney, Cuddy, & Yap, 2010).

In many distress tolerance techniques, clients engage in positive behaviors that differ from the emotions they are feeling, which often causes their emotions to change in the direction of the behaviors (Dijk, 2013; Harvey & Rathbone, 2014; see the discussion of behavioral activation in Chapter 14, Depression).

Acceptance and Commitment Therapy

ACT is based on two propositions that are philosophical as well as psychological. One of these propositions concerns what is valuable in human life, and one concerns the relationship between thoughts and truth.

From an ACT perspective, the purpose of life is not pleasant feelings but valued actions (Eifert & Forsyth, 2005; Hayes et al., 2011; Wilson & DuFrene, 2009). The goal of ACT is not decreasing distress or increasing happiness but living a life that is "vital," "engaged," and worthwhile because the client is involved in activities she values, regardless of whether these activities happen to be accompanied by pleasant feelings. This position differs from the view that, implicitly or explicitly, seems to undergird most other therapeutic approaches, which place a great deal of emphasis on helping clients feel better.

Despite ACT's unusual philosophical position, research on this therapy has assessed outcomes in conventional ways, which means that change in emotional symptoms has been measured. The extensive empirical support for ACT, reviewed ahead in the section on outcome research, indicates that exchanging the goal of feeling better for the goal of doing better facilitates the achievement of *both* goals. Nonetheless, ACT therapists view reduced emotional pain as a desirable by-product but not the goal of their work. A similar conclusion has been reached in a separate area of research—namely, the nonclinical field of positive psychology, where the general finding is expressed in the title of Gilbert's (2007) book, *Stumbling on Happiness*. Sometimes the most effective way to achieve happiness is to forget about it and focus on pursuing valued activities and goals.

ACT is based on a complex theoretical structure called *relational frame theory* (Blackledge, 2003; Hayes et al., 2001; Torneke, 2010). This theory questions the common assumption that the main purpose of thoughts is to ascertain truth and, instead, views cognitions as a function of the operating characteristics of minds and the nature of language. Because ACT therapists believe that minds think thoughts for reasons mostly unrelated to truth, they do not attempt to change clients' unrealistic or maladaptive thoughts by citing reason or evidence. Instead, the objective is to weaken the hold that thoughts have on actions, so values and aspirations can strengthen their hold.

ACT recommends that clients exchange futile attempts to control thoughts and feelings for an endeavor in which success *is* possible: commitment to actions that pursue valued goals (Hayes et al., 2011; Strosahl, Hayes, & Wilson, 2004). Such commitments are resilient when they continue in the face of fluctuating emotional states. Dysphoric emotions might be the price that needs to be paid in order to live a valued life, but it is a price worth paying—especially because attempts to reduce or avoid distress will not work, anyway. Thus, while thoughts and feelings often cannot be changed, they can simultaneously be accepted as experiences and ignored as directives.

While thoughts and feelings often cannot be changed, they can simultaneously be accepted as experiences and ignored as directives.

ACT is an exposure-based treatment in two important ways (Hayes, Luoma, Bond, Masuda, & Lillis, 2006; Strosahl et al., 2004). First, some ACT exercises involve mental exposure to distressing thoughts and feelings, which has the effect of reducing their aversive power. Second, when clients engage in previously avoided activities, they re-encounter the anxiety that prompted their avoidance in the first place. Assuming these situations do not involve actual harm, prolonged exposure results in disconfirmation of fearful expectations, and desensitization occurs (Mowrer, 1960).

The etiological mechanism of experiential avoidance is countered by acceptance of all internal experiences, whether pleasant or unpleasant. Because attempting to suppress thoughts and feelings has the paradoxical effect of increasing them (Clark et al., 1991; Gold & Wegner, 1995; Wegner et al., 1987), when clients give up counterproductive control efforts, this secondary source of distress is eliminated, and some reduction of distress is achieved.

Feelings as Guides for Action

In the history of psychotherapy, there has been a profound shift in the status of feelings as guides for action. The view of client-centered therapy (Rogers, 1951), which became widespread in our field, is that feelings are indices of our truest desires and needs, reliable signals of benefit and harm, and optimal guides for choices and behavior. This is why feelings have been considered so important. However, DBT helps clients tolerate distress by training them to engage in behaviors that are unrelated or even opposite to the emotions they are experiencing. Although 12-step programs are not psychotherapies, it is worth noting that their change strategy called "Fake it till you make it" shares with DBT the notion that behaviors can be performed in a purposeful, contrived way until the corresponding feelings eventually develop.

ACT seems to represent a culmination of this historical trend. DBT includes some strategies that detach behaviors from feelings, but ACT involves a general delinking of internal experiences and behavioral actions. The ACT viewpoint accepts thoughts and feelings as experiences but does not take them seriously as indices of truth, identity, or values, and so does not see them as useful guides for choices. Thus, ACT's view of the optimal role of emotion in human life seems fundamentally different from the traditional view in the psychotherapy field.

Future research is needed to reconcile these two views, perhaps by identifying the conditions under which internal experiences are and are not effective guides for action and/or by identifying individual differences that predict whether internal experiences are useful in this way.

Outcome Research

Mindfulness-Based Therapy

Khoury et al. (2013) performed a comprehensive meta-analysis of 209 outcome studies that examined mindfulness-based interventions. This analysis excluded treatments combining mindfulness work with other CBT components, so DBT and ACT were not included. Most of the studies included only adult participants, and the meta-analysis did not separately examine the few studies with adolescents or children. The basic finding was that mindfulness-based therapy is an effective type of treatment, with medium effect sizes for comparisons to wait-list controls and smaller but significant effect sizes for comparisons with non-CBT therapies (e.g., supportive therapy). There was no difference between the average effect size produced by mindfulness-based therapy and either cognitive-behavioral or behavioral treatments. In comparisons based on type of client symptoms, mindfulness-based therapy produced larger reductions in internalizing than externalizing forms of psychopathology; a similar finding was obtained in a meta-analysis by Hofmann, Sawyer, Witt, and Oh (2010). The reviewed studies that performed follow-up assessments generally found that clients' gains were maintained over time. The interventions consistently produced increased scores on measures of mindfulness, and there were strong correlations between client gains in mindfulness and improvements in their symptoms.

Outcome research on mindfulness-based therapy for youth has begun only recently, but the few studies performed have produced supportive results. Biegel, Brown, Shapiro, and Schubert (2009) conducted an RCT with Kabat-Zinn's (2012) *mindfulness-based stress reduction* (MBSR) program, which was originally developed for adults but was provided to adolescents in this study. Participants were outpatient clients aged 14 to 18 years with a variety of diagnoses. Compared to a TAU control group, teenagers receiving MBSR reported reduced anxiety, depression, and somatic distress, and improved self-esteem, sleep quality, and global functioning. In another study of adolescents, Brown, West, Loverich, and Biegel (2011) found that MBSR produced improvement in several indices of mental health and that increased scores on mindfulness measures correlated with improved mental health.

Mindfulness training for parents has also been examined. This training increased parents' empathy for their children, reduced the degree to which they took their children's behavior personally, calmed their reactions to misbehavior, and increased their child management effectiveness (Coatsworth, Duncan, Greenberg, & Nix, 2009; Goodman, Greenland, & Siegel, 2012).

Dialectical Behavior Therapy

Outcome research has provided a great deal of support for DBT as a treatment for BPD and many other disturbances of emotion self-regulation in adults. According to the criteria by which APA's Society of Clinical Psychology rates interventions, DBT has *Strong Research Support*, the highest possible rating, as a therapy for BPD in adults. A narrative review by Lynch, Trost, Salsman, and Linehan (2006) and a meta-analysis by Kliem, Kroger, and Kosfelder (2010) provide extensive and convincing evidence for the effectiveness of DBT. Kliem et al.'s (2010) meta-analysis indicated an average treatment effect size in the medium range.

A mediation analysis by Neacsiu, Rizvi, and Linehan (2010) found that treatment-associated increases in DBT skills fully accounted for decreases in suicide attempts, decreases in depression, and increases in self-control of anger during the course of treatment. DBT skills partly mediated decreases in self-injury. These results indicate that DBT works through the mechanisms emphasized by its theory.

Outcome research on DBT for adolescents is just beginning to occur. Several preliminary investigations have provided encouraging results, but the weak methodology of these exploratory studies, particularly their lack of control groups, precludes drawing conclusions. MacPherson, Cheavens, and Fristad (2013) performed a narrative review of this research. They noted that most of the studies used Miller et al.'s (2007) treatment manual. These investigations consistently found that adolescent clients who received DBT showed decreases in self-harm and mental health symptoms over the course of therapy.

Mehlum et al. (2014) conducted a multisite RCT that compared DBT to an "enhanced" version of TAU for adolescents with histories of self-harm. The enhancement pertained to the frequency of therapy, not its content; clients received a minimum of one session per week. Compared to TAU, DBT produced larger reductions in self-harm, suicidal ideation, and interviewer-rated depressive symptoms. The two therapies produced similar reductions in scores on measures of depression, hopelessness, and borderline symptoms.

Rathus and Miller (2002) performed a quasi-experimental study (i.e., group assignment was not random) that compared hospitalization and treatment completion rates for a group of adolescents who received DBT and a group who received psychodynamic therapy. The DBT group had fewer psychiatric hospitalizations and higher treatment completion rates, even though this group showed more psychopathology at baseline than the comparison clients. This study did not include pre-/postmeasures of mental health symptoms.

Acceptance and Commitment Therapy

ACT has produced impressive outcomes with adults; clients have achieved significant gains in controlled studies of a variety of internalizing disturbances, with effect sizes typically in the medium range (Hayes , 2004; Hayes, Pistorello, & Levin, 2012). ACT seems less applicable to externalizing forms of dysfunction.

ACT has garnered its strongest support as a means of improving adjustment and quality of life in adult patients with chronic medical conditions. ACT for this population has an APA rating of *Strong Research Support*. ACT for depression, anxiety, obsessive-compulsive disorder, and psychosis in adults has ratings of *Modest Research Support* (the second highest rating). In a meta-analysis by Hayes, Luoma, Bond, Masuda, and Lillis (2006), ACT achieved a large effect size in comparison to wait-list and placebo controls, and also outperformed a number of active, well-specified treatments, achieving a medium-sized effect in these comparisons. In a direct comparison of ACT and CBT for adults with anxiety disorders by Arch et al. (2012), the two therapies produced similar outcomes at termination, but ACT resulted in greater continuing improvement on some measures at a 1-year follow-up.

Lundgren, Dahl, and Hayes (2008) performed a mediation analysis to assess whether treatment effects were produced by the hypothesized mechanisms of change. They found that therapy-associated gains in acceptance of painful emotions and commitment to values did account for substantial portions of treatment effects, which indicates that ACT works largely through the mechanisms emphasized by the theory.

There has been much less research on children and adolescents than adults. An RCT by Wicksell, Melin, Lekander, and Olsson (2009) demonstrated positive outcomes for ACT as a treatment for psychological distress and restriction of activity in adolescents with chronic pain. Research on young clients with mental health problems has been limited to case studies and uncontrolled studies with small samples. Murrell and Scherbarth (2011) reviewed these preliminary results and arrayed some findings with promising implications for ACT with children and adolescents.

Are Attempts to Control Thoughts and Feelings Helpful or Harmful?

Viewed from a broad perspective, there are contradictory implications in the results of research bearing on the question of whether trying to control internal experiences is useful or counterproductive. Investigations performed outside the therapy context, including experimental research (Clark et al., 1991; Gold & Wegner, 1995; Wegner et al., 1987) and studies of individual differences in psychopathology (Howe-Martin et al., 2012; Wegner & Zanakos, 1994), have consistently found that trying to suppress painful internal experience is counterproductive. The positive outcomes produced by ACT also have this implication. However, DBT includes many techniques that purport to reduce painful mental contents, and the strong empirical support for this intervention indicates that these techniques often work. Also, mindfulness exercises involve the mental act of "letting thoughts go," which is a means of terminating unwanted cognitions, and there is convincing evidence that mindfulness practice enhances adjustment and well-being. Finally, CBT for anxiety and depression, as described in Chapters 13 and 14, includes direct attempts to reduce these dysphoric emotions, and there is abundant evidence that these therapies produce benefits for most clients.

Future research is needed to investigate the variables that determine whether efforts to control mental contents are helpful or harmful. It might be that some control techniques are effective and others are not, that some thoughts and feelings are controllable while others are not, or that the effectiveness of control efforts depends on the other strategies with which these efforts are combined (e.g., DBT also includes work on acceptance of emotions).

The Therapist's Style

Therapists who write about mindfulness emphasize that this mental state is beneficial not only for clients but also for ourselves (Morgan, Morgan, & Germer, 2013; Surrey & Kramer, 2013). For counselors, mindfulness entails the recognition that being with the client is the only thing going on in the here and now. Being mindful means clearing our minds of personal concerns and allowing our consciousness to be filled with the experience of working with the client.

The mindfulness approach emphasizes the importance of the therapist's moment-to-moment self-awareness in interactions with clients, which means he is always aware of the feelings and thoughts occurring inside (Bach & Moran, 2008; Brach, 2012). Cultivating a careful, nuanced awareness of our internal experience enables us to pick up on subtle dynamics in a sensitive, intuitive, sometimes preverbal way, as long as we are able to separate out any personal dynamics that are unrelated to the client.

Mindfulness-based therapies generally espouse an authentic, genuine counselor style that deemphasizes differences in the roles of clinician and client (Himelstein, 2013; Surrey & Kramer, 2013). There is no denial of the therapist's status as an expert, but this occurs alongside a willingness to be emotionally present, real, and open in the relationship. This stance involves more willingness to express emotion and disclose personal material than is typical in most other types of therapy, although of course care should be taken to ensure that clinician self-expression never impinges on the client's needs (Morgan et al., 2013). The title of Wilson and DuFrene's (2009) book offers a definition of psychotherapy as this type of encounter between two fellow human beings; the book is called *Mindfulness for Two*.

In DBT, the therapist's style—or rather, styles—fits with this treatment's dialectical orientation. These styles consist of pairs of complimentary opposites, the most important of which is the dialectic between acceptance and change. Linehan (1993a, 1993b, 1997,

2014) recommends that clinicians express acceptance of the client and encouragement of change in an interwoven fashion throughout every session. Client emotions generally warrant validation, but client behaviors sometimes do not. Most clients need a combination of nurturing and challenging, with the optimal proportion depending on the individual; clients who are hard on themselves need a larger proportion of nurturing, and those who are easy on themselves need more challenging (Koerner, 2012). The behavioral/characterological distinction introduced in Chapter 1 provides another way to organize these two types of responses to clients; this would mean expressing acceptance of the client as a person while advocating change in maladaptive behaviors.

In another dialectical practice, DBT therapists use both *reciprocal* and *irreverent* communication styles (Harvey & Rathbone, 2014; Linehan, 1993a, 1993b, 2014). Reciprocal communication includes empathic listening, validation, self-disclosure, and warmth. Irreverent communication involves unexpected, whimsical, possibly humorous verbalizations by the therapist. This playful style prevents therapy from becoming too serious. The element of surprise can disrupt the client's habits and assumptions, thus engendering openness to new input.

Mindfulness Training Exercises

Most youth are not familiar with mindfulness practices or meditation techniques, and it might not be clear to them how these exercises could help with their problems, so it is important to offer a plausible, appealing rationale. Himelstein (2013) presents mindfulness training as a means of strengthening our mental capabilities, just as physical exercise strengthens our bodies. Here is an example of a therapist statement based partly on this parallel:

> "Mindfulness exercises help us become more aware of our minds so we can concentrate, manage our feelings, and control our behavior more effectively. These exercises are kind of like the ones we do in a gym because they make our minds stronger, more flexible and fit, although in another way they're different from physical exercise because there's no huffing and puffing; it's all quiet, gentle, and easy."

Explanations of mindfulness need to be dialectical in that the exercises involve a combination of elements that, on the surface, seem to be opposites. The exercises are goal-oriented—but one of the goals is to be nonjudgmental, *including* about progress toward goals. Mindfulness exercises involve trying, and there is a conception of success, but because everything that happens is accepted as part of the process, there is no such thing as failure. The objective is to direct all attention to one focus, yet no one except advanced practitioners can do this consistently—but the process of redirecting attention from wandering thoughts back to the chosen focus is the mechanism that develops mindfulness. In short, there is a goal, but it is impossible to achieve (at least initially), and that is okay. Success lies in continuing the practice and allowing a natural growth process to unfold. Counselors can say:

> "It's not about doing well or badly; it's just about experiencing the exercises, noticing what happens, and gently guiding our minds toward growth."

Here is an explanation of the process of mindfulness work:

"Mindfulness is about *attention*, controlling and focusing attention. There are different exercises, but they all involve focusing attention on just one thing at a time—for example, focusing on breathing, being completely aware of that.

The exercises are easy in a way but difficult in another way, because our minds wander and thoughts pop up and distract us. This is natural—it happens to everyone—but we're learning to do something different, something special: focus our attention on one thing. So, when your mind wanders to a thought or feeling, just notice it, say something to yourself like, 'Oh, a thought,' let it go, and bring your attention back to the focus of the exercise. That's the game.

Mindfulness is about a certain kind of attitude, an attitude toward yourself and your mind. It's a gentle attitude that doesn't worry about how well you're doing but accepts whatever happens and moves on. You never have to judge yourself, push yourself, or criticize yourself. Of course, your mind wanders—and this lets you make the move of dropping the thought and bringing your attention back to where you want it. That move, done over and over again, is what develops mindfulness."

One obstacle to mindfulness is that our thoughts are usually interesting and compelling, and we get drawn into them. One way to deal with this is to remind ourselves that we can get back to the thought later and that right now, during the exercise, we have an opportunity for the special experience of filling our awareness only with what is happening in the moment.

Mindfulness is about noticing experiences so familiar that our minds normally gloss over them, so we barely notice them at all. Becoming curious about things we generally take for granted helps us engage in the exercises. Therapists can engender curiosity by inviting clients to notice and learn about familiar sensations and experiences and then sharing descriptions of them after the exercise is done.

Himelstein (2013) recommends flexibility about the duration of mindfulness exercises, especially with clients who find it difficult to sit quietly without external stimulation. He suggests starting with periods as brief as two minutes, if this is the most clients can do without becoming restless.

For exercises done while seated, clients should sit in physical positions that combine relaxation with alertness. This means sitting comfortably in an upright position, neither rigidly nor slouching, with good posture and two feet on the floor.

Most exercises are meant to be done with the eyes closed. However, Himelstein (2013) notes that some clients, especially those who have been exposed to violence, feel vulnerable if they cannot see. These clients should focus their eyes downward at a point on the floor a few feet in front of them.

Instructions for Exercises

Instructions for a number of commonly used mindfulness techniques are given next. Two longer procedures, including the widely used exercise called the *body scan*, are described in the website for this book, as Handouts 4.1 and 4.2. I do not cite references for the exercises because the techniques have been described by multiple authors (e.g., Hanh, 1991, 1999; Hooker & Fodor, 2008; Kabat-Zinn, 1994, 2012, 2013; Linehan, 1993b, 2014; Miller et al., 2007; Rathus & Miller, 2014), and most originated through a long process of evolution, largely within the Buddhist and other meditative traditions, without identified inventors. Fontana and Slack's (1997) book offers additional instruction in teaching meditation techniques to children.

Mindfulness of Breathing.   The most basic form of meditation is attending to one's breath in a full, moment-to-moment way. Breathing is the perfect example of a fundamental, omnipresent experience that we ignore because it is so familiar. Becoming aware of the experience means discovering something new in what was there all the time.

The procedure is to sit comfortably, breathe naturally, and allow the experience of breathing to become the focus of awareness. In relaxation training, people purposefully breathe more deeply than usual, but in mindfulness meditation, the idea is not to change one's usual way of breathing but to pay special attention to how one ordinarily breathes. Meditators can choose whether to count their breaths, and the procedure ahead gives a few different ways to do this. Here are the instructions for clients:

"You can begin by sitting comfortably in your chair, sitting straight but not rigidly. It's good to close your eyes, but if you'd rather keep them open, focus on one spot on the floor a few feet in front of you. Breathe naturally, as you normally would, but pay special attention to this ordinary experience—become aware of your breathing.

What does it feel like to breathe? Do you feel the air moving into your nose as you inhale and out through your nose as you exhale? What sensations do you notice in the different parts of your body? What do you feel in your chest? Your stomach? You can become curious about these feelings and really notice them. Mindfulness is all about noticing.

If you want, you can count your breaths to keep your attention focused. Think 'one' as you breathe in and 'two' as you breathe out, then 'three,' 'four,' all the way to 10; then go back and start over at one. (Or, if you want to keep it simpler, just alternate between 'one' and 'two.') You can say the number to yourself as you begin the breath, or you can picture the number in writing, or you can think the number as a long sound happening throughout the breath, like 'Oooonnnne'—whatever you like."

Mindfulness of Everyday Objects.

"Choose any object that you see or use in an everyday way, maybe something from your pocket, purse, or room. Carefully study the object as if you had never seen it before and were wondering about it. See if you can notice things about the object that you have not noticed before. (Pause.) What do you notice?"

Variation: "Choose a penny from a pile of them and study it carefully, noticing its distinctive characteristics such as date, shine, where it is worn down, and so forth. Then, put the penny back in the pile, mix them around, and try to find it again."

Listening to Music.

"Listen to a piece of music one-mindfully—that is, without doing anything else at the time. Carefully observe both the qualities of the music (melody, rhythm, etc.) and your internal responses (feelings, associations, physical sensations, etc.)."

Variation: "Focus on one instrument or type of instrument, such as the woodwinds in classical music or the bass in jazz or rock music. Pick out your chosen instrument as the piece is played and try to stay with it all the way through."

Eating a Raisin.

"Hold a single raisin; carefully observe how it looks, feels, and smells; then eat it slowly and with awareness, noticing the tastes, sensations on the tongue, the muscle movements of eating, and swallowing."

Mindfulness of Thoughts.

"In this exercise, you close your eyes, say to yourself, 'I wonder what my next thought will be,' and wait to see what it is. Then wait for the next thought, as they come one after another. Don't judge the thoughts, try to figure out whether they are true or false, believe the thoughts, or argue with them. The experience is just to wait and see what the thought will be."

Version for young children: "Imagine you are a cat, waiting by a mouse-hole and watching it, only instead of waiting for a mouse, you are waiting for your next thought to come out of the hole. Do you wonder what your next thought will be? Soon you'll find out!"

Noticing Experience.

"Close your eyes and focus on your experience in the moment. Notice the feelings, thoughts, physical sensations, urges, and images as they come and go in your mind. Also, try to notice *how* you know you are having these experiences; in other words, what are the sensations that make up a feeling, a thought, and so forth? Simply observe what goes on inside, with interest but without judgment or evaluation, understanding that inner experience is neither good nor bad but simply is.

You might notice that you like some of the experiences and dislike others—just notice the liking and disliking. Do not get caught up in your thoughts by staying with them, focusing on them, agreeing or disagreeing with them. In fact, don't *think* your thoughts at all—just notice them as they appear and disappear."

Variations: Experiences can be labeled with words, so you can picture words that express your thoughts and feelings. You can imagine these words scrolling across a TV or computer screen. You can picture your thoughts and feelings as words or pictures on leaves floating by on a stream, clouds moving across the sky, balloons or bubbles floating away and, perhaps, popping.

Remembering Past Experiences.

"Think of a recent past experience. Try to remember it as vividly as possible, as if you were back in it. Pay attention to your thoughts, feelings, and physical sensations, and notice whether they were pleasant or unpleasant, but do not judge them as good as bad.

Let the intensity build until it peaks and starts to decrease. Notice how the experience of memory eventually weakens, become pale, dissolves, and breaks up as your mind turns to other things."

Variations: This exercise can be done with both positive and negative experiences, and with events from both the recent past and long ago.

Mindfulness of Movement.

"The idea of this exercise is to become precisely aware of the movements of your body in ordinary activities. The simplest example is walking. Walk quietly across the room, paying attention to the movements of your muscles and the feelings of those movements. Notice your heel making contact with the floor, your toes pushing off the ground, your legs moving, and your arms swinging at your sides."

Variations: This exercise can be done with simple physical actions such as stretching and complex activities such as yoga, physical exercise, and physical work.

Implementation of Dialectical Behavior Therapy

As stated earlier, DBT is a CBT that includes general behavioral and cognitive strategies along with its unique components, but this chapter focuses on what is distinctive to DBT. Skills-training manuals and practitioner's guides by Linehan (2014), Rathus and Miller (2014), Koerner (2012), Moonshine (2008), Harvey and Rathbone (2014), and Dijk (2013) offer guidance for implementing DBT. Dimeff and Koerner (2007) edited a book with chapters describing DBT for a number of specific disorders.

Validating Clients

The foundation of validation is empathy (Linehan, 1997). Validation also includes another component: conveying that the person's thoughts and emotions make sense in relation to her context (history, current situation, and recent events). Validation communicates not only that we know how someone feels but also that we understand why she feels that way (Harvey & Rathbone, 2014; Moonshine, 2008). The metamessage is, "Your feelings make sense."

Clients who characterize their feelings as "crazy" are expressing self-invalidation. This word expresses the client's sense that his feelings do not make sense and are not justified as a response to something that has happened. When clients self-invalidate, therapists can block this action and prompt self-validation by identifying links between the client's emotions and his context. This does not necessarily mean the client's feelings are adaptive, but it does mean they are understandable— for instance:

"Wait a minute—you started off by saying you shouldn't have been so mad, but then you described all those cutting little things he said, and given how he's treated you in the past, I can certainly see why you were angry. Doesn't sound crazy to me."

Sometimes the reasons for the client's feelings have already been made clear, and you can demonstrate her sanity just by citing these links to context. Sometimes the reasons are not yet apparent, so you will need to inquire about them. In the meantime, you can convey that you know the client to be a noncrazy, reasonable person, which means that if she feels there are no reasons for her feelings, that is a failure of introspection, not evidence of insanity— for example:

"Rachel, there've been a few times now when you've come in and said your feelings were 'crazy,' but every time we talked through what happened, we found out the feelings actually made sense. There's something to learn from this: If you feel like your emotions are happening for no reason, that just means you haven't figured out the reason yet."

Disentangling the Valid and Invalid

One of the core dialectics in DBT (and psychotherapy in general) derives from the following conundrum: Clients heal and grow when their experiences are validated, but many of their thoughts, feelings, and behaviors are dysfunctional, and we do not want to reinforce dysfunction. Clients present us with complex mixes of adaptive and maladaptive components of functioning, and it would not make sense to respond in the same way to both. Some clients present with such maladaptive symptoms and session material that it can be difficult to find appropriate targets for validation. What's a therapist to do?

One of DBT's maxims is to validate the valid and invalidate the invalid. Koerner (2012) offers guidelines for identifying valid elements in highly disturbed client presentations. First, it is possible to validate a person's emotions without validating the behaviors that flow from those feelings. Cheyenne's therapist said:

"I certainly understand that it hurt when he didn't want to hang out that night, especially when you'd told him you were going through a rough time. But leaving a message where you just cry over the phone is not going to work out a problem with a boyfriend. How do you think he felt hearing that? How did it probably affect his perception of you?"

It is possible to validate a goal while invalidating the behavior used to pursue that goal—for instance:

- "I understand why you want to be friends with her, but loaning her money that she doesn't pay back is not an effective way to make friends with her or anyone else."
- "There's no doubt—when we're miserable, we want something to make us feel better. But do you think getting drunk really achieves this goal, when you consider all the different consequences that come from it?"

It is always possible to validate the importance of a client's problem, especially when you connect the specifics to the underlying issues. Sometimes self-invalidation occurs because clients do not see this connection— for example:

CLIENT: "I don't know why I'm making such a big deal out of this. It was just one game."

THERAPIST: "Well, I think I see the reason. You worked hard on some different moves in practice, and you were really hoping they'd improve your game, but that didn't happen this time, so you're discouraged about whether the new moves will help. Soccer is important to you, and this season hasn't gotten off to a good start, so it makes sense that you'd be distressed about it."

When it is hard to find material to validate, Koerner (2012) suggests looking to the client's learning history for a way of understanding her maladaptive functioning. You can acknowledge the validity of what she learned from past experiences *and* question the applicability of those lessons to her present life (as discussed in Chapter 2, Behavior Therapy). Here is another example from Cheyenne's therapy:

"I understand that, in the past, showing your mom you were upset and wanted some attention didn't work out well, and you had to escalate into crying, tantrums, and even cutting to get it through her head that you were really hurting and needed some help. Maybe in the past this seemed like the only thing that worked, so you feel like it's the only thing that will work now—but that doesn't take into account how much your mom wants to change this. She wants you to come to her with clear words so she can get this right from now on."

Emotion Regulation Skills

The core purpose of DBT is to help clients develop emotion regulation skills (Neacsiu, Bohus, & Linehan, 2014). This therapy helps clients develop the two basic and opposite capabilities that research by Greenberg (2002; Greenberg & Pascual-Leone, 2006) and others has shown are necessary for effective emotion regulation. The benefits of suppressing emotion are usually apparent to clients. The benefits of processing painful emotions might not be. Therapists can explain:

"Of course I don't want you to feel worse, but I think it could help to sit and talk about this sadness with me instead of laughing it off and moving away. No one likes to feel sad, but if you take a breath and face it, you'll find it won't crush you, and then you won't have to be afraid of it anymore. In the long run, the best way to deal with painful feelings isn't to run away from them—they just get stronger and scarier. The best way is to face the emotions, let yourself feel them, and learn to deal with that experience."

Distress tolerance skills are crisis survival skills that help people maintain emotional control during extremely painful times (Harvey & Rathbone, 2014; Linehan, 1993a, 1993b, 2014; Moonshine, 2008). These are not problem-solving strategies for changing external situations but internally oriented techniques for changing painful emotions (and so would not be part of ACT). Distress tolerance strategies are stopgap measures whose purpose is to help people feel better and get through times of intense stress without being overwhelmed, losing control, or doing something to make the situation worse.

> *Distress tolerance strategies are stopgap measures whose purpose is to help people feel better and get through times of intense stress without being overwhelmed, losing control, or doing something to make the situation worse.*

Work on distress tolerance begins by helping clients appreciate this capability as a goal in itself. Clients might not understand this, initially; they often think of problems in external terms, as negative events or situations that happen to them. Psychological mindedness is engendered by defining problems as maladaptive responses to events or situations. The idea that coping is a learnable skill often intrigues clients and motivates them to take on the challenge of developing this capability—for example:

"I realize that, right now, thinking about your girlfriend with that other guy feels like a knife going through you, makes you want to scream, and getting her back seems like the only important thing in life. But I'm going to offer another goal that I think is actually more important, even though you might not: This goal is learning to deal with the pain of disappointment in relationships. That might not sound like a great goal, but here's why it is: If you can live through romantic disappointment and pain, you can go on to find relationships that *will* make you happy, plus you can develop other parts of yourself. And if you can't live through losing a girl you want … it's going to be tough to make it in life, because this kind of thing happens all the time.

Right now this is a crisis, and our first goal should just be to get you through it. We're going to brainstorm some strategies for helping you feel a little better, so you can get through the night. Once some time goes by and you feel calmer, you can take another look at things, and I bet they'll look more hopeful—as long as you don't do something impulsive to mess yourself up."

Linehan (1993a, 1993b, 2014) and Miller et al. (2007; Rathus & Miller, 2014) compiled lists of distress tolerance techniques, which they organized with the acronym ACCEPTS (even though the techniques are actually attempts to change mental states). Table 4.1 presents these techniques and examples.

Many distress tolerance techniques fit into the general category of *distraction*. Counselors can help clients identify activities with enough stimulus value to pull their attention away from what is disturbing them. Distraction works because the capacity of conscious attention is limited, and filling attentional space with neutral or positive material crowds out dysphoric content.

Some experiences absorb attention simply because of their sensory stimulation, but many distracting activities have intrinsic importance, and their worth lies in channeling attention to sources of value as well as diverting attention away from sources of pain. Engaging in worthwhile activities has value that balances, even when it does not fix, upsetting situations, with the result that we feel better about our lives as a whole. One dramatic example was described by the novelist Anthony Powell, who, during World War II, got through the London Blitz by carefully reading Proust's novel *In Search of Lost Time* through the long nights when bombs rained down on the city, incinerating buildings and killing thousands of people. It was impossible to sleep, and there was nothing Powell could do about whether his building was one of those destroyed by bombs, so he felt the best available option, either way, was to immerse himself in a masterpiece.

Radical acceptance is a direct, psychologically forceful strategy in which the person gives up hope that a negative situation will change and simply makes a decision to accept what had seemed unacceptable (Linehan, 1993a, 1993b, 2014; Neacsiu et al., 2014). It can be a relief to give up a battle that cannot be won. Radical acceptance is a purposeful, self-directed attitude adjustment. The strategy enables people to transfer energy from impossible endeavors to ones at which success is possible. Giving up on relationships that will not work is one important example.

Table 4.1   Distress Tolerance Techniques

<u>A</u>ctivities	*Do something.* Contact a friend, play a sport, card game, or video game, do a hobby, clean your room, go for a walk, go shopping.
<u>C</u>ontributing	*Be kind to someone.* Help a friend or sibling with homework, do household chores voluntarily, hold doors for people, perform random acts of kindness.
<u>C</u>omparisons	*Compare* yourself to people with worse problems and fewer resources than yours, and to yourself during harder times.
<u>E</u>motions	*Create different feelings.* Listen to music, watch funny or inspiring videos and movies, read stories and novels, remember times when you felt differently.
<u>P</u>ushing away	*Push the painful situation from your mind.* Create mental images of distancing or walls between yourself and it, while remembering you can think about it later if you want to.
<u>T</u>houghts	*Change your thoughts.* Read books or magazines about interesting subjects, watch history or science shows on TV, do puzzles, google facts worth knowing.
<u>S</u>ensations	*Create different sensations.* Take a hot or cold shower, stretch, exercise, breathe deeply, pet animals, stroke soft fabrics, eat good foods, smell interesting scents.

From Regulating Emotions to Solving Problems

According to DBT theory, people need to be in the emotionally regulated, cognitively effective, self-aware state called Wise Mind before they can solve problems and plan actions successfully (Linehan, 1993a, 1993b, 2014; Moonshine, 2008). Therefore, DBT therapists teach clients to respond to major stressors with a two-stage coping process: The first step is tolerating distress and regulating emotions, and only when an effective state of mind has been achieved does the person transition to problem solving and planning.

Wise Mind is capable of understanding complicated situations because it can hold onto multiple, and even opposite, partial truths. Dialectical thinking is important to adaptation because human realities are vast in their range, contrasts, and complexity. One example is ambivalence: the common experience of having very different, even opposite, feelings about the same person or thing (van Harreveld, van der Pligt, & de Liver, 2009).

People get "stuck" when they latch onto one side of a dialectic as the absolute truth. Dialectical thinking helps clients get unstuck. There are simple linguistic techniques for teaching clients how to loosen and expand their thinking, such as repeated use of the questions, "What else is true?" and "What are we leaving out?", replacing the word "but" with "and," and using a contrast between "sometimes" and "other times" to link both sides of a two-sided truth— for example:

- "You love him—and he drives you crazy."
- "Sometimes you feel like a strong, capable person—and other times you feel like a mess. Both feelings are part of you, just at different times."
- "I understand you have tons of really boring homework—and also that doing well in school is an important value in your family. We need to come up with a plan that recognizes both truths."

In DBT, problem solving is called *solution analysis* (Linehan, 1993a, 1993b, 2014), which builds on chain analysis and usually follows it. Chain analysis identifies the junctions in dysfunctional sequences where more adaptive responses could change the trajectory and prevent negative outcomes from occurring. At these junctions, therapists and clients draw alternative sequences in which more adaptive behaviors are followed by more positive consequences.

Sometimes the alternative responses are simple behaviors or are already in the client's repertoire, so the challenge is just to remember to do them when needed. For instance, to disrupt a connection between confusion about homework and temper tantrums, a child could ask his parent for help. Sometimes the alternative responses are not part of the client's repertoire, so he needs to learn how to do them. In these situations, cognitive interventions address the thoughts, emotion-regulating strategies target the feelings, and skills training addresses the behaviors that have been identified as maladaptive in the chain analysis. This is the point at which DBT connects with the full array of CBT techniques.

Acting Opposite to the Emotion

In this strategy, the client behaves in a manner opposite to the emotion he is feeling (Dijk, 2013; Linehan, 1993a, 1993b, 2014; Miller et al., 2007; Rathus & Miller, 2014).

For instance, a shy client meeting a new person might stand up straight, make good eye contact, and speak in a strong voice while overriding his impulse to flee the situation. The focus is not on changing feelings but on performing behaviors in the absence of the emotions that normally support those behaviors. The Nike motto "Just do it" conveys the idea of this strategy. Nonverbal aspects of the behavior are particularly important because they may produce physical sensations and even hormonal changes associated with the desired emotion/behavior complex, which helps to create the feeling (Carny et al., 2010). Acting opposite to emotion can be done in therapy sessions, for practice, and in the natural environment, for real.

Because the behavior associated with shame is hiding, opposite action means emphatically not-hiding; this involves self-disclosure accompanied by assertive nonverbal behavior (Linehan, 1993a, 1993b, 2014). DBT therapists treat shame and self-invalidation with opposite action by asking clients to talk about their source of shame in an assertive, unapologetic manner. The contrived nature of the exercise is acknowledged at the outset:

> "I know you don't feel this way about what you did—I know you feel the opposite way—which is why I think this exercise could help. At first it will be acting—acting out a new attitude. You can wear out the shame and begin building the opposite feeling by sitting up straight, looking me in the eye, and telling me what happened in a clear, matter-of-fact way. If you think you made a mistake, say so, but also say *why* you made the mistake by explaining how you felt and how things looked to you at the time. Don't worry if it's hard, because I'm going to ask you to do this over and over until you know in your body that, while you wish you had done things differently, this doesn't change the fact that you're a good person who deserves self-respect."

DBT Use of Operant Conditioning

DBT utilizes principles of operant learning mostly through techniques that are less concrete than those described in Chapter 2 on behavior therapy. DBT clinicians occasionally use charts, tokens, and tangible rewards, but they place more emphasis on three other strategies: using the therapeutic relationship to administer reward and (mild) punishment, teaching clients how to use self-reinforcement to shape their own behavior, and explaining the operation of naturally occurring reinforcement contingencies in the everyday environment (Harvey & Rathbone, 2014; Linehan, 1993a, 1993b, 2014; Miller et al., 2007; Rathus & Miller, 2014).

DBT therapists use explicit expressions of approval and (less so) disapproval to shape clients' behavior, in sessions. The goals are to increase client motivation for adaptive behavior and to provide clear, detailed information about which behaviors are adaptive and which are not. It is especially useful to reward new behaviors, adaptive behaviors that occur in session, and specific skills that are being learned (Koerner, 2012). So, when your clients demonstrate progress, you can visibly brighten, smile, and say something like:

- "I like the way that when you started to invalidate that feeling, you caught yourself—you were like, 'Wait, no, I've got reasons for feeling this way'—and then you told me what those reasons are."

- "Good, Mary—I know it's hard to stay with this feeling, and it's easier to make a joke and move on, but staying with the anger shows you know you don't have to be afraid of it, you can contain and handle it, and now we can explore the feeling to see what we can learn and what you want to do with it."

DBT clinicians use the therapeutic relationship to administer mildly aversive consequences in particularly difficult situations for which no other effective response is apparent. When clients engage in behaviors that seem seriously harmful and highly reinforcing (e.g., drug abuse, sexual promiscuity, and self-injury), therapists clearly state their disappointment and reduce the level of warmth they normally express toward the client. DBT therapists are willing to have phone conversations when clients battle urges to injure themselves or attempt suicide, but if clients give in to these urges and the behaviors occur, therapists withdraw attention and refuse clients' phone calls for brief periods of time.

Cheyenne and her therapist applied this principle to her interactions with her boyfriend, whose urgent provision of attention seemed to reinforce her cutting. In a session with Cody and his mother, Cheyenne behaviorally over-rode her pounding heart and feelings of shame to state, in a dignified, assertive fashion, that she did not want her romantic relationship to depend on pity. She said that, if she were to cut again, she wanted Cody to refuse all contact with her for 48 hours, even if she begged for such contact or escalated her threats.

In DBT, counselors teach clients principles of operant conditioning so they can function as behavior therapists for themselves. As discussed in Chapter 3, Cognitive Therapy, these principles work the same way whether the giver and receiver of reinforcement are two different people or the same person. Setting up explicit reward contingencies is an effective way for people to accomplish changes they have been unable to achieve in the past. For example, clients could plan to buy themselves a desired item contingent on goals such as good school attendance, breaking up with a negative boyfriend or girlfriend, or going for a period of time without self-injurious behavior.

A more complicated example is blocking reinforcement of behaviors that are incompatible with the goal behavior. For instance, Cheyenne's avoidance of homework was often reinforced by spending time on social media. She ended this reinforcement by scheduling blocks of time for homework and then forbidding herself access to social media during these times, regardless of whether she did homework.

Contingency clarification means helping clients understand and predict the consequences of their behaviors in the everyday environment. The technique is especially important when reinforcement contingencies are complicated or ambiguous. When people misunderstand the contingencies in operation, they frequently repeat behaviors that are punished and fail to perform behaviors that would be rewarded. This often occurs when the short-term and long-term consequences of a behavior are different from each other. In Cheyenne's meeting with Cody, it emerged that, although he felt compelled to rush over when she hurt herself, he did not want to have a girlfriend who repeatedly engaged in self-injury. Cheyenne understood, at least on an intellectual level, that while her cutting might pull Cody toward her in the short run, it would push him away in the long run.

DBT therapists disclose their own reactions to clients as a way to teach them how other people are likely to respond to various behaviors they produce (Koerner, 2012; Moonshine, 2008). The therapist uses his internal responses as a source of information about how other people are likely to perceive and react to the client. Here are some examples of this type of self-disclosive feedback from counselors:

- "Whoa, Sue, I know you're upset, but let me give you some feedback: When you yell at me like that, I feel disrespected and mad, and that just gets in the way of my trying to help you."

- "Bob, you've told me you hate the disorganization and forgetfulness that come with ADHD, and I've explained how you could use a to-do list to help with that, but it seems like you just won't do it. I'm confused and frustrated; I don't know whether I haven't given you a good suggestion or there's a reason why you haven't used the suggestion I did give you."

DBT With Parents and Families

DBT with adolescents generally includes work with the client's parents and family (Miller et al., 2007; Rathus & Miller, 2014). Goals for these sessions include increasing parents' understanding of their son or daughter, addressing parents' own emotion dysregulation, improving family communication, modifying disciplinary practices and reinforcement contingencies for the teen, and crisis management (MacPherson et al., 2013). Work with the client's parents and, perhaps, other family members is an important means of facilitating generalization of new skills to the everyday environment (Fruzzetti, Santisteban, & Hoffman, 2007; Miller et al., 2007; Rathus & Miller, 2014). When family work is effective, the members incorporate DBT into their everyday life. One indication of this is family use of the terminology, and it is a good sign if you hear members say things to each other like, "Don't invalidate her," "That's true, but what else is true?," and "Is there a side of this we're leaving out?"

Miller et al.'s (2007; Rathus & Miller, 2014) adaptation of DBT for adolescents added one module, called *Walking the Middle Path*, to Linehan's original treatment manual. This module applies DBT to parenting and helps families understand the dialectics polarizing them so they can find ways to orchestrate the adaptive elements of the polarities. Also, parents are taught child-rearing methods based on operant learning principles.

The module begins by orienting parents and teens to the DBT approach as it applies to the problems between them. A visual metaphor is used: The clinician draws a deep canyon, with the adolescent on one side and the parent(s) on the other. She asks the family to identify the issues that have pushed them to opposite sides of the gulf (e.g., curfew, drugs, homework, and sexuality), and she writes summaries of these polarized views on each side of the divide.

After identifying instances of black-and-white thinking, the counselor explains the disadvantage of viewing complicated issues in simplistic, all-or-none terms: Important truths get left out. The counselor searches for elements of everyone's views to validate and challenges them to identify valid points they have not sufficiently considered, encouraging a "both/and" rather than "either/or" approach. When this exercise works, parents and teens begin articulating points that, previously, had been on the other side of the gulf. (The spectrum technique described in the previous chapter might be a useful tool in this work.)

Therapists can then facilitate a synthesis that integrates input from both ends of the continuum into an evolving middle path for the family. To pursue the graphic analogy, the two sides' work toward resolution can be depicted as a bridge across the gulf, with key words written on the bridge to summarize the steps they took to accomplish this meeting of minds. Here are two examples of syntheses that often need to be achieved in families:

- Rather than viewing discipline in terms of a permissive/strict dichotomy, parents differentiate between important, non-negotiable principles and less important issues suitable for negotiated compromises that acknowledge the youth's preferences.
- Parents maintain insistence on time for homework but negotiate an arrangement that allows for a break after school and time for some enjoyable activity during the evening, even if this means not all the homework is completed.

There is a DBT-based book for parents with the appropriate title of *Parenting a Child Who Has Intense Emotions* (Harvey & Penzo, 2009). The book teaches parents to think dialectically, be mindful of their responses to the child's emotionality, replace judging and blaming with describing and problem solving, and validate the child even when her behavior is difficult. Harvey and Penzo explain how acting out in this population is usually the result of the child being overwhelmed by emotions, even when the parent feels the child is purposely trying to upset him or defy his authority. The book teaches a two-part response to the child's acting out: First deal with the emotion by validating the child's feelings and allowing some time for soothing and calming; later, when the child is ready, shift gears into reviewing what happened, problem solving, planning how to do better the next time and, when appropriate, administering consequences. In Chapter 10, on disruptive behavior, this type of two-part response is elaborated in a presentation of the collaborative problem-solving approach.

Implementation of Acceptance and Commitment Therapy

ACT is based on a complex theoretical foundation. Therapists who want to use ACT strategies without first mastering the theory can consult several practical guides with an emphasis on application, including a skills-training manual by Luoma, Hayes, and Walser (2007), a clinician's guide by Harris (2013), and a primer by Harris (2009). Bach and Moran (2008) and Ciarrochi and Bailey (2008) provide guidance in combining ACT with general CBT.

ACT was developed for adults, and work on adaptations for young clients has begun only recently (Murrell & Scherbarth, 2011). ACT includes complex, abstract, even philosophical ideas, so counselors need to simplify and concretize these ideas for young clients. Recent work suggests that ACT principles and strategies can be presented in forms that youth understand and use, and children's comfort with nonliteral use of language helps them grasp the metaphors used in ACT (Greco & Hayes, 2008). Murrell et al. (2004) provide practical instruction in using this approach with children, with lots of therapy transcripts.

When to Use ACT

The question of when maladaptive thoughts are most effectively addressed by critical evaluation, as in cognitive therapy, and when by acceptance and distancing, as in ACT, is a complex question that can be answered only by future research. Until such research is performed, some practical points warrant consideration. First, whatever the validity of ACT's relational frame theory (Blackledge, 2003; Hayes et al., 2001; Torneke, 2010), persuading clients that it does not matter whether their thoughts are true or false is often difficult or impossible. Also, especially with children, rectifying harmful misunderstandings is often easily accomplished by providing simple information and reasoning in an authoritative, reassuring manner. Sometimes, declining to address cognitive distortions on a reality level would be therapeutically ill-advised and, perhaps, unethical. As examples, if a child blames himself for being sexually abused, his parent's divorce, his sister's illness, or any other event he did not cause, it would seem therapeutically inappropriate to ignore the question of truth and teach the child to watch these thoughts come and go in his mind. In my personal communication with Amy Murrell (September 11, 17, 18, & 20, December 10, 2013), she said ACT therapists generally would address such issues with reason and evidence, like cognitive therapists. However, this type of recommendation is conspicuously absent from the published ACT literature.

The other side of the dialectic is the one described by relational frame theory: To a large extent, thoughts *are* a function of the nature of language and the operating characteristics of minds, rather than truth. The following therapist statement acknowledges both sides of the issue and paves the way for ACT:

> "There are two ways to look at thoughts. One is to view thoughts like windows on reality, which means they are all about figuring out the truth. On the other hand, thoughts are products of our minds, our brains, and they are largely about how our minds work and what our brains happen to be doing at the time we have the thought. This might not have anything to do with truth."

ACT is well suited to clinical situations in which clients are in the grip of disturbing thoughts that are not easily refuted and that become more entrenched when debated.

ACT is well suited to clinical situations in which clients are in the grip of disturbing thoughts that are not easily refuted and that become more entrenched when debated. Even in such situations, the idea that truth does not matter is usually resisted by clients, and I find it more effective to suggest the client's thoughts are probably partly true and partly false, with the more important question being the functional one of how these thoughts affect her life. Words like the following can help clients transition from a focus on truth to a focus on adaptation:

> "I get it that you believe the kids at school don't like you, and you have a lot of reasons for this, so I'm sure there's truth to what you say. But here's something else: Things are usually more complicated than they seem, and things change all the time. If we get locked into a belief, we don't see the possibilities outside it, and it's like we're in a cage made of the belief. Some of the bars in your cage might be made of truth, but I still want to help you get out of it.
>
> It's hard to know what everybody thinks of you. Some kids probably don't like you, some might but you don't know it, some might feel differently about you on different days, and most of the kids probably don't think much about you one way or another.

And that's just today—tomorrow, things could change. So your belief that nobody likes you is probably partly true, partly false, and partly just, who knows? But here's something that seems more solid: You like to sing, you'd like to be in the choir, but your belief is stopping you. What if you didn't let it?"

There are a number of words that, sprinkled through your conversation, can help clients relax their concern about thoughts as truth. Rather than debating, you can respond to clients' distressing beliefs with a shoulder shrug and a statement that these thoughts "might be true and might be false," "might be true sometimes and not at other times," "are probably true in some ways and not true in other ways," "might be true but a lot of other thoughts are true, too," and "are one way to look at it but not the only way," along with statements that it is often impossible to know the full truth about things but we can live our lives successfully, anyway. Referring to cognitions as "what your mind says" or "what your thoughts are telling you" reduces the urgency of the truth issue while acknowledging the reality of mental phenomena. One client distanced herself from her unwanted cognitions by greeting them with the statement, "Hello, thought."

ACT is a distinctively appropriate intervention for the common situation in which clients already know a recurring thought is unrealistic and maladaptive but they cannot stop it from bothering them and influencing their behavior. The ACT insight is that, in situations like these, further struggle with thoughts is usually futile and often counterproductive, and the most empowering option is to let the negative thoughts be but withdraw energy from them so their control over behavior is loosened. In short, when cognitive work seems to have done all it can but dysfunctional thoughts continue to occur, it might be time to switch to ACT. You can explain this to clients by saying:

"When people are bothered by thoughts that aren't true, there's Plan A and Plan B. Plan A is to take a good look at the thought, go over the evidence, and use logic to figure out that this thought is not fair and not right. Sometimes the person is like, 'Okay, I'm done with that thought.' When this happens, Plan A worked and we're finished.

But sometimes the thought keeps coming back and bothering the person. They know it's not true, but they can't get it out of their mind, and it stops them from doing what they want. This situation calls for Plan B. Here, the person stops arguing with the thought, because that just makes it stronger, but she changes the way she *hears* the thought, so it stops having power over her life. I'll explain more about this strategy as we go on."

Accepting (and Demoting) Thoughts and Feelings

In ACT, the bridge between assessment and treatment is made up of inquiry into the client's efforts to reduce his negative feelings and the outcomes of these efforts. ACT assumes that these attempts have not worked in the long run, although they might have worked temporarily, and that a careful review will demonstrate this to the client on the basis of his own experience (Bach & Moran, 2008; Eifert & Forsyth, 2005; Hayes et al., 2011). This assumption is usually valid because, if the client's attempts were successful, presumably he would not be in therapy.

ACT therapists then make a statement to the effect that the client's efforts to control her feelings are hopeless—but this does *not* mean the client and her life are hopeless (Hayes et al., 2011). Murrell (personal communication, September 11, 17, 18, & 20, December 10, 2013) suggests language like the following:

"You're a good kid and a smart kid, but feelings are really hard to change, and sometimes it's just impossible. You've put so much time and energy into trying to make the _____ (e.g., depression, feelings about the divorce) go away, but it keeps coming back no matter how hard you try. And I wonder what your life would be like if you dropped this struggle, let the feelings be what they're going to be, and started going after the things you want, anyway. Maybe you'd still have some _____, but you'd be doing what's important to you and moving toward your goals."

The following quasi-neurobiological account of dysphoric thoughts makes sense to many clients:

"Thoughts don't always tell the truth. Sometimes thoughts have nothing to do with truth, and they come from some quirky little part of our brain, like a negative-thought module or app whose switch gets stuck on 'on,' so it keeps pumping out upsetting signals for no reason other than that's what it does. If you try to shut it off, the little gizmo just gets more agitated and pumps out more negative stuff. It's not like a weed you can pull out by the roots. It's there and it's not leaving.

But there *is* something you can do that works: You can change the way you hear the signals. You can observe your thoughts and feelings like they're just something that happens in your mind, not windows on reality and not the core of who you are. You can let them do their thing, move through you, wash over you like waves crashing on boulders in the ocean, creating lots of noise and commotion but having no effect.

If you decide to live with your thoughts and feelings this way, they will lose their power over you. You don't have to believe them. You don't have to obey them. You don't have to avoid them or argue or fight them. With all the energy and freedom you'll have, you can start doing the things you like and living the life you want, whether they're yapping and growling at you or not. In their *face!*"

ACT's recommended relationship between the self and troublesome mental contents is captured by the African American expression, "Talk to the hand." Clients who know this expression can sarcastically invite their unwanted thoughts and feelings to do so.

The overall strategy of ACT can be explained to clients with the following diagram. With your paper in the landscape orientation, ask the client to draw a representation of herself in the lower right-hand corner. Then, imagine the paper divided approximately in half by a diagonal line from the upper-right to the lower-left corner, and ask the client to use words or drawings to represent her valued activities in the triangularly shaped half of the paper most distant from the picture of herself. Then, ask her to place representations of her dysphoric thoughts, feelings, fears, and rationales for avoidance in the region between the client figure and her goals, and offer the following formulation:

> "This picture shows your situation. You would really like to _____ (e.g., go on sleepovers, play basketball), but there are these painful thoughts and feelings in the way. It's like they are monsters saying, 'You'd better not come toward us, or we'll hurt you.' So you try to stay away from them, but then you have to stay away from the things you like. And the more they intimidate you, the deeper into your corner you go, and your life shrinks.
>
> But there is hope, and this is it: The distressing thoughts and feelings can't actually stop you from moving toward your goals, they can just kick up a fuss while you move through them—which you can! And if you do, they will lose their power to intimidate you, because you'll show they can't stop you from doing what you want. So a really good choice, if you're willing to make it, would be to go for what you want and learn to deal with whatever feelings come along for the ride. Your life will *grow*."

Here is the essence of ACT in one therapist statement:

> "When it comes to painful thoughts and feelings, there's good news and bad news. The bad news is that sometimes we just can't get rid of them. The good news is we don't have to, because they can't stop us from doing what's important and living the life we want."

Here is the essence of ACT in one client's statement: "I am in pain and I can live my life."

Exercises and Metaphors

ACT has a number of strategies for building both the motivation and the capability to accept all experiences, including painful ones. Physical exercise is a useful metaphor for engendering a willingness to try (Murrell et al., 2004). Young people understand that physical training involves pain but produces the benefits of increased strength and stamina, and they know the saying, "No pain, no gain." ACT exercises in particular and all efforts to overcome experiential avoidance in general can be presented as exercises that increase mental toughness and strengthen our ability to pursue valued goals despite pain.

ACT uses a number of exercises and metaphors to depict thoughts and emotions as impermanent phenomena that can be observed without being believed, feared, evaluated, or obeyed. By practicing these exercises, clients learn to step back and look *at* their thoughts rather than *through* their thoughts, as they come to see their cognitions for what they really are (transient products of the mind), not what they say they are (objective truths). Hayes et al. (2011) invite clients to imagine themselves on a bridge overlooking a railroad train moving beneath them, with thoughts and emotions represented as words or pictures on the cars moving into the distance. As in the exercise "Noticing Experience" described earlier, ACT therapists invite clients to imagine their thoughts and emotions as leaves floating on a stream, words crawling across a screen, and so forth. Cheyenne did this with thoughts such as, "No boy will ever love me," "I'll always be lonely," and "There's something wrong with me."

According to relational frame theory, language has a hold on people that becomes maladaptive in situations that concern emotions, and this tyranny is most oppressive when we take language literally (Blackledge, 2003; Hayes et al., 2001; Torneke, 2010). Therefore, ACT includes a number of exercises designed to deliteralize language (Ciarrochi & Bailey, 2008; Harris, 2013; Hayes & Pankey, 2002), which means to recognize that words exist primarily as auditory, visual, and mental phenomena, not objective truths about reality. One example of a deliteralizing technique is to repeat a troublesome thought over and over again, either out loud or silently. The effect is for the emotional power of the words to dim, and we begin experiencing the words as meaningless sounds. In variations of the technique, the words can be repeated slowly or quickly, loudly or softly.

Taking this strategy a step further, clients can achieve distance from their thoughts by externalizing them in a fashion that is not only exaggerated but also whimsical and humorous, which undermines the status of thoughts as truths. Clients can imagine their negative cognitions repeated over and over by silly actors or comedians, people who are singing and dancing, or cartoon characters (Leahy, Holland, & McGinn, 2011). Clients can imagine their negative thoughts vocalized by an announcer on "Bad News Radio," a station whose motto is, "All bad news—all the time" (Hayes et al., 2011). For a version of this metaphor with modern technology, clients can picture their dysphoric mental content as incessant texts or tweets from something like @doomandgloom, #everythingsucks. Cheyenne did these exercises with thoughts like, "Cody is the only boy I could ever love," "I am such a mess," and "My parents hate me."

Feelings are less verbal than thoughts, so different exercises are needed to help clients experience their emotions as finite, limited, and manageable. Therapists can help clients sit mindfully with their feelings by asking them to notice where in their body they feel the emotion and what its physical sensations are. Clients can "physicalize" their emotions by drawing or imagining their shape, size, color, texture, temperature, and so forth (Bach & Moran, 2008; Luoma et al., 2007).

The metaphor called "Monsters on the Bus" presents the ACT view of distressing emotions, valued goals, and choices about which to emphasize in deciding what to do (Hayes et al., 2011). The client imagines she is the driver of a bus that can go anywhere she wants, with destinations that represent the activities and goals she values. Unfortunately, there are monsters on the bus; they are big and scary-looking, and they shout horrible things, such as, "You're not smart enough to do well in school," "Your brother is much more popular than you," and "You're going to make a fool of yourself." The monsters know the client's sensitive issues, so they can really get to her emotionally, but they actually have no physical capabilities, so they cannot stop her from driving where she wants to go. The driver's choice is whether to stop driving, turn around, and argue with the monsters in an attempt to shut them up. The problem is that she has to stop the bus to do this, so she cannot progress toward her destinations, and the monsters only yell louder when she argues with them. The best option is to let the monsters carry on and focus on driving where she wants to go.

Murrell (personal communication, September 11, 17, 18, & 20, December 10, 2013) does role-plays in which she takes the role of the client's mind. The client tries to engage in the activities he values, and the therapist verbalizes the client's troublesome thoughts in an aggressive manner (e.g., "You're going to *fail*," "They're going to *laugh* at you"). If the client is drawn into arguing, the clinician becomes louder and meaner. If the client persists in his chosen activity, the therapist reduces the intensity of her harassment.

Translating Values Into Action

In discussing values with clients, it is important to move from the abstract to the concrete and behavioral (Strosahl et al., 2004; Wilson & Murrell, 2004). For instance, if the value of friendship is taken seriously, this implies the importance of behaviors like sharing, helping, and listening, while behaviors like ignoring, put-downs, and interrupting move us away from friendship.

Murrell et al. (2004) suggest a procedure for helping clients operationalize their values behaviorally. The client writes down or draws behaviors that move her toward valued goals and places the slips of paper in a box decorated with a heart. Then, she writes down or draws behaviors that move her away from goals and places these slips of paper in a bottle labeled with the skull-and-crossbones symbol of poison. (If boxes and bottles are not available, envelopes with these insignia also work.)

Because people must often approach and tolerate distress in order to act in valued ways, ACT includes discussion of the role of courage in striving for change (Wilson et al., 2010; Wilson & DuFrene, 2009). ACT imbues pain with dignity by recognizing the value of actions taken and commitments sustained in the face of distress. Therapists can communicate this to clients with statements like, "I know how stressful it was for you to do that—your courage really inspires me" (Murrell et al., 2004).

Summary

This chapter is about the importation into CBT of the Buddhist concept of acceptance and meditation techniques that build mindfulness. The chapter presents general mindfulness exercises and two cognitive-behavioral treatment packages, DBT and ACT, that have adapted principles and strategies of mindful acceptance for use in psychotherapy.

All three types of psychological interventions have received extensive empirical support as treatments for mental health problems in adults. There is much less outcome research on young people, but the studies that have been conducted have generally produced encouraging results for adolescent clients.

Mindfulness is a mental state in which attention is purposefully focused on chosen aspects of the present moment and all components of experience are accepted in a nonjudgmental fashion. When natural deviations from this focus occur, and the mind wanders to memories of the past, anticipations of the future, or judgments, the person notices the deviation and gently guides her mind back to the chosen focus. As moment-to-moment experiences are accepted, they lose their power to alarm, overwhelm, and control us, and self-regulatory capabilities are strengthened. Neuroscience research demonstrates that mindfulness practice produces beneficial changes in brain structure and functioning.

DBT is a complex, comprehensive treatment for emotion dysregulation. DBT includes the general CBT repertoire of techniques, mindfulness exercises, ideas drawn from dialectical philosophy, and other innovative components. DBT therapists train clients in dialectical thinking, which recognizes that opposing beliefs, emotions, and values usually contain partial truths that can be reconciled in adaptive syntheses.

As one dialectic, DBT therapists try to convey both acceptance of the client and the need for change in every session. As another, clients learn the two opposite categories of skills that research indicates are necessary for effective emotion regulation: the ability to accept, tolerate, and fully experience emotion, and the ability to suppress, distract from, and modify feelings.

DBT teaches distress tolerance strategies that do not address problematic situations but focus on altering internal experiences instead. These strategies inject positive experiences into painful times by using readily available resources, such as music, books, showers, friends, and hobbies. DBT also draws on a variety of CBT techniques, described in other chapters, to strengthen externally oriented problem solving and coping.

ACT is organized around remediation of one etiological factor, experiential avoidance, which it counters with a two-part strategy. Clients learn to accept and fully experience all their emotions and thoughts, both pleasant and painful, and they commit to activities that fulfill their desires, express their values, and pursue their goals. There is a crucial link between these two components: Acceptance training enables people to tolerate distress and overcome experiential avoidance, which is the main obstacle we face in pursuing valued goals.

There is a philosophical premise underlying ACT—namely, that the purpose of life is valued action, not pleasant feelings. Adoption of this premise does not make pain go away, but it reduces the degree to which distress, and (futile) attempts to reduce distress, control choices and behavior. The result is increased freedom to choose desired activities and live a valued life. Also, in a delightful convergence of effects, it turns out that giving up efforts to prevent negative feelings results in improved emotional well-being. Although more positive emotions are not a goal of ACT, outcome research indicates they are usually a by-product.

Case Study

Cheyenne and her parents identified the central dialectic in their conflicts, since her early childhood, as revolving around the question "How bad is it?" regarding the setbacks and disappointments she encountered. Cheyenne had always reacted to ordinary frustrations with an intensity of distress that, to her parents, seemed extremely disproportionate. They had developed a habit of responding with the message of, "It's not that bad," and their expectation of overreaction became so entrenched that they minimized Cheyenne's distress without even investigating what the upsetting events meant to their daughter. The resulting invalidation intensified both Cheyenne's distress and her efforts to communicate how bad she felt, in a cycle that escalated all the way to cutting.

In therapy, both parties worked on understanding and articulating the partial truths on the other side of the gulf between them. The parents learned to see, acknowledge, and empathize with the legitimate pain their daughter experienced in reaction to negative events in her life. Cheyenne learned to say things like, "I know it's not the end of the world, but it really hurts that they didn't invite me to go to the game with them." With both parties verbalizing both sides of the dialectic (albeit to different degrees), there was less to argue about, and conflict evolved into collaborative efforts to understand and cope with problems.

Feelings of loneliness and inadequacy had always been terribly difficult for Cheyenne to endure, and she had desperately pursued romantic relationships as a way to secure affirmation. Therapy involved prolonged exposure to these emotions, using exercises such as Mindfulness of Past Experiences, physicalizing emotions, and deliteralizing thoughts. Socializing had always been intimidating to Cheyenne, but she learned to tolerate this anxiety enough to join a school club and develop some friendships with female peers. Cody was a good guy, but this relationship had been associated with more emotional drama than either teen could handle, and Cheyenne was able to grieve the breakup and then look to other relationship opportunities for the romantic closeness and affection she so deeply valued.

5

Psychodynamic Therapy

OBJECTIVES

This chapter explains:

- *The psychoanalytic model of the mind as a set of distinct structures that sometimes conflict with each other.*
- *The unconscious mind and its role in the etiology of mental health problems.*
- *The mental structures of id, ego, and superego.*
- *The difference between mature and immature ego functioning.*
- *Object relations theory.*
- *The technique of interpretation, which produces insight.*
- *The capabilities and limitations of insight as an agent of change.*
- *The role of psychoeducation in dynamic therapy.*
- *How to provide corrective emotional experiences to clients.*

Case Example
Preemptive Strike

Jennifer's parents did not know whether they felt more sympathy or anger toward their 11-year-old (Caucasian) daughter. They described Jennifer as a bright, competent girl, but nothing made her happy, and she was usually in a bad mood, sometimes crying in response to minor frustrations. Jennifer had no close friends, and she frequently isolated herself in her room, where she watched TV and ate junk food. School came easily to her but, rather than contributing to an enjoyment of learning, this seemed to result in an arrogant attitude toward peers and disrespect for teachers who, she claimed, did not know more than she did. The parents described these problems as long-standing and were unable to locate their beginning at a particular point in time. The therapist, noting that depression in children sometimes manifests itself as irritability more than sad mood (see Chapter 14), made a diagnosis of persistent depressive disorder.

In her first session, Jennifer wasted no time before snickering at the therapist's unfashionable clothing and worn office furniture. She portrayed her behavior in school as justified given how boring and clueless the teachers were. She seemed to enjoy evading questions by turning the spotlight from herself back to the therapist. All attempts to examine her role in problems were met with derision (e.g., "Don't give me your analysis; you're just a Dr. Phil wannabe").

Psychoanalytic Theory

Psychodynamic therapy is a descendent of **psychoanalysis**, which was originated by Sigmund Freud and was the first form of psychotherapy. Modern versions of analysis are practiced today, but not widely, while dynamic therapy is a common form of treatment. Psychodynamic and psychoanalytic therapies are based on the same body of theory; the differences concern practice and technique. Analytic therapy involves four or five sessions a week, and dynamic therapy usually occurs once a week. Analytic treatment frequently takes several years. Dynamic therapy usually takes from several months to 1 year. In analysis, the client lies on a couch with the analyst seated behind her. In dynamic therapy, the clinician and client sit facing each other. (In both types of therapy, children are free to move around and play.)

The term **dynamic**, in "psychodynamic," refers to interactions between different parts or aspects of the mind. According to analytic theory, the mind is not a unified whole, and mental structures differ in their aims, content, and manner of operation. As a result, people often experience **internal conflict** (Fenichel, 1945; S. Freud, 1923, 1933; Hartmann, 1939/1958).

According to analytic theory, the mind is not a unified whole, and mental structures differ in their aims, content, and manner of operation.

Freud created a huge, sprawling theory, many of the tenets of which have been disproved during the last century. However, recent neuroscience research has produce deep-level information about brain functioning that conforms in some fundamental respects to the picture of the mind sketched by psychoanalysis. Westen (2005; Westen & Gabbard, 2002) reviewed psychological and neuroscientific research addressing psychoanalytic hypotheses and identified extensive support for some of the theory's most important postulates.

Perhaps the most important single conclusion of neuroscientific research is this: The mind is modular (Damasio, 1994; Debiec, Heller, Brozek, & LeDoux, 2014; LeDoux, 1998). In other words, the brain is not a single, homogenous entity but is composed of a number of modules or parts. The modules have different anatomical locations, functions, operating characteristics, and, to a considerable extent, *different agendas.* This is why it is possible for conflict to occur within the same brain.

Neuroscientists say that the brain is like a committee—and a fractious one at that, with members frequently arguing about the best course of action to take. When brains are viewed by CAT-scan, PET-scan, and fMRI machines, internal disputes are indicated by high rates of firing in the nerve tracts connecting the modules in conflict (Kehyayan, Best, Schmeing, Axmacher, & Kessler, 2013). There is even a certain brain structure (the anterior cingulate cortex) that functions like a mediator attempting to resolve conflicts between other modules. This neurophysiological account can help clients make sense of their experiences of ambivalence and competing impulses, which emerge as natural aspects of the human condition. Statements taking the form, "Part of me wants X, but part of me wants Y" are not merely analogies—they can be literally true. What neuroscientists call the modular nature of the brain corresponds to what psychoanalysts call the dynamic nature of the mind.

The Core Idea: The Unconscious Mind

In the late 19th century, the scientific view was that "mind" is synonymous with consciousness. But then a young physician named Sigmund Freud, who had never heard of psychotherapy because there was no such thing, observed a demonstration of a new procedure called hypnosis (S. Freud, 1935). A woman was induced into a trance state, and she was given a posthypnotic suggestion that when the hypnotist said a certain word, she would get up from her chair and open a window in the room. The woman was brought out of her trance; the word was said; and the woman walked over and opened the window exactly as she was told to do. But this was not the most interesting aspect of the demonstration to Freud. He was more struck by what the woman said before she got up to open the window. Her verbalization was described as something like this:

" ... hmm, it's getting warm in here.... Boy, is it hot. It's stifling. I could really use some fresh air. Would you mind if I opened that window over there?"

There are two important truths revealed by this sequence of behavior: (1) People sometimes do things without knowing why, and (2) when this occurs, people generally construct plausible reasons for their actions, although these rationalizations have nothing to do with the real reason for their behavior (Fenichel, 1945; S. Freud, 1933, 1943). In this demonstration, the woman's behavior was under the control of her unconscious. However, her conscious mind did not generate thoughts like "I have no idea why I'm doing this" but, instead, generated reasonable (and irrelevant) justifications for the behavior. In the 100 years since Freud developed his theory, research has produced overwhelming evidence that much human cognition, emotion, and behavior are, indeed, controlled by unconscious processes (Damasio, 1994; Debiec et al., 2014; LeDoux, 1998).

Freud's ideas were met with derision by the scientific establishment of his time. The term "unconscious mind" was considered an oxymoron. The opposition was so vehement that the early analysts, in characteristic fashion, thought that people's resistance to the idea of the unconscious was based not on logic but on motivation and emotion. Freud (1943) placed this threat to humanity's collective self-esteem in the context of the history of science:

Humanity has in the course of time had to endure from the hands of science two great outrages upon its naïve self-love. The first was when it realized that our earth was not the center of the universe, but only a tiny speck in a world-system of a magnitude hardly conceivable.... The second was when biological research robbed man of his peculiar privilege of having been specially created, and relegated him to a descent from the animal world, implying an ineradicable animal nature in him.... But man's craving for grandiosity is now suffering the third and most bitter blow from present-day psychological research, which is endeavoring to prove to the "ego" of each one of us that he is not even master in his own house, but that he must remain content with the veriest scraps of information about what is going on unconsciously in his own mind. (p. 252)

Most people in our culture seem to have assimilated the idea of the unconscious and no longer find it threatening or insulting. To me, this underlying layer makes the mind much more interesting and mysterious. Also, as will be discussed later, analytic theory does propose ways for people to come to know their unconscious minds, at least partially.

Mental operations are unconscious for several different reasons. Unconscious processing of physiological and sensory-motor information seems conducive to efficiency; we do not need to be conscious of these mechanisms. Many mental operations are unconscious because they occur automatically and the person has not taken the time to think about them; this is the understanding of unconscious schemas in cognitive therapy. Psychoanalytic theory posits an additional reason for mental contents to be unconscious: Some impulses, emotions, and memories are excluded from consciousness, or **repressed**, because awareness of them is too threatening or painful to be tolerated (A. Freud, 1946a; S. Freud, 1943; Hartmann, 1939/1958). Unconscious material of this type is considered the source of psychological dysfunction.

The anatomy and physiology of the brain are much, much more complicated than the words we non-neuroscientists use to describe the psychological phenomena that result. It is scientifically responsible to acknowledge that our language simplifies real phenomena, and then it is pragmatic to return to the metaphors that enable us to organize reality in a fashion that fulfills our purposes. Here, this means we should stipulate that the conscious and unconscious minds are not literally two places in the brain, one with the lights on and one with the lights off.

A more accurate description would state that the brain includes multiple neural networks that give rise to multiple networks of associations, which vary widely in the degree to which we are conscious of them, from complete awareness to no awareness, with everything in between (Westen, 2005; Westen & Gabbard, 2002). Frequently, we are conscious of the outputs of the networks (thoughts and feelings) without being aware of either the neural connections underlying the outputs or the learning histories responsible for the neural connections. For example, a man whose father frequently belittled him during childhood might find himself extremely anxious with his boss, and the man might not know why, or he might construct a plausible but irrelevant explanation. Sometimes the brain's networks of associations are consistent and coordinated with each other, but sometimes they operate semiautonomously and even produce contradictory cognitions and emotions, which may vary in their degree of conscious representation. As a result, the human mind is prone to conflict, and we do not always know why we feel and behave the way we do. This formulation can be referenced, in a quick and convenient way, by using the shorthand terms "conscious mind" and "unconscious mind."

Freud, working during Victorian times, repeatedly observed his clients repressing sexual and aggressive impulses. However, there are no rules about what feelings might be unacceptable to the conscious mind. Repression often operates against angry, selfish, and jealous feelings, memories of trauma, and sexual desires of which the person disapproves (e.g., homosexual impulses in homophobic individuals).

The difference between the conscious and unconscious minds is not simply that people are aware of the former and unaware of the latter (S. Freud, 1915/1957; Gray, 1994). These two aspects of mind have different properties, content, and ways of operating. The properties of consciousness require less explanation because this is the aspect of mind with which we are already familiar. Consciousness includes those feelings, thoughts, and memories that are acceptable to the individual. This material may be painful, but not to the point of being intolerable.

Cognitively, the conscious mind operates in a manner commensurate with the highest level of development that the individual has attained. In adults, the conscious mind involves adult thinking; in typical 9-year-olds, it involves thinking at this level of cognitive development, and so forth.

The nature of the unconscious mind requires more explanation, because it is not experienced directly. The unconscious includes emotions, cognitions, and memories that are threatening to the individual and that, therefore, have been repressed (Cabaniss, Cherry, Douglas, Graver, & Schwartz, 2013; Cramer, 2006; S. Freud, 1943). There seem to be two main reasons why this occurs: People sometimes cannot tolerate awareness of impulses and fantasies they find morally unacceptable, and people sometimes repress memories of experiences that were extremely painful. Repression can be total, as in amnesia for an event but, more often, it is partial. Frequently, people have some awareness of difficult emotions and painful memories but, as a result of repression, their awareness is incomplete.

According to analytic theory, the nature of cognitive development is dramatically different in the conscious and unconscious minds. The conscious mind becomes more logical and realistic as child development proceeds, but *the unconscious does not mature* (Dewald, 1971; S. Freud, 1957; Horowitz, 1998). Even in adults, its manner of operation remains that of a young child: Feelings are intense and poorly modulated; thinking is impressionistic, illogical, and dominated by emotion; there is little understanding of cause and effect; and there is a blurring of fantasy and reality. This difference between conscious and unconscious functioning is central to the analytic understanding of etiology and therapy.

> *The conscious mind becomes more logical and realistic as child development proceeds, but the unconscious does not mature.*

The Structure of the Mind: Id, Ego, and Superego

To organize its observations of psychological phenomena, analytic theory divides mental functions into a small number of categories. As with any theoretical system, there is a danger of taking the words too literally and thinking of them as concrete things; instead, analytic concepts should be viewed as patterns of mental phenomena.

Freud's (1923, 1943) **structural model** includes three main constructs, as summarized ahead:

- **Id:** the aspect of mind concerned with *what we want*
- **Superego:** the aspect of mind concerned with *what is right*
- **Ego:** the aspect of mind concerned with *what will work*, which includes resolving conflicts between the id and superego

According to analytic theory, most human behavior requires some type of collaboration between these three mental structures. Each aspect of mind is partly conscious and partly unconscious, depending on what has and has not been repressed.

Here is an example of the way the ego manages conflicts between the id and superego. Consider a 5-year-old girl who is enraged with her 2-year-old brother, most immediately because he has taken her favorite teddy bear and, more fundamentally, because he has taken so much of the parental attention that would otherwise be hers. Her conscious wish is to hit her brother so she can regain her bear. Her unconscious wish is to destroy her brother and thereby eliminate the root of the problem. But then come chilling, disturbing memories of the angry faces and harsh words she has received from her parents when she hit the boy, followed by the thought that she does love her brother, and the nice thing to do would be to let him keep the bear. The older sister deliberates between her possible courses of action. Finally, she decides to offer her brother a stuffed dog in exchange for the teddy bear. Although analytic theory has a reputation for being far-fetched, it is about this type of ordinary conflict between what people want and what they believe to be right.

The popular understanding of the id as based on sexual desires oversimplifies Freud's concept. He did not use the word "sex" in this context; he used the word *Eros* (a figure in Greek mythology), which he defined as the desire for pleasure, affection, and connection with other people. Freud viewed Eros as our source of creative energy, and he saw scientific curiosity as a sublimated, sophisticated expression of Eros. He considered sex important not only because it involves pleasure but also because it is perhaps the most direct, intense form of the self's connection with the world outside the self.

The superego has two aspects: the conscience, which is concerned with right and wrong, and the ego-ideal, which represents the type of person one wants to be. The superego is the individual's repository of moral norms and ethical standards learned from parents, other authorities, religious traditions, and society in general. This mental structure is responsible for inhibiting the expression of impulses and motivating prosocial behavior. Harsh superego functioning causes guilt and anxiety, but insufficient conscience development results in actions that hurt other people, and the superego is absolutely necessary for group life and civilization (S. Freud, 1930/1962).

The ego is synonymous with cognition and adaptation; it is the aspect of mind that tries to figure things out and decide what to do (A. Freud, 1946a; S. Freud, 1923; Hartmann, 1939/1958). All perception, memory, reasoning, and planning—all efforts to know and adapt to the external world—are the province of the ego. The ego also has the vital function of mediating conflicts between the id and superego. The ego is *not* necessarily rational and realistic; when thinking is distorted, illogical, and even crazy, that is ego, too.

Because adaptive capabilities develop as children grow up, ego functioning can be characterized as immature or mature. Mature ego functioning involves the type of reasonable thinking and adaptive behavior that are familiar from everyday experience. Immature ego functioning involves thinking that is starkly irrational, unrealistic, and dominated by emotion (Dewald, 1971; Gilmore & Meersand, 2013). The good side of this way of thinking occurs in the lively, elaborate imaginations of young children. The downside of primitive ego functioning, or magical thinking, is that emotions overwhelm reason, and thinking is not constrained by a realistic sense of cause and effect. As a result of their immature ego functioning, young children may, for example, be terrified of monsters that do not exist and be frightened that their secret thoughts will hurt other people.

In older children and adults whose development is unimpaired, mature ego functioning occurs in the conscious mind, and immature ego functioning occurs in the unconscious. (In young children and psychotic adults, conscious ego functioning is immature.) Thus, most adults are conscious only of their adult thinking; most adolescents are conscious only of their adolescent level of cognition, and so forth. But in the unconscious minds of developmentally normal adults and older children alike, there are preserved remains of the disorganized wishes and fears of the person at much younger ages, as (ineffectively) managed by the immature ego of the individual at those ages.

Object Relations

The development of analytic theory did not stop with Freud. The most important ensuing development has been **object relations theory** (Cashdan, 1988; Greenberg & Mitchell, 1983; Kernberg, 1980). Object relations theory does not contradict the older structural model but complements and completes it. While the older theory focuses on conflicts between desires and moral standards, object relations theory emphasizes self-concept and relationships with other people as the foundation of personality.

The word *object*, here, means *other people*, as opposed to the self (as in subject versus object). An object relation has three components—namely, mental representations of:

1. The self.
2. Other people.
3. The relation between the two.

Object relations can be only roughly approximated by words because they exist as internal images, emotions, and experiences of relationships, not conscious thoughts. Nonetheless, we want to present examples to build an understanding of the concept, so here are some examples of object relations translated into words:

- I am valuable and lovable. Dad is caring and affectionate. I feel warm and happy in my relationship with Dad.
- I am unlovable and unimportant. Mom is busy and concerned with herself. In my relationship with Mom, I feel lonely, cold, and sad.
- I am clumsy and unskilled but funny and likeable. My big sister is condescending but good-hearted. If I clown around and don't try to gain her respect, she'll be nice to me.

Object relations are internal images or schemas of the self's relationships with other people, based on past experiences. Because experiences are a joint function of external reality and inner interpretation, object relations are the product of both the behavior of other people and the individual's subjective (possibly inaccurate) perceptions of those behaviors.

Object relations are internal images or schemas of the self's relationships with other people, based on past experiences.

Object relations structure and color people's interpersonal experiences by determining what is expected, desired, and feared (Glickauf-Hughes & Wells, 2006; Greenberg & Mitchell, 1983; Westen, 1991). These templates of relationships govern what people are primed to perceive and what they tend to miss. For example, neglected children sometimes cannot respond appropriately to nurturant caregiving because they have no internal script for this type of interaction, so they cannot recognize it for what it is. Object relations are similar to the schemas emphasized in cognitive therapy.

Object relations have behavioral implications because they govern people's sense of what is possible for them in the interpersonal world. These working models of relationships determine the individual's sense of what she has to offer, what other people want, and what she needs to do to connect successfully with others (Baldwin, 1992; Fraiberg, 1959/1992; Kernberg, 1980, 1993). For example, a child who sees herself as unlovable and her caregivers as self-focused might feel that the only way she can achieve some closeness is by doing whatever she can to meet her caregivers' needs.

People do not have just one object relation; they have many. There may be different object relations for males, females, adults, children, and any other grouping that is salient to the person. To some extent, however, object relations *generalize* and show consistencies across relationships (Cashdan, 1988; Westen, 1991). People form stable concepts of the type of person they are, the typical nature of other people, and recurrent patterns in their interactions with others.

Psychoanalytic theory differs from the other major theoretical orientations by emphasizing the importance of early childhood. The theory is fundamentally historical in nature, viewing the past as a powerful influence on present personality and behavior (Bowlby, 1969; Gilmore & Meersand, 2013; Greenberg & Mitchell, 1983). The basic structures of the mind begin to develop in infancy, and our early experiences are particularly influential because they shape the deepest layers of our learning. As a result, the emotional and interpersonal experiences that laid down the foundations of our personalities were processed, at the time, by ego structures that were immature. This is why the mental functioning of adults contains buried elements of impressionistic, magical thinking and intense emotionality (which can be either positive or negative in valence).

Defense and Coping Mechanisms

Awareness of difficult realities can be painful. External realities hurt when they involve threats to well-being or negative feedback about the self. Internal realities hurt when we experience impulses or emotions that we wish we did not have. When the need to avoid anxiety outweighs the need for reality-based adaptation, people use **defense mechanisms** to avoid being conscious of some painful aspect of their internal or external world (Cramer, 2006; S. Freud, 1923; Klein, 1932).

Defenses represent the best the person has been able to do in her effort to pursue her desires while satisfying her conscience and her effort to see the world realistically while maintaining a sense that life is okay.

There are two important things to understand about defense mechanisms. First, they are relatively ineffective and maladaptive, because they distort the person's awareness of either the world or the self. However, defenses do accomplish something—otherwise, they would not be used. Defenses protect people from anxiety and pain. Thus, defenses represent the best the person has been able to do in her effort to pursue her desires while satisfying her conscience and her effort to see the world realistically while maintaining a sense that life is okay (Cabaniss et al., 2013; A. Freud, 1946a; Hartmann, 1939/1958).

Any unconscious mental operation that protects the individual from anxiety is a defense mechanism. Table 5.1 describes a number of common defenses.

These descriptions of defenses were originally based on clinical observations of clients, but experimental research has since documented many of these processes, including perceptual denial (Broadbent, 1977), projection (Newman, Duff, & Baumeister, 1997), and repression (Cooper, 1992). Some studies have examined sexual emotions. For example, Adams, Wright, and Lohr (1996) tested the psychoanalytic hypothesis that homophobia is a defense against unwanted homosexual impulses. They showed a film depicting homosexual activity to a sample of men who self-identified as heterosexual, and they assessed arousal in a direct fashion using a device that measures penile erection.

Table 5.1   Common Defense Mechanisms

Denial: The person refuses to acknowledge painful realities that are clearly evident. For example, a person who cannot get through a day without alcohol denies that he is addicted to the substance.

Repression: The person pushes painful experiences out of conscious memory, thus forgetting them. Related memories are often lost along with the trauma. For example, an adult survivor of child abuse has no memory of long periods during her childhood.

Devaluation: The person derogates someone or something that stimulates feelings of inadequacy or anxiety. One of Aesop's Fables provides an example: A fox, after unsuccessful attempts to get some grapes from a high vine, decides that the grapes were probably sour, anyway.

Displacement: Feelings toward one object are transferred to a different object. For instance, a woman says nothing while her boss yells at her but later, at home, she kicks her cat.

Projection: The person experiences his unacceptable feelings as located in another person, not himself. For instance, a child who is frightened by the prospect of his parents going away on vacation denies he is scared but insists that his baby sister is terrified and needs the parents to stay home.

Reaction formation: The individual copes with an unacceptable impulse by substituting the opposite feeling or behavior. For example, a jealous brother, resentful of his newborn sister, fawns over the baby and insists that he loves her more than anything.

Splitting: The individual separates and polarizes the positive and negative aspects of her experience in order to avoid the confusion and anxiety of ambivalence. For example, a child of divorced parents feels that his father never does anything wrong and his mother never does anything right.

Participants who gave homophobic responses on a questionnaire exhibited arousal, and participants who did not express homophobia showed no arousal in response to the film. In a study of heterosexual feelings in women, Morokoff (1985) measured sexual guilt with a questionnaire and assessed physiological response to an erotic film using a device that measures genital arousal. Women high in sexual guilt *reported* less sexual excitement in response to the film but *exhibited* more physiological arousal. These studies seem to demonstrate the operation of denial and reaction formation as defenses against sexual impulses that are unacceptable to the superego, as in Hamlet's line, "Methinks he doth protest too much." There are few things as frightening as an unacceptable wish.

Maladaptive defenses account for much of the dysfunction in the world. However, because they perform the necessary function of protecting people from anxiety, defenses cannot simply be eliminated; they need to be replaced by something better.

That something is called **coping**. Like defenses, coping protects people from pain, but it accomplishes this without distorting reality (Gray, 1994; McWilliams, 2011). For example, a child grieving the death of a relative might *cope* by going to her mother for a hug, or she might *defend* against the grief by trying to convince herself that she did not really love the relative, anyway.

As mental operations whose purpose is adaptation, both coping and defense mechanisms are functions of the ego (A. Freud, 1946a; S. Freud, 1943; Hartmann, 1939/1958). Defenses are a product of immature ego functioning, and the mature ego formulates coping strategies. Defenses evolve unconsciously; no one realizes they are using a defense mechanism, or it would not work. Coping strategies are planned and utilized consciously.

What Causes Mental Health Problems?

The analytic understanding of etiology derives from the idea that the unconscious does not mature (Dewald, 1971; Fenichel, 1945; Freud, 1915/1957). When people repress painful experiences, their original understanding and response to those experiences are preserved and never revised in light of future learning—unless the material becomes conscious, and reprocessing can occur. People who repressed painful experiences when they were younger carry those experiences, and the meanings derived from them, in their original raw, disorganized, unrealistic form.

This would not be a problem if the contents of the unconscious were sealed there, hermetically, but they are not. Unconscious material affects people's functioning all the time, although (by definition) they are not aware of this influence. For example, people who were abused as children may experience anxiety in relationships that, in reality, are safe. When a person's reaction to a situation is strikingly inappropriate, that reaction may be based on old learning, preserved unconsciously, that is misapplied to the current reality (Cabaniss et al., 2013; Chethik, 2000; Greenberg & Mitchell, 1983). Such misapplication is similar to the behavioral concept of stimulus generalization presented in Chapter 2 but with the addition of a distinction between conscious and unconscious functioning.

Although unconscious processes affect conscious experiences, the reverse is not true. The conscious mind has no impact on unconscious material—unless that material becomes conscious. Without access, conscious thinking cannot reinterpret and reprocess repressed conflicts and trauma. It is as if these two aspects of mind are separated by a semipermeable membrane that can be crossed in one direction but not the other.

Unless there is severe psychopathology, the conscious ego functioning of older children, adolescents, and adults is relatively effective and mature. Nonetheless, these individuals sometimes experience mental health problems. Psychological disturbance in people who have the ego capabilities for effective functioning is called **neurosis** (Fenichel, 1945). Psychoanalysis was originally developed to treat this level of disturbance.

In neurosis, the person's mature ego has the capability to rethink and resolve old conflicts, but it cannot gain access to these conflicts because they are unconscious.

The development of maladjustment in people who are capable of mature ego functioning is something of a conundrum, because dysfunction generally results from the operation of defense mechanisms and other forms of *immature* ego functioning (Dewald, 1971). The conundrum can be resolved by the idea that neurosis is a problem not of capability but of *access*. In neurosis, the person's mature ego has the capability to rethink and resolve old conflicts, but it cannot gain access to those conflicts because they are unconscious.

The explanation of mental health problems in individuals who do *not* possess high-level ego capabilities is simpler (although their treatment may be more difficult). For young children and seriously disturbed older clients who lack effective ego functioning, psychopathology is less a problem of access than of capability. For these individuals, gaining access to unconscious material will not lead to problem resolution unless there are additional forms of help.

The limited adaptive capabilities of children sometimes make ordinary stressors very difficult for them (Kernberg, Weiner, & Bardenstein, 2000; Klein, 1932). When faced with childhood challenges, such as desiring autonomy but being dependent, feeling small and weak in a dangerous world, feeling jealous of siblings, and experiencing anger toward parents, children sometimes terrify themselves with their misunderstandings and fantasies. If their adaptive tools are limited to primitive defense mechanisms, the result could be the development of mental health problems in the context of a nice, normal family environment.

There are two forms of maladaptive superego functioning: The superego can be too harsh and strict, and the superego can be too lax (S. Freud, 1943; Gray, 1994). Generally, harsh superego functioning produces internalizing disorders, and weak superego functioning results in externalizing disorders.

Maladaptive object relations cause maladjustment by impairing interpersonal functioning (Bowlby, 1969; Kernberg, 1993; Westen, 1991). When internal models of relationships are imbued with a great deal of conflict and pain, and they have not been re-examined by the person's most mature thinking capabilities, these templates may distort the individual's perceptions and expectations of other people. As a result, the person has trouble seeing others for what they really are, he responds to new interactions as if they were old interactions, and his responses are frequently inappropriate.

Jennifer behaved as if interactions with authority figures were battles in which the winner would come out looking smart and the loser would end up feeling stupid. As a result, she experienced ordinary corrections of her behavior or schoolwork as insulting rebukes and was flooded with feelings of failure. She was unable to ask for help because doing so made her feel inadequate, and when someone noticed her need for help, she felt ashamed. Given this stance, therapy seemed like Jennifer's worst nightmare, because it was all about exploring her difficulties.

The Process of Therapy: Resistance

One of the distinctive characteristics of dynamic therapy is its focus on the process of therapy, especially obstacles to progress, and its emphasis on *using* these obstacles as opportunities to learn about client dynamics and create change. In this approach, therapy sessions are not simply occasions for clients to talk about their difficulties and to plan solutions; therapy is a setting in which client issues are manifested in real behavior, emotion, and interaction with the therapist. One example of this in vivo quality of dynamic therapy is the phenomenon of **resistance** (Dewald, 1982; S. Freud, 1943).

Freud discovered resistance as an obstacle that repeatedly blocked his progress. Often, his patients did not welcome his attempts to explore their inner worlds but, instead, resisted the process of therapy and the insights he offered. These patients avoided discussion of painful issues, wasted time on trivialities, and sometimes showed an especially direct form of resistance—being late or failing to show up for appointments.Resistance can be defined as the operation of unconscious defenses in the context of therapy (Cramer, 2006; Dewald, 1982; Horowitz, 1998). In other words, clients sometimes resist becoming aware of uncomfortable truths, even if doing so would improve their adaptation in the long run. An additional source of resistance is clients' fear of change. Even painful situations such as abusive relationships and social isolation may, on some level, involve a secure feeling of familiarity that people are afraid to move past.

Freud was frustrated by his clients' resistance, but eventually he realized that, if handled effectively, resistance can be a therapeutic opportunity. Because clients generally defend against the same issues, often using similar mechanisms, both within and outside therapy, resistance provides clinicians with an opportunity to see the client's defenses in operation. For example, Jennifer often tried to dismiss her therapist's feedback by behaving as if she were superior to him, and she also used this defense in her everyday environment.

The Process of Therapy: Transference

Transference occurs when the client has feelings about the therapist that are the result of his emotional dynamics and past experiences, not the present, external reality of the therapist herself (S. Freud, 1912/1958; Gill, 1982; Westen, 1988). In other words, the client transfers onto the therapist expectations and reactions that actually have to do with other people, often caregivers. The client's internal dynamics function like a lens that colors and sometimes distorts his experience of the counselor.

Transference can be a function of either learning or motivation. Clients' perceptions of therapists are influenced both by their general *expectations* of other people and by their unfulfilled *wishes* for relationships. For example, some neglected children avoid closeness with their therapists because they have learned that positive interpersonal connections do not last, and some neglected children cling to their therapists because they are desperate for nurturance. Learning-based and motivational processes may intermingle in the transference behavior of the same client.

Transference can be either positive or negative in emotional tone. In positive transferences, the client idealizes the therapist and has unrealistic hopes for a gratifying relationship with him. (A colleague of mine, who was raised by two psychodynamic clinicians, remembers a dinner-table conversation in which her father described a female client exclaiming about how charming, handsome, and charismatic he was. Her mother's response: "Now *that's* transference!")

In negative transferences, the client has disappointed, frustrated, or angry feelings toward the clinician. (I remember a very likeable 6-year-old boy who, for a period time, began every session by glowering at the floor and muttering, "I hate you, Shapiro.") There is no prognostic significance to whether the transference is positive or negative. From a dynamic viewpoint, the emotional twists, turns, ups, and downs of therapy are neither good nor bad but are all, equally, grist for the mill. Everything depends on how the material is handled.

Freud initially viewed transference, like resistance, as an obstacle to the progress of therapy. But once again he proved himself to be a master of an intellectual version of judo, turning what appeared to be a problem into an asset for the therapeutic process. Thanks to transference, the therapist does not learn about the client's interpersonal problems only by hearing reports of her experiences outside therapy; the counselor also *sees* these dynamics in action during sessions. Because object relations are manifested in the transference, these blueprints can be changed through work on the therapist-client relationship (Glickauf-Hughes & Wells, 2006; Greenberg & Mitchell; 1983; Kernberg, Yeomans, Clarkin, & Levy, 2008). The child might expect the therapist to treat him as other people have but, in therapy, these expectations will be disconfirmed, and the client will experience new forms of interaction and relationship.

Countertransference, the mirror image of transference, is the effects of the therapist's own issues and dynamics on his experience of the client (Gill, 1982; Schafer, 1983). In general, counselors should attend carefully to their internal responses to clients in a moment-to-moment way, because these reactions can be a sensitive form of information about subtle aspects of the client's functioning. The goal is for these responses to accurately register what the client presents, without being strongly influenced by the therapist's own issues. Countertransference interferes with counseling when it distorts the clinician's perceptions and responses to the client. It is the therapist's responsibility to distinguish between reactions attributable to the client's behavior and reactions deriving from his own dynamics, and it is his job to handle countertransference reactions internally, so they do not distort his work with the client.

Assessment and Case Formulation

Like other clinicians, dynamic therapists assess the child's conscious thoughts, emotions, behavior, and development. Dynamic assessment also focuses on the processes emphasized by the theory, including the client's wishes, fears, conscience, object relations, defense mechanisms, and coping strategies.

The assessment process in dynamic therapy is less straightforward and more interpretive than in the other approaches because the processes of interest are largely unconscious (Cabaniss, Cherry, Douglas & Schwartz, 2011; Chethik, 2000; Klein, 1932). If people could answer direct questions about their unconscious issues, these issues would not be unconscious. Nonetheless, unconscious dynamics are discoverable because they affect the surface of consciousness and behavior.

A psychodynamic counselor might put together observations of the child's play with puppets, his facial expression when he parted from his mother in the waiting room, an odd comment he made several weeks ago, and information about his history to formulate hypotheses about his unconscious conflicts, defense mechanisms, and object relations. Compared to other clinicians, dynamic therapists are willing to make inferences with a greater degree of speculation and a larger conceptual distance between observed behaviors and underlying processes.

It seems useful to engage in the complex, speculative process of dynamic assessment only when the more direct approaches of CBT and systems-oriented therapy fail to explain the client's difficulties. Sometimes, when you ask a young child why he is depressed, scared, or angry, the answer you get is not very helpful, at least not in a direct fashion. The child might say he is afraid a witch will fly through his bedroom window and eat him. Now what? You could ask what evidence he has for this fear—he has none, but he does not care; he is afraid of the witch anyway. Or, a child might say she is afraid her mother will hurt her physically, even though nothing like that has ever happened or been threatened. Immature ego functioning can produce emotional reactions that are divorced from external reality.

In situations like these, your best bet for assessment is probably to enter the child's world of magical, fantasy-based thinking and, for example, ask him to describe the witch, say where she comes from and why she is so mean, draw a picture of the witch, and engage in imaginative play about her with dolls and puppets. In time, this type of work might enable you to trace the fantasy fear back to its source. Such tracing generally leads away from the world of unrealistic fantasy to the much scarier world of real feelings in real relationships. Frequently, young children are not adept at answering direct questions about their emotional issues, but they are often remarkably eloquent in revealing complex paths from their life concerns to their mental health symptoms. The way to facilitate this revealing is to step back, provide the facilitative inquiry and reflection described in Chapter 1, and allow the child's dynamics to unfold.

With young children, this unfolding often occurs in the arena of play. Historically, dynamic therapists were the first to recognize that children's play is more than mere puttering around and sometimes expresses emotional issues and beliefs (Erikson, 1963; A. Freud, 1946b).

Questions to Ask

Psychodynamic clinicians assess the effects of past experiences on present functioning. When clients exhibit emotions or behaviors that do not seem attributable to the immediate situation, which suggests that past learning is having an effect, these clinicians ask questions like:

- "I wonder where those feelings come from. Have you experienced anything like them before?"
- "Wow, you really had a strong reaction to that. Does it remind you of anything that's happened to you before?"

Questions about the child's responses to stress provide information about her coping and defense mechanisms. The clinician can ask parents versions of these questions to hear their perceptions of the child's ways of dealing with stress:

- "What do you do when you feel sad (mad, etc.)?"
- "When things go wrong for you, how do you deal with it? What do you do to try to feel better?"

Dynamic clinicians use their own, internal reactions to the client as a source of information about her functioning (Schafer, 1983; Summers & Barber, 2012). Jennifer's therapist frequently found himself feeling awkward and clumsy with this fast-talking, clever, arrogant client, and he viewed those feelings as information about how Jennifer often made other people feel. Then, he wondered what function this style of relating to others might have for Jennifer.

Therapists need a high level of self-awareness to know when their emotional responses provide information about the client and when these responses are more a function of their own issues. This type of introspective process might be articulated, internally, with words like the following:

"As Mary talks about her parents moving toward divorce, I feel my heart sinking, and I want to implore the parents not to tear this child's world apart. Why am I feeling this way? Is it because, despite her nothing-bothers-me talk, Mary is terrified by the prospect of her parents breaking up? Or are my feelings about my own parents' divorce intruding into my work with this client?"

Self-knowledge has always been considered vital to psychodynamic work, and there is an expectation that clinicians will receive their own therapy. When Freud, as the first analyst, formulated this idea, there was no one to analyze him but himself, so he conducted a formal self-analysis.

Patterns to Look For

Psychodynamic clinicians look for patterns in the client's presentation that connect with analytic theory and help to explain her difficulties. Dynamic clinicians view play, slips of the tongue, transference, resistance, use of language, and nonverbal behavior as reflections of underlying mental structures and processes (Chethik, 2000; Kegerreis, 2010; McWilliams, 2011). They place their observations in the context of information about the child from outside therapy and then try to weave these data into a coherent picture that points toward strategies for helping her.

Compared to other theoretical approaches, the patterns of concern to dynamic therapy are generally less available to direct observation. Dynamic clinicians are interested in psychological phenomena that underlie the surface of behavior and the face value of verbalizations. Assessing these patterns might require complicated inferences, but the process begins with clinical data. Below, I describe three patterns of intermediate depth that lie between in-session behavioral observation and deep-level theoretical constructs.

Discrepancies, or incongruities, occur when client statements or behaviors are inconsistent with each other. For example, a child might insist that he is not anxious about his hockey games but, 3 weeks in a row, he complained of a stomachache on the day of a game and was unable to play. Jennifer claimed she did not care what her teachers thought of her. However, when criticized, she ruminated about the feedback for a long time, refuting the teacher's points but certainly seeming to care about them.

Omissions are noteworthy absences of thoughts or feelings that are "talked around" and never addressed directly. The expression "an elephant in the living room" captures this idea of an obvious but unmentionable issue. Dynamic therapists are interested in what clients do *not* talk about as well as what they do bring up. For example, a youth who has been mistreated but never expresses anger about it might harbor this feeling on some level but be anxious about revealing it.

Excesses are extreme behaviors or expressions of emotion; they are too much of something. For example, a child might become tearful and say, "You hate me" upon being told to play more carefully with a toy. When an emotion seems disproportionate to the event that occasioned it, the true source of that emotion is probably something other than the event. The source is usually an issue that is related to the event but is larger, more threatening, and more difficult to talk about.

When the therapist asked Jennifer what made her feel sad, she rolled her eyes and replied, "Stupid questions like that one." A response of this type does not seem to yield information about the cognitive or behavioral basis of the client's difficulties. From a dynamic perspective, however, this response may provide information about Jennifer's way of dealing with sadness and vulnerability: She avoided acknowledging such feelings and dealt with the threat of vulnerability by trying to turn the tables and make the clinician feel stupid. Further assessment suggested that Jennifer relied on the defenses of devaluation and projection. She was unable to tolerate her weaknesses and imperfections, and she dealt with the threat of personal inadequacy by projecting these qualities onto others and hating them there, as if to say, "*I'm* not bumbling and incompetent, *you* are."

Change Processes

Dynamic therapy pursues its goal of resolving mental health problems in a less direct manner than does CBT. Dynamic therapists not only focus on symptoms but also explore the client's overall development, relationships, and personality because they believe that symptoms arise from deep-level, internal processes.

The objectives of dynamic therapy include the following:

- Increased self-understanding
- Increased acceptance of feelings and wishes
- Replacement of (unconscious) defense mechanisms with (conscious) coping strategies
- Development of realistically complex and positive schemas for relationships between self and others

This chapter describes four change processes in dynamic therapy: Self-expression, insight, a certain type of psychoeducation, and corrective emotional experience. For three of these change agents, the discussion is consistent with mainstream dynamic theory. The discussion of psychoeducation departs somewhat from the traditional approach in a way that, I believe, adds to, rather than contradicts, conventional principles of dynamic therapy.

Facilitating the Expression of Material

One of Freud's (1933) earliest observations was that the act of listening carefully to clients often facilitated the expression of emotional issues underlying their problems, and self-expression, by itself, sometimes reduced clients' symptoms. In the psychodynamic literature, this change agent is called **ventilation** or **catharsis**.

Although based on a different theoretical framework, **emotion-focused therapy** (Greenberg, 2002; Greenberg & Pascual-Leone, 2006) makes extensive use of self-expression as a mechanism of change. Research with adult clients has found that when counselors facilitate the full, intense expression of emotion, particularly feelings that have been blocked from expression by fear or shame, clients often experience a sense of relief and completion. This sequence is conceptualized as a matter of "finishing unfinished business" (Greenberg & Malcolm, 2002). Outcome research reviewed by Greenberg (2002; Greenberg & Pascual-Leone, 2006) indicates that the result is often reduced symptomatology and enhanced relationships. Also, process research on psychodynamic therapy by Ablon, Levy, and Katzenstein (2006) found that outcomes correlate positively with client expression of emotions, especially dysphoric emotions.

Play is an important means of self-expression for young children. In addition to revealing thoughts and feelings, play is a mechanism of change, development, and self-healing through which children experiment with meanings, play out emotional scenarios, solve problems, and work through conflicts (Erikson, 1963; Russ, 2004). In children with mental health problems, defensive inhibitions and developmental blockages often constrain play. Therefore, one way therapists can help children is by supporting and facilitating their expressive play, as described in Chapter 1.

Interpretation and Insight

The core change agent in psychodynamic therapy is **insight** (Dewald, 1971; S. Freud, 1915/1957; Horowitz, 1998). Insight is an increase in self-understanding—specifically, new awareness of previously unconscious material. The central objective of dynamic therapy is *to make the unconscious conscious*. The theory predicts that if clients achieve sufficient insight, their symptoms will resolve.

Interpretation is the therapeutic technique that produces insight in clients. An interpretation is a statement by the therapist that brings an unconscious process to the client's attention (Gray, 1994; Summers & Barber, 2012; Weiner & Bornstein, 2009). Therapists take the lead in the technique of interpretation, figuring out some aspect of the client's unconscious functioning and then offering this new understanding to him. Interpretation involves more than reflection of feelings or meaning; it means telling the client something about herself that she did not know. Interpretations involve causal explanations of feelings, thoughts, behaviors, and symptoms. For example, one interpretation in Jennifer's therapy was that she sometimes tried to deal with her self-doubts by making other people feel the way she felt. If interpretations ring true and have explanatory value for clients, then insight occurs.

The fundamental question about dynamic therapeutic strategy is, why does insight help? The first part of the answer is that accurate self-knowledge is useful and valuable. When people do not know why they feel the way they feel or why they do the things they do, they feel confused and, sometimes, "crazy." Becoming aware of previously unconscious dynamics helps people feel that their emotions and behaviors do make sense, in an augmented version of validation, as described in the previous chapter's section on DBT. Also, accurate self-knowledge is a vital guide for personal planning, choices, and actions (Summers & Barber, 2012; Weiner & Bornstein, 2009). It is hard to know what to do unless we know ourselves.

But that is only the simple part of the story. The full answer to the question of why insight is helpful follows from the analytic understanding of neurosis as a problem not of limited capability but of inadequate access—specifically, access of the mature ego to the unconscious conflicts and misunderstandings responsible for dysfunction. In such situations, insight is the only change agent needed because once the person is able to think consciously about her previously unconscious conflicts, she will be able to resolve them.

Why are clients able to tolerate and utilize knowledge about themselves in therapy when, previously, this knowledge was so anxiety-producing that it had to be repressed? The explanation derives from the different levels of maturity that characterize conscious and unconscious functioning. Usually, when conflictual material is repressed, it is intolerably painful because the person's immature ego capabilities are unable to manage the material. After repression occurs, although years might go by, the unconscious material remains intolerable—but only to the immature aspect of the client's mind. The conscious, mature aspect of mind *would* be able to tolerate, rethink, and integrate the conflictual material—if it could gain access to it. The therapist's interpretations provide this access.

When the unconscious becomes conscious, the mature ego gains access to the problematic material, and it is more capable of managing problems in an effective manner than the immature ego had been.

When the unconscious becomes conscious, the mature ego gains access to the problematic material, and it is more capable of managing problems in an effective manner than the immature ego had been. Insight makes it possible for the client's most rational, realistic, and adaptive thinking to be applied to his long-buried conflicts and misunderstandings for the first time. The person will rethink the old issues and develop more successful strategies for managing them. Defense mechanisms will be replaced by coping strategies. Neurotic symptoms will be replaced by conscious thoughts (S. Freud, 1933).

Dynamic Psychoeducation

I use the term **dynamic psychoeduction** to mean teaching the client about the emotional, relationship, and life issues involved in her difficulties. Psychoeducation is different from interpretation because, while interpretation increases the client's self-understanding, education also involves information about general human functioning. This is the one point in my presentation in which I diverge somewhat from mainstream psychodynamic formulations, although, as discussed later, past writings have included intimations of my recommendation of active, psychoeducational input from the therapist.

The traditional analytic formulation assumed that clients begin therapy with the ego capabilities they need to resolve their problems, once insight is achieved. Since the origination of the theory, some commentators have noted that young children and seriously disturbed older clients usually do *not* have the adaptive capabilities needed to resolve their conflicts, so that insight, by itself, is not a sufficient agent of change. Some authors have proposed that the healing power of play and self-expression, in the context of a supportive therapeutic relationship, is an important change agent in and of itself (Erikson, 1963; Gardner, 1993; Russ, 2004; Winnicott, 1971). However, it seems likely that there are clients for whom mirroring and empathy alone are not sufficient to engender adaptive thinking and coping. In my experience, clients who were not helped by dynamic therapy often complain that this treatment helped them understand their difficulties but did not resolve the problems. Also, the extensive research support for cognitive and psychoeducational interventions suggests that many clients benefit from active, substantive input from their therapists.

Discussions of this type of educative help are scattered in the psychodynamic literature, particularly in the area of supportive therapy (Dewald, 1994; Sugarman, 2003). In her later writings, Anna Freud (1968) expressed concerns about the limitations of insight as a change agent for children, and her work with clients included educative components that taught adaptive skills. Fonagy and Target (1998) proposed that seriously disturbed children often need direct help from their therapists to build ego capabilities. Some dynamic clinicians probably engage in the type of educative work I am recommending, but this form of intervention has received little systematic attention in the literature, and existing discussions have not produced well-articulated recommendations. Such recommendations could contribute to the repertoire of psychodynamic practice.

Counselors can help young children and older clients with limited ego strength to develop the life knowledge, understanding, and skills that clients with mature ego functioning have developed on their own.

Therapists can provide more than empathic reflection and insight. Counselors can help young children and older clients with limited ego strength to develop the life knowledge, understanding, and skills that clients with mature ego functioning have developed on their own. It seems likely that this work would be more effective if done in purposeful, targeted ways, not simply by trusting that an empathic relationship will somehow enable the child to develop the adaptive capabilities she needs but has lacked.

Insights concern the self. The strategy recommended here consists of teaching about life. These lessons generally involve basic, simple knowledge about human nature, relationships, moral values, and the way the world works. As one important example, guilt about angry, selfish, or sexual wishes seems to be an important etiological factor for some children. Two psychoeducational points address this etiology: (1) Wishes, impulses, and desires, in themselves, neither cause harm nor indicate that someone is a bad person, and (2) all people sometimes experience wishes and impulses that, if acted upon, would be morally reprehensible. These points *are not insights* because they concern people and life in general, not the self. Clients who lack this type of knowledge are handicapped in their efforts to adapt, no matter how extensive their self-understanding might become.

Consider this analogy: Dysfunctional emotion and behavior are like the manifestations of a computer software program that does not work properly, and the unconscious is like the program code that governs what happens on the screen. People consciously experience what happens on their computer screen, but they are unaware of the software code responsible for these manifestations. Similarly, people consciously experience behavior, emotion, and symptoms but, ordinarily, they are not aware of the underlying mental structures that govern these phenomena. When things go well, there is no need to become aware either of software code or of unconscious issues, but to fix problems, we need to uncover and change the underlying, governing structures.

Insight reveals something analogous to the program code that controls what happens on a computer screen. If the user is a programmer, then once she becomes aware of the errors in the code, she will need no outside assistance to rewrite them correctly. If the client has mature ego capabilities, then once she becomes aware of her unconscious conflicts, she will need no outside assistance to resolve them. But if the computer user is not a programmer, discovering the errors in the code will not enable him to fix them. And if the client lacks mature ego capabilities, insight will not be enough, and he will need psychoeducational input from his therapist to reprogram the mental structures responsible for his maladjustment.

Insight helps the client make sense of her thoughts, emotions, and behaviors (e.g., "Oh, maybe that's why I feel this way"). Psychoeducation changes the client's picture of the self, other people, and possibilities, often by modifying beliefs concerning good and bad, so that new, more adaptive ways of functioning become apparent (e.g., "Oh, that's a new way to look at it").

As explained in Chapter 2 on behavior therapy, clients' misunderstandings sometimes begin with accurate interpretations of situations but end with overgeneralization of this learning. One important example occurs when children learn to cope with the expectations and demands of dysfunctional parents by developing ways of functioning that work comparatively well with these caregivers. When they take their adaptations to more normal settings, things go badly, because the child's caregivers are not accurately representative of people in general, and these relationships do not provide useful guidance about what generally works in relationships. In a sense, the root of the problem is a type of sampling error. When this is the case, the therapeutic objective is to replace *episodic* knowledge (memory of personal experiences) with *semantic* knowledge (general truths about life) as a basis for perceptions, emotions, and responses in the present.

In a nutshell, insight explains, and psychoeducation corrects. Insight is about why things are the way they are, and life education is about how they could be better. Dynamic therapy also includes a corrective factor that is not cognitive or educational in nature.

Corrective Emotional Experience

Dynamic therapy does not rely only on cognitive understanding and learning to achieve its objectives. Therapeutic *experiences* may be even more important as agents of change because they produce emotional learning and relearning.

Corrective emotional experience begins with the **holding environment** that the therapist creates for the child (Gardner, 1993; Winnicott, 1971). The holding environment is a remarkable setting, different from all other social contexts. The counselor is nondirective, so the child controls the activities and conversational topics. The counselor accepts the child unconditionally, which means that no matter what the child does, the therapist remains locked in her position of trying to understand and help. (Limits are set on dangerous behaviors, but limits are not inconsistent with acceptance.) The holding environment is a refuge where all thoughts, wishes, and fears, no matter how embarrassing they might be in other settings, can be voiced without eliciting disapproval. The counselor reserves only one prerogative: She comments on what the client says and does.

By modeling an accepting attitude toward the client's conflict-laden material and discussing this material in a calm, matter-of-fact way, the therapist detoxifies previously shameful issues (Chethik, 2000; Schafer, 1983). The client learns from experience that his fears and fantasies can be talked about—and, therefore, can be thought about. The child takes in the therapist's calm, constructive attitude toward wishes and emotions that, in the past, had seemed so threatening that they had to be repressed. Thus, the child develops self-acceptance by internalizing the counselor's acceptance of him.

Therapists provide corrective emotional experiences by demonstrating to the child that the interpersonal events she expects and fears will not occur in therapy.

In addition to providing a general atmosphere of empathy and acceptance, corrective emotional experiences should address the specific fears and interpersonal expectations that have impaired the client's functioning. Clinicians can accomplish this by bringing out the dynamics that clients expect will elicit negative reactions and then responding in a way that clearly disconfirms the unrealistic, fearful expectations. For example, the therapist would express heartfelt acceptance of vulnerable, needy aspects of the client if these were the issue, would explicitly express acceptance of angry feelings if these were the problem, and so forth. Therapists provide corrective emotional experiences by demonstrating to the child that the interpersonal events she expects and fears will not occur in therapy (Mallinckrodt, 2010).

From a behavioral perspective, these are counter-conditioning procedures (described in Chapters 2 and 13)—but, rather than targeting concrete fears like spiders or heights, this strategy targets abstract, initially unconscious fears concerning the self and relationships. From a dynamic perspective, this strategy addresses a root source of mental health problems because, if the client's emotions and wishes become tolerable to him, defense mechanisms will become unnecessary, and the etiological sequence will be undone at its origin.

Of course a therapist's acceptance cannot fully repair the emotional damage done to children by caregiver maltreatment, rejection, or disparagement. Nonetheless, corrective experiences show the child that another adult view of her and a different type of relationship are *possible*. Even if the client's caregivers are unable to provide a positive experience, the achievement of one relationship in which the child is fully known, accepted, and cared for may provide a template for similar interpersonal experiences in the future.

Outcome Research

The practice of psychodynamic therapy proceeded for many years without support from research, but recent years have seen a substantial accumulation of supportive evidence. Commentators have noted, however, that proponents of other theoretical orientations, especially CBT, have been slow to assimilate the new findings, and outdated claims that dynamic therapy lacks empirical support continue to appear in the literature (Leichsenring, 2001; Shedler, 2011).

Keefe, McCarthy, Dinger, Zilcha-Mano, and Barber (2014) conducted a meta-analysis of psychodynamic therapy for anxiety disorders in adults. The obtained a medium/large effect size of .64 in comparisons with no-treatment controls. Effect sizes were non-significant for comparisons between dynamic therapy and alternative interventions. Meta-analytic reviews of dynamic therapy for depression in adults by de Maat, de Jonghe, Schoevers, and Dekker (2009) and de Maat et al. (2013) did not include control groups but examined within-client change at pre-treatment, post-treatment, and follow-up. These meta-analyses obtained large effect sizes at termination, and these effects were still larger in magnitude at follow-up. Shedler (2010, 2011) noted that many outcome studies of dynamic therapy have documented this type of "sleeper effect" in which the benefits continued to grow after therapy was completed, which is not generally the case for other types of interventions.

Research directly comparing the effects of dynamic therapy and alternative interventions is less plentiful and especially informative. Most of these studies were conducted with adult clients. Gerber et al. (2011) conducted a systematic review of RCTs that compared dynamic therapy with other empirically supported treatments (mostly CBT and also systems-oriented interventions). Of the 39 RCTs meeting their criteria for methodological quality, six showed dynamic treatment to be more effective, five showed dynamic therapy to be less effective, and 28 showed no difference between the therapies. In an RCT comparing treatments for adults with BPD, dynamic therapy produced benefits that equaled or exceeded those of DBT (Clarkin, Levy, Lensenweger, & Kernberg, 2007). Meta-analyses by Cuijpers, van Straten, Andersson, and van Oppen (2008) and by Leichsenring (2001) compared dynamic therapy and CBT for adults with depression. They found large effect sizes for both types of therapy, with no difference between the two. Similarly, a meta-analysis by Barber, Muran, McCarthy, and Keefe (2013) found no differences between CBT and dynamic therapy in outcomes for adults with anxiety disorders.

Research on the mediation of treatment effects in dynamic therapy for adults has produced extensive support for the hypothesized mechanisms of change (Crits-Christoph, Connolly Gibbons, & Mukherjee, 2013). Studies by Kivlighan et al. (2000), Connolly Gibbons et al. (2009), and Kallestad et al. (2010) found that dynamic therapy helped clients achieve insight (i.e., self-understanding) and that increases in insight predicted ensuing reductions in symptoms. The Connolly Gibbons and Kallestad studies found that dynamic therapy produced larger increases in insight than did cognitive or supportive therapy. Several studies found that dynamic therapy reduced client reliance on rigid, primitive defenses, and that improvements in defensive functioning predicted subsequence decreases in symptomatology (Bond & Perry, 2004; Johansen, Krebs, Svartberg, Stiles, & Holen, 2011; Kramer, Despland, Michel, Drapeau, & de Roten, 2010). In studies by Blatt, Stayner, Auerbach, and Behrends (1996) and by Vermote et al. (2010), dynamic therapy produced improvement in the quality of clients' object relations, and this improvement was associated with reduction of symptomatology.

Research that goes beyond "brand names" by directly measuring therapeutic techniques has produced evidence supporting two psychodynamic strategies: interpretation of transference and interpretation of defense (Ablon & Jones, 1998; Jones & Pulos, 1993). Regardless of whether they believed themselves to be doing dynamic therapy or CBT, the counselors who produced the best outcomes focused more on transference phenomena and defensive avoidance of emotions, compared to less effective counselors.

Abbass, Rabung, Leichsenring, Refseth, and Midgley (2013) performed a meta-analysis of 11 studies ($n = 655$) examining short-term dynamic therapy for children and adolescents with a variety of diagnoses, including depression, anxiety, anorexia, and BPD. Most of the comparisons were to active, bona fide treatments, and these comparisons did not yield significant differences, which is a common finding in outcome research. Within-group analysis of clients receiving dynamic therapy produced a large effect size of 1.07, which increased in magnitude from termination to follow-up ($g = .24$).

A Brazilian study of children aged 6–11 years with a no-treatment control obtained a medium/large effect size of .70 (Deakin & Nunes, 2009). In an Australian study of adolescents with serious mental illness by Tonge, Pullen, Hughes, and Beafoy (2009), psychoanalytic therapy produced larger reductions in overall symptomatology and social problems, compared to a TAU control. An Italian study comparing short-term dynamic therapy to a TAU control found that both groups demonstrated improvement in the study's first 6 months but, at a 2-year follow-up, 65% of the control group and only 34% of the dynamic therapy group still exhibited clinically significant disturbance (Muratori, Picchi, Bruni, Patarnello, & Romagnoli, 2003; Muratori et al., 2002).

Several studies have examined differences between diagnostic groups of young people in their response to dynamic therapy. A large retrospective chart review ($n = 763$) by Fonagy and Target (1996) found that children with internalizing disorders were more likely to complete treatment and to achieve clinically reliable improvement than were children with disruptive behavior problems. In the Italian research cited earlier (Muratori et al., 2002, 2003), internalizing problems were more responsive to treatment than externalizing problems, and outcomes were better for children with "pure" emotional disorders, compared to children who also exhibited behavior problems.

The Therapist's Style

Dynamic therapists generally have a reflective, inquisitive style, with a calm curiosity about all human experiences. Although traditional analysts had a neutral style that precluded expression of their own emotions, modern dynamic therapists make careful exceptions to this rule. In the current understanding of "neutrality," the therapist is fully and equally accepting of all of the client's impulses, emotions, thoughts, and all aspects of self. However, this does not preclude the expression of human responses to the client's experiences (Kegerreis, 2010; Kernberg et al., 2000). Important examples include the expression of compassion when the client is suffering, gladness when the client achieves progress or a victory, and respectful appreciation of efforts or qualities that the client has undervalued because of low self-esteem.

Beneath all the complexities of its theory and technique, the dynamic approach is distinguished by a certain attitude toward mental life. When psychoanalysis began at the end of the 19th century, the prevailing attitude toward mental life in the Western world could be described as judgmental and moralistic. When individuals examined their thoughts and feelings, the main question was whether their mental contents were good or bad. This orientation still seems common today. In contrast, the psychodynamic orientation toward the mind is analytical and naturalistic. When therapists guide clients in examining their thoughts and feelings, the questions are about how they operate and interact, why they evolved the way they did, and whether they are working to produce a good life for the client. This viewpoint permits moral judgments about actions, but internal life is viewed as a natural phenomenon, like chemistry or physics, which operates according to scientific principles, so moral judgments are inapplicable. Just as engineers use principles of physics to build bridges and physicians use principles of biology to treat disease, counselors use principles of psychology to achieve therapeutic goals.

In the psychodynamic viewpoint, people do not choose their impulses and desires, which come into our minds unbidden. Since the flux of mental life is governed mostly by dynamic interactions between subdivisions of the mind that follow mysterious rules and occur unconsciously, it makes no sense to hold people responsible for their wishes and emotions. Also, desires and thoughts, by themselves, cannot hurt others. The core psychodynamic observation is that all people, including very nice ones, frequently have wishes and fantasies that conflict with morality. In contrast to some religious traditions, in dynamic therapy there is no such thing as a sin in thought, because attempting to judge and prohibit mental contents seems to be a fruitless endeavor.

The psychodynamic insight is that mental life is most effectively managed not by simple, forceful efforts to judge and forbid unwanted impulses but by an accepting attitude, self-understanding, and sophisticated self-management strategies.

The psychodynamic insight is that mental life is most effectively managed not by simple, forceful efforts to judge and forbid unwanted impulses but by an accepting attitude, self-understanding, and sophisticated self-management strategies. This scientific, artful approach to mental life seems more effective than a crude, moralistic approach. This attitude toward mental life has been absorbed by the mental health field in general, but it is epitomized by the dynamic approach, which deserves credit for originating this view.

Facilitating Expression of Material

The first objective of dynamic therapy is to bring out the client's issues so they can be reprocessed in the treatment setting. At this stage, the main technique is reflection of feelings and meanings, as described in Chapter 1. The therapist connects with the child on the surface of what he does and says, and then the therapist inquires further, drawing out the emotional themes implied by the child's self-expression. For example, if a child said her father was out of town on business, the clinician might ask whether she misses him. If the child said yes, the counselor might explore further. Was she mad at her father for leaving? Did his leaving have anything to do with her? Was she scared something might happen to him? Or did the child simply miss her dad, with nothing more to it?

Dynamic therapists view the play of young children as a symbolic language, and they try to decode these metaphors in order to understand the child's experiences and mental structures (Gardner, 1993; Russ, 2004; Winnicott, 1971). Dolls, animals, and action figures may represent different elements of the child's internal world, including wishes, fears, possible solutions to problems, and images of self and others. Erikson (1963) proposed that children's play is an early form of the human ability to create model situations in which planning and experimentation can be done in a hypothetical, representational form, and dynamic therapists take children's play seriously, in a sense.

The way to work with play is to relax your reality-oriented set and enter the child's world. Children know their play materials are not really people and animals, but they talk and act as if these symbolic materials *were* real—and you should, too, because playing along communicates understanding and facilitates the emergence of material. This process is like the "suspension of disbelief" that happens when we are drawn into works of fiction or theatre, and we have emotional responses to them even though we know the events are not real.

Reflections of feeling and meaning should not merely echo the client's words and actions but should organize her self-expression and bring out implications that are only hinted at, thus moving the client forward in his conscious processing of emotional issues—for example:

- "The boy tiger is little, but he's so fierce and strong that he scares his father away and does whatever he wants!"

- "It's scary for the rabbit in the woods. All the other animals are bigger, and they're mean. Is there anybody in the woods who might help the rabbit?"

The task of facilitating self-expression with older children and adolescents operates by the same principles, except that talk replaces play as the main mode of communication. Therapists facilitate the emergence of material by connecting with the client's verbalized concerns, demonstrating that therapy is a place where anything and everything can be discussed, and gently pushing toward recognition of patterns and themes that recur or are associated with strong emotions.

Interpretation and Insight

Interpretations link an unconscious process—a defense, wish, fear, memory, or misunderstanding —to the client's conscious experience.

Interpretations link an unconscious process—a defense, wish, fear, memory, or misunderstanding—with the client's conscious experience (Cabaniss et al., 2011; S. Freud, 1915/1957; Hartmann, 1939/1958). This core tool of dynamic intervention makes connections between different aspects of the client's life, including internal processes, in-session events, recurring feelings, past history, current relationships, and presenting problems. Interpretations are causal explanations; they attempt to explain *why* the client feels, thinks, or behaves in some way—for example:

- "Maybe you ran out of the room because you were afraid to hear what the teacher was going to say."

- "Do you think the crying and sadness might be your way of punishing yourself for hurting Mom?"

The achievement of insight is sometimes signaled by an "aha experience," but insights are usually achieved in an incremental manner, with therapist statements gradually increasing the client's level of self-understanding until a point of full insight is reached

(Cabaniss et al., 2011; Summers & Barber, 2010). Insight-oriented work should begin at the surface of the client's conscious self-understanding and then work down into progressively deeper layers of unconscious material.

Weiner and Bornstein (2009) recommend that therapists employ a sequence of three steps to process each new unit of therapeutic material. The steps are: (1) clarification, (2) confrontation, and (3) interpretation.

Clarification, a simple verbal behavior, means asking questions about client statements or behaviors to ascertain what the child meant by his words or actions. The most basic clarification statements are, "Tell me more about that," and "Explain what you mean by _____." Clarification also involves asking for behavioral specification (e.g., "What do your teachers do when they are being 'stupid'?"). Clarification can be applied to the client's play to bring out its meanings (e.g., "Why is the rabbit hiding?").

Confrontation, in dynamic therapy, does not have the aggressive connotation this word has in everyday language. This technique does not involve criticizing or opposing the client. Confrontation means drawing the client's attention to some inconsistency or contradiction within her own beliefs, emotions, and behaviors. Confrontations typically follow the formula of:

"On one hand, you say or do _____, but on the other hand, you say or do _____; how do you put those two things together?"

In confrontation, the therapist connects two pieces of data that the client has not thought to consider in juxtaposition. The two elements are inconsistent with each other, but the client has not noticed this, so the therapist reflects both elements in one statement—for example:

- "You're telling me you're sorry about putting toothpaste on your sister's pillow, but I can't help noticing a smile on your face. I wonder if you actually enjoyed annoying her but don't want to admit it."

- "You're saying you had a good time with your aunt, but it doesn't seem like you want to tell me about it, and you're scribbling awfully hard with that crayon."

The client's new awareness of these inconsistencies alerts him that something confusing is going on. We hope for reactions of puzzlement and curiosity, because these set the stage for new learning.

In the next, final step, interpretations offer explanations of the mystery. We need to be gentle in doing this, because there is a danger of interpretations coming across as presumptuous or intrusive to the client. Interpretations should be offered in a tentative manner rather than with certainty, using stems such as, "I wonder if," or "Could it be that … " (Weiner & Bornstein, 2009). When my interpretations take several sentences to present, I sometimes preface them with requests like, "Could I run something by you?", and I offer permission to disagree by saying, "Now tell me if I'm getting this wrong."

Therapists need words with which to talk about the different, semiautonomous aspects of mind that interact within clients. Terms like "parts of you" and "sides of you" fulfill this function—for example:

- "Right now, I'm seeing a side of you that's small and scared and wants to stay close to Mom, but I know that last week, at the playground, there was another side of you that's strong and confident and wants to go off on your own."
- "It seems like there's a part of you that wants to blow school off and have fun, but there's another part that wants to learn things and succeed, and you haven't yet found a way for those two parts to work together."

Interpretations of resistance and transference can be particularly awkward for clients because, like Freud before he reinterpreted these obstacles as opportunities, clients sometimes feel they have been caught doing something wrong. To make it clear that this is not the case, I sometimes say, "I'm glad this came up, because it's important for us to talk about."

The most basic interpretation of resistance may be, "It seems like you don't want to talk about this." Many interpretations of resistance follow the formula of:

1. "It seems like when I bring up _____ (e.g., your sister, anger), you usually _____ (e.g., stop talking, change the subject)."

Here are two examples of transference interpretations:

1. "Jennifer, you treat me as if I just don't get it, so you're not going to try to explain things to me. What's good about that for you? Does it mean you won't have to worry about anything I say?"
2. "Jason, you seem so concerned about saying something wrong or 'stupid,' like I might judge you for that. Has it ever been this way for you with someone? If you didn't say things just right, they'd make you feel dumb?"

Here are two examples of interpretations of defense mechanisms:

1. "You're really good at forgetting about times you got in trouble, so it's like those things never happened. Your mind erases everything; it's like you have a *mind eraser* for when you do something bad."
2. "I think sometimes you get so mad at your brother that it scares you, and you try to deal with that by bending over backward to be extra, sugary sweet."

Here are two examples of interpretations related to object relations:

1. "Your dad used to promise he'd come visit every weekend, but he usually didn't keep his promise. Could that be one of the reasons why you don't trust people to come through for you?"
2. "Do you feel like the only way to make friends is by doing kids favors and giving them things, like no one will like you unless you do that?"

The increase in self-understanding produced by interpretations may reduce clients' confusion about their experiences. It is a good feeling to realize that one's emotions and reactions make sense. On the other hand, clients often feel some discomfort on hearing interpretations, because these statements generally involve anxiety-producing material and they usually imply a problem with some aspect of the client's functioning (Horowitz, 1998; Weiner & Bornstein, 2009).

Clients sometimes disagree with interpretations. There is an old analytic view that such disagreement constitutes resistance and so supports, rather than weakens, the validity of the interpretation. This may be true sometimes, but it is also possible that the client disagrees with an interpretation because it is inaccurate. The view that the client's disagreement actually proves the therapist is right puts the client in a bind and probably comes across as smug. Usually, it is more useful to consider the possibility that the interpretation was inaccurate.

Insight, as a one-time occurrence, usually does not produce much change. The clinician's initial statement of an interpretation is only the first step in her use of this information. In the process called **working through**, the therapist helps the client *apply* an insight to the variety of experiences and behaviors to which the insight pertains (Cabaniss et al., 2013; S. Freud, 1943). For example, a teen might have an insight such as, "The reason I don't trust people is that my dad physically abused me when I was little." Simply stating this idea would be unlikely to increase the youth's trust in other people. Constructive application of the insight would involve the adolescent remembering and discussing the abuse experiences, other aspects of his relationship with his father, and the experiences with other people that he now realizes might have been affected by the abuse.

Important dynamics manifest themselves in multiple contexts, possibly including resistance, transference, play, fantasy, and a variety of experiences and relationships. When clients discern the response patterns occurring in multiple contexts, and they learn to recognize them *as they occur*, they become able to disrupt their previously habitual responses.

Jennifer's therapist interpreted similar dynamics in his client's functioning with a range of adult authority figures, especially teachers, coaches, and the therapist himself. Authority figures stimulated self-doubts in Jennifer because she knew these adults would be evaluating her. Over time, she learned how her fear of failure caused her to launch preemptive strikes against authority figures in order to put them on the defensive and take the spotlight off her. She also came to realize that the accusations of inadequacy she experienced as coming from others actually originated in her own nagging sense of deficiency. One source of Jennifer's troubled self-concept seemed to be her vacillation between two opposite images of herself: one as powerful and special, and one as a pitiful failure. This dichotomous experience of herself made Jennifer intolerant of her imperfections because any perception of weakness hurled her into an experience of shame.

Once the old, symptomatic ways of operating have been revealed and understood by the client, he is on the road to change, but he has not arrived at his destination until better ways of living have been developed. In the next phase of change, the client learns to substitute new, effective, consciously planned responses for the old, maladaptive, unconsciously driven ones.

Dynamic Psychoeducation

Insight is a lot, but sometimes it is not enough. For example, a child might learn that her low self-esteem is caused by her mother's derogating, rejecting behavior. Understanding the reasons for her low self-esteem would lead to improved self-concept if, but only if, the client has the ego capabilities necessary for reconstructing a positive self-image. Many clients lack such capabilities, in which case something more is needed, and that something is active, substantive input from their therapist.

Insight and psychoeducation should be tightly related, because insight tells counselors what the content of education should be. The sequence should generally be: first insight, then psychoeducation.

When insight reveals a mistaken interpretation that contributes to the client's disturbance, and she lacks the knowledge to correct the misinterpretation by herself, life education can fill this gap by providing valid information. Often, the key to this work is providing an *alternative explanation* of a painful reality. For example, one client achieved the insight that her persistent feelings of being "unimportant" and "small" (despite much academic and social success) stemmed from her father's persistent abuse of drugs despite her entreaties to stop for her sake. This insight was an important step in her therapy; it helped her understand her current feelings of insignificance. However, the insight did not refute her belief in her unimportance because she continued to view her father's continuing drug abuse as convincing evidence of this belief. ("Obviously I'm not important enough for him to make himself stop.") Her self-esteem did not improve until the counselor provided an alternative explanation of her father's drug abuse—namely, an explanation of the causes and consequences of addiction.

Sometimes the client's original, valid learning occurred in the past and is misapplied to the present, and sometimes the valid learning occurs in the family and is misapplied to the larger environment. In both cases, the child has drawn reasonable conclusions from interactions that are not representative of most relationships, so his valid learning becomes maladaptive when it is extended past the domain in which it was acquired. Insight pertains to the reasonable nature of the child's original inferences, and psychoeducation corrects the overgeneralization of this learning, so semantic knowledge overrides episodic knowledge as a basis for emotions and behavior in the present. Here is an example of the insight-education sequence:

"You've always known that, if you want to get your dad's respect, you've got to be that tough kid who is always ready to push back and fight. You learned this way of operating because it worked better than anything else, at least as far as your father was concerned. But the problem is, it's not working in school, and it's messing up your life there.

Your dad's right that it's important to stand up for yourself, but there's a different way of doing that in school. Your father doesn't make the rules in your school—the teachers do, so if you want to do well there, you've got to win at their game. I think you could learn to do this, if you wanted to."

As discussed in Chapter 2, Behavior Therapy, the boundary between dynamic therapy and CBT sometimes blurs when we carefully consider the fabric of therapeutic action, because both theories are concerned with the misapplication and overgeneralization of learning (Dollard & Miller, 1950; Wachtel, 1977). Psychodynamic therapy is distinctive in its emphasis on the unconscious. The foregoing therapist statement was psychodynamic to the extent that the client had been unaware of the connection between his relationship with his father and his aggressive behavior in school.

Because the immature ego is emotion-driven and impressionistic, the life lessons clients need sometimes seem so elementary and obvious that we look past them and do not realize these ideas need to be stated explicitly. Dynamic therapists are alert to primitive cognitions with a degree of irrationality that goes beyond the type of thinking error of concern to CBT. For example, a boy whose father had died of cancer was tormented by images of him crying in pain. The key insight for this client was the realization that, on some level, he felt like his father's suffering was still occurring. The life lesson he needed was a statement of the obvious: When the counselor said the father's suffering was over now, and he was no longer dying because he was dead, the child's empathic agony ceased.

Dynamic therapy hinges on a certain attitude toward emotions and wishes, and psychoeducation socializes clients into this attitude. Therapists help clients develop a constructive attitude toward mental life in which they accept their emotions, examine them without judgment, and make conscious decisions about which ones to express and how to manage the impulses that should not be directly translated into behavior. One client, when asked what had been most helpful to her in therapy, replied, "Learning that the way I felt was okay."

There are innumerable occasions when clients disclose difficult material and then say something like, "It's probably wrong to feel this way," "It might be bad to have this thought," or "I really shouldn't want that." At these times, the psychodynamic attitude toward internal life can be engendered by using words like the following:

- "Well, you're guilty of being human."
- "No one can help what they think; ideas and feelings just pop into our minds."
- "I don't know about 'bad,' but we could look into where that feeling comes from and maybe we'll learn something."
- "Feelings and thoughts don't make people good or bad; that depends on what people do."
- "You criticize yourself for having this wish, which you can't help, but you don't give yourself credit for disapproving and trying to control the wish, which *is* up to you."

Insight-oriented work with internalizing clients often reveals a harsh, punitive superego (S. Freud, 1915/1957, 1943). When this occurs, I sometimes metaphorically describe the client's current conscience as being like a slave-driver with a whip, and I offer an alternative image of a gentler, more effective superego by describing a kind grandparent who helps his grandchild understand her difficulties and do better at being the kind of person she wants to be.

Sometimes (older) clients need to understand the rudiments of object relations theory and how that theory might apply to them. Here is an example:

> "When kids are little, they have no way to know who and what they are—whether they are cute or ugly, lovable or annoying, good or bad. Little kids learn about themselves by seeing how their parents treat them. It's like parents hold up a mirror, and kids see what they are in that mirror. So if parents treat their kids like they're wonderful, that's what the kids figure they are, and if parents treat their kids like they're a pain, kids come to feel like they're not worth much.
>
> There can be a big problem with this: What if the parents are unhappy and angry so much of the time that it gets in the way of their seeing good things in their child? If that happened, when the kid looked in the mirror, he'd feel like he was seeing the truth about himself, but what he'd really be seeing would be his parents' unhappiness and anger.
>
> I know you've always had this feeling that you're just not good enough. But the question is, does this feeling come from reality or psychology? Does the feeling come from the reality of who you are or from that mirror your parents held up? What we see in those mirrors really sticks with us, but it's not fair, because of something very simple that is often hard for kids to believe: Their parents can be wrong."

One of the fundamental dilemmas of life is that investing in new relationships is risky because, the more one likes or loves someone, the more painful rejection and loss are. Three groups who often experience this dilemma in a particularly acute way are foster children, children adopted after infancy, and adolescents who are beginning to date. The safest option might seem to be avoiding all closeness, but this is not a solution—it is a defense mechanism. The adaptive response is to get to know people gradually while assessing their trustworthiness and interest in a relationship, and to let feelings build as the relationship grows. Ascertaining the trustworthiness of other people is both difficult and important, so counselors should offer clients guidance in making these assessments. Of course, our ability to make these judgments is not infallible, but the issue is not our fallibility but whether our input could contribute to the client's capabilities.

When clients fail to recognize the *costs* of their maladaptive behaviors, dynamically oriented psychoeducation can help them understand what they are losing as a result of their accustomed way of operating—for example:

> "People have let you down so many times, you're at the point of saying to *hell* with them. Starting to trust someone is scary, because that's when you can really get hurt. But it's a problem, because you're pushing away good things along with the bad."

Careful thinking about the specific life lessons and skills needed by a client may lead the dynamic therapist to CBT. For example, a child might use maladaptive defense mechanisms to control his anger because he is afraid that, if he allows himself to feel this emotion, his behavior might go out of control. Achieving insight into this dynamic, by itself, will not solve the problem, because there would still be a danger of loss of control. Once insight has revealed the youth's defenses, providing him with anger management training (described in Chapter 12, Aggression) might make those defenses unnecessary. Thus, once the unconscious cause of a symptom is discovered, the therapist's job is to help the client solve the problem that the defense mechanism was originated to solve.

Sometimes, individuals other than the therapist are in the best position to supply the child with the input she needs. When misunderstandings concern family members, it is often useful to move from individual therapy to a parent counseling or family therapy modality (A. Freud, 1946b, 1968).

The central life lesson for Jennifer concerned the nature of human adequacy and inadequacy. Her dichotomous schema needed to evolve into a more complex, calibrated understanding so that failures would not threaten her sense of adequacy. Therefore, the clinician portrayed both Jennifer and people in general as complicated, evolving mixtures of strengths and weaknesses. With this more fluid, flexible view of people, Jennifer came to see herself as a work in progress. Failure no longer seemed like a catastrophe, and Jennifer no longer needed to strike out at others to protect her self-esteem.

Corrective Emotional Experience

Both insight into the self and education about life are cognitively based change processes. Most clients also need interpersonal/emotional experiences to resolve their difficulties. By making skillful use of the therapeutic relationship, counselors can create interpersonal experiences that counter and refute maladaptive lessons about self and others that the client learned in the past (Gardner, 1993; Kernberg, 1980, 1993; Kernberg et al., 2008; Mallinckrodt, 2010; Summers & Barber, 2012).

By making skillful use of the therapeutic relationship, counselors can create interpersonal experiences that counter and refute maladaptive lessons about self and others that the client learned in the past.

Corrective emotional experiences begin with the therapist's own view of the child, proceed to the counselor's communication of this view, and conclude with the child's internalization of the therapist's view of her. Your view of the client becomes a therapeutic experience when it is translated into the way you smile, make eye contact, listen, and speak to her. The metamessage underlying these interactions should be something along the lines of, "I know you don't like parts of yourself, and I also know you are a good kid, and when you understand yourself better, you'll know this, too." Sometimes, stating this message in words might feel awkward or too intense for the child, but at other times, direct statements are the strongest means of getting the message across.

Children with internalizing dysfunction usually need comforting experiences in which they learn that they are okay the way they are. These experiences often involve a two-part sequence. First, the therapist learns of something the child feels guilty or ashamed about. The child might disclose this material, the parent might report it, or the therapist might infer the material from the client's in-session behavior. Regardless of the information source, clients often fear that the therapist will reject them once he realizes how weird, pitiful, or awful they are. Corrective emotional experience occurs when the counselor addresses the shame-associated revelation with the same constructive, helpful spirit he has maintained from the beginning. This exposure-based intervention has the potential to modify harsh superego functioning and make defenses unnecessary.

The therapist's task in implementing this strategy is to be unmistakably clear in expressing two things: full understanding of the shameful or anxiety-producing material, and full acceptance of the child. Neither component, without the other, will produce the needed experience. Generic, nonspecific acceptance does not result in corrective emotional experience. Clients will perceive your acceptance as meaningful only if they believe you know the worst about them and still accept them fully.

One way to begin disconfirming client expectations of disapproval is to respond to new and difficult material with our usual exploratory type of comment:

- "That sounds really important."
- "This sounds like hard stuff."
- "Tell me more about this so I can understand it better."

Providing corrective emotional experiences centrally involves work with the transference. This work often involves the following sequence of six steps. (For the first four steps, illustrative material is included.)

1. Reflection: "You seem afraid that I'll look down on you for feeling this way."
2. Present-oriented inquiry: "Why would I look down on you for this?"
3. Historical inquiry: "Has that happened? Has someone looked down on you for this type of thing?"
4. Therapist provision of realistic feedback to disconfirm transference: "The fact is, I'm not looking down on you at all. What's going on in my mind is that I see how painful this is for you and I'm wondering where that comes from."
5. An interpretation linking past experiences to the client's currently distorted perception of the therapist.
6. Strong disconfirmation of the client's misperception, including a reinterpretation of the client's experience and a statement of the therapist's actual perception of that experience. See ahead.

When maladaptive expectations of relationships are entrenched, they are difficult to disconfirm. With these clients, disconfirmations need to be unmistakably clear and emphatic to break through and produce change. These youth need strong statements that not only deny a negative view of them but also affirm a positive view, and precisely regarding the aspects of self about which they feel most insecure, guilty, and/or ashamed. To accomplish this objective, therapists must provide more than general compliments; they need to articulate specific, insightful appreciation of the client's qualities and strivings—for example:

"Sometimes you wish your big brother would fail at something, because everyone thinks he's perfect and no one seems impressed with what you do. I think it hurts you to have that wish, and you feel guilty and ashamed about it. But I really respect that, even though you can't help feeling jealous and angry, you care about right and wrong, and you care about your brother. It takes character to confront this head-on and try to do better with it."

Insight-Based Child Management

Especially with young children, therapists sometimes make use of their insights into the child's functioning without sharing these insights with the young client, in a strategy I call **insight-based child management**. Counselors can use their understanding of the child as a basis for planning experiences to address her difficulties without increasing the youngster's self-understanding at all.

Insight-based child management can be conducted both by therapists, during sessions, and by parents, at home. In both settings, one important example of this strategy consists of reassuring the child's fears without verbalizing them. When children express anxieties in an indirect fashion through play or fantasy, therapists have a choice between offering an interpretation or bypassing the realm of cognitive understanding to directly allay the fear. For example, if a child's play expressed a fear of being rejected or abandoned by the therapist, the counselor could interpret the connection between this play behavior and the child's real concerns, or the counselor could leave this connection aside and make a reassuring statement about the secure nature of the therapeutic relationship.

As an example of insight-based child management implemented at home, if a counselor ascertained that a client's disturbance derived from his fear that his mother's imminent remarriage might disrupt their relationship, the counselor could pass this information on to the mother, and she could convey to the client, in actions as well as words, that their bond will remain strong in the new family arrangement. If the anxiety at the root of the client's disturbance were allayed, his disturbance might resolve without him ever achieving insight into its genesis.

Summary

Psychodynamic therapy is based on a model of the mind as a set of distinct, semiautonomous structures that interact with each other, usually in a coordinated fashion but, sometimes, with conflict. Much mental activity occurs unconsciously, and people are sometimes unaware of their internal conflicts because their most threatening emotions, impulses, and memories are repressed.

Freud's original model postulated three mental structures: the id, ego, and superego. Since Freud, object relations theorists have proposed a view of personality as composed of internal representations of the self, others, and relationships between the two. Generally, these mental structures are partly conscious and partly unconscious, depending largely on the extent of repression that has occurred.

Outcome research on dynamic therapy lagged far behind research on CBT for many years, but it has begun catching up. There is now considerable evidence that for treatment of internalizing problems, dynamic therapy is similar in effectiveness to CBT and other EBPs. Dynamic therapy does not usually seem to be an effective treatment for externalizing problems.

The psychodynamic understanding of etiology begins with the postulate that the unconscious mind does not mature, and the contents of the unconscious do not change with time and experience. As a result, when conflictual emotions or traumatic experiences are repressed, they remain as threatening, confusing, and unresolved as they were at the time the repression occurred, even if, in ensuing years, the person develops ego capabilities that could resolve the issues.

In this formulation, people are most controlled by what they do *not* know about themselves. Therefore, one fundamental strategy of dynamic treatment is to make the unconscious conscious. When insight is achieved, the client's mature ego gains access to the previously unconscious material and develops more adaptive ways to manage these conflicts and issues.

According to analytic theory, clients' wishes, fears, and object relations are manifested in their experience and behavior during sessions. Defense mechanisms are manifested as resistance to the process of counseling. Emotions and expectations concerning relationships with other people are played out in the transference. Thus, intrapsychic phenomena are translated into interpersonal form. Although these processes might appear to disrupt the smooth flow of counseling, they actually represent valuable therapeutic opportunities, if handled effectively.

Dynamic therapy is conducted in a nondirective, unstructured manner so the client's characteristic patterns of thought, emotion, and behavior are free to emerge. The process of engendering insight is an incremental one; therapists usually do not surprise clients with revelations but gradually increase their self-understanding by offering interpretations of moderate depth and applying these realizations to the details of the youth's experience.

Insight is a lot but, especially for young and seriously disturbed clients, it might not be enough. Psychoeducation is an additional type of help that seems necessary when the client's most mature, conscious level of ego functioning is not capable of resolving her difficulties even when it gains full access to them. Counselors can assist these clients by helping them understand difficult issues and providing guidance in effective coping.

In addition to these cognitively oriented strategies, dynamic therapists use their relationships with clients to create emotional experiences that address the conflicts, misunderstandings, and maladaptive learning that have contributed to the youth's mental health problems. The purpose of these corrective experiences might be to demonstrate that the hurtful relationships the youth has had in the past are not accurate depictions of the types of relationships he could have in the future. Dynamic therapy attends to the youth's history, but its purpose in doing so is to sever maladaptive connections between the past and present, so the client is freed from the harmful effects of his history as he moves into his future.

Case Study

Jennifer was not pleased when the therapist confronted her arrogant stance toward others, but over time there was a decrease in her anxiety about performance as she developed a more resilient image of herself. With a less catastrophic view of failure, she became open to the idea that no one—neither she nor the adult in charge—had to be viewed as deficient when something went wrong. When self-doubts occurred, her lashing out was replaced by problem solving and twinges of anxiety that she learned to tolerate and manage.

The corrective emotional experience Jennifer needed from her therapist was enactment of a balanced, moderate view of her. The counselor was not extremely impressed, intimidated, or disgusted with Jennifer, but consistently viewed her as a good kid who was confused and having trouble with life. One of Jennifer's scripted self-statements (from the cognitive portion of her therapy) was "What's so bad about being a regular kid?"

As Jennifer's self-perceptions became more balanced and stable, she was able to give up the aggressive, attacking stance that had served as a cover for her feelings of vulnerability. Jennifer had fought her war with adults to protect herself from painful feelings of inadequacy. Once she learned to moderate and manage her self-perceptions, there was nothing left to fight about.

6

Constructivism: Solution-Focused and Narrative Therapy

OBJECTIVES

This chapter explains:

- *The philosophy of social constructivism, which states that human realities are constructed by language and talk.*
- *How constructivist therapists use language in subtle ways to change clients' experience of their problems.*
- *The solution-focused therapy techniques of:*
  - *—Identifying and building on exceptions to problems.*
  - *—The miracle question.*
  - *—Surprise enactment of solutions.*
- *The narrative therapy techniques of:*
  - *—Externalizing the problem.*
  - *—Writing and re-writing personal narratives.*

Case Example
Friends and Enemies

Felicia, a 10-year-old African American girl, was brought to therapy because of poor relationships with peers. Her classmates disliked her, and she experienced both social isolation and angry conflict; the teacher said she was usually either arguing with other children or sitting by herself. The social isolation was associated with glum, irritable mood, which often went home with Felicia. Her parents said their daughter had never been well liked by peers, but the problem had worsened at the end of second grade and became severe in third grade, at which time they initiated therapy.

Felicia's mother and father reported no behavior problems with her at home, and her teacher also said she behaved pleasantly when interacting with adults. The parents reported that she got along well with her younger brother and sister, exhibiting none of the social problems apparent in school. These problems were pronounced in her interactions with neighborhood children, however.

True to this pattern, Felicia interacted in a pleasant, engaging way with the therapist. Her description of the problem was that children her age hated her. She imitated her classmates bragging, showing off, and forming little cliques to exclude her. Her explanation of their behavior was that they were snobby and mean. ("They think they're great and I'm nothing.")

Postmodernism and the Social Construction of Reality

Constructivist therapy was developed by practicing clinicians who were also students of philosophy, and the intellectual roots of constructivist counseling lie in the philosophical movement called **postmodernism**. To understand postmodernism, it is necessary to define the worldview against which this movement reacted. Since the 18th-century European Enlightenment, the Western approach to understanding the world has emphasized *objectivity*. According to this framework, which is epitomized by the scientific method, objective observation and reason can produce accurate understandings of reality, including human behavior. In contrast, postmodernists believe that, even if people try to be unbiased, their motives, perspectives, and agendas always influence their perceptions and reasoning, so there is no such thing as objective knowledge (Derrida, 1992; Foucault, 1984).

Postmodernism was influenced by Marxist theory's account of how dominant social classes create spuriously objective descriptions of reality whose function is actually to justify existing societal structures and power inequalities. The scientific question, "What is the objective evidence for this idea?" is replaced by the postmodernist question, "Whose interests are served by this idea?" For example, male-dominated societies might produce scholarly works claiming to prove that males are superior to females in some way, and these writings might be presented as unbiased and objective, but their hidden agenda is to justify the continuing privilege of the people in power. The therapeutic approaches influenced by postmodernism are sensitive and vigilant about the effects of power structures and social inequalities on clients (Madigan, 2010; White, 1995, 2011).

This controversy can be summarized in a formula: In the traditional scientific framework, truth is *discovered*, and in the postmodernist framework, truth is *constructed*. Furthermore, postmodernists believe that truth is *socially* constructed in conversation, written discourse, and the "stories" people create to make sense of their experiences and to further their interests; **social constructivism** is the term for this postmodernist idea (Anderson, 1997; Gergen, 2009). Social constructivists argue that objective "truth" is unknowable and the pursuit of such truth is futile. They advocate replacing this endeavor with efforts to help people create empowering meanings and stories that enhance their lives.

What does all this philosophizing have to do with psychotherapy? There are significant connections. For example, early versions of the *DSM* listed homosexuality as a mental disorder. The authors believed they were presenting objective information, but the postmodernist analysis is that heterosexuals hold power in our society and, in order to perpetuate their power, they construct "science" that defines other sexual orientations as pathological (Laird, 1993). Feminist analyses provide other examples of the complex relations between power, perspective, and claims of objectivity. Feminist theorists have critically analyzed justifications of traditional sex-roles, found fault with family systems theory for failing to consider the societal context in which families live, argued that accounts of wife-battering and rape often blame victims, and criticized etiological theories for holding mothers more responsible than fathers for maladjustment in children (Ballou & Brown, 2002; Lather, 1991; Madigan, 2010).

The constructivist point is that human events are inherently *ambiguous* (i.e., subject to multiple interpretations). Therefore, people interpret their experiences not by perceiving meanings that are already there but by selecting and organizing elements of experience into accounts that fit with their assumptions and agendas (Anderson, 1997; Bruner, 1987; Gergen, 2009). The same set of facts can generate different meanings depending on the way these facts are selected and organized.

The Core Idea: Language Creates Reality

The word **story** is a familiar English term, but it has a special meaning in constructivist theory. This meaning is abstract, broad, and inclusive. As used by constructivists, the word "story" refers to any organized description of experience that goes beyond a literal, indiscriminate report of concrete facts. The key word here is *organized*: Any verbalization that involves selection of some facts over others, a sequence of events, causal explanation, or any inference of meaning is a story in the constructivist sense. The terms **narrative** and **construction of meaning** are synonyms of "story." These terms can refer to an elaborate account of a series of events, like a plot in a novel, and they can refer to a single, simple interpretation. For example, a person whose life includes few friends, a low-paying job, and much time spent in front of the TV might organize these facts into a story that "I am a loser." However, this statement is not a fact—it is an interpretation or narrative, and the same data could be organized into a different story that is equally "true."

People do not have one unitary life story. We have many narratives, large and small; constructivists say that our lives are *multistoried*. For example, a child might have stories of himself as a good baseball player, a poor student, and an effective mischief-maker.

The personal meanings and stories that people construct make an important difference to their quality of experience—for better or worse. Narratives act as filters or lenses that screen out events not fitting the plot line and that shape experiences to fit assumptions (Bruner, 1987). Such filters affect the individual's self-concept and understanding of her past. Narratives also affect people's behavior in the future, because we behave in accordance with what we believe to be possible. If a child's personal story states that "I've always done poorly in school because I'm dumb," she will probably not try hard, and the resulting outcomes will reconfirm the narrative. The idea of **self-fulfilling prophecy** explains how stories affect future outcomes: Expectations create realities.

Social constructivism draws our attention to the fact that therapy consists mostly of talk and invites us to make the most of language as an engine of change.

Psychotherapy emerges from this analysis as well-positioned for its mission of helping people create desired changes in their lives. Social constructivism draws our attention to the fact that therapy consists mostly of talk and invites us to make the most of language as an engine of change.

There are two main types of constructivist therapy: **solution-focused** and **narrative**. There are differences between these two approaches, but there are also important similarities, the differences are complementary, and counselors who use one often use the other, too (Guterman & Rudes, 2005; Selekman, 2010). This book describes solution-focused and narrative therapy in the same chapter because they are related and compatible with each other, both theoretically and practically. Both approaches can be used in either the family or individual modality.

Solution-Focused Therapy

Solution-focused therapy was developed during the 1980s by Steve de Shazer and other clinicians at the Brief Family Therapy Center in Milwaukee, Wisconsin (de Shazer, 1985, 1993). Solution-focused counseling departs radically from one traditional hallmark of psychotherapy: These counselors do not want to talk about problems—they want to talk about solutions (de Shazer & Dolan, 2007; Guterman, 2013; Lipchik, Derks, LaCourt, & Nunnally, 2012). Their sessions do not focus on what has gone wrong in the client's life but on what has gone right. For example, Felicia's therapist wanted to move quickly from talk about how awful things were with her classmates to talk about instances when these interactions were better, even if only a little.

Solution-focused therapists assume that, even when clients are doing poorly, bits and pieces of solutions are already occurring at the time therapy begins (De Jong & Berg, 2012; O'Connell, 2012). Therefore, therapy does not need to start from scratch but should begin by identifying what the client is already doing that is sometimes effective. These seeds of solutions are the raw material of therapy. Solution-focused counseling is based on the idea that talking about positive aspects of the client's life improves self-esteem, engenders optimism, and, most importantly, creates a change process that builds on existing strengths and resources (de Shazer & Dolan, 2007; Lipchik et al., 2012; Kim, 2013).

Solution-focused counseling is based on the idea that talking about positive aspects of the client's life creates a change process that builds on existing strengths.

Bill O'Hanlon and colleagues proposed a slightly modified version of solution-focused therapy called **solution-oriented therapy** (O'Hanlon, 2000; O'Hanlon & Beadle, 1997; O'Hanlon & Weiner-Davis, 2003), which includes more provision for therapists to explore and empathize with the client's experience of problems, even though this subtracts from a pure focus on solutions. It is not clear how important this technical difference is, because there appear to be no outcome studies comparing the two variants. Because there is ample evidence that counselor empathy facilitates the process of therapy (see Chapter 1), the solution-oriented offshoot might be preferable, but the vast majority of writing and research on this type of therapy has been labeled as solution-focused, so that is the term used in this book.

Narrative Therapy

Narrative therapy was developed by Michael White and David Epston at the Dulwich Center in Australia (White, 1989, 1995; White & Epston, 1990). This approach is based on the constructivist principle that **self-stories** organize, interpret, and assign meaning to events and, in so doing, create the experienced realities of people's lives (Denborough, 2014; Epston & White, 1992; White, 2007). Narrative therapy is based on the process of **restorying**, in which clients construct new meanings for the events and situations of their lives.

The goal of restorying is to create "preferred realities" that enhance self-concept, increase sense of empowerment, and make new behaviors, outcomes, and experiences possible.

In the externalization metaphor, "the problem" is not something the client does or is but is like a separate entity with a mind of its own that seeks to oppress and control the client.

For most clients, restorying involves the technique of **externalizing the problem**, in which narrative therapists portray the client's difficulties as a malevolent force that originates outside the person and attempts to assault and dominate him (Madigan, 2010; Payne, 2005; White, 2006). In the externalization metaphor, "the problem" is not something the client does or is but is like a separate entity with a mind of its own that seeks to oppress and control the client. Language such as, "You seem depressed today" portrays depression as internal. Talk such as, "Depression is really weighing you down today" depicts depression as external to the client's core self. Externalizing talk is based on the assumption that problems do not reside in the essential nature of persons but, instead, occur as unwanted processes that impinge upon the self (White & Morgan, 2006).

Narrative therapists use language in careful, subtle ways to change clients' experience of their problems. This change is not accomplished by explicit reasoning or debate, but by indirect, unobtrusive forms of talk. Narrative therapists do not *state* that the client's symptoms are like outside forces; they *portray* problems in this way by talking about them as if they were external entities that impinge on the client. In statements such as, "It sounds like Self-doubt is making it difficult for you to achieve your goals in school," and "Anxiety was really pushing you around yesterday," the problems are not located within the "you" (the person).

Narrative therapists, like solution-focused therapists, make extensive use of questions. The questions are like scaffolding devices around which clients can construct new structures of meaning. Many of the questions prompt clients to expand on and elaborate their descriptions of success so these become more prominent themes in their self-stories. Even when client efforts have not produced success, this type of inquiry brings out accounts of constructive resistance to the problem, which highlights the distinction between the person and her difficulties (Carey, Walther, & Russell, 2009; Denborough, 2014; Furman & Ahola, 1992).

What Causes Mental Health Problems?

In principle, the constructivist position on the etiology of mental health problems is: We don't want to talk about it. Discussions with clients about the causes of their difficulties are considered just the type of problem talk that has kept them mired in an unsatisfactory life experience (De Jong & Berg, 2012; de Shazer & Dolan, 2007; O'Connell, 2012).

Professional or scientific discussions of etiology are not considered any more useful. Constructivists criticize the other therapeutic approaches for positing mechanisms that supposedly exist within clients or families and that "cause" their problems (Gergen, 2009; Payne, 2005; White, 2011). These therapists will not attribute problems to maladaptive beliefs, reinforcement contingencies, unconscious conflicts, or any other mechanism, because they view all such accounts of etiology as "stories" that come from the theoretician's perspective, are no more true than any other story, and do not help clients get better.

Constructivists replace scientific, causal analyses with the belief that the way people talk about their lives sometimes blocks them from getting what they want and makes them unhappy (Anderson, 1997; Madigan, 2010; White, 1995). Constructivists view therapy as a fundamentally *linguistic* activity that consists of talk. (Nonverbal forms of communication such as play and art can easily be accommodated by the same principles.) No underlying process is posited as the source of importance for talk; talk is considered important in and of itself.

Although constructivists do not like the term "etiology," they do see language use as the fundamental source of positive and negative human experience. If we construe the idea of etiology broadly as any process that contributes to a problem, it would be fair to say that constructivism posits the etiologies of problem-saturated talk, focusing on weaknesses instead of strengths, viewing problem sources as internal rather than external, and buying into maladaptive cultural beliefs as causes of the difficulties that bring people to therapists.

Recently, some constructivist therapists have identified findings in neuroscience research that they consider deep-level support for their approach. Beaudoin and Zimmerman (2011) cited findings indicating that the brain is biased toward attending to and retaining negative information and affect (Kensinger, 2007; LeDoux, 2002). At the cellular level, neurons mediating negative affect have thicker axons and more numerous dendrites, compared to neurons mediating positive affect. The brain's high level of engagement with information concerning threat and harm would have survival advantages in the environment in which humans evolved, but this focus on the negative would also lead to anxiety, aggression, and depression. It should be noted, however, that this account does not explain individual differences in adaptation.

Narrative therapy is the most explicitly political of the major theoretical orientations. This approach views harmful cultural narratives as a root cause of maladaptive stories in families and individuals (Madigan, 2010; White, 1995). As two important examples, narrative therapists assert that cultural beliefs are root causes of anorexia in women and violence toward women by men. More broadly, narrative theory generally maintains a critical stance toward the predominant Western culture and attributes maladjustment to social structures of inequality based on race, gender, SES, and so forth (White, 2011; White & Epston, 1990). Again, this formulation does not account for individual differences in adjustment.

Assessment and Case Formulation

In one sense, the idea of constructivist assessment is an oxymoron. Constructivists see no value in diagnosis because they view these labels as stories with no more truth value than any other organization of human experience (Foucault, 1973). Diagnosis is considered irrelevant to the process of constructing solutions, and diagnosis talk with clients is considered potentially harmful because it entrenches them in problem-dominated narratives (Ballou & Brown, 2002; Epston & White, 1992). Constructivists view the medical model as disempowering and espouse a fluid conception of problems and solutions that rejects fixed entities like traits and diagnoses. (Because I do not need to bill insurance for our case study, I can be true to the constructivist viewpoint and decline to assign Felicia a diagnosis.)

However, just as constructivist therapy has its own version of etiology, it includes a form of assessment—namely, assessment of talk. Constructivists are interested in the ways that clients use language to organize their experiences into meaningful narratives (Milner & Bateman, 2011; O'Connell, 2012). They listen for aspirations and seeds of solutions in the midst of problem-saturated talk. They listen for maladaptive cultural narratives that the client may have internalized (Kim, 2013; Madigan, 2010).

In constructivist counseling, there is no assessment agenda separate from the therapeutic one. These clinicians are not interested in discovering things about clients that clients do not know and then using this information as a basis for planning interventions. The process of discovery is shared and simultaneous for client and clinician. Constructivist counseling relies more heavily on questions than any other approach, but the activities of inquiry and discovery are emphasized not because they are sources of information for the clinician but because they are engines of change for the client.

Questions to Ask

Constructivists are similar to behaviorists in that they want to receive clear, concrete descriptions of the behaviors and experiences of concern, and they have little interest in speculation or hypothetical constructs. For example, an adolescent who said he had an anxiety disorder might be asked, "What do you feel and do when you experience what you call an anxiety disorder?" This type of therapist response does not dispute the client's diagnostic narrative but puts that story aside and refocuses the conversation on the client's lived experience.

The most basic solution-focused questions are:

- "When *doesn't* the problem happen?"
- "When do things go better than usual?"

Although simple, these questions might be difficult for parents and children to answer because they are accustomed to focusing on problems and expect therapists to do the same. The process of answering the questions requires attention to the positive and so constitutes therapy as well as assessment.

In keeping with their practical, action-oriented orientation, solution-focused counselors ask clients to put both their complaints and their aspirations into **videotalk**, which describes what an observer would see if she were watching a videotape of the experience in question (O'Hanlon & Weiner-Davis, 2003; Selekman, 2010). Asking clients to translate abstractions and speculations into videotalk provides a clearer picture of the problem and a more potent, self-actualizing picture of desired solutions.

Solution-focused counselors also share with behaviorists an emphasis on formulating specific, achievable goals for therapy, even when clients start out with vague, abstract aspirations. Solution-focused therapists like to know the desired end point of therapy at its beginning—for example:

- "How will you know when the problem is solved?"
- "How will you know when we are done with therapy? What will you see then that you are not seeing now?"

Narrative therapists can be said to assess the stories clients tell about their experiences. These counselors are interested in the meanings, themes, plots, and subplots with which clients organize the events of their lives (Carey et al., 2009; Denborough, 2014; White, 1995).

Rather than inquiring about the causes of problems, narrative therapists ask about the problem's *effects* on the child and family. This inquiry, called "mapping the influence of the problem," illuminates the client's relationship with his difficulties (Payne, 2005; White, 2007). Sometimes the mapping is quite geographical; for example, anxieties sometimes block people from entering feared places. More generally, problem mapping involves delineating the areas of the client's life that have been affected by the problem. This assessment activity also has a therapeutic purpose: It builds the externalization metaphor by portraying the problem as a force that pushes the client away from life domains that he wishes to experience. Examples of this type of question include:

- "What does Depression stop you from doing?"
- "How does Anorexia affect your family at mealtime?"
- "What does Rebelliousness tell you to do?"

Narrative therapy has a literary, not a scientific, quality. These counselors are interested in the metaphors, analogies, and explanatory frameworks with which clients organize the raw data of their experiences into stories. There is particular interest in how clients *select*, from the myriad bits of experience that make up their lives, what to emphasize and what to minimize or ignore—what to include and what to leave out in constructing patterns of meaning (Carey et al., 2009; Denborough, 2014; Winslade & Monk, 2006). There is particular interest in deemphasized experiences that exist as implicit knowledge relegated to the background, because when clients turn toward these inconspicuous aspects of their lives and make them explicit, they often find empowering meanings that counter the discouraging themes formerly dominating their self-stories.

Patterns to Look For

Solution-focused therapists search for positive elements in their clients' lives. Because clients usually begin therapy with problem-saturated talk, identifying positive exceptions may be difficult. The key assessment skill is the ability to discern subtle, perhaps weak intimations of success and then to expand the client's talk about these areas by asking for more and more elaboration. Like behaviorists, solution-focused counselors examine the variables of place, time of day, presence of other people, and any other situational factors that might be associated with patterns of relative success (Epston, Freeman, & Lobovits, 1997; White, 1989).

Solution-focused work seems especially needed by clients who are stuck in rumination about past disappointments while paying little attention to positive possibilities for the future. For example, Felicia's therapist noticed that the child and her parents both focused on the negative aspects of Felicia's interpersonal relationships. It required persistent questioning to bring out other aspects of Felicia's social functioning—namely, the way she got along well with many people, including adults and younger children. Her problems were confined to peers, especially girls, her own age.

Narrative techniques seem called for when clients' accounts of their lives draw large implications from their failures and disappointments while dismissing positive elements as insignificant details. The externalization technique may be useful when the child views the problem as a core aspect of her self and pays little attention to other aspects of self that are separate from the problem and struggle against it. Similarly, the externalization metaphor may help families reduce the prominence of the problem in their overall picture of the child. For example, the therapist learned that Felicia's younger cousins often flocked to her at family gatherings, where she organized their play and read them stories. The parents interpreted this behavior as indicating discomfort with same-aged peers. The therapist reorganized this material into an account that did not reduce Felicia's competent behavior to a by-product of her problems.

Once upon a time there was a girl named Felicia who knew a lot of mean kids. These girls thought they were great and Felicia was nothing. They were so snobby that they didn't see Felicia was just as good as them, probably better. So Felicia didn't have any friends. Just enemies.

Felicia tried to make friends, but it didn't work. She tried to show the girls that the things she did and the things she had were just as good as theirs, maybe better. But they were too stupid to care. It's a sad story. The End.

Figure 6.1   Felicia's first story.

Narrative therapists often ask clients to summarize their experiences by putting them in the form of a story. These stories are then written down. With younger clients, therapists help with organization, spelling, and so forth. Figure 6.1 presents the narrative with which Felicia began therapy.

Change Processes

Constructivist counselors view language and conversation as the tools of their trade, and they use language in strategic ways to sculpt the client's experience.

Constructivists believe that when people are unhappy with their lives, talk is the problem, and when people come for therapy, talk is the solution. These therapists believe that the right type of talk can initiate change in the client's pattern of attention, sense of possibility, self-concept, and behavior. Constructivists are linguistic engineers who view language and conversation as the tools of their trade, and they use language in subtle, strategic ways to sculpt the client's experience in positive directions.

Change Agents in Solution-Focused Therapy

Solution-focused therapy assumes that people have within them the resources they need to solve their problems and live satisfying lives (de Shazer, 1985; de Shazer & Dolan, 2007; Kim, 2013). Since problems occur when problem-saturated talk dominates the client's sense of her life and self, therapists can help by engendering a focus on solutions that nourishes and launches the client's capabilities.

For example, a parent and adolescent with a long history of conflict might discover, in response to solution-focused questioning, that they get along a little better than usual when they play tennis together. While many therapists would consider it important to investigate the issues and history underlying the conflict, a solution-focused therapist would consider it more useful to build on the positive exception that already exists. This would mean playing more tennis and, perhaps, watching tennis on TV, attending tournaments, subscribing to a tennis magazine, talking about tennis, and trying to transfer the tennis-associated style of being together to other activities and settings.

The fundamental change strategy of solution-focused therapy is to discover what has already worked and then to do more of it. Behaviors that work in one setting are transferred to other settings. Small successes are considered capable of initiating change processes that disrupt entrenched patterns, generate their own momentum, create ripple effects, and eventually become important solutions. Therefore, the therapist's initial task is just to get the ball rolling, because a snowball effect often follows. There is a suggestion commonly made to clients that is the title of one of O'Hanlon's (2000) books: *Do One Thing Different.*

Solution-focused therapy involves an optimistic attitude toward life. O'Hanlon playfully refers to himself as "a psychotic optimist." Although humorous, this expression is based on a belief in the self-fulfilling effects of expectations. The core sequence of events in solution-focused therapy is this:

1. The therapist talks positively.
2. The client talks positively.
3. The client thinks, feels, and acts positively.

Solution-focused counseling emphasizes the future, not the past. Sessions focus on what the client *wants*, not on what he has already experienced, because talk that elaborates the person's desires and goals is expected to lead toward actualization of those visions. (See Chapter 1's discussion of envisioning.)

Solution-focused therapy is generally brief. Successful interventions can occur in several sessions and even in just one. Brevity is possible because solution-focused therapy is practical, action-oriented, and unconcerned with complex, underlying processes. However, there is no rule that these interventions *must* be brief. Bill O'Hanlon told a story about a client he had been seeing for over a year. The client picked up a brochure in the waiting room that extolled the virtues of brief therapy and wondered why his therapist, the author of the brochure, was not providing this form of counseling to him. O'Hanlon's response was, "Some people's brief therapy takes only a few sessions, and your brief therapy is taking more than a year."

Change Agents in Narrative Therapy

In the narrative therapy formulation, people with "mental health problems" tell self-stories dominated by themes of disappointment, failure, and inadequacy. Narrative therapists assume that these problem-saturated themes do not capture all the events and actions of the client's life. These counselors assume that other, unacknowledged bits and pieces of life data are scattered inconspicuously in client stories but have not been selected for inclusion in the dominant themes. These counterexamples, or **sparkling outcomes** (Denborough, 2014; Epston et al., 1997; White & Epston, 1990; White & Morgan, 2006), contradict or, at least, modify the client's dominant story. The main narrative therapy change agent consists of drawing out, recognizing, and amplifying these instances of strength, and then organizing them into new plots and themes. The result is a new self-story.

The goal is not to create stories that are more "true." Constructivist counselors are not concerned about logic or evidence. Instead, the goal is to construct new narratives that the client experiences as coherent and meaningful, like a good novel, not a scientific proof. The value of narratives depends on their effects on the client's sense of self and life experience. A new narrative is considered successful if it increases the client's appreciation of her past strivings and empowers her to pursue future possibilities more effectively.

Narrative counselors help clients add new meanings and themes to their personal narratives in order to balance the old, problem-saturated accounts with more complex, empowering self-stories.

Narrative counselors help clients add new meanings and themes to their personal narratives in order to balance the old, problem-saturated accounts with more complex, complete, empowering self-stories. Old meanings are not so much refuted as reframed. There is less reliance on narratives internalized from the dominant culture and construction of more authentic meanings based on personal experience (Epston & White, 1992; White, 2007, 2011). Narrative therapists talk about self-stories becoming "thicker": more complex, nuanced, and balanced.

The therapeutic strategy of problem externalization can have several helpful effects (Epston et al., 1997; White & Epston, 1990; White & Morgan, 2006). Portraying the problem as an external, malevolent force often motivates clients to resist and oppose the problem. Social psychological research on **reactance** indicates that people often respond to coercive external influences by trying to assert the choice they perceive as threatened (Brehm, 1993). By portraying the problem as a constraint on the client's freedom to do what he wants, the externalization narrative may recruit reactance into striving for therapeutic change.

Portraying the source of the problem as outside the client may reduce guilt and shame. The externalization narrative increases client awareness of the many aspects of self that have struggled against the problem and have achieved small victories, although not final triumph. The externalization metaphor de-pathologizes the client's sense of self by moving the perceived source of the problem outside the self, as if it were a situational factor. For example, instead of thinking of herself as a depressed person, the client could think of herself as a person who is battling depression. This might seem like a "semantic" difference, but if language creates human realities, semantic differences matter a great deal.

Externalization also provides the client's family with an adaptive way of viewing the problem. This construction of meaning often reduces blame and disagreement among family members about who is responsible for the problem because, in effect, the problem is held responsible for the problem. The externalization metaphor may facilitate cooperation among family members as they unite against what is now seen as their common enemy.

Although the truth value of externalization narratives is not a concern of constructivists, if we were to slip into the scientific framework that takes truth seriously, it would be reasonable to make several points. First, it is not literally true that psychological problems exist outside the people who experience them. However, it is also not true that problems define people or constitute their essences. Because clients have many characteristics that exist outside and even in conflict with their symptoms, there is a sense in which problems are external to their core selves. Neurobiological research may provide a scientifically valid way of understanding symptoms that preserves the empowering value of the externalization metaphor without de-emphasizing truth. Beaudoin and Zimmerman (2011) suggest that therapists present symptoms to clients as particular brain-states that involve only parts of their brain (e.g., the amygdala). The counselor could say that a problem-associated brain-state is "not your friend" and, rather than identifying with it, the client could oppose this brain-state and increase his identification with others.

Use of Questions.   Narrative therapists do not make explicit attempts to persuade clients to adopt the externalization story. Instead, they ask the client questions. However, the purpose of the questions is not to elicit information but to change the client's experience by restructuring her use of language.

Narrative therapists construct the externalization story by embedding it, as an *assumption*, in the questions they ask clients. Clients cannot answer these questions without adopting the externalization framework (at least temporarily). The process of answering the questions shapes the client's talk about his problems in the direction intended by the therapist. For example, the question, "When did Rage first invade your life?" assumes that rage is like an external force that has victimized the client, rather than an emotion that is part of him. Other questions asked by narrative therapists encourage clients to notice and appreciate the courageous, successful, and empowering elements of their selves (Anderson, 1997; Carey et al., 2009; White, 2007).

The externalization narrative assumes that clients do not want to have their problems. This assumption is generally valid for clients with internalizing difficulties. The situation is more complicated for clients with externalizing problems, but with them, too, narrative therapists talk as if the client engages in the problem behaviors only because an external entity has forced or manipulated her into doing so. Thus, rather than trying to persuade an adolescent that complying with her curfew is a good thing to do, the therapist would assume the client realizes this on some level and would depict all anticurfew arguments and impulses as not really belonging to the client (e.g., "What has Rebelliousness said to convince you that you shouldn't have a curfew?"). Thus, the therapist assumes what he is trying to prove and begins the conversation from that assumption.

The narrative therapy way of using questions seems to involve a method of persuasion, however subtle. Because narrative therapists do not explain the purpose of their questions, there seems to be an element of well-intentioned manipulation in their work, but clients have the final level of control because therapists abandon stories that do not move clients forward (Nichols, 2012; White, 2007). The subtlety of narrative techniques, which might operate at preconscious levels of linguistic processing, probably contributes to their effectiveness.

Constructivist Therapy and Truth

Nichols (2012) noted that one limitation of the constructivist approach may be that its postmodernist disavowal of objective truth does not match the orientation of most clients. Constructivists argue that talk does not reflect but actually constitutes reality (Anderson, 1997; Bruner, 1987; White & Epston, 1990). This idea is inconsistent with the experiences of many people with mental health problems and with a great deal of research that has identified correlates of maladjustment besides maladjusted talk, including distinctive neurophysiological states.

Average people, like scientists but unlike postmodernists, usually care about objective truth (Held, 1995). Anxious children care whether their fears are realistic. Depressed clients want to know whether they really are as inadequate as they think they are—or as okay as their therapist thinks. Parents want to know whether it is true that negative attention can reinforce child misbehavior. These client needs are not met by the construction of stories, no matter how empowering, that provide no information about the validity of the relevant propositions.

Nichols (2012) also noted that one limitation of the narrative approach may be that the externalization metaphor varies in its applicability to different problems. Although some difficulties may be like outside forces, negative emotions and behaviors often signal that something important is wrong in the individual's life. If so, directing attention away from that issue, toward a metaphorically external force, might lead away from the changes that are needed. There are often *reasons* why people are depressed, frightened, or angry, and creating a metaphor of invasion by Depression, Fear, or Anger may do little to address these factors.

There seems to be little support for narrative therapy's general contention that the oppressive nature of our society is a root cause of mental health problems. Although this argument seems plausible in regard to eating disorders and male violence against women, there is little evidence for this contention outside these specific problem areas. To be convincing, an explanation of psychological problems as the result of harmful cultural narratives requires evidence that other, less oppressive societies have lower rates of mal-adjustment. I am not aware of findings documenting the existence of such societies. Also, positing a societal etiology does not help to explain individual differences in adjustment.

Overall, there seems to be much of value in the constructivist approach to ther-apy. Although talk does not seem to be the sole creator of reality in human life— neurophysiology provides one counterexample, and infants provide another—language certainly shapes experience and influences behavior in important ways. Therapists can make good use of constructivist insights and techniques without necessarily buying into the radical aspects of postmodernism that reject the idea of objective truth.

Outcome Research

The constructivist therapies have an ambivalent relationship with outcome research. From a postmodernist philosophical perspective, such research is an invalid endeavor that pur-sues the illusion of objective truth by standing outside the lived experiences of people and claiming to assess those experiences. However, constructivist therapists are typically more pragmatic than postmodernist philosophers, and they want general knowledge about the effects of their interventions on clients. Outcome research on constructivist therapies has begun, although it began later and has progressed less far than research on all the other the-oretical orientations in this book. There has been much more research on solution-focused counseling than narrative therapy.

Solution-Focused Therapy

Gingerich and Peterson (2013) performed a comprehensive, qualitative review of con-trolled outcome studies of solution-focused therapy, both published and unpublished. Most of the studies focused on adult clients, but results for youth were generally similar. Overall, 74% of their 43 studies reported significant benefits resulting from solution-focused ther-apy, with an additional 23% reporting positive nonsignificant trends. Ten studies compared solution-focused therapy with some alternative treatment, either a therapy or a medication. In nine of these investigations, there was no significant difference between the treatments. In one study, solution-focused therapy produced better outcomes than paroxetine.

Kim (2008) conducted a meta-analytic review of 22 outcome studies. Again, most of the studies had adult clients, but the results for those including youth were generally sim-ilar. The meta-analysis indicated a nonsignificant effect for problems in the externalizing category and a small, significant effect of .26 for both internalizing dysfunction and family problems.

Bond, Woods, Humphrey, Symes, and Green (2013) conducted a careful review with clear methodological criteria to examine outcome research on solution-focused therapy for children. Of the 38 studies they identified as meeting minimal methodological standards, 32 provided some form of supportive evidence for the intervention, with 2 indicating solution-focused therapy was ineffective and 4 producing neutral results. However, only eight of the studies demonstrated that clients receiving solution-focused therapy achieved better outcomes than a control group. Also, their review included many different types of interventions and clients, some of which are of limited relevance for our purposes. Some of the research examined solution-focused techniques in nontherapy settings (classrooms and child welfare); in some, solution-focused techniques were combined with other therapeutic and educational strategies, making it impossible to isolate their impact on outcomes; and the studies' dependent variables included academic outcomes as well as measures of mental health.

The studies reviewed ahead are limited to those in which solution-focused counseling was provided without other intervention components, compared to a control condition, and evaluated in terms of mental health outcomes. In research conducted in schools, Franklin, Moore, and Hopson (2008) compared solution-focused therapy and TAU for children who had been identified by teachers as exhibiting behavior problems. Solution-focused therapy produced significant reductions in both internalizing and externalizing dysfunction, with effect sizes in the medium range and average group scores moving from the clinical to the normal range.

In another school study, Corcoran (2006) found no difference between solution-focused therapy and TAU, although there was a nonsignificant trend favoring solution-focused counseling. Corcoran noted that TAU, in this study, included empirically supported cognitive-behavioral and family therapy techniques, so the lack of difference did not indicate that solution-focused therapy was ineffective.

A Lithuanian study of adolescents in foster care found that clients who received several sessions of solution-focused therapy showed greater reductions in behavior problems than did an untreated control group of similar adolescents (Cepukiene & Pakrosnis, 2011). Thirty-one percent of the therapy clients showed statistically reliable and clinically significant improvement in behavior problems, and 29% showed this level of improvement in somatic and cognitive difficulties.

A study in Norway by Kvarme et al. (2010) compared a group of socially withdrawn children who received solution-focused group therapy to a no-treatment control group of similar children. The therapy produced improvement in scores on a self-efficacy measure.

Bond et al. (2013) concluded their review by noting that the research base for solution-focused therapy is progressing but does not yet include a substantial number of methodologically strong studies. Most of the results that have been obtained are encouraging, and it seems clear that solution-focused therapy can be helpful to many clients. Further research is needed to compare the impact of this therapy to other types of intervention and to assess whether its effectiveness varies for different types of clients.

Solution-focused techniques generally do not take a long time to implement, so this approach is often associated with brief therapy. For clients who need more assistance, these strategies can easily be combined with other therapeutic procedures. From a research perspective, using solution-focused techniques in this way is problematic, because the effects cannot be isolated. From a clinical perspective, however, eclectic therapists can probably add something valuable to their repertoire by using solution-focused techniques.

Narrative Therapy

There has been very little research on narrative therapy. Ahead, I review the few studies I could find that examined pre-/postintervention change in a sample of 10 or more clients who received a narrative intervention that was psychotherapeutic in nature (i.e., not an educational or experiential activity). This review includes studies that do not meet the methodological standards of the outcome research sections of the other chapters of this book.

Vromans and Schweitzer (2011) measured the effects of narrative therapy on depressive symptoms in a sample of adults with major depressive disorder. This study did not include a control group. The clients showed reductions in depression, with a large effect size of 1.36 and clinically significant improvement in 53% of the sample. Gains were maintained at a 3-month follow-up assessment.

Cashin, Browne, Bradbury, and Mulder (2013) performed a study of narrative therapy for 10 young people with mild autism. There was no control group. The participants showed decreases in several measures of emotional distress, including cortisol level.

Silver, Williams, Worthington, and Phillips (1998) conducted a retrospective chart review of therapy for children with encopresis, some of whom received narrative therapy and some of whom received TAU at the same clinic. The narrative therapy group demonstrated a larger reduction in soiling, and these parents rated therapy as more helpful, compared to families receiving TAU.

In a study conducted in Malaysia, Looyeh, Kamali, and Shafieian (2012) provided narrative therapy in a group format to a sample of girls with ADHD and compared their behavior to a wait-list control group. Post-treatment ratings by teachers indicated improvement in the girls who received narrative therapy. Gains were still in evidence at a 1-month follow-up.

Narrative therapists publish many case studies, qualitative investigations, and process studies, but they do not conduct much research that allows generalizations to be made about typical responses to this type of therapy. The lack of emphasis on research in the narrative therapy field is consistent with postmodernist skepticism about science as a means of discovering truth about human beings.

However, some cognitive-behavioral therapists have imported narrative techniques into their interventions and evaluated the packages in outcome studies. One important example is Cohen, Mannarino, and Deblinger's (2006) intervention for traumatized children, which has received extensive support from outcome research, as described in Chapter 15.

The Therapist's Style

Because constructivists do not believe in objective knowledge, they are skeptical about the idea of expertise. Constructivism replaces the view of the counselor as an expert with a collaborative model of therapist-client interaction (De Jong & Berg, 2012; Lipchik et al., 2012; White & Epston, 1990). These therapists do not believe they know anything about the client's functioning that the client does not know himself. Anderson (1997) recommends that therapists adopt a position of **not-knowing** and engage in open-minded conversations with clients.

Constructivist therapists make no claim to scientific knowledge, but they offer something they consider more valuable—namely, an ability to *create conversations* that mobilize the client's own resources for positive change. Constructivist counselors believe they are experts in one thing: the change process.

These counselors do not teach, train, interpret, or give directives (Epston & White, 1992; O'Hanlon & Weiner-Davis, 2003; White & Morgan, 2006). However, their subtle insistence on focusing on solutions and portraying problems as external can be construed as directive, in a sense.

The nonhierarchical, nonauthoritarian spirit of constructivist therapy should be visible in the counselor's style of interacting with clients. Conducting this type of therapy means conveying, both verbally and nonverbally, that you are not there to figure out the client's problems and make professional recommendations. Instead, the counselor's function is to "host therapeutic conversations" (Furman & Ahola, 1992)—to create an atmosphere and conversational structure in which the client's own strengths and ideas can be brought out and applied to the solution of her problems.

As one ramification of this nonhierarchical relationship, constructivists believe in being human and real with their clients, rather than trying to keep their personalities and issues out of the conversation. These therapists are willing to disclose personal material when it seems relevant to the client's concerns. They behave in a natural, informal style, rather than a conventionally professional one, and are sometimes playful, even boisterous. Constructivist counselors join children in their natural style of inter-action, getting on the floor with them and playing with toys (Berg & Steiner, 2003; Selekman, 2010).

Solution-Focused Techniques

In everyday conversations about personal difficulties, people often spend much more time and energy talking about the problem than talking about possible solutions. People often focus on analyzing the causes of a problem, tracing its development, trying to decide who is to blame, and anticipating future consequences of the problem. The solution-focused insight is that such problem-saturated talk, even when factually correct, often entrenches people in their problems rather than moving them forward (De Jong & Berg, 2012; de Shazer & Dolan, 2007; Guterman, 2013; Kim, 2013).

Solution-focused therapists begin counseling by directing the client's attention to what is already going well in his life. One technique for doing this is called the **formula first-session task**, because it is a traditional homework assignment given at the end of the first meeting (de Shazer, 1985; Furman & Ahola, 1992; Lipchik et al., 2012). The therapist says:

> "Between now and the next time we meet, I would like you to observe, so you can describe to me next time, what happens in your (family, life, marriage, relationship) that you want to continue to have happen." (de Shazer, 1985, p. 137)

As well as focusing clients' attention on what they have to be thankful for, solution-focused counselors direct clients' attention to what they want—which results in talk that is different from complaints about what they do not have. Talk about desires and goals, even when not based on a clear understanding of the problem, tends to focus attention, energy, and creativity on the development of solutions. Even when the topic or issue is identical, problem-talk and solution-talk are not the same:

> PROBLEM TALK: My son never does his homework without a fight. He argues when I try to get him to do it and, if I force him, he cries and says he hates school. It's been this way for months. Nothing works. I've tried rewarding him, punishing him, begging him—it's all futile.
>
> SOLUTION TALK: I've got to think of some new strategies for motivating my son to do homework. I should probably talk to other parents, and there are books and magazine articles with ideas for accomplishing this. Maybe if I found a way to make it like a game, that would improve things.

These two samples of conversation involve no disagreement about facts or logic, but they seem quite different in their potential for producing positive change. The problem talk seems to lead more deeply into discouragement. The solution talk moves toward hope and innovation (Milner & Bateman, 2011; O'Connell, 2012; O'Hanlon, 2000).

When clients describe upsetting situations, therapists can spend some time on acknowledgment and empathy, and then shift gears by means of simple questions that change problem-talk into solution-talk:

- "What would you like to see happen in this situation?"
- "Any thoughts on what could be done to improve things?"

Problem-talk and solution-talk have different time frames: Problem-talk is about the past, and solution-talk is about the future. Solution-talk can generate compelling images that pull the client forward into the reality he envisions.

Compliments are considered a therapeutic technique in solution-focused work, which is not the case in other theoretical orientations. Compliments are different from the praise that behavior therapists use as a positive reinforcer because they are not contingent on desired behavior. Compliments are used to expand positive aspects of clients' self-images and to nourish and energize their capability to do even better in the future (Berg & Steiner, 2003 Lipchik et al., 2000).

Compliments may have underutilized potential as a therapeutic technique. This type of counselor statement has received very little attention in the literature, perhaps because it does not seem sufficiently technical in nature. However, on a simple, human level, receiving a compliment from a respected person generally feels good, is encouraging, and supports self-esteem. Compliments are probably most therapeutic when they are insightful—when they tell the client something about himself he did not already know and address aspects of self deeper than aptitudes and talents. Because therapists presumably know their clients more deeply than most people do, we are in a good position to offer meaningful observations about their efforts, concern for others, aspirations, the courage and integrity of their struggles, and their striving to understand and improve their life in the face of obstacles and stress. Compliments probably need to be sincere in order to be effective. There is no point saying something you do not mean but, if you notice something importantly positive about your client, a compliment might be therapeutically useful.

It is worth noting that the technique of focusing on solutions can be useful in many situations outside therapy. In families, relationships, and on the job, setbacks often cause people to fall into intensive, detailed talk about why the problem occurred and who is to blame. While a certain amount of such problem-talk may be useful, people often continue well past the point of diminishing returns. At these times, it may be possible to turn the conversation in a more useful direction by asking, "What are we going to *do* about this? What are our options?"

Breaking the Connection Between Past and Future

Solution-focused therapists reject the idea that people's pasts determine their futures. They view these connections as a matter of self-fulfilling prophecy: If people believe there is an iron connection, there will be, but if people believe in the possibility of change, the future can be different from the past (de Shazer & Dolan, 2007; Metcalf, 2008; Selekman, 2010).

At the same time, solution-oriented (as opposed to solution-focused) therapists believe it is important to hear and acknowledge clients' descriptions of their problems. These therapists combine empathy for the client's past experiences with hope for future change by means of a strategy called **possibility-laced acknowledgment** (O'Hanlon, 2000; O'Hanlon & Weiner-Davis, 2003), which involves careful, subtle use of language.

To implement this strategy, the therapist uses time-related aspects of language to break the client's sense of a deterministic connection between her history and future possibilities. Counselors use the past tense to talk about problems, and they use the future tense to discuss goals and plans. Small, inconspicuous words like "so far" and "yet" convey the clinician's belief that the future can be different from the past. Clients may not be aware of the little phrases with which solution-talk is sprinkled, but this therapeutic use of language can shape their sense of possibility nevertheless. These subtly potent little phrases include:

- "Hmm, so far."
- "Well, up 'til now."
- "So, that's how it's been in the past."

In possibility-laced acknowledgment, therapists reflect client statements, but they reframe complaints as goals, and they change the time orientation from the past to the future. Many of the examples ahead are drawn from O'Hanlon and Beadle (1997).

CLIENT: The kids in my class don't like me.
THERAPIST: You haven't made friends yet this year.

The technique of changing a complaint about the past into a goal for the future is widely applicable, because almost any complaint can be reauthored into a desire or objective:

- "So, you want to feel more confident when you take tests in school."
- "You'd like to have a girlfriend, but that hasn't happened yet."

Reflecting clients' *global* statements as *partial* statements is another tool of possibility-laced acknowledgment. These reflections include enough of the client's expressed meaning to provide acknowledgment while modifying that meaning sufficiently to suggest a crack in the wall of negativity. Because it is unlikely that things really are 100% awful, this technique generally moves clients toward greater realism as well as optimism—for example:

> CLIENT: I'm nervous about everything.
>
> THERAPIST: You've been worried about lots of things.

The next technique is to reframe the client's claims about reality as perceptions or beliefs. These therapist statements do not convey disagreement but, by portraying the client's statements as personal views rather than facts, the implication is that reality might not be as definitively awful as the client feels it is:

> CLIENT: I just wasn't meant to be happy.
>
> THERAPIST: You've come to feel that it's not your destiny to be happy.

Solution-focused therapists try to induce hope not by making explicitly optimistic predictions, which might elicit disagreement, but by letting their assumption of eventual improvement shape their language in small, unobtrusive ways. When talking about positive change, they say "when," not "if." These counselors try to generate conversation about what life will be like when the problem is solved, because clear, elaborated expectations have a way of actualizing themselves—for instance:

- "When you're feeling better, and the depression is manageable or gone, how will your life be different? Will you be paying closer attention in class? Playing softball more? Doing more activities after school?"
- "When you start making friends with the girls in your class, what games do you think you'll play with them?"

The Miracle Question

The first session of solution-focused therapy often includes use of **the miracle question** (De Jong & Berg, 2012; de Shazer, 1985; Murphy, 2008). This technique asks clients to envision their goals for change in a detailed, vivid way. Introductions like the following create the mindset needed to answer the question:

> "Let's say that a miracle occurred, and the problem just went away. Let's say you went to bed tonight and, while you were sleeping, a miracle took place, so that tomorrow, when you wake up, the problem is gone, and things are exactly how you want them to be. My question is, how would you know? What would be different?"

Follow-up questions should be used to fill in the details of the miracle (de Shazer & Dolan, 2007; Murphy, 2008). Examples include: "Who would be the first person to notice that the miracle happened?" "How would your father react? Your teachers?" "How would the miracle affect your grades? The way you play after school? The way you get along with other kids?"

With young children, concrete symbols and images facilitate the process of visualizing the desired change. Berg and Steiner (2003) suggest asking children what animal they are like when the problem is happening and what animal they will be like when their behavior and feelings become the way they want them to be. Aggressive children might want to change from an angry crocodile to a cool cat, and timid children might want to change from a scared mouse to a brave tiger. Berg and Steiner also suggest asking children to find images of the changes they desire in sports, celebrities, cars, and characters in books and TV programs.

Solution-focused therapists use art therapy techniques. Clients can draw a picture of the problem, a picture of the solution, and pictures of steps in between. Therapists ask clients to draw pictures of activities they do well, favorite toys and places, and what they want to be when they grow up (Berg & Steiner, 2003; Milner & Bateman, 2011; Selekman, 2010).

Felicia's initial picture of a solution showed her jumping rope in front of a group of impressed, admiring peers who had to admit she was a better rope-jumper than any of them. Then, the therapist asked her to remember a time in her past when she did have some fun with peers. Although it took some thinking, Felicia recalled an experience at day camp of playing cooperatively with a small group of girls. The counselor asked her to remember this experience in as much detail as possible and then to draw a picture of herself as part of a group having fun together as equals, with no one standing out. Although this picture did not produce the first drawing's feeling of triumph, when Felicia imagined what it would be like to be in the picture, she did notice some good feelings.

Building on Exceptions to the Problem

Another solution-focused technique is the use of **exception questions** (de Shazer, 1985; de Shazer & Dolan, 2007; Lipchik et al., 2012). Exception questions ask when the problem does *not* happen. If the client says the problem happens all the time, the counselor asks when the magnitude is a little less.

Exceptions do not have to be dramatic in order to be therapeutically useful; hints or bits of exception will do. For example, you could ask the parents of an oppositional child to remember when the child did one thing she was told. Other examples for parents include:

- "When is Harvey's behavior with other children a little less aggressive than usual?"
- "In taking me through a typical day with Debbie, you described lots of trouble in the morning and evening, but you didn't say much about the afternoon. Tell me about her behavior in the afternoon."

Examples of exception questions for clients include:

- "Tell me about a time when the problem could have happened but didn't."
- "Has there ever been a time when you could have given in to the problem, but you didn't?"
- "Let's take a look at what you're already doing right."

The following questions for children combine inquiry about positive exceptions with the externalization metaphor:

- "When does Nervousness let up on you, so you can relax a little bit?"
- "Tell me about a time when you tamed the Anger Beast for a while so you could get along with your brother."

At the beginning of therapy, clients sometimes find it difficult to think of even minor exceptions to the problem. However, such exceptions must exist, because behavior always shows some variability, and clients never experience an identical level of failure across all situations. Therapists should identify, articulate, and build upon the most adaptive instances of the client's functioning, even if these seem to be the result of random variability, because positive exceptions provide a starting point and raw material for change.

Solution-focused counselors value small changes, and therapeutic conversations need a terminology with which to discuss such changes. The procedure called **scaling** supplies that language (De Jong & Berg, 2012; de Shazer & Dolan, 2007; Metcalf, 2008). Therapists ask clients to rate the severity of problems on a scale from 1 to 10, with one end of the scale defined by the client's response to the Miracle Question and the opposite pole defined as the worst the problem has ever been.

Counselors home in on small differences to increase the client's appreciation of variation in his functioning and to expand on positive movements. We should respond with interest and brightened affect to all reports of upward movement, even if small and low on the scale (e.g., from 1 to 2). The next question is, "How did you do that?" If there is no improvement at all, unless there is deterioration, clinicians can note that the client prevented the problem from getting worse. If deterioration does occur, unless the client gives a rating of 1, the therapist can point out that the client has maintained a problem level above past low points.

Perhaps the most essential skill for solution-focused therapists is the ability to find glimmers of success in the midst of problem-saturated talk. In this thought process, the critical strategy is to extend your sense of possibility *downward*, as far as it can go, so you are more able to perceive differences between the client's functioning and the bottom of this dimension. By having a clear sense of how bad things could be, you will be able to see the ways in which the client is doing better than she might. The question to ask yourself, as clients describe their problems, is "How could things be worse?"

For example, if one's internal definition of acceptable grades is limited to As and Bs, there is little difference between Cs, Ds, and Fs. But if one believes that only straight Fs represent a truly zero level of accomplishment, it makes sense to ask a child, "How were you able to get a D in math?" With a concept of failure that extends low enough, it is possible to look at a test with 19 of 20 items wrong and ask the client, "What did you do to get this question right?"

People do not appreciate accomplishments that they assume will happen. The more we assume, the less we celebrate. Therefore, the key to being a connoisseur of positive exceptions is to assume as little as possible. Just as behaviorists reinforce minor instances of positive behavior, solution-focused counselors portray the slightest exceptions to problems as notable.

Consider this mother's report on her teenage daughter:

"Her behavior in school is a disaster. Her grades have gone from Bs to Ds and Fs in everything but gym. Whatever homework she can't do in study hall doesn't get done, and that isn't much because she spends most of her time passing notes to her friends. I've talked to her teachers, and they say she interferes with the learning process for the other students because she asks questions that are off the point of the lesson. In class, when teachers correct her, she argues. On days when there's no play rehearsal, she cuts school and hangs out with kids whose parents aren't home and don't care enough to check on where they are. I've seen those kids, and I can't prove it, but I'll bet they're either drinking alcohol or smoking pot or both."

Therapists with a sense of possibility extending far enough downward will be able to discern, in this description, the following positive elements:

- The girl earned good grades in the past.
- She still gets good grades in gym.
- She does homework in study hall, indicating some motivation and capability.
- She has friends, indicating the presence of social skills.
- Her note passing, while against the rules, shows she likes to write and can express herself in writing.
- She asks questions in class, indicating interest in learning and respect for the teacher as a knowledge source.
- When arguing with teachers, she controls her behavior enough to avoid explicit disrespect, screaming, and violence.
- She cares about being in the school play and is disciplined enough to attend school on the days there are rehearsals.

When it is especially difficult to find positive exceptions in a bleak description of problems, **coping questions** provide therapists with a technique to fall back on. The idea behind this technique is that as long as the client continues to walk around and live, he has not been totally defeated by the problem, and some form of coping is taking place. Such coping represents a form of strength, and it should be noticed and amplified. No matter how negative the client's description of her situation, therapists can ask how she kept the situation from getting worse (de Shazer & Dolan, 2007; Guterman, 2013; O'Hanlon & Beadle, 1997)—for example:

> CLIENT: I'm so depressed. I'm miserable, exhausted, no energy at all.
>
> THERAPIST: And feeling as awful as you do, how did you manage to get up this morning to come here?

When framed in the right way, even the client's distress can be viewed as an aspect of her striving in a positive direction, because discomfort with a negative situation bespeaks both good judgment and motivation for change. (See the discussion of the extendincorp strategy in Chapter 8, Atheoretical Techniques.) For example, a therapist could portray a youth's complaints about a parent as evidence that the youth recognizes the problems in the relationship and wants to improve the situation. Clients' unhappiness with almost any element of their own functioning can be portrayed as the result of a constructive desire for self-improvement (e.g., "You're here because you want to work on this").

When exceptions to problems are found, we want clients to take credit for them. Making clients aware of how their effective behaviors lead to positive outcomes has two beneficial effects: improving self-esteem and increasing their ability to reproduce the outcome in the future. If the client knows what he did right, he will be able to do it again—for example:

> CLIENT: School's been a little better lately.
>
> THERAPIST: Oh, what happened?
>
> CLIENT: I don't know. My teacher has been nicer to me.
>
> THERAPIST: What did you do to get her to be nicer?
>
> CLIENT: Nothing. She just got nicer.
>
> THERAPIST: I don't think that would happen by itself. Think back. What have you been doing differently that might have helped her get nicer?

Clients may initially believe that solutions will require brand-new behaviors and abilities, but solution-focused questions often reveal that the only thing needed is to do more of the same, or to do it more consistently, or to do it in new situations. Felicia's therapist asked her to notice and report any peer interactions, no matter how small, that did not involve conflict or unpleasantness. Initially, she could report only routine, task-oriented interactions. But although these exchanges did not involve friendship, the therapist pointed out that she was sometimes able to get along with other students and that, if she did more of whatever she did in those interactions, she could move toward making friends.

Clients often have difficulty identifying what they did to produce exceptions to their problems. It might seem to them that their anomalous success "just happened," but this cannot really be the case. In these situations, counselors should guide clients in performing a close-up, slowed-down examination of their thoughts, feelings, and behavior prior to and during the positive exception. If clients can remember exactly what they did, they will be able to do it again.

Changing the Doing

Once the client has a vision of the solution she wants, therapy turns to the process of designing steps toward that goal (De Jong & Berg, 2012; Furman & Ahola, 1992; Lipchik et al., 2012; O'Hanlon, 2000). These steps involve action-oriented assignments that build on exceptions to the problem. The therapist identifies anything that is working in the client's life and looks for ways to expand that element. For example, if a traumatized adolescent feels a little safer when in church, the counselor might suggest he join a church youth group. This type of intervention shrinks the domain of problems while enlarging the domain of successful functioning.

Felicia's therapist worked with her teacher, who noted that Felicia was less competitive with boys than girls and did less showing off and arguing with male peers. Therefore, when the class did small-group activities, the teacher placed her with boys. Once appropriate interaction patterns began to develop, the teacher introduced increasing numbers of girls into the groups.

The therapist identifies anything that is working in the client's life and looks for ways to expand that element.

If it is difficult to find positive exceptions within the domain of the problem, you will need to search in related areas. Given that the client has probably functioned comparatively effectively in some domain, you can identify connections between the more successful area and the problematic one. For example, consider an adolescent girl who is anxious about initiating relationships with boys and complains that "I don't know how to flirt; I can't think of anything to say." You could ask such a client how she has initiated friendships with girls, what she has talked about with boys she did not view as potential dates and, if necessary, what she talks about with her family. Finally, you could suggest that she talk to potential dates using the same conversational behaviors that have served her well with other people. Once she achieves comfort with this type of interaction, she might become ready to add the final element of romantic flirtation.

It is more difficult to make connections between domains of success and failure when these areas are dissimilar. Nonetheless, there are usually indirect connections between the competencies involved in different realms because basic human abilities apply to many situations. Even the skills involved in recreational activities are not completely different from the skills needed to succeed in school and work. For example, playing video games requires motivation, concentration, learning rules and strategies, repeated practice, and dealing with the possibility of failure—all skills required by school. Therapists can assist low-achieving children who are good at video games by showing them that they already possess some of the skills needed in school and by helping them transfer those skills to academic work. Even negative behaviors such as gang involvement include some of the abilities needed for prosocial behavior. Success in gangs and success in work both involve being motivated by money, following directions from leaders, and working toward goals as a member of a team.

Here is a three-step formula for finding ways to bridge existing competencies and new challenges:

1. Identify a specific activity (no matter how trivial) in which the client is relatively successful.
2. Construct an abstract definition of the ability involved in that success.
3. Think of concrete forms this abstract ability could take in the problem area.

This cognitive sequence can be summarized as moving from the concrete to the abstract and then back to the concrete. In terms of the video game example, the counselor would ask the child to specify exactly what he does when he plays successfully. Then, the therapist and child would label the capabilities involved (motivation, practice, etc.). Finally, they would translate those capabilities into the specific behaviors needed in school. This work might involve changing the way the client thinks about school to identify parallels with video games. The therapist might talk about academics in terms of "getting high scores" and "figuring out the trick to winning."

The **miracle day technique** described by Berg and Steiner (2003) can be used as an intervention for disruptive behaviors. (The technique is less applicable to internalizing forms of dysfunction.) In this procedure, the therapist and family plan for the child to conduct "a miracle day" during which the answer to the miracle question will be enacted in the home. The child is not to tell the parents when this occurs; the parents just wait to see what happens. The child has control over the timing of the miracle; she can prepare for as long as she wants and do the miracle when she is ready. Once the miracle day is over, the child is under no obligation to continue the desired behavior.

This intervention seems to work for several reasons. The procedure is dramatic and fun, with an element of surprise. The arrangement gives the child a great deal of control, and, because the timing of the miracle is up to him, there is not too much pressure. Clients do not have to make substantive internal changes to do the miracle; they simply *enact* the solution. The procedure is like an experiment in which the child tries out the new behavior to see how it feels. Clients usually enjoy the interactions and consequences that occur on their miracle days, and this enjoyment motivates future changes.

Narrative Therapy Techniques

The next sections describe the four main strategies of narrative therapy. For most clients, externalizing the problem provides a new, destigmatizing, and empowering perspective on their difficulties. The search for sparkling outcomes is similar to solution-focused therapy's search for positive exceptions and demonstrates the link between these two constructivist therapies. Work on cultural narratives is based on narrative therapy's distinctive emphasis on societal sources of problems for people, with the goal being to help clients free themselves from the harmful effects of cultural messages. The last section describes the writing and rewriting of personal stories as a therapeutic activity.

Externalizing the Problem

The central strategy of narrative therapy is externalizing the problem (Epston et al., 1997; White & Epston, 1990; White & Morgan, 2006; Winslade & Monk, 2006). The first step in this work is to create a name for the problem. The act of naming, in itself, portrays the problem as something separate from the client. Early in therapy, the therapist asks the client for a shorthand term:

"What should we call this problem? Let's think of a simple name that sums it up."

Table 6.1   Questions for Constructing the Externalization Metaphor

1. When did _____ (the externalized problem) first invade/come into your life?

   "When did Anxiety first invade your life?"

2. When does _____ (the externalized problem) control you, and when doesn't it?

   "Does Procrastination control you more when you're trying to practice the piano or when you're trying to do homework?"

3. Has _____ (the externalized problem) changed/affected _____ (a life area)?

   "Has the Ruminating interfered with your conversations with friends?"

4. How has _____ (the externalized problem) convinced/coerced you to _____ (the presenting problem)?

   "What has Jealousy said to get you to insult the girls in your class?"

If the client cannot think of a name, the therapist should brainstorm possibilities, and the client should choose the one that makes the most sense to her. Older children and adults usually use conventional terms, such as "the Depression," "the Rebellion," and "the Tantrums." With young children, less conventional terminology may resonate more closely with the client's experience of the problem. In a famous case of White's (1989), the client's encopresis was named "Sneaky Poo." Other examples of problems named in child language would include "the No-I-Won'ts" and "the Anger Monster." For Felicia, the label that seemed to capture her competitiveness and distress about seeing peers excel was "the Jealousy" or "the Jealousy Monster."

The questions used by narrative therapists to engender a process of externalization take several forms that can be expressed as formulae. These questions are presented in Table 6.1.

Narrative therapists do not explicitly describe, explain, or justify the idea that problems are external to people. This type of counseling is not an exercise in reason and evidence but in subtler, stealthier forms of influence and persuasion. Narrative counselors induce belief in the externalization metaphor by using questions to create thought processes that lead to this view of problems. Specifically, they embed the externalization metaphor as an assumption in the questions they ask clients, which requires clients to adopt the assumption in order to answer the question. Thus, narrative therapists do not ask questions like, "Does your rebellion against your parents seem like an external force?" Instead, they ask questions like, "How has Rebellion convinced you to break your parents' rules?" The idea of externalization is stated as a given, and the question is about the effects of the externalized problem.

Therapeutic conversations translate internalized versions of problems verbalized by clients into externalized versions offered by counselors—for example:

CLIENT: I get so nervous when I try to talk to a girl. Then I start tripping over my words, and she must think I'm a dork.

THERAPIST: It sounds like Self-Doubt really comes after you when you talk to a girl. It trips up your talking and even convinces you the girl won't like you.

CLIENT: My science teacher is this dried-up old guy with a droning voice—really boring. I can't stand listening to him, and there's no way I'm going to pay attention in that class. His homework assignments are stupid, and I'm not going to do any work for him.

THERAPIST: It sounds like Contempt really invades your life in science class. Even though you don't want to flunk, Contempt makes you focus on what you don't like about the teacher instead of your own goals. Maybe that's its strategy for screwing up your plan to go to college.

The externalization narrative encourages clients to develop a different relationship or stance toward the problem (White, 2007, 2011; Winslade & Monk, 2006). Words like the following can galvanize and organize the client's motivation for change:

- "I think you're getting tired of running away, and you're ready to stand up to the Fear."
- "This War with your father is making both of you miserable. Every time you start calming things down, the War steps in and gets a big fight going. When are you going to decide you've had enough and put a stop to this?"

Felicia's therapist explored the many ways in which Jealousy disrupted her efforts to make friends with girls her age. Jealousy had convinced Felicia that the way to be liked was to show other kids how great she was, even though the effective way to socialize is actually to be friendly and appreciative of other people. With the counselor's guidance, Felicia drew a picture of the Jealousy Monster as a puppeteer and herself as a puppet.

Butler, Guterman, and Rudes (2009) suggest another way to use puppets in narrative therapy: by making the puppet a physical objectification of the problem. The therapist asks the child to select a puppet that looks like the problem and then asks her to verbalize what the problem would say, both to herself and to other people. In their case example with an oppositional child, the client selected an insect puppet that verbalized his oppositional impulses, "bugged" his mother, and interfered with their relationship. The child had the puppet express his "annoying" side, and he also talked to the puppet. He took it home, where the puppet continued to exert its annoying influence until he and his mother united against it and eventually defeated the Annoyance.

In a family therapy context, therapists can use the externalization metaphor to create positive changes in the functioning of the system. By portraying the problem as something outside the client that distresses her as well as the family, blame and anger toward the client might be reduced. The client's perception might then change from the family being against her to the family being against the problem. With this reconfiguration, a new pattern of alliances and conflict becomes apparent. Counselors can invite the youth and family to consider a new system of allegiances by using words like the following:

"I guess in the past it was Alex and the OCD against the family, but it doesn't have to be that way. Alex, you can think about whose side you want to be on. You don't have to be loyal to the OCD—you can switch sides, team up with your parents and sister, and then it will be your whole family against the OCD."

The narrative therapy literature does not focus on the issue of what to do if clients question the externalization metaphor, but this issue sometimes comes up. If it does, I would suggest borrowing a technique from psychodynamic therapy and talking about "parts" of the self, or you can talk in neurobiological terms. In this scaled-back version of the externalization narrative, the problem is presented as a peripheral and temporary part of the client, and core aspects of the self are described as opposed to the problem. This spatial metaphor for the relationship between (peripheral) problems and (core) strengths is more plausible to some clients than the idea that their problems originate outside them. Therapist statements like the following can be useful when clients say something like, "But Irresponsibility *isn't* some outside thing that attacks me; it's what *I* want to do."

> "That's true, but Irresponsibility isn't all of you, it's just one part. There are other parts of you that want to take care of business and succeed, so you can get your driver's license, graduate from high school, get a good job, and be something in life. The Irresponsibility part has been in control of you a lot lately, but there's more to you than that."

Finding Sparkling Outcomes

Narrative therapy generally includes solution-focused work (Guterman & Rudes, 2005; Payne, 2005; Selekman, 2010). The therapist's ear is tuned to elements in the client's account that are inconsistent with the dominant, negative theme of his narrative (Carey et al., 2009; Denborough, 2014). Positive elements in the client's initial self-story, even if few and small, undercut the theme of failure. Narrative therapists ask questions that help clients become more aware of their successful efforts to oppose the problem— for example:

- "Have there been times when the Arguing could have ruined hanging out with a friend, but you prevented that from happening?"
- "Tell me about a time when you refused to let Pessimism stop you from trying your best."

Clients typically include these little bits of data in their descriptions but glide right by them, recognizing no significance to these positive counterexamples because they are not part of the dominant theme. Therapists can induce change in such stories by slowing the client down, redirecting his attention to the neglected territory, and asking for elaboration of the element he had been ignoring:

> CLIENT: I get too nervous when I do my homework—I keep thinking about how we're going to have a test, I'll forget everything, I'll flunk, and I just hate the whole thing. All I want is to run down to the playground to see if there's a basketball game. But that's no good because the next thing you know, two hours have gone by, I'm all sweaty, my mom is mad because I said I'd be back in an hour, I haven't gotten any homework done, and I'm even more worried than before. I can't concentrate because I'm too worried about screwing up.
>
> THERAPIST: Tell me more about playing basketball.

Narrative therapists combine work with sparkling outcomes and externalization in single questions—for example:

- "How did you overcome Depression enough to earn all these merit badges?"
- "Tell me about a time you stopped Rage from making you explode, so you could keep your cool even though people said things you didn't like?"

Sparkling outcomes are reauthored from stray bits of behavior to important elements of identity.
One technique for moving positive exceptions from the periphery to the core of the client's self-story is to ask what these sparkling outcomes mean about the type of person she is. In this way, sparkling outcomes are reauthored from stray bits of behavior to important elements of identity—for instance:

- "What does this discovery say about what you really want for your life?"
- "What does it mean about you as a person that you are sometimes able to face down the Anxiety and talk to a boy?"

Therapists can ask family members the same type of question in regard to the client:

"What personal qualities must Felicia have to be able to fight back against the Jealousy and get along with Tanisha?"

Narrative therapists are more willing than solution-focused therapists to focus on the past. Reworking historical narratives is considered important because of the potential effects on the client's feelings about the life she has lived.

Narrative therapists help clients construct self-stories that integrate setbacks and frustrations with efforts to overcome obstacles and achieve success. It is important to highlight the client's efforts to succeed even when those efforts have failed, because such attempts demonstrate the courageous aspects of the person that strive for a better life. The externalization metaphor makes it possible to change stories of shameful or pitiful defeat into narratives of struggle against powerful, harmful forces. Pitiful inadequacy and courageous efforts to overcome difficulties are not the same story, even if these efforts have not yet produced success:

"There have been a number of times when you struggled against the dark cloud of Depression even though it had crushed most of the energy out of you. Depression can be miserable. You must be a strong, determined person, or you wouldn't have been able to fight back like that despite the pain."

Narrative therapists do not try to convince the client that his original story was "wrong." The assumption is that the initial story expresses some elements of the client's experience and, in that sense, has validity. The objective is to fill gaps in the client's understanding of his life by recruiting ignored elements into prominent themes. The emphasis is not on replacing story elements but on adding new ones to fill out the narrative. For example, a narrative like, "I am an anxious person who is scared of almost everything," could become a story like, "Anxiety attacks me in many situations, but I fight back as hard as I can and, sometimes, I overcome the anxiety." Successful therapy results in narratives that are more complex, multifaceted, nuanced, and balanced than the pretherapy stories.

In the process called **reauthoring**, the client tells and retells important sections of her self-story, perhaps in writing and perhaps to an audience of other people (Denborough, 2014; Epston et al., 1997; White, 2007). These retellings build successive layers of narrative about courageous efforts and partial successes. Facts whose significance had gone unrecognized are reorganized into new themes. Even if the new stories do not depict more success than the old ones, they depict more struggle, courage, and strength. Narratives that are touching or moving, even if they are not happy, increase the client's appreciation and respect for herself and her life.

Resisting Harmful Cultural Narratives

With relatively mature clients, it is sometimes useful to include attention to harmful cultural narratives in the general effort to locate problem sources outside the client (Madigan, 2010; White, 1995, 2011). This political aspect of therapy seems particularly relevant to eating disorders and maladaptive aspects of sex-roles. Here are some examples of questions designed to externalize harmful cultural narratives:

- "Who persuaded you that asking for help is a weak, pathetic thing for a guy to do?"
- "Where did you get the idea that only thin girls are pretty?"
- "Who says you have to be pretty to have a boyfriend?"
- "Who says you must have a boyfriend to be happy?"

To be more polemical about issues related to eating, weight, and looks, counselors could say something like:

"Where do kids get their ideas about how girls have to look to be pretty? Mostly from the media. But fashion websites and magazines with skinny women on the cover aren't showing regular people; they're showing models who usually starve themselves to look that way.

What are the websites up to, what's their agenda? They want to make girls and women feel insecure about their bodies, like there's something wrong with them, so they'll buy the stuff the websites advertise. First they convince everybody there's a problem, and then they offer to sell you the solution. They're just trying to make money, but you don't have to buy into it."

Interactive Storytelling

Narrative therapists use storytelling as a counseling activity (Denborough, 2014; Epston et al., 1997; White, 2006; White & Morgan, 2006). These stories are not fictional—they are autobiographical. The client is the main character in the story. Sometimes children are comfortable giving the central character their own name, and sometimes they prefer to give the main figure a different name. Young children sometimes intermingle fantasy elements with their stories (e.g., animals whose characteristics correspond to the child's issues).

Berg and Steiner (2003) present detailed recommendations for a complex story structure, with a solution-focused emphasis, that can be used with older children and adolescents. To simplify, the basic structure of these stories consists of a beginning, middle, and end. In the beginning, the client is oppressed by the problem. In the middle, which is usually the longest part of the story, the child engages in problem-solving efforts and/or exerts her will in attempts to resist and defeat the problem, often with help from other people. In the end, the child either overcomes his difficulties or, at least, succeeds in building a more satisfying life around a reduced version of the problem.

Stories provide a format in which clients can plan new strategies, depict new behaviors, and experiment with possible solutions in fantasy form, without the risks present in real life. Envisioning a successful behavior can be a form of practicing the new skill. Constructing alternative endings allows clients to explore possible contingencies between actions and outcomes.

Symbolic solutions sometimes lead to practical problem solving. For example, a story about a frightened rabbit who learns to jump over a pursuing wolf might empower a child to face and overcome a fear. To translate this fantasy image into a practical strategy, the therapist could ask, "What could you do, when Fear is coming after you, that would be like the rabbit jumping over the wolf?"

Collaboration between therapist and client usually produces the most helpful stories, with the amount of therapist input varying in accordance with the client's needs. If the client is intimidated or stymied by the problem, so she has trouble moving the story forward, the therapist can come to her assistance with suggestions. The client's response to the suggestions should determine which ones are incorporated into the developing story. Suggestions are most likely to feel right to the client if they are plausible within the story's reality and they lead toward resolution of the problem.

Because of their capacity for magical thinking, children sometimes relate to physical symbols of emotional phenomena as if they were the phenomena themselves (see Chapter 5, Psychodynamic Therapy). In a technique that makes use of magical thinking, the therapist encourages the child to attack and destroy a picture of the problem. Thus, clients might tear up pictures of the Anger Monster, the Math Fear, and so forth; paper shredders work very well for this purpose. The accompanying emotion is usually delighted and triumphant.

In the later stages of narrative therapy, the counselor asks questions about how the new story elements will change the child's and family's relationship with the problem in the future—for example:

- "How will this new understanding influence your relationship with Anger in the future?"
- "How will these discoveries change the way you deal with Jealousy if it tries to attack you again?"

Narrative therapists often suggest that clients tell their new stories to **outsider witnesses** (Payne, 2005; White, 1995; Winslade & Monk, 2006). The purpose of this technique is to solidify and strengthen the new narrative by making it public. These retellings can take place either during or outside the sessions, and can occur with family members, friends, teachers, and so forth. The audience can add their own input to the narratives by providing observations and memories that corroborate the new story.

Narrative work often involves written records that track the client's evolving self-story over the course of therapy (Denborough, 2014; Epston & White, 1992; White & Morgan, 2006). When significant new versions of the evolving story are produced, they should be written down. The final version of the client's self-story is an important document that the child should keep to help her maintain therapeutic gains.

Therapeutic documents can take the form of letters, lists, and essays as well as stories. The use of therapy diplomas as a technique to facilitate termination fits well with the narrative approach. The externalization metaphor can be incorporated into the certificate.

Summary

Constructivist therapy is based on the idea that people create meanings through their talk about events and experiences. A given narrative is only one of many possible ways to organize a sequence of events, but these constructions of meaning have important effects on the quality of people's lives. When people are demoralized by self-stories emphasizing disappointment and failure, therapists can help them develop more self-enhancing, empowering narratives.

Constructivists view talk as the root cause of the problems for which people seek therapy, and they view language use as the essence of counseling. These therapists have devoted careful attention to inconspicuous features of language that shape attention, experience, and meaning, and they make use of these aspects of language to create therapeutic effects on clients' talk. Their linguistic strategies are subtle and unobtrusive, with reliance on questions containing implicit assumptions rather than statements containing explicit assertions.

Solution-focused therapy differs from other therapeutic approaches in its conversational focus. While there may be acknowledgment of the client's distress, the counselor avoids dwelling on the nature and causes of the client's problems and, instead, focuses attention on possible solutions. Analysis of etiological processes is considered counterproductive because change can be achieved through the type of choices, planning, and action that are familiar to people from their everyday lives, without addressing esoteric, hidden mechanisms.

There has been less outcome research on constructivist therapy, and most of the studies have been methodologically weaker, compared to the other theoretical orientations covered in this book. There has been some investigation of solution-focused therapy, mostly but not only with adults, and the results have been encouraging. Narrative therapy deemphasizes research, and few outcome studies have examined this type of counseling.

Solution-talk includes conversation about past successes the client has achieved, even if those successes were partial, as well as discussion about what he wants in the future and what he could do to create the desired changes. The miracle question stimulates clients to envision, in a concrete way, the state of affairs they want to bring about. Solution-focused therapists help youth and parents identify the exceptions to the problem that generally exist at the time counseling begins. Then, by moving back and forth between abstract conceptualization and situation-specific application of the client's strengths, therapists help children expand their instances of success and transport their strengths to new areas of functioning. Miracle days are used to show families that they can achieve solutions simply by enacting the new behaviors and interactions they want to enjoy. When problems are severe, solution-focused counselors draw attention to the coping demonstrated by the client as she continues with her life despite the emotional pain caused by the problems. Even the client's distress can be portrayed as evidence of striving for positive change.

The main technique of narrative therapy is externalizing the problem. This strategy involves talking about the problem as if it were a malevolent entity or force that exists outside the client and seeks to impair his life. Externalizing the problem in this way often reduces parental blame of the client and strengthens the youth's appreciation of the many aspects of his life and self that are distinct from his difficulties. The externalization metaphor often galvanizes the client's and family's motivation to resist and overcome the problem.

Narrative therapists help clients construct new self-stories that integrate the events and situations of their lives into more complete, balanced, and empowering structures of meaning. As in solution-focused therapy, elements of success are highlighted. Self-stories of failure and defeat are reconstructed as narratives of courageous struggle against powerful, harmful forces. The new narratives may be preserved in written documents, and these stories may be presented to witnesses.

Figures 6.2 and 6.3 present the story with which Felicia's therapy concluded and the graduation diploma she received at termination.

Friends and Enemies

Once upon a time there was a girl named Felicia who wanted to make friends. Felicia should have been able to make friends because she was just as good as the other girls, with more of some things and less of others. But Felicia couldn't make friends, because a Jealousy Monster put himself right in between her and the other girls her age.

The Jealousy Monster was very slick. He didn't say he was a Jealousy Monster. He said he was Felicia's friend, and he wanted to help her make other friends. He was wearing a *disguise* that made him seem like a nice person. But it was a trick.

The Jealousy Monster told Felicia it wasn't okay to be as good as the other girls. He said she had to be *better*, or she wouldn't make friends. So Felicia tried very hard, for a long time, to be better than the other girls. When she did something well, she wanted everyone to look. If they didn't, she got mad.

When another girl did something well or had something pretty, Jealousy put an evil magic glass in front of Felicia's face. The glass made the other girl look like Felicia's enemy, because if everyone looked up to her they wouldn't look up to Felicia. So she tried to tear the other girl down. Then there were fights and misery.

One day a therapist came, and she didn't like what the Jealousy Monster was doing. She yanked the monster's disguise off, and Felicia saw how mean and ugly he was. Felicia got mad at the monster and broke his evil magic glass. She saw that girls who did things well weren't her enemies; the *monster* was her enemy.

Then Felicia started refusing to listen to Jealousy. The more Felicia ignored him, the smaller he got. His voice sounded like a little pip-squeek. Now Felicia doesn't even care if he tries to trick her because she's onto his tricks and she knows she doesn't have to listen to him.

The less Jealousy there is, the more friends there are. Felicia doesn't need to be better than people anymore. She likes being one of the girls. Everybody is better at some things and not better at other things, and friends are fine with that.

Figure 6.2   Example of a story written at the conclusion of therapy.

Figure 6.3   Example of a graduation diploma.

7

Family Systems Therapy

OBJECTIVES

This chapter explains:

- *Systems theory's focus on interactions in families, not characteristics of individuals.*
- *Nonlinear, reciprocal causality.*
- *The differences between functional and dysfunctional families.*
- *Positive feedback loops, in which people unintentionally elicit behaviors they do not want from each other.*
- *How to translate a family member's statements into words the others can hear, understand, and accept.*
- *How to reframe aversive client behaviors so the family responds with understanding, not anger.*
- *How to arrange deals in which family members solve each other's problems.*
- *Therapeutic strategies for repairing disrupted attachment relationships between parents and adolescents.*

Case Study
Good Intentions

Nicolle, a 14-year-old girl, was the older of two daughters of a Korean American father and a European American mother. The parents described her as an unhappy, discontented child who complained constantly, had angry outbursts about seemingly trivial matters, resisted directives, performed much below her potential in school, and frustrated their efforts to figure out what was wrong by being closed and secretive. The therapist's diagnosis was disruptive mood dysregulation disorder.

The client's mother expressed sadness bordering on grief about Nicolle pushing her away. She felt she hardly knew her older daughter, although she was close with her younger one. Nicolle got along better with her father, although she did not disclose much about her feelings to him, either.

There was a mental health history in the family. Nicolle's mother suffered from postpartum depression after she was born, and her depression recurred intermittently, sometimes with high severity, for about 8 years after her daughter's birth. During the next 6 or so years, the mother's depression was an occasional problem but was fairly well controlled with medicine and occasional psychotherapy. Nicolle's father and younger sister, 9 years old, exhibited no mental health problems.

Nicolle was adamantly opposed to therapy. Her opening statement to the clinician was, "I have nothing against you, but this is just one more way my mother is trying to pry into my life, and it isn't going to work."

Systems Theory

Sometimes the term **family therapy** is used simply to designate the family modality of treatment—that is, working with two or more family members, using any theoretical approach. The term **family systems therapy** has a more specific meaning that identifies a well-defined theoretical approach: The theory emphasizes *patterns of interaction* among family members, rather than their individual, internal characteristics. This chapter describes family systems therapy as a theoretical orientation, not simply a modality in which two or more family members participate in sessions.

The Core Idea: Problems Exist in Families, Not Individuals

Family systems therapy is based on a distinctive paradigm: While the other theories of psychotherapy focus on individuals, systems-oriented therapy focuses on interactions and relationships between individuals (Goldenberg & Goldenberg, 2012; Haley, 1963; Minuchin, 1974; Nichols, 2012). Systemic therapy views the family, not the individual, as the basic unit of analysis and treatment, and this paradigm views relationships and interactions as more important than the internal characteristics of persons (Bateson, 1972; Jackson, 1965). In order to do family therapy effectively, it is necessary to adopt the mental set of a systems thinker and to look at clinical issues through these eyes.

> *While the other theories of psychotherapy focus on individuals, systems-oriented therapy focuses on interactions and relationships between individuals.*

The core idea of the systems approach is that, while mental health problems may be manifested or expressed by individuals, the true *cause* of problems lies in patterns of family interaction, and family members other than the person exhibiting disturbance are involved in the maintenance of that disturbance (Becvar & Becvar, 2012; Minuchin et al., 2014; Satir, 1967). The systems-oriented understanding of etiology has obvious implications for treatment strategy: In order to help an individual with mental health problems, it is necessary to work with and help his immediate family members. If what looks like individual psychopathology is really a manifestation of disturbed family interaction patterns, therapy needs to change the set of relationships in which the individual's problems are embedded.

What Is a System?

The word *system* is commonly used in everyday language, but family therapists mean something special by it. Systems theory is used to describe information flow and control mechanisms in biological organisms, machines, and computers, as well as to describe interactions within human groups (Bertalanffy, 1968; Jackson, 1965). Because systems theory differs from our ordinary way of thinking about people, it takes a little pondering to understand the formulation, but once you get it you will really get it, and the world of human behavior will never look quite the same again.

The basic idea of the theory is that there is more to a system than the individual characteristics of its component parts; the components behave the way they do not just because of their own internal properties but also because of their interrelationships with other components. This idea is captured by the saying that "the whole is greater than the sum of its parts." The word *gestalt* involves the same idea.

Buckley (1967) defined a system as a set of parts with two essential features: (1) The components are interconnected and interdependent, with each influencing and being influenced by every other part, and (2) Over time, the parts evolve relatively consistent, recurring patterns of interaction. Systems theory states that it is impossible to predict the nature of interactions solely from knowledge about the component parts, because individual entities arrange themselves into gestalts or structures in complex and unpredictable ways (Bateson, 1972, 1979; Minuchin, 1974; Minuchin, Lee, & Simon, 1996).

The properties of systems that are not predictable from the characteristics of their components are called **emergent properties**, because they emerge from the arrangement or interaction of individual elements. For instance, a pile of automobile parts is not a car; only a precise arrangement of those parts will result in a working vehicle. Emergent properties are fundamental to the nature of biological and machine systems (Bateson, 1979; Bertalanffy, 1968). No biochemist could look at a collection of the elements of which living things are made (carbon, hydrogen, oxygen, etc.) and predict the resulting tree, rabbit, or family systems therapist. The concept of emergent properties applies to human beings because we have many more behavior potentials than we exhibit in any given situation, and a slight change in situation can cause a major change in behavior.

In a clinical context, the concept of a system means that we cannot understand the functioning of families as a straightforward combination of the individual, internal characteristics of the family members (Haley, 1963, 1996; Jackson, 1965; Minuchin & Fishman, 1981; Minuchin et al., 2014; Nichols, 1999). For instance, there are siblings who fight like cats and dogs with each other but have positive interactions with all their friends. These clinical data cannot be explained by saying that the siblings are angry, aggressive children, because they do not exhibit this behavior except with each other. Instead, the cause of the behavior must be located in the *relationship between* the two children, which exists, in turn, in the context of the full set of family relationships.

The simplest subsystem within a family is a **dyad**, which is a relationship between two people. At the next level of complexity, there is the **triangle**, which consists of the relationships among three people.

When relationships between two people become problematic, they sometimes (perhaps unconsciously) look to a third person to add an element to the relationship that will return the dyadic subsystem to a viable equilibrium. This third person is said to be **triangulated**, which means that the members of the dyad behave toward him in ways that are helpful to the dyadic relationship, even though possibly harmful to the third person (Bowen, 1978; Colapinto, 1991). For instance, when Nicolle and her father experienced tension in their usually amicable relationship, they found that if they joked about the mother's foibles, they regained their feeling of seeing things the same way and having a lot in common. When triangulation involves denigration or purposeful cruelty toward the third person, it is called **scapegoating** (Ackerman, 1966).

Triangulation is particularly serious when two parents triangulate a child. For example, two parents involved in a power struggle might bring their child into the conflict as a means of asserting their authority in the family. Such interactions might sound like this:

FATHER: It's warm in here. Kathy, please open that window.

MOTHER: It is not warm in here. Kathy, don't open the window.

FATHER: Young lady, I said open the window, and I mean now.

MOTHER: Sit back in your chair; you are *not* to open that window.

Interactions like these put the child in a no-win position. When parents triangulate a child, which frequently happens in situations involving marital conflict or divorce, they lose sight of her needs as a separate individual, and they use her as a tool in their efforts to accomplish some objective in their relationship with each other.

Reciprocal Influence: The Web of Causality

The concept of mutual, **reciprocal causality** is central to systems theory. Reciprocal or circular causality means that two or more individual entities influence each other in a back-and-forth fashion (Bednar, Burlingame, & Masters, 1988; Bertalanffy, 1968; Watzlawick, Weakland, & Fisch, 1974). The opposite of reciprocal causality is **linear causality**, in which one entity influences the other in a unidirectional sequence. Linear causality can be diagrammed as A → B, while reciprocal causality can be diagrammed as A ↔ B.

All schools of child and adolescent therapy recognize that parents exert powerful influences on their children. The family systems approach is unique in its emphasis on the influence that children exert on their parents (Goldenberg & Goldenberg, 2012; Kerr & Bowen, 1988; Minuchin & Fishman, 1981). Thus, the other approaches generally discuss parent-children interactions in terms of linear, unidirectional influence (parent → child), while systems-oriented counselors think about these relationships in terms of reciprocal influence (parent ↔ child). In regard to Nicolle, an individually oriented therapist might hypothesize that intrusive questioning by the parents has caused the daughter to become secretive, and a systems-oriented therapist might share this hypothesis, but he would also consider the possibility that Nicolle's secretiveness had caused her parents to become intrusive in their questioning.

The notion of reciprocal causality has implications for the way that clinicians conceptualize the development of problems in time. If causality is linear, it makes sense to think of well-defined causes, which occur first, and discrete effects, which occur second (cause → effect). However, when causality is reciprocal, the roles of cause and effect flip back and forth continuously, like this:

$$\to A \to B \to A \to B \to A \to$$

In such situations, it does not make sense to locate "the cause of the problem" in one person and to view the other person's behavior as the effect or result of that cause. Family systems theorists view causality as a chain, with links provided by both parents and children. The origins of such chains are buried in the mists of the past and, often, are undiscoverable (Bowen, 1978; Haley, 1963, 1996; Watzlawick et al., 1974). Fortunately, according to the theory, it is not necessary to discover the origin of problems in order to solve them. Instead, it is important to discover the interaction patterns that *maintain* the problems at the present time. If these patterns are changed in a positive way, the problems will get better regardless of what initially set the chain of events in motion. Systemic therapy is an ahistorical approach to treatment, focusing on the present, not the past.

For instance, one sometimes sees families in which the parents are overprotective and controlling, and the child is immature and helpless; the parents do all sorts of things for the child, and the child seems unable to do much for himself. Investigation of the experiences of the family members might suggest a pattern such as: (a) The parents wish the child were more self-sufficient, but they feel they must perform daily self-care tasks for him because he cannot do these tasks for himself, while (b) the child longs to be more independent but cannot develop skills because he has so few opportunities to practice. Does the cause of this interaction lie in the child or parents? The answer is neither and both, as diagrammed here:

Child immaturity ↔ Parental overcontrol

In reciprocal causality, the distinction between cause and effect breaks down. Each person's behavior simultaneously results from and causes the behavior of the other members of the system. Responsibility emerges as a complex, subtle issue (Gladding, 2014; Rigazio-DiGilio & McDowell, 2013).

As if things were not already complicated enough, systems theory views two-person relationships as just the simplest subsystems within families, and things get more complex when all the relationships are considered together. Influences flowing among the members of a four-person family are diagrammed in Figure 7.1.

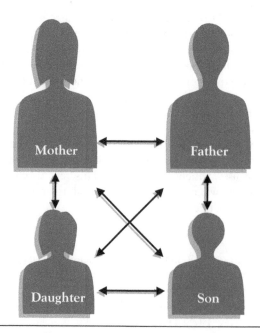

Figure 7.1   A four-person system.

In families, each person influences every other person, and each relationship influences every other relationship. As a result, a change in any part of a system will produce **ripple effects** that change every other part of the system (Buckley, 1967; Jackson, 1965; Smith-Acuna, 2010). For instance, a change in the mother/son relationship would cause change in the father/daughter relationship. According to systems theory, causality is not merely a chain; it is a web.

Functional and Dysfunctional Families

Systems theory states that families evolve their relationships to achieve and maintain an **equilibrium**, which means an arrangement of stable roles and interactions that enables the system to continue intact over time (Bateson, 1972, 1979; Bowen, 1978; Watzlawick et al., 1974). Family equilibria are not consciously planned but evolve naturally over time, as the members strive to meet their needs and find ways to fit together. Equilibria are disturbed both by external events that have an impact on the family and by developmental changes in any of the members. When something happens to disturb families' customary ways of interacting with each other, the system makes adjustments to restore the status quo (Hoffman, 1981; Lindblad-Goldberg & Northey, 2013; Minuchin, 1974).

A system equilibrium represents the best the family has been able to do at meeting the needs of its members while maintaining the stability of the system. Whether needs are mostly met or mostly unsatisfied varies widely. In **functional** families, individual needs are mostly satisfied in ways that do not threaten the stability of the system but, in **dysfunctional** families, the maintenance of equilibrium requires distortion of the healthy functioning of at least one of the members (Colapinto, 1991; Jackson, 1965; Minuchin et al., 1996). According to systems theory, this is an important cause of mental health symptoms.

The term **identified patient** is a hallmark of family therapy. The qualifier "identified" expresses skepticism because it is the family, not the therapist, who identifies one person as a "patient." According to the theory, it is arbitrary which member of a dysfunctional family happens to become the bearer of symptomatology. The person who expresses the system's pathology is not viewed as genuinely more disturbed than the other participants in the network of relationships that produced a mental health problem in one of the family members (Becvar & Becvar, 2012; Satir, 1967, 1972; Weakland & Fisch, 1992).

Often, the family's initial view of treatment is that there is one member who needs to be dropped off at the clinic to be "fixed." But part of the work of systemic therapy is to help the family recognize that change is needed not only by the identified patient but also by all other family members (Bowen, 1978; Goldenberg & Goldenberg, 2012). This therapy always has two goals: improvement in the overall functioning of the family and, as a consequence, resolution of the identified patient's presenting problems.

Feedback Loops

When something happens to disturb a family's equilibrium, the system may respond by developing patterns of reciprocal behavior called **feedback loops** (Bateson, 1972, 1979; Jackson, 1965; Nichols, 2012). Family therapists distinguish between two, opposite types of feedback loops: negative and positive. These terms, here, do not mean good and bad. Instead, the terms identify how the feedback loop responds to a disturbance of equilibrium, whether by moving the system *back toward* a stable state (negative feedback), or by accelerating change and moving the system *away from* equilibrium (positive feedback).

A negative feedback loop occurs when a system responds to a disturbance of equilibrium by undoing the change and returning to its previous state. Negative feedback loops keep things the way they are. In families, negative feedback loops occur when an individual's behavior acts to rein in escalating instability in the family's relationships (Colapinto, 1991; Minuchin, 1974; Minuchin et al., 1996). For instance, when parents and adolescents become distant from each other, the teen may break family rules, the parents' attention may come rushing back to its previous level, and the rule breaking may then cease, with the equilibrium of the system restored.

Positive feedback loops have the opposite effect: They do not reverse but accelerate change, and they move system functioning away from equilibrium (Haley, 1963, 1996; Madanes, 1991; Micucci, 2009; Watzlawick et al., 1974). One example of this process sometimes occurs in international relations: In an arms race, each country builds more weapons because the other country is building more weapons, resulting in a self-perpetuating cycle that both countries honestly believe is caused by the other nation. In positive feedback loops, each party's response to a disliked behavior of the other has the unintended effect of *increasing* that behavior. For example, the more Nicolle's mother questioned her about the reasons for her anger and depression, the more closed off the girl became, which left the mother feeling even more in the dark, so she intensified her inquiries, and the cycle continued and escalated.

Communication Patterns

Communication theory has a central role in systemic therapy (Haley, 1963, 1996; Jackson, 1965). The emphasis here is not only on the content of communication (what people say) but also on the *form* or pattern of communication. For instance, systems-oriented counselors are interested in which family members speak directly to which, whether there are frequent interruptions, who speaks first when a new topic is broached, and whether difficult issues are confronted or avoided.

Communication patterns are governed by **rules**, which are neither said out loud nor consciously planned but which, nonetheless, exert a pervasive influence on family life (Bateson, 1972, 1979; Satir, 1972). An example of a rule would be "Whenever we notice Father's alcohol addiction, we must make a joke about it so that it is viewed as a funny eccentricity, not a serious problem."

Communication theorists distinguish between *explicit* and *implicit* communication (Watzlawick, 1978; Weakland & Fisch, 1992). Explicit communication consists of the obvious content or meaning of the words the speaker says. Implicit communication is not contained in the overt message but, instead, comes through via small, interspersed bits of language and, especially, by nonverbal communication; listeners perceive implicit messages by "reading between the lines." Implicit meanings are communicated mostly by tone of voice, facial expression, and body language, in the context of the listener's preexisting knowledge about the speaker (Kerr & Bowen, 1988; Watzlawick et al., 1974).

In well-functioning communication systems, implicit messages may modify what is explicitly said, but implicit communication does not contradict the surface meaning of statements. In the dysfunctional communication pattern called the **double bind**, the implicit message is the opposite of the explicit one, and the two levels of communication contradict each other (Bateson, 1972, 1979). In addition, the speaker behaves as if there is no contradiction, and he implicitly forbids the listener to point out the inconsistency.

For example, a father who is jealous of a close relationship between his wife and daughter, but who believes it would be wrong to discourage this closeness, may explicitly support the relationship while subtly, implicitly discouraging it. When told the wife and daughter plan to spend a Sunday afternoon at an art museum (an activity he does not enjoy), he forces a smile and says, "Oh, great," but his jaw seems clenched even though he is smiling, and he is digging his thumbnail into his chair. The mother and daughter may not be able to say why, but a pall has been cast over their mood as they set off on their afternoon together.

Double binds are hurtful and damaging to people not because they are blatantly cruel but because they are insidious and unnerving. Double binds are invalidating; the speaker behaves as if the listener's gut feeling about the interaction has no basis in reality. The listener feels uncomfortable, but the speaker, if questioned, acts as if she does not know what the questioner is talking about. As a result, double binds feel "crazy-making." The people involved in these transactions have no opportunity to work on solutions to the underlying problems because the existence of the problems is denied.

What Causes Mental Health Problems?

Within the systems theory field, **structural** family therapists (Aponte & DiCesare, 2000; Colapinto, 1991; Lindblad-Goldberg & Northey, 2013; Minuchin, 1974) have contributed a great deal to our understanding of the differences between functional and dysfunctional families. The descriptions below are based largely on their work.

In functional families, the members find a comfortable balance between their needs for closeness and independence. Dysfunctional families can be found at both extremes of this spectrum. In **disengaged** families, the people are highly independent and distant from each other, with insufficient warmth and mutual support in the family. At home, they spend most of their time in different rooms, meals are microwaved one at a time, and they show little interest in what is going on in each other's lives. There are also problems at the other extreme of the spectrum. In **enmeshed** families, there is excessive, unhealthy closeness, with insufficient autonomy and separation. Family members spend most of their leisure time together, there is little concern about privacy, and people respond to each other's experiences almost as intensely as if these experiences were their own. Enmeshed families are smothering. Thus, a moderate, flexible balance between connection and autonomy is an important characteristic of positive family functioning. Aristotle was right about families, too.

Functional families communicate clearly. In dysfunctional families, communication is typically ambiguous, overly complex, or contradictory, so that it is difficult to infer what people mean from what they say. Sometimes there is a belief that explicit communication is unnecessary because people in close relationships should know how the other feels without being told, as if they can read minds. Maladaptive communication also involves a lack of attentive listening, sometimes because people are too focused on composing their next statement to listen carefully to what the other person is saying. As a result of these factors, members of dysfunctional families do not understand each other well, and their behavior is based more on assumptions and misconceptions than on accurate information about the other family members.

Dysfunctional families are often characterized by **subsystem alliances** or coalitions in which some people are extremely close and others are excluded. Alliances involve rigid boundaries between subsystems. Nicolle was closer with her father, and her sister was closer with the mother; when disputes arose, the family members usually divided into these sides. In more functional families, coalitions are not lined up against each other, there is a basic level of closeness involving everyone, and positive relationships in subsystems contribute to the health of the family as a whole.

Healthy families have a hierarchy of authority that reflects the different capabilities and needs of children and adults. In other words, the parents are in charge, and they give directives, establish rules, and enforce the rules with consequences (Alexander, Waldron, Robbins, & Neeb, 2013; Parsons & Alexander, 1973; Sexton, 2011; Szapocznik, Hervis, & Schwartz, 2003). Parent-child role reversals, in which children fulfill age-inappropriate functions for adults (e.g., advising the parent), disrupt the family structure that children need for healthy development. Minuchin found that this departure from an appropriate hierarchy of authority played a central role in many of the families he treated (Minuchin, 1974; Minuchin et al., 1996; Minuchin & Fishman, 1981). Accounts of the etiology of conduct disorder, described in Chapter 11, emphasize the role of impaired parental authority in families.

Positive feedback loops seem to play a role in many family disturbances (Haley, 1963, 1996; Micucci, 2009; Watzlawick et al., 1974). In this interaction pattern, two (or more) people behave in ways that the other person dislikes, and each tries to change the other's behavior, but these attempts not only fail but also backfire: Each person's attempt to reduce the other person's behavior has the unintended effect of increasing that behavior. When these cycles continue over time, they result in an escalating spiral of dysfunction, anger, and distress.

Clinically, it seems that the positive feedback mechanism sometimes interacts with the continua described in Chapter 3, Cognitive Therapy, to produce a reciprocally polarizing effect on the content of disagreements between family members. When two people hold positions at different locations on these spectra, and their disagreement leads to debate, several factors seem to drive them further and further apart. When people in an argument become emotionally aroused, their perceptions of the other side's position seem to become simpler and more extreme, as if the other opinion moves away from theirs toward the opposite extreme of the spectrum. As the arguers become more and more struck by how wrong the other person is, they selectively focus on the points supporting their own view while discounting the opposing points. If a similar process occurs in the other person, the result is increasing polarization. (This pattern is frequently apparent in political arguments.) The two parties might not start out all that far apart, but as the argument intensifies, their positions become more and more distant from each other. Diagrammatically, the progression looks like this:

|....| → |.........| → |................| → |.........................|

Clinicians can convey this idea of escalating polarization to clients by using another visual tool: their hands. To symbolize two opinions that, initially, are only somewhat different, hold your hands up and a little bit apart. Then, as you describe the reciprocal effects of conflict and argument, move your hands further and further away from each other.

For Nicolle and her mother, the relevant spectrum was this one:

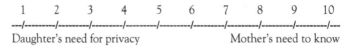

Daughter's need for privacy   Mother's need to know

The reciprocal escalation of their positive feedback loop had reached the point that, when the mother responded to a visibly bad mood in her daughter by asking what was wrong, Nicolle's typical response was, "What's wrong with you?" Desperate for some idea of what was going on in her daughter's mind, the mother searched her room for drugs or a diary, found neither, and figured out how to monitor her phone and social media pages. Nicolle found out, was enraged, changed her user names and passwords … and so forth.

Assessment and Case Formulation

In its theoretically pure form, systems-oriented therapy does not value diagnosis, because diagnosis locates problems in individuals, not systems (Kerr & Bowen, 1988; Nichols, 2012; Satir, 1972). Systems theory posits a number of mechanisms by which family dysfunction results in individual symptomatology, but there is no specific correspondence between mechanisms and disorders. (There are no rules of thumb stating, for instance, that positive feedback loops result in depression, while triangulation causes oppositional child behavior.) Diagnosing the identified patient, while possibly important for other reasons, is not a focus of family assessment. Instead, family evaluation attempts to identify the interaction patterns that are central to the family's dysfunction.

Systems-oriented assessment begins when the family enters the room. Seating arrangements and physical proximity provide clues to family structure (Aponte & DiCesare, 2000; Colapinto, 1991; Patterson, Williams, Edwards, Chamow, & Grauf-Grounds, 2009). Who sits next to whom? Who makes eye contact with whom? Such information provides a quick sense of coalitions within the family. Observing clients' use of physical space helps to assess boundaries, disengagement, and enmeshment. It is useful to note people's reactions to changes in physical proximity. If the mother reaches over to take the son's hand, how does he react? How does the father react?

Family members sometimes give radically different descriptions of their interactions, with each person completely sure of the validity of his perceptions. Typically, the crux of the difference is that each person thinks his behavior was appropriate and the other person's unreasonable behavior was the cause of the problem. In such situations, one useful rule of thumb for counselors is that, no matter how glaring these discrepancies might be, there is almost always some truth to each individual's view, and each person's perception captures an aspect of what occurs in the family. The task of assessment is to figure out how the viewpoints of different family members fit together, like the pieces of a puzzle, and to formulate a synthesis that integrates the different perceptions into one complex whole. Treatment will then involve helping family members move toward a shared understanding that includes elements of each individual's viewpoint.

The task of assessment is to figure out how the viewpoints of different family members fit together, like the pieces of a puzzle, and to formulate a synthesis that integrates the different perceptions into one complex whole.

At first, it might appear that the family is divided into healthier and more disturbed individuals, or even good guys and bad guys, but this initial impression usually gives way to a more balanced conceptualization as assessment and therapy proceed. Generally, the more we understand a family's dynamics, the more we appreciate the reciprocal effects of individual behaviors. Behaviors that had seemed reprehensible are often revealed to be understandable responses to difficult family situations, and individuals who had looked like innocent victims may in time come to be seen as engaging in subtly selfish or harmful behaviors. Usually, the basic reality is that everyone is doing the best they can under confusing and difficult circumstances.

Questions to Ask

As in individual work, the first question to ask clients is something like "What brings you here?" It is vital to ask for each person's view of the problems. Sometimes families have a quasi-official spokesperson who will respond first, consider the question answered, and be prepared to move on. Nonetheless, it is useful to move around the room ascertaining whether the other views are similar or different, and assessing whether family members feel free to disagree with each other (Lindblad-Goldberg & Northey, 2013; Micucci, 2009; Smith-Acuna, 2010).

At some point in the assessment, it is useful to broaden the focus by moving the discussion away from symptomatology. Questions about everyday life help paint a picture of the family's functioning at home. Therapists can say, "Tell me about life in your family." It is useful to inquire about routines, mealtimes, and use of leisure time (Gladding, 2014; Goldenberg & Goldenberg, 2012).

Some clinical situations call for therapeutic attention to persons outside the client's immediate or nuclear family. One example would be when a relative provides a significant amount of childcare for the identified patient. Another occurs when a father-in-law's or mother-in-law's negative feelings about their adult child's spouse cause conflict in the marriage or undermine that spouse as an authority figure for the child. A third example occurs when distinctive types of marital or parent-child conflict seem to occur repeatedly across generations.

The **genogram** is a visual method of diagramming webs of nuclear, extended, and multigenerational family relationships. Genograms are like family trees. Large amounts of information are captured in a simple format by means of a conventional set of geometric symbols, including squares for males, circles for females, Xs indicating death, solid lines for marital and parent-child relationships, broken lines for divorces, straight lines for positive relationships, and jagged lines for conflictual ones. McGoldrick, Gerson, and Petry (2008) provide instruction in this symbol system. Nicolle's genogram is presented in Figure 7.2.

Patterns to Look For

Systems theory offers valuable guidance about what to look for in exploring family interaction patterns. Effective assessment requires the ability to translate theoretical concepts into observations of behavior and so to recognize triangles, double binds, positive feedback loops, and so forth, when we see them (Becvar & Becvar, 2012; Kerr & Bowen, 1988; Minuchin et al., 2014; Patterson et al., 2009).

The nature of family communication is of central importance to systems-oriented assessment. Do family members listen to each other or look out the window while others are speaking? Do they talk in order to share thoughts and emotions or in order to dominate, derogate, or manipulate each other? Does conversation focus on the topic at hand, or are frequent tangents used to avoid difficult issues? Patterns of agreement and disagreement provide information about coalitions. Does the daughter nod while her mother talks but roll her eyes when the father speaks?

Because double binds generally occur on an unconscious level, they cannot be ascertained by direct questions and answers (Bateson, 1972, 1979). Sometimes, the implicit

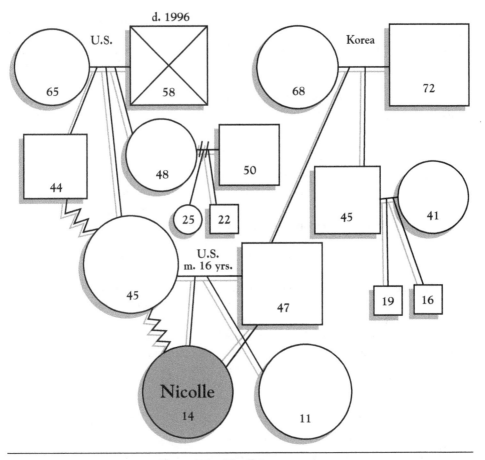

Figure 7.2   Nicolle's genogram.

messages consist of subtle parental encouragement and reinforcement for the very child behaviors that make up the presenting problems. For instance, parents who were disinterested and rebellious in school often feel it is their job to push their child to be a better student than they were, but their heart might not be in this job, and they might get a secret kick out of the child's rambunctious behavior. The result is an explicit message that they want the child to be a good student but an implicit message that they like his spunk when he mouths off to his teachers. The child is left in a no-win situation, and he cannot ask for guidance, because the existence of the conflict is denied. Sometimes children pick up on their parents' inner hopes for them even when these hopes are explicitly denied.

At times, the contradiction in messages occurs not between two levels of communication from the same person but between the explicit statements of two parents who have conflicting desires for their child. While not constituting a true double bind, such situations subject children to disturbing quandaries in which they can please one parent or the other but not both. Clinicians should assess the degree of consistency between the two parents' expectations for their child (Gladding, 2014; Minuchin et al., 1996; Rigazio-DiGilio & McDowell, 2013).

The paradoxical feature of positive feedback loops is that, although they do not realize it, the people are causing precisely the behavior they dislike in each other.

The paradoxical feature of positive feedback loops is that, although they do not realize it, the people are causing precisely the behaviors they dislike in each other (Haley, 1963, 1996; Madanes, 1991; Micucci, 2009). Each person believes the cycle was started by the other and she herself is only reacting; each believes the other person's behavior is the cause, and her behavior is only an effect. It might seem to the clinician that someone must be wrong in the way she portrays the interactions. However, the paradox can be resolved by systems theory, which transcends simplistic notions of linear cause and effect with the idea of reciprocal causality.

Whether a behavior is the problem or an attempted solution looks different from the two perspectives: In fact, each individual's attempted solution is viewed *as* the problem by the other person. The coping response of Person A is the stressor experienced by Person B, and vice versa. People respond to the failure of their efforts not by rethinking their approach but by intensifying the same type of attempts they have been making—which causes the other person to reciprocate with her own "more-of-the-same" attempted solutions.

Positive feedback loops seem to drive many problems between parents and adolescents. In one example, the teen rebels against restrictive rules; the parents respond by becoming stricter and allowing less freedom; the teen escalates her defiant and/or sneaky breaking of rules, and so on. In situations like Nicolle's, adolescents' efforts to achieve separation and parents' efforts to learn about their teen become more and more intense as they become less and less successful. Both parties' behavior is perfectly logical and counterproductive at the same time. Their argument boils down to the following:

MOTHER: If you told me how you are doing and what is going on, I wouldn't ask so many questions and snoop around your room.

NICOLLE: If you left me alone and didn't treat me like I was up to no good, I might feel like talking to you.

Change Processes

The mechanisms of change postulated by systems theory follow logically from the understanding of etiology held by this theoretical orientation. Since behavioral and emotional problems are considered to be the result of disturbed family interaction patterns, the way to resolve these problems is to achieve positive change in the family system. The question becomes, what kinds of experiences in therapy could change the way that family members relate to each other in everyday life?

Facilitation of communication among family members is usually the first change process that therapists set in motion when families begin counseling. Effective communication increases mutual understanding, so family members become more aware of each other's feelings, needs, and views. When families experience lots of anger and conflict, their perceptions of each other often become simplistic, with a focus on behaviors they dislike and little understanding of the thoughts and feelings behind those behaviors. When emotionally important information is communicated, family members' views of each other become more complex, nuanced, and three-dimensional. This may result in the replacement of anger by empathy.

The change process of insight sometimes plays a role in family therapy, but not in the same way as in dynamic therapy. Systems-oriented counselors might help family members develop insight into themselves, but they place more emphasis on helping the family better understand each other and the way their system operates (Hoffman, 1981; Nichols, 2012). This systemic form of insight might lead to the development of more adaptive patterns of interaction in the family. Also, systems-oriented therapists believe that behavior change can lead to insight, as well as the other way around (Gladding, 2014; Satir, 1972).

Family therapists use the technique of **reframing** to change the way that family members interpret each other's behavior. To reframe a behavior or event is to change its perceived meaning, generally by providing a new explanation for the behavior or event (Alexander & Parsons, 1982; Minuchin et al., 2014; Sexton, 2011; Weakland & Fisch, 1992). It is especially important to reframe behaviors that are viewed as negative or reprehensible. Reframes do not dispute the facts of a situation, but they reinterpret them by offering an understanding that preserves a positive, or at least a neutral, evaluation of the person behind the behavior. In particular, reframes usually posit benign or even positive motives behind troublesome behaviors. For example, a therapist might acknowledge that a son becomes flippant and sarcastic when his parents try to discuss his problems, but, instead of joining the parents in attributing this to obnoxiousness, the therapist might wonder whether the boy is so embarrassed by his symptoms that he needs to disrupt discussion of them in order to protect his pride. A reframe is like a new theory for old data.

Reframes usually posit benign or even positive motives behind negative or upsetting behaviors.

One fundamental type of reframe is based on the distinction between *motivation* and *capability* as factors in hurtful or undesirable behavior. When family members attribute a person's negative behavior to malevolent motivations, such as cruelty, disrespect, or selfishness, they typically become angry and respond in a punitive or aggressive manner. When they attribute the same behavior to inadequate capabilities, such as weak psychosocial skills or disruption by emotional distress, family members usually respond to the same behavior with sympathy and concern. An attribution to inadequate capabilities implies that the person cannot help engaging in the undesirable behavior and might be suffering as much as the people on the receiving end. Attributions to inadequate capabilities explain why good people sometimes engage in hurtful behaviors.

Emotions affect capabilities. Emotional distress can disrupt the effectiveness of behavior so that even well-intentioned people sometimes become harsh, caustic, and even mean. This phenomenon occurs verbally and also on a nonverbal level: Distress often produces facial expressions, body language, and tones of voice that look and sound like withdrawal, irritability, and/or hostility. As additional examples, when youth are upset, they may refuse to speak, pull away when touched, defy directives, shout insults, and even engage in seriously dysfunctional behaviors, such as drug use and violence. In such cases, the person does not *want* to be hurtful to others, even though his behavior has those effects. Family members understand this intuitively, so they do not become angry in response to this type of behavior *if* they believe it is caused by emotions too strong to control.

This effect is so reliable it can be produced in the laboratory. In a social psychology experiment by Zillmann (1993), participants were subjected to an irritable research assistant who gave them instructions and supervised their work in an impatient, rude manner. The independent variable was this: For half the participants, a second research assistant came by when the first was out of the room and, in an offhand way, said something like,

"I sure hope Bob is okay—he just found out his father has terminal cancer." When the procedure was over, participants had an opportunity to retaliate against the research assistant by giving him negative ratings on an evaluation form. Most of those who did not receive the foregoing information did so. Most of the participants who believed the assistant was understandably upset give him neutral or positive ratings. This experiment illuminates the change process of reframing in family therapy: The identified patient is like the distressed research assistant; the therapist is like the second assistant who came by with transformative information; and the family is like the experimental participant who judged the first assistant.

Of course, hurtful behavior *is* sometimes the result of selfish or cruel motivations. If this is the case, reframing will not be an effective therapeutic technique. But it seems much more frequently the case that, when family members hurt each other, they do so because they are caught in a web of interpersonal and emotional pressures they do not understand and cannot manage effectively. (We return to this distinction between motivation and capability as factors in dysfunction at a number of points in this book, especially in Chapters 10, 11, and 12 on externalizing disorders.)

Systems-oriented clinicians often direct families to try new ways of interacting, sometimes without first figuring out the reasons for the old, maladaptive patterns, and sometimes without even explaining why the behavioral experiment might be helpful (Haley, 1963, 1996; Madanes, 1991). The rationale for such therapist directives is that new *experiences*, even if unaccompanied by analysis, can produce positive change. Therapist directives are a quick, efficient way to get new types of interaction to happen, and once they do, these experiences may disrupt old habits, prove to be self-reinforcing, and take on a life of their own.

Systems-oriented therapists try to disrupt positive feedback loops that drive painful, dysfunctional interactions between family members (Patterson et al., 2009; Santisteban, Mena, & Abalo, 2013; Szapocznik & Kurtines, 1989). One way to do this is by giving directives that short-circuit the loop's operation without explaining the rationale to the family (Haley, 1963, 1996). Another strategy is to reveal the feedback mechanism. Family members are often struck by the logical yet counterproductive nature of these cycles in which they elicit exactly the behaviors they dislike from each other. Once this systemic insight is achieved, the way out is usually clear: Each person needs to stop reacting to the other's unwanted behavior in ways that perpetuate this behavior and, instead, initiate new actions that give the other person what she needs to behave in the desired fashion. Positive feedback loops are just as capable of driving desirable as undesirable interaction patterns, because the more Person A does what Person B wants, the more Person B will do what Person A wants, and so on, back and forth.

Attachment-based family therapy (ABFT; Diamond, 2014; Diamond, Diamond, & Levy, 2014; Diamond, Siqueland, & Diamond, 2003) is designed to repair disrupted attachment relationships between parents and adolescents. ABFT has been used primarily to treat depression and suicidal ideation in adolescents, but its understanding of etiology and its therapeutic techniques may also apply to a wider range of ages and presenting problems. ABFT uses three core therapeutic strategies: relational reframing, eliciting expression of primary emotions and unmet attachment needs, and facilitation of corrective attachment experiences. In relational reframing, the therapist redefines the main purpose of therapy from treating the adolescent's symptoms to repairing his attachment relationships with his parents (Diamond & Siqueland, 1998). Then, there is work on "primary" emotions, based on L. S. Greenberg's (2002; Greenberg & Pascual-Leone, 2006) distinction between surface feelings (e.g., anger about a particular action) and the underlying or primary emotions that are the basis of immediate reactions (e.g., feeling unloved). When deep-level emotions are expressed openly, although there might be pain, positive change in both internal difficulties and relationship problems is often initiated (Ablon, Levy, & Katzenstein, 2006; Greenberg & Malcolm, 2002). Following the expression of primary emotions by parents and children, ABFT counselors try to elicit interactions that repair past damage to their attachment relationships.

Outcome Research

Shadish and Baldwin (2003) summarized the results of 20 meta-analytic reviews of marital and family interventions. Their review did not focus on child treatment, but it included numerous studies of family therapy that measured outcomes in child clients. Averaging across the meta-analyses, they obtained an effect size .65 for assessments conducted immediately post-treatment and an effect size of .52 for follow-up assessments conducted 6–12 months later; these effect sizes are in the medium range. Shadish and Baldwin concluded that there is abundant evidence for the effectiveness of systems-oriented therapy.

In general, while older research examined family systems therapy as a broad category of treatment, recent studies have examined more specific interventions, which are generally defined by treatment manuals. Because family therapy has received more empirical support as a treatment for externalizing than internalizing problems (Nichols, 2012), most of these manualized interventions are for youth with conduct disturbances and histories of delinquency. Chapter 11, Disruptive Behavior in Adolescents, summarizes the outcome research on functional family therapy, multisystemic therapy, and parenting with love and limits. Overall, outcome studies have provided extensive support for these three interventions for youth with conduct disturbances.

Baldwin, Christian, Berkeljon, Shadish, and Bean (2012) performed a meta-analysis of 24 studies examining brief strategic family therapy, functional family therapy, multidimensional family therapy, or multisystemic therapy as treatments for adolescent substance abuse and delinquency. When results for the four therapies were combined, there was a small but significant effect size of .21 for comparisons with TAU, a similar effect size of .26 for comparisons with active, alternative therapies, and a medium/large effect size of .70 for comparisons with no-treatment control groups. The analysis did not produce evidence that the four therapies differed from each other in effectiveness.

Brief strategic family therapy (BSFT; Santisteban et al., 2013; Szapocznik et al., 2003; Szapocznik & Kurtines, 1989) is an intervention for behavior problems and drug abuse in adolescents. BSFT was designed to be culturally specific for Latino/a youth, but it has also been used with other groups. Szapocznik et al. (1989) found that BSFT and psychodynamic therapy were similarly effective at reducing child emotional and behavioral problems, and both were superior to a recreational activity control. Santisteban et al. (2003) compared the effects of BSFT and a placebo-type group therapy for Latino/a adolescents with conduct disturbances. BSFT produced more improvement in parent reports of adolescent conduct problems, adolescent reports of marijuana use, observer ratings, and self-reports of family functioning. In an effectiveness study performed in a community setting by Coatsworth, Santisteban, McBride, and Szapocznik (2001), Hispanic and African American adolescents with conduct problems and their families were randomly assigned to BSFT or TAU. BSFT achieved higher rates of engagement (81% vs. 61%), and retention (71% vs. 42%), and BSFT was especially effective at retaining teens with severe behavior problems. However, there were no differences between the two types of intervention in their effects on behavior problems. Nickel et al. (2006) recruited a sample of female bullies from the general population and randomly selected half of them to receive BSFT. Compared to the no-treatment control group, girls who received BSFT achieved reductions in bullying, anger, aggression, and risk-taking. Most of the gains were maintained at a 1-year follow-up.

ABFT is an exception among the empirically supported family therapies in that it focuses on internalizing disturbances—namely, depression and suicidal ideation. Diamond et al. (2010) randomly assigned adolescents with suicidal ideation to ABFT or TAU. ABFT produced more reduction in suicidal ideation, with a large effect size of .97. After therapy, only 13% of the AFBT clients continued to express significant suicidal ideation, compared to 48% of the TAU clients. Effects on self-reported and clinician-rated depressive symptoms were similarly strong. Retention rates were much higher in AFBT, with these clients participating in more than three times as many sessions as clients in TAU. In a previous, smaller RCT, adolescents with major depressive disorder were assigned to ABFT or a wait-list control. Following therapy, 81% of the teens who received ABFT no longer met criteria for this diagnosis, compared to 47% of the controls. ABFT also reduced anxiety symptoms and family conflict.

Process research on ABFT has obtained support for the theory underlying the intervention. Postsession interviews with parents showed that the therapist's relational reframes led them to revise their understanding of the problem from internal dysfunction in the adolescent to a parent-child issue (Diamond & Siqueland, 1998). A second study found that relational reframes led parents to focus their attention on impasses in their relationships with their teens (Moran, Diamond, & Diamond, 2005). A third study found that, when this shift occurred, parents adopted a less critical, more empathic posture toward their sons and daughters (Moran & Diamond, 2008).

The Therapist's Style

Systems-oriented counselors generally have an active, "out there" style of working with families (Colapinto, 1991; Goldenberg & Goldenberg, 2012; Nichols, 2012). Typically, compared to dynamic therapists, their manner is less quiet and analytical, and more directive and active. Like constructivist counselors, they are willing to be somewhat emotive, dramatic, and self-disclosive with clients. These therapists may talk about their personal experiences, including their reactions to the sessions taking place, when such disclosures serve a therapeutic purpose.

The value of a strong, active style has been supported by research on the process of family therapy. Allen-Eckert, Fong, Nichols, Watson, and Liddle (2001), and Nichols and Fellenberg (2000) found that highly experienced, effective counselors were quite active and directive in their work with families, and this approach seemed to facilitate change in relationships and patterns of interaction.

The roles of the counselor in family therapy include being a referee, teacher, model, and coach. As a referee, the therapist restrains family members who tend to dominate the conversation and encourages hesitant family members to speak up. As a teacher, the counselor explains patterns of interaction and their effects on the identified patient and other family members. Family therapists model adaptive ways of relating and provide clients with feedback about their behavior. They direct clients to experiment with new ways of relating both within and outside the sessions.

Combining Family and Individual Modalities

Therapists do not need to choose between the family and individual modalities of treatment; we can blend them in a variety of ways. Actually, child and adolescent therapy includes more than two modalities. There is a menu of options from which to choose, some of which stand in between individual therapy and seeing the whole family together. Much child and adolescent treatment involves work with parents, often the mother, without the client present. Parent training and guidance occur in this modality. Much family work involves the parent(s) and the client, without the siblings. At the other end of the spectrum, when members of the extended family seem either to be involved in the client's problems or able to contribute to solutions, it is useful to bring these individuals into the therapeutic mix.

Therapists have the freedom to mix and match different modalities both from session to session and within each appointment. Counselors can go back and forth to the waiting room, bringing in family members that seem needed at each juncture of the work. Diamond and Liddle (1996) refer to this process as "shuttle diplomacy."

Often, there is a certain sequence to the use of individual and family modalities. At the beginning of treatment, it is often useful to spend time with the child and parents separately. For many young people, individual time with a counselor has a special power to facilitate the development of a trusting relationship and encourage the expression of previously hidden concerns. Often, young clients will say things to their therapists that they would not initially say in front of their parents. During this phase of treatment, therapists can help both children and parents clarify their views of the difficulties, gain insight into their roles in the problems, and develop an understanding of what they need from each other. Frequently, this individual work helps young people formulate specific questions, messages, and requests for their parents, and the parents often accomplish something similar, too. Then it is time to bring the family members together, ask them to present their different perspectives, and begin integrating their viewpoints. (Sometimes clients prefer their therapist to provide a summary of their concerns, and this is an effective option as long as the client is willing to interject any corrections that need to be made.) This sequence from individual to family work is part of the design of ABFT and is also common in systems-oriented work in general.

Facilitating Communication

When family communication is poor, people sometimes produce torrents of words that contain a good point but this point is obscured by disorganization, confusion, and detail. Just because someone is inarticulate does not mean he is wrong, and people who have trouble expressing their thoughts often have valuable things to say. Counselors can help by discerning the valid points usually contained in everyone's words, stripping away exaggerations, hostility, and extraneous content, and presenting the distilled result to the group. By rephrasing family members' statements in more moderate terms and presenting their arguments as one valid side of a two-sided issue, counselors can often help listeners perceive useful points that had been obscured by extreme rhetoric.

On an interpersonal level, therapists can translate family members' verbalizations into more palatable terms by finding tactful words to express the message that the speaker needs to communicate. Therapeutic translations downplay the accusatory elements and emphasize the emotions and needs contained in the speaker's verbalization, thus composing a type of I-statement for her (see Chapter 12, Aggression). These translations should be offered in a tentative spirit, so, before you begin, turn to the person for whom you are speaking and say, "Now tell me if I'm getting this wrong" and, after you are done, ask, "Have I got that right?"

When people are sure they already understand each other, they are neither interested in listening nor open to learning, and they are likely to remain stuck in their misunderstandings. Curiosity is a constructive emotion. To motivate curiosity, counselors can offer the following observation of human nature:

> "As people, it's natural for us to be intensely aware of our own feelings, and yet we're often pretty clueless about the emotions happening in the minds of the people we see every day. We're very aware of their behavior but often unaware of the feelings behind those behaviors. One of the services I want to provide you with is this: When you leave our sessions, you should know more about the feelings of the people in your family than you did when you walked in. And I hope you keep this up when you go home."

One useful tactic is to ask each family member what the others do not understand about her. Surprises, even if small, usually produce forward motion.

It is useful to ask family members questions about *other* people's feelings and views (Aponte & DiCesare, 2000; Patterson et al., 2009). For instance, you can ask the parent how the child feels when she gets a bad grade on a test, and you can ask the child why it is important to the parent that he complete his chores. In addition to these dyadic examples, you can ask the son how the mother feels about the father's temper outbursts, and you can ask the daughter how the father feels about the son's drug use. After the other-directed question is answered, you can turn to the person who was the subject of the question and ask, "Is that right?"

This procedure, in which you move around the room asking family members why the others feel and behave the way they do and then going to the source for feedback about the answer, is a staple of family therapy.

This procedure, in which you move around the room asking family members why the others feel and behave the way they do and then going to the source for feedback about the answer, is a staple of family therapy. The technique has the effect of pulling family members out of their own, individual perspectives and helping them view situations through each other's eyes.

Families' maladaptive communication styles occur in sessions just as they do in everyday life, and this can make the clinician's work difficult. However, just as dynamic therapists try to turn the potential obstacles of resistance and transference to therapeutic purposes, family therapists view disruptions of the therapeutic process as instances of the communication problems that make life unhappy at home, and they approach these problems as grist for the mill. This idea can be conveyed to clients with words like the following:

> "It seems like every time Dad starts talking about changes he would like to see in the family, Lily changes the subject to something less serious, and people start talking about that until they forget about the changes Dad was talking about. Let's take a look at this because, if it happens in our sessions, it probably happens at home, too."

Interrupting is a common communication problem. Interrupting may be an individual problem (it is symptom of ADHD), but when it occurs family-wide, it is probably a systems issue. People who interrupt often have reasons for doing so. For instance, sometimes speakers hurt listeners with their words, in which case interruption is a self-protective behavior. Another reason for interrupting is that sometimes it is the only way to break into a conversation. If so, counselors can note that if speakers do not give others an opportunity to talk, they are virtually forcing them to interrupt. On the other hand, if speakers control the length of their statements appropriately, it is the listener's job to wait for them to finish before responding.

One way to circumvent the obstacles to communication that sometimes erupt in arguments is to suggest that family members put personal statements in writing for each other. Following preparation with the counselor, family members can write constructive statements that are free from exaggeration and personal attack and that clearly state their points and express their emotions. The advantages of this technique are that writers can put their thoughts and feelings into words in an unhurried manner, and then readers can take it in and think about the entire statement before responding.

Chapter 12, Aggression and Violence, focuses on interpersonal conflict between peers, but much of its material also applies to conflict-related emotions and behavior in families. Counselors can integrate training in Chapter 12's communication and conflict resolution techniques into their systemic work with families.

Systemic Insight

Sometimes facilitating communication, with no additional action by the counselor, increases mutual understanding in the family. At other times, families can go only so far by themselves, but they could go further if the clinician provided input by explaining the processes occurring in the family, in a systemic version of interpretation. One technique is to make implicit family rules explicit, by stating them out loud (Bateson, 1972, 1979; Haley, 1963, 1996)—for instance:

One technique is to make implicit family rules explicit, by stating them out loud.

> "Oh, I think I see how things work here: Mom and Dad keep saying they want Noah to be more independent, but when he offers ideas for things he'd like to do on his own, there's always some reason why it won't work. It's like there's a rule that he's not allowed to get involved in activities outside the family, but there's another rule that no one can talk about the first rule, so everyone pretends he stays home all the time because he can't think of anything else to do." (Note the double bind.)

One common obstacle to communication in families occurs when logical content and emotions about relationships get tangled up and mixed together. If the emotions are strong, the logic often gets lost. When people accumulate resentment, this feeling often flows into the way they express their arguments, even when the topic has nothing to do with the relationship issue. The person on the receiving end might feel the negative emotion so strongly that she hardly processes the logic of the argument but fights back reflexively. As one important example, when parents are angry with their children, they sometimes state reasonable directives with reasonable explanations but speak in bitter, insulting, or sarcastic tones of voice—and then get more angry when the child resists their directive.

If asked about the reasons for their behavior, the parent and youth might answer on two completely different levels: The parent might answer on the level of logical content and say the youngster's refusal to comply makes no sense and is totally unacceptable, and the youth might answer on an interpersonal-emotional level by saying he will not comply with a parent who talks to him in such a nasty fashion. This dynamic is signaled by parents who describe their children's behavior as grossly illogical and youth who say things like, "My father treats me like garbage." These two sentiments are not inconsistent with each other—they might even be reciprocally linked. The parent attributes his insulting tone to the youth's noncompliance, the youth attributes his noncompliance to the parent's insulting tone, and the positive feedback loop spirals upward. The same pattern can occur with the parent and child roles reversed: Sometimes youngsters make reasonable requests that they support with logical points, but when they do so in an angry, disrespectful manner, parents usually refuse to cooperate. Counselors can help by making the following points:

- The level of logical content and the level of interpersonal emotion are distinct, separate, and equally important.
- Being right about content does little good when one is disrespectful interpersonally; these interactions usually go badly.
- It is best, although difficult, to consider valid input even when it is stated in an angry fashion.

Interaction patterns operate across time and remain in force even when nothing happens for a while, because people remember each other's behavior, take up where they left off, and respond to behaviors that might have happened days or weeks before. This causes confusion when people think a behavior must have been caused by what happened right before it. In the previous example, the impatient tone with which the parent first stated his directive might have been due to the headache his teen gave him the last time he tried to get her to clean her room, but if the teen did not realize this, her father's angry tone would seem to come out of nowhere for no reason. Or, the adolescent's resistance to cleaning her room might have resulted from the insulting way the father talked to her the last time he gave her this directive, but if the father did not realize this, his daughter's refusal would seem like pure, pointless obnoxiousness. In this pattern, each person's behavior is based on an *anticipation* that the other person will behave as he did before, so there is a self-fulfilling prophecy in which the people elicit the behavior they expect and then believe their angry responses were justified by the other person's behavior.

Here is a rule of thumb for therapists: If a person's behavior seems inexplicable as a response to present stimuli, it is probably a response to past stimuli that the person sees as relevant to the present situation. Explaining this to families may help them understand why people do things "for no reason."

Reframing

A reframe is a reinterpretation of a behavior of one family member, largely for the benefit of the others. The purpose of the technique is to change the way family members see each other—to change the meanings they perceive in each other's actions (Haley, 1963, 1996; Sexton, 2011; Szapocznik & Kurtines, 1989; Weakland & Fisch, 1992). Specifically, reframes change explanations or attributions for behaviors: They identify a different reason or cause for the behavior in question. Reframes generally take the form, "Oh, I thought she did that because of x, but now I see she did that because of y." These reinterpretations may have an impact on judgments, emotions, and relationships, because the reasons for behaviors often matter more to people than the behaviors themselves. Reframing is a staple technique of family therapy.

Reframing positive behaviors is not usually a high therapeutic priority. Counselors focus on reinterpreting behaviors that are aversive, upsetting, or hurtful to family members. Reframing is useful when family members perceive negative meanings in behaviors the therapist believes might actually have benign or even positive meanings. When this technique works, it changes people's reactions to each other from disappointment, blame, and anger to sympathy, understanding, and, sometimes, respect.

The therapist's challenge is to formulate reframes that are both true and kind. The focus is generally on the second characteristic, because this improves the emotional tone of family relationships. Nevertheless, benevolent fictions are unlikely to work for long because family members will see through them, while valid reframes not only help people see each other more favorably but also provide a basis for more realistic planning and problem solving in the future.

In family therapy, the most basic reframe involves changing the perceived meaning of the identified patient's symptoms from an internal characteristic of that person (e.g., "something wrong with him") to a manifestation of a systemic process in the family (Alexander et al., 2013; Diamond, 2014; Haley, 1963, 1996; Minuchin, 1974; Sexton, 2011; Szapocznik et al., 2003). The youth's symptoms are reframed from a "disorder" that he "has" to one facet of a systemic family pattern that might involve the parents' marital difficulties, parent-child conflict, and fighting between siblings. All the major types of family therapy use these *individual-to-system reframes* to reduce blame of the identified patient and guide families toward acknowledging and changing the dysfunctional patterns that have resulted in the youth's symptoms and their own unsatisfying interactions with each other.

> *In family therapy, the most basic reframe involves changing the perceived meaning of the identified patient's symptoms from an internal characteristic of that person to a manifestation of a systemic process in the family.*

There are also reframes that address meanings within the confines of one individual's behavior. Many of these reframes are based on the motivation/capability distinction: Aversive behavior that seems voluntarily chosen elicits more anger than equally aversive behavior attributed to factors that the other person cannot control. When people do not know how to handle a difficult situation, all sorts of dysfunctional behaviors might result—even though the person desires neither those behaviors nor their consequences. The most important capability-related impediments to effective, considerate behavior appear to be weak psychosocial skills, disruptively painful emotions, misunderstandings (often due to a lack of information), and medical (including mental health) conditions. Here are examples of each:

- People who have trouble managing and expressing themselves in emotionally charged situations sometimes avoid such situations (e.g., in a new blended family) not because they do not care but because they feel they cannot handle the interactions or express their feelings in a way the others will accept.
- Emotional distress disrupts effective behavior in many different ways, including by producing behavior that looks angry but is actually based on pain, and by producing withdrawal or "clamming up."

- One common type of misunderstanding derives from the motivation/capability distinction itself: When we do not know what others are up against, we might attribute hurtful behavior to a lack of caring when, in fact, the person was unable to do better.
- Medical conditions, whether serious or minor, often cause irritability, unresponsiveness, or demands that other people might mistake as indications of meanness, disinterest, or selfishness.

Capability deficits are often difficult for other people to see. One reason is that many people are embarrassed by their skill deficits and vulnerable emotions, so they conceal them to protect their pride, preferring to present their maladaptive behaviors as freely chosen and embraced (e.g., school truancy in youth with learning problems and substance abuse in adolescents who self-medicate their depression). Aesop's fable about the fox and sour grapes is a perfect example of a capability deficit transformed into a motivational preference; *can't* was disguised as *don't want to*.

When families interpret the hurtful behavior of one of their members as motivated by selfishness, disrespect, or cruelty, it is often useful to reinterpret this behavior as the result of painful emotions that the person did not choose and cannot manage effectively. The therapist's task is to figure out how a benign human motive, when implemented in a disorganized, distressed fashion, produces dysfunctional behavior. When family members grasp this, their view of the person as bad is changed to a view of him as upset and confused, and acrimony dissolves into compassion and problem solving. Empathy is an antidote to anger.

When people witness actions that seem to have no reason and serve no purpose—when they cannot figure out *why* the person does what she does—they typically respond with frustration and anger (Sukhodolsky & Scahill, 2012; Yeager, Trzesniewski, Tirri, Nokelainen, & Dweck, 2011). Effective reframes explain the seemingly inexplicable by attributing these behaviors to motives, thoughts, and emotions the family members recognize as understandable but have not connected with the behaviors in question. When a person's negative behaviors *make sense*, this individual is humanized in the others' eyes. For example, Nicolle had trouble understanding her parents' "prying" and "snooping" because she did not grasp what it is like for parents to see their child suffer from depression. When her parents explained the desperate feelings behind their intrusive behavior, Nicolle could see their intentions were good, although she continued to disagree with their methods. Similarly, Nicolle's parents were angered by her secretiveness because they did not understand how embarrassed she was about her problems and how humiliating it felt to have them discovered and discussed. When these feelings were brought out, the parents' anger decreased.

The motivation/capability distinction is not an absolute dichotomy. Sometimes capability-related factors do not make it literally impossible for the person to behave appropriately; they just make it difficult, with "difficulty," here, consisting of the amount of effort the person must exert, the amount of pain he must tolerate, and/or the amount of sacrifice he must make to behave in a desirable way. In some cases, a high level of motivation can compensate for a low level of capability. In other cases, certain behaviors are simply impossible for the person to do; they are beyond her capabilities.

One important category of understandable motive is young people's need for a balance between dependence on their parents and autonomy. Functional family therapy (FFT; Alexander et al., 2013; Alexander & Parsons, 1982; Parsons & Alexander, 1973; Sexton, 2011) places a great deal of emphasis on this source of parent/child conflict, which is also a focus of family systems therapy in general. In FFT, reframing (or "relabelling") usually seeks to identify the **function**, or social-emotional goal, of behaviors. According to FFT theory, young people's behavior with their parents often involves one of three functions: (1) increasing connection and closeness, (2) increasing separation and independence, and (3) finding a balance between the two, which is called **midpointing**. In FFT, client behaviors toward family members are usually interpreted as attempts to achieve one of these three goals. Nicolle's therapist helped her parents understand that her anger about their questioning, although expressed in unacceptably disrespectful ways, was related to a valid, age-appropriate desire for more privacy and self-sufficiency.

When behavior is adaptive, its function is generally clear: A child who says, "Mommy, come play with me" probably simply wants to connect with his mother. In contrast, the functions of maladaptive behavior are often ambiguous and disguised, and it is an assessment task to discern them. For example, one adolescent's depressed behavior might serve the closeness function by eliciting parental nurturance, while another teen's depressed behavior might be a way for her to separate from the family.

Research on the process of FFT has found that therapist reframes of the youth's problem behaviors are usually followed by reduced parent-child conflict and positive therapeutic movement, apparently because the youth feels more understood and supported (Robbins, Alexander, Newell, & Turner, 1996; Robbins, Alexander, & Turner, 2000). FFT does not ask family members to change the functions or goals of their behavior; it uses psychosocial skills training to help them replace ineffective efforts with adaptive behaviors that are capable of achieving their goals.

Family Translations

One of the most common counselor activities in family therapy involves a certain blend of facilitating communication, engendering systemic insight, and reframing. In this work, the therapist translates the verbalizations of family members to make their messages more understandable and acceptable to the other people in the family. The verbalizations are organized, clarified, softened, and made less extreme and angry, so the essential messages are easier to receive, and the dignity of family members is preserved, but the meaning of the statements is not altered in any important way. Here is an example from a session focusing on parent/adolescent conflict about managing the teen's chronic medical condition.

The therapist translates the verbalizations of family members to make their messages more understandable and acceptable to the other people in the family.

SARAH: I can't stand it when you talk to the doctors like I'm 6 years old instead of 16. They look right at me and ask questions about my symptoms, and *you* answer like you know better. And I hate when you say, "We" and you're talking about me, like, "When we start taking this medication, are there going to be side effects?" *I'm* the one taking the medicine. It's like you're on some kind of power trip, you have to be in control of everything, and my only job is to have my body poked at.

MOTHER: I can't believe the way you look at things. From the time you were diagnosed, this illness has been so scary for both of us, and I've been on the case 100% of the time, watching you like a hawk, getting all the information for the doctors, doing everything as well as I can. It *has* been we—and that's a term of endearment, not an insult—I've been so tuned into you—it *is* like it's happening to me. And you think I'm on a *power* trip ... (becomes tearful) ...

THERAPIST: Let me break in for a minute. I think I see what Sarah is saying ... (to the girl) ... now stop me if I'm getting this wrong, okay? (Sarah nods; therapist turns to the mother.) You've had your experience of Sarah's illness, but she's had her experience of it, too, because the illness is happening to her. When you answer the doctor's questions about her symptoms, she feels like, "What am I, a nonperson? I'm the one who has the damn symptoms—I know more about this than you do—let me talk. Maybe I couldn't express myself clearly when I was 6, but I can now." (Turns to Sarah) Is it something like that?

SARAH: That's it.

THERAPIST: (To the mother) Now you let me know if I'm not getting this right, too, but (turning to Sarah), I think where your mother is coming from is that the information for the doctors and the way your regimen is carried out need to be really precise and correct, there's no room for mistakes, and this doesn't seem like something a kid can handle on her own, so your mother has poured her heart and soul into it, and the only thing she cares about is how you're doing, so to hear you take all that effort and caring and call it a power trip.... I think she feels horribly misunderstood and hurt.

MOTHER: It's like a kick in the stomach.

THERAPIST: Maybe there just needs to be some change in how you two manage your communication with the doctors now, based on Sarah being older and more capable than when she was younger.

To translate family members' words and behavior in an accurate, tactful fashion, therapists function as a bridge between the speaker's experiences and what the listener can understand and accept. Sometimes, family members need translations like these to grasp the meanings and emotions contained—and obscured—by the words with which they have tried to communicate in the past.

Treating Enmeshment and Disengagement

Since enmeshed and disengaged families function at two, opposite extremes on the continuum of closeness versus autonomy, the Aristotelian goal for both types of families would be movement toward the middle of the spectrum (Micucci, 2009; Minuchin, 1974; Minuchin et al., 2014; Smith-Acuna, 2010). It is often useful to help enmeshed families develop insight into their discomfort with separation and to help disengaged families better understand the ways in which they feel threatened by closeness. In both cases, these threats usually seem more manageable once they are acknowledged openly. Conscious thought and open discussion usually enable families to develop more adaptive compromises between these conflicting needs.

The spectrum technique can help families understand and master the two-sided issue with which they are struggling. Therapists can use this visual tool to acknowledge the validity of the side the family has overemphasized, point out the validity of the side they have underemphasized, and develop their conception of the adaptive middle of the continuum, where the best of both worlds is located. This work can begin by presenting the following diagram to the family:

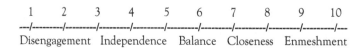

Then, the concept should be fleshed out by citing the behaviors and emotions that correspond to different points on the scale. The question is, what does family life look like and feel like in the different regions of the spectrum?

Sometimes families feel that any departure from their familiar position will hurl them toward the other end of the continuum, which is the one they fear. Counselors can help enmeshed families understand that autonomy does not imply isolation, and they can help disengaged families understand that closeness does not imply smothering. The therapist should provide behavioral, experiential descriptions of the alternation between connecting and separating that occurs in balanced family life. Here is an example for an enmeshed family:

> "It's not a big deal when people have parts of their life that they do on their own, because they'll come back and, when they do, maybe they'll bring something that can add to life in the family."

Enmeshed and disengaged families share an implicit view that families can have either closeness or individuation but not both. This view is a form of dichotomous thinking, and, as discussed in Chapter 3, such cognitions are usually unrealistic and maladaptive (J. S. Beck, 2011; Egan, Piek, Dyck, & Reesa, 2007; Oshio, 2009). According to object relations theory, intimacy and individual identity not only are compatible but also can reinforce each other (Scharff & Scharff, 1987). When families are comfortable moving back and forth between connection and autonomy, both types of experiences are enhanced, as when a base of security enables people to venture assertively into the world and when outside activities enrich family relationships. Dinner table conversation is livelier when family members have interesting, separate experiences to report. The therapeutic message for both enmeshed and disengaged families is that they do not have to choose between closeness and independence, because they can have both.

Therapist Directives

Direct therapist input helps families go beyond the limitations of their own resources to develop new forms of relating (Haley, 1963, 1996; Madanes, 1991; Patterson et al., 2009; Santisteban et al., 2013). The purpose of therapist directives is to initiate experiences that introduce families to new and more satisfying ways of interacting. If these behavioral experiments are reinforcing, they will be repeated voluntarily and become part of the family's everyday repertoire.

It might or might not be useful to explain the reasoning behind directives. Families whose style is thoughtful and intellectual may want to know the reasons for their assignments, but this is less important for families whose style is action-oriented and concrete. Also, explanations can come either before or after the new, therapist-directed experience. Sometimes, new experiences have more impact when people jump in without thinking about it too much first. The message is, "Just try it—you might like it."

Therapists can use in-session directives to alter maladaptive communication and interaction patterns (Minuchin & Fishman, 1981; Satir, 1967; Szapocznik et al., 2003). Coalitions can be broken up by changing the seating arrangements so that distant family members sit next to each other. Therapist directives can disrupt habitual patterns of interruption or domination of the conversation by some individuals and can help family members listen to each other more effectively than they have in the past.

One useful technique is to ask family members to provide explanations or express certain feelings to each other—for example:

- "Mrs. Fischer, have you explained to Joey why you haven't been able to come see his plays?"
- "Sally, would you tell Mom how you feel about her decision to move the family to Cleveland?"

This type of directive is useful when family members harbor thoughts and feelings about each other that they have not expressed and that the family could benefit from hearing, or when certain types of communication seem needed to balance the relationships in the family system. For instance, family members who constantly criticize each other can be asked to say what they admire, like, or love about each other. People who present themselves as totally confident can be asked to talk about their fears and self-doubts. Parents whose disciplinary behavior is consistently stern and authoritarian can be asked to share their soft side with the youth, perhaps by describing memories of warm interactions in the past.

Therapist directives can push people into unfamiliar territory as they try new behaviors outside their familiar roles. The result may be greater system flexibility. Clients may discover unexpected benefits: Quiet family members may find they can get their points across without negative consequences, and previously dominant talkers may find they can learn valuable things by listening to family members who, in the past, have not spoken up much.

For example, consider a family in which the father constantly corrects the child and pushes for behavioral improvement, while the mother consistently voices appreciation of what the child is able to do and makes excuses for her mistakes and weaknesses. One appropriate intervention might be to present this observation to the family and then ask the parents to switch roles. This directive would require both parents to focus their attention on aspects of the child's behavior opposite to their usual focus. Two benefits might flow from this intervention. The couple might broaden their capabilities for performing different parental functions, so the child would have two sources of correction and two sources of support, instead of just one apiece. And even if the parents maintain the old division of responsibilities, their appreciation of each other's role will probably increase, and they will see their two functions as complementary and equally necessary, rather than conflicting.

Therapist directives for family interactions outside sessions fulfill the same functions. Perhaps the most common purpose of these assignments is to bring estranged family members closer together by directing them to share pleasant activities, thus strengthening connections across the boundaries of coalitions. This type of directive is a common component of therapy for conduct disturbance in adolescents, as described in Chapter 11.

It is not essential that the shared activities have the same level of interest for both people. In a subtype of these assignments, one family member takes part in a hobby or special interest of the other. Thus, you can suggest that a parent help a child build model airplanes or receive instruction in his favorite video game. By the same token, you can suggest that a child accompany a parent to work, join him on the golf course, or take a close look at her scrapbook. The technique is equally applicable to siblings. By joining in each other's favorite activities, family members may be pulled out of their usual interaction patterns, discover new things about each other, and find new ways of relating.

Because of the busy nature of modern family life, often with both parents working and children as overscheduled as parents, family dinners are not the common routine they once were. Research does not portray this development as progress: Youth who frequently eat dinner with their families have lower rates of obesity, eating disorders, and depression, compared to young people who have few family dinners, and these effects remain when variables such as SES and general family functioning are statistically controlled (Meier & Musick, 2014; Musick & Meier, 2012). Therapists can sometimes bring families closer by suggesting they eat dinner together more often.

Treating Positive Feedback Loops

Work on positive feedback loops can begin with systemic insight: helping families discover the mechanisms that have driven the problems making them unhappy. Families are often struck by how different the situation looks from different perspectives and yet how neatly the two perspectives fit together, as mirror images, to make up the whole. The previously confusing situation suddenly makes sense, and everyone's behavior emerges as understandable (Gladding, 2014; Micucci, 2009; Smith-Acuna, 2010).

Nicolle and her parents had evolved polarized ways of dealing with the problems she experienced. Their pattern was a common one: When adolescents try to hide their problems, the parents get nervous about what they do not know, and they often interrogate the teen and snoop in her room, phone, and social media sites, while the teen, in a desperate, angry effort to protect her privacy, redoubles her self-concealment and secrecy. Nicolle, like many adolescents, tried to hide her difficulties to make it seem like everything was okay—so her parents over-reacted to any indication of a problem that did leak out. The cycle went like this:

> MOTHER: She hides her problems from us, and it's nerve-wracking to be in the dark about what's going on with your kid. When something does come out, it's usually the tip of an iceberg, so of course we get upset. If she told us how things were going day to day, we wouldn't get so alarmed when we discover a problem.
>
> NICOLLE: If I tell them I missed an assignment or did bad on a test, they freak out, tell me I can't go on the Internet, and try to make me study for hours. It just makes things worse, so of course I'm not going to say anything. If they didn't have a fit about it, I could tell them when I'm having trouble in school.

Therapists can bring these perspectives together using words like the following:

> "Your perspectives are so different, and yet they actually fit together. To understand, just put yourself in each other's shoes. (To Nicolle) You *have* had trouble in school, so when you're secretive about what's going on, your parents fear the worst. When the little bit they find out is bad, they figure it's a small part of a big problem—and they're usually right. (To parents) It's upsetting for Nicolle when you have a big reaction to what she sees as a small problem, and she regrets telling you. From her perspective, it would be

better to hide the problem, work harder in class, and hope it eventually works out, so there's nothing you need to know.

The remarkable thing is that you are each doing exactly what it takes to produce the behavior you don't like in the other. (To Nicolle) If you *wanted* to make your parents overreact, you couldn't find a better way to do it, and (to parents), if you wanted to make Nicolle hide her school problems, there's no more effective way than what you've been doing up till now."

Diagrams provide a useful way to help families understand the operation of positive feedback loops because the geometry of these visual tools conveys the circular, chicken-and-egg nature of the process more clearly than words can. Nicolle's diagram is presented in Figure 7.3.

There are four points to make in the accompanying explanation:

1. No one's behavior is malevolent or arbitrary; both people's behavior is logical and reasonable, so no one deserves blame.
2. Each person views his behavior as a response to the other person's behavior.
3. Each person is contributing to the problem and is, in fact, eliciting exactly the behavior she dislikes.
4. The interaction pattern is self-perpetuating and will go on forever if nothing is done to change it.

If movement in a conciliatory direction is initiated by either party, the positive feedback mechanism will cause reciprocation and escalation of the desired behavior in the other.

The transition from explaining the problem to planning a solution can occur in a moment, because the logical connection is usually so clear. Feedback loops are just as capable of driving desirable as undesirable interaction patterns: If movement in a conciliatory direction is initiated by either party, the positive feedback mechanism will cause reciprocation and escalation of the desired behavior in the other, because the more

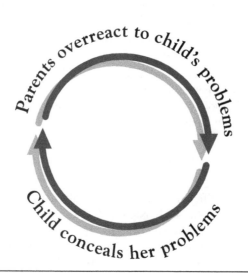

Figure 7.3   Diagram of a positive feedback loop.

Person A does what Person B wants, the more Person B will do what Person A wants, and so on—for example:

"So I guess there's good news and bad news. The bad news is that, if you don't change what you've been doing, things are not going to get better, because this cycle can go on forever. But the good news is that you can make this circle go *in reverse*; you can get the other person to do more of what you want by doing more of what he wants."

Interpretations of positive feedback loops often defuse power struggles. When this mechanism is operating, both people believe that the only way to win is to overcome the other person and get her to come around to their position. They are like two people in a tug-of-war, both believing that if they stop pulling as hard as they can, the other person will defeat them. Often both believe that if they give the other person an inch, he will take a mile. However, the reality is usually the opposite, and the way to get the other person to move toward them is to move toward the other person. Usually, either both people get what they want, or neither does; the only way for each person to get what he wants is to give the other at least some of what she desires; and neither person can solve his own problem but each can solve the other person's problem. The only solution is to replace battling with collaboration or, in tug-of-war terms, to drop the rope.

Often, positive feedback loops have a polarizing effect on the language used in arguments. As the exchanges escalate, the parties perceive and misperceive each other's positions as more extreme than they really are and, in response, they state their own views in intensified form, as they drive each other toward the opposite ends of the continuum. Therapists can address conflicts driven by polarized, dichotomous thinking with diagrams that define the disagreement in quantitative terms. Nicolle's counseling involved a 10-point scale depicting the range of possibility for the cleanliness versus messiness of rooms. Initially, the mother said Nicolle wanted her room to be "a pigsty" (a "1.5"), and she "has a fit" when told to clean up. Nicolle's initial view was that her mother wanted "a spotless room that looks like nobody lives in it" (a "10") and that her mom "freaks out" when there is an article of clothing on the floor. Both descriptions turned out to be exaggerations, which the counselor translated into more accurate, moderate terms by saying that the mother wanted a "more orderly" room (a "7"), Nicolle's preference was for a "more casual" setting (a "4"), and both became "angry" when they disagreed about how clean the room should be. Similar conversations revealed that the mother did not really want to know "everything" about her daughter's life and emotions, nor did Nicolle want a relationship in which she was "a stranger" to her mother. Both wanted something in between (although not exactly the same).

The spectrum procedure can enable both parties to acknowledge the validity of each other's points without abandoning their own. When family members cite arguments for their own side of the debate, therapists can nod in agreement and then add the DBT question, "What else is true?" When the two-sided nature of the issue becomes apparent to both parties, they can collaborate on developing a balanced synthesis in the mid-range of the spectrum. The parties do not usually meet at one exact point on the scale, but, as they move toward the middle, the final distance between them becomes manageable.

The next step is for the two parties to make a deal in which each gives the other what she wants and, in return, receives what he wants. These solutions do not usually require much self-sacrifice because, once Person A ceases her unwanted behavior, Person B no longer needs to continue his unwanted behavior, and vice versa.

Nicolle and her parents agreed that, each Sunday evening, she would inform them of all school assignments and tests coming up that week and, each Friday evening, she would tell them how she did on those assignments and tests. The parents agreed that they would not ask their daughter about school at other times during the week and they would not contact her teachers. The same principle was applied to the parent's desire to know how Nicolle was feeling, emotionally. Scheduling these inquiries seemed too artificial, but the parents agreed to minimize their questions, and Nicolle agreed to provide honest, though brief, answers. The parents agreed to control their reactions and end the inquiries once Nicolle provided a reasonably informative response. In negotiations between parents and children, the symmetry should not be complete: The parents reserved the right to determine whether the new method was working or required revision.

If the family members do not think of the needed bargain on their own, the clinician should look at Person A and ask whether she would be willing to do what Person B wants *if* Person B would do the same for her; then, the therapist should ask the same of the other party. Both people will usually say yes. Then, the only thing necessary is for someone to make the first move. Counselors should suggest that both parties do this simultaneously.

Therapists can give families a diagram of the old, dysfunctional feedback loop and also a diagram of the loop consisting of the new, self-reinforcing solution to the problem. For Nicolle's family, the content of this loop was: Parents respond calmly to daughter's problems ↔ Daughter is open about her problems. A third piece of paper can also go home with the family after being copied for the chart—namely, a written contract stating each person's side of the bargain.

Unlooping Hurt and Anger

There is a type of positive feedback loop that combines the systemic process discussed earlier with an internal mechanism called **aggressive response to shame** (Shapiro, Dorman, Burkey, Welker, & Clough, 1997). In this mechanism, being treated with disrespect causes feelings of shame, which are transformed into anger, and the individual strikes back at the person who humiliated him in an attempt to repair the damage to his self-esteem. (This process is discussed further in Chapter 12, Aggression.)

Consider what happens when the individual mechanism of aggressive response to shame occurs in a two-person system. When Person A's hurt and shame are transformed into aggressive behavior toward Person B, the second individual is likely to feel disrespected and injured. If Person B also deals with shame through this mechanism, she will strike back at Person A, resulting in more hurt for this individual, which may be translated into more aggression toward Person B, and so on, back and forth. This positive feedback loop has four parts, with an emotional and behavioral step for each of the two people:

A's Shame → A's Aggression → B's Shame → B's Aggression → A's Shame →

To provide a circle diagram for families, just wrap this four-part sequence around in loop form. Each of the two semicircles then includes an emotional step and a behavioral step.

Much of the acrimonious conflict that occurs between parents and children, spouses, and siblings seems to fit this pattern of aggressive response to shame in a feedback loop. This mechanism is signaled by angry exchanges in which the family members respond to criticism or insult by criticizing or insulting the other person back. These exchanges take the form of, "I'm _____ (e.g., sloppy, selfish)? You're *twice* as _____ as I am!" These interactions fit the norm of reciprocity (Gouldner, 1960) and can be summarized as, "You hurt me, so I'll hurt you." Families have to do better than this.

The solution is simpler than the problem. It is simpler to express hurt directly than to transform it into aggression and hostility. The simplest thing to say when someone hurts our feelings is some version of, "Ouch." A direct, honest response is also more likely to be effective than aggressive response to shame, because expressions of hurt usually elicit compassion, or at least concern, rather than retaliation and escalation (Shapiro, 2003). Expressions of concern and compassion are likely to elicit similarly kind and constructive responses—and a new positive feedback loop has been initiated in the direction of reconciliation.

Simpler does not mean easier. Many people, especially males (Jansz, 2000; Kring & Gordon, 1998), find it difficult and uncomfortable to express pain and vulnerability, while expressing anger seems to preserve pride and dignity. Therapists must be gentle and skillful in encouraging family members to forego vengeful counterattacks and take the risk of expressing the pain beneath the anger. We can support clients' undisguised communication of distress by explaining the defensive aspect of the aggression/shame mechanism and portraying the open, transparent expression of hurt as a difficult act that requires strength and contributes to improved relationships in families.

ABFT (Diamond, 2014; Diamond et al., 2003, 2014) is based on this strategy, with a focus on the hurt associated with disrupted attachment relationships between youth and their parents. This intervention helps parents and adolescents express their pain about past relationship difficulties and come together in efforts to achieve more trust and closeness in the future.

The first step is individual sessions with the adolescent and parent. The counselor's goals, for both parties, are: (a) to encourage the experience and expression of existing disappointment, anger, and unhappiness about the parent-child relationship, (b) to identify the obstacles and disruptions that have impaired this relationship, and (c) to access the longings for a warm, affectionate relationship that usually exist beneath the bitterness and even hopelessness that have accumulated through the years.

This work includes delving into the past, as the primary emotions of hurt and pain are brought into consciousness and words. For youth, individual sessions explore the events and experiences responsible for injuring or rupturing the attachment bond. For parents, this work often includes inquiry into their own childhood experiences and relationships with parents, with exploration of possible intergenerational patterns. It is also important that the therapist prepare the parent to hear and validate the child's expression of hurt and anger without reacting defensively. Therapists help adolescents and caregivers clarify and articulate these core emotions in individual sessions so that, with this preparation, they can communicate their feelings to each other in an effective fashion. Following this emotion-focused work based on L. S. Greenberg (2002; Greenberg & Pascual-Leone, 2006), ABFT becomes solution-focused (De Jong & Berg, 2012; de Shazer, 1985, 1993), and encourages parents and teens to talk about the kind of relationship they want to have in the future. Counselors facilitate this communication by quelling argument and refutation and encouraging the participants to listen and learn how each other feels.

Through this work, Nicolle and her parents discovered the pivotal and damaging role that the mother's depression, which began postpartum and continued intermittently until Nicolle was about 7, had played in their attachment relationship. Nicolle began with vague but deeply painful feelings that she was barely able to articulate and quite unable to organize. What she knew was that her mother had often been unavailable to her—sometimes physically, when the mother was in bed, and more often emotionally, when her mom was withdrawn, too tired to play or talk, and impatient with her daughter's efforts to connect. The only interpretation available to Nicolle as a child was that her mother did not want closeness with her. She had coped by trying not to care, making the most of her relationship with her father (who did not spend much time at home), and trying to be self-sufficient by creating her own activities and interests. In later years, when her mother increased her attempts to enter Nicolle's world, this felt like a disruptive intrusion that reminded her of what she had missed—it seemed too little, too late, and her mother's efforts only reignited Nicolle's old hurt and anger.

ABFT involves simple, pure questions with which therapists facilitate the evolution and expression of attachment-related emotions and desires in adolescents and caregivers. Therapists ask parents and children what they want, what they wish for, what has gotten in the way of closeness, what would make it more comfortable to connect, what they know about the other person's experience of the relationship, and what they want the other person to know about theirs. Here is what the counselor said to Nicolle and her mom:

> "So much has happened that can't be undone, but you both want a relationship that makes you feel close, warm, and happy. (To Nicolle) We can figure out what gets in the way of your trusting your mom and work through those obstacles so you don't need to push her away anymore, and it's easier to turn to her for help and comfort when you're upset, without embarrassment, because kids should be able to get a hug from their parents when life is hard. And you (Mom) have made it so clear that this is what you want, to reach her when she's in distress, to listen so you really hear her and are there for her through all the ups and downs."

One goal of these conjoint sessions is for the parents and child to hear and understand each other's feelings. Another goal is to begin envisioning and planning the relationship they want to have in the future. But on a deeper level, the purpose of these sessions is not discussion or even planning but the enactment of attachment experiences. With all its terminology, theory, and diagrams, in the final analysis, family therapy is about love.

Summary

Systems theory emphasizes patterns of interaction in families, rather than individual characteristics of family members, as the unit of analysis most important to understanding behavior, problem etiology, and therapy. Families exhibit emergent properties and nonlinear, reciprocal patterns of influence, with changes in any part of the system having an effect on everyone in the family. Because the theory views family dysfunction as the root cause of child psychopathology, the goal of resolving the identified patient's symptoms is pursued by working with family members in addition to the child client.

Family dysfunction takes a variety of forms, including enmeshment, disengagement, and maladaptive patterns of communication, such as the double bind. In positive feedback loops, each person's response to a disliked behavior of the other has the unintended effect of *increasing* that behavior, and yet the more the attempted solutions fail, the more strenuously the people try to implement them.

Generally, outcome research provides the same level of support for family systems therapy as for most EBPs. Most of this research has examined therapy for disruptive behavior problems in adolescents and is reviewed in Chapter 11. As an exception, ABFT has been shown to be effective for depression and suicidal ideation in teens.

The therapist's first objective is to help family members communicate more effectively with each other. Systems-oriented interpretations provide clients with insights into their family's patterns of interaction. Family therapists also use directives to disrupt engrained patterns of dysfunctional interaction.

Systems-oriented counselors reinterpret problematic behaviors so family members understand both their own and others' functioning more accurately and sympathetically. Perhaps the most basic reframe involves changing the perceived meaning of the identified patient's symptoms from an internal characteristic of that person to a manifestation of a systemic process in the family. Reframes typically attribute troublesome behaviors to a combination of a benign motive and an inability to translate this motive into adaptive behavior. Important capability-related factors include weak psychosocial skills, disruptive emotional distress, misunderstandings, and medical conditions. Effective reframes depict a positive image of the person despite her undesirable behavior and, by providing an accurate understanding of the reasons for the problem, offer an effective basis for problem solving.

In positive feedback loops, each person's response to a disliked behavior of the other has the unintended effect of *increasing* that behavior, and yet the more the attempted solutions fail, the more strenuously the people try to implement them. Therapists can treat positive feedback loops by helping families understand this cycle (perhaps with the aid of a circle diagram) and then proposing that each person could elicit the behavior he wants from the other by providing the behavior that person wants from him. Then, the feedback mechanism will cause reciprocation and escalation of the desired behaviors in both people, because the more Person A does what Person B wants, the more Person B will do what Person A wants. In these situations, neither individual can solve her own problem but both can solve the other's, and if they focus on constructing the future instead of reacting to the past, solutions will be generated.

Positive feedback loops in which hurt is transformed into aggression may cause especially severe damage to relationships. ABFT treats disrupted parent-adolescent attachments by helping both parties experience and express their painful feelings of being unloved, first in individual sessions and then together. The therapist helps caregivers and children share their longings for a warmer and closer relationship in the future. Obstacles that have prevented affectionate relations are identified, and plans are made for dissolving or overcoming those obstacles. In successful ABFT sessions, parents and teens not only analyze problems and plan solutions but also enact attachment-repairing experiences that heal their injured relationships and strengthen their feelings of love.

Case Study

Attachment-related work brought out the issues that had disrupted Nicolle's relationship with her mother and contributed to her anger, irritability, and depression. The mother expressed frustrated longings for closeness with Nicolle, and she described her past experiences with depression as obstacles to the relationship that she had been unable to overcome at the time. At first, these explanations sounded like excuses to Nicolle, but a combination of the therapist's explanations of depression, some reading to provide an objective perspective, and, especially, the mother's courageously honest descriptions of what those times were like for her eventually enabled Nicolle to understand that her mom had done the best she could.

These increases in Nicolle's understanding of her mother and the parents' understanding of Nicolle went a long way toward resolving the anger and withdrawal that had wounded their lives together. Some behavioral adjustments were also needed. Because of Nicolle's strong need for privacy, she was very uncomfortable with her parents monitoring her exchanges with friends on social media, and the attachment work did not change that. The parents promised to forego this type of monitoring as long as Nicolle treated their inquiries about her mood-state as legitimate questions and provided informative answers.

The mother and daughter had some real catching up to do—to some degree, they had missed significant portions of each other's lives. Nicolle had some penetrating questions about her mother's depressive episodes that the mom found intrusive and embarrassing, but she made the effort necessary to help Nicolle know her as well as she wanted to know her daughter.

8

Atheoretical and Transtheoretical Techniques

OBJECTIVES

This chapter explains:

- *Therapeutic diagrams of several types.*
- *Techniques for bringing adaptive states of mind into problematic situations.*
- *How to help clients find new routes to their original goals.*
- *How to help parents work through psychodynamic obstacles to their use of behavioral techniques.*
- *How to apply the idea of balance within continua to a variety of clinical problems.*
- *Basic neuroscientific findings that are useful for clinicians (and some parents and clients).*
- *How to accommodate therapy to the client's genetically based style.*
- *A simple value system that can be used in therapy.*
- *Ways to extend clients' structures of meaning and incorporate problematic experiences into them.*
- *How to help clients overcome fear of failure.*

This is the one chapter of the book in which I unmoor myself from the theoretical frameworks and outcome studies that govern most of my recommendations in order to share some techniques I have developed on the basis of general psychological research and clinical experience. Because outcome research is generally a stronger basis for treatment planning, I recommend supplementing, not replacing, empirically supported interventions with these strategies.

The major therapeutic approaches provide our field with large chunks of theory and technique. However, psychotherapy also includes small and medium-sized chunks—that is, ideas and techniques that do not fit into extensive theoretical structures but provide useful components of therapy with some clients in some situations. Individually, these ideas and techniques are not large or complicated enough to require a chapter for their description, so they are gathered together in one chapter here. The applicability of these techniques generally does not depend on the client's diagnosis but on the presence of the issues and processes addressed by the techniques. Some of the strategies are atheoretical in that they are not closely related to any therapeutic orientation, and some are transtheoretical in that they involve change agents that crosscut theories.

Miscellaneous Techniques

A *Spoonful of Sugar Helps the Medicine Go Down*

Therapists can sometimes find ways to bring things the client likes into the situations or tasks she does not like. In other words, we can try to find ways to bring pleasant, encouraging, or empowering contents into domains that have troubled and even defeated the client.

For example, children can choose a favorite character from a book or movie and then imagine what that character would say to cheer them on in their efforts to overcome a problem. One 7-year-old girl with school phobia was able to venture back into her classroom with the voice of Wonder Woman shouting encouragement in her ear. Children who have trouble getting up and going in the morning can turn on their favorite music to stimulate them to move through their routine. Therapists can ask clients to identify a song or two that could motivate, inspire, and guide their efforts to make a change they want to make. When youth feel intimidated by problems, playing their theme song, either literally or in their minds, provides a source of encouragement that they always have with them.

Structured Drawing and Diagrams

Therapists sometimes use artistic activities in a free, expressive fashion, and they can also use drawing in a structured way to accomplish specific objectives. Structured drawings and diagrams supplement verbal reasoning with visual representations of psychological content. These crystallizations can help clients understand both the dysfunctional processes that have contributed to their difficulties and strategies for functioning more effectively. I wrote a brief Kindle ebook called *Psychotherapeutic Diagrams* that describes how our 10-point scales, circle diagrams of positive feedback loops, and other structured drawings can be used in counseling. The ebook can be found at Amazon.com.

Structured drawings and diagrams supplement verbal reasoning with visual representations of psychological content.

While diagrams can take any form, certain structures seem to fit many of the situations and challenges faced by young people. The 10-point scales and positive feedback loops presented in previous chapters are important examples of therapeutic diagrams, and some additional structures are described below. Therapists can use these descriptions as templates, filling them in with the specifics of their clients' issues.

Lines representing paths or roads to destinations can depict sequences of events and action/consequence relationships. Choices can be represented as forks in the road, with each path representing an option and the endpoints indicating predictable results. I suggest drawing positive behaviors on lines with an upward slope that lead to positive results and negative behaviors on lines with a downward slope that lead to negative consequences. Obstacles to goal attainment can be drawn on the path, and strategies for circumventing them can be indicated graphically (e.g., fear might block a path toward sports participation, and deep breathing might circumvent this obstacle). Here is a simple example of this type of diagram:

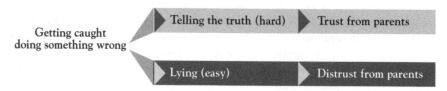

Upward and downward slopes of horizontal lines can depict improvement and deterioration in the client's mood or situation. This technique can be used to diagram the costs and benefits of gratification delay, in their characteristic order. For instance, starting homework might be drawn as the line dropping sharply; doing homework could be drawn as a plateau at this low level; finishing homework could be drawn as a line shooting up higher than the starting point; and the rest of the evening could be represented as a high plateau defined by the good feeling of earned relaxation.

Arrows are conventional symbols of causality that can be used to show how one event leads to another (e.g., "Mom says no → You nag Mom → Mom gets mad"). As described in Chapter 7 on family therapy, double arrows can be used to depict reciprocal causality (e.g., feeling depressed ↔ watching TV). Branching lines of arrows indicate alternative courses of action and their predictable results.

Walls that separate people can represent obstacles to closeness. The walls can be filled in with words or pictures that describe the difficulty (e.g., past arguments, fear of rejection). Different responses to obstacles can be symbolized by the actions of figures toward the wall (e.g., breaking a hole through the wall or going around the barrier).

The client's ability to protect herself from negative influences can be drawn as a *shield*. For example, a girl who was prone to losing her temper in response to teasing drew a shield repelling the taunting words of her peers; behind this protective barrier, she maintained self-control.

Emotional situations can be drawn as *places* that are happy, unhappy, scary, and so forth. Details of the pictures, or words written into them, can be used to describe and explain the nature of the place for the client.

Clients and therapists can draw a *picture of the problem*, a *picture of a solution*, and steps that can traverse the space in between. These steps might involve thoughts or actions.

Transporting Adaptive States of Mind

Research on **mood-dependent memory** (Balch, Myers, & Papotto, 1999; Lewis & Critchley, 2003) has shown that memory works best when learning and recall occur under similar emotional conditions. When people acquire information during a depressed mood, they are most able to retrieve that information when feeling depressed, with the same pattern for positive moods. Life looks different depending on the emotional state we are in.

Mood-dependent memory becomes relevant to clinical work when clients develop adaptive intentions and plans during sessions but do not follow through with them in everyday life. For example, aggressive youth might verbalize determination to control their tempers and depressed clients might list good things about themselves in sessions, but when back in their everyday environments, the situations that elicited maladaptive functioning might do so again, with no apparent effect of the therapeutic work. These clients seem to lose access to an adaptive state of mind they had achieved in the past. Therapists can address this problem by helping clients *transport* their wise, healthy states of mind from the reflective experiences in which they developed to the difficult situations in which they are needed.

The important process here is memory—not only for information but also for emotion and intention. If clients remember their in-session thoughts and feelings when in difficult situations, they are more likely to follow through with the intentions they expressed in therapy rather than succumbing to the pressures of the immediate environment. The first step in building this connection is to ask the client to remember and describe her problematic experiences, with emotional detail, so therapeutic conversations connect with those experiences in a substantive way.

The goal is to create a two-way street between therapy and the problematic situations, so the client can both remember and anticipate each when located in the other. Clients generally think about their problem situations while in therapy sessions; the additional exercise here is to remember and anticipate therapy sessions while in problematic situations. Once the mental connections develop, situations associated with past dysfunction become cues for the recall of adaptive strategies (e.g., "The next time one of your friends says 'Hey, let's cut school,' a red light could go off in your mind to remind you that this is exactly the situation we've been preparing for in therapy"). Clinicians can help clients integrate therapy into their everyday lives by weaving memories and anticipations of counseling around their problematic experiences (e.g., "You'll get up in front of the class, remember our talks, do your plan, and come back to tell me how it went").

Paper or digital documents provide a physical medium of connection between counseling and everyday life. Therapy notebooks can go back and forth with the client. Counselors can write homework assignments, messages, and reminders in these notebooks and, when clients are home, they can write accounts of their experiences, thoughts, and topics they want to remember to discuss in sessions. Or, therapists can construct a very simple chart consisting of one row of blank space for each day of the week. The parent and possibly the child write a brief summary of the day's behavior in each row for the counselor to read at the next appointment. For children who want to please their therapist, this exercise is a potent reminder and motivator for positive behavior.

Techniques for young children can make use of the type of magical thinking that is characteristic of children below age 6 or so. Dolan (1998) suggests that clients select or make a small object associated with confidence and strength (e.g., "a power bracelet," or "a safety stone"). Therapist and client bring this object into their times of security and warmth to create associations with good feelings. When symptoms or stressful situations occur, the client can hold his talisman tightly to experience some of the confidence with which it was imbued. If the client has a phone, a picture of the therapist, or a picture of the therapist with the client, might serve a similar function.

In older children, talismans are usually replaced by written materials (see Chapter 1) and self-statements prepared in advance (see Chapter 3, Cognitive Therapy). During calm, clear-headed times, youth can compose brief phrases that encapsulate their new intentions and then memorize these self-statements for future use. The mantras may reinvoke the mental state associated with therapy:

- "Remember your goals."
- "I always feel better eventually."
- "There are a million rationalizations but not one good reason to take a drug."
- "This is what I've been waiting for: a chance to put what I've learned into practice."

Journal writing can be an effective tool for integrating thoughts, feelings, and behaviors across time and situations. Youth who are not interested in writing on an ongoing basis might still benefit from preserving their key ideas and resolutions in written form. Clients should anticipate situations in which it will be helpful to examine these messages from the self to the self. The messages can be placed in an envelope, computer file, or phone, and the time for opening them can be identified—for example, "To be opened when I'm depressed." Then, when the time comes, the client will have a preset plan to implement and will need only to follow his own directions.

New Routes to Old Goals

Many behavior problems can be conceptualized by assuming that, when people are unable to meet their needs through adaptive behavior, they have recourse to dysfunctional strategies. And many therapeutic procedures can be based on a corresponding general strategy: figure out what goals the child is trying to achieve with her disturbed behavior and then help her develop alternative, adaptive routes to those same ends.

A general strategy: figure out what goals the child is trying to achieve with her disturbed behavior and then help her develop alternative, adaptive routes to those same ends.

Most of the goals pursued by clients are healthy and positive—at least in principle. Children with mental health problems, like other youth, typically want attention from parents, respect from peers, success experiences, and so forth. Legitimate needs like these motivate a great deal of maladaptive behavior. The solution is not to eliminate such motivations but to respect their presence in the dysfunctional behavior and help clients find adaptive ways to meet these valid needs.

This treatment strategy draws a distinction between specific, *concrete* goals, which are defined by particular events and outcomes, and general, *abstract* goals, which are defined by underlying needs. Clients' concrete objectives are frequently maladaptive, but their abstract goals usually are not. For example, a boy might bully weaker children in an attempt to feel powerful and earn respect from peers. His counselor cannot support his concrete objective, but she would support and help him achieve his abstract goals.

The first step is to discover what the client's underlying goals are. In this assessment task, the therapist's thought process needs to move from the concrete to the abstract ("What is she trying to accomplish with this behavior?"). Then, treatment planning requires movement from the abstract back to the concrete ("How could the same goal be accomplished in a healthy way?"). To continue with our example, the bully's counselor might suggest adaptive ways to earn respect from peers and feelings of power—for instance, by taking a leadership role in a school activity. Often, the most effective way to eliminate dysfunctional behavior is to replace it with a more effective route to the same goal.

Route/goal conceptualizations can be expressed in diagrams. The client's initial effort to meet his needs can be depicted as the shortest, simplest route toward the goal—but this avenue is blocked by the negative consequences associated with the presenting problems. Strategies developed in therapy can be depicted as longer routes that circumvent obstacles and, therefore, provide a more reliable means to the client's ends.

The distinction between specific objectives and general goals can be useful in helping clients recover from disappointments. Although people's hearts are often set on specific objectives, quality of life is usually more dependent on abstract goals that, if not achievable in one way, are attainable in another—for example:

- "I get that smoking weed helps you relax and it's something to do with friends. Those are good things—but there have to be ways to relax and hang out with friends without taking drugs."

- "Maybe you should give up on Jessica, but you don't have to give up on the kind of relationship you wanted to have with her. You'll just have to pursue that dream with another girl."
- "If your mom can't find a job that pays as much as her old one, your family will need to be more careful with money and more creative about activities so you can have just as much fun with less expensive stuff."

When clients become aware of the higher-order goals that underlie their particular objectives, they become more able to respond to disappointments with fallback plans. Fallback plans, by definition, are never our first choice, but they prevent helplessness by providing alternative avenues for striving when the first one is blocked. The more abstract the clients' goals, the better she will be able to bounce back from disappointment by pursuing other objectives. In anticipation of challenges, knowing that one has fallback plans prevents the frightening feeling that everything depends on a single outcome. Counselors can work through the particulars of contingency planning with their clients, applying a framework stating that if Plan A does not work, they can go to Plan B, and if that does not work, they can move to Plan C, and so forth, so that all will never be lost.

Money and Materialism

Money-related issues often create problems in people's lives, and these issues come up in therapy. Therapists can do little about families' income, but there are other ways to help: We can use research on the psychology of money and happiness to help families develop adaptive attitudes toward material things and manage their spending without feeling deprived—an accomplishment described by the title of my Kindle ebook for non-professionals, *How to Get More Happiness From Less Stuff* (available at Amazon.com).

High levels of materialism are associated with unhappiness, low self-esteem, and disinterest in helping others (Kasser, 2002; Opree, Buijzen, & Valkenburg, 2012; Schor, 2005). As in the tolerance phenomenon in addiction, showering children with toys and treats probably results in habituation to a high level of indulgence, so less enjoyment is derived from a given amount of consuming and larger quantities are required for stimulation and satisfaction. Conversely, responsible spending and consuming are examples of the broad skill set called self-control (Baumeister & Tierney, 2011; Oaten & Cheng, 2006, 2007). In her review of research on happiness, Lyubomirsky (2008) reviewed a number of studies demonstrating the old-fashioned truth that we enjoy material things most when we wait, work, and save for them.

For parents, managing children's materialism is sometimes a challenging child-rearing task—and is the topic of my Kindle ebook called, *The Child Psychology of Money and Happiness: A Guide for Parents*. When children whine for purchases in stores, the immediate question is how to stop the nagging, but the larger question is how to shape the child's development as a consumer. Parenting techniques that structure children's consuming may contribute to the development of self-control, moderate the development of materialism, and enhance young people's appreciation of the possessions they do have.

Maintaining a **wish list** is an effective way to expand children's sense of time and strengthen their ability to delay gratification. When youth make requests that parents do not want to fulfill immediately, parents can suggest adding the item to the list. In the future, these lists will provide ideas for birthday and holiday presents. Parents can share the lists with relatives looking for gift ideas. The lists provide parents with something to say in addition to "no," so the child does not feel totally stymied and she has something to look forward to.

Wish lists provide clients with a tool for organizing their desires. When they look back at their wishes after the passage of some time, youth often find that some of the items do not even seem familiar, let alone desperately needed, and they discover that urgently felt desires sometimes dissolve. When occasions approach, they can rank their gift preferences. Parents can provide information about the items' prices and the budgets of potential gift givers, so youth who do the arithmetic can propose exactly how they would like to allocate their finite resources. This exercise in prioritization prompts clients to think about translating money into happiness in an optimally efficient way—a skill they will need all the time as adults.

Allowances provide children with practice in managing their own money. Parents step back, allow youngsters to make decisions about spending versus saving, and let them experience the consequences of their decisions. As a guideline, one dollar per year of the child's age seems about right. Saved allowance money provides an option in addition to gifts for purchasing items on wish lists.

With adolescents, parents can reduce power struggles and control spending by using a variation on the allowance—namely, a budget for a specific category of purchase. For example, instead of repeatedly arguing about purchases of clothes, parents can establish a total clothing budget for a given period of time, such as one school semester. The youth can draw down this suballowance at will, without justifying his purchases to the parents—until he runs out of money, when he must stop until the time period is up. With this strategy, the expensive tastes that used to be the parent's problem become the teen's problem. Youth who used to resent their parents for being cheap begin to resent the producers of designer labels for selling overpriced merchandise.

With these strategies, parents can respond to requests for purchases with answers in between "yes" and "no." The strategies transform potential arguments into learning opportunities by giving youth substantial control, providing guided practice in planning and prioritizing, and creating conditions that enhance appreciation of possessions and treats while moderating appetites for material things.

Parent Counseling

Most work with parents focuses exclusively on the child. However, parents' emotional issues sometimes interfere with their implementation of therapeutic recommendations (Blatt & Homann, 1992). Parental objections to therapist suggestions might also be the result of unwise recommendations or inadequate explanations, but in this section I discuss what to do when the parent's emotional issues seem to interfere with her functioning as a caregiver.

One option is to refer the parent for his own therapy. Regardless of whether this occurs, it is sometimes necessary for child treatment to include a component of **parent counseling**:

a type of work in between parent training and treating the parent as an individual therapy client. Parent counseling addresses the caregiver's emotional concerns and history while focusing on how these issues affect her functioning with her child.

There are a variety of dynamics that sometimes interfere with this relationship. Sometimes, caregivers have negative feelings toward the client because of anger toward the other biological parent (often, an absent father). When the client's behavior is difficult, the parent may attribute this to his being "just like his father." Therapists can help caregivers separate their feelings about ex-partners from their reactions to the child by pointing out that no one chooses his parents, and children have no control over what traits or tendencies they inherit. Also, counselors can remind parents of the biological fact that half of the child's genetic makeup comes from the father and half comes from the mother.

Parents' emotional concerns sometimes disrupt their implementation of behavioral techniques. Some parents object to replacing their reliance on punishment with the reward-oriented procedures central to behavior therapy, which they might view as "spoiling" the child (Barkley, 2013). Discussion sometimes suggests that the parent's underlying concern is the contrast between her own upbringing and the child-rearing methods recommended for use with the client. These concerns may be revealed in questions like, "Are you saying my parents didn't raise me right? Are you saying my parents didn't love me? Didn't I turn out okay without these fancy techniques and rewards you are recommending?" To these caregivers, using the recommended practices feels like a repudiation of the way they were brought up by their own parents.

When differences between the parent's upbringing and the recommended methods seem to be merely a matter of technique, counselors can point out that the parent now has an opportunity that his own parents might not have had: a chance to rethink child management practices and learn some new strategies. Furthermore, it is possible that the parent's parents *would* have taken advantage of new ideas for child management, if someone had offered to provide explanations of them. If so, the parent's adoption of the new techniques, while a departure from his parents' concrete behaviors, would actually be an affirmation of their belief in finding better ways to do things—and so would not be a betrayal at all. As analogies, therapists can cite other technological advances that are widely used by the parent's generation but not by older people.

It sometimes seems necessary to do psychodynamic work with the parent in order to implement behavioral interventions with the child.

When differences between the parent's upbringing and the suggested methods concern more than technique—for instance, when the parent's childhood involved maltreatment, reliance on corporal punishment, or indifference—it might be useful for the parent to discuss her upbringing and its effects on her current functioning as a caregiver. When parents become more aware of the issues underlying their responses to the child, their mastery over these issues may increase, and they may become more able to make conscious choices rather than responding reflexively.

These parents may need to grieve disappointing or hurtful aspects of their own childhoods before they can put this pain aside and focus on the child. Thus, it sometimes seems necessary to do psychodynamic work with the parent in order to implement behavioral interventions with the child. This work might enable the caregiver to embrace a profoundly difficult goal: providing her child with an upbringing more effectively nurturing than her own.

Therapists can facilitate this process by helping parents understand and respect the meaning of what they are trying to do—for example:

"In parenting, the easy and natural thing is to raise your children the way your parents raised you. It's like we record what our parents do while we are growing up, and then, when we're parents ourselves, we hit the Play button and say what we heard. This is the default mode—it's normal and natural—but it's possible to do better by stopping and thinking about it, getting good input, and trying to raise our children better than we were raised ourselves. I don't think you'd be here if you didn't want to do that."

Choosing to parent more lovingly and effectively than one's own parents might sound like the obvious decision to make, but for parents whose own childhoods included maltreatment or serious caregiver dysfunction, making this choice can be excruciatingly difficult. Every use of a supportive child management technique contrasts with the threats and slaps they received growing up and, consciously or unconsciously, reminds these parents of the difference between their own childhoods and what they want to provide for their child. Enduring these painful reminders is the price some parents must pay to end the intergenerational transmission of unhappiness. Giving what one never received always involves hard work and often involves suffering. Doing the right thing even when it hurts is a definition of everyday heroism. Therapists can support parents' adherence to this path by offering this definition, so parents can appreciate the meaning of what they do. Credit should be given where credit is due.

Balance Between Extremes

Therapists can use visual depictions of spectra (e.g., 10-point scales) to help clients understand ranges of emotional and behavioral possibility and develop adaptive styles in the middle of these ranges. This schema is a flexible tool that can be applied to all sorts of client problems. Figure 8.1 provides a sampling of functional dimensions characterized by maladjustment at the extremes and successful adjustment around the midpoint. These spectra were constructed with clients using the procedure presented in Chapter 3, Cognitive Therapy.

The spectrum procedure can be used to accomplish DBT's twin objectives of conveying acceptance and the need for change at the same time (Linehan, 1993a, 1993b, 1997, 2014). This formula, followed by examples, combines both messages in single questions:

- "How could you continue to _____ (client's end of scale) while also _____ (other end of scale)?"
- "How could you continue striving for excellence while also accepting that you're human and sometimes make mistakes?"
- "How could you continue being independent while also making use of the help that's available to you?"

Openness About Emotion: How Much Is the Right Amount?

1	2	3	4	5	6	7	8	9	10
	Cut off from others	Distant	Reserved	Selectively open		Saying more than people want to hear			Attention whore
Secretive about everything				Sharing important things with important people				Spilling guts to anyone	
	Closed, emotionally alone		Hard to get to know		Open in good relationships		Burdening people		No dignity
"You're just there."		Blank face			Choosing with whom and when to be open		Laying everything on table		Hiding nothing

Getting Help From Other People

1	2	3	4	5	6	7	8	9	10
No help ever		Help as a last resort	Help when needed		Help when appropriate		Help when unnecessary		Help to avoid work
	No help even if it means failing			Doing what you can and then getting help				Getting help before trying	
	Self-destructively independent			Using resources skillfully			Lazy	Needy Dependent	Helpless
	Living with one arm tied behind back				Knowing when you need help and when you don't				Can't do anything on own

Figure 8.1 Dimensions of functioning.

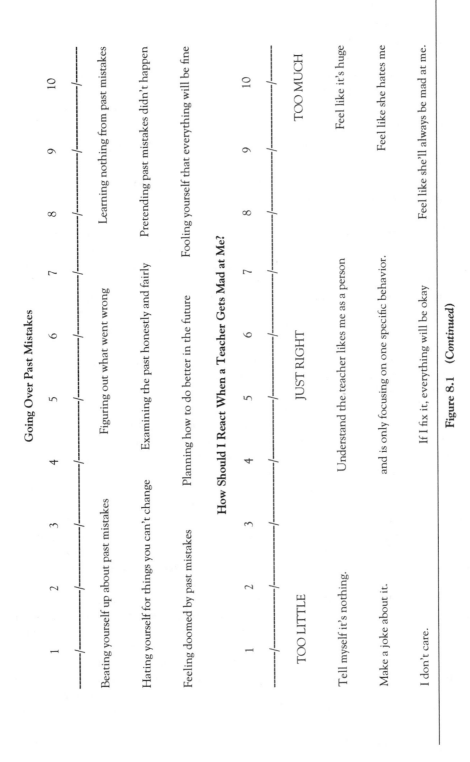

Going Over Past Mistakes

| 1 | 2 | 3 | 4 | 5 | 6 | 7 | 8 | 9 | 10 |

Beating yourself up about past mistakes   Figuring out what went wrong   Learning nothing from past mistakes

Hating yourself for things you can't change   Examining the past honestly and fairly   Pretending past mistakes didn't happen

Feeling doomed by past mistakes   Planning how to do better in the future   Fooling yourself that everything will be fine

How Should I React When a Teacher Gets Mad at Me?

| 1 | 2 | 3 | 4 | 5 | 6 | 7 | 8 | 9 | 10 |

TOO LITTLE   JUST RIGHT   TOO MUCH

Tell myself it's nothing.   Understand the teacher likes me as a person   Feel like it's huge

Make a joke about it.   and is only focusing on one specific behavior.   Feel like she hates me

I don't care.   If I fix it, everything will be okay   Feel like she'll always be mad at me.

Figure 8.1 (*Continued*)

Similarly, therapist statements to parents can both recognize what they have accomplished with their children and identify changes that need to be made. Parents sometimes feel affirmed and relieved when they are reminded of problems on the *other* end of the continuum—for example:

- "I know you're concerned about how cautious and inhibited Aaron is, and we're going to work on that, but in a way you could count your blessings, because I've got other parents with impulsive, reckless children who *wish* their kids were more like Aaron."
- "David has a really strong conscience. Now we have to help him go a little easier on himself."
- "Sue is really good at going after what she wants. Now we have to help her become more considerate of other people."

Why would there be a general relationship between moderation and adaptive functioning on a variety of dimensions? The reason might be that, although moderation does not necessarily involve flexible, versatile functioning, such functioning *would* be summarized as a location in the middle portion of a spectrum. This conclusion is explained ahead.

People do not and should not behave the same way all the time. Although an individual's overall style can be summarized as one point on a scale, such summaries collapse a great deal of information into simplified form. Adaptive functioning is generally situation-specific because it responds to the context in which it occurs. Because situations vary, adaptive functioning varies, too. For example, a generally assertive person would probably behave submissively if held up at gunpoint, assertively in most everyday conflict situations, and aggressively if physically attacked. Although moderation can be rigid as well as flexible, flexibility can only be summarized as moderation.

Moderation is difficult to achieve because extreme forms of functioning are simple, usually involving only one side of a two-sided issue, while balance is inherently complicated, because it requires integration of both sides. For instance, in the interpersonal realm, a guarded stance preserves emotional safety while closing off connections, an uncritically trusting stance allows many connections to be made but incurs risks of being exploited or hurt, and healthy interpersonal functioning balances caution and friendliness to provide both relationship possibilities and emotional safety.

Evolutionary psychology provides a framework for a speculative explanation of the adaptive value of moderation on many functional dimensions. Cognitive, emotional, and behavioral styles evolved and persisted in human populations because they had adaptive advantages. Because our early ancestors faced a wide variety of challenging situations that required markedly different responses for success and survival, contrasting and even opposite styles of functioning have been selected and passed on to future generations (Barrett, Cosmides, & Tooby, 2007; Cosmides & Tooby, 1994). The adaptive value of most psychological traits and processes, even those generally considered positive (e.g., optimism, forgiveness, empathy), varies markedly depending on the situation (McNulty & Fincham, 2012). If opposite styles of functioning confer advantages in different types of situations, natural selection would produce stylistically opposite emotional and behavioral potentials (e.g., the parasympathic and sympathetic nervous systems). Our genetic inheritance, rather than being internally consistent, would include bases for a diverse array of thoughts, feelings, and actions. The superordinate adaptive advantage would lie in flexible, situation-specific responding—which would be summarized as the midpoint of a spectrum.

Framing treatment objectives as a matter of versatility provides an affirming way to present these objectives to clients. In most clinical situations, therapists can say that the goal is not to remove or replace aspects of the client's personality or customary way of doings things but, instead, to introduce new skills, ideas, or techniques that provide more options. When objectives are presented as an expansion of existing repertoires, clients feel they can pursue change without repudiating valued aspects of self. One useful exercise is to differentiate between situations in which the client's existing responses work well and situations in which new ways of functioning could work better.

Psychoeducation

In **psychoeducation**, the clinician provides new information about human behavior to children or parents. This is not an academic exercise: The therapist *applies* his general knowledge about child development, psychology, and other social sciences to the unique situation of the client. This information provides a framework within which the child's difficulties become more understandable and manageable. Here is an example for a parent:

> "Most adolescents want to develop an identity of their own, with tastes and interests different from their parents'; it's part of growing up. Anne's attraction to these styles of dress and music don't mean she's rejecting you; she's just trying to become more of her own person."

Here is an example for a child:

> "Kids with ADHD usually have trouble getting their homework done. This doesn't mean they're lazy or dumb; it means their brains work a little differently from kids who don't have ADHD. We're going to talk about strategies for helping with this."

Many older children and adolescents, including some who are not academically inclined, are interested in psychology and the social sciences, which they see as inside information about how people think, why people do what they do, and how people can improve their lives. To invite clients into the psychoeducational process with a light spirit, counselors can say, "I'm going to give you a little Psych 101 course along with your therapy." To invite collaborative application of the material to the youth's own situation, counselors can say, "Now be a psychologist (or therapist) with me."

Psychoeducation is an inherently normalizing technique, because the fact that a problem has a name and there are books about it proves that other people experience that problem, too. Placing clients' difficulties in the context of general knowledge about human functioning may reduce their sense of deviancy and stigmatization; this can be a profound relief to clients who have lived with a sense of being "the only one." Also, the

Psychoeducation is an inherently normalizing technique, because the fact that a problem has a name and there are books about it proves that other people experience that problem, too.

existence of strategies that have proven helpful for people similar to the client implies that her problems are solvable, too.

Even though reference groups defined by a diagnosis are not "normal" in the usual sense, diagnostic groups can provide the basis for a certain type of normalization. Statements like, "Well, that's OCD," and "This is a normal part of anxiety" make problems seem more manageable by implying that other people have gone down this road before.

Normalizing, like everything else, can be taken too far, and this occurs if there is an implication that the client's current way of functioning cannot or should not change. Normal does not mean optimal. Counselors can say:

> "You reacted to that situation in a normal, natural way—but I don't mean that as a compliment. The possibility of failure is scary, and it's a relief to get out of these situations by deciding you don't care, but that doesn't help things get better. You could make it a goal to respond in a better than normal way."

In another type of psychoeducational intervention, the counselor helps the client understand the behavior of an individual other than herself. For example, after listening to a client's account of an interaction, a counselor might provide feedback about whether the other person seems trustworthy, seems to like or dislike the client, and how the client could deal with the person more effectively. Of course, therapists cannot be sure their interpretations are accurate, but their coaching might still add something useful to the client's thinking:

> "I understand that she's been friendly in some ways, but she has so many favors she wants you to do for her, and some of those favors are just not cool, so to me it doesn't sound like she wants to be a real friend. She might be trying to take advantage of you."

Another service sometimes provided by therapists is giving feedback to clients about how they come across to other people and why their behavior might produce the responses they receive. Just as we can rely on our friends to tell us when we have food stuck between our teeth, clients should be able to count on their counselors to say things like:

> "Telling friends that you feel like killing yourself might scare them and, after a few times, might drive them away, because they don't know what to do about a problem like that. I know you want more support from your friends, but I don't think this is an effective way to get it."

Sometimes, the information needed by clients does not come from the human sciences but pertains to some other aspect of the world. As examples, clients might need information about the biology of human sexuality, academic and career options, recreational resources in the community, and legal issues. When clients lack information about an issue of significance, counselors can help by explaining some aspect of how the world works. Although this type of input might not be considered "therapy" in a narrow sense, creative clinicians are alert for opportunities to use any knowledge they have to benefit clients.

Making Use of the Therapist Role

The literature does not include much discussion of how psychotherapists can explicitly utilize their role, as seen through clients' eyes, to achieve treatment objectives. Counselors might be uncomfortable about using their status as experts because they see this as elitist and because it departs from the reliance on evidence, not authority, that is central to science. Nevertheless, the therapist role can be a powerful asset because it imparts trustworthiness and credibility, and while some professionals might be sheepish about this power, most clients seem to embrace it. This is why, from the first time they meet us, clients often confide the most intimate concerns in their lives, sometimes telling us things they have never told anyone before.

Therapists can invoke their role with statements that begin, "I've talked to a lot of kids, and ..." This implies the counselor has encountered the client's issues before and has some understanding of them. Beginning counselors are not in a position to say this, but children probably have lower thresholds than adults for considering something "a lot," so newbies need not wait too long to make this statement. In the meantime, it makes sense to say, "We therapists have talked to a lot of kids, and . . . ."

Invoking the therapist role is particularly effective when addressing guilt or shame about experiences that clients perceive as deviant but that, in fact, are not. One important example concerns the ordinary self-doubts and insecurities, concealed behind a confident persona, that most people acknowledge having (cf. the "Barnum Effect"; Forer, 1949), and that seem especially common in adolescents. Other examples include the feelings and thoughts emphasized by psychodynamic therapy—namely sexual, aggressive, selfish, and jealous impulses. There seems to be a massive group phenomenon in which common awkward experiences are concealed from others because they are perceived as deviant, but the reason they are believed to be rare is that everyone else is concealing them, too, and for the same reason. This positive feedback loop on a mass level can be summarized as: concealment from others ↔ shame within self.

The institution of psychotherapy is ideally suited to exploding this cycle. Clinicians can bring common, awkward, human experiences out of the shadows and into the light by saying something like this:

> "One good thing about being a therapist is that people are usually open with us, so we get to find out the truth about what's going on. One of the things I know is that *lots* of people _____ (e.g., worry that they're a loser). But each person feels like he's the only one, because he never hears anyone else talking about it—and because of that, *he* never says a word, so no one hears it from him, either. Everyone puts on a façade, their Facebook pages make it look like they've got it all together and are having a great time, so there are millions of people who have the same self-doubts, but they're all fooling each other into feeling like the only one. It would probably be better if we gave it up and just admitted being human, which includes feeling _____ sometimes."

Statements of this type can expand clients' conception of the normal human condition in such a way that their own experiences are included, so they no longer feel inferior to others. Clients generally expect their therapists to have this type of knowledge, or at least to have more of it than they do, in the same way that they expect auto mechanics to know how cars work. We can use the confidence clients have in us to provide credible reassurances that they need to receive.

The Role of Genetics in Mental Health Problems

In recent years, there has been an explosion of knowledge about the role of genetic factors in human behavior. This complex field has been summarized in nontechnical books by Plomin, DeFries, Knopik, Jenae, and Neiderhiser (2012), Tabery (2014), and a wonderful book by Pinker (2002), which examines the broad implications of behavior genetics for our understanding of human nature. Here, we focus on therapeutic handling of one basic fact: Genetic factors play a large role in developmental psychopathology.

The "nature/nurture debate" is over, at least scientifically. Hundreds of studies of twins and other genetic relatives, adoption, and molecular genetics have demonstrated that heredity and formative environment both exert strong influences on human development. The importance of genes means that children are not blank slates whose developing personalities are purely a function of the experiences provided by parents and other people. Children come into the world with their own temperaments and personality tendencies that unfold over time, unless the environment is extremely unusual. Parenting practices and other formative experiences influence children's personalities, but they do so in interaction with the nature of the child that is already there. Parents do not form their children in the way that a potter forms a pot, because infants have many more preset characteristics than wet clay.

If genetic factors influence the development of psychopathology, then parents are not necessarily to blame for their children's mental health problems. Historically, therapists have been guilty of a great deal of parent blaming, much of which was both hurtful and scientifically invalid.

The importance of genetic factors in the etiology of some disturbances does not make parenting inconsequential but shapes the specific child-rearing challenges and opportunities that parents face. Therapists can say:

> "This doesn't mean there's nothing you and your husband can do to help your son—far from it. If he had a genetically based medical condition, you would do everything you could with diet, rehabilitation, et cetera, to help him as much as possible. It's the same thing with behavior problems. We'll come up with strategies to compensate for Eric's vulnerabilities and help him learn better ways of behaving. He may need more help than other kids but, if you put in the extra effort, he'll be able to learn organized, cooperative behavior."

The importance of genetics in personality development does impose some constraints on change efforts. Such efforts, including therapy, generally cannot reverse temperament. Fortunately, major improvements in adaptation can often be accomplished by relatively small adjustments in the client's personality style. The spectrum/moderation idea provides therapists with a strategy for working with, rather than against, clients' genetically based styles. In these terms, when clients move from a 9 to a 7 or from a 2 to a 4, their basic style is preserved, but it becomes more adaptive as it moderates. In this way, anxious youth become cautious, oppositional youth become independent, and so forth.

One interesting ramification of genetic factors in psychopathology is that parents and children sometimes experience similar mental health difficulties. Also, during their childhoods, parents sometimes experienced problems similar to those their children are experiencing currently. Therapists can make use of this parallel. Parents' memories of their childhood experiences can provide a basis for empathy with the child. Also, because of their genetic similarity, strategies that worked for parents during their childhoods are likely to work for their children, too. Therapists can encourage parents to share such strategies.

Neuroscience for Therapists (and Clients)

Neuroscience research has produced profound insights into the workings of the human mind. Counselors with knowledge of these findings bring a scientifically valid understanding of the brain to their therapeutic work. Parents and older clients are often interested in basic neuroscientific knowledge, which can help them make sense of their experiences and behavior.

In this chapter, I present some fundamental conclusions of this research that are relevant to clinical issues across a wide range of diagnoses. My citations are mostly secondary sources—books by researchers written for nonneuroscientists—because it is generally unnecessary for clinicians to wade through neuroscience research articles; we just need to get the basic ideas. Books by LeDoux (1998, 2002), Damasio (1994, 2010), and Pinker (2009) provide excellent summaries of what neuroscientists have learned about the brain.

As discussed in Chapter 5, Psychodynamic Therapy, the most fundamental conclusion of neuroscience research is that the brain is a *modular* entity composed of subsystems with different locations, functions, characteristics, and, sometimes, aims. Of course the modules work together, and usually they do so in a smooth fashion, but their heterogeneity creates the potential for internal conflict—which sometimes brings clients to therapists.

While a large number of distinct brain structures and systems have been identified, there are two that are particularly central to clinical work. The **limbic system** includes the amygdala, which is involved in fear and aggression, and the nucleus accumbens, which is involved in reward-seeking and pleasure. The **cerebral neocortex** is a large structure covering the entire top of the brain; its prefrontal and frontal lobes are of special importance in the story told next.

In many ways, the limbic system and cerebral neocortex are a pair of complementary opposites. The limbic system is the seat of emotion and motivation, including drives for food and sex. The human capacity for rational, logical thought resides in the prefrontal and frontal lobes of the cortex. Information processing operates differently in the two systems: Conditioning produces learning of associations in the limbic system, while the cortex is capable of abstract, conceptual thought. Limbic cognition is simple, approximate, and categorical, while cortical cognition can be complex and precise. The limbic system is extremely fast, performing operations in milliseconds. The cortex is comparatively slow and deliberative. The workings of the limbic system are mostly unconscious, while we are more conscious of our cortical processes. Anatomically, the structures of the limbic system are concentrated in the central portion of the brain, while the cortex makes up the top, outside layer. Developmentally, the limbic system matures faster than the cortex, both prenatally and postnatally, and the cortex's development continues for a longer period of time, with maturation reaching completion only in the late twenties. Evolutionarily, the human limbic system is comparatively "old" and primitive, in that it is not extremely different from the limbic systems of lower animals (and was once known as "the reptilian brain"), while the human neocortex, as its name implies, is evolutionarily new and unlike anything found in other species.

The resemblance between the limbic system and Freud's concept of the id is obvious. Clients who feel guilt or shame about their impulses might benefit from understanding the brain system from which these desires arise as well as the system that evaluates and influences the expression of limbic output—for instance:

> "Yes, there's a part of you that wants to do some pretty troubling things, but there's also a part of you that evaluates these possible actions, decides whether they fit with your values, and blocks the ones that seem wrong, so you go forward only with those behaviors that seem okay. "

There are strong, fast neuronal connections between the limbic system and the body, which are mediated by the endocrine and autonomic nervous systems. Limbic activation quickly affects the cardiovascular, respiratory, muscular, and digestive systems. This is why emotions cause physical feelings. When people contrast what they know in their "head," versus when they feel in their "gut" or "heart," they are actually contrasting the outputs of their cortex and limbic system.

There are nerve fibers connecting the limbic and cortical systems, which is why our feelings affect our thoughts and our thoughts affect our feelings. However, the connections are not symmetrical: There are many more neurons running in an upward than downward direction, which is why emotions exert strong effects on thoughts while it is difficult, although not impossible, for reason to overcome emotion.

Different therapeutic strategies target different brain systems. Behavior therapy procedures involving classical and operant conditioning, as well as the corrective emotional experiences emphasized by dynamic therapy, seem to work in a bottom-up direction by reconditioning limbic responses, which might then lead to changed thoughts. Cognitive, insight-oriented, and constructivist methods seem to work in a top-down direction by targeting cortical processes, which might then lead to changed feelings. In all types of therapy, clinicians collaborate with clients in this uniquely human process of the brain changing the brain.

The different speeds with which the limbic and cortical systems operate present a formidable obstacle to the achievement of self-control. Many maladaptive behaviors occur as a result of impulsivity, and many would be prevented if the person could delay his response by the second or two needed for the cortex to shift into operation. The self-statement "Stop and think," or variants thereof, is a staple of this type of work.

Neuroscience research has illuminated adolescent brain development and revealed mechanisms underlying some familiar characteristics of this age. Jetha and Segalowitz (2008), Spear (2009), and Weinberger, Elvevåg, and Giedd (2005) summarize research on factors that contribute to the emotional and behavioral intensity, impulsivity, and risk taking associated with the teenage years.

The rapidly maturing limbic system approaches full development during adolescence, while the more slowly developing cortex does not nearly complete its maturation during this time. As a result, adolescents experience adult-like drives and emotions before they have the cognitive and inhibitory capabilities to control them effectively. One useful analogy is that teens are like cars with fully developed engines but incomplete steering systems and brakes. Levels of the excitatory neurotransmitter dopamine increase markedly during the teenage years, without commensurate increases in inhibitory neurotransmitters. Also, during early adolescence, there is a surge in the formation of new synaptic connections, followed by a pruning of connections during late adolescence. This pruning eliminates unnecessary and counterproductive associations and consolidates learning that is reliable and useful, resulting in more effective mental functioning.

These factors make adolescence an exciting, vivid period of life, and also a somewhat dangerous time. Adolescents are often passionate, creative, and insightful, but their leaps of imagination and initiative may not be adequately structured by critical thinking and good judgment. These features of adolescent brain development sometimes contribute to impulsive, risky behaviors that involve jumping to conclusions, intense pursuit of rewards, and little concern about consequences.

The Neuroscientific Orientation. Beneath all the complexities of the numerous brain structures and functions that have been identified, neuroscience involves one idea so general that it represents an orientation toward mental life. Because the brain and mind are one, brain functioning governs human experience in a fundamental, inescapable way. The ultimate reason why we think a thought or have a feeling is that the brain module that produces the thought or feeling has been activated. This is not the way people typically explain the occurrence of their thoughts and feelings. Typical explanations are of two types: Emotions and cognitions are generally attributed either to external events or to person characteristics, such as character, personality, and intelligence. The neurobiological orientation does not mean external events or person characteristics are irrelevant but that their effects on experience and behavior are mediated by brain functioning.

Counselors can use the neuroscientific orientation to produce therapeutic effects for clients. This does not depend on using technical terms for brain structures but on conveying the idea that the mind is modular and modules may function in either an adaptive or maladaptive way. The concept can be diagrammed by sketching an outline of the brain, drawing the relevant module as a small, irregularly shaped circle within it, and picturing the module's output as arrows pointing outward, with words expressing the messages thus imposed on the rest of the mind (e.g., for the amygdala, "Danger!," "She hates me!," etc.).

The neurobiological paradigm can help clients make sense of confusing experiences. Clients sometimes complain of thoughts and feelings they believe are "crazy" or "stupid," which usually means they recognize the unrealistic nature of these mental processes but cannot get rid of them, so their internal experiences seem disconnected from external realities (e.g., "I know there's nothing to be afraid of, but I'm scared anyway"). When clients recognize that all anxiety results from the activation of relevant brain modules, which might or might not be in synchrony with external events, the disconnection no longer seems so bizarre. Older clients can understand statements such as:

"I don't think you're crazy, but you have a limbic system, and everybody's limbic system is crazy."

The neuroscientific idea can be integrated into several different theoretical orientations. From its inception, psychodynamic theory was based on semiautonomous mental structures, which Freud presumed had an anatomical basis, although the science of his time did not permit him to know what it was. The neuroscientific idea fits neatly with ACT, with its emphasis on thoughts and feelings that the self did not produce and cannot control. Representing the source of these mental contents as brain modules provides clients with a conception that seems less abstract, easier to picture, and more scientifically based than most ACT metaphors.

Narrative therapy's externalization metaphor might initially seem incompatible with a neurobiological location of unwanted emotions and impulses, because our brains are obviously not external to us in a literal way. However, the boundary between inside and outside is not a simple matter. People seem to think about this boundary in highly abstract, complex, and variable ways, with some mental contents identified as belonging to our core selves and others perceived as, comparatively, external. This is why some emotions and impulses are experienced as incongruent and unwanted. Unwanted by whom? By the core self—which does not include the brain module responsible for the ego-dystonic emotion or thought.

Therapists can make use of the neuroscientific orientation to help clients who blame themselves for having mental health problems. Counselors can explain that we do not choose the genetically based, neurobiological characteristics of our brains, including activity levels of neurotransmitters and brain structures. Sometimes brains are just sad; sometimes they wake up in the morning with a high level of anxiety; and sometimes they are wired with a low threshold for angry responses. This does not mean neurobiology is the only factor, or necessarily the primary one, but it is an important factor in mental health.

The neuroscientific orientation might initially seem to imply helplessness, but it does not. Mental contents affect neurobiology as well as the other way around. As discussed in Chapter 3, numerous studies have demonstrated that psychotherapy changes the brain. Purposeful self-change efforts, whether therapeutic or not, are possible because of the miraculous yet commonplace ability of the brain to change the brain. Clients who suspect that a particular structure is overactive or underactive can recruit other mental capabilities to balance or compensate for it. This neurobiological form of insight often points toward effective strategies for self-management. I refer to this type of therapeutic work as "developing a user's manual for your brain."

Values in Psychotherapy

Traditionally, psychotherapists have attempted to be value-neutral and have maintained a stance of **moral relativism** toward the ethical dimension of client actions. In keeping with 20th-century developments in philosophy, especially postmodernism and deconstructionism, the view has been that values are inevitably relative, subjective, and dependent on perspective. In this view, there is no objective basis for judging the morality of an action, so there is no point in trying to change someone's moral standards. As a result, therapists have traditionally been loathe to impose their values on clients, and counseling has not included work on moral issues beyond nonjudgmental exploration of the beliefs the client already holds.

The philosophical question of whether morality is subjective, objective, or some combination of the two is beyond the scope of this book. However, the clinical question of the role of values in therapy is difficult to avoid because these issues sometimes present themselves in ways that cannot be ignored. Our concern here is with moral choices that affect the welfare of other people, not morality in the sense of sexual practices or religion.

As a practical matter, the moral judgments germane to therapy are often so clear that arguments about subjectivity and objectivity, however interesting they might be in a philosophy seminar, seem beside the point. For example, it seems obvious that a bully who victimizes other children should stop this behavior even if he believes in a value such as, "Wimps deserve to get beaten up," and it seems clear that perpetrators of sexual abuse should change any aspect of their value system that supports this behavior.

Some therapists hesitate to provide input on moral issues because they (rightly) believe that they have no special claim to authority in this area. However, in clinical work, the relevant question is not whether our thinking is infallible but whether it may be more valid and useful than the child's or parent's current view of the issue in question. In morally clear-cut situations like those just cited, I would recommend that therapists speak up unless there is reason to believe that doing so would interfere with some aspect of the counseling.

A commonsensical moral system, practical for use in therapy, can be based on the idea that all human beings are of equal value, so their welfare is equally important. This idea is supported by the observation that virtually all people strive for their version of happiness and suffer when they are victimized or hurt. There is no apparent basis for deciding that one person's well-being is more important than another's. Both historically and in individual situations, judgments that one group's or one person's welfare is more important than others' generally turn out to be self-serving rationalizations for unfair or cruel actions. Therefore, when moral choices are made, the effects of possible actions on the well-being of all the people involved need to be considered and given equal weight.

A commonsensical moral system, practical for use in therapy, can be based on the idea that all human beings are of equal value, so their welfare is equally important.

This crude formulation leaves out all sorts of interesting complexities and ambiguities. (What about people who misunderstand their own needs? What about masochists?). Nonetheless, this framework seems to provide a workable basis for moral judgment and decision making in the vast majority of situations that present themselves in child therapy. In everyday life, the most common threats to prosocial behavior seem to lie not in abstruse moral quandaries but in the common human bias toward weighting one's own interests differently than those of others. This bias is most frequently of concern in therapy for youth with externalizing disorders. These youth sometimes behave as if they consider their own needs to be more important than other people's, and they may be willing to manipulate, intimidate, and even injure others in order to gain relatively small benefits for themselves. In psychopathy, this inequality of concern for self versus others goes to alarming extremes. Youth with internalizing problems sometimes show the opposite inequality by weighting other people's needs more heavily than their own, so they sacrifice their own interests to those of others.

Balancing the Needs of Self and Others

One therapeutic tool for helping both externalizing and internalizing clients move toward balance in their valuation of self and others is our familiar method based on 10-point scales. The spectrum method provides a way to integrate work on the moral issues of concern in externalizing and the self-care issues of concern in internalizing. The relevant spectrum is presented in Figure 8.2 and included in this book's website as Form 8.1, so therapists can print it for use with clients.

In behavior on both sides of this continuum, human beings sustain damage to their welfare. The only difference is the *location* of the damage: self or others. If all people are of equal worth, the location of damage is not fundamental, because the damage is equally regrettable.

The diagram depicts the clear, stark nature of some choices and the quantitative nature of other decisions. Some moral judgments are black-and-white, while in the grey areas

Figure 8.2 (scale: 1 — 2 — 3 — 4 — 5 — 6 — 7 — 8 — 9 — 10)

Scale	1–2	3–4	5–6	7–8	9–10
	Totally selfish and self-centered. Harms and uses others for personal gain. Cold, uncaring and callous.	Big ego. Dominant. Good at speaking up for self and asking for things.	Fair to self and others. Respects and values self and others equally. Looks for win-win solutions or compromise.	People-pleaser. Accommodating. Guilt-prone. Self-denying.	Only cares about others. Won't stand up for self. Won't accept gifts or help. Doormat. Sucker.
	"In a conflict of interest, I must win."				"In a conflict of interest, they must win."
	Sees self as more important than others.		Sees self and others as equally important.		Sees others as more important than self.
	Only takes	Mostly takes	Gives and takes	Mostly gives	Only gives
	Kind only to him/herself	Stingy	Kind to self and others	Over-generous	Kind only to others

Figure 8.2 Balancing the needs of self and others.

there is a fine line between vigorously pursuing one's goals and encroaching on the rights of others, and another fine line between being very generous and subverting one's needs to those of others.

There is one therapeutic message that addresses problems at both ends of the continuum because it articulates the balance-point in the middle. This message may draw people toward balance from both directions:

"I think you are exactly as important as every other person in the world—no more and no less."

This statement expresses a moral ideal that few people achieve, but it is useful as a standard to strive for, and it usually makes sense, at least abstractly, to young people. Clients often have trouble with its specific implications for their actions, but the activity of applying principles to situations seems central to the process of moral development, and this work is a worthwhile therapeutic activity.

In work with externalizing clients who hurt other people, the therapeutic challenge is to facilitate the development of a sense that other people's welfare is as important as one's own. Selfishness and cruelty are based on a lack of empathy (Decety, 2011; Hoffman, 2001), and interventions that strengthen empathy contribute to the development of prosocial behavior in children (Schonert-Reichl, Smith, Zaidman-Zait, & Hertzman, 2012). Empathy is based on a sense that oneself and others are fellow human beings with more similarities than differences and, behind their eyes, other people have an inner reality with experiences of happiness and pain that are just as real as one's own.

There are several strategies that counselors can use to facilitate the development of this sense that other people are as real and important as the self. Because emotional self-awareness facilitates awareness of emotions in others (Asendorpf, Warkentin, & Baudonnière, 1996; Beitel, Ferrer, & Cecero, 2005), the basic counseling techniques of reflection of feelings and meaning, described in Chapter 1, may contribute to the development of empathy. The simple question, "How do you think that made her feel?" prompts the client to think about others' experiences. Because the skill of perspective taking depends on the ability to simulate another person's experience in one's own mind (Chambers & Davis, 2012; Preston & Hofelich, 2012), it is useful to ask clients to imagine how they would feel if they were in the position of another person in an interaction with them—for example:

- "How would you feel if someone said that to you?"
- "How would you feel if you had just lost the game and someone said that to you?"
- "How would you feel if you got teased a lot, and you had just lost the game, and someone said that to you?"

It may also be useful to ask clients how they did feel in any similar situations they experienced themselves. Finally, there is evidence that reading fiction contributes to the development of empathy and emotional intelligence (Mar, Tackett, & Moore, 2010;

Oatley, 2011), so this might provide another useful form of practice. Chapter 12, Aggression and Violence, presents additional information on mechanisms that can cause clients to dehumanize others and strategies therapists can use to counter these mechanisms.

The technique of perspective switching can be used both to help externalizing youth become kinder to others and to help internalizing youth become kinder to themselves. For example, if a client castigated himself because he made a mistake that cost his team a ball game, the counselor could ask how he would feel about a teammate who made a similar mistake. Clients usually say that, as long as the teammate tried his best, they would not be angry at him. The counselor could then ask why the client does not view his own mistake in the same way he would view someone else's, and could add, "It's not fair to be harder on yourself than you are on other people."

When internalizing youth fail to value their own interests sufficiently, therapists should help them identify and question this type of discrimination against the self. Counselors should advocate for the importance of the client's own needs in the same way that, with externalizing clients, they speak up for the importance of other people's welfare.

If all human beings are equally valuable, there are deep commonalities among harming others, harming oneself, and allowing harm to oneself. In work with clients who are excessively self-sacrificing, therapists can offer a variation of the Golden Rule that preserves its logic while extending its reach to the self:

- "But if it's not right for you to take advantage of other people, how can it be right for other people to take advantage of you?"

- "Isn't it right to treat ourselves as well as we treat others? Not better, but just as well—because aren't we equally important?"

A similar line of questioning can be used with clients who feel uncomfortable about receiving help. First, the counselor can ask the youth how she feels about helping others and whether she looks down on people who need help. Most clients' answers will put therapists in a position to say, "If you are glad to help other people, and you don't look down on them for asking, why shouldn't you feel the same way about asking others to help you?"

Children generally develop values less through their own reasoning than by internalizing the values and expectations of important figures in their lives (Eisenberg, Fabes, & Spinrad, 2006; Hoffman, 1983). When therapists have positive relationships with their clients, they can make use of this same internalizing process. By letting clients know our thoughts about values-related behaviors, we can exert a positive influence on their moral development. Of course, a preachy or disrespectful style is counterproductive, but clear input in the context of a collaborative thought process and caring relationship may facilitate the development of positive values and behaviors that benefit both our clients and other people with whom they interact.

While the purpose of kind behavior is to benefit other people, such behavior often produces side benefits for the self. Children's helpful behaviors often elicit praise and rewards from adults as well as reciprocated help and positive relationships with peers (Eisenberg, 2000; Layous et al., 2012). Both organized volunteer work and informal acts of altruism produce feelings of connection with others, increased happiness, and even moments of joy (Aknin, Dunn, & Norton, 2012; Borgonovi, 2008). Long before these studies were conducted, Alyosha, the hero of Dostoyevsky's novel *The Brothers Karamozov*, exclaimed, "How wonderful life is when one does something good and just!"

Incorporating Experiences Into New Structures of Meaning

Finding Words Both True and Kind

In the nitty-gritty, moment-to-moment process of counseling, there is no aspect of therapeutic skill more fundamental than responding to clients with words both true and kind. Therapists should not deny, minimize, or sugarcoat their discussion of client problems, but we also need to maintain a spirit of hope. Generally, it is not difficult to think of accurate statements, and it is not hard to think of affirming statements—it is not hard to be realistic, and it is not hard to be optimistic—but the challenge is to think of statements that have both qualities at the same time. This is a verbal skill, so let's consider some words and phrases that make it possible to accomplish our dual purpose.

Enlarging clients' time frame supports the adaptive combination of being realistic about the present and optimistic about the future—for example:

"This isn't the end of the story; it's the middle of the story."

The phrase "in the process of" communicates that the situation is in flux, not in final form—for instance:

"You're in the process of getting used to your new blended family, and they're getting used to you. It might take a while."

If clients can project themselves into the future, they can imagine looking back on their present situation, which will then be in the past. This type of time travel builds a sense of perspective that contains the current source of distress within a more positive gestalt:

"Someday you'll look back on this and see a tough time you went through once."

Sometimes reframes can be accomplished with a single word. The words "challenge" and "struggle" acknowledge the undesirable nature of situations while also connoting dignity, an active orientation, and the possibility of overcoming the difficulties—for example:

CLIENT: Those kids are so cliquish, but I thought, I've got such cool stuff on my Tumblr page, if I could just get them to take a look at it, so I showed it to a couple of them, and they were like, "Oh, we are so done with Tumblr." It was a disaster.

THERAPIST: Ouch—what a disappointment. Getting in with that group is definitely a challenge, but you're just starting to get to know them, and there's more to you than your Tumblr page.

Other words that reframe defeats as solvable problems include "setback," "obstacle," "twists and turns," and "rollercoaster." One particularly useful phrase is, "difficult but not impossible."

The word "wounded" acknowledges client self-perceptions of being damaged while implying that healing can occur. The word "mistake" can be used to reframe actions about which clients feel debilitating guilt. Therapists can modify client perceptions of themselves as losers by acknowledging that there are psychosocial skills they do need to learn.

True-and-kind combinations do not all hinge on the possibility of the future being different from the present. There may also be a more fair and affirming way to interpret the current situation. For instance, clients who do not fit in with their peers can be described as "a nonconformist" or "your own person." These terms can repair the client's sense of dignity without denying the issue of concern.

As another example, let's consider possible responses to clients who call themselves "crazy." These clients are rarely psychotic. Instead, their emotions are usually intense, painful, and, especially, confusing. Sometimes these emotions are expressed in behaviors that are erratic or disruptive. Unpacking the client's concept of "crazy" into these components does not deny the seriousness of the problem but reduces self-derogation and normalizes the client's experience. On a simple level, it can be reassuring for clients to hear a therapist state unequivocally that they are not crazy—but, to maintain credibility, we must follow with an alternative explanation of the experiences that make them feel this way. We need to supply a new theory that accounts for the old data. The concept of low self-esteem is a versatile tool for this type of work because it provides an alternative explanation for all sorts of negative self-perceptions that, otherwise, might be attributed to truth—for example:

"You're not dumb—you think you are because you have low self-esteem."

The challenge of finding words both true and kind is different in work with internalizing and externalizing clients. When internalizing clients self-criticize, the task is to acknowledge the elements of truth in their negative self-perceptions while adding elements that change the overall structure to one that is compatible with positive self-esteem—for example:

"I understand that you totally blew it with Jeff, and I agree that what you did is no way to handle a problem with a guy. But that doesn't mean you don't have what it takes to get a boyfriend; it just means you're learning how to do this and you're not done yet."

With externalizing clients, the challenge is to show kindness by avoiding personal criticism and empathizing with attraction to antisocial behaviors while also truthfully presenting the likely consequences of those behaviors:

"People take drugs for reasons, and the main one is that drugs make people feel good at the moment, but that doesn't change the fact that you have a life to live, and the drugs you've been taking will make it harder for you to live a good life."

The worse the situation described by the client, the more difficult it is to be encouraging without denying painful truths. When clients are convinced an event or situation is wholly negative, therapist efforts to find positive elements might come across as unsympathetic or even phony. Sometimes these clients are right: There is nothing positive in the situation. But even in these cases, it is possible to identify the potential for good in the client's *response*. As discussed in Chapter 15 on trauma, research on post-traumatic growth provides information about last-resort possibilities for good in the forms of increased personal strength, spiritual growth, learning, closer relationships, and mutual support.

Even when we must give up on finding anything "good," we can help clients see the place of their troubles in the context of their life. Sometimes this results in an appreciation of their personal story. Experiences can be perceived as interesting, remarkable, dramatic, touching, or moving without being pleasant or desirable. Providing a broad, philosophical, or spiritual context for misfortune and pain sometimes helps clients appreciate the meaning of their struggles and supports their sense of dignity in suffering. Many great works of literature demonstrate this transformation of painful, even terrible occurrences into moving stories of courage, nobility, and beauty.

The Extendincorp Strategy

The next sections are about one particular type of inference—namely, inferences in which people view a specific, concrete outcome as a manifestation of a large, general, abstract pattern. For instance, a teenage girl who is rejected by a boy she likes might interpret this outcome as the result of a large reality such as, "I am unattractive," or the result of a different overarching reality such as, "In dating, sometimes things work out, and sometimes they don't." The girl's experience would be influenced by her belief about which generality included the rejection as an instance.

In this type of interpretation, the person implicitly asks the question, "What whole is this event a part *of?*" The importance of the event lies in what it signals or indicates about a larger, deeper reality that is not apparent. In science, there are parallels to this type of part/whole connection in the relationship between a sample and a population, and also in the relationship between data and theory. For scientists and nonscientists alike, viewing a specific outcome as an instance of a general class of events is one operational definition of the word *meaning*.

The extendincorp strategy addresses these part/whole connections by means of a two-part procedure: (1) expanding the client's conception of some aspect of positive functioning (a whole), so she is then able to (2) integrate problematic or painful elements of her functioning (parts) into this conception. Thus, the two steps in this cognitive operation are *extending* a structure of meaning and *incorporating* experiences or behaviors into the expanded structure.

For example, a child who fails a test in school may be extremely upset if he believes this outcome cannot be part of a whole consisting of long-term academic success (i.e., "Only lousy students fail tests"). However, this outcome will not be perceived as a disaster if the child's therapist expands his understanding of the long-term process of school success to include occasional poor performances (i.e., "Some good students fail tests once in a while"). Thus, one way to help clients cope with failure is to extend their concept of success so that it allows for negative outcomes along the way.

In cognitive, constructivist, and some types of family therapy, counselors help clients reframe the meaning of events and behaviors (Alexander & Parsons, 1982; Haley, 1963;

The counselor adds elements to the client's general conception of positive attributes and successful endeavors in order to encompass problematic aspects of his personal experiences.

Minuchin, 1974). The present formulation involves no disagreement with these approaches but seeks to further develop their analyses and implications for treatment. The distinctive feature of the extendincorp strategy is that the therapist seeks to change the structures of meaning into which the client fits his personal events and situations. The counselor adds elements to the client's general conceptions of positive attributes and successful endeavors in order to encompass problematic aspects of his personal experiences. Frequently, this means describing the endeavors of strong, competent people as typically including some errors, misfortunes, and reversals. Thus, while other approaches attempt to change the assignment of parts to wholes, the extendincorp strategy seeks to change the wholes into which the parts are fit.

The extendincorp strategy necessarily involves talking about people in general as well as the client as an individual. The technique attempts to normalize the client's experiences by changing the norms in relation to which she evaluates herself and her life—for example:

"Crying a lot doesn't mean you're having a nervous breakdown. Sometimes, crying is part of coping: It's one way people release tension and get their feelings out. There are very strong people who cry sometimes because it's part of how they deal with things."

As you listen to clients describe upsetting experiences, the question to ask yourself is, "What emotionally acceptable whole could this bad experience be a part of?" Helpful structures of meaning generally have two characteristics. These frameworks must be *plausible*; the client's experiences must fit into the proposed structure in a realistic, believable way, which means there can be no denial. Also, these conceptions must be *adaptive*; they should support positive self-perceptions, be optimistic in their implications for the future, and be conducive to effective behavior. Again, we search for words both true and kind.

The extendincorp strategy can be implemented in forms ranging from brief comments to philosophical discussions. Sometimes, a single word can incorporate a problematic experience into a new, positive structure of meaning—and resolve an Oedipus complex, too. A 6-year-old boy who had battled with his father over his mother's attention suddenly put this acrimony behind him and bonded warmly with his dad. When his father asked about the change, the boy said:

"I used to get mad when Mommy paid attention to you instead of me, but then one day I thought, hey, we can *share* her."

Everyday language includes a number of sayings expressing the idea that negative events can be part of a benign, even a positive, gestalt—for example:

- "Win a few, lose a few."
- "That's life."

- "One step backward, two steps forward."
- "Using lemons to make lemonade."
- "It's usually darkest right before the dawn."

Using the Extendincorp Strategy to Enhance Self-Concept

The extendincorp technique can be used to improve clients' self-esteem. This work hinges on the relationship between the attributes the client already possesses and the qualities she views as valuable and admirable. While cognitive therapy helps clients identify personal attributes that fit into their existing conception of strengths, the extendincorp strategy seeks to expand conceptions of admirable qualities until they take in characteristics the client already possesses but does not value. The expression "making a virtue of a necessity" describes this cognitive operation. Consider the example of a teenage boy who is shy, studious, and not athletic, and who lives in a peer culture that values sports, self-confidence, and extroversion. If the boy's conception of admirable qualities is limited to the view prevalent in his social environment, there is no way for him to think well of himself. But if his conception of winners were broadened to encompass the qualities he already has, he would not have to consider himself a loser. His therapist could say:

> *The extendincorp strategy seeks to expand conceptions of admirable qualities until they take in characteristics that the client already possesses but has not valued.*

"Being athletic, confident, and sociable is one way to be cool; being quiet, thoughtful, and intelligent is another."

Counselors can use reason and evidence to widen the range of human attributes that the client considers valuable. To continue with our example, the therapist could point out that introverted, studious individuals have made major contributions to society that helped many people in substantial ways (Cain, 2012).

Peer cultures sometimes have narrow conceptions of valuable human qualities, and it is difficult for youth to appreciate personal attributes that are not respected by their peers. Fortunately, conceptions of success and attractiveness often diversify as people grow older, and clients may feel better if they believe that time is on their side—for example:

"Do you think Bill Gates was popular in middle school? I doubt it. A lot of smart kids who are considered nerds when they're young become extremely successful when they grow up. So, no, I don't think you're a loser; I just think the game you're going to win hasn't started yet."

Utilizing Achievement Motivation in Therapy

Achievement motivation is the desire to demonstrate excellence in the skillful performance of a challenging task (Atkinson & Raynor, 1974; McClelland, Atkinson, Clark, & Lowell, 1953). This motive is about the desire to perform well for its own sake, as a matter of pride in a job well done, not about extrinsic rewards, such as money or grades, although these often accompany excellent performance. Traditional operational definitions of achievement situations have included school, work, entrepreneurship, and sports. However, the definition is abstract and psychological, not a matter of concrete particulars, which means that anything can be an achievement situation if it engages a person's desire to perform well.

Achievement motivation can be an empowering source of energy for coping, personal improvement, and work toward therapeutic goals. Counselors can help clients make use of this internal resource by extending their conception of achievement to include adaptive responses to any difficult situation they face. Stressful situations can be portrayed as opportunities to develop and demonstrate coping skills and related personal strengths. As examples, a client with separation anxiety could view overnight camp as a chance to use his new self-soothing skills, and a depressed youngster could view setbacks as opportunities to practice generating realistic, adaptive thoughts. It is only in tense situations that a person can stay cool under pressure, and it is only when the going gets tough that the tough can get going.

Anything can be framed as a skill, including dealing with undesirable situations in an adaptive manner.

Anything can be framed as a skill, including dealing with undesirable situations in an adaptive manner. For instance, in school, learning from bad teachers is a skill—and a more impressive one than learning from good teachers, which most students can do. Dealing with obnoxious people is a skill. So is recovering from romantic disappointment, maintaining commitment to values in the midst of antisocial peers, and coping with a disability.

By focusing on the client's use of skills and strategies, rather than the environment's response (which is less reliable), therapists can encourage clients to strive for personal development rather than merely wishing for desired outcomes. In turn, clients can become more autonomous and grounded in a strong sense of self, rather than being dependent on external outcomes for their sense of well-being. For example, a client who is invested in effective use of an anger management technique can feel good about her maintenance of self-control even if an obnoxious peer continues to harass her. This is a fundamental strategy for finding the potential for good in the midst of bad situations, because the possibility of personal growth exists under virtually all circumstances. People who are invested in this type of growth are well positioned for the development of resilience.

Therapists should be careful not to overstate this case or we will come across as unsympathetic and phony. People's first choice is to enjoy good fortune and get the things they want. Personal growth is a consolation prize—but it is much better than nothing. Here are examples that address both sides of this issue:

- "If you need to have that surgery, I hope you'll try to be a good patient and work hard on your rehabilitation. That's your challenge now."

- "I'm sorry your step-siblings are so annoying. I guess the most constructive thing to do in this type of situation is to figure out how to make the best of it. This could be an opportunity to develop new skills, like getting along with people who are hard to like. That's actually a very useful skill in life."

Even failing, in the right way, is a skill. For example, one client was afraid of making outs in his Little League games because he believed this meant he was a bad player. By portraying outs as an inevitable part of the game, discussing how to conduct oneself in this situation, and asking the client to observe the behavior of major league players when they made outs, the counselor extended the client's conception of being a good baseball player to include "making an out like a pro." Similarly, a girl stopped having tantrums in response to homework she could not do when she came to view staying calm in this situation as more of an accomplishment than getting the problems right. In both examples, the extendincorp strategy transformed events that had been considered pure failures into opportunities for successes of a certain type. Therapists can achieve reframes like these by identifying the behavior they want the client to acquire and then constructing a conception of success *around* that behavior.

The Extendincorp Strategy With Externalizing Clients

The extendincorp strategy needs to be implemented in different ways depending on whether the target of intervention is internalizing or externalizing dysfunction. When internalizing is the focus, the framework to enlarge is the client's conception of a positive life and self, and the objective is to incorporate his failures and disappointments into this framework. When externalizing is the focus, and the client has a negative view of prosocial functioning, the framework to enlarge is his conception of appealing, attractive behavior, and the objective is to shoehorn prosocial functioning into this framework.

Sometimes, clients persist in maladaptive behaviors not because of the goals they hope to achieve but because of the meanings they perceive in these behaviors. For example, an aggressive youth might agree that fighting results in more negative than positive consequences, but he might continue to fight because he believes that violence is the only honorable response to disrespect from other people. A youth might resist working hard in school, even though she sees the benefits associated with success, because she views academic striving as an uncool, submissive attempt to win adult approval. When the point of an action is its meaning, not its consequences, therapists will be unable to dissuade youth from engaging in the behavior by demonstrating that it does not "work." Instead, it is necessary to change the meanings that the client perceives in these behaviors and the alternatives to them.

The meanings valued by clients, like the abstract goals they pursue, are usually positive, but problems sometimes lie in the way that youth operationally define the meanings they value. Striving for personal honor is potentially positive, although this striving sometimes takes the form of violence, and wanting to be an independent, fun-loving person can motivate positive behavior as well as refusal to work in school.

One strategy for addressing this type of situation is to agree with the client about the meanings or personal qualities he values but to challenge his behavioral definitions of these qualities. Such challenges involve: (a) questioning whether the client's dysfunctional behaviors are truly consistent with the meanings he intends those behaviors to have and, perhaps more importantly, (b) extending the operational definitions of meanings the client already values so that the behavioral goals of treatment fall under these new definitions. For example, youth whose violent behavior is motivated by a desire to prove themselves strong and tough may become motivated to learn conflict management skills if their conception of strength is extended to include the type of self-control and "street smarts" that enable people to handle difficult situations without violence. These discussions can begin with open-ended questions, such as, "What is strength?" and "What is toughness?," and can proceed to discussion of different types of strength. Here are two more examples:

- "If you're as tough as you say you are, you'll be able to listen to my feedback about your behavior and have an intelligent conversation about whether you really want to continue this behavior."

- "I suppose you can let your teachers flunk you and keep you in eighth grade next year, while your friends move up to high school. But I wonder if there's a part of you that would like to show them they can't beat you so easily."

Metaphorically, the therapist paints the behaviors that are the goals of treatment with colors the client already likes.

Metaphorically, the therapist paints the behaviors that are the goals of treatment with colors the client already likes. Thus, if the client values strength, the therapist depicts peaceful behavior as strong. This type of intervention allows clients to continue adhering to their principles while changing only the concrete, behavioral definition of these principles.

Meanings of Emotional Pain

The extendincorp technique can be applied to clients' emotional distress to help them tolerate, manage, and even utilize their pain. Counselors can facilitate effective coping by helping clients incorporate their suffering into adaptive structures of meaning.

From an evolutionary perspective, pain has information value as a signal that something is wrong, with physical pain pertaining to our bodies and psychological pain signaling that something is wrong in our lives. However, the system does not work perfectly. Physical pain is sometimes misleading as a signal about the state of the body (there may be pain with no other pathology), and emotional distress is sometimes misleading as feedback about behavior. Not infrequently, positive actions are accompanied by pain. (As discussed in Chapter 4, ACT is based on this premise.) Combinations of positive actions and painful experiences occur, for example, when people undergo painful medical procedures, withdraw from addictive substances, change maladaptive habits, confront fears, and address difficult issues in therapy.

One important example of the link between positive behavior and negative affect is self-control. When self-control is exerted at high levels, discomfort inevitably results. In the short term, giving in to impulses feels better than resisting them, which means the ability to tolerate discomfort is necessary for self-control (Baumeister & Tierney, 2011). Clients who want to change maladaptive behaviors often need to increase this ability, and therapists can help by explaining the positive meaning of some negative affect, so clients can respect their constructive choices even when these choices cause distress. This combination of goodness and pain may be confusing, but it is actually central to what is admired about human behavior in the moral sphere—for example:

- "Anyone can do the right thing when it's easy, but it takes something to do the right thing when it's hard. That's my definition of heroism."

- "In a way, the more it hurts, the more respect you deserve—from me, from other people, and from yourself."

When good behaviors feel bad, the danger is that people will quit before their struggle bears fruit. Therapists can help clients persist by portraying their distress as a necessary and temporary part of a worthwhile whole, rather than an indication of being on the wrong track. Counselors can use a metaphor of a tunnel going through a mountain to convey this idea to clients:

"It's like you want to get from a bad place to a better one, but there's a mountain blocking your path, and the only way through is a long, dark, cramped tunnel. As you move into it, the tunnel gets darker and darker, and stuffier and stuffier. The further you go, the worse you feel—and you think, 'Maybe this is a mistake; I'd better turn back.' But you should still keep going forward because, even though things feel worse, actually they are getting better, since you are moving closer and closer to your goal. If you keep going forward, you will move through the tunnel and come out the other side, into the sunshine and the better place where you want to be."

Figure 8.3 describes a sequence that often happens when people work on a problem such as overcoming a fear or changing a habit: Things feel worse before they feel better, even though in the underlying process, things are moving forward and getting better all the time. Therapists can use this graph with older clients. At the beginning of change efforts, people are located on the steep, upward portion of the curve, where the going is tough. We can draw a straight, downward-slanting, dotted line from the graph's start-point to its endpoint, where distress has abated, thus cutting off the hump, and then we can say, wistfully:

"Wouldn't it be great if the pain started decreasing as soon as people started working on the problem? Unfortunately, no one knows how to do that. If you and I figure out a way, we'll win a Nobel Prize. In the meantime (pointing to the curve), this way involves some pain and takes some strength, but it does work."

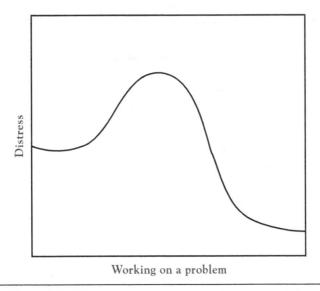

Figure 8.3   Distress as a temporary part of a positive whole.

Emotional pain sometimes signals an adaptive response to a negative situation. For instance, distress in response to a setback indicates strong motivation to succeed. Being upset about problems in a relationship signals constructive motivation to improve the relationship. These types of distress have positive meanings because they indicate an early stage of a larger process that could lead to a good outcome.

When people begin looking into their difficulties, especially those they had previously tried to ignore, emotional pain often results. This is true on an individual level and, in family therapy, on a systems level. Although the client's current *position* might be revealed as worse than she had thought, she is engaged in positive *movement* toward a better position in the future. It helps to know this. Therapists can say:

- "Sometimes, finding out how bad things are is the first step toward making them better."
- "When people overcome problems, there is usually some struggle and pain, especially at the beginning."

In externalizing youth, guilt is a positive prognostic sign because it indicates appropriate discomfort with irresponsible or hurtful behavior, and such discomfort is a step toward change (Frick, Ray, Thornton, & Kahn, 2014). When these youth begin developing self-control, they often experience frustration, strain, and even depression, because inhibiting impulses and delaying gratification are hard work, especially for youth who are not accustomed to exercising these capabilities. It is important for these clients to understand that, counterintuitively, their distress is a sign of progress, not an indication that they are on the wrong track. The expression "no pain, no gain" provides a positive framework of meaning that includes discomfort. Counselors can also say:

- "I'm glad you're smart enough to feel bad about what you did, because it shows you're getting ready to do better. That anger at yourself can become energy for positive change."
- "Sometimes behaviors that *feel* bad actually *are* good, because those behaviors will make things better in the long run."
- "What you're experiencing is the feeling of changing from an old way to a new way of doing things; it's not easy and, at first, it hurts."

There is a saying in learning theory that "learning depends on failure." This means that people (and animals) generally develop new capabilities not when their existing repertoire of behavior meets their needs but when things go wrong and new responses become necessary. An older, more philosophical version of this idea is expressed in the saying that "Suffering is good for the soul," and in Nietzsche's statement, "That which does not destroy me strengthens me." Obstacles and setbacks require people to develop new strengths, and these strengths might prove valuable in the future—for example:

- "Maybe going through this will make you a stronger person, and you'll be more able to handle other problems that come your way in life."
- "When things go well for people, they usually roll along without thinking too much, but when they're hit with problems, they often stop and do some serious thinking about life. So I'm glad we've met, because if we put our heads together, I bet we'll figure something out."

Sometimes negative events and situations add to our ability to help others:

"Once you've worked out some ways to handle life in a wheelchair, maybe you'll be able to help other kids dealing with it for the first time. You could become an expert in this."

Meanings of Being a Therapy Client

The extendincorp technique can address youngsters' feelings about being psychotherapy clients. Some youth believe that having mental health problems means they are weak, weird, crazy, or inadequate in some way. The source of this belief might be that the client's conception of strong, sane people excludes the possibility of behavioral or emotional difficulties. If so, therapists can help by expanding the client's conception so it does include admirable, capable people with this type of problem. Authoritative, psychoeducational statements are sometimes useful here:

"Some of the finest people in the world have psychological problems."

To elaborate this point, counselors can provide information about people with mental health problems who made major contributions to society and, in fact, achieved greatness (e.g., Lincoln, Beethoven). On a more down-to-earth level:

"There are plenty of kids who are smart, nice, and good in all sorts of ways—but you know what? They have a psychological problem, too."

Young people do not usually want to become therapy clients, but, once in this position, therapists can help them view counseling as an honorable endeavor with the potential to produce benefits. Counselors should explain that therapy can help people learn and grow in response to troubles. Youth who become interested in understanding and overcoming problems can be comfortable and even enthusiastic about the role of therapy client—for instance:

> "Therapy is an opportunity—although one you didn't ask for—to learn some things about yourself and about life."

Some clients, particularly males, feel that accepting help for personal problems is a weak, pitiable thing to do. Therapists can respond by extending the client's conception of strength to include the ability to make use of help:

- "Sometimes people feel uncomfortable about receiving help because they think it means they're weak. But people who feel secure about themselves have the strength to do whatever it takes to make things better, and they use every tool they can."
- "No one is completely independent except hermits who live alone in the woods. Help from other people is out there—it's a resource in the world—and I don't see what it accomplishes to live with one hand tied behind your back. If you're sick, is it weak to call a doctor? If your house catches on fire, is it weak to call the fire department? Making use of help from other people is a skill, and you're better off with it than without it."

When client progress is interrupted by a resurgence of symptoms, counselors can prevent undue discouragement by extending the youth's conception of therapeutic progress to include such reversals. Therapists can explain that symptoms do not usually decrease in a consistent manner but, instead, *typically* exhibit ups and downs. Setbacks can be portrayed as opportunities:

> "We're both sorry you had another panic attack, especially after you were doing so well for a while. But this doesn't mean you're back to square one. In a way, this is a good opportunity, because setbacks are bound to happen sooner or later, and now you have a chance to practice bouncing back from one."

Overcoming Fear of Failure

Fear of failure is not a diagnosis; it is a type of anxiety and a psychological dynamic that impairs the functioning of clients across diagnostic categories. Research in the areas of achievement motivation (Atkinson & Raynor, 1974; Covington, 2000; McClelland et al., 1953) and sports psychology (Conroy, 2004; Passer, 1983) has illuminated the causes and consequences of fear of failure. This research has produced findings that apply to a wide range of life issues and are sometimes useful in therapy.

Fear of failure does not help people do better; it causes them to do worse. Failure anxiety impairs concentration by causing a distracting focus on the self, which reduces attention available for the tasks to be performed. For instance, fear of failure might absorb the attention of a child working on an arithmetic test with thoughts like, "I wonder how many of these I've gotten wrong so far.... I don't know whether I'll pass this test.... Flunking would mean I'm no good at math." In contrast, children with little fear of failure could devote most of their attention to the activity of solving the problems, so their minds would be filled with the mechanics of math. Children can redirect their attention from self-evaluation to the content of the test with self-statements like, "I can worry later about how well I did on this test; right now, I just need to focus on the material I learned in class."

Although this might seem counterintuitive, fear of failure reduces effort at challenging tasks. The key to understanding this finding is to recognize that "failure," here, concerns the effects of poor task performance on perceptions of the self ("ego" in the lay sense), not external *Fear of failure reduces effort at challenging tasks.* consequences of failure, such as poor grades. People with strong fear of failure may believe they have a great deal of potential, but they are afraid to test their ability by seeing what would happen if they made a full effort to succeed. As a result, they want to avoid tasks unless they are sure of success. When avoidance is not feasible, they invest as little effort as possible, so failure will not reflect badly on their abilities. Low effort is equivalent to partial avoidance. People who are anxious about failure feel that if they do not try, they cannot really fail, because they might have succeeded if they had tried; thus, they preserve their belief in their raw ability. This dynamic is an important factor in procrastination (Haghbin, McCaffrey, & Pychyl, 2012).

Whether the context is school, sports, or dating, reduced effort protects self-esteem in the event of failure, but at a high cost: missing out on opportunities to pursue goals, develop skills, and succeed. Counselors can explain that "You miss every shot you don't take." Learning to cope with failure in small doses, as part of everyday life, actually reduces the likelihood of long-term failure.

People are not usually aware of the mechanisms by which they avoid risk of failure, because these mechanisms involve self-deception. Clients sometimes derogate the challenges they avoid to preserve their belief that they could succeed, if they did try. Statements that "I don't care" sometimes reflect fear of failure, because caring about a goal involves vulnerability and risk. People sometimes try to save face by saying, "I don't want to," when their real feeling is, "I can't."

Client insight into this dynamic is an important step toward change, because when clients take a clear-eyed look at the trade-off, they usually realize that sacrificing real possibilities for success to protect self-esteem is not truly in their best interests. Nonetheless, the realization that one is afraid of failure does not necessarily reduce the fear.

Detoxifying Failure

Research on the development of achievement motivation suggests how fear of failure can be reduced: Parents of children with low levels of this anxiety usually emphasize effort, not outcome, in their feedback (Gunderson et al., 2013; Pomerantz & Kempner, 2013). These parents praise their children for trying hard, express disapproval for lack of effort, and do not place undue emphasis on whether the child succeeds or fails at particular tasks. Classroom studies of teachers and students also indicate that praise for effort results in high levels of persistence and achievement, while praise for intelligence or talent makes children feel pressured and actually undermines their motivation and performance (Haimovitz & Henderlong, 2011; Mueller & Dweck, 1998; Ricci, 2013). Extreme praise (e.g., "You're a genius!") makes children especially anxious because they doubt their ability to sustain the extraordinary performances their parents seem to perceive. Therapists can explain to parents that saying, "I'm proud of you for working so hard on this project" is more effective than saying, "I'm proud of you for being so smart." Clients who internalize these reinforcement contingencies learn to self-reinforce for effort and gain an ability to persist in the face of failure.

Research by Carol Dweck and colleagues has demonstrated the adaptive value of fluid conceptions of ability that emphasize the possibility of growth, versus static conceptions of ability as a fixed trait, which has maladaptive consequences (Dweck, 2007; Romero, Master, Paunesku, Dweck, & Gross, 2014; Ricci, 2013). Children with **growth mindsets** believe they can become smarter by working hard in school; these youth are less anxious about failure and more persistent when they encounter difficulties, compared to youth with **fixed mindsets**, who believe that people are born with a set level of intelligence. Both mindsets result in self-fulfilling prophecies, because effort and practice really do produce increases in ability, while people who do not believe in this possibility will not make the efforts that could prove its existence. Dweck's school program teaches that the brain is like a muscle that becomes stronger when it is exercised, and the more the better. (An online version for middle and high school students is available at www.brainology.us.)

Therapists who utilize these findings can help clients overcome fear of failure and unshackle their motivation to achieve. The essential idea is that a young person's skill set is always a work in progress. If abilities really were unchangeable, it would make sense to interpret failure as an indication of permanently weak ability. However, while genetic factors play a role, skill development *is* a process, and viewing it as such changes the meaning of failure to one in which we encounter limits to our abilities and then have an opportunity to push, stretch, and strengthen these abilities. Just like in the gym, we strengthen ourselves most when we struggle and strain against difficult challenges.

Fear of failure is based on a view of achievement-related tasks as assessments that *reveal* how capable we are. In the growth mindset, these tasks are viewed as practice opportunities that *change* our capabilities, regardless of whether we succeed or fail. In the course of developing abilities, direction of change is more important than level of ability at any particular time. Counselors can explain that how good we are today is not as important as how good we become tomorrow:

> "If you try and fail, you might not be good yet, but you're in the process of getting better—and if you keep going, it's only a matter of time before you get good."

Counselors can help clients develop growth mindsets by extending their conception of long-term success to include short-term failure. Two well-known examples are Albert Einstein, who did poorly in elementary school, and Michael Jordan, who was cut from his high school basketball team. More examples can be found at http://www.onlinecollege .org/2010/02/16/50-famously-successful-people-who-failed-at-first/. If the therapist has encountered a setback similar to the client's, self-disclosure may provide a demonstration that childhood difficulties are not necessarily the first stage of long-term failure.

Failure is frightening to the degree that it is viewed as predictive of more failure. The two mindsets involve different views of the predictive power of short-term outcomes. In the fixed mindset, current performance is viewed as an indication of whether we have what it takes to succeed. The growth mindset involves a long time frame in which immediate outcomes are not viewed as very predictive of the future.

When clients are highly anxious about an exam, therapists can ask them to calculate the number of tests they will take during their academic careers (tests per class × classes per year × years in school). With this number as a denominator, the test currently making them nervous emerges as a tiny fraction of their overall academic record.

With older clients, therapists can use graphs with a sawtooth form (see Figure 8.4) to portray a process of long-term success that includes short-term setbacks. Counselors can explain that the process of achieving real-world goals (in business, etc.) *typically* exhibits this sawtooth form. Also, this complicated type of trajectory toward success certainly provides the basis for more stories, novels, and movies than a simple, straight line going up, because it is more likely to be interesting, moving, and even inspiring.

Failure is not merely survivable; it has the potential for good. The key variable is not whether or how much we fail but how we respond when we do. Failure can always produce learning and lead to improvement, so its value for the future might more than offset its disappointing meaning in the present. Whether clients are working on academic or psychosocial skills, the process of trying, failing, learning, and trying again will eventually lead to some form of success, and this process is more important than the particular outcomes occurring along the way. Therapists can say:

- "Everyone fails sometimes—unless they never try anything hard. The thing that separates the men from the boys and the women from the girls is what people do after they fail."
- "A low grade on a test means something bad about what you know now, but if you figure out what went wrong and how to do better the next time, making good use of this failure will help you succeed in the future—and that's what counts."

The meanings and values people associate with failure influence their responses to setbacks. The question is, what does failure mean? The simplest answer is that failure

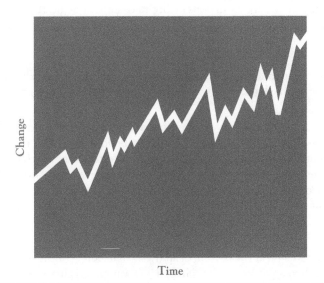

Figure 8.4   Short-term failures within a process of long-term success.

indicates personal inadequacy—but that is not a sophisticated or insightful answer, as explained ahead.

Many of the factors that determine success or failure at particular tasks are beyond the individual's control. No one chooses the conditions in which she grows up, and no one chooses her natural abilities. Our inborn talents, or lack thereof, are essentially a matter of luck, so there is no valid justification for taking credit or blame for them. Effort is under our control, at least to a considerable extent, so it is a truer index of character. Persistence in the face of failure requires willpower, resilience, tolerating emotional pain, and resisting the temptation of self-deception. When you think about it, the courage to try seems a more substantial basis of pride than the good fortune of having natural ability. Taking pride in this form of strength can reduce fear of failure because it provides a dimension on which success can be achieved even while failure is occurring on others. People who value this form of character know that no one who tried his best has anything to be ashamed of.

As discussed earlier in this chapter, everyone's first choice is to enjoy the good fortune of easy success, and the arduous process of developing complex strengths like persistence is a consolation prize. Nonetheless, when asked, most clients say they *envy* people for whom success comes quickly and easily, but they *admire* people who overcome obstacles in order to succeed. Tenacity in the face of setbacks thus provides a valid basis for positive self-esteem.

Skill development depends on repeated practice, and the skill of coping with failure is no exception. It is impossible to practice persistence without encountering difficulties, so it is both ironic and true that failure is an opportunity to develop an important skill. Therapists can ask clients how people get better at soccer, math, and so forth, and then ask how people get better at failure.

The principles governing fear of failure can apply to any endeavor, including therapy. Fear of failing at personal change often presents, in a disguised way, as denial of the need for change. Clients who are afraid they might be unable to overcome difficulties sometimes attribute them to temporary, quirky factors that will not recur and so can be ignored. These youth give their parents unconvincing reassurances while they hope for a magical turnaround and avoid the hard work of change. Counselors can address this issue by saying:

> "What do you want to do? Cheer yourself up by convincing yourself that things are already okay, or think about what you could do to make things better for real?"

People do not enter therapy to develop abilities that come naturally to them. Counseling is about facing weaknesses in order to build strengths in those areas. When clients gain an understanding of their problems, they often discover that they must lean into their most sensitive issues and strengthen their least developed capabilities to achieve therapy goals. Counselors can encourage clients in this arduous work by recognizing the nature of its difficulty, so the client respects the significance of what she is trying to do and sees the virtue in the necessity–for example:

> "So I guess what we find at the bottom of all this is that feeling of embarrassment, which you hate more than anything. It looks like, if you want to go after the things you want, you'll have to steer right into the danger of embarrassment, because trying your best puts

you out there like that. You are being called on to learn and grow in exactly the area that's given you the most trouble. It will be a great achievement, if you can do it—and I believe you can."

The same principle applies to parents:

"You wouldn't be here if your natural style of parenting worked with Emily. You are being called upon to grow as a parent, learn new skills, and add some techniques to your repertoire."

The current culture of business, especially high-tech start-up companies, supports adaptive attitudes toward failure. Zafar (2011) described how Silicon Valley entrepreneurs wear their business failures as badges of honor, include bankruptcies in their resumes, and discuss their failed projects on blogs and in talks at conferences. This is not an exercise in masochism; these businesspeople understand that innovative, ambitious projects always involve risk of failure, and the only way to know which projects will work is to try them. In this environment, failure is viewed as a step on the path to success—as long as it is mined for information and lessons about how to do better the next time. Children and adolescents benefit from adopting this attitude toward their own endeavors.

Summary

This chapter describes an array of therapeutic techniques that do not fit neatly into any theoretical orientation. These strategies, which are based on clinical experience and general psychological research, are small in scope and do not make up complete treatments, but they might fill gaps in what the major therapeutic approaches offer to clients.

The chapter includes suggestions for constructing therapeutic diagrams, transporting in-session intentions to the everyday environment, identifying new ways to meet needs that have motivated maladaptive behavior, and helping parents manage money-related problems with their children. I described how parents' psychodynamic issues can block their implementation of behavioral child management techniques, and I suggested ways to help parents reprocess these issues. Our procedure for developing balance between opposite extremes was extended to a number of additional clinical problems.

Psychoeducation is an information-based type of intervention that illuminates the client's situation by applying general knowledge about human functioning. For example, research in neuroscience and behavior genetics has produced important insights into mental health, and some parents and older clients find this information useful.

Moral issues are sometimes unavoidable in therapy. This chapter includes a simple, practical framework that therapists can use to help clients make sense of moral issues. The framework can be used to help externalizing clients value others more and to help internalizing clients value themselves more.

The question for therapists to ask themselves as they use the extendincorp technique is, "What is the structure of meaning that, if properly extended, could incorporate a problematic aspect of this client's functioning in a therapeutic way?" Many client problems fit into one of the frameworks listed in Table 8.1.

Table 8.1   Problems and Frameworks of Meaning Into Which They Can Fit

Problem	Conception to extend
Overreaction to setbacks	Vicissitudes of successful long-term endeavors
Low self-esteem	Range of positive human qualities (to include client's)
Self-perceived weakness (e.g., crying)	Forms of strength (to include client's)
Overreaction to failure	Forms of achievement (to include coping with failure)
Externalizing	Appealing behavior (to include prosocial behavior)
Guilt	The process of self-improvement (to include guilt)
Unalterably negative events	Opportunities to demonstrate and develop coping
Emotional distress	Feelings associated with positive processes

The last item in Table 8.1 requires elaboration because there are several types of positive processes that can result in emotional pain. The client's distress:

- May be a short-term component of a process leading to long-term success.
- May indicate positive motives and qualities in the client.
- May contain useful information for the client.
- May indicate the client is doing things right, not wrong.

The abstract issue underlying the extendincorp strategy is the relationship between good and bad in human life. The strategy makes sense because bad things are sometimes indications or parts of good things. People's experience of negative situations can be transformed in a therapeutic way when they see the relationship of a negative part to a positive whole that would not be the same without it.

Fear of failure reduces effort at challenging tasks because people with this anxiety feel that, if they do not try, they cannot really fail. Failure can be detoxified by reframing it from an indication of personal inadequacy to a transient, normal experience and an opportunity for learning and skill development that can contribute to future successes.

PART II

THE NEEDS OF CLIENTS

PART II

THE MEDIA OF CULTURE

9

Cultural Factors in Therapy

OBJECTIVES

This chapter explains:

- *Important dimensions of culture.*
- *Psychotherapy's historical development in the context of European American culture.*
- *The components of cultural competence for therapists.*
- *Basic features of European American, African American, Latino/a, Asian, and LGBT cultures.*
- *How to assess the cultural identities of minority clients.*
- *How to modify therapy to fit the cultures of clients.*
- *How to help clients adapt to the culture of therapy.*
- *Ways to talk about experiences of prejudice and discrimination with clients.*
- *How to use spirituality and religious principles in therapy.*

Case Study
Between Two Worlds

Carlita, a 12-year-old Mexican American girl, was brought to therapy by her parents because her school principal told them to do so. Carlita's teachers reported that her school performance had recently declined from below average to unsatisfactory. The teachers said this decline was accompanied by nervousness and complaints of stomachaches and feeling faint. Carlita seemed worried and preoccupied, and she bit her nails. After a medical examination found no physical basis for her complaints, the therapist made a diagnosis of Generalized Anxiety Disorder.

Carlita was born in Mexico and came to the United States with her family when she was 6 years old. She had three siblings who were considerably older than she. Spanish was the language used at home, but Carlita's school and neighborhood were ethnically diverse, she had English-speaking friends, and language limitations did not play a role in her academic problems.

The parents seemed confused and distressed about being in a mental health clinic. When asked why they had come, they said the principal told them they needed to do so to avoid a special school placement for their daughter. The mother seemed open but unenthusiastic about therapy, and the father seemed offended by the idea. Both parents believed Carlita's problems could be solved by serious, concerted prayer and participation in Catholic religious practice, but they were willing to participate in therapy if that was needed to satisfy the school.

The Role of Culture in Psychotherapy

A **culture** can be defined as a set of meanings, norms, values, and customs that are shared by members of a large social group or society. Culture can be contrasted with *personality*, which involves individual differences that are not a function of group membership. Membership in cultural groups is associated with feelings of belonging, a sense of similarity and common fate with other members, and shared traditions.

In groups defined by race, ethnic group, and religion, cultures are transmitted through the generations largely by parenting practices (Cole, Bruschi, & Tamang, 2002; Sue & Sue, 2013). In groups defined by sexual orientation, ability/disability status, social class, and age, cultural influences are transmitted largely by peer groups and media.

Especially in diverse societies, such as the United States, most people's cultural identity includes multiple components rather than one single, defining feature (Pantalone, Iwamasa, & Martell, 2010). When we refer, for example, to Asian Americans, Catholics, gay people, or the poor, we are not fully describing the cultural makeup of any one individual but, instead, are choosing to discuss one cultural characteristic at a time.

Stereotyping is a crude cognitive operation that ignores the reality of individual differences and defines people by their group (Franzoi, 1996). Research indicates that experiences specific to individuals have stronger effects than large-group experiences on psychological characteristics, behavior, and adjustment (Bale et al., 2010; Foster & MacQueen, 2008). Therefore, knowledge of an individual's cultural background does not necessarily provide reliable information about that person.

Thus, there is a dilemma at the heart of our endeavor to be culturally competent: Cultures have characteristics, which means that groups of people share commonalities, but generalizations about groups ignore individual differences (Lee, 2006; Pantalone et al., 2010). We want to achieve a balance that combines valid generalizations about cultural tendencies with attention to individual variation. To do this, we need to understand that there is nothing wrong with "making a generalization" as long as we know it *is* a generalization, not a factual statement about any particular individual.

Sue and Sue (2013) offer a tripartite conceptual scheme that is based on an old saying: "All individuals, in many respects, are (a) like no other individuals, (b) like some individuals, and (c) like all other individuals" (p. 41). In other words, a person's characteristics can be partitioned into: (a) unique qualities, (b) characteristics shared with individuals who are similar to the person on some dimension, which includes culture, and (c) universal attributes of human nature. This framework provides therapists with a useful way of organizing client attributes.

Acculturation is the process by which people internalize elements of new cultures. Acculturation is an important process for immigrants, who typically internalize their new culture gradually and progressively over several generations (Kohatsu, Concepcion, & Perez, 2009). Acculturation is a stressful process that requires "psychic effort" and can cause anxiety symptoms (Barrett, Sonderegger, & Xenos, 2003). **Assimilation** involves an exclusive identification with the host culture and a loss of the original ethnic identity. Writers in multicultural studies generally advocate **biculturalism**, because this synthesis is typically associated with good self-esteem and successful adjustment (Sue & Sue, 2013).

In immigrant populations, different rates of acculturation in parents and children can lead to conflict between the generations (Sonderegger & Barrett, 2004). This was the case in Carlita's family. The client was a bicultural child, but she experienced conflict and confusion about combining Mexican and American components in her identity. Because her parents were much less acculturated, Carlita's characteristically adolescent conflicts with them were intertwined with her internal conflicts about cultural identity. The therapist observed that these conflicts seemed to contribute to Carlita's anxiety and distress.

In immigrant populations, different rates of acculturation in parents and children can lead to conflict between the generations.

Cultural influences flow in multiple directions, because immigrants influence their host culture and minority groups influence the predominant culture, as well as the other way around. For example, African Americans have probably had more impact on American popular music and culture than any other minority group. Observation of schools and playgrounds in the United States quickly reveals the influence of African American culture on the dress, music, language, and gestures of youth of all American ethnicities, as 7-year-old White boys greet each other by saying, "Whatup, man?" Culture is a rich, evolving story, not a matter of static categories.

Culturally Competent Therapy

Historically, psychotherapy originated in Europe and North America. For approximately the first 100 years of our field's development, it evolved within the framework of the Western or European American worldview (Laungani, 2004). There certainly were non-Caucasian therapy practitioners and writers during this time, but these professionals were generally members of minority groups who had assimilated the European and American cultures in which they lived. The theory and practice of therapy developed with little awareness of the different perspectives that other cultures could bring. During the 1980s, this began to change, and now most therapists are aware of the important effects that cultural factors have on human behavior, mental health problems, and psychotherapy.

Nevertheless, it is still the case that the culture of therapy is based on Western culture (Lum, 2011). This is apparent in the basic assumptions of the therapeutic endeavor that are so familiar we might not notice them. For example, there is belief in the value of science, practitioners become credentialed by completing courses of university study, and clients disclose intimate details of their lives to strangers in an attempt to get help. These are not self-evidently valid practices or universal features of human societies but characteristically Western practices.

There are problems associated with practice and research conducted within one cultural framework. **Ethnocentrism** means mistaking one's own cultural perspective and norms as universal principles of human life, so ideas from outside this framework are considered objectively wrong and behaviors not normative in this context are considered deviant and maladaptive (Arnett, 2009; Hays, 2008). Ethnocentrism might not involve conscious or intentional hostility toward members of other groups, but an inability to step outside one's frame of reference leads to pathologizing and stigmatizing culturally different individuals.

Ethnocentrism is based on a lack of awareness of other cultures. Because of the learning process called habituation, people are unresponsive to familiar, unvarying stimuli, and awareness depends on novelty, contrast, and change (Pinker, 2009). This concept is expressed in the saying, "If you ask a fish to tell you about his environment, the last thing he'll mention is water." This cognitive situation has characterized most of the history of therapy because most participants have been European or American, and culture was not recognized as a salient variable because it did not seem to vary (Laungani, 2004; Sue, 1999). To unreflective European Americans, Western culture may be as invisible as water is to a fish; it just seems like the way things naturally are.

If mental health research and practice are characterized by ethnocentrism, misunderstandings of minority group members are likely to result (Sue, Zane, Nagayama Hall, & Berger, 2009). There is evidence that criteria of normalcy are biased toward European American norms, which means that cultural differences are liable to be misconstrued as psychopathology (Arnett, 2009; Brammer, 2012). If European American behavior patterns are viewed as the standard of normalcy, data may be misinterpreted as indicating deficits in minority groups when only differences exist. Or, if a higher incidence of dysfunction in minority group members is found, it may be misattributed to genetic, familial, or cultural factors when the dysfunction is due largely to the harmful effects of discrimination and prejudice (Fisher et al., 2002; Hwang & Goto, 2009).

Mismatches between the implicit culture of psychotherapy and the cultures of minority clients undoubtedly contribute to underutilization of mental health services by these groups (Thurston & Phares, 2008). Minority individuals attend fewer sessions and are more likely to drop out of therapy before their goals are met, compared to their White counterparts (Fortuna, Alegria, & Gao, 2010; Lester, Resick, Young-Xu, & Artz, 2010).

Because of the congruence between the cultures of therapy and the West, the structure and procedures of counseling make sense to most European American clients (with exceptions discussed later). However, there are major differences and even potential incompatibilities between some cultures and the traditional framework of therapy (Anderson & Middleton, 2011; Lum, 2011; Rice & O'Donohue, 2002). It is important for therapists to think carefully about cultural issues and to adjust service provision accordingly when working with clients from these minority cultures.

Therapists need to shape their interventions to be as congruent as possible with clients' cultural frameworks to optimize the acceptability and effectiveness of services (Ridley, Mollen, & Kelly, 2011; Sonderegger & Barrett, 2004). Therapists who fail to take cultural factors into account when working with clients from non-Western backgrounds are likely to use therapeutic procedures that clash with the client's culture and so seem pointless, nonsensical, or even offensive to the client (Parham, Ajamu, & White, 2011). The purpose of this chapter is to help therapists avoid this type of mistake so they can provide interventions that fit with clients' culturally based values, assumptions, beliefs, and preferences. The ability to provide such therapy is called cultural competence.

Racism, Prejudice, and Discrimination

The multicultural approach to therapy does not constitute a theoretical orientation with a distinctive model of etiology, and there is nothing about this approach that conflicts with other formulations of how mental health problems develop. The multicultural approach has, however, described one type of etiological factor that is not specific to any disorder but threatens the well-being of many minority group members. Encounters with racism, prejudice, and discrimination are potent risk factors for mental health problems in minority individuals (Kelly, 2006; Saez-Santiago & Bernal, 2003; Seaton, Caldwell, Sellers, & Jackson, 2011).

Racism and the broader concept of **prejudice** can be defined as holding negative stereotypes of people because of the group to which they belong. According to Hays (2008), racism is produced by a combination of bias, stereotyping, and power. Racial/ethnic minorities and other marginalized groups (e.g., LGBT and disabled) are often subjected to individual and institutional forces that demean, disadvantage, and deny them opportunities. Many minority youth suffer prejudice-based teasing and both psychological and physical violence, which result in racial mistrust, anxiety, depression, anger, and lowered self-esteem (Fishbein, 2002; Hwang & Goto, 2009).

Privilege, the mirror image of discrimination, consists of advantages people have because of their membership in a dominant group (Ridley et al., 2011; Sue et al., 2009). Many different groups of people have some form of privilege in our society, including Caucasians, males, wealthy people, heterosexuals, and able-bodied individuals. Because a number of different cultural dimensions are salient, many people are privileged in some ways and discriminated against in other respects.

Minority status, in an abstract sense, is not about population size but about fairness and power. One useful operational definition of a minority group member is a person whose access to power is limited by the dominant culture (Hays, 2008).

Cultural Portraits Painted With a Broad Brush

For therapists, one aspect of cultural competence is knowledge about ethnic groups with significant representation in their practice (Sue & Sue, 2013). Such knowledge involves useful generalizations not only across individuals but also across related cultures. There are so many different cultures in the world that an individual description of each one would exceed the capacity of any book. To keep the amount of information manageable, the section ahead aggregates related cultures into broad clusters or categories. The terms *Hispanic* and *Latino/a* combine the many countries of Latin America, and *Asian* combines people from the different nations of that continent, which contains about half the world's population. The terms *European American*, *Western*, and *the predominant culture* meld diverse groups of Caucasian or White people in North America, Europe, Australia, and other countries. Examining these extremely broad ethnic categories necessarily results in a loss of information about specific groups, but the descriptions provide a beginning for the study of cultures.

European American Culture. European American culture is generally described as *individualistic*, in contrast to the more collectivist and familial orientations of many non-Western peoples (Lum, 2011; Pedersen & Pope, 2010). Western culture highly values the free choice, autonomy, and authenticity of the individual, and de-emphasizes loyalty and duty to the family or group. This culture is pragmatic and optimistic, with the belief that individuals can control their destinies if they try hard enough, in contrast to the more fatalistic orientation of many other cultures, in which outcomes are viewed largely as a function of unchangeable forces to which people must adapt. Western culture encourages verbal directness and self-assertion, in contrast to the valuation of modesty and tact common in many other cultures.

In Western societies, the family unit of primary importance is the nuclear family, while most non-Western societies emphasize extended family and kinship networks (Sue & Sue, 2013). European American parents are typically willing to tolerate open (if civil) expressions of disagreement by their children, and sometimes compromise between parent and child is viewed as a desirable outcome of a disagreement. In many traditional cultures, family harmony based on parental authority is the highest priority, and the desired outcome of a conflict is for the child to accept parental authority and control his rebellious impulses (Lum, 2011; Organista, 2006).

African American Culture. African Americans share a history of slavery, oppression, and struggle against racism that has combined with their African heritage to produce their culture. The poverty rate in this community is three times the rate of European Americans, and large numbers of African Americans, especially males, are imprisoned (U.S. Census Bureau, 2012).

Currently, most African American children are born to single mothers and, particularly in low-income groups, most families are headed by women (Child Trends, 2010). Writers on multicultural issues have argued that this difference in family structure should not necessarily be viewed as a deficit (Saez-Santiago & Bernal, 2003). Extended family relationships are an important resource in the African American community, and childcare is often shared among mothers, grandmothers, and other female relatives (Kelly, 2006). The strong bonds and flexible arrangements made possible by the extended family have enabled African Americans to cope with severe adversity during their history (APA, 2008). This culture values unity, cooperation, and a group orientation.

The African American style of communication has been described as animated, intense, direct, and, when strong emotions are involved, passionate (Richardson, Bethea, Hayling, & Williamson-Taylor, 2009; West-Olatunji & Conwill, 2011). This style is sometimes misinterpreted as aggressive and threatening by European Americans who are not knowledgeable about cultural variation (Kelly, 2006). When people recognize that cultures differ in the way that emotions are translated into behavior, they are able to infer emotions from behavior in a more accurate fashion. A tone of voice or decibel level that, in a European or Asian context, would signal a danger of aggression might indicate only a strong opinion in an African American context.

Compared to youth from other ethnic groups, African Americans are more likely to be diagnosed with externalizing or psychotic disorders and less likely to be diagnosed with depression (Dupree, Spencer, & Bell, 1997). However, experiences of racial discrimination are associated with depression and low self-esteem in these youth (Seaton et al., 2011). In school, Black students are more often perceived negatively by teachers, and these youth often see the school environment as unsupportive (Tucker & Herman, 2002).

Coping with racism is a significant part of life for most African Americans (Dupree et al., 1997; Hays, 2008). Many of these parents believe that teaching their children how to cope with prejudice is an important task of socialization (Franklin, Boyd-Franklin, & Draper, 2002). They try to help their children develop sufficient self-esteem and confidence to insulate them against the damaging effects of racism (APA, 2008). Therapists working with African American clients should be cognizant of the harmful effects of racism and should be ready to help clients cope with this stressor, if such help is needed.

Latino/a Culture. Hispanic or Latino/a culture emphasizes group solidarity, mutual aid, and relationships more than individualism (Hernandez, Garcia, & Flynn, 2010; Organista, 2006). Family loyalty, cohesion, and obligation are paramount values (Falicov, 2009; Kuhlberg, Pena, & Zayas, 2010). For example, while European American parents often expect their children to move out of town when they become adults, Latino/a parents usually want and expect their adult children to stay close to the family. This emphasis on family cohesion over individual desires is called **familism**.

Especially among lower-SES Latino/a families, who are likely to be recent immigrants, the parenting style is typically authoritarian in nature, and children are expected to obey their parents without questioning their directives (Lum, 2011; Miville, 2009; Organista, 2006). Fathers usually hold the position of highest authority in the family, in accordance with the traditional gender roles common in Latino/a societies, which emphasize machismo (Lefkowitz, Romo, Corona, Au, & Sigman, 2000; Lopez-Baez, 2006). Latinos/as with strong ethnic identities are most likely to adhere to traditional gender roles. Therapeutic work on parenting practices and assertiveness needs to be cognizant of the hierarchical structure traditional in Latino/a families (Pantalone et al., 2010).

Latinas exhibit higher rates of depression than European American women (Diaz-Martinez, Interian, & Waters, 2010). Hispanic children respond similarly to European American youth on most anxiety measures, but they show higher rates of separation anxiety (Ginsburg & Silverman, 1996), which might reflect the familism of this culture.

Latino/a students have school dropout rates that are twice as high as African Americans' and 3 times as high as Whites' (Fry, 2010). This lack of school connection and success seems attributable largely to low rates of English language proficiency and family histories of limited education, which results in an absence of academic role models for Hispanic students. For example, it was difficult for Carlita to imagine herself excelling in school and going to college because she knew of no one in her family who had done so.

Asian Culture. Asian Americans make up a minority group that, overall, has achieved levels of socioeconomic success above the U.S. average. However, Asian immigrants have many different countries of origin, and specific Asian American groups show pronounced variability in average income and educational levels, with some having poverty rates above the national average (U.S. Census Bureau, 2012). Also, despite being viewed by some as a "model minority," Asian Americans have long been exposed to racism and discrimination, which continue to the present day (Sue, Bucceri, Lin, Nadal, & Torino, 2007).

The cultures of most Asian countries are described as collectivist, with high valuation of harmonious relations among people, especially in families (Chen, 2009; Kim, 2011). Children are expected to respect and obey their parents and other adult authority figures without questioning them (Lau, Fung, & Yung, 2010; Yeh & Kwong-Liem, 2009). Mutual obligations are considered crucial, and fulfilling duties to others is valued more than pursuing personal desires. The type of individuation and autonomy considered healthy in European American culture is considered selfish in Asian cultures (Sue & Sue, 2013). For example, consider a teenager who loves theatre but passes up a part in a school play because the evening rehearsals would prevent him from helping his younger siblings with their homework. From a Western perspective, this situation might suggest treatment goals such as increasing independence and assertiveness, but from an Asian perspective, the adolescent is a responsible, loving brother who is doing the right thing.

The Asian emphasis on family closeness can have the effect of decreasing treatment utilization. Receiving outside help may be viewed as a source of shame or "loss of face," so

Asian Americans often resist seeking services until every effort has been made to manage the problem inside the family (Chen, 2009; Liu & Clay, 2002).

Communication styles differ in the West and East, with different preferences for frankness versus tact. European American cultures emphasize the freedom of speakers to express their feelings, and Asian cultures emphasize protecting listeners from words that would upset them. Asian communication is typically polite and considerate, which often means that messages are stated in indirect, subtle ways that must be decoded by listeners to be understood (Chen, 2009; Kim, 2011). The straightforward expression of emotions valued by Caucasians and African Americans often strikes Asians as crude, rude, and insensitive (Sue & Sue, 2013). Asian cultures emphasize modesty and humility, in contrast to the European American valuation of high self-esteem. In therapy, these cultural factors may affect the way Asian families respond to interventions such as facilitating open communication, assertiveness training, and parent-child negotiation.

Lesbian, Gay, Bisexual, and Transgender Individuals.   It is estimated that 3.5% of the U.S. population is lesbian, gay, or bisexual, with transgender individuals making up .3% (Gates, 2011). Societal attitudes toward the LGBT population are characterized by conflict, contradiction, and major historical change. Overall, acceptance of LGBT people has increased markedly in recent years, with the most positive changes occurring in young people, a majority of whom support legal recognition of same-sex marriage (Newport, 2011).

As gay and lesbian youth grow up and form their identity, they often struggle with a painful sense of being "different" (Wilton, 2009). Portrayals of romantic love in the media and other cultural forums are almost invariably heterosexual. LGBT youth do not see their emotions and desires depicted anywhere, and they sometimes interpret this as indicating that there is something wrong with their feelings. Bisexual youth experience even higher levels of identity confusion and distress, perhaps because they have less of a coherent community than consistently gay and lesbian people (Balsam & Mohr, 2007). LGBT youth face high levels of harassment, bullying, and physical assault from peers, which may combine with their self-doubts to produce high rates of depression, anxiety, and substance abuse (Rienzo, Button, Sheu, & Li, 2006) and a rate of suicide attempts 5 times greater than their heterosexual peers (Hatzenbeuhler, 2011).

The struggle to conceal aspects of their sexuality perceived as unacceptable to others is a constant, oppressive burden for many LGBT youth (Wilton, 2009). The open, accepting atmosphere of therapy seems to provide exactly what these clients have been missing. Counselors often need to address not only the heterosexism of others but also the internalized heterosexism that many LGBT youth carry within themselves (Scott, 2011). While coming out might be a client-determined goal of therapy, counselors should be aware that the development of sexual identity is usually a complex, fluid process during adolescence. Sexual experimentation is common, and the occurrence of same-gender sexual attraction or experience does not necessarily indicate a stable LGBT orientation or identity (Sue & Sue, 2013). Counselors can best serve LGBT youth in the same way they should serve all clients: by putting preconceptions aside to provide a nonjudgmental, facilitative setting in which the client's emotions, beliefs, and aspirations can unfold and evolve in adaptive directions.

Culture and Socioeconomic Status, History, and Politics.   Social class and classism have been cited as important but overlooked issues in mental health (Smith, 2010). Low social class is associated with depression (Lorant et al., 2003), low sense of control

(Chen, Matthews, & Boyce, 2002), poor physical health (Gallo & Matthews, 2003), and exclusion from educational, occupational, and social opportunities (Smith, 2010).

Clinicians exhibit biases against impoverished individuals and attribute more psychopathology to them than similar persons of higher social class (Liu et al., 2004). Middle-class therapists often have trouble grasping the difficult and uncomfortable day-to-day effects of poverty on clients' lives, which limits their ability to understand clients' experiences (Liu, Pickett, & Ivey, 2007). While counselors typically value self-exploration and insight, low-income individuals across ethnic groups usually do not see much value in this, because their focus is on solving practical problems (APA Task Force on Socioeconomic Status, 2007).

While our concept of ethnicity is based on geographical origins, the dimension of time or history also seems to be an important cultural variable. I would suggest that many aspects of what is commonly called Western culture could also be described as *modern*, and many aspects of what is called non-Western culture could be described as *traditional*. Premodern European and American cultures valued emotional self-control, kinship networks, respect for elders, and duty to family in ways that are now considered characteristic of non-Western cultures. As a result, European American families that seem "old fashioned" may have much in common with non-Western cultures, and non-Western families that seem very modern may be culturally similar to typical European American families.

The prototype of a successful therapy client has never matched a typical European American person but instead corresponds to a certain type of modern individual who is introspective, psychologically minded, and open about emotions (Sundberg, 1981). Schofield (1964) described promising therapy clients with the acronym YAVIS (young, attractive, verbal, intelligent, and successful). For many urban, well-educated people, therapy is an accepted part of life that most of their friends have experienced (as per the films of Woody Allen). In contrast, many rural, less educated, poor, and/or working-class Caucasians, with more traditional values, continue to view therapy as a strange, overly emotional activity appropriate only for "crazy people." The view of therapy held by these large sectors of Western society seems to have more in common with non-Western views than with those of typical YAVIS individuals. Also, prior to 50 or so years ago, most people of all social classes were uncomfortable about therapy participation. Historically, the view that counseling is the normal, sensible thing to do when one has a personal problem seems quite recent, even in Europe and America.

The political beliefs of therapists represent an interesting cultural issue that has received some research attention. Most of the research in this area has focused on psychologists, but it seems likely that other mental health professionals have similar sociopolitical views. Both content analyses of journal articles (Redding, 2001) and surveys (Inbar & Lammers, 2012) indicate that psychologists are overwhelmingly liberal in their political beliefs, in contrast to the general American population. Gartner, Harmatz, Hohmann, Larson, and Gartner (1990) found that therapists have more empathy for clients who share their political orientation. Clinicians should be alert to the possible occurrence of this bias in their work so that self-awareness can limit its impact.

What Does It Take to Be a Culturally Competent Therapist?

Because there are so many different cultures in the world, the achievement of cultural competence might seem like a daunting task, since no therapist could possibly acquire an understanding of all the cultures she might encounter in her work. However, we can define cultural competence in a practical, achievable way that is within the capability of real therapists. A number of writers and professional organizations have addressed the question of what is needed to be a culturally competent clinician (American Psychological Association, 2003; National Association of Social Workers National Committee, 2001; Rice & O'Donohue, 2002; Sue et al., 2009). In Table 9.1, I present five essential therapist capabilities and attitudes that can be distilled from these discussions.

Cultural competence does not depend primarily on detailed knowledge of specific cultures. While such knowledge is certainly helpful, the ability to work with culturally different clients depends mostly on the therapist's self-awareness, attitudes, and conceptual understanding of cultural factors. The major threat to cultural responsiveness is ethnocentrism, and the main resource for developing cultural competence is interest in learning about other cultures.

Therapists should plan their reading and training in accordance with the clients they see, learning most about the cultures they encounter frequently in their work. When clinicians encounter the inevitable limits of their knowledge, a culturally responsive attitude should guide their response. Clients from cultures that are new to us present both a learning task and resources from whom to learn, because families can teach us about their beliefs and practices. Therapists should ask questions to learn about differences and similarities between the culture of therapy and the culture of the client. Benish, Quintana, and Wampold (2011) found that it is especially valuable to discuss clients' ideas about the causes of their disturbances and change strategies that can address those causes.

A conceptual understanding of therapeutic principles is an important tool for the provision of culturally competent therapy. Therapists who have learned procedures in a mechanical way cannot vary their implementation of procedures in a flexible manner to fit client preferences, while a conceptual understanding of change agents enables clinicians to gear an intervention's language, materials, and activities to the client's culture. In other words, if you understand why and how a technique works, you can alter its form to suit the client's culture without sacrificing the change agent on which the technique is based. For example, parents from cultures that do not emphasize careful record keeping may have trouble completing detailed behavior charts on a daily basis, especially if they have several children and numerous demands on their time. Counselors who understand principles of reinforcement on an abstract level will be able to adapt charting procedures to the parent's culture by reducing the technique's complexity while preserving the fundamental mechanisms of operant learning.

Finally, cultural competence requires that we become aware of our own prejudices, so we can manage them effectively and prevent our biases from negatively affecting the services we provide to clients with backgrounds different from our own (Hays, 2008; Pantalone et al., 2010). Most therapists probably consider themselves free of overt racism

Table 9.1 Components of Culturally Competent Practice

1. An awareness of one's own cultural background, including its similarities and differences from other cultures, and including one's culturally relevant experiences and biases.
2. An attitude of respect for other cultures and a desire to learn about them.
3. A general, conceptual understanding of cultural variables in therapy.
4. The ability to discuss cultural issues with clients in a comfortable, insightful manner.
5. Some specific knowledge about commonly encountered client cultures.

and prejudice, but research indicates that covert, implicit stereotyping is extremely common in people who consider themselves unprejudiced. In laboratory studies, unconscious biases exert pronounced, negative effects on perceptions of minority group members (Carlsson & Björklund, 2010; Sekaquaptewa, Espinoza, Thompson, Vargas, & von Hippel, 2003). Implicit biases might have especially pernicious effects precisely because people are unaware of them (Boysen & Vogel, 2008).

Especially if they are unexamined, biases are likely to cause **microaggressions**: commonplace, often unintentional indignities, such as subtle insults and invalidation, which are usually embarrassing and disturbing to minority individuals (Sue et al., 2007). Counselors should be scrupulously careful about such behaviors, because microaggressions damage therapeutic relationships and probably contribute to premature terminations in minority clients (Sue & Sue, 2013).

There is a psychodynamic principle that can help therapists with this challenge. Whether dealing with countertransference or unconscious prejudices, the solution to unwanted thoughts and feelings is not self-punishment but self-acceptance and self-awareness, which are the foundations of self-control. The harboring of cultural stereotypes, like the existence of internal conflicts, seems to be a characteristic of human nature, but both potential problems become manageable when we are conscious of their effects and correct for them, so our perceptions of clients are minimally distorted by our own issues and biases. Our efforts to become more culturally competent should include self-assessment of our own biases, messages we have received, experiences that have shaped us, and beliefs we hold about different groups of people (Ridley et al., 2011; S. Sue et al., 2009).

Whether dealing with countertransference or unconscious prejudices, the solution to unwanted thoughts and feelings is not self-punishment but self-acceptance and self-awareness, which are the foundations of self-control.

Assessment and Case Formulation

Culturally responsive assessment is not a matter of using certain tests to measure cultural factors but, instead, involves approaching assessment in an informed manner. One important principle is that reliability and validity are not intrinsic characteristics of tests but are characteristics of tests *for specific populations*. It is quite possible for a measure to be reliable and valid for one population but not for another. The cultural appropriateness of an instrument for a particular client depends on the comprehensibility and meaning of the items for her cultural group, psychometric data obtained from her group, and representation of the client's population in the test norms (Rice & O'Donohue, 2002; Sonderegger & Barrett, 2004).

Although there are more normative data for European Americans than for any other ethnic group, the most carefully researched and widely used assessment instruments, such as the Child Behavior Checklist and Youth Self-Report (Achenbach & Rescorla, 2000, 2001), usually have been validated with African Americans and Hispanics as well, and the availability of normative data for these groups makes valid score interpretation possible. Achenbach and Rescorla (2007, 2010) have collected and analyzed a great deal of data from diverse youth populations, and they offer empirically based guidance for clinicians who use their measures with youth from a variety of ethnic groups.

The problem of test applicability is generally more serious with numerically small ethnic groups because there may be no ethnically specific normative data for them. In these situations, one option is to forego using the test, but this might result in a loss of potentially useful information. Instead, I would suggest that clinicians jointly consider what they know about the instrument and what they know about the client's culture and then judge whether responses to the measure might have different meanings or correlates in the standardization sample and the client's group. If the answer to this question is yes, the test results might be misleading and should probably be foregone. If there is no evident reason to believe the measure is invalid for the client's group, the results should be considered but interpreted cautiously.

Questions to Ask

It is sometimes difficult for children and parents to answer direct questions about their culture because it is so close and familiar to them. (For example, ask yourself how you would answer a question like, "How do people express anger in your culture?") Some children and parents can provide answers, and some cannot. Often, it is more useful to inquire about culture-related aspects of clients' lives without talking explicitly about "culture." Salient topics include religious beliefs, values, explanations of psychological problems, familiar forms of help-seeking, and preferred methods of problem solving. Clinicians can devote a portion of their interviews to cultural issues, but it is probably more effective to weave these questions into the general assessment process.

Asking the client about differences she has noticed between her own group and the predominant culture is often useful because the human mind habituates to constancy and sameness while responding to contrast, change, and the violation of expectations (Pinker, 2009). Client reactions to the majority culture provide information about their own, especially the types of behaviors they consider normative. Often, the client's culture has characteristics opposite those she finds most surprising or difficult in the predominant culture. For example, clients who perceive European Americans as loud are likely to be soft-spoken; clients who perceive Caucasians as self-centered are likely to be family-oriented; and those who perceive the predominant culture as unrestrained and exhibitionistic are likely to be reserved and private.

Clinicians should be careful and tactful in asking direct questions about culture, because there is a risk of such questions coming across as silly, clumsy, or insensitive (e.g., "Tell me about being African American). Cultural assessment is sometimes most effectively accomplished by unobtrusively discussing issues related to culture and noting the information that emerges. In addition, with parents and older clients, carefully crafted, explicit questions can sometimes contribute to the assessment.

It is difficult to describe one's culture without comparing and contrasting it with a different one, so clinicians can juxtapose the client's culture with salient aspects of the predominant culture—for example:

- "Have you noticed some differences between how most Black people act and how most White people act?"
- "Do you think your family and other Mexican people look at some things differently from how Anglos look at them?"
- "Are there things Korean people really care about that other Americans don't seem to consider important?" "Are there things non-Korean Americans think are really good that Korean people don't think are good?"

Cultural assessment involves two levels of information, one pertaining to the cultural groups to which clients belong and the other pertaining to the degree to which they have internalized these norms and values. In other words, individuals vary in the degree to which they are prototypical members of their groups versus acculturated members of the predominant culture (Bernal & Saez-Santiago, 2006; Kim, 2007). Making matters more complex, individuals sometimes embrace different aspects of their culture to different degrees, so there is not one assessment question here but several. For example, Carlita showed some rebellion against the traditional hierarchical structure of authority in Latino/a families, in that she sometimes verbalized rejection of the idea that parents know more than their children, but she adhered to her tradition's emphasis on the importance of closeness and mutual devotion in families. She wanted to be close to her family, but she also wanted to be treated as more of an equal by her parents.

The counselor's knowledge about the client's culture helps him know what to expect and what to look for, but these expectations must be checked against direct knowledge of the client to determine whether they have predictive value. Clinicians can inquire about the degree to which the client shares the beliefs, values, and behaviors of her cultural group by asking questions like:

- "Is being _____ (e.g., Puerto Rican, Pakistani) an important part of who you are?" "In what ways?"

- "What do you like best about being _____?" "Are there things you don't like about it?"

- "What do you like best about the overall American culture?" "Are there things you don't like about it?"

- "Is it pretty easy and comfortable being both _____ and American, or is it sometimes hard to put the two together?"

The questions in Table 9.2 are based largely on recommendations by Friedberg and McClure (2002) and Liu and Clay (2002) and apply both to immigrants and to minority clients who were born in this country. These assessment issues can be investigated either by direct questions or general inquiry.

Differentiating Culture and Dysfunction

Unsophisticated clinicians sometimes mistake culturally based behaviors for evidence of psychopathology, which can result in misdiagnosis and pathologizing of minority clients (Bernal & Saez-Santiago, 2006; Rice & O'Donohue, 2002; Sue, 1999). The assessment ambiguity is that culture and individual personality both produce *behavior*, which is all clinicians can see. The *DSM-5* (American Psychiatric Association, 2013) recognizes that diagnostic assessment must consider both individual and cultural factors to separate their effects. The fifth edition of the DSM includes much more material on culture than the previous editions, including sections on cultural syndromes or symptom clusters, culturally based ways of expressing distress, culturally based explanations of mental health problems, and a Cultural Formulation Interview (for adults).

Eye contact is an example of a behavior that is a function of both cultural norms and individual differences (Cartledge & Milburn, 1996; Hays, 2008). In Western culture, making direct eye contact is interpreted as indicating interest, engagement, and assertiveness,

Table 9.2   Questions for Cultural Assessment

What is the child's ethnocultural identity? Is there more than one important dimension or component?

To what extent does the child share the family's ethnocultural identity, beliefs, values, and traditions?

What is the family's level of acculturation to the predominant culture? Are there generational differences in degree of acculturation?

What are the family's desires for acculturation? Do they perceive conflicts between their ethnic identity and the majority culture?

Are client behaviors that are perceived as disturbed by members of the predominant culture (e.g., teachers) viewed as acceptable by the client's own culture?

What languages are used by the client and family? Do English language limitations contribute to their difficulties?

How is psychotherapy viewed from the perspective of the family's culture? Do these procedures make sense to the family? Are there analogues to therapy in the client's culture (e.g., consultation with elders, advice from clergy)?

How do members of the client's culture view talk about personal issues and emotions? Are the therapist's questions experienced as embarrassing?

What are the family's culturally based beliefs about achieving change?

What forms of prejudice and discrimination has the family experienced?

while avoiding another person's gaze is seen as indicating shyness, lack of confidence, or, possibly, evasiveness. However, in many Asian and American Indian cultures, direct eye contact is viewed as a challenging, aggressive behavior, and looking away from the speaker while listening is seen as conveying respectful, thoughtful attention to his words. A clinician who mistook Western norms for healthy human behavior would erroneously perceive interpersonal disconnection in these clients.

In most Asian cultures, parents expect their children to maintain high levels of respect and obedience, while European American parents accept some questioning of their directives and opinions (Canino & Spurlock, 2000; Lau et al., 2010; Liu & Clay, 2002). Unsophisticated Western therapists might misinterpret typical Asian child behavior as passive, constricted, and fearful. The concrete behaviors in question—the words, tones of voice, and body language—might in fact indicate anxiety or intimidation in the average European American child but, nonetheless, might merely indicate respect for parents in the Asian cultural idiom.

Cultural factors affect children's behavior in school. For example, Asian children are sometimes taught that it is disrespectful to ask the teacher questions following a presentation because this implies that her teaching was incomplete (Chen, 2009). Asian American students sometimes do not raise their hands in class even when they know the answer because they do not believe in showing off, standing out, or drawing attention to themselves. They may refrain from expressing their opinion, especially when they disagree with the teacher. Teachers from the predominant culture might view this pattern as reflecting disinterest, lack of comprehension, or inhibition, while the students and their families might view the same behaviors as appropriately modest and respectful.

"Woofing," also called "the dozens," is a verbal game of competitive banter, repartee, and creative insults that is played by African Americans. Woofing can be a sophisticated form of wordplay involving quick thinking, humor, playful aggression, and nonviolent discharge of tension (Jenkins, 1982). However, "to the outsider, it may appear cruel, harsh, and provocative" (Sue & Sue, 2013, p. 226). European American teachers might consider woofing an unacceptable form of verbal aggression and might respond to it with disciplinary consequences or even a mental health referral, while the youngsters involved might believe they were engaged in a normal type of play.

While knowledge about cultures should prevent clinicians from overdiagnosing minority children, culturally competent practice does not necessarily mean saying, "It's just cultural" and taking no action, because it is also possible to misunderstand real problems as reflections of cultural norms. Careful assessment is often necessary to disentangle cultural, systemic, and personality factors in the child's behavior (Laungani, 2004; Rice & O'Donohue, 2002). To continue with our examples, it is possible that the African American students engaged in "woofing" do have problems with aggression, and it is possible that the Asian American student who does not question the teacher has anxiety about speaking in class. Also, parents who have trouble accepting the existence of mental health difficulties in their children may attempt to portray these difficulties as culturally appropriate behaviors that are misunderstood by representatives of the predominant culture. The cultural factors we discuss should be considered in assessments, but the occurrence of these factors does not rule out the possibility of significant mental health problems.

Culturally competent assessment requires clinicians to synthesize a variety of considerations. It is important to evaluate the child's distress, the parents' concerns, and the effects of the behaviors in question on the child's overall functioning and development. Another consideration is that minority group members need to be bicultural, at least to some extent, in order to adapt successfully to their host culture, and problems in achieving such an adaptation may warrant clinical attention regardless of whether the difficulties are attributable to cultural factors or individual psychopathology.

Outcome Research

In the past, there was tension between the mental health field's growing emphasis on evidence-based practice and the multicultural counseling movement because most therapy outcome research paid little attention to cultural variables (Fisher et al., 2002; Huey & Polo, 2008). Few outcome studies compared results for different ethnic groups, many studies did not even report the ethnic composition of their samples, and when sample composition was reported, the overwhelming majority of participants were White. As a result, it was difficult to know how most outcome research applied to minority individuals (Alvidrez & Arean, 2002; Bernal & Scharron-del-Rio, 2001). This situation left multicultural counseling advocates in a bind, because the research base was not multicultural, and little of it applied to non-White clients.

Fortunately, in recent years these two currents of thinking have converged to a considerable extent, as reflected in the title of an article by Morales and Norcross (2010), "Evidence-Based Practices With Ethnic Minorities: Strange Bedfellows No More." The APA Presidential Task Force on Evidence-Based Practice (2006) states that research-based considerations should be integrated with cultural factors in planning treatment. However, the convergence is not complete, and multicultural counseling advocates continue to express reservations about the Western bias toward individualism, pathologizing of other cultures' norms, and the comparative lack of research attention to minority clients (Bernal & Saez-Santiago, 2006; Sue et al., 2009).

A review of the literature on outcome research and cultural variables yields two general conclusions that might initially seem inconsistent with each other but actually are not. First, even though many EBPs were initially developed with European American client samples, the overwhelming majority of outcome studies that examined demographic variables have *not* found that EBPs were less effective for minority group clients, although when occasional small differences were obtained, these did usually indicate better outcomes for Whites (Bohart & Wade, 2013; Huey & Polo, 2008). Nevertheless, a meta-analysis of outcome studies comparing EBPs that were and were not modified to fit minority clients' cultural backgrounds found that adapted EBPs were somewhat more effective than non-adapted ones and that the most effective treatments had been most extensively revised in accordance with cultural considerations (Smith, Rodriguez, & Bernal, 2011). Similarly, in their meta-analysis of both published and unpublished studies, Benish et al. (2011) found that culturally adapted interventions were more effective than nonadapted treatments for ethnic minorities. In short, a great deal of outcome research supports the following two conclusions:

1. Most EBPs are similarly effective for European American and minority clients.
2. EBPs for minority clients are generally more effective when adapted to their culture.

EBPs adapted for minority cultures have been used successfully with Latino/a and Haitian American adolescents (Duarte-Velez, Guillermo, & Bonilla, 2010; Nicolas, Arntz, Hirsch, & Schmiedigen, 2011), Latino/a adults with depression (Aguilera, Garza, & Munoz, 2010), African American teens with histories of delinquency and substance abuse (Cunningham, Foster, & Warner, 2010), American Indians with trauma symptoms (BigFoot & Schmidt, 2010), and Chinese immigrant families (Lau et al., 2010).

The APA has developed a list of EBPs for ethnic minority clients (2003), women and girls (2007), and lesbian, gay, and bisexual clients (2012). These guidelines can be consulted when planning therapy for clients from these groups.

Different cultural groups seem to vary in their preferences for different types of therapy, which means that providing treatment of equal value sometimes requires differentiating among cultural groups (Choudhuri et al., 2012; Ivey, D'Andrea, & Ivey, 2011; Ridley et al., 2011). The nondirective, collaborative style of therapy seems most compatible with European American culture, while many persons of color prefer to receive help that includes authoritative instruction and advice, as they do when they see a medical doctor (Lum, 2011; Organista, 2006). Therapy involving personal analysis, emotional exploration, and insight seems most congruent with Western culture, while Latino/a, Asian, Native American and African American clients seem more responsive to active, directive, practical approaches (Brammer, 2012; Guzman & Carrasco, 2011). Socioeconomic status is also related to preferences for different styles of therapy (APA Task Force on Socioeconomic Status, 2007), with the preceding characterization of European American preferences actually applying to urban and middle- and upper-class individuals, while low-income and/or rural Caucasians typically prefer the same active, directive style that most minority clients prefer. In summary, these findings suggest the following two conclusions:

1. Nondirective, introspective forms of therapy, including client-centered, emotion-focused, narrative, and psychodynamic therapy, seem more appropriate for urban and middle- and upper-class European American clients.

2. Active, directive forms of therapy, such as CBT and solution-focused therapy, seem more appropriate for minority clients and low-income and/or rural European American clients.

Another broad generalization suggested by the evidence is that the individual therapy modality seems well suited to the individualistic orientation of Europe and North America, while the familism of most other cultures would support a systems-oriented approach (Falicov, 2009; Organista, 2006). Szapocznik et al. (1989) found that Hispanic boys with conduct disturbance achieved greater gains in response to family treatment, compared to individual therapy. Shapiro, Welker, and Jacobson (1997) compared the effectiveness of different therapeutic approaches with different subgroups of adolescent clients and found that cognitive therapy was more effective with Whites, while family systems therapy was more effective with African Americans. Sweeney, Robins, Ruberu, and Jones (2005) found that involving extended family in CBT for depressed African American youth improved their compliance with treatment.

Clinical Considerations

There are two main strategies for incorporating cultural considerations into treatment planning for clients of different ethnic groups. Clinicians can select approaches based on the clients' culture—for example, by selecting a culturally specific treatment package or taking the client's background into account when choosing which types of therapy to emphasize. Also, therapists can choose approaches based on diagnostic and individual variables and then adapt their implementation to fit clients' cultural characteristics. Thus, cultural variables can be used as a basis for *selecting* an approach or for *tailoring* an approach to the client and his family. There is no contradiction between these two strategies, and counselors could use both depending on the clinical circumstances.

When planning treatment for minority youth, therapists should address cultural beliefs concerning utilization of mental health care and other forms of help (Anderson & Middleton, 2011; Benish et al., 2011; Sue et al., 2009). Treatment planning should also be cognizant of situational stressors and practical barriers that might block therapy utilization, such as transportation problems, financial limitations, and time constraints (APA, 2003; Smith, 2010). Culturally based protective factors (e.g., extended family networks and community institutions) should be sought out and incorporated into the treatment plan whenever possible.

Cultural considerations have implications for therapeutic materials. Clinicians should have dolls and puppets of different ethnicities so their child clients can use figures that look like them (Gil & Drewes, 2005). Pictures of faces showing different feelings should include diverse ethnic appearances. Storytelling techniques may be most useful when the stories are selected from the client's own cultural tradition (Malgady, 2010; Malgady & Costantino, 2003). Cartledge and Milburn's (1996) book provides references to stories and biographies from all over the world that address specific cultural and gender issues.

In planning Carlita's treatment, the therapist thought first of cognitive-behavioral techniques both because there is empirical support for CBT as a treatment for anxiety and because the active, problem-solving style of this approach is compatible with Latino/a culture. Because of the familism of Carlita's Mexican heritage, much of the cognitive work was done in a family treatment modality. Her parents and, in some sessions, her siblings joined in the process of evaluating the thoughts and beliefs contributing to Carlita's anxiety and school problems.

The Therapist's Style

Conducting culturally competent therapy means adapting your style, to some extent, to fit the expectations and preferences of your clients. Just as accommodating to the client's personality helps to build rapport, adapting to the client's culture facilitates the development of a positive therapeutic relationship. If taken too far, both types of adaptation become inauthentic and unworkable, but moderate degrees of accommodation are feasible. As discussed in Chapter 1, therapists can compromise between maintaining an unvarying style across clients and trying to mirror clients in a chameleon-like manner. My suggestion is not to try to behave as if you were a member of the client's group but to be mindful of behaviors that clients might misunderstand or find offensive and to selectively emphasize behavioral styles from your repertoire that make sense in the client's cultural framework. For example, with Asian American clients, this would mean talking in the manner that you would use to be tactful, careful about the other person's feelings, and, possibly, indirect.

Parham et al. (2011) found that Black clients seem most comfortable with helping professionals who are authentic, emotionally real, and somewhat self-disclosive in their interactions. B. Kim (2011) observed that Latino/a and Asian American clients typically are less comfortable with therapist self-disclosure, compared to European American and African American clients.

Culturally competent therapy includes appropriate therapist **self-identification**. This consists of the clinician giving the client basic information about his cultural background (Hays, 2008; Ridley et al., 2011). Cultural self-identification by the therapist models open conversation about group identity and tells the client something about who the therapist is.

If the client has beliefs or feelings about the therapist's ethnocultural group, these should be discussed as openly as possible (Park-Taylor et al., 2009; Smith, 2010). Honest, straightforward talk about the therapist's background and the client's feelings about her cultural group usually takes care of these issues. Sometimes, clients' concerns about their counselor's background reflect worries, which might be conscious or unconscious, about whether the clinician will be able to work effectively with them. If so, it might be useful to offer an interpretation of the transference (e.g., "Maybe you're wondering if I'm too different from you to understand what you're going through and think of good ideas to help").

Sometimes, when clients wonder about the therapist's ability to understand their ethnic group, it is useful to reframe the issue from a matter of counselor capability to an issue of client-counselor collaboration—for example:

> "I'm not _____ (client's ethnic group), and there's a lot I don't know about being _____. But I promise to listen carefully to everything you say and to do my best to understand. If I don't understand something, I'll ask you questions. If you think I'm missing something, I want you to let me know—don't worry, you won't hurt my feelings. Then I'll ask you to explain some more, and we'll go back and forth until you think I get it."

Not being knowledgeable about a client's culture is a manageable problem unless the therapist acts as if he *is* knowledgeable. The important thing is to be respectful and interested, not presumptuous. Clients usually appreciate an honest acknowledgment of limited familiarity with their culture if the acknowledgment is accompanied by expressed interest in learning more about their customs, values, and way of life.

Connecting the Cultures of Therapy and Client

Given that psychotherapy first developed in a European American context, its use with minority group members represents, to some extent, a meeting of two cultures. This meeting can be either successful or unsuccessful. If no common language or understanding is developed, the client will experience counseling as a strange, possibly offensive endeavor, with dropout as the most likely outcome. The counselor is responsible for creating an effective translation process.

In work with minority clients, the culturally competent therapist is like a bridge traversing the gap between the European American culture of counseling and the client's own tradition. In a sense, this bridging is a variant of the therapist's usual position with clients, which involves connecting theories of psychotherapy with the specifics of the client's personality and situation. Therapy always involves a meeting of minds; culturally competent work also involves a meeting of cultures.

In work with minority clients, the culturally competent therapist is like a bridge traversing the gap between the European American culture of counseling and the client's own tradition.

This is the case even when the clinician's own background is not European American. Therapists from non-Western backgrounds have already traversed the cultural divide by completing their professional training, which represents acculturation into the therapeutic sector of the European American tradition. These counselors have an advantage in bridging the cultural gap with members of their own tradition, but they still face challenges in doing so with members of non-Western cultures other than their own.

Culturally competent therapists explain how therapy works, acknowledge differences between counseling practice and the client's traditions, and figure out ways to manage these discrepancies (Choudhuri et al., 2012; Sue & Sue, 2013). For example, direct inquiry about personal issues is an integral part of therapy, but such discussion may feel intrusive and embarrassing to people from Asian, Latino/a, and American Indian cultures, many of whom are uncomfortable with self-disclosure outside the context of a close relationship (Kim, 2011; Lau et al., 2010; Organista, 2006). Clients who feel uncomfortable discussing problems with people outside the family might benefit from an explanation of confidentiality, the reasons for personal questions, the uses to which this information will be put, and, if needed, a therapist statement to the effect that his respect for families is not marred by learning about the real-world problems they face. It should be made clear that, outside the boundaries of counseling, the therapist will fully honor the family's belief in privacy. Thus, basic principles of therapeutic practice can be used to alleviate culturally based discomfort with the treatment process just as these principles can be used to help clients whose discomfort is caused by noncultural, individual factors.

The cultural divide separating minority clients and therapy can be traversed by moving in either of two directions: Counseling practice can move toward the client's tradition, and the client can move toward the therapeutic culture. Of course, these two strategies can be combined, resulting in a meeting halfway. Because clients are customers, the therapist should go first in accommodating to their preferences. However, sometimes clients must accommodate to therapy if effective treatment methods are to be employed. In this situation, the therapist's job is to help clients accomplish the adjustments they need to make.

Empathic acknowledgment of the family's perspective is generally the best way of introducing a new viewpoint:

"My goal for this meeting is to learn about the problems Lee has been having and anything that might be causing those problems, so we can figure out the best way to help him. To do this, I will need to ask some questions about Lee's life, which of course includes life in your family. Some of these questions might seem personal, and that might feel quite different or even uncomfortable because you're not used to talking about private things with strangers, so I want you to understand the reason why I'm doing this. Also, if any of my questions seem *too* personal, just let me know, and I'll try to find another way to get the information I need."

Our requests that families venture outside their cultural comfort zones are likely to be more acceptable if they are combined with expressions of respect for the positive attributes of their culture. Research by Cardemil and Battle (2003) and Owen, Tao, Leach, and Rodolfa (2011) found that clients from ethnically diverse backgrounds reported better experiences when therapists acknowledged the strengths of their cultures and when therapists seemed to understand the effects of cultural variables on the process of therapy.

The emphasis on rationality in cognitive therapy has been critiqued from a multicultural perspective (Dowd, 2003; Hays, 2008). While objective evidence and logic are valued highly in the West, many non-Western cultures also value intuition and emotion as guides to understanding and action. If there is concern about the cultural suitability of terms like "rational" and "realistic," cognitions can also be evaluated by reference to criteria such as "balanced," "useful," and "helpful"; these terms have less of a dry, intellectual quality and so may be effective with a wider array of cultural and personality groups.

Friedberg and McClure (2002) discussed ways in which cultural factors sometimes affect implementation of the cognitive therapy strategies of collaborative empiricism, guided discovery, and Socratic dialogue. These techniques involve an egalitarian relationship between the therapist and client in which the counselor does not provide authoritative guidance but asks the client to judge the usefulness of cognitions. For clients who believe in deference to authority, this type of collaboration might seem insufficiently respectful of the therapist's status as an expert. Clinicians can address this potential problem in two ways. First, counselors can conduct therapy in a more authoritative style, with more direct suggestions, than they usually use, thus changing their style in the direction of the client's preference. Second, therapists can encourage client movement toward the culture of cognitive therapy by explaining that the function of client feedback is not to judge the quality of the counselor's input but to assess whether this input is right for the individual client, which means that saying a suggestion is not useful does not express disrespect for the therapist—for instance:

"It's like trying on a pair of shoes: They might be the greatest shoes in the world, but if they don't fit your feet, you need to try on another pair. So, you can help me by saying which of my ideas feels right and would work for you, and which don't seem like a good fit."

All forms of therapy are facilitated by a positive relationship between child and therapist. In Western culture, interpersonal warmth is conveyed by eye contact and occasional touching. However, in many Asian and Native American cultures, these behaviors feel intrusive, especially when not in the context of a close relationship (Cartledge & Milburn, 1996; Liu & Clay, 2002). In work with children from these backgrounds, culturally responsive therapists would reduce their usual eye contact and touch, but rather than reducing their efforts to establish positive relationships, these therapists would seek *other* behaviors with which to convey warmth, perhaps by using an especially gentle tone of voice. The therapeutic strategy here was described in Chapter 8: Identify the abstract goal to be achieved and then find the specific route or behavior most likely to reach that goal. Eye contact and touch are merely two possible means to the end of good rapport, so they are replaceable.

Concrete aspects of therapeutic work can often be changed to accommodate clients' preferences without sacrificing the abstract or theoretical basis of a technique. Many cultural features that have not typically been part of counseling practice can be incorporated into it. For instance, even though spiritual beliefs have not been integral to cognitive therapy, a religious client struggling with guilt might want to write the self-statement "God will forgive me if I have faith in Him" in the column for adaptive cognitions in her thought record. This modification of typical practice leaves the change agents of cognitive therapy quite intact.

Different cultures have different views of time and different beliefs about how time should be spent. European Americans usually believe in using time for specific, constructive purposes, while Latinos and American Indians tend to be less hurried and more concerned about relationship quality than task completion (Canino & Spurlock, 2000; Hernandez et al., 2010; Kuhlberg et al., 2010). When members of these cultures begin interactions, they spend some time in pleasant, friendly conversation before getting down to business (Falicov, 2009). Therapists should bear this in mind when beginning sessions with families from these cultures.

Modifying therapeutic practices to accommodate client cultures is not always this easy. As a more difficult example, suppose a therapist working with a Chinese family discovers that the child harbors suppressed anger toward his father. Adopting a family systems approach, the counselor might plan to help the son express his anger in a therapeutic context. Without appropriate modification, this technique would probably be ineffective. If cultural norms are violated, both parents and child might feel the therapist has encouraged rude, disrespectful behavior. The solution would be for the counselor to find a culturally appropriate form for the change process needed by the family. The therapist could change his usual language in order to model a tactful, indirect style of communication that the family finds acceptable but that can be decoded so that the son's message gets across. For example, instead of saying, "It sounds like Jiang gets angry at Dad for being away on business so much of the time," the therapist might say, "I know Jiang appreciates the hard work of traveling that Dad does for the family but, because he misses his father so much, there might be difficult feelings of frustration at times." The second statement would probably achieve the goal of clear, assertive communication in an Asian family (although in a Caucasian or African American family, the message might not get across).

Some aspects of therapy are difficult or impossible to modify for purposes of cultural accommodation. In such cases, adaptation on the part of the family is needed. Culturally competent therapy does not mean viewing all family cultural patterns as unchangeable; such a view would underestimate the capabilities of minority families. Instead, therapists should help families assimilate elements of the therapeutic culture that would be of use to them. For instance, if a family is convinced that their child's problems are caused by supernatural forces, divine punishment, or inborn evil, they would not be interested in any therapeutic effort, no matter how modified or packaged. The existence of such beliefs would necessitate some movement of the family toward the culture of therapy, particularly in its emphasis on observable evidence and a pragmatic approach to human problems. It is not advisable to assault a family's worldview, and a way can usually be found for the new ideas to be integrated with, rather than to replace, the family's traditional beliefs—for instance:

> "I understand that you think Rene's anxiety problems are a punishment from God, and that might be true, I don't know. But in my experience, I have seen that the thoughts in kids' minds have a big effect on how they feel. So I think we could help Rene by working on those thoughts. Since God knows everything in our minds, maybe our work on thoughts will help Rene put things right with Him, too."

Conflicts Between Client Cultures and the Predominant Culture

Culturally competent therapy can facilitate management and even resolution of conflicts between client traditions and the expectations of the majority culture. These resolutions can involve change on the part of the client, modification of the expectations of representatives of the predominant culture (e.g., teachers), or a combination of both. Counselors can assist with this process by helping the family accommodate to the expectations of the host culture, advising them how to negotiate with representatives of this culture, and functioning as a go-between (e.g., by having a phone conference with the client's teacher).

The routes/goals strategy discussed in Chapter 8 can be applied to problems related to cultural differences. Typically, even when the family and the predominant culture differ in their specific behavioral expectations for the child, they concur about basic, abstract goals. For instance, in principle, both Asian and Western cultures value respect for teachers and engagement in class activities, but they operationally define these goals differently enough to diverge in their views of students asking questions of teachers. The appropriate strategy would be to identify the abstract goals of both cultures, note their similarity, and then develop practical arrangements capable of managing the relatively superficial conflicts that sometimes exist between behavioral definitions of these goals.

Sometimes it is possible to package the behaviors expected by one culture in the values emphasized by the other (see Chapter 8). For the Asian American student, the therapist might suggest to teachers that they frame their invitations for questions in terms emphasizing the modesty, respect for authority, and sense of duty valued by Asian cultures—for example:

> "If there are parts of the lesson you don't understand, your job is to let me know, so I can tell which parts were hard for you. I'll know this doesn't mean you think I did a poor job of teaching, it just means you need a little more help from me to understand the lesson."

Carlita, like many Hispanic students, was uncertain about how academic striving fit into her ethnocultural identity because no one in her family had advanced far in school.

School was conflictual and anxiety-producing for her because she believed that trying to excel would imply an attempt to outdo or place herself above her family and relatives ("I don't want to be better than the people in my family").

Therapists and educators can make use of Hispanic familism to motivate these students to work hard in school (Guzman & Carrasco, 2011; Sue & Sue, 2013). Instead of individually oriented forms of praise, such as, "Good work, you should be proud of yourself," they suggest praise like, "Good work, your family will be proud of you." Carlita's counselor conveyed this information to her teachers, who used it to increase the effectiveness of their efforts to motivate the child. In addition, the therapist tried to help Carlita and her family come together in their thinking about academic achievement.

Based on information that, although Hispanics have high rates of school dropout (Fry, 2010), most Latino/a parents want their children to succeed academically (Lopez-Baez, 2006), the therapist hypothesized that an open family discussion of these issues might reveal misunderstandings and free Carlita of the burden of mistaken assumptions about what her family desired for her. In the ensuing family sessions, Carlita learned from her parents and older siblings that the reason her relatives had not advanced far in school was lack of opportunity, not disinterest in education. The parents said they were excited about Carlita's educational opportunities because they wanted her to advance the family's dreams for a better future. Far from feeling that their daughter's success would represent outdoing them, the parents emphasized that they had worked hard to establish a new home in the United States, and it would feel like a slap in the face if Carlita did *not* make use of the opportunities they had obtained for her.

At home, Carlita's family members sometimes spoke angrily about Anglos who looked down on Latinos/as for lacking education, and they spoke harshly about Mexican Americans who advanced economically and then turned their backs on old friends, neighbors, and customs. These conversations had made a strong impression on Carlita, but she had not understood them. Her parents and siblings explained the difference between two distinct views: They thought poorly of people who disvalued others because of a lack of education, but they considered educational achievement itself to be a fine thing. They believed strongly in the traditional values of their culture, but they rejected the idea that education and professional achievement were culturally Anglo, not Hispanic. Carlita learned that her family would view her success in school not as outdoing them but as expressing their values in a new form and providing a source of shared pride for the family ("You couldn't do this without us, so your accomplishments will be ours, too").

Addressing Prejudice and Discrimination

Culturally competent therapists discuss clients' experiences of prejudice, racism, and discrimination, and they help clients cope with these stressors. Ignoring the roles played by these pernicious forces may result in the counselor blaming the client for problems caused primarily by factors beyond her control (Fisher et al., 2002; Hwang & Goto, 2009; Ridley et al., 2011). Coping with prejudice means finding self-enhancing ways to resist and oppose discrimination (APA, 2003; Ivey et al., 2011).

Culturally competent therapists discuss clients' experiences of prejudice, racism, and discrimination, and they help clients cope with these stressors.

Dealing with prejudice, like coping with other forms of adversity, can result in the development of psychological strengths and resiliency, as well as emotional harm (Anderson & Middleton, 2011; Hays, 2008). Minority group members often support each other by drawing on resources of self-knowledge and self-esteem to resist the unfair messages they receive from prejudiced people (APA, 2008). Clinicians can join with these forms of support to help clients deal with prejudice—for example:

> "You need to remember who you are and not let your opinion of yourself and your people be affected by the garbage they say. They don't know a thing about you."

Across minority groups, positive ethnic identity is associated with high self-esteem, successful school performance, good family and peer relationships, and positive views of other ethnic groups as well as one's own (Pierre & Mahilik, 2005; Vedder & Phinney, 2014). Thus, positive ethnic identity is not linked with chauvinism or prejudice but, instead, with good mental health. These findings suggest that negative views of one's own ethnocultural group may be a clinical problem for some minority clients. If so, therapeutic efforts to increase the client's positive regard for his group would be useful. Counselors could work toward this objective by inquiring with interest about the ethnic group's history, achievements, and unique characteristics, and also by adding to the client's knowledge about positive features of her group. Resources such as prominent individuals or elders in the client's community and relevant books, museums, and websites can contribute to the achievement of this objective.

Culturally Specific Adaptations of Therapeutic Approaches

It seems likely that core features of empirically supported interventions would be helpful to minority clients as long as implementation of these therapies is geared to their cultures.

Therapists have developed a number of interventions for specific ethnocultural groups. In general, these interventions are based on the major theoretical orientations discussed earlier in this book, with the operational details of the interventions tailored to the groups for whom they are intended. It seems likely that core features of EBPs would be helpful to minority clients as long as implementation of these therapies is geared to their cultures (Pantalone et al., 2010; Park-Taylor et al., 2009; Rossello & Bernal, 2005). Next, I present several important examples of empirically supported therapeutic packages geared to specific cultural groups of youth.

Self-empowerment theory (SET; Tucker & Herman, 2002) is a culturally specific approach to strengthening the academic, emotional, and social competencies of African American youth. There is a focus on important life tasks, such as achieving in school, managing emotions, selecting friends, handling conflict, and performing well in job interviews. The parent training portion of the program focuses on use of praise, high expectations for grades, and anger management. The program collaborates with important sectors of the African American community, such as churches, political organizations, and businesses, to provide positive role models and stimulating experiences for participants. The principles of SET have been applied in health-care settings to increase medical compliance and positive health-related behaviors among African American youth (Tucker, Daly, & Herman, 2010; Tucker, Nghiem, Marsiske, & Robinson, 2013).

Tell me a story (TEMAS) therapy. Malgady and Costantino (2003; Malgady, 2010) developed an intervention to strengthen the psychosocial skills of Latino/a youngsters and help them acculturate to North American society. The culturally specific materials are most closely geared to youth from Puerto Rico. There are different versions of the program for youth of different ages. The intervention utilizes a narrative approach and includes biographies of heroic Puerto Rican historical figures as well as stories, folk tales, and pictures related to common themes in Hispanic life. Clients role-play the behaviors of positive role models and create stories from their own life experience. Therapists reinforce adaptive strategies depicted in the stories and offer alternatives to maladaptive coping responses. There is work on coping with prejudice and discrimination. The activities include positive portrayals of both Hispanic and Anglo values and behavior patterns, because the intervention aims both to affirm participants' traditional culture and to facilitate acculturation in their new home. Outcome studies have found that the intervention produced significant improvement in participants' anxiety symptoms, conduct problems, and social judgment (Constantino, Malgady, & Cardalda, 2005; Malgady, 2010).

Brief strategic family therapy (Robbins, Horigian, Szapocznik, & Ucha, 2010; Santisteban et al., 2003; Szapocznik et al., 1989) was originally developed to treat conduct disturbance and drug abuse in Hispanic adolescents, and, while it has been extended to other youth populations, it remains highly congruent with Latino/a culture. Familism is emphasized in that both the youth's behavior problems and their resolution are viewed as manifestations of the network of family relationships. The intervention combines elements of structural family therapy (Minuchin, 1974) and strategic family therapy (Haley, 1963; Madanes, 1991). The therapist targets maladaptive interaction patterns in an active, directive way—for example, by supporting parents as authority figures, strengthening appropriate boundaries, and challenging coalitions within the family. When implemented with Latino/a youth, the intervention draws on the norms, values, history, and customs of this culture.

Rossello and Bernal (1999, 2005) constructed a treatment package that integrates CBT and interpersonal therapy in a Puerto Rican cultural context. The treatment manual was written in Spanish, and it provides metaphors, sayings, and images drawn from Puerto Rican culture. In keeping with Hispanic familism, there is a focus on family relationships and obligations as the basis of a successful life and positive self-esteem. The manual acknowledges the poverty experienced by many of the families in treatment and identifies community resources (e.g., recreational activities) that can be used to counter some of the effects of poverty.

Bringing Spirituality Into Therapy

Religion and spirituality are important aspects of human culture that can affect mental health and therapeutic processes (Hays, 2008; Sue & Sue, 2013). Religion is the narrower term because it connotes institutional systems of belief and practice. Spirituality, the broader concept, may or may not occur within the framework of an organized religion. For most people, religion and spirituality are important sources of moral values, beliefs about the meaning of life, and experiences of connection with God.

During most of the history of our field, therapists considered spirituality to be outside their purview. Recently, this view has changed to a significant extent, due largely to the work of therapists interested in multicultural issues (Shafranske, 2013). A meta-analysis of outcome studies with religious, adult clients found that interventions were more effective when there was explicit attention to spiritual issues, compared to interventions that did not address spiritual matters (Smith, Bartz, & Richards, 2007). A number of commentators (e.g., Post & Wade, 2009) have recommended that counselors acknowledge clients' spiritual beliefs, assess their effects on problems and coping, and try to utilize spirituality as a resource for change.

Counselors might be concerned that if they do not share the client's religious beliefs, they would be in a poor position to work on spiritual issues with them. However, Wade, Worthington, and Vogel (2007) found that religious and nonreligious therapists provided similarly effective counseling to observant Christian adult clients as long as they discussed religious issues openly and provided interventions the clients perceived as congruent with their religious beliefs and values.

If clients' religious beliefs either contribute to their difficulties or have the potential to be sources of coping and healing, bringing spirituality into the therapeutic process would probably increase its effectiveness.

Therapists should not introduce spiritual matters into counseling if these issues are not a concern of the client. However, if clients' religious beliefs either contribute to their difficulties or have the potential to be sources of coping and healing, bringing spirituality into the therapeutic process would probably increase its effectiveness.

Religious activities such as prayer, ritual, and attendance at services are effective coping mechanisms for many youth (Balk & Hogan, 1995). Prayer has the asset of being available at all times. Counselors should encourage religious clients to turn to these practices in times of trouble and to make the most of the comfort they offer. Also, from a CBT perspective, brief prayers can be used as self-statements and tools for self-regulation of emotion.

Of course, therapists should not try to persuade clients to alter their religious beliefs. There may be occasions in which therapist self-disclosure of spiritual beliefs is appropriate, especially if the client asks, but this should be a matter of sharing experiences, not proselytizing. However, I would suggest one limiting condition to a completely nondirective stance: When clients seem to misunderstand the meaning of their own religious tradition in a manner that causes them distress or dysfunction, therapists can help clients examine how they are applying their religious beliefs to their own situations. Sometimes these beliefs are applied in a maladaptive fashion that is both harmful to the client and inconsistent with an accurate understanding of their tradition (Walker, Reese, Hughes, & Troskie 2010).

The most important type of example occurs when clients' religious beliefs contribute to debilitating guilt or self-hatred. Research by Pargament (1997) found that religious adults who believe in an angry, punitive God experience more distress, compared to equally religious adults who believe in a caring, loving God. When clients with the punitive concept of God transgress their moral standards, they may believe they have earned God's opprobrium, deserve to suffer, and are irredeemably bad. These clients sometimes feel their sins have made them unworthy of God's concern and of being part of a religious community. Their religious beliefs, which could be a source of strength, have become a source of self-laceration.

Counselors can help by pointing out that this type of guilt is *inconsistent* with the understanding of human error and sin found in the world's major religions, particularly the Judeo-Christian tradition, which emphasizes the fallibility of people, the importance of repentance, and God's willingness to forgive. These religions do not push people out of the community for erring or sinning but, instead, help people to redeem themselves. As the saying goes, "Church is for sinners, not saints."

On one hand, it might seem presumptuous to correct a client's understanding of his own religion's principles, but, on the other hand, it sometimes seems clear that a hurtful misunderstanding has occurred and that continuation of this misunderstanding will result in continuation of the client's distress. These situations do not involve complicated or controversial theological points but basic, simple, readily apparent principles. Therapists should be humble and tactful but not reticent about addressing this type of clinical situation—for instance:

> "I don't know more about God than anyone else does, but I can read, and the Bible says that all human beings make mistakes and do things they shouldn't. God totally understands this, and He's planned for it: This is why He wants us to admit our sins, repent, and ask Him for forgiveness. There's no way you could be the first person in the history of the world who has done things so bad that God won't forgive her. God's forgiveness is way bigger than your sins. But He wants you to ask."

Clients who experience terrible misfortunes sometimes feel they must have done something wrong or God would not punish them or permit them to suffer so terribly. But this notion, while common, is not a correct reading of the mainstream Judeo-Christian tradition, which holds that divine justice (in the sense of reward for virtue and punishment for unrepentant sin) does not occur on earth but only after death. (Calvinism is a historical exception but one that has little to do with today's young people.) For instance, the story of Job makes a clear statement that misfortune and suffering are not signs of God's rejection but happen to good people as well as bad. The prophets of the Old Testament and Jesus in the New Testament state repeatedly and in many different ways that God's love embraces people who suffer misfortune, including terrible misfortune. Counselors who understand these basic religious principles are in a position to make strong, spiritually based statements from within clients' own religious traditions.

There is a deep-level connection between the emphasis on effort, as opposed to outcome, central to work on fear of failure (see Chapter 8) and the religious view that God knows everything that happens inside individuals' minds. Therapists can make use of this commonality:

> "You've gotten dumped and kicked around so much, it's no wonder you feel like there must be something about you that makes it happen, like you're bad inside, or God just doesn't want you to be happy. But I know that through all those awful experiences, while you made mistakes and lost your temper sometimes, you tried, hard, and you did the best you could with what you had. Whatever things looked like from the outside, that's what was happening on the inside. And God sees the inside."

This is not the type of thing you should say if you do not mean it, but neither should you refrain from saying such things if you do mean them. The spiritual principle that God values every human being can be used to support healthy self-valuation in children whose life experiences have not taught them this:

> "God loves you, so it must be right for you to love yourself. Or, do you think He's wrong to love you?"

The theology here is simple and basic, but, for most clients, the psychology is complex and individual. Generic statements about God's forgiveness may not help clients feel better. To help youngsters resolve guilt or self-hatred, it is necessary to address the specific experiences behind these emotions, including actions they believe were selfish or wrong. Clients are most able to forgive themselves, and most able to believe in God's forgiveness, when they understand what they need forgiveness for.

Several sources of credibility beyond the therapist can be used to counter maladaptive beliefs and a sense of being unworthy or irredeemable. Counselors can cite scripture and ask the child's parents to give their views. When sources with more theological expertise are needed, therapists should refer clients to their own clergy, who generally support understandings of religious doctrine that enhance client well-being (Walker et al., 2010).

Summary

Culture and personality jointly influence human behavior. Pronounced individual differences exist within cultures, and statements about groups of people should always be recognized as generalizations, but knowledge about a person's cultural background often contributes to an understanding of that person.

Historically, psychotherapy originated in a European American cultural context, and therapy is still largely a product of modern Western culture. As a result, therapeutic activities might feel more comfortable to members of this culture than to people from other traditions unless suitable accommodations and assistance are provided.

Counselors who are unaware of the culturally based assumptions embedded in therapeutic practice and their own thinking are poorly equipped to facilitate a comfortable fit between minority clients and therapeutic activities. Ethnocentric clinicians might misinterpret behaviors consistent with non-Western norms as manifestations of psychopathology, and their implementation of interventions might strike minority clients as confusing, insensitive, and offensive. Culturally competent therapists respect and learn about cultures different from their own, and they function as bridges between the cultures of clients and the culture of therapy.

This chapter provides schematic descriptions of the African American, Latino/a, Asian, and LGBT cultures in the United States. Non-Western cultures differ in many respects, but most seem to share two characteristics that contrast with prevailing European American norms. First, while Western culture is individualistic, most other traditions place greater emphasis on the harmony of the family and group. Second, therapies that emphasize introspection and insight seem congruent with urban, middle- and upper-class Western culture, while most non-Western groups and low-income and/or rural Caucasian clients seem to prefer more active, directive forms of counseling that focus on problem solving.

In most outcome studies, client samples have been predominantly European American, and outcome research has not devoted sufficient attention to cultural factors. Nonetheless, the available evidence generally supports the effectiveness of psychotherapy for minority youth, although modifying interventions to fit client cultures increases their effectiveness.

Counselors have not developed fundamentally different treatment strategies for clients from different cultural groups. Instead, culturally competent therapy involves selecting appropriate strategies from among the major therapeutic approaches and customizing their implementation to fit clients' cultures. There are a number of published treatment packages that tailor the techniques of major theoretical orientations to specific ethnocultural groups.

Until recently, most therapists considered religious and spiritual issues to be outside their purview, but there is research evidence and a growing recognition that these issues can contribute both to maladjustment and to therapeutic change. Counselors can integrate clients' religious strivings and beliefs into therapeutic interventions. When clients misunderstand their religious traditions in self-punishing, harmful ways, therapists can draw their attention back to the spiritually supportive, forgiving, and enhancing foundations of these traditions.

When there is dissonance between the culture of therapy and the culture of the client and family, accommodation can be achieved by movement in either of two directions: The counselor can modify therapeutic practices to make them more acceptable to the family, and he can help family members augment their attitudes, beliefs, and behaviors so they become more able to participate in therapeutic work. Frequently, the cultures of clients and the culture of therapy differ less in fundamental principles than in particular behavioral forms. When this is the case, relatively superficial adjustments to either therapeutic practice or culturally based client views can resolve inconsistencies, expand the reach of therapy, and enrich the cultural endowment of our field.

Case Study

Carlita's therapy consisted partly of straightforward application of CBT strategies. Relaxation training was used to address the physiological aspects of her anxiety, and her somatic complaints resolved. Her worries also involved some abstract concerns, and cultural issues played an important role in these.

Carlita's therapy included family sessions in which the group listed features of Mexican and majority American culture, compared the features, and discussed choices between these cultural alternatives. One frequent question was whether the different cultural forms were incompatible with each other or were merely different. The family, led by the parents, came to several conclusions as these issues were sorted out. The family decided that some aspects of the two cultures could simply coexist (e.g., Latino/a and American music), so that new components could be added without replacing traditional ones. The parents believed that other aspects of their culture, such as Catholicism and devotion to family, were nonnegotiable and should be part of their children's lives. As discussed previously, the family concluded that any perceived incompatibility between Latino/a culture and educational achievement was an artifact of lack of opportunity and was illusory.

This work clarified the parents' expectations for Carlita, modified some of these expectations to permit more exploration of Anglo cultural forms, and corrected some of the misconceptions that had contributed to her anxiety symptoms. Carlita became more comfortable in school when she understood that there were no unmanageable conflicts between her identities as student, daughter, Mexican immigrant, and American resident. The family emerged feeling both more committed to their core Mexican values and more confident about partaking of their new, European American culture, including the remarkable endeavor called psychotherapy.

10

Disruptive Behavior in Children

OBJECTIVES

This chapter explains:

- *Integration of behavioral and systems-oriented therapy in treatment for disruptive child behavior.*
- *How subtle reinforcement contingencies can lock parents and children into aversive interaction cycles.*
- *Behavioral parent training as a treatment for disruptive behavior caused primarily by motivational factors.*
- *Collaborative problem solving as a treatment for disruptive behavior caused primarily by capability deficits.*
- *"Special Time": A technique for improving parent-child relationships.*
- *How to conduct timeouts.*
- *The "1-2-3" method of replacing parent-child arguments with child compliance.*
- *A structured, five-step method of solving problems.*

Case Study
Getting Noticed

Ricky was a 6-year-old European American boy whose mother (a single parent) looked exhausted and frustrated when she brought him for treatment. She described his behavior as "impossible—whatever I say, he does the opposite, and 'no' is his favorite word in the English language." She reported that Ricky got into mischief when he was left unattended, turned everyday routines such as getting dressed into prolonged ordeals, had temper tantrums, and made scenes in public places when he did not get his way. The mother complained that, even when he was not acting out, Ricky was "a constant pest," frequently annoying her and his two sisters, who were a number of years older and not interested in playing with him.

Ricky's behavior was better controlled when he was supervised by adults other than his mother. His teacher described him as "strong-willed" but not a serious problem in the first grade. Ricky's father lived in a different city and was not involved with him. The clinician made a diagnosis of oppositional-defiant disorder.

The mother described parenting Ricky as an aggravating, draining experience, complaining that "It's hard to enjoy being with him when he fights everything I try to do." She expressed the hope that therapy would help Ricky bring his behavior under control so she could enjoy an occasional moment's peace to read a book without needing to have her son out of the house.

Diagnoses Treated in This Chapter

Oppositional-Defiant Disorder

As defined by *DSM-5* (American Psychiatric Association, 2013), ODD identifies a pattern of resistant, noncompliant behavior in children. The hallmark of the disorder is disobedience to adult directives; children with ODD do not do what they are told, and they argue with adults who try to structure or inhibit their behavior. These children have frequent temper tantrums, and they are both easily annoyed and frequently annoying to other people. Cognitively, children with ODD are impulsive, and they have weak problem-solving skills, with deficient ability to anticipate the consequences of their actions.

Attention-Deficit/Hyperactivity Disorder

Children with attention-deficit/hyperactivity disorder (ADHD) have trouble controlling the direction of their attention. These youth find it difficult to stay focused on tasks and activities. They are highly distractible, disorganized, and restless, and they change activities frequently. School is an especially difficult setting for children with ADHD because they lack the concentration ability, self-control skills, and goal-directedness necessary for academic success. *DSM-5* includes a subtype of the disturbance in which hyperactivity does not accompany the disordered attention and organization. The diagnosis requires that some symptoms be present before the child is 7 years of age.

Clinical Presentation and Etiology

The next three chapters of this book make up a section on externalizing problems. There are chapters on disruptive behavior in younger children (up to age 11 or so) and in adolescents, followed by a chapter on aggression and violence. These chapters address related client problems with related therapeutic techniques that are often combined in work with individual clients.

This first chapter is about **noncompliant behavior**—children refusing to do what adults tell them to do. Noncompliance in its various forms is the most common reason for referral to child mental health centers, especially for boys (Hinshaw & Lee, 2003; Patterson, Dishion, & Chamberlain, 1993).

The etiology of disruptive behavior problems, like most forms of psychopathology, includes an important genetic component that, beginning in infancy, manifests itself in child temperament (Nigg, 2006). Babies and toddlers who show irritability, inattentiveness, and poor habit regulation (e.g., of sleeping and eating) are more likely to develop disruptive behavior patterns at older ages (Stifter, Spinrad, & Braungart-Rieker, 1999). Child temperament has such strong effects that it can initiate the development of dysfunctional parent-child interaction patterns when the same caregiver, with a more typical child, would not develop dysfunctional parenting practices (Martel, Gremillion, & Roberts, 2012). Explaining this research to parents often helps to alleviate self-blame for their child's difficulties.

Typically, ODD is diagnosed in children under age 12. When this developmental path continues into adolescence, a diagnosis of conduct disorder (CD) often becomes warranted (Burke, Waldman, & Lahey, 2010; Moffitt et al., 2008). If this developmental trajectory continues uninterrupted, the typical outcome is antisocial personality disorder and criminal behavior in adulthood (Hann & Borek, 2002). There is a high degree of association between all three diagnoses and ADHD (Biederman et al., 2008; Matthys & Lochman, 2010).

Oppositionality in children is not a unitary dimension but includes two fairly distinct factors, one predominantly emotional and one predominantly behavioral (Kolko & Pardini, 2010; Stingaris & Goodman, 2009). The emotional dimension involves a type of mood disturbance consisting of irritability, sensitivity to frustration, and quickness to anger. The second dimension is made up of defiant behavior, social conflict, and a propensity for rule breaking, with associated characteristics of impulsivity, excessive exploratory activity, and hyperactivity, all of which are summarized by the term *headstrong*.

Neurobiological Etiologies

Because most neuroscientific research on disruptive behavior disorders other than ADHD has focused on adolescents, this research is reviewed in the next chapter. In brief, as summarized in narrative reviews by Kimonis, Frick, and McMahon (2014) and Knafo, Jaffee, Matthys, Vanderschuren, and Schutter (2013), children and adolescents with ODD and CD exhibit abnormally *weak* biological responses to the prospect of punishment and to punishment itself. They show reduced cortisol reactivity to stress and reduced amygdala response to aversive stimuli. This biological under-reactivity may explain why negative consequences do not seem to bother them much and may account for their weak ability to learn associations between negative behaviors and punishments.

Neurobiological research has produced a counterintuitive understanding of ADHD: these children are underaroused and underreactive on a neurophysiological level.

Neurobiological research has produced a counterintuitive understanding of ADHD: As indicated by their electroencephalograms (EEGs), these children are underaroused and underreactive on a neurophysiological level (Loo & Makieg, 2012; Monastra, Lubar, & Linden, 2001). ADHD is associated with abnormal functioning of the neurotransmitter dopamine in brain pathways that mediate response to incentives, reward, and pleasure (Fan, Xu, & Hess, 2010; Swanson, Baler, & Volkow, 2011; Volkow et al., 2009). Dopamine receptors are under-responsive, and dopamine levels at synapses are low, resulting in low levels of response and activity in this brain circuitry. This may be why people with ADHD do not experience as much interest, engagement, or excitement from a given quantity of stimulation as do people without this disorder.

If people with ADHD are underaroused, why are they often hyperactive? The reason seems to be that their motor overactivity represents an attempt to *compensate* for their neurophysiological underactivity. In other words, because they often feel bored and restless, children with ADHD move around and look around a lot in an attempt to liven up their experience.

This formulation explains why amphetamine medications (a slang term for which is "speed") reduce, rather than increase, ADHD. Medicines like Ritalin and Adderall work by blocking the reuptake of dopamine at synapses, so that more accumulates and less additional dopamine is needed to reach the threshold for neuronal firing. As a result, these medicines cause dopamine pathways to become more active. The person feels more alert, so stimuli hold his attention more effectively, and he does not need to fidget and move around as much to feel interested and engaged (Swanson et al., 2011).

ADHD is also characterized by abnormally low levels of activity in regions of the prefrontal cortex that mediate inhibition and control of behavior and in the circuits that connect these prefrontal regions with the limbic system (Hendren, De Backer, & Pandina, 2000; Tannock, 1998; Yeh et al., 2012). In other words, ADHD involves weak activity in brain structures that control behavior and in connections between these structures and the emotion centers of the brain. Underactivity of the brain systems that perform executive cognitive functions seems to account for the deficits in attention regulation and impulse control that are characteristic of youth with ADHD.

Behavioral-Systemic Etiologies

Rather than describing behavioral and systemic therapies separately, both of our chapters on disruptive behavior disorders describe interventions that integrate these two theories into one approach to treatment. This integration mirrors the therapies with the most empirical support (Barkley, 2013; Funderburk & Eyberg, 2011; Henggeler et al., 2002; Kazdin, 2005; McMahon & Forehand, 2005; Patterson, 1982). These treatment packages combine behavioral and family systems theory in a synthesis so seamless that it does not make sense to separate the two formulations.

One ramification of the role of genetics in etiology is that parents often exhibit adult versions of the difficulties exhibited by their children. Youngsters with ODD and/or ADHD often have parents with mental health problems, including impulsivity, inattentiveness, hostility, antisocial personality disorder, and depression (Harvey & Metcalf, 2012; Nigg, 2006). These parents are more likely to have trouble empathizing with their children, have low frustration tolerance, and show disrupted synchrony in their parent-child interactions, compared to parents of children without these diagnoses (Deault, 2010).

Research has documented strong associations between disruptive behavior disorders in children and maladaptive child management practices in parents (Patterson & Chamberlain, 1994; Harvey & Metcalf, 2012; Pardini, Fite, & Burke, 2008). These parents often vacillate between providing insufficient supervision and exploding with anger when the child does something wrong.

Noncompliant behavior presents an explanatory challenge to behavioral theory because these parent-child interactions are usually so unpleasant for everyone involved that it is difficult to see what the reinforcers could be. Everyone seems to be getting punished, no one seems to be receiving rewards, and yet the pattern of behavior persists and persists. Parents often experience this confusion themselves; they do not understand why the child continually engages in behaviors they believe they punish. The operant question is: What is maintaining the pattern?

Behavioral-systemic analysis has developed an ingenious answer to this question. G. Patterson (1982) launched this analysis by describing **cycles of coercive behavior**

Table 10.1   Sequence of Parent-Child Interaction in Disruptive Behavior Disorders

1. The parent gives a directive.

2. The child disobeys the directive.

3. The parent repeats the command several times.

4. The child ignores the command and continues doing what she was doing before.

5. The parent escalates his level of insistence, anger, and threat.

6. The child argues back in a hostile manner, escalating along with the parent.

7a. The parent gives up, because trying to get the child to comply seems like more trouble than it is worth.

Or

7b. The parent reaches a climax of rage and threat, possibly with physical aggression, and the child finally complies.

between parents and children, and later authors built on Patterson's foundation. The empirically supported treatment programs (cited earlier) are based on the analysis of parent-child interaction sequences presented in Table 10.1.

Hidden reinforcements for both parent and child are revealed by examination of this cycle. The key is to understand the time period just prior to the parent's statement of a directive. Noncompliance typically occurs when the parent directs the child to switch from an enjoyable activity (e.g., play) to a nonenjoyable one (e.g., putting toys away). When the parent gives up and **acquiesces** to the child's defiance, so the command goes unfulfilled (outcome 7a), the child avoids the unpleasant task she was told to perform (negative reinforcement), and she continues the enjoyable activity she was doing prior to the command (positive reinforcement). For the parent, acquiescence is maintained by negative reinforcement—namely, termination of the child's argumentative, unpleasant behavior. In the short run, parents experience relief after giving up on their directive, perhaps with a thought like, "It just isn't worth it." Parental acquiescence is the most common response to child noncompliance. But even when the parent eventually forces the child to comply (outcome 7b), the *delay* in compliance involves reinforcement for the child because, during the interim, he was engaged in the enjoyed activity. Outcome 7b reinforces the parent for escalating the level of threat and aggression in her commands to the child. However, when parents rely on a high level of escalation to secure compliance, directives that are not stated aggressively lose credibility with the child, so that nothing but intense escalation works. Thus, the parent receives negative reinforcement for one maladaptive child management behavior (acquiescence), positive reinforcement for another maladaptive child management behavior (aggression), and punishment for child management attempts that fall in between the two.

The negative attention pattern explained in Chapter 2, Behavior Therapy, contributes to the cycle of behavior described by Table 10.1. Parents often reduce their supervision of oppositional children to avoid the unpleasant experience of confronting and trying to correct their misbehavior. As interaction decreases, the child becomes more desperate for attention and more willing to engage in negative behavior the parent cannot ignore; this then increases future parental avoidance of interaction with the child. The parent's maladaptive child management practices produce oppositional behavior in the child; the child's oppositional behavior produces maladaptive child-rearing practices in the parent; and the positive feedback loop continues indefinitely (see Chapter 7, Family Therapy).

The result is a system of interlocking, learned responses in which nothing works well and yet no better alternative is apparent to the child and parent. In this cycle of coercive behavior, the child uses refusal and defiance to delay or escape unwanted tasks and to elicit attention, while the parent uses threats and force because these behaviors receive intermittent reinforcement and seem to work better than anything else at eliciting child compliance (Forgatch & Patterson, 2010; Patterson, 1982).

The main learning mechanism driving the coercive cycle is operant conditioning, described by behavioral theory, and the overall pattern of interaction is the positive feedback loop, described by family systems theory.

Thus, the main learning mechanism driving the coercive cycle is operant conditioning, described by behavioral theory, and the overall pattern of interaction is the positive feedback loop, described by family systems theory. This formulation provides an example of how processes described by different theories sometimes interweave in everyday life and clinical problems.

Cognitive Etiologies

Cognitive factors also play a role in childhood noncompliance. Kendall (1993) distinguished between cognitive *distortions*, which involve flawed reasoning and misunderstandings of evidence, and cognitive *deficiencies*, which involve an insufficient quantity of cognition in situations requiring some type of thought. Depression and anxiety typically involve cognitive distortions, while in disruptive behavior disorders, the problem is less that these children have the wrong thoughts than that they do not think enough.

Both ODD and ADHD are associated with deficits in **executive cognitive functioning**, which includes emotional self-regulation, anticipating consequences, and problem solving (Frick & Viding, 2009; Greene, Ablon, Goring, Fazio, & Morse, 2004). Youth with disruptive behavior problems are impulsive; they react quickly and without thought to stimuli and emotions. For example, Ricky knew his mother's rule against touching breakable objects in the sense that he could state the rule verbally, but when something grabbed his attention, he reached for it so quickly that he had no time to access the relevant information in his memory.

Oppositional children exhibit skill deficits in problem solving and **consequential thinking**—that is, anticipating the likely consequences of actions (Kazdin, 2010; Matthys, Cuperus, & Van Egeland, 1999). Consequential thinking takes the form of questions like, "If I do _____, what will probably happen?" Noncompliant children often fail to expect consequences that seem obvious to others (e.g., if you take a peer's possession, he will respond angrily). Their social cognition tends to be inflexible, unsophisticated, and unimaginative. When they confront interpersonal problems, they typically think of only one or two possible actions to take, while socially skilled youngsters think of multiple options. The options disruptive children do generate are usually simple, physical, and direct, which is unfortunate, because problems are more often solved by responses that are verbal and somewhat complex.

Psychodynamic Etiologies

Psychodynamic theory emphasizes the individual nature of etiology and views oppositional behavior as a result of any number of internal, dynamic processes, with the important question being the role played by defiance in the child's interpersonal and emotional functioning. Kernberg and Chazan (1991) observed that many children with oppositional behavior seem unable to express themselves in words and can only use actions. Oppositional behavior may be defensive, serving to ward off unconscious feelings and thoughts that cause anxiety (Klein, 1932; Wachtel, 1994). For example, some boys use defiant behavior to project a "tough guy" stance and protect themselves against fears of vulnerability and weakness (Chethik, 2000). Sometimes, children burdened with guilt use oppositional behavior to provoke punishments they feel they deserve, because the experience of punishment relieves their feelings of guilt (Gardner, 1993).

Oppositional behavior may also indicate impaired object relations. For example, some children seem to misperceive appropriate directives from parents as attempts to deprive them of all personal control. In such cases, the child's noncompliance preserves a fragile sense of autonomy that he feels would crumble if he became obedient to adults (Wilson, 1999). Dynamic therapy for disruptive behavior involves addressing deep-seated misunderstandings and disturbances of personality development such as these.

Assessment

Observation of parent-child interaction is an important assessment method for children with disruptive behavior problems because noncompliance is generally a characteristic of interactions between the child and authority figure, not a purely internal attribute of the child. In observing these exchanges, clinicians should be equally interested in the parents' behavior toward the child and the child's response to the parent.

McMahon and Forehand (2005) recommend that clinicians assess two types of parent-child interaction. In one, the therapist asks the parent to allow the child to direct the activity, and the parent's task is to accompany the child in his play, providing attention and positive comments but no direction or correction. In the second type of interaction, the therapist asks the parent to take the lead and attempt to structure the child's behavior in the play activity or game. Observation of the first interaction assesses the parent's ability to attend to the child. Observation of the second interaction assesses the child's compliance with parental directives.

Behaviorally oriented questions about noncompliance should follow the guidelines presented in Chapter 2, Behavior Therapy, with clear operational definitions of problems and careful attention to antecedents and consequences:

- "What usually happens when you tell him to do something?"
- "Are there certain directions she's more likely to obey, and others she's less likely to obey?"
- "What do you do when he complies?" "When he doesn't do what you tell him?"
- "Who is she more likely to obey?" "Who is she less likely to obey?"
- "Are there certain situations in which she's more likely to do what she's told?" "More likely to be disobedient?"
- "How does he do with following rules?" "What rules is he relatively good at following?" "Which ones does he usually not follow?"

Assessment of noncompliance depends more on parent interviews than child interviews, because oppositional children often deny their misbehavior or blame it on other people. Nonetheless, interviews with these children sometimes yield information about their perceptions of parental and family functioning and possible relationships between these factors and the noncompliance. Information from teachers and other adults can help clinicians determine whether the problems are situation-specific.

ADHD assessment relies primarily on teacher reports, parent reports, and behavioral observation, but it can also be useful to inquire about the child's experience of his attention problems. Clinically, the emotional hallmark of ADHD seems to be boredom, which probably results from the underactivity of dopamine pathways characteristic of this disorder (Fan et al., 2010; Swanson et al., 2011; Volkow et al., 2009). Children with ADHD describe feeling understimulated much of the time, and their daydreaming and hyperactivity seem to be restless efforts to seek stimulation. It is useful to ask these clients how often and under what conditions they feel bored, and what they do in response.

Treatment Planning

Treatment planning occurs at the nexus of two types of information: general, scientific knowledge about categories of clients and individual, personal information about the child sitting in front of you. Therapists need to integrate these two types of knowledge to plan their work with clients. Accordingly, the treatment planning sections of the chapters to follow include two subsections: outcome research and clinical considerations.

Research is about groups, and clinical decision making is about individuals. Clients are members of groups defined by diagnosis, age, cultural group, and so forth, and they are also unique individuals with no group member exactly like them. Research on groups provides vitally important information about clients, but this information is never complete and, sometimes, it may be outweighed by person-specific data.

Counselors need to understand both the value and the limitations of outcome research findings to use this information most effectively. The most empirically well supported interventions never produce improvement in all or nearly all of the clients who receive them. In typical outcome studies, the experimental intervention produces improvement in approximately 75% of participants, and the comparison therapy produces improvement in fewer of them. This means that, all things being equal, therapists should use the experimental intervention with clients who share diagnostic and demographic characteristics with the study sample. However, all things are not always equal. Therapists need to consider the question of whether the client in their office seems more likely to respond to the EBP like the 75% of study participants who showed improvement or the 25% who did not (Shapiro, 2009).

Another difficulty is that outcome research often provides support for more than one type of therapy. When the effects of active, bona fide therapies are compared, the results do not usually indicate that one is superior to the others (Wampold, 2010; Wampold & Imel, 2015). When this is the case, outcome research does not provide complete guidance for treatment planning, and clinical reasoning is our only apparent means of filling the gaps.

Child and family assessment often provides information with implications for treatment planning. Different types of psychotherapy are based on different understandings of etiology, and they utilize different change processes to address the etiologies they emphasize. Assessment often reveals patterns and processes that contribute to the presenting problems. *Outcome research + assessment information = treatment planning.* Clinical observations that illuminate etiology should be considered in conjunction with outcome research to customize therapy for clients. In short: Outcome research + assessment information = treatment planning. Clinical considerations should supplement and sometimes even outweigh outcome research when an EBP does not seem to address the etiological factors responsible for a client's disturbance, when the family is uncomfortable with the procedures making up the EBP, and/or when the EBP has been tried but has not sufficiently helped the youngster.

The interventions examined in outcome studies usually consist of one type of therapy based on one theoretical orientation or one package of techniques that does not vary in the study. In a sense, research examines therapy in large chunks. In community settings, most clinicians are eclectic, and they usually mix components of therapy from multiple theories in an attempt to match their clients' needs (Shapiro, Welker, & Jacobson, 1997; Weisz & Jensen, 1999). Sometimes we can settle on one type of intervention at the beginning of therapy and find that it resolves the client's problems. At other times, one type of therapy does not seem sufficient, and treatment planning is a matter of ongoing assessment, experimentation, and midcourse correction (Clarkin & Levy, 2004; Persons, 2008). We should certainly try to plan ahead, but we can also try different things to see what works.

Outcome Research

Outcome research on treatment of childhood noncompliance provides its most extensive support for behavioral-systemic interventions based on parent training in child management techniques.

Outcome research on treatment of childhood noncompliance provides its most extensive support for behavioral-systemic interventions based on parent training in child management techniques (Anastopoulos et al., 1993; Chacko et al., 2009; Curtis, 2010; Gerdes et al., 2012; Nixon et al., 2004; Rejani et al., 2012; Thomas & Zimmer-Gembeck, 2007). These interventions are based primarily on operant learning principles and secondarily on family systems theory. Parents who participate in these training programs usually report improved child behavior, with increased obedience to parental directives, reduced tantrums, more independent play, and more emotionally positive interactions. In direct comparisons, behavioral parent training has achieved larger improvements in child compliance than has nondirective, relationship-based play therapy (Brestan & Eyberg, 1998; Weisz & Jensen, 1999). Follow-up studies have found maintenance of treatment gains for one or more years after termination (Eyberg et al., 2001; Nixon et al., 2004; Patterson, Reid, & Dishion, 1992; Pisterman et al., 1989).

Outcome research provides not only general support for behavioral interventions but also separate, specific support for most of the techniques packaged together in these treatment programs. Table 10.2 lists a number of components of parent training programs that have been shown to be effective.

Behavioral interventions produce positive changes in parents as well as children. In addition to improving child management practices, behavioral parent training results in more positive attitudes toward the children, decreased stress, and improved self-esteem in parents (McMahon & Forehand, 2005). These interventions have positive spillover effects on aspects of family functioning that were not even targets of treatment, such as improved behavior in the client's siblings (Brestan, Eyberg, Boggs, & Algina, 1997) and improved marital and family functioning (Kazdin & Wassell, 2000).

Outcome studies generally find that behavioral parent training programs produce clinically significant improvement in 60%–75% of the children treated (Barkley, 2013). Research has identified several predictors of outcome. Parent factors seem to be more predictive than child factors (Reyno & McGrath, 2006). Dropout and poor outcomes have been associated with parental psychopathology (Patterson & Chamberlain, 1994), social isolation (Dumas, 1984), single-parent families (Drugli, Larsson, Fossum, & Morch, 2010), marital discord (McMahon & Forehand, 2005), anger control problems, and low SES (Fernandez & Eyberg, 2009). For parents with mental health problems, the

Table 10.2   Empirically Supported Components of Behavioral Parent Training

Reducing attention to negative child behavior while increasing attention to positive behavior (Kaminski, Valle, Filene, & Boyle, 2008; McMahon & Forehand, 2005).

Stating directives or commands in an effective fashion (Gerdes et al., 2012; McMahon & Forehand, 2005).

Shaping increases in the child's independent, appropriate play behavior (Anastopoulos et al., 1993).

Time-out (Curtis, 2010; Kaminski et al., 2008).

Response cost (Anastopoulos et al., 1993; Little & Pisterman, 1989).

Proactive structuring of the child's environment and activities (Gerdes et al., 2012; Pisterman et al., 1989).

Use of structured reinforcement systems with carefully defined target behaviors and consequences is a fundamental behavioral method that has received support in numerous studies, including most of the above investigations.

addition of training in problem solving and anger control to child management training has produced better outcomes (Chacko et al., 2009; Webster-Stratton & Reid, 2003).

Younger children (<6 years old) typically benefit more from parent training interventions than do older children (Anastopoulos et al., 1993; Dishion & G. Patterson, 1992). Children whose main problem is noncompliance, who do not exhibit other forms of psychopathology (e.g., ADHD or autism), and whose families are not seriously dysfunctional show the highest rates and largest degrees of improvement from treatment. Many children with comorbid disorders and family dysfunction do benefit from intervention, but they typically continue to exhibit significant disturbance after program completion (Anastopoulos et al., 1993; Chacko et al., 2009; Drugli et al., 2010). With these parents, it is most realistic to present the techniques as ways to ameliorate their child's problems and help them cope with these difficulties, rather than as a "cure."

Beauchaine, Webster-Stratton, and Reid (2005) performed a mediation analysis with pooled data from six RCTs of the Incredible Years treatment program (Webster-Stratton & Reid, 2003). They found that decreases in harsh, critical, and ineffective parenting practices accounted for reductions in children's externalizing problems, thus indicating that this behavioral-systemic intervention worked largely through the change process emphasized by its theoretical basis.

Parent-child interaction therapy (PCIT: Brinkmeyer & Eyberg, 2003; Funderburk & Eyberg, 2011; McNeil & Hembree-Kigin, 2011) is a parent training program that is largely similar to the programs described earlier but also uses client-centered play therapy techniques, taught to parents, as a way of enriching parent-child interactions. A meta-analysis by Menting, de Castro, and Matthys (2013) examined studies comparing PCIT to control treatments and found a medium-sized effect of .50 for parent reports of reduction in children's disruptive behavior. PCIT has produced clinically significant improvement in both reported and observed child behavior and parent functioning in a number of studies (Chase & Eyberg, 2008; Eyberg et al., 2001; Nixon et al., 2004).

When the parents of children with both ODD and ADHD receive child management training, the ODD typically improves, but the ADHD usually improves less or not at all (Anastopoulos et al., 1993; Pelham & Fabiano, 2008). While parents become more skilled at directing their children's attention, and the children become more able to function effectively when their parents help them, the core symptoms of dysregulated attention are not effectively treated by parent training interventions. At the present time, medications are the only reliable treatment for the core attentional deficit of ADHD (Connor, 2006; Pelham & Fabiano, 2008). Behavioral-systemic therapy does seem to address the academic, behavioral, and emotional problems often associated with ADHD in a fashion that is not duplicated by medications (Pelham & Waschbusch, 1999; Wells, 2004).

The *collaborative problem solving* approach (CPS; Greene, 2001, 2010; Greene, Ablon, & Goring, 2003; Greene, Ablon, Goring, Fazio, et al., 2004) represents something of a dissenting view within the parent training field because it places less emphasis on securing immediate compliance with caregiver directives. In this approach, therapists train parents to respond to noncompliance by providing support, helping the child problem-solve, and even by negotiating compromises. CPS was developed specifically for the type of child who typically achieves less positive outcomes in response to standard parent training—namely, children with disturbances in addition to noncompliance. Greene, Ablon, Goring, Raezer-Blakely, et al. (2004) compared CPS to traditional behavioral parent training in a sample of 4- to 13-year-old children who, in addition to ODD, were diagnosed with either major depression or bipolar disorder. CPS produced stronger positive effects on a number of outcome variables, thus outperforming a well-established treatment.

Martin, Krieg, Esposito, Stubbe, and Cardona (2008) conducted a 5-year, prospective study of seclusion and restraint on an inpatient psychiatric unit serving children and adolescents. There was no control group but, after three years of data collection, unit staff were trained in CPS, and they consistently used this approach thereafter. The results were dramatic: Prior to introduction of CPS, restraints were used 263 times per year, and afterwards, restraints were used seven times per year. Seclusion of patients occurred at a rate of 432 times per year before CPS and 133 times per year after CPS. In a similar study by Greene and Ablon (2006), there were 281 restraint episodes during the 9 months prior to introduction of CPS, and there was *one* restraint episode during the 15 months afterwards.

Thus, there is a large body of outcome research that supports behavioral parent training for noncompliant children without prominent psychopathology, and there are a few studies that support CPS for youth with both disruptive behavior and high levels of comorbid depression or mental illness warranting hospitalization. From a "scorecard" perspective, behavior therapy is the obvious winner. However, the few studies on CPS have produced impressive results for the subset of noncompliant youth who typically respond less well to behavioral intervention.

There is also a type of cognitive therapy that has received substantial empirical support. *Problem-solving skills training* (PSST; Kazdin, 2003, 2010; Shure, 1996; Spivack & Shure, 1982) teaches children simple, practical formulas for thinking through problems, anticipating likely consequences of alternative behaviors, and planning responses to difficult situations. In a meta-analysis of 40 studies of youth with anger-related problems, Sukhodolsky et al. (2004) obtained a medium/large effect size of .67 for comparisons between children receiving PSST and a variety of control groups. Kazdin, Bass, Siegel, and Thomas (1989) compared PSST to a nondirective therapy emphasizing discussion of feelings and found that PSST produced larger decreases in disruptive and aggressive behavior. In a study by Kazdin, Siegel, and Bass (1992), PSST and parent training, delivered alone, were similarly effective at reducing disruptive behavior in children, and the combination produced better outcomes than either separately. However, Bushman and Peacock (2010) found that a problem-solving intervention for children did not add effectiveness to child management training for their parents.

As discussed in the outcome research section of Chapter 5, there is little empirical support for psychodynamic therapy as a stand-alone treatment for externalizing dysfunction, and several studies have indicated that it is not an effective intervention for this form of disturbance (Fonagy & Target, 1996; Muratori et al., 2002, 2003). Clinical considerations might suggest that dynamic techniques could be included as elements in a primarily behavioral-systemic and/or cognitive approach.

Clinical Considerations

One important purpose of assessment, both at intake and throughout therapy, is to identify etiologically significant processes that correspond to the change agents emphasized by our repertoire of therapeutic strategies. Clinicians should consider several types of information in deciding which strategies to use. If the parent's child management practices share features with the coercive behavior cycle described earlier, behavioral-systemic parent training would be useful and might be the only intervention that is necessary. If the caregiver's child management techniques already seem competent and similar to what is taught by parent training programs, a different therapeutic strategy is needed. If the child becomes so overwhelmed with distress that she seems unable to respond to consequences, CPS seems called for. If the child is unable to think of reasonable responses to problem situations even when calm, PSST would be an appropriate intervention. In a sense, we are looking for broken processes that we know how to fix.

In Chapter 7, the distinction between motivational and capability-related factors in maladjustment was introduced. In that chapter, this distinction was discussed as a source of family members' attributions and emotional responses to aversive behavior by the identified patient. In this chapter, we return to this distinction but as an etiological issue for the client, not an attributional issue for her family members.

Treatment planning for disruptive behavior disorders depends, in large part, on the clinician's answers to two etiological questions: (1) To what degree does the source of problems lie in the parent's child management practices versus the child's internal processes? (2) If processes within the child seem important, to what extent are these factors motivational in nature, and to what degree do they concern the child's capability for compliant behavior? Motivational factors pertain to the child's willingness or desire to behave compliantly. Capability-related factors pertain to the child's ability to behave in a controlled and compliant fashion, if that is her goal. Executive cognitive functioning, especially self-control, is the most important capability to assess in therapy for disruptive behavior disorders.

If motivation is the source of problems, the client could behave appropriately, but this is not his choice, because his desire to engage in proscribed behaviors is stronger than his desire to comply with adults. If incapability is the source of problems, the child is unable to behave appropriately, even if he wants to. For example, some temper tantrums occur because parents reinforce this behavior with acquiescence to the child's demands, and some tantrums occur because intense distress, perhaps due to trauma, overwhelms the child's controls. The difference between capability-related and motivational etiology is the difference between *can't* and *won't*. This is not an either/or question, because many youth exhibit both types of etiologies. If both seem present, therapeutic strategies should be proportioned to match the importance of the etiological factors they address.

Parent description and therapist observation of disruptive behavior episodes often suggest answers to the motivation/capability question. A cool, calculating quality to the child's misbehavior suggests the salience of incentives and choice, while physiological hyper-arousal (red face, hyperventilation, etc.) suggests the child is overwhelmed with emotion and incapable of bringing her behavior under control. However, motivation-based and capability-related acting out sometimes look the same while they are occurring. Behavior that looks "out of control" might, in fact, be manipulative, which means it is actually under control. Additional types of information need to be considered to make this determination.

Assessment should investigate patterns in the context, timing, antecedents, and consequences of misbehavior. For example, if disruptive behavior occurs more frequently when the client is tired, ill, or stressed, capability factors are suggested. If misbehavior is more frequent with a caregiver who often gives in to the child, a motivational mechanism seems probable. Another test occurs when, in the midst of a tantrum, the child achieves his objective. An immediate cessation of distress suggests a motivation-based mechanism, because if hyper-arousal were the problem, it would probably take some time to dissipate. The continuation of distress after the youngster achieves his objective suggests that intense emotions do disrupt his capability for self-control, even when he gets what he wants.

Both motivational and capability-related factors include internal characteristics of individuals and person-environment interactions. In other words, the motivation/capability distinction is independent of the internal/external dimension. A youngster's general desire to behave in a compliant, controlled manner is an internal motivational factor. Reinforcement contingencies are a situation-specific motivational factor. A child's general level of executive cognitive functioning is an internal capability-related factor. External factors that influence children's capability for controlled behavior include the effectiveness with which caregivers structure the environment and provide directives and prompts as well as the effects of caregiver behavior on the youngster's level of emotional distress.

Thus, misbehavior that occurs across diverse situations might be due either to a client's lack of prosocial motivation or to weak executive functioning. Situation-specific misbehavior might be due either to variation in incentives and reinforcement contingencies or to variation in environmental factors that affect a youngster's ability to behave in a cooperative, organized manner. For example, a child might be disruptive at home but not in school either because the parents inadvertently reinforce this behavior or because they provoke emotional reactions that overwhelm the youngster's self-control. These different etiologies call for different therapeutic approaches.

Behavioral-systemic therapy addresses situation-specific factors of both the motivational and capability-related types. Motivational factors are addressed by altering incentives and reinforcement contingencies. Capability-related factors are addressed by teaching parents how to give effective directives, prompts, and cues. This type of therapy places less emphasis on stable, cross-situational factors of both types (although positive indirect effects might occur). Capability factors are addressed not by strengthening the child's executive cognitive functioning but by teaching the parent how to compensate for the child's weaknesses in this area by providing strong environmental support for compliant behavior. In essence, the parent's strong child management skills compensate for the child's weak self-management skills.

PSST, a narrower intervention, targets the internal, capability-related factor of weak executive functioning by teaching the client problem-solving skills. Because these skills are portable, PSST might produce more cross-situational change than does behavioral-systemic therapy. PSST does not address motivational factors in a direct way.

CPS focuses on capability-related factors of both the internal and situational types. This intervention trains the parent in child management practices that both support positive behavior in an immediate way and facilitate the development of the child's emotion regulation and problem-solving skills. Like PSST, CPS does not emphasize motivational factors.

One final note: When parents harbor strong problematic emotions (e.g., anger) toward their child, they sometimes provoke emotional distress that results in non-compliant, disruptive behavior. This behavior might be neither desired by the child nor reinforced by the parents, thus representing a situation-specific, capability-related etiology. In these cases, parent counseling would be an appropriate intervention.

Behavioral-Systemic Parent Training

In behavioral-systemic parent training, therapeutic activities focus on the parent (although the child often participates in the parent's practice of techniques). The strategy is to make the child's home environment a source of prompting and reinforcement for compliant behavior. In a sense, the parent is the direct provider of therapeutic experiences to the child, and the counselor's job is to teach the parent how to do this.

Counselors should balance directive and nondirective styles in their work with parents (Barkley, 2013; McMahon & Forehand, 2005; Patterson & Chamberlain, 1994). While training is generally didactic in nature, clinicians are most likely to be successful if they interact in a collaborative way that stimulates parents to think the material through. These authors recommend using the parents' own experiences as a resource for evaluating alternative child management techniques. For example, questions about the best and worst bosses a parent has had may guide her thinking toward an appreciation of positive reinforcement as the main strategy for inducing desired behavior. Counselors should ask parents what they think about the new techniques, and they should invite parents to modify and embellish the procedures to optimize their fit with family preferences.

If parents seem to resist adoption of the new practices, therapists can respond with a combination of motivational interviewing techniques (Miller & Rollnick, 2012; Miller & Rose, 2009; Rosengren, 2009), as described in Chapter 1, and scientific information about the utility of behavioral child management strategies. For example, parents who have relied on corporal punishment could list the advantages and disadvantages of this approach and the alternatives recommended by the therapist.

Although the various parent training programs differ in details, they are based on a shared set of principles. These principles are presented in Table 10.3.

All of the major parent training programs place more emphasis on reward than punishment. From an operant learning perspective, the reason is that reward is generally a more effective method of controlling behavior (Kodak, Lerman, Volkert, & Trosclair, 2007). From a systems theory perspective, these interventions create change in the parent's experience of the child by reversing the parent's previous focus on the child's misbehavior and directing his attention to the child's positive behavior.

Table 10.3   Principles of Parent Training Programs

Consequences should be immediate, specific, and consistent so they provide the child with clear, detailed information about behavioral expectations.

There is a stronger emphasis on reward than punishment.

Behavioral targets or standards are low enough to allow the child to succeed and high enough to stimulate growth in competence.

The parent provides prompts and external structure to support positive behavior.

The parent is calm and firm, not emotional, when disciplining the child.

The parent always delivers the consequences she says she will deliver.

Increasing warm, positive interactions between parents and children is a central goal of treatment.

Parent training sessions focus on the learning of behavioral skills. Therapists should model the new techniques for the parent and then should provide detailed feedback as the parent practices the new procedures in the sessions with the child (Barkley, 2013; Forgatch & Patterson, 2010; Kazdin, 2005). It might initially seem artificial to practice child management techniques in an office setting, but this is generally not a problem, and the opportunity for live, hands-on practice is invaluable. The goal of therapy is not for the parent to understand child management techniques but to *do* them effectively.

The sections to follow present the steps of parent training in the order of their recommended implementation. The sequence reflects a building block approach in which utilization of the first techniques is a prerequisite for the effectiveness of the later techniques.

Special Time

The single most important change agent in behavioral-systemic treatment for noncompliance is parental use of positive attention as a reinforcer. However, at the beginning of therapy, there is usually a serious problem with this strategy: The parent's customary way of attending to the child has been critical and punitive for such a long time that the child has come to associate this attention with anger and threat, and it has lost reinforcement value for the child. As a result, a key tool for creating change in the child is often broken at the beginning of treatment. The first therapeutic objective is to fix this tool.

The parent-child activity used to accomplish this objective has different names in different programs. I will use Barkley's (2013) term: **Special Time**. (Funderburk & Eyberg, 2011, use the term "child-directed interaction," and McMahon & Forehand, 2005, use the term "child's game.") Special Time is a method for increasing the reinforcement value of the parent's attention and, more broadly, for improving the parent-child relationship.

Special Time is a method for increasing the reinforcement value of the parent's attention and, more broadly, for improving the parent-child relationship.

Special Time consists of 15 to 20 minutes of time per day (or as much as feasible) during which the parent attends to the child's free play, with no directives or correction, and with expression of interest and support for the child's activity. The child chooses the activity, within reason. The parent's role is to observe and to *narrate* the child's play by describing it, in detail and out loud, as it proceeds.

In instructing parents, it is just as important to explain what *not* to do as what to do. There should be no directions, advice, teaching, criticism, or quiz-type questions. Many parents find it difficult to relinquish these functions because they are so accustomed to trying to improve their child's behavior that, without this job, they feel they have nothing to do. However, Special Time is not about improving the child's behavior; it is about appreciating the child's behavior just the way it is. Nevertheless, there *is* something important for the parent to do: Communicate positive attention to the child by expressing moment-to-moment awareness of her activities.

The analogy used to explain this type of narration is that of a sportscaster describing a game. The idea is to verbalize, with interest and occasionally some excitement, the details of the action. For example: "You're getting ready to build something with these blocks—hmm, you're putting the red block on top of the green one." As another example: "You're having the girl dinosaur jump up and down … Now the mother dinosaur comes over and gives a big roar—look at that!"

At intervals, the parent should offer some praise for the child's activity. The praise can refer to the play itself (e.g., "What a big tower of blocks you built"), and can refer to the interpersonal interaction (e.g., "I like it when we play quietly together like this"). If the child behaves negatively, the parent should turn away and ignore the behavior. If the misbehavior persists, the parent should announce that Special Time is over because it cannot continue while the child misbehaves. The website accompanying this book includes a handout for parents (Form 10.1) that summarizes these instructions.

Initially, observing and narrating their child's play might seem like a trivial, silly activity to parents, but the idea is actually quite substantial: entering the child's world by sharing in something important to her. The goal of therapy is to help the child do things the parent's way (i.e., compliance), but the process is initiated by the parent joining the child, following his lead, and doing things his way—just as therapists should begin their effort to influence clients by listening and empathizing with them. Special Time has one additional benefit: Most children really enjoy it.

Special Time and similar procedures were developed and validated with play activities involving physical toys. What about the video games that are so popular with children, especially boys, above age 6 or so? There are competing considerations. Most video games involve less latitude for free, creative play than old-fashioned toys, and they do not lend themselves as well to being narrated by parents. On the other hand, many children genuinely value their video games, and they seem to experience adult interest in their play as validating and gratifying. In the absence of guidance from research, my suggestion is based on the principle underlying Special Time: When parents pay close and respectful attention to what is important to children, they gain access to their worlds, and the relationship usually improves. If so, the Special Time procedure can be adapted to video games or any other play activity.

Parents should generalize the practice of positive attention beyond the confines of Special Time to their everyday interactions with the child. Of course, caregivers cannot do this all the time, but counselors should explain that attending to and praising the child's positive behavior contributes to a warm parent-child relationship, and this type of relationship is the foundation of child compliance.

Giving Effective Directives

One reason for noncompliance is that the parent's commands are stated in an ineffective fashion, so the child is unable to process them effectively. The solution is to teach parents how to give effective directives. Commands are effective when their cognitive level of difficulty matches the child's attention and memory capabilities. This component of the intervention teaches parents how to reduce the difficulty level of their directives by minimizing distractions, facilitating the child's attention and memory, and breaking complicated commands into simple components (Barkley, 2013; Forgatch & Patterson, 2010; Kazdin, 2005). This strategy addresses limitations in the child's capabilities, but not by remediating them (as in CPS and PSST). Instead, the parent learns how to compensate for these limitations by becoming more skillful, herself, in child management.

Guidelines for effective commands are presented in Table 10.4. You can go to our website for a parent handout (Form 10.2) that summarizes these guidelines.

When parents have a directive to give, they have a decision to make about timing—namely, whether the child needs to perform the action immediately or could wait until she is ready. Which option is appropriate depends on the situation. If a task needs to be performed right away, caregivers should make that clear, and should treat procrastination as noncompliance. However, there are many directives that do not need to be followed immediately (e.g., cleaning a room), and in these cases, parents should show the child the

Table 10.4   Guidelines for Effective Commands

1. Eliminate distractions when giving the directive (e.g., turn off the TV).

2. Begin by securing the child's attention and establishing eye contact, perhaps by saying something like, "I have something to tell you now."

3. State the directive politely but as a command, not a request or question. Words such as, "Could you put your toys away?" are ineffective because they implicitly give the child permission to disobey. Words like, "Please put your toys away now" are more likely to be effective.

4. Instructions should be given one at a time as simple directives for individual behaviors. If a series of steps needs to be performed, the parent should wait until one task has been completed and reinforced before stating the next one.

5. Sometimes it is useful to have the child repeat the directive back to the parent, to make sure she understands what she is supposed to do.

same consideration they would show an adult—for example, by allowing her to finish what she is doing before complying with the directive.

Compliance Training Periods

The next step is positive attention to the child's compliant behavior. However, the problem might be that the parent has little obedient behavior to attend to, because the child rarely complies with directives. As discussed in Chapter 2, Behavior Therapy, the solution is to make the desired response as easy as possible for the child, so reinforcement and then learning can occur. Compliance training periods set the child up to succeed (Barkley, 2013; Forgatch & Patterson, 2010).

This procedure involves a few minutes of time and takes place two or three times per day for a week or two. The parent initiates the training periods only when the child is in a good mood and is not engaged in an absorbing activity. Then, the parent gives simple commands that are chosen to be easy for the child—for example, "Please pet the kitty," "Now, hand me that magazine," and "Please put this plate on the table." When the child complies, the parent rewards the compliant behavior immediately, using praise for older children and small bites of a favorite snack for younger children. If the child does not obey, the parent ignores the noncompliance and gives a different command.

Behavior therapy is concrete, with nothing left to chance, so parent training includes specific words to use in praising children. Praise such as "good boy/girl" is ineffective because it is too global to provide useful information to the child about what he did right. Effective praise is specific. The following phrases can be adapted to praise many different child behaviors:

- "I like it when you _____" (e.g., "do what I say").
- "It's nice when you _____" (e.g., "help your little brother").
- "I am proud when you _____" (e.g., "put your toys away without being asked").
- "You did that all by yourself—way to go!"
- "Good job!" "You did it!"

Shaping Independent Play

Noncompliant children often have trouble playing by themselves, and, as a result, they frequently pester their parents. In the behavioral intervention for this problem, parents are trained to ignore minor misbehavior and to attend positively to independent play, thus reversing the past contingency between child behavior and parental attention. The key ingredient in this technique is the parent's initiation of positive attention at times when, in the past, such attention was least likely to occur—namely, when the child *was* playing quietly on her own (Barkley, 2013; Kazdin, 2010; McMahon & Forehand, 2005).

The first step is for the parent to prompt the desired behavior by making this request explicitly and also suggesting an activity for the period of time involved, because it is more effective to tell children what *to* do than what not to do. Thus, the parent says something like:

> "I'm going to make dinner now. Please do not interrupt me. While I'm cooking, color me a nice picture with these crayons, and I'll come look at it in a little while."

Then, the parent begins her separate activity. But after just a bit of time, she breaks the previous pattern by walking into the room where the child is playing and expressing appreciation for the independent behavior.

How long should the parent wait before administering the reward? Based on principles of operant learning, the time interval should be short enough so the child can succeed approximately two thirds of the time. At the beginning of therapy, these time periods might need to be quite short. As the child's capability increases, the time intervals should be lengthened. As children become more secure in the knowledge that their positive behavior is appreciated by the parent, they need less and less demonstration of this appreciation to keep going, although there should always be some reinforcement for positive behavior.

Structuring the Environment

This type of intervention is particularly useful with children who are young and/or have limited self-control capabilities, because the technique relies on external structure provided by the parent, not internal controls of the child. This proactive strategy focuses on antecedents, not consequences, of behavior.

First, the therapist and parent identify situations in which the child's behavior tends to be more disruptive and less disruptive. Then, the parent maximizes the frequency of the situations that go well and minimizes the frequency of situations that are difficult for the child. The parent structures the child's environment to steer his behavior in desirable directions (McMahon & Forehand, 2005; McNeil & Hembree-Kigin, 2011). Like effective commands, this strategy addresses capability-related etiology not by remediating the child's limitations but by compensating for them.

Structuring the environment is a useful technique for children whose disruptive behavior is occasioned by boredom or "not having anything to do." This problem is common in children with ADHD, who become restless if not provided with stimulation. Unstructured situations are often recipes for trouble with these children, because their search for stimulation often leads to problems (e.g., fiddling with breakable objects and pestering siblings).

To return to our case study, after Ricky's mother came home from work and took care of dinner, she collapsed in a chair, and she did not have the energy to comply with her son's requests for active play. Ricky gradually learned, through trial and error, that if he made a mess or tipped something over, his mother would come rushing into the room—angry, but there, and intensely focused on him. Based on this analysis, the therapist and parent developed a procedure combining elements of structuring the environment and shaping independent play. The mother got to relax in her favorite chair, but she prepared by setting out toys and giving her son little assignments to complete on the floor in front of her. She provided positive attention when Ricky sustained appropriate behavior for a period of time corresponding to his level of capability (e.g., "I like relaxing together like this—I get to see you play and read my book, too").

Posting household rules and step-by-step instructions for daily routines is another strategy for structuring the child's environment. If the child does not read, rules and instructions can be posted in picture form, perhaps with a large X crossing out proscribed behaviors. Also, children should be asked to repeat rules and instructions often enough to maintain their day-to-day awareness of them. Parents can replace nagging around morning and bedtime routines with copies of written instructions that the child checks off as he completes each step. In general, maintaining consistent routines (e.g., for bathing and bedtime) provides structure that helps children organize their behavior.

In **redirection**, the adult responds to a minor misbehavior not by presenting a consequence but by moving the child's attention from the stimuli that prompted misbehavior toward stimuli likely to prompt positive behavior. Often, this can be done by physically turning and moving the child. Redirection addresses negative behavior with guidance, not discipline. For example, if a child is playing roughly, instead of saying "No!" or "Stop it," the parent could tell the child to play more gently, present an attractive toy, and demonstrate gentle play with this toy. The parent's voice should be cheerful, not stern, because her focus is on encouraging a positive behavior, not discouraging a negative one.

Here is a technique that parents can use in those common situations in which children make requests that are reasonable in principle, but the timing is wrong (e.g., requests for ice cream before dinner). The parent can teach the child to add the word "when" to requests for treats and privileges. Thus, rather than asking *if* she may have an ice cream cone or toy, the child asks *when* she could have these things. The different type of question elicits a different type of answer: Parents can respond by saying when they will give the child what she asked for. This technique may build children's sense of the future and help them tolerate the frustration of not having requests fulfilled immediately because, instead of being thwarted by a simple "no," they find out when they will get what they want.

Homework is often an ordeal for children with disruptive behavior problems, especially ADHD. Books by Canter (1993) and McNerney (2011) offer suggestions for helping children manage this challenge. The recommendations ahead draw on these books. Form 10.3 on our website provides a handout that summarizes these recommendations for parents.

Structuring the environment is crucial for helping youngsters succeed at homework. Parents should establish a routine, with the same time for homework every weekday (when practical), to reduce decision making about when to start, which is often a source of agitation. The best times are late afternoon and/or early evening, because children need a break from work after school, and they need time for relaxation before going to sleep. Thus, the child's afterschool sequence of activities should be play, work, play.

Many children with ADHD seem more able to focus after they have had some physical exercise. If little time is available, doing push-ups or other strenuous calisthenics helps to discharge some restlessness.

Youngsters should do their homework at one set location in the house to facilitate habit formation and build environmental cues for focusing on work. This location should be supplied with all the materials they need for homework. Distracting stimuli should be minimized by creating a quiet environment without TV, other people's conversation, or uncontrolled access to electronic devices.

With young children and older ones who need help with organization, parents should begin the sessions by stating the tasks to be completed, perhaps in checklist form, so the child can keep track of his progress. Youngsters should be offered choices about the order of tasks, when practical. There should be short breaks at intervals corresponding to the child's attention span, which for some children means a break every 15 minutes, although this varies widely. Large projects should be broken down into smaller chunks. Parents should shape independent work with the same methods they use to shape independent play, as described in the previous section. Some children benefit from receiving a small tangible reward (e.g., a poker chip) when they are halfway through.

Game-like elements can increase engagement. For instance, each time the client completes a task, she can add a block to a tower or make a mark in a tic-tac-toe game with her parent. Some children enjoy teaching their parent something they learned from their homework.

Offering Children Choices

Parents can provide children with cues for positive behavior while also allowing some latitude for personal control by offering them choices between two behaviors—and making sure both of the options are appropriate. Thus, the child gets to decide what to do, but the parent chooses the choices. Here is an example for a young child:

> "It's time to get dressed now. Would you like to wear your green shirt or your blue shirt?"

Here is an example for an older child:

> "Your father and I have decided that we want you to do one organized activity besides school, so you can have a new experience and maybe make some friends and learn a new skill. You can choose any reasonable activity you'd like—a sports team, a play, a musical instrument—it's up to you."

With this technique, parents and children share control in a certain way: The parent's control occurs first, and it circumscribes the domain within which the child's control can operate. This arrangement meets the child's needs for both structure and autonomy.

Contingency Contracting

Parent training programs generally include organized systems of reinforcement using charts, symbolic reinforcers such as poker chips and stickers, and backup, tangible reinforcers. Chapter 2, Behavior Therapy, presented detailed instruction in setting up contingency contracts, which will not be repeated here.

Parents of oppositional children often voice several objections to reward-based contingency contracting, and therapists should be equipped to deal with these objections. The suggestions ahead draw from the behavioral parent training programs cited earlier, with especially large debts to Barkley (2013), and McMahon and Forehand (2005).

BOX 10.1

Consulting With Teachers to Help Children With ADHD

Children with ADHD need extra help from teachers to structure their behavior in accordance with classroom expectations, but teachers point out that they are responsible for many children and cannot devote extensive attention to each one. Therapists can help by suggesting strategies that are both time-efficient for teachers and beneficial to children. Here are three techniques that teachers can use to help children with ADHD focus their attention more effectively:

1. Seat the child as close to the teacher's desk as possible. (The adult's physical presence prompts on-task behavior.) If this is not feasible, the child should be seated as far from distractions as possible.

2. Break long tasks into a series of short tasks for the child and provide a bit of social reinforcement at the completion of each step.

3. Arrange for a secret signal, known only to the teacher and child, that the teacher can use to communicate positive attention to the student's on-task behavior. For example, if the child is listening attentively, the teacher could tug on his left ear to convey that he appreciates the child's good listening. This technique has the effect of drawing the child's attention to the teacher, to see if some social reinforcement is forthcoming.

Parents sometimes object that formal reinforcement systems constitute "bribery." Therapists should respond with the dictionary definition of this term, which is paying someone to do something illegal or immoral. Behavioral reinforcement systems reward children for performing positive behaviors.

Some parents object to children being rewarded for behaviors that they simply "should" do, based on the idea that no incentive ought to be necessary for doing what is right. One quick response is to ask the parent how long she would continue going to work if she did not receive a paycheck. A more substantive response asks parents to think about the developmental process that begins with an infant, whose behavior is motivated only by desires for immediate pleasure, and culminates in a disciplined, moral adult. It seems clear that people are not born knowing how to exert self-control and that children gradually acquire this capability through a long process of learning. The purpose of reinforcement systems is to provide clear, detailed incentives and information about positive behavior. Tangible rewards provide motivation to engage in behaviors that need to be practiced and increase the power of information. Structured reinforcement systems differ from ordinary child-rearing practices chiefly by being explicit about what is usually implicit and by being clear and detailed about what is usually vague.

Parents sometimes complain that normal children (i.e., those without behavior problems) behave appropriately without receiving rewards in return. Therapists can respond by saying that normal children actually receive frequent privileges and material rewards, and these are contingent on their positive behavior in an approximate way. Children with behavior problems need more detailed, specific reinforcement that is rich in information to facilitate their learning process. Formal systems are analogous to a prosthetic device for a physically handicapped child, which enables the child to do things that normal children can do without help. Finally, therapists can say that contingency contracts are used to get children back on track and, over time, as the external source of control is internalized, reinforcement systems can be faded out; the analogy here is training wheels on a bicycle.

Some parents have personal issues that interfere with their use of behavioral child management techniques. Chapter 8 offers suggestions for helping parents with these issues.

Negative Consequences

In behavioral-systemic therapy, the procedures for positive consequences are always established first, and the procedures for negative consequences are implemented later. This sequence facilitates children's buy-in to the program, which for older children is important. Once the pleasant intervention components have been established, it is time to target misbehaviors in a strong way.

Behavior therapy does not involve "punishment" in the strict, technical sense of administering an aversive stimulus; the negative consequences involve *removing* some type of pleasurable experience. Nonetheless, children do not like it when positive reinforcers are removed, so behavioral parent training does include procedures that feel punitive to children. Punishment is not a dirty word in behavior therapy. Its purpose is not to make children suffer but to provide clear, experiential information that teaches children how to behave appropriately.

Effective negative consequences have four characteristics: They are strong enough that the child cares about them but are not severe, and they are immediate, consistent, and understood by the child (Barkley, 2013; Kazdin, 2005; Patterson, 1982). Severe punishments cause intense distress and anger, which disrupts the learning process that is the purpose of the procedure.

Ignoring. Ignoring is the mildest and most commonly used negative consequence in behavior therapy. Parent training programs teach caregivers that the best response to minor, annoying child behaviors is the withdrawal of attention.

Ignoring does not work if the child does not know he is being ignored. Therefore, this procedure should be enacted in a clear, unmistakable fashion: The adult should stop speaking to the child, break eye contact, and turn away.

Effective attending and ignoring require caregiver *agility* in switching from one to the other in response to a change in behavior from the child. When a period of negative child behavior is followed by positive behavior, the adult should immediately express cheerful approval, with a quick change in emotional tone. These nimble changes require a high degree of self-control, particularly if the parent felt anger toward the child during a long, preceding period of negative behavior. Although understandable, the problem with persistent anger is that it punishes whatever the child is doing at the time, including changing his behavior in a positive direction, which is what we want to reinforce. There is no holding grudges in behavior therapy.

Response Cost. Response cost, the reverse of reward, should be part of a contingency contracting system: When the child misbehaves, the parent takes away a predetermined number of poker chips or points. This technique is like a monetary fine. The child should be told, in advance, what the fines are for various negative behaviors.

Therapists and parents should plan the response cost system so the child cannot lose more chips or points than he would be able to earn with 2 to 4 days of positive behavior. The fines should be large enough so the child cares about the loss but not so large that accumulated rewards for substantial amounts of positive behavior can be quickly wiped out.

There should be only one response cost per negative behavior by the child. If the behavior does not stop, it is time to implement the next type of negative consequence.

Time-Out. The full term for this procedure is "time out from positive reinforcement." This technique consists of a complete absence of opportunities for rewards or fun for a specified length of time. Time-out is the appropriate consequence only for comparatively serious misbehaviors, such as physical aggression and defiance of a parental directive. My guidelines for this procedure closely follow Barkley's (2013) recommendations. Table 10.5 presents the time-out procedure.

When time-out is first introduced, it often elicits a firestorm of anger and defiance from oppositional children. There should be preparation for this firestorm. Therapists should predict difficult child reactions and assure parents that this is par for the course, not a sign that something has gone wrong. Time-out should be introduced on a week-end, and no activities should be scheduled during this period, so there is plenty of time to wait out the child's possible resistance to the procedure.

During the first couple of weeks after introducing time-out, parents should be judicious about its use because, if they implement it every time the child misbehaves, the result might be whole days spent in time-out. However, following this phase-in period, defiance of a parental directive should be followed, 100% of the time, by time-out. (Otherwise, noncompliance will be maintained by a partial reinforcement schedule.) Parents should adopt the position that every directive they give will either be obeyed or will be followed by time-out; there is nothing in between. Parents should keep this guideline in mind when

Table 10.5   The Time-Out Procedure

1. The parent states her command, once.

2. The parent counts backwards from five. During the first few weeks, this is done out loud, so the child understands what is occurring.

3. If the child does not comply with the directive, the parent gives one warning, raising her voice moderately and saying something like, "If you don't do what I say, you will go into time-out" (or, "sit in that chair").

4. The parent counts backward from five once again. If compliance has not occurred, time-out is initiated: The parent takes the child by the arm and walks him to the time-out chair. Children sometimes promise to comply at this point, but it is too late; once time-out has begun, it must be completed.

5. The time-out period should be 1 minute per year of the child's age for minor misbehaviors and 2 minutes for serious misbehaviors. This period does not begin until the child sits appropriately. A timer can be used to show the child how the time elapses. If the child sits appropriately for a while and then misbehaves or attempts to leave, the timer is put back to zero. The child must demonstrate fully quiet behavior for about 30 seconds at the end.

6. Then, if practical, the child must comply with the original command; this is the final step in the time-out procedure. If the child complies, the parent should respond with a cheerful expression of approval. If the child does not comply, the time-out procedure starts over at the beginning.

deciding whether to give a command. Some directives will be skipped as a result, but this is better than allowing a child to disobey a directive.

The time-out chair should be in a place where no reinforcing experiences are available. There should be no toys within reach and no interesting sights within view. Corners are good places for time-out chairs. No one should talk to the child during time-out. Television and music should be turned off. Time-out is supposed to be boring.

If the child refuses to sit in the time-out chair, the parent should physically put her in her room and close the door. The room must be prepared in advance, with no toys, electronics, or enjoyable activities available. If the child's pulling on the door creates a problem, the parent should install a device for locking the room from the outside.

If the parent cannot easily handle the child physically, she should not attempt to do so. There should be no wrestling around because this might be exciting and subtly reinforcing for the child and also might detract from the parent's aura of authority. The other option is to make sure that all enjoyable activities (TV, games, eating, etc.) cease for the child until he complies and then to wait him out. Because time-outs do not end until the child completes his part, it can take hours to conduct the procedure. Generally, this occurs only when time-out is first introduced, because once children realize their parents will never acquiesce to their refusal to do time-outs, they learn to get the procedure over with as quickly as possible. Patience is a vital resource for caregivers determined to win power struggles and establish themselves as authority figures.

No explanations should be given during time-out, because children experience the resulting argument as a stimulating activity that delays the negative consequence. The reasons for rules and the consequences for breaking them should be explained in advance and, if necessary, after the time-out is over.

Time-out is easier to implement at home than in public places, where the combination of a child having a tantrum and strangers watching may be embarrassing for the parent. Parents should establish time-out as a familiar routine at home before extending it to public places. Then, several modifications make the procedure portable. First, to be proactive, parents should have children state the rules for behavior in public places before going out. A photograph of the child in the time-out chair at home can serve as a visual reminder of the contingency in place. Appropriate places for time-out include empty corners of rooms and inside the family car. The time period should be shortened to one-half minute per year of the child's age. Our website provides a handout for parents (Form 10.4) on how to implement time-out both at home and in public places.

The time-out procedure is set up to ensure that noncompliance always backfires on the child, and the only way to succeed is with compliant behavior. This strategy establishes the parent as the authority figure who makes the rules and must always be obeyed, sooner or later. The parent should do no arguing, cajoling, or threatening but should simply conduct the procedure. Caregivers should understand that, as long as they implement the behavior management system, nothing can go wrong, because no matter what the child does, the caregiver has an effective response. A child's tantrum, while unpleasant, is not a negative outcome if the parent's response helps the child learn more appropriate behavior. Therapists can portray the screaming as "the sound of a child learning—he's learning that he can no longer fight his way past Mom's directives."

When parents are secure in the knowledge that they can handle anything the child presents, they replace emotional arguing with calm, methodical implementation of procedures.

When parents are secure in the knowledge that they can handle anything the child presents, they replace emotional arguing with calm, methodical implementation of procedures. This change in emotional tone is a central purpose of behavioral-systemic therapy. When discipline is infused with anger, it is usually ineffective and often counterproductive, because the child feels the parent is trying to defeat and hurt her, not help her. Clients sometimes report that this type of discipline makes them feel their parent hates them and makes them even more determined to fight back against their parent's directives. Children need to experience discipline as firm teaching, not angry revenge, to develop positive associations with prosocial behavior and gradually internalize their parents' expectations.

The 1-2-3 Technique

Phelan's (2014) *1-2-3* procedure is not a component of the major parent training programs (although it is based on the same principles), and it is described in his book for parents. This procedure is a simple child management technique that warns children about a possible time-out, helps them change their behavior, and corrects most misbehaviors before negative consequences become necessary. The method provides parents with a replacement for emotional debating with the child.

The technique works like this. When a child disobeys a directive or begins arguing, no matter what the child says, the parent's single verbalization is, "That's 1." If the child does not comply, the parent pauses a few seconds and says, "That's 2." If the child still does not comply, the parent says, "That's 3—time-out." If the parent gets to 3, time-out must occur, even if the child then complies.

The power of the 1-2-3 technique lies as much in what does not happen as in what does. The procedure short-circuits the counterproductive arguing that typically occurs between oppositional children and their parents. Consider the following examples of parent/child exchanges before and after adoption of the 1-2-3 technique:

CHILD: Mom, would you buy me this video game, please?

PARENT: (Looks at game) No. This game has too much fighting and blood, and that's not good for kids.

CHILD: Oh, come on, this is a great game. Look how many of them the store has!

PARENT: It's not a great game. It teaches kids that fighting is fun. And the reason the store has a lot of them is to make money, not to do good things for kids.

CHILD: It's not going to make me fight, I promise! If you buy me the game, I'll promise never to fight again.

PARENT: Violent games like this DO get you fighting more; remember what happened at Kevin's house?

CHILD: That had nothing to do with the game! I can't believe you're being so mean. You just don't want me to have any fun; you HATE it when I have a good time.

PARENT: Honey, of course I want you to have fun. Let's look for another video game that doesn't have violence.

CHILD: But this is the one I want! This is all because of the divorce—you've been so mean since the divorce!

PARENT: This has NOTHING to do with the divorce. Daddy and I explained to you …

The same conflict, after the 1-2-3 procedure has been put in place, would go like this:

CHILD: Mom, would you buy me this video game, please?

PARENT: (Looks at game) No. This game has too much fighting and blood, and that's not good for kids.

CHILD: Oh, come on, this is a great game. Look how many of them the store has!

PARENT: That's 1.

CHILD: It's not going to make me fight, I promise! If you buy me the game, I'll promise not to fight any more.

PARENT: That's 2.

CHILD: I can't believe you're being so mean. You just don't want me to have any fun; you HATE it when I have a good time.

PARENT: That's 3. Time-out is going to happen in that corner over there.

The "1" and "2" counts are there to provide the child with some time to bring her behavior under control before a time-out must occur. For misbehaviors of high severity (e.g., breaking a known rule), the first two counts are skipped, and the parent says: "That's 3—time-out."

Phelan (2014) also recommends use of a kitchen timer as a tool for parents trying to enforce children's performance of everyday tasks, such as getting dressed and doing chores. Rather than cajoling or threatening, he recommends the parent state the directive, set the timer for a period of time sufficient for task completion plus a small allowance for procrastination, state the consequences that will follow compliance or disobedience, and leave. Then, there is no one for the child to argue with but the timer.

Abbreviating Behavioral-Systemic Interventions

The child management techniques recommended by parent training programs are fairly labor-intensive, and, even after discussion with the therapist, some parents feel they cannot implement all the procedures. This is a situation in which the therapist must weigh research findings against clinical considerations. Outcome studies have supported parent training programs that were implemented in their entirety, but if the reality is that the caregiver will not conduct all the procedures, clinicians need to develop flexible alternatives that, although not empirically supported in the strict sense, seem capable of helping the child. Clinical experience suggests that abbreviated versions of these interventions can be effective.

It is important to think carefully about which techniques to keep and which to let go. Barkley (2013) advises that, if only two techniques can be implemented, the parent should use praise for positive behavior and time-out for noncompliance. In addition, busy parents could learn those techniques that require them to develop new skills but do not involve significant amounts of time. These strategies include praise for positive behavior, ignoring negative behavior, stating directives effectively, and Phelan's (2014) 1-2-3 technique.

Contingency contracting cannot be done without some investment of time, but if necessary for the sake of feasibility, it can be pruned of its charts, point systems, and reward menus, and simplified into a procedure with three components. The parent:

1. Defines the behavior he expects from the child.
2. Identifies a time frame, such as an afternoon or a full day.
3. Provides an incentive, such as dessert or computer time, for satisfactory behavior during this time.

Child management procedures can usually be modified without severe loss of effectiveness as long as the modifications are consistent with the theoretical principles on which the procedures are based. Table 10.2 summarizes these principles.

Collaborative Problem Solving

This section must begin with a note about labeling. The collaborative problem solving (CPS) approach was originally developed primarily by Ross Greene (2001), but due to a lawsuit with an appeal pending at the time of the writing of this book, Greene is unable to use this title for his approach, which he has relabeled "collaborative and proactive solutions." The result is confusing. Greene's approach is generally known in our field as "collaborative problem solving," and that is how I refer to it in this book. However, if you google the term, you will find books and articles by Greene but the website of the organization on the other side of the lawsuit. (Ironically, the two sides have not been able to solve their problem collaboratively.)

CPS is a parent training intervention, but it differs from the behavioral-systemic therapies described previously by placing less emphasis on securing immediate, consistent child compliance and more emphasis on remediating the deficits in emotion regulation and executive cognitive functioning that contribute to noncompliance (Greene, 2010; Greene & Ablon, 2006; Greene, Ablon, Goring, Fazio, et al., 2004; Greene et al., 2003). The CPS understanding of etiology is based less on principles of reinforcement than on cognitive, developmental, and neurobiological research on disruptive behavior disorders. The child for whom CPS is intended defies directives not because she chooses to do so in order to maximize reinforcement but because she is upset, cannot think clearly, becomes disorganized, and overflows with distressed and/or angry emotions. CPS focuses on capability, not motivation.

CPS dissents from traditional parent training programs by advocating discussion and negotiation with children during conflicts, even when this delays compliance. CPS teaches parents and other authority figures both to work around the child's weaknesses and to facilitate the development of strengths she lacks; thus, CPS both compensates for and remediates deficits in executive cognitive functioning. Overall, this approach has a softer, gentler quality than the more strictly behavioral forms of parent training. Later in this section I will discuss which clients are appropriate for CPS, but first I will describe how it works.

The intervention begins with psychoeducational work with the parent. The counselor explains the child's noncompliance as the result of a "learning disability." The clinician explains that, while some disobedient behavior is willful, much is not, resulting instead from dysfunction in the areas of the brain responsible for managing emotions and controlling behavior—for example:

"When Susie is told to do something she doesn't want to do, her experience isn't like yours or mine. She can't look at the situation objectively. She fixates on the thing she wants, and it fills her mind until it seems like the most important thing in the world—she feels like there's no reason for someone to stop her from getting it unless they're just *mean*—and she just wants to scream and fight. It's like her brain goes into a spasm, and there's no real thinking going on, it's just intense emotion, so when your voice comes in, she can hardly hear it. It isn't that she's a bad kid because, for one thing, she didn't ask to have a brain that works like that, and for another, these experiences are pretty miserable for her, too."

The collaborative approach trains parents to be proactive by examining the antecedents of their child's disruptive behavior and structuring the environment to minimize their frequency, as discussed earlier. For example, if a child and his sister often get in each other's way while brushing their teeth before bed, it might be easier to prevent crises by having them do this separately than to manage the crises that occur when they are in the bathroom together.

CPS teaches caregivers to choose from among three types or "baskets" of responses when their child begins to misbehave. Basket A includes responses that impose the adult's will on the child by enforcing compliance (e.g., time-out). The disadvantage of Basket A is that these responses sometimes increase oppositionality and elicit outbursts. Basket C responses remove the expectation that is eliciting the noncompliant behavior. Basket C responses usually prevent outbursts, but at the cost of leaving the adult's expectation unmet and, possibly, reinforcing oppositional behavior. Basket B responses combine emotional support and collaborative problem solving provided by the caregiver to the child.

The collaborative approach acknowledges that all three types of parental responses have advantages and all provide appropriate options in some situations. Basket A responses are called for when there is a danger of harm or severe inconvenience, so it is imperative that the child comply with the directive immediately. Basket C responses make sense when the directive is not important and attempting to secure compliance would result in a major battle that is not worth the trouble. Basket B responses apply to the largest number of situations and also have the major asset of facilitating the development of stronger executive functioning in the youngster. CPS is mostly about Basket B responses.

For parents, this type of response begins internally, with the establishment of a collaborative *attitude*. The parent's agenda expands from the simple objective of securing immediate compliance to the broader goal of helping the child learn self-management skills.

The parent's agenda expands from the simple objective of securing immediate compliance to the broader goal of helping the child learn self-management skills.

If the child becomes upset, whether in response to a directive or for some other reason, the parent is taught to empathize and to help the child organize her emotions by putting them into words. The parent labels the child's feelings, connects these emotions to the events eliciting them, and acknowledges desires of the child that are frustrated by the directive. Thus, therapists teach parents how to use the basic counseling skills described in Chapter 1—for example:

- "You don't like going to bed when you're having fun playing."
- "You really want that toy, and you don't understand why I won't buy it; you feel like I'm just being mean."
- "You're really mad at Anne for saying that, and you feel like hitting her."

If the child needs more help to calm down, the parent coaches him in emotion regulation techniques, perhaps by suggesting deep breathing, taking a break from the conflict, or providing a pleasant distraction. If the child is soothed by physical affection, the parent could stroke his arm or offer a hug. If the child is soothed by food (and eating issues are not a concern), the parent could offer a snack.

Once the child calms down, problem solving can begin, with the parent guiding the process. Therapists can teach parents the same problem-solving technique they teach children (described later in this chapter). The routes/goals strategy presented in Chapter 8 can also be applied here.

The parent verbalizes both his expectation of the child and the child's reaction to this expectation, thus accomplishing two things simultaneously: validating the youngster's feelings and conveying that the expectation will not go away. Then, the caregiver thinks out loud as he leads the search for a way to enable both of them to get most of what they want, with brainstorming and evaluation of possible solutions. If the child becomes upset again, the parent switches back to empathy and coaching in stress management (e.g., "I know this is frustrating; maybe it will help to stretch and take a deep breath").

Ideally, this type of negotiation results in a win-win outcome. Perhaps a chore could be delayed, or an element of fun could be added to make it more palatable, or an incentive could be offered for completing the task. Compromises are appropriate if caregiver expectations are negotiable. Most importantly, this parental coaching provides in-home training for the child in precisely the capabilities she needs: emotion regulation and executive cognitive functioning.

Authoritative Versus Collaborative Responses to Noncompliance

The markedly different responses to child noncompliance recommended by CPS and traditional parent training represent a challenge for therapists planning treatment. Careful consideration of the outcome research supporting these two types of intervention can help with this decision making. While behavioral parent training has received support from a much larger number of studies, there is some evidence that CPS is more effective with the subset of noncompliant children who exhibit serious depressive symptoms and/or deficits in executive functioning.

Behavioral parent training programs are predicated on the assumption that the client is responsive to environmental contingencies and will change his behavior if those consequences are altered. The firm, no-nonsense spirit of these interventions seems well suited to the treatment of noncompliance that, to a significant degree, is voluntary, chosen, and initiated by the child. The gentler nature of the collaborative approach, with its emphasis on support rather than consequences, may be vulnerable to manipulation by youth who are in control of their behavior, but CPS seems well suited to the treatment of youngsters whose disruptive behavior is a function of emotional flooding, misinterpretation of situations, and an inability to think of adaptive options. The difference is not absolute–behavioral-systemic therapy includes some provision for supporting the child's self-control capabilities (e.g., reducing caregiver yelling and increasing the clarity of directives), while CPS acknowledges that some directives should be non-negotiable and consequences are sometimes useful–but the difference in emphasis is extensive and fundamental. As a result, behavioral parent training seems appropriate to the degree that misbehavior is a function of motivation, reinforcement, and incentives, while CPS seems appropriate to the degree that misbehavior results from weak capabilities in emotion regulation, problem solving, and self-control.

When children behave in an agitated, disruptive, and/or aggressive manner, the behavioral and CPS approaches suggest caregiver responses that, in some ways, are not merely different but are opposite to one another. The question is whether comforting a misbehaving child would be more likely to reduce the distress impairing her self-control or to reinforce the noncompliant behavior. From a behavioral perspective, the support and negotiation recommended by CPS would have the effect of rewarding dysfunctional behavior. From a CPS perspective, administering a negative consequence to a youth already in distress would further reduce his capability for self-control and result in even more disturbed behavior. In some situations, the recommended response of each approach is viewed not merely as ineffective but as counterproductive by the other formulation. (It is interesting to note that this dilemma of whether to respond to maladaptive behavior with negative consequences or support also appears in social policy discussions. Controversies about whether criminals should be punished or rehabilitated and whether welfare dependency should be addressed by increasing services or cutting benefits seem to hinge on the empirical question of whether these behaviors are primarily a function of motivation or incapability.)

This quandary cannot be resolved on theoretical grounds but should be approached as an assessment question for each client. The caregiver, with guidance from the therapist, needs to determine whether the misbehavior is primarily the result of motivational or capability-related factors, so she can gear her response to the type of factor most responsible for the disturbed functioning. Clinical decision making need not be black-and-white. If both types of factors seem to be involved, some combination of CPS and behavioral techniques might be optimal. It is possible to blend the assets of the firmer and the gentler approaches, rather than choosing between them. Achieving an effective blend requires the parent to maintain a boundary between collaborating with the child and acquiescing to her. Parents can respond in different ways to the same child in different situations, depending on whether the misbehavior seems more due to manipulation or incapability. Within single episodes, caregivers can achieve a balance in which they alternate between comforting the child and insisting on compliance. The message is, "I will help you manage this situation, but I will not let you escape the situation." Often, directives have a "bottom line," and, above this line, there can be give-and-take about details.

Individual CBT With the Child

Although outcome research provides support only for medicines as treatments of the core attentional symptoms of ADHD (Connor, 2006; Pelham & Fabiano, 2008), clinically, there are a couple of techniques that seem to help some of these youth. First, putting tasks and plans in writing, whether on paper or digitally, seems to concretize and organize

thoughts that, otherwise, often slip away from youth with ADHD. To-do lists are an important tool for this population, and the positive reinforcement of checking off items as they
are completed seems to help clients stay on track. Use of these lists can extend beyond
homework assignments and chores. Complex plans can be broken down into lists and sub-
lists in a hierarchical manner (i.e., tasks unpacked into subtasks).

ADHD is characterized by deficits in self-monitoring (Barkley, 2006; Rickel & Brown,
2007). These clients frequently lose the thread of what they are doing and find themselves
off-task. Cognitively, in a moment-to-moment way, what they seem to lack is the mental
habit of checking on their intention for the period of time involved to see if their immediate behavior connects to that plan. Therefore, it is valuable for these clients to cultivate
the habit of frequently asking themselves the question, "What is the best thing for me to
be doing right now?" Use of this self-statement results in discoveries such as, "Oh: I wanted
to type an email to my friend, but I seem to be playing this video game again." Such discoveries may bring clients out of daydreams or extraneous activities and back to the tasks
they wanted to focus on.

Social Problem Solving

Training in social problem solving (Kazdin, 2003, 2010; Shure, 1996; Spivack & Shure,
1982), an empirically supported cognitive intervention for children aged 7 years and older,
treats some of the deficits in executive functioning that are common in children with disruptive behavior problems. This type of therapy consists of teaching the client a structured
technique for thinking problems through and planning responses, and then guiding her
practice and application of the technique.

There are several different formulae that can be used, but they all share central features. First, the cognitively demanding nature of the procedures requires the child to slow
down in order to perform them; rather than responding quickly, the child must talk himself
through a procedure with several steps. This feature of problem solving is probably helpful
in itself, regardless of content, because step-by-step thinking is inherently incompatible
with impulsivity.

Table 10.6 presents a step-by-step formula similar to the one originated by Spivack and
Shure (1982). The technique consists mostly of a series of questions that the child asks

Table 10.6   The Problem-Solving Procedure

---

1. *What is the problem?* This first step simply asks for a concise verbal statement of the situation
   being faced.

2. *What are possible solutions to the problem?* This step requires the child to brainstorm at least two
   options for what she might do about the problem.

3. *What are the probable consequences of the options?* In this step, the child switches from
   brainstorming to critical, realistic thinking, as he projects his options into the future and
   anticipates their consequences.

4. *Choose the best option and do it.* Clients choose the option with the best probable consequences,
   as assessed in Step 3.

5. *Did it work?* If Step 4 solves the problem, the procedure is over. If it does not, the child goes
   back to her remaining options from Step 2 and chooses the one with the consequences she
   likes best.

---

herself and answers. Our website includes a handout (Form 10.5) that clients can use to apply the technique to situations in their lives.

Problem-solving techniques require clients to **brainstorm**—that is, to think of multiple possibilities for a given situation. In brainstorming, the premium is on the quantity not the quality of ideas, and the goal is to free up the thought process so it produces numerous possibilities. Critical thinking, in which good ideas are separated from bad ones, comes later. This separation of generative and critical thinking is consistent with research on the creative process, which is most effective when people first allow their minds to roam and play and then, later, subject the products of their imagination to critical evaluation (Guilford, 1984).

Counselors can help clients increase the range and productivity of their brainstorming with instructions like, "In this step (#2), the goal is to think of as many ideas as you can, and it doesn't even matter whether they're good or bad; we'll deal with that later." In Step 3, the client switches gears to a more stringent type of cognition: consequential thinking. Clients picture their different options and the consequences likely to result, which usually consist of the reactions of the other people in the situation. An example therapist instruction would be, "Now let's think about this realistically; if you go with that option, what do you think would probably happen?" In the evaluation step (#4), clients add up the probable consequences associated with each option and determine which provides the most favorable sum. Clients' responses to questions 2, 3, and 4 should parallel each other, as they first generate and then evaluate the same set of possible solutions. If implementation of the first chosen option does not work, Step 5 sends the child back to Step 2 to select another option.

For younger children, most of the reasoning involved in this technique is a matter of common sense, with the main point usually being that disruptive behavior generally leads to negative consequences, while cooperative behavior usually leads to positive ones. PSST is useful because it provides a structure that funnels children's thinking toward common-sense decisions. With older, more cognitively advanced youth, the technique provides a structure for organizing complicated, creative reasoning and planning.

To help youngsters learn the technique, counselors should model the steps by using them to think through problems out loud. Then, to help clients practice the technique, therapists should guide clients through applications to a variety of situations. Additional examples should be done as homework. The technique is widely applicable, and clients can use it to generate and evaluate possible solutions for problems depicted in books, movies, television programs, and even current events in the news.

Children who are young or intellectually limited need a simplified version of the problem-solving technique. I use a stripped-down procedure that consists of asking and answering three questions:

1. What is the problem?
2. What could I do? (Must think of at least two options.)
3. What should I do?

For clients who think visually, diagrams of branching paths can be used to visually represent the likely consequences of alternative behaviors. Choices are like a fork in the road; they lead, predictably, to different consequences. The essentials of problem solving can be diagrammed as two basic options: The aggressive or oppositional one that is the child's typical way of responding, and the cooperative behavior that is the goal of therapy. Two lines drawn from this choice point can lead to written or drawn depictions of predictable out-comes. I always draw the prosocial path going up and the disruptive one going down.

Psychodynamic Therapy

Although the dynamic approach does not have empirical support as an intervention for disruptive behavior, it may be useful as a component of therapy for some clients. Dynamic therapy may be helpful for clients whose noncompliant behavior is caused by internalized relationship dynamics or conflicts that are not accessible to conscious, reality-oriented thinking. This approach differs from the interventions presented earlier by viewing dis-ruptive behavior not only as a symptom to be eliminated but also as an informative piece of the puzzle of the child's development.

Kernberg and Chazan (1991) provide a manual for treating children with oppositional and conduct disorders. Their approach utilizes dynamic principles in three treatment modalities: individual and group therapy using play, and parent guidance. The material to follow also draws on Chethik (2000), Gardner (1993), and E. Wachtel (1994).

Dynamic therapists assume that noncompliance has some meaning for the child. Interpretations help the client discover the meaning of this behavior, its defensive purpose, and the conceptions of self and others on which the noncompliance is based. Then, dynamic psychoeducation corrects any misunderstandings or unrealistic thinking that has contributed to the problems.

Dynamic therapists set limits on misbehavior like other clinicians do. In addition, they inquire and comment—for example:

> "Whatever I say, you do the opposite; you just don't want to do what I say. Does some-thing like that happen with Mom and Dad?"

For some children, noncompliance is motivated by a fear of helplessness and depen-dency. In the defense mechanism called **overcompensation**, the person goes in the opposite direction from her fear in order to allay that fear. This defense usually has an overdone, extreme quality. In noncompliance, it is as if the child has the thought, consciously or unconsciously, that the way to prove he is not a dependent baby is to defy parental direc-tives and do whatever he wants. Thus, noncompliance may function as a defense against the anxiety of feeling weak and powerless. This pattern can be interpreted with statements like the following:

> "I guess when you listen to adults and do what they say, you feel like a baby who can't do things on his own. Maybe that's why you fight with Mom so much; to prove you're not a mama's boy by being the opposite."

Anxious concern about being dependent sometimes derives from a schema in which control is viewed as an all-or-nothing phenomenon. In these object relations, adult author-ities are perceived as tyrants who want to have complete control over children. Given this concept of the Other, children have only two, opposite alternatives: They can submit and receive adult approval at the price of relinquishing all independence, or they can say no and refuse to comply in an effort to preserve their autonomy. Interpretations like the following address the client's concept of adult authority figures as well as her representation of self:

> "Is that what you think grownups (or your parents, teachers, etc.) want? To tell you what to do all day long, like you're a dummy or a robot who can't think for yourself? It must make you want to fight back by not doing anything they say. It's a war—and the war is no fun, but I guess you don't see any way out."

Because children with such object relations lack a schema for power sharing with their parents, they feel that compliance equals humiliating defeat and/or helpless dependency. But both extremes—helplessness and defiance—are unsatisfactory, and the need is for a third alternative that stands in between.

Providing disruptive children with insight into the dynamics beneath their behavior might not be enough to enable them to develop new, adaptive responses to adult authority. Many of these clients also need psychoeducational input to help them develop new schemas for positive responses to directives—for example:

- "You've been stuck in this problem where you feel like you can either make Mom happy or make yourself happy. But what if both of you could be happy? There's enough time for you to do the things Mom wants and the things you want to do yourself."
- "It's like how grownups have work time and play time. For kids, doing what parents and teachers tell them is work, because it's not usually fun but it needs to be done, and then, during play time, you get to do what you want."

Clinicians should operationally define the new, recommended conceptions of authority and compliance so the client can picture them—for instance:

> "I wonder what would happen if you took all that 'I'm not listening to you' energy and used it to learn what Dad is trying to teach you about baseball; I bet you'd improve your game."

The type of therapeutic input contained in these statements might help clients modify their schemas for interacting with authority figures in ways favorable to the development of compliance. These modified schemas could involve a compromise or synthesis that the client had not previously been able to envision, in which age-appropriate degrees of self-direction and compliance coexist in a comfortable balance.

Summary

Noncompliant behavior is generally caused by a combination of genetic factors, deficits in executive cognitive functioning, and cycles of coercive behavior between parents and children. Behavioral-systemic analyses have identified subtle patterns of reciprocal reinforcement occurring between parents and children who are stuck in aversive interaction cycles.

Outcome research provides extensive support for behavioral-systemic parent training and considerable support for PSST as treatments for disruptive behavior in children.

The CPS approach has some strong support for the subset of noncompliant children with serious comorbid depression.

Behavioral-systemic therapies teach parents how to provide nondirective, positive attention to their child in an activity called Special Time; this technique improves parent-child relationships and increases the reinforcement value of parental attention. Parents learn how to address the antecedents of noncompliant behavior by structuring the child's environment and providing clear, easily understood directives. Behavioral parent training programs reverse the reinforcement contingencies associated with noncompliance by training parents to ignore minor misbehavior; provide social, symbolic, and tangible rewards for positive behavior; and administer time-outs and response costs contingent on significant misbehavior.

When disruptive behavior is mostly under the voluntary control of the child, firm implementation of consequences, with a minimum of conversation, seems to be the most effective parental response. In other words, when disruptive behavior seems mostly a function of motivational factors, behavioral parent training seems to be the most appropriate intervention. When misbehavior results from breakdowns in emotion regulation that the child cannot control, parents seem to be more effective when they help the child calm down, think the situation through, and negotiate a mutually acceptable solution. In other

Table 10.7   Key Concepts in Treatment of Disruptive Behavior Disorders

Therapeutic Approach	Etiologies	Treatment Techniques
Behavioral-systemic	Cycle of coercive behaviors between parents and children.	Behavioral-systemic parent training.
	Environmental antecedents of misbehavior.	Structuring the child's environment.
	Parent's directives are complex and unclear.	Guidelines for effective commands.
	Insufficient positive interaction between parent and child.	Special Time.
	Parent ignores positive and attends to negative behavior.	Parent ignores negative and attends to positive behavior.
	Insufficient positive reinforcement.	Contingent praise and contingency contracting.
	Excessive negotiation.	The 1-2-3 technique.
	Punishments are harsh, delayed, and/or inconsistent.	Time-out and response cost.
Cognitive	Deficiencies in emotion regulation and executive cognitive functioning.	Collaborative problem solving led by the parent.
	Impulsivity and weak consequential thinking.	Problem-solving training for the child.
Psychodynamic	Compliance threatens the child's sense of autonomy.	Build schema reconciling compliance and autonomy.

words, when disruptive behavior seems mostly a function of inadequate self-regulatory capabilities, CPS is probably the most appropriate intervention.

PSST strengthens executive cognitive functioning. These step-by-step problem-solving procedures teach children how to respond to difficult situations by generating options, anticipating consequences, and planning what to do.

Table 10.7 summarizes the causes of disruptive behavior disorders and the treatment techniques designed to address these etiologies.

Case Study

Ricky's therapy consisted entirely of behavioral-systemic parent training, and his treatment was straightforward and uncomplicated. The assessment revealed that his mother had fallen into some of the traps that commonly block parents from translating their child-rearing intentions into everyday practice. Ricky's mother learned and applied the new child management techniques she was taught by the therapist. The child's cooperative, pleasant behavior increased as it was nurtured by his mother's positive attention and tangible rewards, and his annoying, recalcitrant responses diminished as the arguments that had fueled them were replaced by withdrawals of attention and consistent use of time-outs.

11

Disruptive Behavior in Adolescents

OBJECTIVES

This chapter explains:

- *The breakdown in parental authority associated with disruptive behavior disorders.*
- *The roles played by motivational factors and self-control capabilities in conduct disturbances.*
- *The importance of clear, consistent rules.*
- *A hierarchy of consequences and fallback plans that parents can use with adolescents.*
- *Effective ways for parents to talk to teens about disciplinary issues.*
- *How to make prosocial behavior more appealing to rebellious youth.*
- *How parents can rebuild trust and warmth with conduct-disordered teens.*
- *Interpretations that help clients see the discrepancies between their object relations and real behavior by adults.*

Case Study
Control

Jack, a 16-year-old European American adolescent, had become impossible for his parents to control. Jack was often truant from school, had all but stopped doing homework, and had grades ranging from Cs to Fs. His mother and stepfather were certain he shoplifted because he had more clothes and knick-knacks than could possibly be purchased with the money they gave him. If they stayed up late enough on weekend nights to be there when he came home, they often smelled alcohol or marijuana.

The parents and teen had terrible arguments in which Jack screamed, swore at them, and, on several occasions, destroyed household objects. During these arguments, he sometimes blamed his mother for divorcing his father who, 8 years previously, had moved to another state and did not maintain consistent contact with his son; Jack claimed the loss had ruined his life. This accusation often reduced his mother to tears, which enraged the stepfather, who counterattacked with insults that sometimes precipitated violent responses from Jack.

His mother and stepfather had been married for 4 years when the family came for treatment. When Jack was home, he was unsociable with the family, refused to do chores, and monopolized the one large TV set, showing little consideration for the parents, his younger sister, or stepbrother. The diagnosis most appropriate for Jack was conduct disorder, adolescent-onset subtype.

During the assessment, the therapist repeatedly had to remind Jack to keep his feet off the office furniture. Jack occasionally snorted in response to her inquiries, saying, "That question is irrelevant." More frequently, he yawned and said he did not know. The therapist found herself wondering angrily how this low-achieving, obnoxious adolescent could act as if he considered himself so superior to others.

Diagnoses Treated in This Chapter

Conduct Disorder

Conduct disorder (CD) is a pattern of behavior in which the rights of other people or major societal norms are repeatedly violated. Three of the following four features must be present: aggression against people or animals, destruction of property, serious rule violations, and deceitfulness or theft. DSM-5 differentiates between the childhood-onset and adolescent-onset subtypes of this disturbance. CD is a type of externalizing dysfunction that usually causes distress to others and may or may not involve distress for the youth himself.

Adjustment Disorder With Disturbance of Conduct

This diagnosis differs from CD in that it originates in response to a stressful external event. In order for the diagnosis to be made, the disturbed conduct must appear within 3 months of the occurrence of the stressor, and after the stressor and its situational consequences come to an end, the disturbed conduct must abate within 6 months. This diagnosis does not require as high a severity level as CD.

Clinical Presentation and Etiology

This chapter is about adolescents who break societal rules and hurt other people. It is the middle chapter of our three-chapter sequence on externalizing problems.

CD occurs at the interface of the mental health and juvenile justice systems, and these youth are involved sometimes in one, sometimes in the other, and frequently in both (Lourie & Hernandez, 2003). Conduct disturbances are like mental health problems in some ways and like juvenile delinquency in other ways.

ODD in early childhood often develops into CD in later childhood and adolescence (Burke, Waldman, & Lahey, 2010; Moffitt et al., 2008). Without effective intervention, this developmental trajectory often ends in adult antisocial personality disorder and incarceration (Beauchaine, Hinshaw, & Pang, 2010).

CD tends to have a different etiology, symptom pattern, and prognosis, depending on when, in the course of development, it first appears (Frick & Viding, 2009; Moffitt, 2003). The **childhood-onset** subtype of CD is associated with more risk factors, including neuropsychological deficits, family dysfunction, ADHD, and rejection by peers, as well as a worse prognosis for both mental health and adult criminal outcomes. The **adolescent-onset** subtype is more common and less severe, and is associated with antisocial and aggressive behavior committed in groups, such as gangs. These youth may be popular, especially with antisocial peers. This subtype of CD often dissipates in adulthood.

The childhood-onset subtype is associated with more severe psychological dysfunction, while the adolescent-onset subtype is largely a matter of rebellion and rejection of conventional norms, especially compliance with adult authority (Dandreaux & Frick, 2009; Kimonis, Frick, & McMahon, 2014). This subtype can be viewed as an exaggeration of developmentally normal adolescent rebellion and experimentation with forbidden activities. Although occasional experimentation with rule breaking is a common part of adolescence, frequent occurrence of these behaviors leads to negative developmental outcomes.

CD is associated with a long list of risk factors, including genetic, familial, socioeconomic, maltreatment-related, peer, and neighborhood factors (Kimonis et al., 2014; Murray & Farrington, 2010). Genetic predisposition is a significant factor of moderate magnitude (Bornovalova, Hicks, Iacono, & McGue, 2010). Genetic factors are more important to the childhood-onset subtype, while environmental risks are more important to the adolescent-onset subtype (Moffitt, 2003).

If youth with CD are asked about the reasons for their behavior, they typically say they just want to have fun, which requires them to defy adults' restrictions so they can cut school, steal desirable possessions, refuse to do chores, have sex, use drugs, and so forth. Given that activities of this type do naturally involve pleasure, it is useful to ask why most youth do *not* develop CD. The short answer is that their parents won't let them.

Young people frequently do not want what is best for them in the long run, and it is natural for them to prefer candy over vegetables, video games over schoolwork, and taking what they want over sharing with others. As a result, compliance with adult authority plays an essential role in the development of prosocial behavior. In the beginning, children engage in positive behavior largely because their parents require and reinforce such behavior. Over time, they develop the values and skills necessary to maintain prosocial functioning on their own. CD involves a breakdown in the normative authority structure in families, in which the parents are in charge of the children (Barkley & Robin, 2014; Henggeler, Schoenwald, Rowland, & Cunningham, 2002; Sells, 2004). In families where the parents are not in charge, the youth's impulses toward immediate gratification overpower the requirements of socialization, and developmental trajectories end in disruptive behavior disorders.

CD involves a breakdown in the normative authority structure in families, in which the parents are in charge of the children.

Youth with CD exhibit psychological abnormalities that make them difficult to parent. In laboratory experiments and in real life, these youth are under-responsive to negative consequences (Frick, Cornell, Barry, Bodin, & Dane, 2003; Frick, Cornell, Bodin, et al., 2003). They have particular difficulty reversing their responses when reinforcement contingencies change from reward to punishment (Budhani & Blair, 2005). Their lack of fear in response to threat may give these youth an appearance of "having ice water in their veins," and this insouciance reduces the effectiveness of punishments threatened by authority figures.

Along with under-responsiveness to punishment, youth with CD show a heightened sensitivity to rewards (Frick, Cornell, Barry, et al., 2003; Frick, Cornell, Bodin, et al., 2003). In laboratory experiments, they are willing to risk strong aversive consequences for the chance to obtain small rewards. In everyday life, they are willing to risk getting in serious trouble for the chance to experience brief excitement and pleasure.

Although internalizing and externalizing are very different forms of psychopathology, they can co-occur. Youth with CD have high rates of depression and anxiety (Boylan, Vaillancourt, Boyle, & Szatmari, 2007; Frick & Nigg, 2012). Their nonconforming, antisocial behaviors generally seem motivated by the pursuit of fun and excitement, but these attempts do not usually work past the short term, and most youth with CD are not happy. The existence of dysphoria is a potential source of treatment motivation.

Motivational and Capability-Related Factors

Youth with CD exhibit below-average cognitive capabilities, scoring about 8 points below average on IQ tests (Hogan, 1999). Their verbal IQs are lower than their performance IQs (Lynam & Henry, 2001). CD often co-occurs with ADHD and deficits in executive functioning (Angold, Costello, & Erkanli, 1999). These weaknesses in language and attention contribute to the deficits in self-control, problem-solving, and social skills associated with CD (Hastings, Zahn-Waxler, Robinson, Usher, & Bridges, 2000; Jaffee & D'Zurilla, 2003).

At the extreme end of CD-associated motivational abnormalities are youth with **callous and unemotional traits**. These youth show a lack of empathy for other people, do not feel guilty about hurting others, and engage in especially severe and aggressive forms of antisocial behavior that often persist into adulthood (Frick, Cornell, Barry, et al., 2003; Frick, Ray, Thornton, & Kahn, 2014). Youth with callous and unemotional traits can injure people in a disturbingly calm, cool way, without being angry or upset, as if the behavior comes easily to them and is not opposed by their conscience.

There is also a subtype of youth with CD who show the opposite pattern of emotional responding: Their feelings are unmanageably intense. Youth with CD but without callous traits are highly *reactive* to negative emotional stimuli and other people's distress (Kimonis, Frick, Fazekas, & Loney, 2006; Loney, Frick, Clements, Ellis, & Kerlin, 2003). They feel distress and remorse when they hurt others and have high rates of anxiety (Pardini, Lochman, & Powell, 2007). These young people act out because they get so upset in response to problems that they are unable to maintain self-control. The presence of internalizing dysfunction in youth with CD has positive prognostic implications and predicts improvement in response to intervention, perhaps because it suggests discomfort with antisocial behavior (Jarrett, Siddiqui, Lochman, & Qu, 2014; Kernberg, Weiner, & Bardenstein, 2000; Lahey & Waldman, 2003).

These research findings in conjunction with clinical observation suggest two different types of factors in CD. When motivational factors are primary, the youth does not *want* to behave in a prosocial manner: These adolescents are attracted to antisocial forms of pleasure, do not find the associated punishments highly aversive, and are not very concerned about transgressing moral standards or hurting other people. They are capable of behaving appropriately, but they frequently choose not to, because they find that disruptive behaviors "work" in the sense of getting them what they want. Their disruptive behaviors are planned, proactive, freely chosen, and enjoyed. In contrast, when self-control capabilities are weak, the youth might want to behave in a prosocial manner, but a combination of weak psychosocial skills and intense emotional pressures often disrupts his intention to behave appropriately. The disruptive behaviors that result are typically undesired and aversive to the youth, and might even feel involuntary. These are the adolescents about whom it could be said that "They can't help it." Their disruptive behaviors are reactive, dysphoric, and regretted afterward. Research on CD subtypes indicates that childhood onset is associated with weak capabilities and adolescent onset is associated with antisocial motivations, but for treatment planning purposes the important consideration is not age of onset but which set of factors is primarily responsible for the pattern of disruptive behavior.

For example, adolescents with either type of CD often resist doing homework, but the reasons and dynamics would be quite different. If motivational factors were primary, typical reasons would be that the youth does not care about school or pleasing her parents and she prefers playing video games and chatting with friends, while if capability factors were primary, typical reasons would be that weak concentration abilities, low frustration tolerance, and anxiety about failure make homework such a miserable ordeal that it cannot be sustained for long without a meltdown. As another example, teens with either type of CD get into a lot of fights, but as explained in Chapter 12, proactive and reactive aggression have different causes and call for different therapeutic responses.

The motivation/capability distinction mirrors the different views of disruptive behavior presented by Greene and Ablon (2006) on one hand and traditional behavior therapists on the other, as discussed in the previous chapter. The collaborative problem solving approach applies to emotionally impaired teens who cannot help acting out in response to overwhelming distress. The behavioral approach applies to young people who have been responding to reinforcement contingencies that support disruptive behavior but who can also respond to therapeutically designed contingencies that reinforce prosocial behavior. Table 11.1 summarizes the factors associated with motivation-based and capability-based etiologies of disruptive behavior.

Neurobiological Etiologies

Neurobiological research has identified abnormalities in brain anatomy and physiology that help to explain many of the behavioral, emotional, and interpersonal characteristics of youth with CD. These abnormalities are most consistently found in the subset of youth who exhibit callous and unemotional traits, which can be viewed as indicating a severe form of CD (Frick & Viding, 2009). Many of the abnormalities involve low levels of activity and responsiveness in systems that regulate functioning related to the consequences of actions (Passamonti et al., 2010).

Table 11.1   Capability-Related Versus Motivational Factors in Conduct Disturbance

Cause of disturbed conduct	Inadequate capabilities	Dysfunctional motivations
Disturbed behavior is:	Reactive	Proactive
Emotional quality:	Agitated and remorseful	Callous and unemotional
Reaction to negative feedback:	Excessive	Insufficient
Age of onset:	Childhood	Adolescence
Parents should:	Offer support	Administer consequences
Treatment should emphasize:	Skills training	Reinforcement contingencies

Youth with callous and unemotional traits perform poorly in reversal learning tasks, which require the person to stop a previously rewarded response when the reinforcement contingency changes to punishment (Budhani & Blaire, 2005; Fisher & Blair, 1998). Neuroimaging research demonstrates that, during reversal learning, these youth show atypical functioning in the orbitofrontal region of the cortex, which processes information related to rewards and punishments (Finger et al., 2008). Apparently, their brains do not function in a way that enables them to effectively foresee consequences and modify their behavior in accordance with changes in reinforcement contingencies.

Raine (2011) found that, compared to normal controls, youth with CD have a smaller volume of gray matter (neuronal dendrites) in the amygdala, a structure that mediates fear conditioning. In studies by Jones, Laurens, Herba, Barker, and Viding (2009) and Marsh et al. (2008), children and adolescents with callous, unemotional traits showed less right amygdala activity in response to pictures of fearful faces, compared to normal controls. Youth with CD exhibit reduced functioning of the autonomic nervous system and the hypothalamic-pituitary-adrenal (HPA) axis, the brain/endocrine system that mediates arousal and fear (Cappadocia, Desrocher, Pepler, & Schroeder, 2009). In response to experimentally induced stress, they produce less cortisol, a stress hormone, compared to normal controls (Stadler et al., 2011). Because fear, stress, and threats of punishment elicit less of a physiological response in youth with CD, compared to other youth, it is not surprising that negative consequences have weaker effects on their behavior. The phrase, "I don't care" is a verbal expression of this unconcerned, blasé physiological state.

Behavioral-Systemic Etiologies

This chapter, like the preceding one, provides a single, integrated presentation of behavioral and family systems approaches because this is generally how the empirically supported interventions are constructed. For most clients with conduct disturbance, the main ingredients of effective treatment are appropriate consequences for behavior and improved parent-child relationships.

The behavioral-systemic formulation of the etiology of CD is similar to the explanation of disruptive behavior disorders in children, as described in the previous chapter. In adolescents as in children, genetically based temperament and neurophysiology exert significant influences on conduct problems (Bornovalova et al., 2010; Moffitt, 2003). Central nervous systems that feel irritable, crave immediate gratification, and react with frustration to ordinary obstacles are not comfortably adapted to a life consisting largely of sitting quietly, obeying adults, and concentrating on school material. As a result of this uncomfortable fit, these young people often clash with their caregivers, and youth with CD are difficult to parent (Fite, Colder, Lochman, & Wells, 2006). Another ramification of genetics is that the parents of these teens often have similar temperamental and cognitive characteristics (Capaldi, Conger, Hops, & Thornberry, 2003).

CD is associated with numerous familial risk factors, including low SES, parental separation, maternal depression, and social adversity (Frick & Viding, 2009). Family dysfunction, conflict, and lack of cohesion are strongly associated with CD (Reid, Patterson, & Snyder, 2002). The most important familial risk factor is dysfunctional parenting, which, to a substantial degree, mediates the association between conduct problems and other risk factors, such as poverty and family conflict (Lavigne, Gouze, Hopkins, Bryant, & LeBailly, 2012). In other words, when parents maintain effective child-rearing practices despite poverty and family conflict, the likelihood of adolescent CD is reduced. Dysfunctional parenting includes lack of involvement, rejecting behavior, inadequate supervision, and inconsistent discipline (Murray & Farrington, 2010; Patterson et al., 1992).

The social ecology perspective (Brofenbrenner, 1977) can be applied to any type of child dysfunction, but it has been most emphasized in treatment of CD. The clinical implication of this model is that therapists should broaden their work beyond the nuclear family by working, for example, with extended family, schools, neighbors, and peers (Henggeler et al., 2002; Henggeler, Cunningham, Schoenwald, Borduin, & Rowland, 2009).

When young people are not bonded to their families, they often bond with their peers. Association with antisocial peers is a strong predictor of disruptive behavior disturbances (Granic & Dishion, 2003; McCabe, Hough, Wood, & Yeh, 2001). When these youth congregate, they often encourage each other to explore risky, forbidden behaviors that promise a quick thrill (Dishion, Bullock, & Granic, 2002; Vitaro et al., 2000).

Cognitive Etiologies

Cognitive factors are frequently involved in the development of adolescent disruptive behavior disorders. In this book's three-chapter section on therapy for externalizing problems, there are sections on cognitive etiologies in Chapter 10 (on disruptive behavior in children) and Chapter 12 (on aggression). Because these clinical problems overlap so extensively with adolescent CD, the chapters immediately preceding and following this one include descriptions of the cognitive factors that contribute to conduct disturbance in teens, and readers are referred to those chapter sections for this information.

Psychodynamic Etiologies

Dynamic formulations of the causes of CD emphasize impaired parent-child attachment and inadequate superego development. Research indicates that insecure attachment to caregivers during infancy and early childhood predicts later development of conduct disturbance (Greenberg, DeKlyen, Speltz, & Endriga, 1997; Speltz, DeKlyen, & Greenberg, 1999).

Attachment theory proposes that the quality of children's attachments to their parents influences their willingness to comply with parental expectations (Sroufe, 2005). When the attachment relationship is secure and affectionate, children are willing to give up immediate gratification to gain their parents' approval. When the attachment relationship is insecure or ambivalent, children are less willing to make this trade.

The quality of the attachment relationship governs the degree to which children internalize their parents' values and moral standards. When children have loving internal images of their parents, they usually make parental norms and values their own. When internal representations of caregivers are rejecting or hurtful, children are less likely to internalize caregiver values and ethics (Greenberg et al., 1997; Speltz et al., 1999).

According to dynamic theory, the behavior of youth with CD makes sense as a response to the interpersonal world they see through the lenses of their object relations (Bleiberg, 2001; Kernberg & Chazan, 1991). These adolescents typically view adults as selfish and uncaring, if not hurtful and cruel. As a result, lying, manipulation, and intimidation seem like reasonable ways to deal with authority figures.

Although the terminology is different, the more closely one examines the dynamic and behavioral-systemic explanations of the etiology of disruptive behavior disorders, the less different they seem. The two theories provide similar descriptions of parent-child relationship disturbances and the consequences of these disturbances.

Assessment

Asking youth to report on their own behaviors may not be an effective way to diagnose conduct disturbance because these disorders often involve denial, externalization of blame, and lying. Clinicians typically rely on adult informants to report the extent of the youth's behavior problems. However, interviews with the youth are important for assessing the causes, functions, and meanings of the disturbed conduct.

Once the diagnosis has been made, one of the most important assessment questions is the degree to which the conduct disturbance is a function of motivational or capability-related factors. When disturbed conduct is caused by overwhelming emotions and weak coping skills, clients are likely to exhibit anxiety and internal conflict, and their acting out is related to these painful emotional states. When disturbed conduct is caused by rejection of societal norms, lack of concern about others, and an unwillingness to delay gratification, the client will not be disturbed by her behavior, although she might be unhappy about getting in trouble.

The presence of genuine remorse or guilt about past antisocial behavior suggests that capability-related factors play a primary role in the youth's conduct disturbance. Self-blame is a positive prognostic sign that indicates conscience development and concern about others (Kernberg & Chazan, 1991; Lahey & Waldman, 2003). The presence of anxiety predicts a positive response to therapy in adolescents with CD (Frick, Lilienfeld, Ellis, Loney, & Silverthorn, 1999; Kernberg et al., 2000). The assessment question is whether the client feels conflicted or comfortable about his antisocial behavior.

The motivation/capability distinction is sometimes difficult to assess. In principle, youth who choose disruptive behaviors for hedonistic purposes should present as cool and calculating, while youth whose emotional distress overwhelms their controls should be recognizable by their emotional outbursts and eventual expressions of remorse. Sometimes, however, both etiological processes are present and hard to disentangle. Also, youth with motivation-based CD sometimes learn that acting as if they are overwhelmed with distress is an effective manipulation technique. In these situations, assessment is an ongoing process of discovering the functions of behavior by noting sequences of precipitating events, client responses, and consequences, as described in the previous chapter.

Questions like the following can be used to assess client motivation to change disruptive behavior patterns:

- "Do you have any regrets about things you've done? Do you ever feel guilty about them?"
- "Is the problem that you *did* those things, or is the problem more that you got *caught*?"
- "What do you think of your behavior? Is there anything about it that you'd like to change, or is the problem in the way that adults react to your behavior?"
- "What do you think of the rules most kids have to follow these days? If it were up to you, what would the rules be?"

Here are some questions for examining conflict about impulses and ability to control emotional reactions:

- "Do you ever want to do things that you believe are wrong? Is it pretty easy to stop yourself, or is that hard?"
- "When you want to do something that could get you in trouble, can you put it away and move on, or is it like the desire gets stronger and stronger until you just have to do what it says?"
- "When upsetting things happen, are your emotional reactions ever so intense that they practically take over and make you do things? Like there's no way you could stop yourself?"
- "Do you wish you could do things that make your parents happy, or do you wish they'd just lay off you?"

DBT chain analysis (Linehan, 1993a, 1993b, 2014), presented in Chapter 4, is a useful assessment strategy for CD as well as BPD. This means asking the client to narrate two or three recent examples of her disruptive behavior in a detailed, moment-moment-way, with equal attention to what happened internally and externally, so you can gain a sense of the typical sequence of events.

Jack vacillated in his responses to these questions, and the clinician had trouble reading him. His bravado seemed to stop him from acknowledging any regrets about his behavior, but his tone of voice and body language suggested that there might be a part of him that was unhappy with the way he had been living. The therapist's assessment was that Jack's desire for quick, effortless forms of enjoyment, his limited degree of concern about other people's feelings, and his weak self-regulation capabilities probably all played contributory roles in his CD.

Treatment Planning

Outcome Research

Outcome research on CD has consistently failed to support unstructured, nondirective interventions, such as psychodynamic and client-centered therapy (Lipsey, 1995; Lochman, Powell, Boxmeyer, & Baden, 2012). Treatments that consist entirely of efforts to work through emotional issues, with no skills training for either youth or parent, are unlikely to help teens with CD.

Nondirective, process-oriented group therapy for youngsters with conduct disturbance actually makes their problems worse, because the group members encourage and reinforce antisocial behaviors in each other (Dishion et al., 2002; Dishion, McCord, & Poulin, 1999). Restrictive approaches, such as residential treatment, inpatient psychiatric hospitalization, and incarceration, while they temporarily get youth "off the streets," show little effectiveness at changing behavior and are extremely expensive (Henggeler & Santos, 1997). Incarceration brings antisocial youth together in groups, and the peer influence processes that result generally make their problems worse (Granic & Dishion, 2003).

Outcome research on CD indicates that two main ingredients are nec- *Outcome research on*
essary for effective therapy: behavioral parent training and family systems *CD indicates that*
work. The interventions with the most empirical support use this com- *two main ingredients*
bination of approaches. Psychosocial skills training for the adolescent *are necessary for*
is also an element of therapy in some of the treatment packages. Thus, *effective therapy:*
effective therapy for conduct disturbances generally combines CBT and *behavioral parent*
family systems therapy. *training and family*

Multisystemic therapy (MST; Henggeler et al., 2002; Henggeler, *systems work.*
Cunningham, et al., 2009) is an intensive, in-home intervention
combining behavioral parent training, family therapy, social-ecological interventions,
and psychosocial skills training for the youth. MST has produced positive outcomes
with severely disturbed and delinquent youth populations in over 20 published outcome
studies. A meta-analysis by van der Stouwe, Asscher, Stams, Deković, and van der
Laan (2014) found small but significant, positive effects on delinquency, out-of-home
placement, psychopathology, substance use, and family functioning, with no significant
treatment effects for youth skills or cognitions and an interaction effect indicating greater
effectiveness for youth under 15 years old.

In an efficacy trial with a sample of chronic, violent juvenile offenders followed for
14 years, MST improved family relationships, decreased mental health symptoms in
both youth and parents, and produced more than a 50% reduction in youth rearrests and
incarcerations, compared to usual juvenile justice services (Schaeffer & Borduin, 2005).
Rowland et al. (2005) compared MST to Hawaii's continuum of care for treatment of
youth with serious emotional and behavioral disturbances and found that MST produced
larger reductions in mental health symptoms and days in out-of-home placement. In a
quasi-experimental study of youth with serious emotional disturbance who were at risk
for out-of-home placement, MST produced larger decreases in mental health symptoms,
more improvement in youth functioning, and larger decreases in placements, compared
to wraparound services (Stambaugh et al., 2007). In a study with clients referred from
behavior intervention classrooms in public schools, Weiss et al. (2013) found a lower
level of effectiveness than most past investigations: Compared to TAU, MST produced
reductions in two of four outcome measures of externalizing problems.

Research on mediation of treatment effects has produced evidence for the mechanisms
of change emphasized by the theory underlying MST. Huey, Henggeler, Brondino, and
Pickrel (2000) showed that MST's positive impact on delinquent behavior was mediated by improvement in family relationships and reduced association with negative peers.
Henggeler, Letourneau, et al. (2009) found that MST's effects on antisocial behavior were
mediated by improved caregiver discipline and reduced association with negative peers.

Functional family therapy (FFT; Alexander & Parsons, 1982; Alexander, Waldron,
Robbins, & Neeb, 2013; Sexton, 2011) combines systems-oriented strategies, parent
training, work on family communication patterns, and reframing of the adolescent's
behavior. In one of the first randomized trials to show positive outcomes with youth in the
juvenile justice system, Parsons and Alexander (1973) found that FFT was more effective
than three comparison conditions in improving family interactions and decreasing recidivism for status offenses, but not criminal offenses. Barton, Alexander, Waldron, Turner,
and Warburton (1985) compared previously incarcerated delinquents who returned home
and received FFT to delinquents in group homes and found lower rearrest rates in the FFT
group over a 15-month period (60% vs. 93%). In a quasi-experimental study, D. Gordon,

Arbuthnot, Gustafson, and McGreen (1988) compared FFT with probation services and found that, 2.5 years post-treatment, FFT produced an 84% reduction in recidivism. A subsequent follow-up by D. Gordon, Graves, and Arbuthnot (1995) showed that the FFT group's reduced recidivism was sustained for an additional 32 months.

Outcome research on FFT has not produced uniformly positive results. In one of the largest RCTs ever conducted with juvenile offenders (917 clients in 14 countries), Sexton and Turner (2010) compared home-delivered FFT with traditional probation services. At a 12-month post-treatment follow-up, rearrest rates were 22% in both treatment conditions, although therapist adherence to the FFT protocol was inversely associated with recidivism. The importance of therapist adherence was further demonstrated in a study of adolescent offenders by Sexton and Turner (2011), who found that, compared to usual probation services, high-adherence therapy reduced reoffending, while low-adherence therapy was associated with increased reoffending.

In a study that directly compared two EBPs, Baglivio, Jackowski, Greenwald, and Wolff (2014) assessed outcomes in juvenile offenders who received either MST or FFT. There were no differences between treatment groups on most of the measures, but there were two exceptions that favored FFT: Females who received this intervention had lower recidivism rates, and comparatively low-risk youth who received FFT had fewer probation violations, compared to low-risk offenders who received MST.

Parenting with love and limits (PLL; Sells, 2004, 2009) combines parent training and systems-oriented intervention in family and group sessions. PLL was examined in a pilot test with a sample of 102 adolescents referred by juvenile court for substance abuse and a comorbid diagnosis of either ODD or CD (Smith, Sells, Rodman, & Reynolds, 2006). The study did not include a control group. Clients' attitudes toward drugs and alcohol did not change, but there was a reduction in self-reported substance use, and 85% of the adolescents did not relapse for a year following the end of treatment. Sells, Winokur-Early, and Smith (2011) compared youth in the juvenile justice system who were randomly assigned to either PLL or usual probation services. PLL produced significant reductions in CBCL scores on the externalizing, aggression, depression, and ADD scales. Over a 1-year follow-up period, the PLL group had a 16% recidivism rate, compared to a 55% rate for the control group. In a quasi-experimental investigation with youth re-entering the community following confinement, Winokur-Early, Chapman, and Hand (2013) found that PLL resulted in lower recidivism rates than standard aftercare services over a 1-year follow-up period. The effect sizes, while significant, were small, with values of .11 for rearrest and .22 for readjudication.

Barkley and Robin (2014) combined their two interventions into one manualized treatment package for adolescents with ODD or ADHD (not CD). Barkley's parent management training (PMT), described in the previous chapter, teaches behavioral child management techniques to caregivers, and Robin's problem-solving communication skills training (PSCT) teaches these skills to parents and adolescents, in a family therapy format. PSCT for adolescents and their parents has received support from research by Robin (1981; Robin & Foster, 1989). Barkley, Edwards, Laneri, Fletcher, and Metevia (2001) compared PSCT alone to a combination of PSCT + PMT. Both interventions produced positive change in the two groups of families that received them, with no difference between the two treatments. Approximately 70% of the teens' scores on outcome measures moved from the abnormal to the normal range.

Overall, research suggests that treatment outcomes for adolescent CD are somewhat less positive than outcomes for the other categories of disturbance discussed in this book.

Of course each client's prognosis is a function of multiple factors besides diagnosis, with severity being a particularly important one, but, as a generalization, CD seems to be more difficult to treat than most other nonpsychotic, nonorganic mental health problems.

Clinical Considerations

Assessment of the relative importance of motivational versus capability-related factors in the client's problems provides important information for treatment planning. An emphasis on strict enforcement of rules and consequences is appropriate when the adolescent seems to choose defiant behaviors. I refer to this as the "hard" approach to treatment. To the extent that the youth's disturbance results from emotional distress and weak coping abilities, therapy should also emphasize individual work with the adolescent, an effort to increase parental nurturance and support for the teen, and, when appropriate, negotiation about disciplinary issues. I refer to these as "soft" therapeutic techniques.

Effective treatment planning for conduct disturbance depends largely on deciding how to proportion the hard and soft components of treatment and how to orchestrate their implementation. Some youth do best with an approach that emphasizes the hard aspect of therapy, some respond best to an approach emphasizing the soft aspect, and for some clients, an even combination seems most effective. When both types of techniques are used, the clinician (and parent) must move back and forth between thinking of the client as a troubled youth who needs support and a self-serving adolescent who needs limits and consequences.

Effective treatment planning for conduct disturbance depends largely on deciding how to proportion the hard and soft components of treatment and how to orchestrate their implementation.

Thus, if a teen's arguing seems attributable primarily to poorly regulated emotional distress, it may be appropriate for the parent to provide empathy, support, and negotiation along with limit setting, as in the CPS approach. Individual therapy, including both cognitive-behavioral and supportive components, may be useful with these adolescents. If there are indications that the teen is confused or conflicted about his emotions and behavior, dynamic techniques might be useful as a supplementary aspect of therapy.

However, if the teen's arguing represents a manipulative attempt to defeat the parent's authority, which is the traditional behavioral view of noncompliance and is emphasized by PLL, the parent should resist being drawn into discussion or negotiation and should firmly implement the planned consequences. Operant conditioning-based systems of reward and punishment should be emphasized in therapeutic work with youth exhibiting callous and unemotional traits.

The social ecology perspective provides a framework for selecting environmental systems for intervention (Brofenbrenner, 1977; Henggeler et al., 2002; Henggeler, Cunningham, et al., 2009). A broadly based assessment should discover where both problem sources and positive resources are located, and treatment should attempt to make use of resources and reduce the impact of negative influences on the adolescent. If the parent either lacks a social network or relies on individuals who do not support effective parenting, the therapist should help the parent explore sources of more helpful relationships. If the client either lacks a social network or has friends who support antisocial behavior, the counselor should guide the youth in making new friends. Positive and negative consequences might be necessary to motivate the client to improve her social network.

If the client has problems in school, the therapist should coach the parent in working effectively with teachers, perhaps by role-playing effective interactions, calling the school, or participating in conferences there. If the client has positive interests or abilities that have been underutilized, counselors can explore ways to increase the scope of these activities. For example, Jack was a good athlete, although not at a high school varsity level, and his therapist encouraged his participation in a basketball team at a youth recreation center.

Behavioral-Systemic Therapy

Therapy for adolescents with CD may involve a number of different strategies—more than can be described in one chapter. Some of these strategies are also useful with populations whose characteristics overlap with adolescent CD. Thus, Chapter 10, Disruptive Behavior in Children, presented a problem-solving technique, and Chapter 12, Aggression and Violence, will describe skills training in communication, assertiveness, and anger management. All these strategies are appropriate components of therapy for adolescents with CD, depending on their individual needs.

Barkley and Robin (2014) offer a user-friendly manual for treating ODD and ADHD in teenagers. The first half of the intervention is an adaptation for adolescents of Barkley's (2013) program for younger clients. This half of the program teaches parents how to implement effective directions, behavior contracts, point systems, consequences, and shared enjoyable activities with their adolescent. The second half of the program, based on Robin and Foster's (1989) work, trains parents and teens, together, in problem-solving and communication skills, and then guides families in applying these skills to negotiable issues concerning the adolescent's activities and behavior. Kazdin (2010) offers a similar combination of training in child management for parents and training in problem-solving skills for youth.

As its name implies, PLL has a dual emphasis on firm limit setting and warm nurturing for parents of adolescents, thus combining hard and soft aspects of parenting. Sells's (2004, 2009) method for limit setting uses detailed contracts rather than the charts, tokens, and/or point systems that are more traditional in behavioral parent training. PLL guides parents in using active techniques for rekindling warmth in their relationships with adolescents at the same time that they are taking strong, forceful steps to bring the acting out under control. Sells seems to have peered deeply into the combative, tricky thought processes that enable many youth with CD to defeat their parents, and he offers parents clever techniques to counter their teens' manipulative efforts. The therapy methods presented ahead draw heavily on Sells, Barkley and Robin, FFT, and MST.

The empirically supported interventions for adolescent CD share one core idea: The parent must be established as the authority in the family.

The empirically supported interventions for adolescent CD share one core idea: The parent must be established as the authority in the family. The behavioral-systemic insight is that no matter how complex the individual and family dynamics might be, if the parents do not achieve control over the youth's behavior, nothing good will happen, and the adolescent's life will continue downhill. If the parents do establish their authority, and the youth accepts the hierarchy that is normative in human families, progress can be made not only behaviorally but also on emotional and relationship problems.

Because some degree of parental control is a prerequisite for useful work on emotional issues, establishing rules and consequences is the first therapeutic priority. It is also possible to initiate soft elements of therapy at the beginning of treatment. Thus, at the same time that limits are placed on the client's behavior, and the parents and counselor stand firm in the face of the angry protests that typically result, the adults should look for opportunities to intersperse elements of nurturance, support, and gratification in their approach to the teen. The hard and soft aspects of parenting and therapy must not be allowed to negate or disrupt each other. This is easier said than done, but the hard and soft elements can occur on parallel tracks that eventually converge in the synthesis of limits and love that defines effective parental authority.

The main treatment modality of behavioral-systemic therapy is parent training. While family sessions are part of the mix, and individual sessions may be included, treatment consists largely of the counselor training the caregivers in parenting techniques that are effective with conduct disordered youth. This work consists of explaining the principles behind the strategies, planning the details of implementation for each client, anticipating problems that might occur and planning how to deal with them, and practicing the techniques in role-plays. In these exercises, the therapist plays the part of the adolescent and does his best to confront the parents with every argument, manipulation, and provocation that the youth might use in her attempt to defeat their authority. This practice prepares the parents to deal with the difficult behaviors they are likely to encounter when they implement the techniques at home.

As discussed in Chapter 1, youth with externalizing disorders typically do not want therapy because they do not view their behavior as a problem, and their desire is for other people to change (Clarkin & Levy, 2004). The suggestions presented in Chapter 1 might initiate the development of treatment motivation in these youth. Counselors should attempt to "work both sides of the fence" so both parents and adolescents can view therapy as a means of achieving desired changes (Selekman, 2010). Sometimes, however, this effort is not successful, and it is necessary for the parents to enforce the youth's participation and define the goals of therapy. Hopefully, as counseling progresses, the youth will begin to see ways in which he could benefit from changing his behavior, and the parents might also identify changes they could make to improve the teen's experience in the family.

Rules and Consequences

Effective treatment for CD requires parents to establish clear rules that are enforced by consequences (Forgatch & Patterson, 2010; Henggeler et al., 2002; Henggeler, Cunningham, et al., 2009; Sells, 2004, 2009; Sexton, 2011). The rules must be defined carefully and in some detail because, like a lawyer more concerned with the letter than the spirit of the law, youth with CD often pounce on any loophole or ambiguity they can find in order to manipulate things to their advantage. Parents must define positive behaviors, rewards, negative behaviors, and punishments in a concrete manner so that everyone knows what to expect of each other. Everything must be put in writing, with one copy for the parents, one for the teen, and one for the chart.

Rules and consequences should be constructed in a two-stage sequence. First the parents, in consultation with the therapist, develop the rules. Then the youth is brought in, and the adults present the rules, possibly responding to objections by making some modifications but cutting off negotiation if the youth descends into disrespectful arguing. Teens should not take part in the first stage of the process because they often disrupt the discussion with objections. The sequence of this procedure supports parental authority and draws a healthy boundary between the adults and teen (Sells, 2004, 2009).

The details of the rule-making process might be complicated, but there is simplicity at its core: When parental decisions or rules mean that the adolescent is not going to get something she wants (e.g., the freedom to stay out late at night), she will not like it. Usually no amount of explanation and discussion will be good enough to convince the teen to change her mind and embrace the rule. If so, discussions quickly become counterproductive. Many parents make the mistake of believing that if they cannot persuade the teen of the fairness of a rule, they have no right to enforce it. These caregivers misunderstand what goes on when parents and youth argue. The youth is not engaged in a search for truth and fairness; she is trying to attain an objective. To these parents, I sometimes say, "This isn't like Plato and Aristotle arguing about the nature of justice; your daughter is just trying to get something she wants." Or, with a satirical tone, I ask, "What do you expect your son to say? (I conk my forehead with my palm, as if the proverbial lightbulb just went off.) 'Oh, now I get it! You want me to come home on time to make sure I stay safe and learn responsibility!'" Parents generally laugh at the absurdity of this hope.

To be effective, a system of rules and consequences should have six characteristics (Sells, 2004; see Table 11.2).

1. *Preset rules and consequences*: Preset rules seem more principled to adolescents than improvised ones. Discussing consequences in advance enables youth to begin learning the rules while in a calm state of mind, and this prepares them for the more emotional situations that, eventually, will call for their compliance. With everything established in advance, it is possible to say to the youngster, "When you choose the behavior, you choose the consequence."

2. *A manageable number of rules*: I recommend starting therapy with between three and five rules. More can be added later. Parental control can be established with a small number of rules if they are sufficiently broad in scope. Generally, there should be one rule stating that the teen must comply with immediate directives and one requiring a minimal level of respectful behavior (i.e., no swearing, threatening, or insulting). The first rules should concern safety issues (e.g., drug use) and behaviors that, if unchecked, will result in natural consequences harmful to the adolescent (e.g., expulsion from school).

3. *Clear operational definitions of rules*: When rules are vague, adolescents frequently look for ways to violate their spirit without receiving a punishment. The solution is to define rules in enough detail so that it is clear whether a violation has occurred. Rules such as, "Come home at a reasonable hour" are vague. Curfews should be defined with a specific time for each day of the week.

Provisions for exceptions and judgment calls should be written into the rule definitions to the greatest extent possible. Flexibility is useful when it means acknowledging

Table 11.2   Characteristics of Effective Rules and Consequences

1. The rules should be explained to the youth in advance.
2. The rules should be few enough in number for the client to remember them.
3. The rules should be defined in detail, with provision for complications and exceptions.
4. The consequences, both positive and negative, must matter to the client.
5. The consequences should be administered with consistency.
6. The consequences should be arranged in a hierarchy, so the adolescent's refusal to accept one punishment is followed by another.

Adapted from *Treating the Tough Adolescent: A Family-Based, Step-By-Step Guide* by S. P. Sells, 2004, New York, NY: Guilford Press.

complexities and good faith efforts, but flexibility is harmful when it means backing down because the adolescent pleads or argues. For instance, if the parents are willing to allow a 10-minute grace period around curfew, that should be stated in advance, with the understanding that 11 minutes of tardiness will result in a negative consequence. Homework rules can state an amount of time for work that, once done, will allow the client to be finished for the night, even if some assignments are incomplete. This amount of time can be reduced for nights with special activities if the youth obtains permission from the parents in advance.

Rules need to state how the youth's compliance will be measured or monitored. The parent should *expect* the youngster to try to circumvent rules and should make plans to overcome this threat to her authority. Caregivers should accept that gaining control over a misbehaving teen requires detective work, and they should be unapologetic about their suspiciousness, which is the result of the youth's past misbehavior and which will change once the youth achieves a track record justifying trust. Parents should monitor the teen's functioning in school by checking homework, looking at test grades, and communicating frequently with teachers; most or all of this can be accomplished online. Other behaviors can be supervised by checking in with the adolescent by phone, including at unpredictable intervals, and by obtaining reports from other adults. Jack's parents monitored his compliance with the rule against shoplifting by making a complete inventory of his possessions and requiring him to show them a receipt for anything new he brought home.

4. *Consequences that matter to the adolescent*: When possible, each rule should be associated with a positive consequence for compliance and a negative consequence for noncompliance. When behaviors are linked to consequences from the same domain, the logical connection often helps youth feel that the rules make sense. For example, if an adolescent is late coming home for dinner, he could have to prepare his own meal. A contract could state that coming home after curfew will result in grounding on the next night, while a week of coming home on time could be rewarded by extending curfew by one hour on the following weekend night. If the youth destroys property, she should pay for it to be replaced, if necessary by selling some of her possessions and/or by doing chores at a reasonable hourly rate.

As discussed in Chapter 2, Behavior Therapy, noncontingent rewards must be limited if reinforcement systems are to work. Food, clothing, shelter, medical care, education, and parental love are rights and so should not be on a reward list. Everything else is on the table. Telephones, transportation, material possessions, spending money, and so forth are not rights. If the adolescent thinks they are, that is part of the problem, the technical term for which is **sense of entitlement**. (The lay term is "spoiled.") It is therapeutic to reframe supposed rights as privileges that must be earned with responsible behavior. Youth often protest. Therapists should help parents portray the new system as an unchangeable fact of life. The parents must patiently and consistently demonstrate that the teen can gain nothing by fighting the system but can prosper by making it work for him.

Grounding is a basic negative consequence. Grounding can be defined as forbidding the adolescent to leave the home, and it can also be defined to include the loss of enjoyable activities in the home.

5. *Consistent implementation of consequences*: In planning consequences, parents should make realistic plans that they will be able to follow through on. Parents often make two, opposite mistakes that are particularly harmful in combination: They threaten too much, and they deliver too little. For example, parents might angrily tell the teen that she is grounded for a month but, as the days grind by, they realize this punishment is excessive and end the grounding after a week. Failure to follow through on either promises or threats teaches the adolescent that the parent does not mean what he says, thus setting the stage for more misbehavior in the future. Grounding should not last longer than two weeks; other punishments can be added for serious misbehaviors.

Parents should be careful not to announce excessive punishments out of anger, because this sets up an untenable position from which they will have to retreat when they realize they went too far. Also, parents should resist temptations to reduce promised punishments because they feel sorry for the adolescent. Effective child-rearing requires an ability to tolerate the youngster's distress, as when parents take children to physicians for injections. When this ability is lacking, some teens use the parent's sensitivity to their pain as a means of controlling the parent.

Jack's behavior contract is presented in Figure 11.1. Because this set of rules and consequences addresses issues that arise in therapy with many youth, the contract is on our website (Form 11.1), where therapists can customize and print it for their own use. The website also includes Jack's narrower contract for the specific goal of homework completion (Form 11.2).

6. *Hierarchy of consequences*: One important form of noncompliance is refusal to accept punishments. For instance, a youth who has been told she is grounded might get up and walk out of the house. Parental use of force is generally not the best way to deal with these situations because the adolescent might have more physical strength and because wrestling with a teen, no matter what the outcome, detracts from the dignity of the parental role. Adolescent challenges to parental authority represent a showdown, and it is crucial that parents win these power struggles. In order to do so, parents need to be equipped with a hierarchy of consequences to deal with refusals to accept punishments.

The hierarchy should include several levels. The first consists of the negative consequences already discussed. Second-level punishments are usually escalated versions of first-level punishments. For example, time-outs can be increased in length if the teen refuses to comply, and they can be reduced if he complies immediately.

Parents should use punishments they can control as a means of enforcing compliance with punishments that the adolescent controls. Parents should use punishments they can control as a means of enforcing compliance with punishments that the adolescent controls (Sells, 2004, 2009). For example, if the teen has lost his television-watching privileges but he defies the punishment and sits down in front of the TV anyway, the parent should not attempt to wrestle the remote control from his grasp. Instead, the parent should announce a consequence he can control, such as withholding the youth's allowance.

At the next level up, punishments become more creative. Parents can target the adolescent's possessions—for instance, by confiscating or discontinuing payment for her phone and making its return contingent on improved behavior. Caregivers can also remove favorite articles of clothing or other possessions. For girls, confiscation of makeup is often an effective consequence.

"Parental strikes" are a high-level consequence. In a strike, parents stop providing some of the services they normally do for their children, such as transportation, laundry, and cooking. The message to the adolescent is that the parent will do fewer things for her if she refuses to fulfill minimum expectations as a member of the family.

As a consequence for repeated misbehavior in school, Sells (2004) recommends that the parent accompany the youth throughout his school day, going with him to classes, lunch, gym, and so forth. Most youth find this embarrassing, which makes the consequence aversive and effective.

Rules and Consequences

Rule 1: Jack will come home by his curfew time. Sunday through Thursday, curfew is 5:00 P.M. On Friday and Saturday evenings, curfew is 10 P.M. Jack will have a 10-minute grace period during which lateness will not result in a negative consequence, although arrival during this period will not count as a positive behavior deserving reward, either. Arriving home 11 or more minutes late will result in negative consequences.

Positive Consequences

If Jack comes home on time, his curfew on the next afternoon or night will be made later by one-half hour, up to 5:30 on school days and 10:30 on weekend nights. If Jack achieves a full week (Sunday through Saturday) of perfect performance, he will receive an extra hour of time on the following Saturday night, resulting in a curfew of 11:30 P.M.

Negative Consequences

If Jack returns home after curfew, he will be grounded the next day. In addition, for every minute he is late, his curfew on the following weekend night will be made earlier by two minutes. If the penalty time exceeds the amount of time in a weekend night, Jack will be grounded for that night and also have an earlier curfew the next night, until the penalty time is paid.

Rule 2: Jack will attend school all day every day school is scheduled, beginning at 8:15 and ending at 3:10, and will attend every class during this time. All scheduled school activities—homeroom, study hall, lunch, and so on—are considered classes and must be attended. Parental permission to miss school for a medical reason must be given in advance. If Jack feels ill on the way to school, he is to go there and tell the nurse how he is feeling. If the nurse determines that Jack is ill, she will call a parent who will take him home.

Positive Consequences

Following each day of full school attendance, Jack will be rewarded with 2 ½ hours of screen and phone time. In addition, one week of full attendance will be rewarded with $5.00 of credit toward his weekly allowance, to be paid on Friday at 6 P.M.

Negative Consequences

If Jack is truant from school for a full day, he will be grounded on the next three weekday afternoons and one full week-end, during which times a parent will confiscate his phone, iPad, and laptop, except when needed for homework. He will receive no allowance that week. If he cuts classes, he will lose two hours of screen time and $1.00 of allowance for each class missed. Each instance of tardiness for a class will result in the loss of 30 minutes of screen time and $.50 of allowance.

Rule 3: Jack will not take illegal drugs or drink alcohol. The parents will monitor substance use, at any time they choose, by administering a breathalyzer test for alcohol and/or a urine test for illegal drugs.

Positive Consequences

If test results indicate that Jack has been clean for a month, the parents will take him and a friend to a reasonably-priced restaurant (entrees under $17.00) of Jack's choice for dinner. If test results indicate that Jack has been clean for 6 months, the parents will take him and a friend to a professional basketball game.

Figure 11.1   Jack's rules and consequences.

Negative Consequences

If the breathalyzer test indicates alcohol consumption at a time when Jack has not been driving, he will be grounded and lose his allowance for two weeks. If the breathalyzer test indicates alcohol consumption at a time when Jack has been driving, in addition to the above consequences, the parents will call the police and ask that Jack be arrested. If the urine test indicates illegal drug use at a time when Jack has not been driving, in addition to 2 weeks of grounding and loss of allowance, the parents will go on strike for 2 weeks, and Jack will lose his cell phone for one month. If the urine test indicates illegal drug use at a time when Jack has been driving, in addition to the above consequences, the parents will call the police and ask that Jack be arrested.

Rule 4: Jack will behave respectfully toward his parents, as defined below:

1. Telling the truth is respectful. Lying is disrespectful.

2. Obeying a spoken directive at the time it is given is respectful. Refusing to obey a directive is disrespectful.

3. Speaking in a civil fashion is respectful. Words such as "I totally disagree with you," "This makes no sense to me," and "This really makes me mad" are angry words, but they are civil. Swearing, insulting, and mocking are disrespectful.

(There are no specific positive consequences for showing respect to parents because this is a basic expectation. Jack's parents will show respect to him by telling the truth and speaking to him in a respectful fashion at all times.)

Negative Consequences

If Jack behaves disrespectfully, he will be given a verbal count to three; if he ends the disrespectful behavior, there will not be a negative consequence. If the disrespectful behavior continues, he will be given a 10-minute time out. If Jack cooperates immediately, the time out will be shortened to 5 minutes. If he refuses to go to time out, every 5 minutes of refusal will result in the loss of $1.00 of allowance. If his refusal continues past the point of using up 2 weeks of allowance, the parents will implement additional backup consequences.

Figure 11.1   (*Continued*)

In a hierarchical arrangement of consequences, the youth can bring high-level, parent-controlled punishments to an end only by complying with the lower-level consequences he had previously defied. As an example, consider the following sequence of events: (1) The parent tells the youth to take out the garbage, and he refuses; (2) the parent attempts to implement a time-out, but the teen refuses to comply; (3) the parent tells the youth he is grounded for the weekend, but when Saturday night arrives, he walks out of the house and gets into a car with his friends. At this point, the parent switches to consequences that do not require the youth's cooperation: (4) The caregiver removes several of the youth's favorite possessions, and when this does not bring him under control, (5) the parent goes on strike. Then, for the youth to regain his possessions and the parent's services, he must backtrack through all the consequences he had defied and comply with them. Thus, he must accept a weekend of grounding, at the end of which he must complete the time-out he was assigned earlier, and, finally, he must take out the garbage. By moving through the sequence of consequences in reverse order, the youth learns that he would be wise to obey his parents' directives the first time they are stated, because he will have to obey them eventually.

Some clients can be treated with contracts less complicated than the type described earlier. Counselors and parents can begin with relatively simple contracts, continue their use if they are effective, and increase their detail if the adolescent attempts to find loopholes

Behavior	Consequence
1. Acceptable behavior.	Allowance.
2. Yelling, insulting, or disobedience toward parents.	Grounding.
3. Swearing at or threatening parents.	Parents on strike.
4. Violent behavior.	Police called.

Definition of Terms

Acceptable behavior = A minimum degree of respect, compliance with rules and directives, and the absence of the unacceptable behaviors listed in #2–#4 above.

Allowance = $15.00 per week, paid on Fridays at 6:00 P.M.

Grounding = No leaving the house except to go to school, work, the doctor, and church. At home, no visitors or screen time except for homework. Listening to music is permitted.

Parents on strike = Parents will not cook meals, do laundry, or provide transportation to places other than the ones listed in the item above.

Figure 11.2   A simple behavior contract.

or exploit ambiguities. Simple contracts sometimes produce quick results that make more complicated ones unnecessary. Figure 11.2 presents an example of a simple contract, which is also on our website (Form 11.3), so therapists can customize and print it for their clients.

Calibrating Supervision of the Adolescent.   Counselors should help parents choose their battles wisely, rather than attempting to micromanage details of the youth's behavior. Parents should be firm about behaviors related to safety, important values, and preparing for adult life (e.g., school), but they should be flexible about more superficial choices concerning styles of dress, hair, and entertainment. Parents sometimes hate adolescent styles in these areas, but not everything is important enough to be a disciplinary issue. Also, the process of establishing an independent identity generally involves some type of rebellion against parents. Hopefully, these rebellions occur in areas where the teen can win without doing herself any harm. Such victories contribute to the separation process and reduce the adolescent's need to oppose parents on issues where more is at stake.

It is also counterproductive to make rules about the youth's *manner* of complying with directives. Many parents reprimand youngsters for exhibiting "a bad attitude" through nonverbal behaviors such as muttering, scowling, or stomping. However, if youth convey this attitude while complying with a directive, punishing one will punish both, and I suggest that caregivers reframe the youth's manner of complying as, "A First Amendment issue of freedom of speech—if he's doing what you said, doesn't he have a right to express how he feels about it?" (Of course, this does not apply to explicit disrespect.)

Adolescents need to believe in the possibility of earning back their parents' trust or they become hopeless about treatment (Micucci, 2009). Teens feel they are regaining their parents' trust when they receive more freedom. The dilemma for parents is that freedom also provides youth with opportunities to engage in negative behavior. To manage both sides of this dilemma, parents should allocate freedom in an incremental, flexible manner that matches the youth's level of self-control. Parents can allocate different degrees of freedom in different areas, depending on the adolescent's level of functioning in those areas.

Infractions by the teen should be followed by tightened supervision. Responsible behavior should be followed by gradual loosening of supervision.

Parents need a range of options with which to calibrate their level of supervision. Caregivers can require teens to provide a written schedule of where they will be, with names and phone numbers of responsible adults in the vicinity, and then can call the adolescent at unpredictable intervals. For a lower level of supervision, parents can require the youth to check in by phone once or twice a night. For school functioning, parental supervision can range from nightly checking of homework and reports from teachers to weekly or monthly feedback from the school. In contrast, trustworthy youth need only a low level of supervision, which might consist of specific times to be home, quarterly review of report cards, and no other form of checking on the youth's behavior.

Young people need to understand that irresponsible behavior *elicits* restrictions. In a sense, youth need a certain, fixed amount of control in their lives, and this total amount is divided between them and their parents. The more self-control an adolescent exercises, the less external control the adolescent needs to receive from her parents. Normally, as children grow up, the proportion of self-control increases and the proportion of parental control decreases, so the total remains constant. When clients complain about parental restrictions that, in fact, are a response to their lack of self-control, therapists can reply that the only solution is to "put your parents out of business" by demonstrating enough personal responsibility to make some of their constraints unnecessary (with the proviso that zero parental control becomes appropriate only when the youth is grown up).

Point Systems

Behavioral contracts and point systems are two clinical applications of operant learning. The change agent is the same, while the procedures are different. My presentation of point systems is based on Barkley and Robin (2014) and is similar to the contingency contracting procedure described in the previous chapter.

Point systems are generally more complicated and labor-intensive than contracts, and they provide a more flexible linking of behaviors and consequences. Contracts directly link specific behaviors to specific consequences. In point systems, all positive target behaviors earn points, and points can be exchanged for all rewards that are part of the system.

Barkley and Robin recommend using point systems for less mature or younger adolescents (up to about age 13) and contracts for more mature teens, who are likely to become impatient with the careful monitoring and record keeping required by point systems. Therapists should also consider the family's style and preference. Some youth are put off by complicated systems, and others are intrigued by the details.

The procedure for designing contingency contracts was presented in Chapter 2 on behavior therapy. While charts and poker chips are appropriate for younger children, ledger systems are appropriate for adolescents. The ledger has four columns to keep track of daily changes in the client's points. There are columns for recording when the teen:

- Earns points with positive behaviors.
- Loses points as a consequence of negative behaviors.
- Spends points on rewards.

The fourth and last column is for the running total. Only the parent is permitted to write in the ledger, but the teen can look at it any time she wants.

The most complicated task is determining the number of points for target behaviors, response costs, and rewards, with the goal of aligning the three in a way that produces a moderately difficult, feasible system for the client. This means that reasonably positive behavior should produce enough points to purchase everyday privileges and to bank about one third of the points toward purchase of larger rewards. Table 11.3 presents an example of a complex, comprehensive point system. This example is on our website (Form 11.4) so counselors can adapt it for their own use.

Point systems should include a spontaneous element called **bonus points**. Bonus points are not preplanned but are given by the parent whenever she feels the client has behaved in a particularly positive or pleasant way. Parents must be careful to use this technique sparingly, at most twice a week, or the client will come to expect it and the technique will lose its power.

Point systems should be implemented in three stages. First, for 2 weeks, only positive behaviors receive consequences from within the system. During this time, the parents ignore minor negative behaviors and respond to serious misbehaviors with punishments unrelated to the point system. Second, the parents introduce the response cost component. There is an initial, 1-week training period during which the parents do not subtract points for misbehaviors but inform the teen that this contingency will begin soon (e.g., "Now that's what I mean by disrespectful behavior. Starting next week, if you behave disrespectfully, you will lose 35 points."). Third, the parents implement the response cost procedure. Adolescents often react with frustration and anger. To soften the blow, parents should introduce the reward-oriented bonus point technique at this time.

Because clients typically improve their behavior in response to point systems, one possible problem is that success becomes too easy for them, in which case learning would come to a halt. Parents should implement two modifications of the system in response to this encouraging development. These modifications should be presented to the youth as recognition of the important progress she has achieved. The first modification is to increase the level of positive behavior that is required to earn a given number of points. The second modification is to add new, highly attractive incentives to the reward menu. Here, as in general, youth should have two internal responses to the reinforcement system:

1. The system puts pressure on the youth to improve her behavior, and there may be regret about enjoyable negative behaviors that are slated for extinction.
2. The youth should realize that, if he plays the game well, he will win; that is, it should be within the youth's capability to obtain more rewards and more privileges than he had before the system was modified.

Preparing for Setbacks

Even when treatment is eventually successful, its course is rarely smooth. There is often a delay between the beginning of therapy and improvement in the teen's behavior. Then, change usually occurs unevenly, with ups and downs. However, the important variable is not whether setbacks occur but how parents respond when they do (Forgatch & Patterson, 2010; Kazdin, 2005).

The important variable is not whether setbacks occur but how parents respond when they do.

Adolescents who are accustomed to riding roughshod over their parents' attempts to control them do not easily accept their parents' recovery of authority, and they fight back. Although teens with CD often exhibit intellectual

Table 11.3   Example Point System

Positive Behaviors	Points Earned
Full day of class attendance	5
Full week of class attendance	10 (+ daily points)
One and a half hours of homework in a day/night	3
Teacher report of 1 week's full homework completion, per class	3
One week of school-reported satisfactory behavior	15
Grades for a school quarter, per class: A	150
B	100
C	50
Coming home on time, per day	5
Full week of coming home on time	10 (+ the above)
Okay relations with sibs (no yelling, swearing, or fighting), per day	7
Setting the table, each time	3
One month without use of alcohol or drugs	25
Six consecutive months without use of alcohol or drugs	50 (+ the above)

Reward Menu	Point Cost
1/2 hour of screen time (including phone, not including homework)	5
1/2 hour of playing pool	3
1/2 hour of time out beyond usual curfew (limit 1 hour)	10
Use of the car, per afternoon or evening	10
$.25 of allowance, up to $10, per week	1
New skateboard (up to $80)	100

Negative Behaviors	Points Lost
Cutting a class	15
A day of truancy	75 (+ the above)
Refusal to do $1^1/_2$ hours of homework, per day	5
Negative behavior report from school	40
School suspension	100
Failing a class	150
Coming home after curfew, per quarter hour	5
Verbal aggression or cruelty toward siblings, per incident	15
Physical aggression toward siblings	100
Disrespect toward parents (swearing, insulting, lying)	35
Physical threat toward parents	100
Destruction of family property	50 and pay to replace
Evidence of alcohol use when not driving	50
Evidence of alcohol use when driving	125 and police called
Evidence of drug use when not driving	100
Evidence of drug use when driving	150 and police called
Evidence of shoplifting	50 and police called
Physical aggression toward parents	150 and police called

limitations in school, many of them seem highly skilled at disrupting their parents' plans to bring them under control (Sells, 2004, 2009). From a learning theory perspective, these adolescents do not believe that reinforcement contingencies have changed just because the parents say they have, so the teens continue or escalate the behaviors that have worked in the past (Henggeler et al., 2002; Henggeler, Cunningham, et al., 2009). When new rules and consequences are put in place, things often get worse before they get better, because it takes time to learn new reinforcement contingencies. It is critical that parents do not become discouraged and that they maintain their new practices even though the practices are not yet being reinforced by improved adolescent behavior. Therapists can help parents cope with setbacks by depicting the teen's escalation of misbehavior not as an indication that something has gone wrong but as a normal part of the process:

"In the beginning of therapy, my concern is with your behavior, not Jack's. He is not going to believe the rules have changed until he tests them with negative behavior. This will not be a pretty sight, but it's not a problem for treatment; it's a normal part of the process. We are going to show him that, no matter what he does, you can handle it. If he acts out, that's a learning opportunity, so figure out what you want to teach him. As long as you respond skillfully, that's a success, no matter what he does. In time, the effects of your skillful parenting will kick in, and Jack's behavior will improve."

It is impossible to tell right away whether a new behavioral system will work. However, although persistence is important, at some point it becomes counterproductive to cling to a system that is not working. Generally, if a reinforcement system produces no improvement in a youth's behavior after 3 weeks or so, it should be revised or abandoned (Barkley & Robin, 2014).

If behavioral techniques produce little or no improvement, the clinician should consider the possibility that factors other than those addressed by the intervention are at work. One possibility is that the youth is using drugs. Surprise drug tests are the most effective way to assess this danger. It is also possible that neurobiological problems are contributing to the teen's self-control problems. Referral to a psychiatrist for medication evaluation is an appropriate response. The possibility that the youth is being physically or sexually abused could also be investigated.

Talking Effectively With Defiant Adolescents

Sells (2004, 2009) recommends that counselors prepare parents to remain calm and effective in confrontations with adolescents by identifying their areas of emotional sensitivity in advance. This type of self-knowledge helps parents maintain composure when their hot buttons are pushed. Examples include accusations of hypocrisy, variations of "you don't love me," references to mistakes the parent has made, and insults that cause shame because they contain elements of truth. Jack often counterattacked with heartrending statements about how his parents' divorce ruined his relationship with his father (a concern he never voiced at other times). One way to reduce the power of these wounding statements is to become desensitized to them, using a version of an exposure procedure. Parents can conduct role-plays with the therapist and with each other in which they verbally stab at each other's most vulnerable areas until these insults lose the power to produce a loss of self-control.

Being firm does not mean being harsh. The difference is largely a matter of nonverbal behavior. There is research from the business world that has useful implications for the parents of defiant teens. In a study of supervisors giving negative performance feedback to their employees, Newcombe and Ashkanasy (2002) found that when critical words were delivered with friendly, supportive tones of voice and facial expressions, employees had positive overall feelings about their feedback session even though the content was negative. Delivering negative verbal material with a positive nonverbal tone does not come naturally. The researchers trained the supervisors to separate these two dimensions of communication, and counselors can do the same for parents. Adolescents are more likely to accept critical input and even punishment when these are communicated with tones of voice and body language that convey sincerity and caring as well as firmness. Thus, the hard aspect of parenting can be delivered verbally while the soft aspect is communicated nonverbally.

In parent-adolescent communication about discipline and limits, there is such a thing as talking too much. Parents and therapists should develop a plan for how much discussion to have around disciplinary confrontations based partly on their assessment of the relative importance of motivational versus capability-related issues in the client's problems with limits. As per Greene and Ablon's (2006) recommendations, discussed in the previous chapter's section on CPS, if the youngster's difficulty with limits seems to be the result of disruptive emotions, cognitive distortions, and/or confusion, parents should provide explanation, support, and, possibly, negotiation. But when arguments become a matter of manipulation, power struggle, or personal attack, parents should take control by ending the conversation. This means resisting the desire to get in the last word, announcing that the discussion is over, and, if necessary, walking away. Sometimes, parents need to do a quick, decisive shifting of gears from a debating mode to an enforcement mode. Parental statements like the following combine empathy for the youth with control over the interaction:

> "I've thought about what you said, but my decision is still the same: You can go to the play tonight, but you cannot go to the party afterward. I know you're disappointed, but that's the way it is, and there's no point arguing about it anymore. Now you have a choice about what you're going to do and what the consequences will be."

Sells (2004) recommends that parents use **deflectors** to make the transition from empathy to firmness. Deflectors are words like "nevertheless," "still," and "even though you feel that way." In essence, statements using deflectors mean, "I heard what you said, but I'm not changing my mind." Such statements help parents empathize without backing down or leaving the door open to endless discussion—for example:

> "I know you're upset about missing the game, plus you think I'm being unfair. But even though you feel that way, you must meet us at Aunt Rose's at 1 o'clock, or you will be grounded for the next two days."

Here is a technique for controlling the length of arguments while ensuring that the youth has an opportunity to state her points. When debate reaches the point of diminishing returns, the parent gives the teen a final opportunity to argue for the option she wants. During this time, the parent does not interrupt or even speak but listens attentively to the teen until she says she is finished, perhaps even jotting down a few notes. Then, the parent goes into another room, alone, and thinks for a few minutes. Finally, the parent returns and announces his decision, which is now final. Because the parent has heard all of the adolescent's arguments, clearly there is no point in additional debate.

Marketing Prosocial Behavior

Youth with disruptive behavior disorders often perceive prosocial behavior as unappealing, and this perception is an obstacle to progress even when incentives for good behavior are present. It is not easy to sell these youth on the appeal of self-control, schoolwork, and obedience to parents, but trying to persuade clients of the legitimate, valuable nature of prosocial behavior is part of the nitty-gritty work of therapy with this population.

As discussed in Chapter 1, motivational interviewing techniques (Miller & Rollnick, 2012; Rosengren, 2009) and listing the pros and cons of options (Fishbein & Izjen, 2009) are effective strategies for exploring the reasons for clients' attraction to problem behaviors. Sometimes these nondirective techniques engender an evolution of client attitudes in a prosocial direction, with increased readiness to change. At other times, clients show no movement in this direction without input from the counselor.

Many clients complain that they will never need to know the information taught in school for any job they can envision having or for any other purpose, so they see no reason to go through the laborious process of learning the information. This is a reasonable and formidable objection, and answering it requires us to think about the value of school. Two points might help, one for content and one for process. First, the main purpose of school is not job preparation but learning about the world, which is not a means but a worthwhile end in itself. The content areas taught in school describe basic dimensions of existence, with the sciences describing the natural world, social studies and humanities illuminating our society and other cultures, and so forth. Second, the process of education develops skills through guided practice in learning, thinking, organization, discipline, and working with others. As an analogy, counselors can say that weight-lifting and calisthenics are not part of football games, but players spend lots of time on these exercises to strengthen the abilities they do use in games. Similarly, schoolwork is exercise for our minds—it makes us smarter. (See Chapter 8's discussion of Dweck's research.)

Another objection that some clients have to our recommendations is that their parents are frequently wrong, are no smarter than they are, and have made serious mistakes of their own; as a result, these clients do not see why they owe their parents respect and obedience. Answering this question requires us to think hard about the rationale for parental authority over children—for example:

> "I have no trouble believing that sometimes you're right and your parents are wrong, but that's not the important point here. What's important is this: Families work well when the parents are in charge and the kids cooperate, and families are miserable when kids disrespect their parents and fight with them. I've never seen a happy family where the kids disobeyed the parents a lot. So the real question is, what is your job in your family, and how well are you going to do it? I think your job is to be a good son. This job is just as important as being a good parent, and just as hard, but it's different. When you disagree with your parents, you might be right about the specific thing, but that doesn't change the fact that if you do what they say, you'll make things better for everyone in your family, because it will be peaceful and respectful in your house, while if you fight with your parents, there will be tension and disrespect, which makes things worse for everyone."
>
> "I don't think you've ever put your mind to the job of being a good son—but you could."

Conduct disturbance involves a rejection of the hierarchical relationship between parents and children that generally exists in families (Fite et al., 2006; Henggeler,

Cunningham, et al., 2009; Sells, 2004, 2009). One client's perception was that "Parents are like kings, and kids are like serfs." Since the strategy of behavioral-systemic therapy is to establish or reestablish the traditional hierarchy of families, counselors can help by explaining this arrangement in a way that portrays it as sensible and fair:

> "There's a certain kind of deal between parents and kids that's been going on since the beginning of people. The parent's job is to give the kid everything he needs from the day she's born until she's grown up—food, clothes, medicine, transportation, and any kind of care the kid needs. It may be easy or it may be hard, but the parent has to come up with the time and money to do those things. Actually, it's a law: Parents can be arrested if they don't take care of their kids, because they owe it to them. What do parents get in return? Kids owe their parents respect and cooperation, doing what they say—being a good daughter. That's the kid's side of the bargain."

When youth disagree with their parents' directives, compliance is more comfortable if the youngster believes it is possible that the parent's age and experience enable him to understand things the youth does not understand, so it is conceivable that the parent really does "know better," even though the youngster cannot see why. To increase the plausibility of this idea, therapists can ask clients to recall baby-sitting or childcare experiences in which they denied requests or gave directives to young children. When clients recall the reactions of anger and frustration that sometimes resulted, they realize that they, too, have been in the position of an authority figure who knows what is right but cannot convince a younger person of this.

To youth with CD, problem behaviors often *seem* to work quite well. Behaviors like lying, stealing, and drug use do have high success rates, in the sense that adolescents who are good at them rarely get caught. However, there are two serious drawbacks to these behaviors that young people need to understand. First, some clients who enjoy the benefits of behaviors like lying and stealing do not feel okay about the identity of being "a liar" or "a thief," and therapists can sometimes motivate change by confronting them with the self-concept implications of what they are doing (e.g., "I understand that it 'works,' but is this the kind of person you want to be?"). Second, many antisocial behaviors that usually work have extremely high costs when they do not: Getting caught shoplifting or using drugs can result in a juvenile offense record; substance use has the additional dangers of overdose and serious mishaps resulting from impaired judgment; and liars are not believed even when they tell the truth, because the other person has no way to know when they do which. Therapists can say that lying, stealing, and drug use are terrible practices, because you can have a 99% success rate and still wreck your life.

The final marketing point is simple but effective: Compliance with authority makes life easier and more pleasant, because constant battling with parents results in a stressful, unsatisfying existence. Clients sometimes come to this understanding on their own when they realize, for example, that cleaning their room or taking out the garbage would be much less time-consuming and annoying than arguing with their parents about these chores. One client turned himself around with the following realization: "I said to myself, 'Stop complaining and just fucking do it. It's actually easier. You'll like your life better.'" In ensuing conversations, we referred to this as "the Nike strategy."

The Soft Side of Therapy: Rebuilding Trust

The hard side of behavioral-systemic therapy is complemented by a soft side that emphasizes warmth, affection, and trust, and seeks to increase the youth's sense of well-being (Alexander et al., 2013; Sells, 2004, 2009; Sexton, 2011). Repairing and improving parent-teen relationships is a central goal of this type of treatment (Barkley & Robin, 2014; Henggeler et al., 2002). As a result of this soft side, even teens who are angry about the restrictions placed on their behavior often find something they like about therapy.

When parental reprimands include denigration of the youth, receiving correction is an aversive experience (e.g., "My parents make me feel like a stupid, worthless piece of shit"). Teens are likely to reject and fight back against this type of input, which infuriates their parents even more.

To disrupt these feedback loops, parents should intersperse warm, positive experiences for their teen in the midst of the limit setting and confrontations that are often prominent in therapy for CD. This is not a matter of contingent reinforcement but of noncontingent, loving behavior. Parents can look for opportunities to provide little treats and favors. Even small, casual gestures can break up what might otherwise seem to the adolescent like an unremitting effort to control him. These parental gestures, which occur apropos of nothing, provide the adolescent with a pleasant, if initially confusing, surprise. We hope for interactions like the following:

> *Parents should intersperse warm, positive experiences for the teen in the midst of the limit setting and confrontations that are often prominent in therapy for CD.*

PARENT: I got you something.

TEEN: What's this for?

PARENT: Nothing. You like those, right?

TEEN: I don't get it.

PARENT: There's nothing to get.

Therapists, too, should punctuate the generally serious tone of sessions with interludes in which they joke, share interests, compliment, and express caring for the client. The combination of therapy's hard and soft aspects presents youth with an exchange they are often willing to make: They lose the freedom to shirk responsibilities, behave impulsively, and seize immediate gratification, but they gain warm relationships with adults and a growing appreciation of their own competence. This is the trade-off that, regardless of whether youth are in therapy, generally motivates the process of socialization (Bowlby, 1969; S. Freud, 1930/1962; Greenberg et al., 1997).

As discussed in Chapter 7 on family therapy, facilitated communication about feelings may reduce anger when family members learn about the pain and distress underlying the behaviors they had found offensive. The technique of reframing helps parents understand the valid emotional-interpersonal goals their children sometimes try to pursue, albeit ineffectively, through maladaptive behavior (Robbins, Alexander, Newell, & Turner, 1996; Robbins, Alexander, & Turner, 2000; Sexton, 2011).

Solution-focused therapy provides techniques for increasing pleasant aspects of the parent-adolescent relationship. This work could involve asking the parent and teen to remember good times they have shared in the past and asking them to envision, in detail, the types of interactions they want to enjoy in the future (Milner & Bateman, 2011; Selekman, 2010).

The warm side of the parent-adolescent relationship is difficult to reinstate after an argument, but it is important to do so (Sells, 2004, 2009). The parent's first step should be to separate from the teen for some time, so they both can calm down. Then, the parent should make an attempt at reconciliation. There should be no rehash of the argument; it's over. Once the adolescent complies with the parent's requirements, even if harsh words were said, the caregiver should make sure not to convey any sense of gloating about her victory in the power struggle. Instead, the parent should approach the teen with warmth, a portrayal of the bigger picture, and anticipation of happier times to come. The parent can come into the adolescent's room, sit down, and say something like:

> "I know you're mad about missing the party. Parents and teenagers bump heads about things like this; it's always been that way. Anyway, I've got both hamburger and chicken in the refrigerator, and I was wondering which you'd rather have for dinner."

Efforts to build more affectionate relationships between parents and adolescents should include making plans for shared, enjoyable activities (Barkley & Robin, 2014). The youth should choose the activities (within reason and affordability), which could include going out to eat, movies, bowling, and so forth. Even if the youth participates solely because she enjoys the activities and does not value spending time with the parent, this component of treatment might help to rehabilitate their relationship. The activities should be scheduled to occur every week or two and should occur on schedule regardless of the youth's behavior, because they are an expression of parental love, not a contingent reward. Thus, the activities should take place even if the youth is grounded or the parents are on strike. The reliable occurrence of these scheduled activities sends the message that the parent's love is a constant, although his approval of the youth's behavior is not.

Social-Ecological Strategies

MST (Henggeler et al., 2002; Henggeler, Cunningham, et al., 2009) has a larger quantity of empirical support than any other treatment package for adolescent conduct disturbance, with positive outcomes for youth with histories of juvenile delinquency, substance abuse, serious emotional disturbance, sex offending, and other disorders. MST is an extremely time-intensive, in-home intervention that can be provided only under special (and well-funded) conditions. For therapists, providing MST requires training and supervision by a purveyor organization, MST Services. Most readers of this book will never provide MST (nor have I), but, nonetheless, we should all learn what we can about this treatment package because of its high level of success with difficult client populations.

In developing MST, Scott Henggeler and his colleagues brought together as many empirically supported techniques as they could (Henggeler & Borduin, 1990; Henggeler & Santos, 1997). Most of these techniques came from the family systems, parent training, behavioral, and cognitive approaches. MST's most distinctive element is its social-ecological emphasis, which involves active intervention in any aspect of the client's environment that either contributes to her problems or might contribute to solutions.

MST clinicians have a very broad definition of therapist responsibilities and a willingness to cross the boundaries of traditional mental health work. When they discover a salient factor in the client's environment, they do not shrug their shoulders and think,

"Not my job," or "Nothing I can do about that." Instead, they try to recruit all available social resources into the therapeutic effort, and they seek to overcome all environmental obstacles to the client's progress. There is no boundary between therapy and the rest of the client's world.

MST therapists attend school with clients, go to church with the family, talk to neighbors, meet the client's friends, and so forth. They try to connect the family with any community resource that could be helpful to them. If the family's electricity is turned off, MST therapists help the parent get it turned back on. They identify prosocial individuals potentially accessible to the client and family and try to facilitate new connections with these individuals. In their efforts to track problems back to their sources, MST therapists attempt to terminate the client's and family's connections with antisocial influences. When appropriate, these therapists accompany clients to gang meetings to inform the group that, because of the youth's enrollment in MST, often as a condition of probation, he will not be able to participate in gang activities any more.

Few therapists can reproduce these aspects of MST, with the main practical reason being that insurance companies generally reimburse only for office-based services. Nonetheless, if we expand our definition of therapy toward a social-ecological conception, we may discern new opportunities to help clients. Counselors can seek out positive social resources and encourage the development of these connections, perhaps by making suggestions to parents and perhaps by being more personally involved. Families benefit when they reduce their association with dysfunctional individuals and create or strengthen connections with people they meet in the context, for example, of church, community groups, adult education, the arts, and recreational activities. For therapists, phone calls are usually more practical than visits to the community, and we can also (with parental permission) invite into our offices people in the client's life beyond the traditional nuclear family members, including extended family, neighbors, nannies, peers, coaches, and so forth. The MST insight is that positive relationships with positive people are the building blocks of a successful life, and no developmental variable of this importance should be beyond the purview of a psychotherapist.

Psychodynamic Therapy

Psychodynamic therapy is appropriate for clients with CD only if they show significant conscience development, and their acting out seems attributable largely to emotional distress, internal conflict, and weak coping ability (Bleiberg, 2001; Gabel, Oster, Pfeffer, & Marlier, 1988). In other words, dynamic intervention seems appropriate only if the conduct disturbance is due primarily to deficits in ego functioning, not superego development.

Although dynamic therapy does not include the detailed guidelines for rules and consequences supplied by behavioral treatment, this approach certainly supports firm limit setting. In fact, dynamic theory posits that, unconsciously, youth with CD are frightened by their out-of-control behavior and wish their parents would demonstrate concern by setting limits, so they would no longer be at the mercy of their impulses (Gabel et al., 1988).

According to dynamic theory, many youth with conduct disturbances have had negative attachment-related experiences, expect mistreatment or abandonment by adults, feel vulnerable to harm in close relationships, and cannot tolerate critical examination of their behavior because their self-esteem is fragile (Kernberg & Chazan, 1991; Kernberg et al., 2000; Wachtel, 1994). Therapy, by its nature, pushes their most sensitive buttons.

The transference relationship is an ideal place for clients to discover the differences between the disappointing, hurtful behavior they expect from adults and the decency and caring that also exist. By repeatedly pointing out the discrepancies between the therapist's real behavior and the client's expectations and perceptions of him, transference interpretations can reduce the distorting effects of the past on the client's responses to people in the present—for instance:

> "Look at what's going on here: I'm asking you questions about school so we can figure out how you're going to pass the 11th grade, and you're looking out the window and acting like my questions are boring and stupid. What am I doing to get that reaction?"

In the object relations typical of CD, adults are viewed as uncaring and malevolent (Rinsley, 1980). Clients behave toward authority figures in accordance with these blueprints; this behavior angers the adults and causes the punitive responses the youth expects. When clients become aware of this positive feedback loop, new ways of interacting with adults become apparent. Interpretations should address both the history and the present effects of the client's object relations:

> "Maybe you think the only way to get things from adults is to be sneaky and dishonest because, in the past, when you asked for things in a simple, straight way, your foster parents wouldn't do anything for you. But not everybody is like that. I'm not, for one."

The self-concepts of youth with CD are typically fragile and brittle. Self-esteem might seem high, but pride is only skin deep, and experiences that suggest some flaw or mistake often result in a painful collapse of self-esteem (Bleiberg, 2001; Wachtel, 1994). When things go wrong, these youth cannot tolerate critical self-examination, and they need to defend against threatening feelings of inadequacy by blaming and even attacking other people. (See the discussion of aggressive response to shame in Chapter 12.) Therapists can say:

> "When something goes wrong, no matter what happened, you find some way to believe you didn't do anything to cause it and it's all someone else's fault. So instead of figuring out what you did that was part of the problem, you get mad. This might make you feel better for a moment, but it will stop you from doing better in the future."

To identify the life lessons a client needs to learn, ask yourself what she does not understand about people that she needs to understand. Many youth with CD need to realize that most adults are more trustworthy than their past experiences led them to believe and, therefore, they will do better if they stop fighting with adults and join them in pursuit of shared goals (e.g., school success and family harmony). With this type of realization, clients can stop pushing nurturance away and recognize caring behavior from other people when it occurs:

> "I know you've been kicked around a lot, which you never deserved, but I also know there are good people in the world, and you'll get along with them if you give them a chance. Let's talk about how you can tell the good ones from the bad ones and how you can link up with the good people."

Parent Counseling

Parents of youth with disruptive behavior disorders frequently feel discouraged, angry, and beaten down by the defiance and hostility they typically endure from their adolescents. The term "parent abuse" is sometimes an accurate description of what these caregivers go through. In addition, they often feel frightened and helpless as they watch their offspring go down paths that predictably lead to poor life outcomes. Parents might be partly responsible for their son's or daughter's problems, but this does not mitigate their distress or their need for an effective therapeutic response.

Counseling can create positive changes in the parent's feelings toward her adolescent. It can be useful to ask questions and solicit memories of the child from better times in the past, even from as far back as the child's birth and infancy. Solution-oriented questioning about positive experiences in the relationship can provide seeds for a rejuvenation of warm parental feelings toward the youth (Milner & Bateman, 2011; Selekman, 2010). Two years prior to therapy, Jack came through in a helpful manner when his stepbrother broke his leg, and his parents became more aware of their son's nurturing side when the therapist asked for a detailed description of this behavior.

It is the parent's job to take the lead in developing more positive styles of interaction in the family (Barkley & Robin, 2014). Frequently, parents need to persist with their leadership efforts for some time before the youth starts responding positively to them. During this time, the adults must suppress their emotional reactions to the adolescent's provocations and hostility. If they are unable to do so, and they strike back at their children like angry peers hurling insults back and forth, this undermines their authority. Young people can sense when disciplinary responses are infused with vindictive attempts to hurt them, and they often recoil and counterattack in reaction to this type of parental input. Teens might not enjoy any type of discipline, but if based on efforts to teach and help, most teens gradually come to accept this structuring influence on their life.

It is difficult to help a person when she responds by hurting you, but demonstrating love in the face of mistreatment and rejection is frequently the challenge faced by parents of youth with conduct disturbance. Sustaining this type of unselfish devotion in the absence of reinforcement is part of how parents earn the status of authority figures with their children.

Demonstrating love in the face of mistreatment and rejection is frequently the challenge faced by parents of youth with conduct disturbance.

Therapists should help parents stand above the fray, without their egos on the line, so they can focus on the task of raising the adolescent without being disrupted by the obnoxious and/or alarming behaviors these youth sometimes produce. One visual image that concretizes this position is that of waves (the teen) crashing on rocky cliffs by the ocean (the parent), creating lots of sound and fury but not moving or damaging the cliffs at all. Another visual image is that of the parent high on a hill, looking down at her son or daughter going through adolescent turbulence, while thoughtfully stroking her chin and deciding what to do next to facilitate the teen's development—for example:

> "The thing to understand about George is that he doesn't really know what he's doing. He's a confused kid, angry and frustrated, thrashing around and making everyone miserable, including himself. The thing to do isn't to hurt him, though—it's to help him by teaching him what's what."

Summary

Adolescent conduct disturbances are generally due to combinations of genetic and environmental variables. Some teens engage in antisocial behavior because their needs for immediate impulse expression and pleasure are stronger than any inhibitions resulting from empathy, moral principles, or fear of punishment. Others exhibit disturbed conduct because intense, disruptive emotions overwhelm their self-control capabilities. Many clients exhibit a combination of motivational and capability-related etiological factors. Counselors should attempt to address each client's needs with the right proportions of the hard and soft aspects of therapy, which correspond to the hard and soft aspects of parenting.

Disruptive behavior disorders often develop in families in which the parents do not fulfill the role of authority figures, and the children exercise developmentally inappropriate levels of power. Therefore, one central goal of therapy is to help the parent establish her control over the adolescent's behavior. Parent training is the primary treatment modality for achieving this goal. The empirically supported interventions generally involve combinations of systemic and behavioral theory and technique. It is also useful to address social-ecological factors outside the family. Other theoretical approaches can play supplementary roles but do not have empirical support as stand-alone interventions for CD.

Implementation of effective rules and consequences is a central aspect of therapy for disruptive behavior disorders. Therapists should help parents function as detectives who stay one step ahead of their offspring, anticipating and countering manipulative attempts to break rules and escape consequences. Counselors should train parents in skills for monitoring the adolescent and calibrating supervision to the level of responsibility she has achieved. Written contracts and point systems are vital tools for providing structure and predictability of consequences.

Therapists should equip parents with a hierarchy of negative consequences so that if the youth refuses to accept one punishment, caregivers can implement another that is under their control. Parent-controlled consequences should remain in place until the youth complies with the entire sequence of escalating punishments that preceded the high-level consequence.

Because adolescents' arguments against rules and consequences generally have less to do with seeking justice than with trying to fulfill a desire, parents need to learn when and how to terminate these debates. Therapists can provide tools, such as deflectors, for parrying manipulation attempts and maintaining control over arguments.

Youth with CD often perceive prosocial behavior as unappealing, so marketing positive behavior is one aspect of counseling with this population. Explaining the nature, value, and challenges of the son or daughter role in families may provide a self-enhancing justification of compliance with parental authority.

Treatment for disruptive behavior also includes work on repairing and enhancing the parent-adolescent relationship. Here, the emphasis is on the parent's unconditional love for the teen, not on contingencies between behavior and reinforcement. Parents should schedule enjoyable, shared activities with the client and should occasionally provide small favors and treats as spontaneous, affectionate gifts that the adolescent did not earn and did not need to earn.

To reclaim control over their adolescent's behavior, parents need to demonstrate unselfish devotion by tolerating whatever personal distress attends implementation of their disciplinary measures and persisting with loving, nurturing behavior even when the youth responds with anger, contempt, and rejection. When parents consistently demonstrate that their devotion to the adolescent does not depend on whether their own needs are met in the relationship, it may eventually dawn on the teen that the adults taking care of him are legitimate authority figures to whom he owes respect and obedience.

Case Study

Therapy resulted in substantial improvement in Jack's behavior, with an end to the serious problems of shoplifting, truancy, recreational drug use, and defiance of his parents. There was less improvement in the emotional tone of his relationships with family members, and he never developed a warm relationship with his stepfather. Jack continued to show much more concern about his own desires than about the needs and feelings of other people in his family.

Incentives and consequences elicited some effort in school, but it was clear that Jack had little aptitude or taste for academic work. The therapist and family identified a vocational course of study that Jack much preferred because the hands-on work offered more stimulation, and the incentive of a well-paying job was not too distant in the future.

Jack attributed his behavioral improvement to the consequences his parents administered. He seemed more comfortable viewing his compliance as a matter of "working the system" than as the result of his relationship with his parents or his own values. Because Jack did not have much intrinsic motivation for positive behavior, his parents recognized the need to remain vigilant in their supervision of him. Their hope was that prosocial behavior would gradually become habitual by the time Jack left home to live on his own.

12

Aggression and Violence

OBJECTIVES

This chapter explains:

- *The difference between reactive and proactive aggression.*
- *The myth that low self-esteem causes violence.*
- *Hostile attributional bias: misreading social cues so that offense is taken when none was intended.*
- *A definition of cruelty for bullies: making yourself feel better by making other people feel worse.*
- *A four-step anger management technique.*
- *Assertive behavior as the midpoint between passive and aggressive behavior.*
- *Communication and conflict resolution techniques.*
- *When and why to walk away from fights.*

Case Study
Strength

Miguel was a 17-year-old Latino adolescent whose parents immigrated from El Salvador before he was born. His parents brought him to therapy because of his fights in school, which had resulted in several suspensions and, recently, a threat of expulsion. Miguel hung out with a group of guys that he called his "gang," but they did not appear to engage in illegal activities beyond underage drinking and occasional truancy. The parents said their son had a bad temper but generally complied with family rules and did enough work in school to pass. Because Miguel's aggression did not fit any specific pattern of disturbance in *DSM-5*, the therapist made a diagnosis of unspecified disruptive behavior disorder.

School staff reported that Miguel had a long record of starting fights. Other students complained that Miguel reacted violently to minor conflicts and playful teasing. Staff complained that he did not take responsibility for his behavior and always blamed the other person for starting the fight, while witnesses usually reported that Miguel threw the first punch.

Miguel's accounts of his fights differed markedly from other people's reports. He insisted that he did not want to fight but was forced to do so by arrogant, obnoxious peers who tried to push him around. He was not interested in therapy because he saw no alternative to fighting as a way to respond to the mistreatment he believed he received: "I am not going to let people disrespect me, and nothing you say is going to change that."

Diagnoses Treated in This Chapter

Intermittent Explosive Disorder

Intermittent explosive disorder should be diagnosed when the client has had several episodes of serious aggression that were grossly disproportionate to precipitating stressors, that involved either assault on another person or destruction of property, and that cannot be accounted for by another mental health disorder, substance use, or a medical condition. This disorder is distinguished by a pattern in which a buildup of tension is followed by an explosive release of anger and aggression. Thus, the person vacillates between two extremes: excessive inhibition of anger and violent outbursts.

Disruptive Behavior Disorders

Most aggressive clients meet criteria for ODD, ADHD, or CD (Connor, 2002). Descriptions of these diagnoses were given in the preceding two chapters. A number of the diagnostic criteria for ODD and, especially, CD involve aggressive behavior (American Psychiatric Association, 2013).

Clinical Presentation and Etiology

Aggression has two possible components: forcefulness and cruelty. In some contexts, such as sports and business, forcefulness is a positive attribute, and being aggressive has connotations of strength and effectiveness. However, when aggression involves harm to other people, it is a dysfunctional behavior. This is the meaning of the term in clinical contexts, where the concern is with maladaptive aggression.

Violence is a simpler concept in that it always involves an intention to harm and so is generally considered maladaptive (with the exception of self-defense, discussed later). Although people sometimes refer to verbal aggression, the word *violence* usually connotes physical force.

Because aggression often co-occurs with disruptive behavior disorders, it is typically associated with the same socioeconomic variables, forms of family dysfunction, and maladaptive parenting practices that contribute to the development of those disorders. The reviews of etiological research presented in the preceding two chapters generally apply to aggression, too, and will not be repeated here, in this last chapter of our sequence on externalizing disorders.

Genetic factors play an important role in aggression. Studies of twins and adoption have produced high heritability estimates for aggressive and violent behavior (Buchmann,

Hohmann, Brandeis, Banaschewski, & Poustka, 2014). In addition to this general relationship, genetic studies have identified specific gene/aggression links, including mutations associated with abnormal serotonin transport and monoamine oxidase metabolism (Baker, Raine, Liu, & Jacobsen, 2008; Moffitt, Ross, & Raine, 2011).

Rates of physical aggression peak at ages 2–3 years and decline thereafter (Bongers, Koot, der Ende, & Verhulst, 2004; Tremblay, 2014). This finding might seem counterintuitive because toddlers are not physically able to do much damage, but they push, hit, and kick each other quite frequently. The developmental course of aggression suggests that, while it is a learned behavior to some extent, violence is also instinctive under some conditions, and the primary effect of socialization is to reduce aggression. Like externalizing dysfunction in general, physical aggression reflects immature self-control capabilities. However, verbal and other complex, indirect forms of aggression increase in the course of development.

Violent behavior shows a significant degree of stability over time, with correlations in the .25 to .50 range (Buchmann et al., 2014; Hofstra, van der Ende, & Verhulst, 2000). Thus, aggressive children are at risk to become aggressive adolescents and adults. Aggression at young ages is especially predictive of violence later in life if the youth also experiences family disruption and a negative mother-child relationship. Childhood aggression predicts a number of later problems, including mental disorder, academic failure and dropout, substance abuse, and unemployment (Tremblay, 2014).

Depression, including bipolar disorder, is common in violence-prone youth (Buchmann et al., 2014; Knox, King, Hanna, Logan, & Ghaziuddin, 2000). In contrast, most anxiety disorders seem to lower the risk of violence, perhaps because anxiety is associated with anticipation of consequences, inhibition, and conflict or regret about antisocial behavior (Connor, 2002; Jarrett, Siddiqui, Lochman, & Qu, 2014).

Types of Aggression

Research has identified subtypes or categories of different kinds of aggressive behavior. One important distinction is between **reactive** and **proactive** aggression (Dodge & Coie, 1987; Dodge, Laird, Lochman, Zelli, & Conduct Problems Prevention Research Group, 2002; Polman, de Castro, Koops, van Boxtel, & Merk, 2007). Reactive aggression is an angry, defensive response to a perceived threat, provocation, or injury. Reactive aggression can be elicited by *mis*perceptions of threat, without any real danger from the environment, but the person's experience is still that she is defending herself. Reactive aggression is characterized by physiological hyperarousal, intense feelings of fear and anger, and disorganized attacks on the perceived source of threat or injury (Williams, Lochman, Phillips, & Barry, 2003). This type of aggression is associated with higher levels of depression than proactive aggression (Card & Little, 2006). Miguel's aggression seemed to be predominantly of the reactive type.

Proactive aggression (also called instrumental and predatory aggression) is not a response to threat but is purposefully initiated in order to achieve a goal, such as intimidating, exploiting, or stealing from another person. Proactive aggression does not involve anger or emotional upset; it is a planned, goal-directed behavior. This type of aggression is usually conceptualized in social learning theory terms (Card & Little, 2007), which explains behavior as a function of observational learning and reinforcement history (Bandura, 1977, 1986).

Proactive aggression has a "cold-blooded" quality, while reactive aggression feels "hot"; these terms are not merely metaphors but reflect different degrees of biological arousal. The difference between the experiences of reactively and proactively aggressive people lies in their perception of whether they or the other person started the fights they were in. Instrumental aggression often "works" in the sense that it gets youth things they want, in the short term, while reactive aggression usually does not lead to positive outcomes, even in the short term. Proactive aggression is associated with juvenile delinquency, while reactive aggression is not related to delinquency (Raine et al., 2006; Vitaro, Brendgen, & Barker, 2006). Reactive aggression is clearly a mental health problem, while this is less true of proactive aggression, which might be viewed as a criminal justice issue. Finally, reactive violence is due to deficient self-control capabilities and feels involuntary or, at least, undesired by the person, while proactive violence is a function of motivational factors and is a freely chosen behavior.

There is also an aggression typology associated with gender differences. Males are generally more aggressive than females, and this sex difference is reliably found in overt verbal aggression and physical violence. However, gender differences in aggression depend on the type of behavior that is measured. Females exceed males in **relational** aggression (Card, Stucky, Sawalani, & Little, 2008; Crick & Werner, 1998). This type of aggression attacks the victim's relationships with other people by snubbing her, organizing peers to ostracize the victim, and spreading rumors that damage her reputation. Thus, while boys' aggression typically takes the form of *assault*, girls more frequently work behind the scenes to *exclude* the victim from her social group.

Neurobiological Etiologies

Neurobiological research has identified links between abnormalities of brain anatomy and violent behavior (Raine, 2013; Raine, Buchsbaum, & LaCasse, 1997; Yang & Raine, 2009). Brain imaging studies have documented low volumes of gray matter (dendrites) in the prefrontal cortices of adults with serious violence histories. This abnormality is highly specific: The overall brain volumes of violent individuals are not abnormally low; the volumes of white matter (axons) in their prefrontal cortices are not low; and control groups of substance abusers and psychiatric patients without violence histories do not show low volumes of prefrontal cortex gray matter. This anatomical finding makes psychological sense: The prefrontal cortex is a key brain area for conscience, forethought, and self-control, so low levels of the biological circuitry needed for these functions would plausibly lead to violent behavior.

Histories of violent behavior are also associated with abnormal responses in brain areas involved in aggression and its inhibition (Meyer-Lindenberg et al., 2006; Raine, 2013). Under conditions of emotional arousal, violent individuals exhibit hyperresponsiveness of the amygdala, a brain structure involved in fear and aggression, and underresponsiveness of prefrontal and anterior cingulate cortex, brain areas involved in behavioral inhibition and management of competing impulses. On a neurophysiological level, violent individuals exhibit both more intense aggressive impulses and weaker cognitive controls, compared to people without histories of violence.

Exposure to neurotoxins, such as nicotine, alcohol, and cocaine, during embryological development is another biological cause of violence (Connor, 2002; Raine, 2013). Childhood exposure to lead also results in neurobiological harm that increases risk for aggressive behavior.

Cognitive-Behavioral Etiologies

Psychosocial skills deficits are a fundamental etiological factor in the reactive type of aggression. Reactively aggressive youth do not know how to manage interpersonal problems in a nonviolent way, so they lack alternatives to aggression in conflicts, and they get into fights because they do not know what else to do in the situation (Dodge et al., 2002; Lochman, 2004). These youth show faulty social judgment, and their behavior often antagonizes their peers, resulting in retaliation and rejection. When conflicts occur, they have difficulty using verbal assertion and compromise to solve problems (de Castro, Merk, Koops, Veerman, & Bosch, 2005; Powell et al., 2011). Their social-cognitive deficits are not simply the result of slow intellectual development but make an independent contribution to aggressive behavior. Thus, deficient psychosocial capabilities play a central role in the etiology of reactive aggression.

Reactively aggressive youth do not know how to manage interpersonal problems in a nonviolent way, so they lack alternatives to aggression in conflicts.

The etiology of proactive aggression is more a function of motivational factors. Many violence-prone youth see violence as a way to achieve their goals and meet their needs, particularly needs for safety, power, excitement, and self-esteem (Camodeca & Goossens, 2005; Salmivalli & Peets, 2009; Shapiro, Dorman, Burkey, Welker, & Clough, 1997). When conflicts occur, these youth identify dominance and revenge as goals, and they view violence as an acceptable, effective strategy for solving problems.

Self-concept factors play an important role in violence, but this role is different from what is commonly assumed. The belief that low self-esteem causes violence is widespread among professionals and laypeople alike, but this connection is a myth, because research has consistently indicated that most violent individuals do *not* have low self-esteem (Baumeister, Campbell, Krueger, & Vohs, 2005; Baumeister, Smart, & Boden, 1996; Moeller, 2001). There is an element of truth to the widespread view, but the reality is more complicated than the simple association commonly believed to exist. There are two steps in the sequence. First, the self-esteem of most violent individuals is not low but rather unstable and fragile. These individuals often express an arrogant, swaggering sense of self, but when their self-concept is threatened by failure or disrespect from other people, their self-esteem quickly falls from very high to very low. When this occurs, violence-prone individuals often strike out aggressively in an attempt to repair the damage to their self-esteem by attacking the perceived source of the damage (Bushman et al., 2009; de Castro, Brendgen, van Boxtel, Vitaro, & Schaepers, 2007; Shapiro, Dorman, et al., 1997). If they beat up the person who humiliated them, they feel better about themselves.

Aggressive and nonaggressive youth show consistent differences in the way they interpret the behavior of other people. Aggressive youth exhibit **hostile attributional bias:** They perceive others as more hostile than is really the case (de Castro et al., 2002; Dodge et al., 2002; Lochman & Wells, 2002). This disturbance in social perception causes aggressive youngsters to take offense when no offense was intended. Hostile attributional bias played a major role in Miguel's aggression. He often felt that others were laughing at him or trying to push him around when, according to observer reports, the other student's behavior was not truly hostile. Miguel was not lying, but he was incorrect when he attributed his fights to aggressive behavior by the other person.

There has been a great deal of controversy about the question of whether violent media, especially violent video games, causes aggressive behavior in young people. Studies have produced markedly conflicting results. There is a meta-analysis indicating these games cause aggression (Anderson et al., 2010) and another meta-analysis finding no such effect (Sherry, 2007). Methodological criticisms have flown back and forth. A narrative review by Markey and Markey (2010) brought together evidence that violent video games increase aggression in individuals with preexisting, personality-based proneness to violence but do not have this effect on people without vulnerability. For clinicians, the most reasonable integration of this set of findings might be to forego blanket proscriptions of violent video games but to inquire carefully about their effects on individual clients, and if the games sometimes seem to be antecedents of aggressive behavior, to recommend that parents restrict their use.

Psychodynamic Etiologies

Dynamic explanations of violence emphasize both ego and superego factors (Dewald, 1971; Gray, 1994). Without adequate conscience development, people are willing to hurt others in order to obtain personal gratification. Inadequate ego development results in difficulties tolerating frustration, regulating emotion, and inhibiting aggressive impulses. Thus, from a psychodynamic perspective, proactive aggression is the result of inadequate superego development, and reactive aggression is the result of inadequate ego development.

In the defense mechanism called **identification with the aggressor**, victims identify with the person who controls, dominates, or abuses them (A. Freud, 1946a; McKenzie, 2004). This defense seems related to the common desire to be on the side that is winning—even if the loser is you. Through the alogical processing characteristic of immature ego functioning, the victim comes to adopt the viewpoint of his victimizer. In the short-term, this defense reduces emotional distress because it makes the abuse seem more acceptable, perhaps because the victim internalizes the view that he deserves the abuse. The defense's lasting effects are likely to be harmful, because identification with the aggressor causes victims to behave as their perpetrators behaved.

In the related mechanism called **turning passive into active**, the person defends against emotional pain by doing to other people what was done to her (A. Freud, 1946a; Gardner, 1993). Violent individuals sometimes feel as if hurting another person discharges their pain into the victim and thus rids them of it (Shapiro, 2003). In revengeful actions, the pain is sent back to the person from whom it originated. In the defense mechanism of **displacement**, the individual expels his pain into people other than those who hurt him in the first place. In these defenses, violence brings the individual temporary relief, but at the price of causing more pain to others.

Systemic Etiologies

Family dysfunction is a significant etiological factor in violence (Frick & Viding, 2009; Lochman, 2004; Moeller, 2001). Dysfunctional mother-child attachments, particularly those of the disorganized type, predict the future development of aggression (Carlson, 1998). Harsh, coercive, inconsistent parenting styles of the type discussed in the chapters on disruptive behavior disorders also contribute to the development of aggression (Harvey & Metcalf, 2012; McMahon & Forehand, 2005; Patterson & Chamberlain, 1994). Divorce increases rates of child aggression, as do high levels of conflict between parents who stay together (Hetherington & Stanley-Hagan, 1999).

Research on "the cycle of violence," or the intergenerational transmission of aggression, indicates that physical abuse and corporal punishment increase aggressive behavior in children (Lansford et al., 2014; Taylor, Manganello, Lee, & Rice, 2010). Witnessing domestic violence between parents is also associated with increased aggression in children (Tremblay, 2014). Children seem to learn and imitate the aggressive behaviors modeled by their parents regardless of whether they are victims or witnesses of these behaviors (Moeller, 2001).

Aggression is associated with maladaptive peer relationships. During the elementary school years, reactive aggression is associated with rejection by peers (Dodge et al., 2002; Card & Little, 2006). During adolescence, there is a change in the social lives of many aggressive children, as they dissociate from prosocial age-mates and form groups (or gangs) with other rejected, aggressive youth (Granic & Dishion, 2003; McCabe et al., 2001). Coming together with peers who have shared similar experiences provides a sense of belonging, but these youth often encourage each other to engage in antisocial behavior (Dishion et al., 1999).

Assessment

Assessment of aggression in children and adolescents should begin with a tabulation of the type, frequency, severity, and history of the youth's violent behavior. The assessment should examine the broad domains of psychological functioning that influence likelihood of violence, including cognitive and academic functioning, the presence of other disorders such as ADHD and substance abuse, possible biological abnormalities, impulsivity, empathy, self-concept, and relationships with parents, other family members, and peers. Because aggressive youth tend to deny, minimize, and rationalize their behavior, it is important to obtain observations from multiple informants.

Family and peer influences should be assessed to gauge the amount of modeling and support for aggressive behavior present in the client's social environment. This part of the evaluation should inquire about exposure to family and neighborhood violence.

Reports by parents, teachers, and other adults in the client's environment can provide data for a functional behavioral assessment to illuminate what the client attempts to accomplish with her aggressive behavior. Antecedents and consequences should be identified in a search for actionable information. For example, if aggression tends to co-occur with schoolwork that is too difficult for the child, acceptable alternatives might include asking for help, receiving more time to do the work, or taking a break if frustration mounts.

One basic assessment question is whether the client's aggression is reactive, proactive, or both. In reactive aggression, the antecedents are social misperceptions, hyperarousal, and emotional distress. The consequences are usually negative, but it does not matter, because reactive aggression is driven primarily by antecedents. Proactive aggression is primarily a function of consequences, which are perceived by the youth as positive, and which typically include reinforcers such as material gain, the excitement of dominance and victory, and admiration from peers.

Aggressive youth often believe that disclosing their negative behavior will elicit disapproval from the therapist and get them in trouble. To maximize their openness, clinicians should provide face-saving ways for clients to disclose problems. It helps to phrase questions in language consistent with the client's perspective—for example:

- "I don't think you got into all those fights because you woke up in the morning and decided you just wanted to be violent that day. I think there were reasons for those fights, and that's what I want to ask you about."
- "When someone disrespects you, is it easy to control your temper, or is it hard?"
- "What kinds of situations make you feel like you have to fight?"

Violence assessments should investigate the client's repertoire for dealing with anger and conflict. Open-ended questions like, "What do you do when you get mad?" provide information about the youth's range of responses. (One 7-year-old boy responded to this question with a pause, a puzzled expression, and a reply of, "Do you know why I'm here?")

It is important to evaluate the client's level of comfort with her past aggressive behavior. The question is whether violence is acceptable to the youth's conscience, so she makes little effort to control it, or whether there is guilt about this behavior, but she is unable to inhibit her violent impulses—for example:

- "How do you feel after you've been in a fight? After fights you've lost? After fights you've won?"
- "Is fighting something you *decide* to do, or is it more like you just go off and, before you know it, you're in a fight?"
- "Do you ever wish there was a way you could stay out of fights? Or do you feel like something would be missing from your life if you never fought again?"

Therapy cannot address the appeal of aggressive behavior unless assessment first discovers the substance of this appeal. To learn about the functions of violence in the client's life, ask:

"I don't think there would be so much violence in the world if there wasn't something about it that people liked. So my next question is, what's good about fighting? What can it do for you?"

Treatment Planning

Outcome Research

Because aggression is a common symptom of disruptive behavior disorders, the outcome research reviewed in the previous two chapters is generally relevant to the question of which interventions are effective for violent behavior. Treatment planning for aggressive youth should make use of outcome research on any related problems exhibited by the client.

There has been a historical trend in the results of research on therapy for aggression. Studies done prior to the 1980s consistently indicated that therapy failed to ameliorate conduct disturbances and violence, and there was doubt about whether these disturbances were treatable (Shamsie, 1981). The early research evaluated the approaches in common use at the time—namely, client-centered, psychodynamic, and nondirective forms of family therapy. The negative results produced by the early research indicate that these approaches are not effective with most aggressive clients. Also, recent research on dynamic therapy has found that this approach is less effective with externalizing than internalizing problems (Fonagy & Target, 1996; Muratori et al., 2002, 2003).

While nondirective approaches apparently do not work, outcome research supports cognitive-behavioral therapies for aggression in young people.

While nondirective approaches apparently do not work, outcome research supports cognitive-behavioral therapies for aggression in young people. Smeets et al. (2014) performed a meta-analysis of 25 studies of CBT for aggression in adolescents. They obtained a medium-sized effect of .50. Sukhodolsky et al.'s (2004) meta-analysis of 40 outcome studies examined CBT for anger-related problems in children and adolescents. They obtained an overall effect size of .67, which is in the medium/high range. Some techniques were found to be more effective than others. The strongest results were produced by anger management skills training, work on hostile attributional bias, problem-solving skills training, and assertiveness training. Smaller improvements were produced by affective education, self-monitoring, and relaxation training. Effect sizes were larger when the therapies involved rehearsing techniques in sessions and practicing them as homework assignments, compared to therapies that explained the procedures but did not emphasize practice.

McCart, Priester, Davies, and Azen (2006) performed a meta-analytic review that compared two approaches to aggressive behavior problems in youth: behavioral parent training (described in Chapter 10) and group and individual CBT delivered to young clients. They obtained effect sizes of .45 for parent training and .37 for CBT, which were not significantly different from each other and are in the small to medium range. In addition, McCart et al. found that the comparative effectiveness of parent training and CBT depended on the client's age: Parent training was more effective with children aged 6–12 years, while CBT was more effective with older clients. The authors interpreted this result as consistent with the idea that young children are more dependent on and influenced by their parents, compared to adolescents.

One of the most extensively researched CBT packages is the Coping Power program (Lochman, Boxmeyer, Powell, Barry, & Pardini, 2010; Lochman, Wells, & Lenhart, 2008), which is usually provided in schools to groups of children identified as having problems with aggression. This intervention has achieved positive results in a number of studies, demonstrating reductions in aggressive behavior, delinquency, and substance use (Lochman et al., 2013). In an RCT conducted by Lochman and Wells (2004), the intervention resulted in less teacher-reported aggressive behavior and less parent-reported substance abuse, compared to a TAU control. Mediation analysis supported the theory underlying the intervention: Improvement in behavior was mediated by changes in social-cognitive processes, including decreases in hostile attributions and reduced belief in the instrumental utility of violence (Lochman & Wells, 2002). Gains were maintained at a 1-year follow-up (Lochman & Wells, 2004). In an RCT by Stoltz et al. (2013), a modified version of the program reduced both proactive and reactive aggression as reported by children, parents, and teachers. Effect sizes were generally small but significant, ranging from .11 to .32.

Training in social problem solving, described in Chapter 10 on disruptive behavior, has been supported as a stand-alone treatment for adolescent aggression in studies by Guerra and Slaby (1990) and Larson and Gerber (1987). These studies also produced evidence that the effects of therapy were mediated by improved problem-solving skills in the adolescents.

Violence prevention programs in schools have made up a great deal of the work done on youth aggression. Wilson, Lipsey, and Derzon (2003) conducted a meta-analysis of these interventions and obtained effect sizes ranging between .20 and .33, which are small but significant in magnitude. Interventions for high-risk youth produced larger effect sizes than universal prevention programs. Demonstration projects achieved stronger results than routine program implementation. Because the content of most school violence prevention programs overlaps with CBT, their results provide indirect support for the cognitive-behavioral approach.

Clinical Considerations

Because risk of violent behavior is determined by an interaction of child-level variables and contextual, especially family factors, treatment is most likely to be effective when it includes work with both the child and parents (Conduct Problems Prevention Research Group, 2002; Lochman & Wells, 2004). McCart et al.'s (2006) meta-analysis provides therapists with guidance about how best to proportion the parent training and child CBT components of therapy: Typically, parent training is most important for younger clients, and individual CBT is most useful for adolescents. Of course, individual client factors might override the implications of these findings for large groups of youth.

Parent and family work in aggression treatment is usually similar to parent and family work in therapy for disruptive behavior disorders. This chapter will not repeat previous descriptions of these interventions, but it should be understood that the individual therapy techniques presented in this chapter are frequently combined with the parent training and family therapy strategies described in the previous two.

Reactive aggression is caused by deficits in emotion regulation and psychosocial capabilities (Dodge et al., 2002; Polman et al., 2007; Williams et al., 2003), so therapy for these clients should generally be based on skills training. Specifically, because reactive aggression is associated with hostile attributional bias, therapy for these clients should include work on interpreting the behavior of other people. Because reactively aggressive youth experience surges of anger and arousal when provoked, they would probably benefit from anger management training. Since these youth are often disorganized and unskilled in conflict situations, training in social problem solving and assertive communication would be helpful to them. Miguel's therapy was based on training in these skills.

Proactive aggression is a motivation-based problem that is a function of operant learning, values, and attitudes related to violence (Dodge et al., 2002; Polman et al., 2007). Therefore, treatment for proactive aggression should emphasize reinforcement contingencies and work on attitudes and values (Card & Little, 2007). Many youth exhibit both reactive and proactive aggression, so their therapy should be designed to strengthen both motivation and capability for nonviolent behavior.

Several therapeutic ingredients in addition to CBT, parent training, and family therapy may add useful elements to counseling for some clients. Violence-prone youth who have histories of trauma might benefit from the interventions described in Chapter 15. Solution-focused techniques can be used to expand on strategies the client has used to manage conflicts nonviolently in the past. Narrative therapy may increase the client's motivation for nonviolent functioning by depicting aggression not as an aspect of self but as an external force that sometimes takes control of his behavior. Psychodynamic therapy may be useful when the client's violent behavior seems related to unconscious processes, learning, and defenses, as well as unrealistic beliefs about self and others that do not respond to reason and evidence.

Addressing Decisions About Fighting

Most interventions for aggressive behavior emphasize training in the psychosocial skills necessary for skillful, nonviolent responses to conflict. These interventions generally assume that aggressive youth want to live nonviolently but have been unable to do so because they lack the necessary skills. This assumption seems valid for reactive aggression, which is based on capability deficits, but invalid for proactive aggression, which is based on motivational factors.

Research on violence-related attitudes and values suggests that some youth believe violence is an effective, honorable response to insults and other interpersonal problems (Bushman et al., 2009; de Castro et al., 2007; Shapiro, Dorman, et al., 1997) as well as an effective strategy for pursuing goals (Slaby & Guerra, 1988; Smithmyer, Hubbard, & Simons, 2000). With attitudes and beliefs favorable to violence, clients would probably not be motivated to learn new, nonviolent conflict management skills. Therefore, especially with proactively aggressive youth, therapy probably needs to address the issue of client motivation before moving on to skills training.

It is often useful to discuss the consequences of fighting at the beginning of interventions for violence (Glick & Gibbs, 2010; Prothrow-Stith, 1987). Aggressive clients are usually quite capable of stating the advantages of fighting. It is also easy for them to see the disadvantages of fights they lose. However, these discussions often encounter a macho form of resistance when the youth assures the counselor that he always wins fights. It is probably not effective to question the client's fighting skills, but it is useful to question the reliability with which these skills can produce victories:

> "Street fights aren't like boxing matches, where there are rules and the best man wins. If your foot slips, or the other guy picks up a bottle, something really bad could happen to your face. Fights aren't necessarily won by the better fighter; half the time they're won by the luckier fighter or the dirtier fighter, and it's not worth the risk."

For violence treatment to be effective, clients must learn about the negative consequences that flow from *winning* fights, an outcome they may initially view as completely positive. The counselor can point out that fighting is a bad idea, even if one wins, for the reasons stated in Table 12.1.

Table 12.1   Negative Consequences of Winning Fights

Fights do not solve the problems that caused them; those problems are still there, and they are usually worse after a fight.

Winning a fight proves nothing about who was right or wrong about the conflict that led to the violence.

The winners of fights often receive injuries and, although these might be less severe than the loser's, these victories are not worth the risk of permanent physical damage.

Winning a fight often leads to future retaliation from the other person or her friends and relatives. Sometimes the winner's friends and relatives are victimized in an escalating cycle of violence.

Violence often gets people in trouble in school and with the law, resulting in the loss of opportunities to pursue goals much more valuable than winning fights.

It is important for clients to understand that, although violence sometimes seems to work in the short term, a social adaptation based on fighting generally leads to negative outcomes in the long run—for example:

- "You might win 99 fights in a row—but the 100th one could be the end of that nice face of yours."
- "Jails, hospitals, and cemeteries are filled with people who thought they could fight their way through life."

Motivation for violent versus peaceful behavior is an issue of values as well as a question of what works. Moral development influences rates of violent behavior (Eargle, Guerra, & Tolan, 1994; Gibbs, 2003; Guerra, Nucci, & Huesmann, 1994).

As discussed in Chapter 8, values-related issues sometimes arise in counseling, in which case clinicians should address these issues in a therapeutic manner. Pro-violence values are often promulgated by clients' peer groups, families, and/or the mass media. Given this reality, it would be unfortunate for people who are against violence to muzzle themselves on the grounds that value judgments are subjective and therefore should be avoided. Therapy should address values-related issues in a respectful manner that emphasizes helping the client do better in the future, not judging her behavior in the past. It is possible to combine acceptance of the youth as a person, empathy for the emotions behind her actions, and advocacy of values and strategies that will be better both for the client and for other people she encounters.

As discussed in Chapter 8, the Golden Rule provides a moral framework that is practical for work with young people. The Golden Rule addresses a social-cognitive deficit common in aggressive individuals—namely, difficulty looking at their own behavior from other people's perspectives (Berkowitz, 1993; de Castro et al., 2005). The Golden Rule is an exercise in perspective switching. It can be applied to virtually any situation.

All of the major world religions include some version of the Golden Rule. Because this principle makes sense on both religious and humanistic grounds, its therapeutic use can be either connected to or independent from the client's spiritual tradition. For Miguel and his family, the Golden Rule provided a connection between their therapeutic work and their Catholic faith. Miguel's counselor did not try to change his religious beliefs, but neither would she go along with maintaining those beliefs as platitudes with no relation to his everyday actions. The therapist challenged Miguel to apply his religious convictions to specific situations and to put his values into action in the way he lived his life.

The Golden Rule directly addresses a social-cognitive deficit common in aggressive individuals— namely, difficulty looking at their own behavior from other people's perspectives.

Discussions of right and wrong in regard to violence sometimes come down to the issue of self-defense. Therapists might feel they face a quandary in these discussions because clients insist that they must fight in self-defense, but counselors might not want to accept any justification of violence.

Self-defense is a two-sided issue, and both sides need to be considered. On one hand, therapists who maintain a blanket opposition to fighting risk losing credibility with their clients, who might see such adults as unable to understand what goes on in their neighborhoods. On a commonsense level, it seems unreasonable to advise clients not to fight back while being beaten up. Also, the law explicitly recognizes the legitimacy of violence used in self-defense.

On the other hand, violence-prone youth frequently abuse this concept by invoking an expansive, careless definition that justifies all sorts of aggressive behavior that is not true self-defense. These clients justify their violence with distorted cognitions, such as, "He looked like he was going to hit me; it was self-defense." At the beginning of therapy, Miguel viewed confrontational behavior from peers as tantamount to assault, and he justified his ensuing violence as self-protection.

Fortunately, there is a way to prevent misuse of the self-defense concept without adopting an unrealistically pacifist position. This stance consists of acknowledging a right of self-protection while *shrinking* the youth's concept of self-defense down to its true, valid size (Shapiro, 2003). Self-defense means fighting back when one is literally, physically being assaulted, after having tried everything possible to avoid violence. Self-defense must involve the minimum amount of aggression necessary to achieve safety; continuing to hit someone after her attack has been stopped is revenge, not self-defense.

Therapists who acknowledge the legitimacy of fighting under certain narrow conditions can propose a policy that is both consistent with peaceful values and acceptable to most youth. This policy consists of a resolution never to throw the first punch, plus a willingness to fight, in self-defense, if attacked. If an individual adopted this policy, he would never be responsible for starting a fight.

Mental health and school professionals who work with aggressive youth often complain that parental influences oppose their efforts, and young people do often report their parents saying that, if someone hits them, they are to hit the person back. If this parental advice is understood accurately, it presents no problem for aggression treatment because it is based on a valid concept of self-defense. The advice implies that, if someone has *not* hit the client, she has no justification for becoming violent. In these situations, the task for therapists is to help clients understand their parents' guidelines more accurately. In Miguel's Salvadoran culture, issues of self-assertion, pride, and aggression are considered particularly salient for males, and boys generally take their cues from their fathers more than from their mothers. Therefore, the counselor made an effort to schedule sessions at times when Miguel's father could participate.

Violent and Peaceful Foundations of Self-Esteem

While interventions designed to increase self-esteem in a simple, straightforward fashion are not likely to reduce aggressive behavior, techniques based on a more accurate understanding of self-concept factors in violence can be effective (Shapiro, Burgoon, Welker, & Clough, 2002). Nonviolence is most effectively supported not by extremely high self-esteem but by moderate, realistic self-esteem that is resilient in the face of setbacks, failures, and, especially, disrespect from others (Baumeister et al., 1996, 2005; Bushman et al., 2009; de Castro et al., 2007).

The difference between violent and nonviolent youth is less in the level of their current self-esteem than in the content of their self-concept *aspirations* (Shapiro, Dorman, et al., 1997). In other words, the important issue is not how proud of himself the youth is but what he wants to be proud *of*. If a person's self-esteem is based on his ability to be aggressive, violence makes sense as a means of repairing damaged pride. But if a person has invested in an image of himself as a fair, nonviolent person, violence would do nothing to repair his self-esteem. Therapists who are comfortable with self-disclosure can explain this concept by using themselves as an example (e.g., "If someone said I was a lousy therapist, that would make me feel bad about myself—but would it make sense for me to beat them up to get my pride back?"). The idea of the counselor assaulting someone to protect his self-esteem strikes most clients as absurd, and the meaning of this absurdity is that violence can be completely unrelated to a person's worth.

Initially, the self-esteem aspirations of many aggressive youth, especially males, emphasize physical strength and fighting ability. Prosocial motivation increases when clients expand their concepts of strength beyond physical capabilities to more abstract "inner strengths." One technique for initiating this process is to ask clients about people in their lives who have helped them feel better and do better, or who have helped others and made the world a better place in some large or small way (Shapiro, 2003). Then, ask the client to describe the strengths of these individuals. The descriptions that emerge usually emphasize virtues like kindness, loyalty, and wisdom, not strengths related to physical dominance. This exercise may increase clients' investment in prosocial self-esteem components, and such aspirations motivate clients to develop nonviolent conflict management capabilities.

Bullying

Although this chapter focuses on conflicts in which the two parties have comparable levels of power, some forms of aggression involve a unilateral victimization of one person by another. Bullying is not a matter of self-protection, retaliation, or even anger toward the target, but of intentional cruelty practiced for its own sake (Olweus, 1993; Olweus & Limber, 2010). Bullying is a common problem in childhood that is associated with an increased likelihood of mental health problems and negative life outcomes for both victims and bullies (Arseneault, Bowes, & Shakoor, 2010; Arseneault et al., 2006).

Cyber bullying seems similar to face-to-face bullying, especially in its relational form, but the anonymity and distance of cyber bullying make it possible to promulgate hurtful messages on a grand scale, and this type of cruelty has some characteristics that distinguish it from the face-to-face type (Jose, Kljakovic, Scheib, & Notter, 2012; Modecki, Minchin, Harbaugh, Guerra, & Runions, 2014). Cyber bullying is associated with even higher levels of internalizing dysfunction, for both bullies and victims, compared to face-to-face bullying (Bonanno & Hymel, 2013).

To a large extent, bullying is a function of group norms and peer culture, which means that interventions should operate on the level of schools or other youth-serving organizations when possible (Garrity, Jens, Porter, Sager, & Short-Camilli, 2000; Olweus & Limber, 2010). Nonetheless, therapists should do what we can to reduce bullying by working with individuals.

Research has identified two important individual-level factors in bullying: (1) proactive aggression as a means of achieving social status and power (Camodeca & Goossens, 2005; Salmivalli & Peets, 2009), and (2) callous-unemotional traits and a lack of empathy for victims (Ciucci & Baroncelli, 2014; Muñoz, Qualter, & Padgett, 2011). Bullies do not have low levels of social intelligence, but they lack compassion for other people (Gini, Pozzoli, & Hauser, 2011). These findings and others can be distilled to their essence in a formulation simple enough to be understood by the clients whom the theories are about: In bullying, and in cruelty generally, the individual tries to make himself feel better by making other people feel worse (Shapiro, 2003). This statement is not an explanation, but it is an accurate description that identifies two basic attributes of cruelty: It is morally wrong, and there is something pathetic about it.

In bullying, and in cruelty generally, the individual tries to make himself feel better by making other people feel worse.

Therapists can confront clients who bully with this description and invite them to think about the meaning of what they have been doing. Bullies often generate rationalizations for their cruel behavior, and some exploration of these rationalizations might be useful at times, but, more frequently, these discussions are beside the point. Therapists should focus on the bottom line, which is that bullies try to make themselves feel good by making other people feel bad. Bullies seem to operate on the basis of a zero-sum schema of well-being in relationships, in which the pleasure and pride of one person must be purchased by the pain and humiliation of the other. Form 12.1 on our website presents a visual metaphor of a seesaw to explain this process and depict the cognitions underlying bullying (e.g., "If I can make her feel stupid, then I will feel smart," "If I can make him feel weak, then I will feel strong"). Therapists need to help bullies find ways to deal with their emotional pain without inflicting it on others.

When people behave selfishly or cruelly, they often rationalize their actions by blaming the victim of their hurtful behavior (e.g., "She deserved it"; Olweus, 1993; Olweus & Limber, 2010). Clinicians can confront these rationalizations by identifying them as self-serving excuses for violating the principle of the equal value of human beings. It may be worth adding that, historically, crimes against humanity have always been justified by this type of denigration of scapegoated groups, which allows sadistic impulses to be cloaked with the mantle of justice. Clients can learn to recognize such rationalizations as warning signs of cruel behavior, and they can view efforts to control these impulses as part of the hard work of being a good person.

Cognitive-Behavioral Therapy

There are several manuals that delineate cognitive-behavioral therapy packages for anger, aggression, and violence (Glick & Gibbs, 2010; Larson, 2005; Lochman et al., 2008; Sukhodolsky & Scahill, 2012). Much work on aggression also takes the form of violence prevention programs in schools. These curriculum-based interventions generally include a great deal of cognitive-behavioral content that is similar to the material in clinical manuals (Committee for Children, 2002; Conduct Problems Prevention Research Group, 1992; Gordon, 2009; Shapiro, 2003). The recommendations ahead draw on these sources.

CBT generally has a large psychoeducational component. We want clients to become experts on the problems for which they are in therapy, and we want them to apply this expertise to their experiences and behaviors. As discussed in Chapter 8, nurturing clients' interest and ego involvement in how they respond to difficult external situations often galvanizes constructive coping efforts. The practice of making anger ratings on a 0–10 scale facilitates this process of locating the problem internally, where it can be controlled, rather than externally, in the form of uncontrollably difficult or even obnoxious people. Sukhodolsky and Scahill (2012) suggest that clients keep an anger log in which they describe situations that made them angry, what they said and did, the outcome, and what they could have done differently.

Violence rarely erupts suddenly and unpredictably; most violence occurs as the last step in a process of escalating conflict and anger (Prothrow-Stith, 1987). The way to understand aggressive outbursts is to track them back through their antecedent sequence of events. Identifying the steps involved in violent incidents provides important information

Table 12.2   Sequence of Violence Prevention Strategies

1. Conflict avoidance.
2. Conflict management.
    a. Anger control.
    b. Problem solving.
    c. Assertive communication.
    d. Conflict resolution.
3. Leaving the conflict (i.e., walking away).

for treatment because different prevention strategies are applicable at different stages of the process, as shown in Table 12.2.

The sequence of strategies shown in Table 12.2, which is depicted graphically on our website (Form 12.2), can be explained to clients as a matter of "what to do when." If a strategy works, the sequence terminates, because success has been achieved. If a strategy does not work, the youth should move to the next one in the sequence. Safety lies in having multiple options, so there is always a fallback plan.

Step 2 in Table 12.2 lists conflict management techniques in a sequence that goes from the inside out, which is the order in which the techniques should be used, if possible. First, anger management brings emotions under control, which enables people to think effectively and plan how to solve problems. Then, assertive communication can be used to implement conflict resolution plans in collaboration with the other person in the conflict.

Conflict Avoidance

Conflict avoidance is the least effortful violence prevention strategy because when it works, conflicts do not occur and therefore do not need to be managed. Conflict avoidance can be explained to clients as an intelligent way to "look down the road" and "steer clear" of the type of situation that might lead to violence. Many aggressive youth need this type of training in proactive thinking because without it, they often fail to realize when they are on a path toward violence, and they are surprised by confrontations that could have been anticipated (Loeber & Hay, 1997; Shapiro, 2003; Sukhodolsky & Scahill, 2012).

One proactive strategy consists of avoiding places and people that predictably occasion conflict and violence (Canada, 2010; Prothrow-Stith, 1987). Practical planning based on past experience and observation of certain street corners, groups of people, and so forth can sometimes accomplish significant violence prevention all by itself.

One important conflict avoidance strategy is to inhibit behaviors that are likely to offend or provoke other people. It is useful to ask clients to identify behaviors that anger them when they are on the receiving end and then have them notice when they engage in these behaviors themselves. This strategy for avoiding inflammatory behavior is a variation of the Golden Rule. Therapists can say:

"Use yourself as a guide to decide: Before you say or do something, put yourself in the other person's shoes and ask the question, 'How would I feel if someone said or did that to me?'"

The following example helps clients get the idea:

> "Let's say you see a kid come running into class, he's almost late, carrying a bunch of things, and he trips and falls, splat, and his stuff goes flying everywhere. Then, you think of something really funny you could say, that would crack everybody up. The question is: Should you say it?"

Based on what we know about shame and aggression, a humorous comment in this situation might bring the target into an angry confrontation with the comedian, perhaps with a retort such as, "What's so funny?" Clients who imagine themselves in the target's position quickly realize that a humorous comment would be hurtful and likely to start a fight. In this scenario, conflict avoidance consists simply of foregoing the comment and gliding by what would otherwise be a situation with the potential for violence.

Forethought can help youth identify and avoid other behaviors that predictably lead to conflict. Examples include walking through crowded hallways in a domineering fashion, teasing others about sensitive concerns, spreading rumors, pestering, and engaging in rough games with unclear rules.

Hostile Attributional Bias

Aggressive youth need to learn how to interpret the behavior of other people in an unbiased way. Attributional biases usually manifest themselves in perceptions of *ambiguous* social stimuli—that is, behaviors that could be interpreted in more than one way. Aggressive youth are biased toward perceiving hostility and disrespect in the behavior of other people (de Castro et al., 2002; Dodge et al., 2002). When these misperceptions occur, youth often respond with real hostility, and the interactions may deteriorate in the direction of violence, as an illusion becomes a reality. Interventions that treat hostile attributional bias decrease violent behavior in young people (Lochman & Wells, 2002, 2004; Stoltz et al., 2013).

The difference between violence-prone and nonaggressive youth is not simply that the former attribute hostile intentions to others while the latter infer benign motives. Instead, the pattern is that nonviolent youth posit *a larger number* of possible motivations, including both benign and hostile intentions, while aggressive youth posit a smaller number of mostly malevolent motives behind the behavior. Nonaggressive youth typically feel that they are not sure why the person did what he did, because there are so many possibilities, while violence-prone youth quickly jump to angry conclusions. Therefore, treatment of hostile attributional bias involves teaching clients to generate a larger number of possible interpretations, so their degree of certainty about the meaning of ambiguous behaviors is reduced. Social perception, like social problem solving, is more effective when the person thinks of a number of different possibilities, even if many of the possibilities are incorrect. It is difficult to know why people do what they do, and it is adaptive to know when we do not know.

Table 12.3 describes four ambiguous situations that sometimes precipitate violence in aggressive youth. The client's task is to answer the question, why might the person have done this?

Table 12.3   Ambiguous Situations

1. Someone bumps into you in the hallway.

2. You say hi to someone, and she doesn't say hi back.

3. Someone seems to be staring at you.

4. You are writing on the board with your back to the class, and someone starts laughing.

Table 12.4   Plausible Attributions for Table 12.3's Ambiguous Situations

1. Someone might bump into you accidentally, perhaps because he was talking to someone else, getting something out of his pocket, or looking at something.

2. Someone might not return a hello because she did not hear it, did not see you, or she was absent-minded, preoccupied, or just too tired to notice what was going on.

3. Someone might seem to be staring at you because he is spaced out and unaware of where his eyes are focused. It is also possible that the person noticed something about your appearance but without intending to challenge or disrespect you.

4. Someone might start laughing while you are doing something for reasons that have nothing to do with you. Her friend might have said something funny, or she might have read something humorous.

Aggressive clients typically posit a hostile or disrespectful intention behind these behaviors and then feel they have answered the question. If this occurs, the counselor's initial objective is to show the youth that she has not given an adequate answer. You can respond to hostile attributions by saying that these are certainly possible, but other reasons for the behavior are possible, too, and the client should try to think of them. After the client has thought of all the possibilities she can, you can fill in the additional ones. Table 12.4 presents plausible, benign attributions for the ambiguous situations shown in Table 12.3.

The common theme shared by these benign interpretations is that, frequently, other people's behavior has nothing to do with us, even though it might appear as if the behavior is sent in our direction. In addition to the previous examples, other people's behavior is sometimes rude or angry for reasons originating within them, such as that they are depressed, upset, or angry at someone else. Hostile attributional bias frequently has an element of egocentrism, even paranoia, and aggressive clients often overestimate their role in other people's behavior.

There are two main options for responding to ambiguous behaviors: investigate the behavior or let it go. If the incident is important, the appropriate response is to look into the behavior and attempt to determine its meaning. It might be useful to ask the other person nonconfrontational questions (e.g., "Why did you do that?" or "What was so funny while I was writing on the board?").

If the incident is unimportant, the adaptive option is to let it go and move on. The therapeutic message here is that life is filled with little things that can aggravate us if we let them but will do us no harm if we forget about them. It is useful to portray the option of moving past the incident as based on a position of strength, not weakness. Helpful therapist statements that can become helpful self-statements include:

- "Little things like that aren't worth your time."
- "Don't sweat the small stuff."
- "Move on to bigger and better things."

Empathy and Perspective-Switching

When people receive aversive behavior from others, their understanding of the reasons for this behavior influences their response. This person-perception issue is related to the motivation/capability distinction: The issue is whether the other person's aversive behavior is attributed to malevolent motivations or inadequate capabilities. As discussed in Chapter 7, Family Systems Therapy, frustrating or hurtful behavior that is attributed to a selfish or cruel motive elicits anger, while equally aversive behavior attributed to deficient capabilities often elicits constructive or even compassionate responses. Reactively aggressive individuals have little ability to infer how other people's behavior derives from their experiences of situations (Berkowitz, 1993; Olson, Lopez-Duran, Lunkenheimer, Chang, & Sameroff, 2011). These youth lack a well-developed "theory of mind," with deficits similar in some respects to those associated with autism (McHugh & Stewart, 2012; Mitchell, 2011). As a result, reactively aggressive individuals are unlikely to attribute others' aversive behavior to capability-related factors and more likely to make simpler attributions to malevolent motivations (e.g., "evil"). Accordingly, many violence prevention programs include training in empathy and perspective-switching (Committee for Children, 2002; Feindler & Engel, 2011; Glick & Gibbs, 2010; Gordon, 2009).

One important capability-related factor is situation-specific information—that is, what the other person in the conflict knows about the situation. If the other person is operating on the basis of incomplete information or a misunderstanding, she might say or do something hurtful to the client, not because she wanted to but because she was incapable of responding more adequately. For example, the person might inadvertently joke about something that is a sore subject for the client or might mistakenly believe a possession of the client's is hers. In situations like these, if the client understands how unwanted behaviors can occur when nonmalevolent people lack the information necessary for desirable behavior, the conflict will be viewed as a problem to be solved, not a battle to be won.

Therapists can help clients develop empathy and perspective-taking ability by providing guided practice in this skill. This can be done by asking questions about other people's feelings and thoughts in hypothetical and real situations. These questions should ask the client to look at a situation from another person's perspective, based on the information she has—for instance:

"Now wait a minute: *You* know her boyfriend doesn't like you that way, and *you* know you don't feel that way about him, but if Jessica *didn't* know that, and she had a fight with her boyfriend that day, and then she saw the two of you having lunch together, couldn't that have upset her and made her mad, even if she isn't a nasty, bitchy person who wanted to walk all over you?"

Another type of question asks how the other person's emotions might have affected his actions, with particular reference to how those internal pressures might have affected his capability for positive behavior. Sometimes it is useful to move back and forth between the client's own experiences and those of the other person. Empathy is possible because human beings are generally more similar than different, which means we can use introspection to gauge how another person might feel in a given situation. Therapists can also use self-disclosure to fill in gaps in the client's understanding of others—for instance:

> "When you're really worried about something, maybe feeling desperate about it, and someone interrupts you with something unrelated—might you react in a way that seems grumpy and mean? I know I do that sometimes."

One application of empathy is awareness of how one's own behavior is perceived by others. Reactively aggressive youth are typically weak in this ability (de Castro et al., 2005; Polman et al., 2007; Powell et al., 2011). One way to work on this is to provide clients with immediate feedback about how we receive and experience their behavior (e.g., "Wow, that felt insulting to me," "It's frustrating for me when you don't let me talk"). Also, when clients' accounts of incidents portray the emotional quality of their behavior, we can provide feedback about the impression created by their words and nonverbal behavior, so they gain a sense of how they probably came across to the other person in the conflict, and then we can ask how receiving this type of behavior would make them feel.

Anger Management

This section presents a structured, step-by-step anger management technique based on past research in this area (Ecton & Feindler, 1990; Kassinove & Tafrate, 2002; Larson & Lochman, 2011; Lochman et al., 2010; Novaco, 1975). The procedure addresses several important aspects of aggression in an efficient fashion. The impulsivity aspect is addressed by slowing down the youth's response to provocation. The technique uses deep breathing to counter the physiological overarousal associated with anger. Finally, there is a self-talk component to counter the thoughts that produce aggression.

The technique can be introduced by explaining that anger is a natural response to conflict and is not necessarily a bad thing. In fact, anger can be useful because it signals that something is wrong and provides energy for solving problems. (Historical figures like Martin Luther King Jr. provide useful illustrations of this idea.) Anger management is not about eliminating anger but about controlling it so its usefulness is maintained while its damaging consequences are prevented. The first step in breaking the connection between anger and violence is to help clients recognize that their feelings do not have to dictate their behavior. Therapists can say:

> "When you get mad, there are reasons for that, and you might need to do something about those reasons. The goal isn't for you to stop getting mad—it's for you to manage your anger effectively, so it doesn't get you in trouble. The idea is for you to control your anger, instead of your anger controlling you."

The idea that connections between emotions and behavior can be severed has been most extensively developed by ACT (Eifert & Forsyth, 2005; Hayes, Strosahl, & Wilson, 2011; Murrell, Coyne, & Wilson, 2004; and see Chapter 4). In ACT terms, the purpose of aggression treatment is to help clients free their conflict-related behavior from control by their feelings and place this behavior under the control of their values. Technically, ACT for aggression could include techniques such as picturing one's anger as a monster shouting violent orders in a repetitive, exaggerated manner that eventually becomes absurd and so ceases to be compelling.

Therapists should help clients identify their **anger triggers**—that is, experiences that reliably make them mad. Common anger triggers include disrespect, teasing, unfair treatment, and frustration. The process of identifying, listing, and discussing triggers helps clients achieve some distance from their automatic reactions, recognize that these reactions are neither universal nor inevitable, and realize that their reactions, not the situations eliciting them, are the true causes of their aggressive behavior. Clients who know their triggers can quickly recognize situations that call for use of the anger management technique. Teaching the procedure is a straightforward task. The technique consists of a sequence of four steps, which clients should memorize:

1. Stop and think.
2. Take deep, slow breaths.
3. Count.
4. Use a personal reminder.

1. *Stop and Think.* The step consists of this self-statement. The purpose of the step is to recognize that one's anger has been triggered, to inhibit impulsive reactions (e.g., "Don't do anything for a moment"), and to recognize that this is the type of situation that calls for use of the anger management technique. Sukhodolsky and Scahill (2012) also recommend that the client visualize a stop sign and imagine putting on emotional brakes.

2. *Take Deep, Slow Breaths.* This step can be introduced by saying, "Anger happens in our bodies as well as in our minds." Then, ask the client what happens in her body when she gets mad. Most youth will identify some features of the physiological anger response caused by arousal of the hypothalamic-pituitary-adrenal axis: rapid breathing and heartbeat, increased blood pressure, feeling hot and sweaty, clenched muscles, and release of adrenaline and cortisol into the bloodstream. Then, explain that deep, slow breathing literally counteracts the physiological effects of anger. Finally, guide the client in taking several deep, slow breaths, expanding the rib cage and taking air into the lungs all the way down to the diaphragm. Most clients experience some immediate relaxation.

Deep, slow breathing literally counteracts the physiological effects of anger.

3. *Count.* Counting to oneself is a simple cognitive technique with the purpose of occupying the mind and crowding out other, anger-producing thoughts. There are different options for counting: Clients can count forward or backward, and they can go from 3, 5, 10, and so forth. Therapists can invite clients to choose what they think would work best for them. Counting is most useful when it is cognitively demanding enough to soften the youth's reaction to the situation but not so difficult that it is frustrating. Plans for counting should be cognizant of the different types of situations that occur. In the midst of a back-and-forth exchange, it is impractical to use a number larger than three. When the client is out of the situation, larger numbers should be used. It can also be helpful to intersperse self-talk such as, "I'm breathing calmness in and anger out," or "I'm more relaxed at 9 than I was at 10," and so forth as the countdown proceeds.

4. *Use a Personal Reminder.* In this final step, the youth engages in self-talk with preplanned sayings that express his intention to maintain self-control in angry situations. This is the one creative step in the technique, and clients should choose or compose sayings that feel right to them. Therapists can help clients brainstorm possibilities for these little "mantras." Personal reminders should emphasize calm, self-direction, and resolution to maintain nonviolence. Some clients prefer simple reminders, such as, "Chill out," "Easy now," "Remember your goals," and "I can handle this." Others prefer more involved, substantive reminders, such as simple prayers or asking what a loved one would want them to do in the situation.

This anger management technique has features that seem capable of addressing the neurobiology of aggressive behavior by activating the prefrontal lobes of the cerebral cortex and controlling limbic system overarousal. The self-statement "Stop" might delay the effects of fast, reflexive amygdala responding. The word "think" is the most cortical word in the English language. The deep breathing component would reduce physiological overarousal. The personal reminder would activate long-term memories of intentions to control impulses and translate valued intentions into behavior. All of these effects would serve the purpose of violence prevention, because the general advice to "go with your gut" is pop psychology at its worst. This input might benefit individuals at the overinhibited end of the spectrum, but it is bad advice for impulsive youth in general and aggressive youth in particular. Self-control is a matter of the prefrontal cortex inhibiting limbic impulses (Damasio, 1994; LeDoux, 1998), and therapy for externalizing disorders is all about helping clients learn to do this.

One of the persistent problems in therapy for aggression is that clients verbalize nonviolent intentions when in the calm environment of the therapy office, but in the midst of a conflict in the very different environments where problems occur, those intentions sometimes seem to disappear from their minds (Larson, 2005; Larson & Lochman, 2011). Personal reminders can help by connecting the client with her own best intentions for herself, so she is not "like a puppet on a string," controlled by the other person's provocative behavior or her own emotional reactions. As discussed in Chapter 8, this type of technique is designed to transport the client's intentions from the therapy room to the everyday environment, and from an emotional context of calm resolution to a context of agitation and confusion, in which it is more difficult to preserve nonviolent intentions.

The other half of this integration is to transport experiences associated with aggression and violence from the everyday environment into the therapy room. This is a matter of emotional memory and full sharing with the counselor. By doing so, clients make it possible for therapy to touch the raw, intense, painful experiences associated with their violent behavior. It is useful for clients to report their aggression-associated emotions, thoughts, and behaviors as fully as possible, including quotes of what they said. These reports can make clients wince, especially when they honestly describe aggressive behavior toward their parents, so therapists should explain that the purpose of the exercise is not to embarrass the youth but to bring her therapy state of mind into contact with her problematic experiences, so her best intentions can gain mastery over previously uncontrolled reactions and impulses. Clients can also write down their aggressive verbalizations, either in therapy or on their own, as another means of increasing cortical control over behaviors originating largely in the limbic system.

As with all CBT techniques, repeated practice is key to the effectiveness of anger management training (Glick & Gibbs, 2010; Sukhodolsky et al., 2004). The technique should be memorized and overlearned. Therapists and parents can quiz clients on the steps. Young children and their parents can do the procedure collaboratively: For example, the parent can breathe while the child counts, and vice versa. Clients should practice not just verbalizing the steps but doing them both in sessions and at home. To move toward application of the technique, clients can begin by imagining their anger triggers being pushed, and then they can go through the procedure in the settings and with the individuals most associated with their triggers. Parents can prompt clients to implement the technique, perhaps by using a secret code that siblings do not know.

Clients should be on the lookout for opportunities to use the technique in real situations. Their successes or failures should be reviewed during sessions so that learning and improved plans are derived from the outcomes, whether positive or negative.

Social Problem Solving

Teaching clients structured techniques for planning solutions to interpersonal problems is an effective intervention for aggressive behavior (Glick & Gibbs, 2010; Guerra & Slaby, 1990; Kazdin, 2003, 2010; Shure, 1996). A structured problem-solving technique was presented in Chapter 10 on disruptive behavior, and that description will not be reiterated here. In therapy for violence-prone youth, the technique should most frequently be used to analyze and plan responses to problems involving interpersonal conflict and anger triggers.

Sukhodolsky and Scahill (2012) suggest asking youth to do the problem-solving procedure's first step, problem identification, twice: once from the perspective of the self, which is the usual way of doing this step, and once from the perspective of the other person in the conflict, which is more difficult. If the client responds that the other person has no legitimate perspective but is simply evil, therapists can acknowledge that this is within the realm of possibility, but it is much more likely that the other person is operating from some perspective quite different from the client's, and the key to conflict resolution is to figure out how things look from this perspective. Generally, rumination about the evil nature of the other person has an inflammatory effect, which increases the likelihood of violence, while trying to figure out how understandable psychological processes might have produced the person's behavior makes violence less probable and increases the likelihood of constructive problem solving (Sukhodolsky & Scahill, 2012; Yeager, Miu, Powers, & Dweck, 2013).

Assertiveness Training

In my experience, aggressive clients' most common objection to violence prevention techniques is that the recommended behaviors seem like submissive, ineffective responses to conflict (e.g., "You're saying I should let people push me around"). The dichotomous thinking underlying this objection includes one category for aggressive, domineering behavior and one for passive, "wimpy" behavior. The balanced, effective option lying midway between these two extremes is called **assertiveness**. Aristotle was right.

Therapists should state emphatically that they do not advocate passivity. Assertiveness training is an important component of aggression treatment because it provides a prosocial alternative to the option that high-risk youth most want to avoid—namely, submission (Feindler & Engel, 2011; Huey & Rank, 1984; Shapiro, 2003; Sukhodolsky & Scahill, 2012).

It is useful to use the word "fairness" as a synonym for assertiveness because it describes prosocial behavior without having any connotation of weakness, and because the concept includes both fairness to others and fairness to self. The idea of being fair usually seems more attractive to high-risk youth than the idea of being "good" or "nice" (which they often believe is the therapist's recommendation). Even street gang members usually believe in being fair, at least in principle.

The idea of a spectrum, with ineffective behaviors at the poles and adaptive behavior in the middle, is the conceptual framework of assertiveness training. This idea can be conveyed to clients by drawing the continuum on paper and filling in the characteristics of passive, aggressive, and assertive behavior, or by using the handout provided on our website (Form 12.3). As simpler terminology for young children, therapists can use the words "soft," "mean," and "fair."

The spectrum conveys the idea that in problem situations, there is often a conflict of interest between self and others, with the two extreme behaviors involving a choice to pursue one priority or the other but not both. The complex, sophisticated behavior in the middle of the spectrum combines respect for self and respect for others. Passivity means giving in to the other person, as if one's own needs do not count. Aggression means attacking the other person, as if his needs do not count. Assertiveness, or fairness, means treating both people's needs as important and "standing up for yourself without pushing the other person around."

Therapists should demonstrate the body language of self-assertion, which consists of standing straight and tall, with both feet planted squarely on the ground, shoulders back, arms at the sides, and head held high in a posture combining calmness and strength. Assertiveness also includes direct eye contact (in most American cultural groups), a steady and moderate distance from the other person, and a tone of voice conveying sincerity, perhaps intensity, but not threat. It may be helpful to demonstrate passive and aggressive behavioral styles, for purpose of comparison. Another useful exercise is to say the same words in a passive, aggressive, and assertive tone of voice, and then to ask the client which style would be most likely to work with her in a conflict situation. Therapists should demonstrate assertive behavior in role-plays with clients, and then should switch to a provocative role and have clients demonstrate assertiveness with them.

> *Assertiveness, or fairness, means, "Standing up for yourself without pushing the other person around."*

In intermittent explosive disorder, there is an oscillation between two opposite extremes: excessive inhibition of anger and its explosive release. These two opposite ways of functioning may produce each other through the mechanism of reciprocal causality (described in Chapter 7, on family therapy), which can be summarized as: extreme inhibition of anger ↔ aggressive explosion. In this etiological mechanism, extreme inhibition results in a buildup of anger that occasionally explodes in an outburst of aggression—which then frightens the person so much that she redoubles her efforts to inhibit her anger.

When each extreme causes the other, the solution is usually to help clients develop the moderate, adaptive portion of the relevant dimension of functioning. When the pendulum stops swinging to one extreme, it does not need to swing to the other. Specifically, when clients learn to express anger in an assertive, well-modulated fashion, their anger does not build to the point at which explosions occur, and without such outbursts to fear, clients are not unduly anxious about expressing anger, so they do not feel the need for extreme inhibition. Reciprocal causality will then drive the situation in a positive direction.

In addition to being a component of aggression treatment, assertiveness training is an important intervention for passive, inhibited youth who get pushed around by their peers. Although they start out at opposite extremes, bullies and victims need to move toward the middle of the same continuum; they both need to develop assertiveness.

Martial arts training seems to reduce maladaptive aggression in many youth who learn these skills, perhaps by increasing control over aggression and strengthening self-confidence, so the youth has less need to demonstrate his toughness to others

(Lakes & Hoyt, 2004; Lamarre & Nosanchuk, 1999). Martial arts experts generally teach that rigorous self-control is the responsibility of anyone who learns these arts and that illegitimate violence is a shameful abuse of this training. Martial arts training may also help passive, submissive children, including victims of bullying, because increased self-confidence might change the way these children carry themselves so they no longer elicit bullying by radiating a sense of anxious vulnerability (Olweus, 1993).

Communication Skills

Conflict management is mostly a matter of communication. As a result, most empirically supported violence prevention programs train participants in communication techniques for conflicts (Committee for Children, 2002; Glick & Gibbs, 2010; Gordon, 2009; Lochman et al., 2008; Shapiro, 2003).

Communication is the means by which people exchange perspectives and collaborate to solve problems. Therapists can explain:

- "When you're in a conflict, trying to beat the other person down just makes things worse. The way to make things better is to communicate: Tell the person where you're coming from, and find out how she sees the situation."

- "If you haven't listened carefully to the other person's side of the story, how can you be sure you're right?"

- "If you haven't carefully explained your side of the story, how do you know the other person wouldn't agree with it once he understood?"

Communication has two parts: Talking and listening. Clients are usually more interested in talking, but this is because they underestimate the skill involved in effective listening and the difference this makes in conflicts.

Effective listening benefits both the speaker and the listener. The listener learns about the other person's experience of the conflict. For speakers, the experience of being heard usually has a calming effect, even before steps are taken to solve the problem. Poor listening, the epitome of which is interrupting, usually makes speakers angrier and angrier.

Effective listening does not necessarily mean we agree with what the speaker says. The essence of good listening is *interest*—a desire to understand the speaker's points. The listener's interest must be conveyed, behaviorally, to the speaker. Nonverbal behavior is important, especially eye contact, nodding, and facial expressions indicating concentration.

Effective listening in conflicts has much in common with the type of listening that therapists do, as described in Chapter 1. Such listening involves a certain type of talking. Asking questions conveys interest and elicits needed information. Statements that reflect or summarize what the speaker has said enable listeners to check out the accuracy of their evolving understanding. Our website includes a handout (Form 12.4) that summarizes the behaviors involved in effective listening.

The concept of assertiveness provides a framework for instruction in effective talking. The passive style of talking is ineffective because it does not get one's message across. The aggressive style is ineffective because it causes anger that disrupts listening. Assertive talking has the highest likelihood of success in conflicts. In other words, the client should: "Say what you've got to say without putting the other person down."

As in parental discipline of children, conflict-related criticisms and complaints can be useful when they concern the other person's *behavior*, but they will be counterproductive when they concern the individual's *personality* or character (see Chapter 1). Derogation of the other person (e.g., "You're stupid") and statements that the person "always" or "never" does something cause anger, are rarely accurate, and reduce focus on the problem at hand. In contrast, talk about behavior is informative and has action implications. Clients should "stick to the facts" when trying to work out conflicts.

Statements about personality can be translated into statements about behavior. These translations generally preserve the speaker's valid points while shedding the insulting, inflammatory aspects of statements about character. Communication training should include practice in making these translations, as illustrated in Table 12.5.

Violence prevention and treatment programs often include training in **I-statements**. These statements take forms like, "I feel _____ when … " The opposite of an I-statement is a You-statement, which make assertions about the other person in the conflict. You-statements are usually presumptuous in that they make definitive statements about the other person, and these statements are often insulting. As a result, You-statements frequently make conflicts worse. In I-statements, the speaker is on firmer ground, epistemologically, because he is making a statement about something he knows about—namely, himself. I-statements are not usually insulting, and they provide the other person with important information about the conflict—namely, the speaker's perspective.

Sometimes there is a problem with the touchy-feely tone of I-statements, which might seem artificial to clients. High-risk youth often feel awkward saying things like, "I feel angry when you call me a bitch," and they may resist using such statements on the grounds that talking like a therapist does not work on the streets.

The problem here is an issue of wording. The solution is to modify the language of these statements so they become more similar to the way young people naturally talk (Shapiro, 2003). Small variations in language make a difference. For Miguel, the words, "It makes me mad when … " were easier to say than the words, "I feel mad when … ", and sometimes it felt most natural for him to say, "It pisses me off when … " Also, saying, "I don't like it when … " sometimes felt more natural to him than using emotion words.

The challenge here, as often in aggression treatment, is to package socially competent content in the casual, tough style that many high-risk youth desire. I-statements are not defined by a gentle sound but by the function they fulfill, which is to give the listener information about the speaker's perceptions, emotions, and goals without insulting her. Any statement that fulfills this function is, for all practical purposes, an I-statement (even if it does not have the word "I" in it.)

Often, the most effective communication is the simplest, most immediate translation of an internal state into words. I suggest to clients that, if they do not know how to explain

Table 12.5 Translating Criticisms of Personality Into Criticisms of Behavior

Personality Statement	*Behavioral Statement*
"You're a thief."	"You took my radio without asking."
"You're selfish."	"You're not looking at how this affects me."
"You're stupid."	"You're not getting my point at all."
"You're crazy."	"I don't understand why you did that."

something, they say, "I don't know how to explain this." If they are afraid something they have to say will make the other person mad, their I-statement could be, "I've got something I want to say, but it might make you mad, and that's not what I want." If something comes out wrong, the client could say, "That didn't come out the way I meant it."

Another useful communication technique in conflicts is to work in some type—any type—of positive comment. Agreeing with one point made by the other person sometimes changes the tone of the argument, even if disagreement about the main point remains. If the client is in conflict with someone she knows, any reference to a past positive experience together may place the current problem in a more benign perspective (e.g., "Remember the time when we … ").

In conflicts, when youth think of something they could say, they need a *test* to determine whether making that statement would be a good or bad idea. This test pertains to the reason for making the statement. There are three common reasons for saying things in conflicts that are natural and understandable but sometimes counterproductive. Youth might want to make a statement because: (1) It expresses the anger they feel, (2) they believe the other person "deserves" to hear the statement, and/or (3) they believe the statement is true. The trouble with these reasons is that sometimes they lead to insulting or inflammatory verbalizations. In conflicts, the useful criterion for a possible statement is whether it would be likely to make the situation better, with improvement defined as reduced acrimony and movement toward resolution. Only statements that pass this test should be made. Part of skillful conflict management is thinking of possible statements that are true but would be destructive to the problem-solving process, and not saying them.

Conflict Resolution

This section presents five conflict resolution techniques used in violence prevention and treatment programs: focusing on solutions, agreeing to disagree, compromise, apology, and restitution (Bodine & Crawford, 1997; Glick & Gibbs, 2010; Kreidler, 1997; Lantieri, Miller, Lieber, & Roderick, 1998; Shapiro, 2003). Clients' most frequent objection to these techniques is that they might not work. This is a valid objection. However, therapists should explain that violence prevention does not depend on finding some magical technique that resolves all conflicts because, unfortunately, no such technique exists. The key to violence prevention is to be equipped with a repertoire of different strategies to try so that, if a strategy does not work, there is always a fallback plan.

Solution-Focused Conflict Resolution. The insights of solution-focused therapy (De Jong & Berg, 2012; de Shazer, 1985, 1993; O'Hanlon & Weiner-Davis, 2003; Selekman, 2010), discussed in Chapter 6, can be applied to conflict resolution. In conflicts, people sometimes become stuck in problem-talk, which usually means the argument focuses on the question of how the conflict started and who is to blame for its origin. Frequently, these arguments are futile because the people will never agree about what happened. Fortunately, it is often possible to agree about what to do in the future without ever agreeing about what happened in the past. For example, if a boy says a girl spread a rumor about him, but the girl insists she did not, one possible solution would be for the girl to promise that she will never spread a rumor about the boy in the future and that she will clear up any misunderstandings that are brought to her attention. The girl could offer this contribution to a solution without admitting any past wrongdoing. The question, "Why did this happen?" is often less useful than the question, "What should we do now?"

Agreeing to Disagree. Sometimes, youth get into conflicts and even fights about trivial differences of opinion (e.g., which athlete or singer is better). Such conflicts escalate because the participants feel it is extremely important to get the other person to agree with their opinion. However, disagreements do not necessarily indicate either that one's position is wrong or that the other person is deficient; disagreements usually result from different perspectives or tastes. Typically, there is nothing particularly beneficial about achieving agreement and nothing disastrous about failing to do so. Conflicts like these can be resolved simply by dropping them and moving on. The phrase "agree to disagree" provides a realistic, palatable description of this conflict resolution technique.

Compromise. Negotiated agreements can resolve conflicts by providing each person with some or most of what she wants from the situation. Therapists can make two points to motivate clients to try this strategy: Compromise often enables people to get more of what they want than they would get by insisting on having everything, and compromise is usually fair to both people in the conflict. Thus, like violence prevention in general, compromise serves both enlightened self-interest and ethical values (Bodine & Crawford, 1997; Kreidler, 1997; Lantieri et al., 1998).

One procedure for constructing compromises involves orchestrating four elements: what each person truly needs from a resolution and what each would be willing to concede. The strategy is to juxtapose and, if necessary, modify these elements until they fit together into a workable compromise. These four components, worded from the client's perspective, are presented in Table 12.6.

Therapists should guide clients in working through several examples of conflicts using this framework. The formula can be used as a tool in private thought, and it can also be used in collaboration with the other person in the conflict. One way to elicit cooperation from recalcitrant people is to model the behavior by offering to go first. The formula is: "Let's make a deal: I'll do this if you'll do that."

The process of developing compromises depends on the distinction between what people want and what people need. Conflict resolution is facilitated by a broad perspective that enables clients to give up fixations on specific desires (e.g., a certain place in line) in favor of larger goals, such as getting along with others and being a socially intelligent person.

Apology. Violence-prone clients often resist the idea of apologizing. Many of these youth view words like "I'm sorry" as submissive and self-abasing. Therapists can address this problem by portraying apology as an intelligent, effective strategy for resolving conflicts, rather than a demeaning behavior. This type of packaging is feasible if apology is defined as an

Table 12.6 Four Components of Compromise

What I need to get;
What the other person needs to get;
What I am willing to give;
+   What the other person is willing to give.
A fair compromise.

expression of regret for upsetting the other person and a plan to avoid doing so again, rather than a derogation of self.

As with I-statements, subtle differences in language sometimes make a big difference to young people's view of apology because, often, they feel uncomfortable with the word but not the concept (Shapiro, 2003). For instance, Miguel viewed saying, "I'm sorry" and "I apologize" as whimpering, cowering statements, but he had no trouble saying "my fault" or "my bad" to express regret for something he did. The solution to this type of problem is to help clients find jaunty, youth-oriented language they feel comfortable using to perform socially competent functions.

Apologies should be specific and should express regret only for what is truly regretted. Sometimes people do not regret the intentions behind their behavior but do regret the consequences that occurred—for example, "I didn't intend to put you down by saying that, but I'm sorry that's the way you took it."

Restitution. Restitution takes apology a step further by repairing injuries to the other person. This concept can be explained to clients as "fixing things," or "making things right." Examples of restitution include replacing a possession that was lost or broken and correcting misinformation disseminated by a rumor (Bodine & Crawford, 1997; Kreidler, 1997; Lantieri et al., 1998).

Restitution is difficult for the same reason that apology is difficult: Both behaviors threaten the pride of people whose self-esteem is fragile. Counselors can address this problem by portraying the behavior they recommend as imbued with meanings that the client values (see Chapter 8). If apology and restitution are viewed as strong, intelligent behaviors that repair problems between people, then performing these behaviors will support, not threaten, the client's self-esteem. This idea can be explained in words like the following:

> "Everybody makes mistakes. The difference between strong people and weak people is that when strong people hurt someone, they fix it. So when you make things right, you have a right to feel proud, because it's not an easy thing to do."

Violence Prevention Under Difficult Conditions

Clients in the midst of therapy often complain that they tried to use their new violence prevention strategies, but the other person continued his disrespectful, aggressive behavior, so they abandoned their new learning and responded in kind. Although socially competent behavior works more frequently than anything else, it does not work all the time, because the outcomes of conflicts are largely a function of the other person's behavior. Clients need to develop self-reinforcement capabilities to bridge the gap between socially competent behavior and the positive consequences that usually occur eventually but might not happen immediately (see Chapter 3 on cognitive therapy). This type of self-directed autonomy is especially difficult but necessary when the other person responds to positive behavior with insults, taunts, and threats (Shapiro, 2003).

The norm of reciprocity (Gouldner, 1960) works against violence prevention when it causes reciprocal deterioration of behavior (e.g., "I insulted her because she insulted me"). Paradoxically, such reciprocation is an *imitation* of the person whose behavior is viewed negatively. When clients justify their aggression by citing the other person's hostility and disrespect, counselors can respond by saying:

> "Let me get this straight: You thought his behavior was stupid and disgusting—so you imitated him."

Clients who overcome their natural tendency to strike back can turn the norm of reciprocity to the advantage of violence prevention by initiating positive, fair behavior toward people who behave in the opposite fashion. Such initiation, in which the youth's behavior is under the control of her values and goals rather than the other person's, constitutes leadership in a conflict (Shapiro, 2003). Counselors can say:

> "If someone acts in a nasty, threatening way, you've got a choice: You can sink down to her level, or you can try to raise her up to yours. If you follow her down, you'll end up rolling around in the dirt with her. If you try to lead her up, you might be able to work out the conflict, and at least you won't make things worse."

Leadership often requires the ability to tolerate pain. Maintaining positive behavior in the face of disrespect and threat usually results in frustration, wounded pride, and suppressed anger. Clients need to recognize that positive behavior does not always feel good.. The experience of pain in the process of doing the right thing constitutes strength and courage. Clients who understand this can reinforce themselves for peaceful behavior in the absence of reinforcement from the environment.

This concept of leadership played an important role in Miguel's therapy because it enabled him to bring together two sets of values that he had not previously been able to integrate. His culture valued strong, brave, "macho" behavior in males, but his Catholic religious tradition emphasized kindness and peace. Therefore, Miguel's therapist painted nonviolent behavior in the colors of strength and effectiveness. The counselor pointed out that violence, like breaking things, requires no skill, while leading a process of conflict management, like repairing or creating things, requires self-control, intelligence, and determination. This portrayal influenced Miguel toward viewing nonviolent, effective behavior in conflicts as being "more of a man" than someone who falls into violence in response to provocation.

The experience of pain in the process of doing the right thing constitutes strength and courage.

Walking Away From Fights

Many adults view walking away as a basic conflict management technique that should be initiated when problems begin to escalate. However, for most youth, walking away is the most painful, difficult violence prevention strategy of all, because they view it as a humiliating submission. Therapists should present this strategy as a last resort to be used only when other techniques have failed and the other person seems likely to become violent (Shapiro, 2003). Work on walking away should not begin until there has been training in other, more palatable techniques, and the client has developed some investment in the goal of violence prevention.

Persuading clients that walking away from a fight is sometimes the best thing to do requires them to rethink the meaning of this action. The question is, who has lost and who has won when someone walks away from an imminently violent confrontation? In the absence of intervention, violence-prone youth typically believe that people walk away from fights because they are afraid they would lose, so the threatening individual has defeated them. Therapists should offer an alternative analysis in which the question of whether one should go or stay depends on whether anything can be accomplished by remaining in the situation. If the other person is behaving in a manner that is controlled and at least somewhat reasonable, the client should try to talk to him. If the person seems to be unreasonable, losing control, and about to become violent, the client should go. Therefore, walking away does not indicate cowardice in the person who leaves but a lack of self-control in the person left behind. Walking away from a violent person means overcoming his provocation, living up to one's own values, and taking control of the situation by refusing to be provoked into violence. Winning, abstractly understood, is not a matter of beating people up. Therapists can say:

> "The point isn't whether you're afraid to fight; we both know you're not. The point is whether the other person has enough sense and self-control, at the moment, to make it worth your time to try to work out the problem. If he does, you should stay. If he doesn't, and it looks like he's going to become violent, then he's unworkable, he's impossible to talk to, and you have a right to get away from people like that. This doesn't say anything bad about you—it says something bad about him."

Clients who are considering whether to fight should weigh two priorities against each other, as if on a scale. On one hand, there are the client's goals, values, and what she has to lose by fighting (the risks of injury, getting in trouble, etc.). On the other hand, there is whatever benefit she would gain by proving to an obnoxious person that she can fight. If the client considers her own goals most important, the best choice is to walk away.

Therapists should try to help clients with their anger toward people who, in many cases, really have behaved terribly toward them. It may help to explain that the best response to a bad person is generally to *avoid* him, while fighting is actually an approach behavior. As an analogy, you can say that if you get mud on your shoes, you don't beat it up, you wipe it off. Some clients are consoled by the idea that people whose behavior is harmful generally do not do well in life, and negative consequences usually accrue to them without intervention by the client. Thus, counselors can recommend the client "stay away and let her self-destruct." Another advantage of avoidance is that it allows clients to turn their energy away from the obnoxious person and toward the good things in their lives. This idea is expressed by the saying, "Living well is the best revenge."

Because walking away requires intense inhibition of anger, use of this technique often leaves youth feeling extremely stressed. Therapists can help by suggesting coping strategies, such as self-praise, seeking social support, distraction with an enjoyable activity, and self-reward (Glick & Gibbs, 2010; Larson & Lochman, 2011; Sukhodolsky & Scahill, 2012). DBT distress tolerance strategies (Linehan, 1993b, 2014; Miller, Rathus, & Linehan, 2007), presented in Chapter 4, may be helpful here. Therapists can explain that when the client is in pain as a result of doing the right thing in a tough situation, he deserves to treat himself well.

Psychodynamic Therapy

As discussed earlier, outcome research does not support dynamic therapy as a primary intervention for aggression, but these techniques may provide useful components of treatment for aggressive clients whose issues it is suited to addressing. P. Kernberg and Chazan (1991) and Bleiberg (2001) describe psychodynamic methods for treating CD and aggression.

These methods can address violence caused by the defense mechanisms of identification with the aggressor and turning passive into active. Interpretation of these defenses provides clients with an understanding of the reasons for their anger and aggression. The next step is to help clients develop adaptive, conscious strategies for coping with their painful experiences, so maladaptive defenses become unnecessary (A. Freud, 1946a; Gray, 1994).

Dynamic techniques can be useful for addressing the fragile self-concepts characteristic of violence-prone youth (Bushman et al., 2009; de Castro et al., 2007; Shapiro, Dorman, et al., 1997). Aggressive clients might experience their mistakes, failures, or weaknesses as devastating because of object relations in which other people are viewed as harsh, judgmental, and/or cruel, with a readiness to humiliate, reject, or victimize the client for falling short in any way. The corrective emotional experiences these clients need can occur most powerfully when their issues are recapitulated in interactions with their therapists. Then, counselors can provide new ways of experiencing mistakes, failures, and weaknesses by discussing them in the same matter-of-fact, empathic spirit with which they discuss all material. Rather than responding to clients' vulnerabilities in the way they expect, counselors can disconfirm clients' expectations and begin the development of new ones by saying things like:

- "Ouch, damn, I'm really sorry that happened to you."
- "He called you that in front of all those people? It must have been awful."
- "I guess you screwed up. Want to take a look at what happened so you can do better the next time?"

From a dynamic perspective, patterns of violent behavior may reflect internal blueprints of relationships based on domination, intimidation, and force. Youth who grow up in violent homes and neighborhoods may come to see this interaction pattern as a normal part of life, with the main variable being whether they are in the role of winner or loser in these interactions. Such clients need to develop new schemas of relationships that are free of victimization. The concept of assertiveness would furnish some of the psychoeducational input these youth need to develop object relations involving neither victims nor perpetrators.

Systems-Oriented Intervention

Physical punishment seems to increase aggression in children, probably because it creates anger and models violence as a way of responding to problems (Lansford et al., 2014; Moeller, 2001; Taylor et al., 2010). Therefore, counselors treating young people for aggression should recommend that parents eliminate or, at least, substantially reduce their use of corporal punishment. Many parents will resist this recommendation unless they have child management strategies to replace what they have been doing, so therapists should fill this gap by providing appropriate training, as described in the chapters on behavior therapy and disruptive behavior disorders.

Peer pressure is an important factor in youth violence (Dishion et al., 1999; Granic & Dishion, 2003; McCabe et al., 2001). When peers push each other to fight, it is difficult for youth to resist this pressure, even when they have no internal desire for violence.

Therefore, violence prevention efforts need to help youth deal with peer pressure (Gibbs, 2003; Prothrow-Stith, 1987; Shapiro, 2003).

Peer audiences influence the outcome of conflicts. Too often, onlookers form a circle around the disputants and egg them on to fight. Therapists should provide clients with an understanding of the crowd's motives in this type of situation. Although onlookers might claim to be offering well-intentioned advice, youth in conflicts should understand that the crowd does not have their best interests in mind and is essentially trying to elicit some free entertainment. I suggest that clients ask onlookers how much money they would pay to see the fight, on the grounds that boxers won't fight for free, so why should the client? (I have never heard a report of the crowd taking a client up on this.)

Clients need to understand that succumbing to peer pressure means being pushed around by peers and behaving in accordance with their values, not the client's own. Research on reactance (Brehm, 1993) suggests that framing the situation this way may recruit the client's desire for self-determination to the purpose of violence prevention.

Summary

The distinction between reactive and proactive aggression mirrors the distinction between capability-related and motivational factors in behavior. Because proactive aggression is freely chosen, intervention should emphasize positive and negative consequences as well as efforts to change attitudes and values that support violence. Therapy for reactively aggressive youth should emphasize training in the emotion regulation, self-control, and social skills that youth need to handle interpersonal conflicts in a nonviolent, competent fashion. Many clients need both types of help.

The Golden Rule has two important uses in therapy for aggression: It contains a clear statement of positive values, and applying this rule is an exercise in perspective-switching. In their work with bullies, therapists should provide direct, honest descriptions of the nature of cruelty, because this description confronts clients with the immoral and unattractive nature of this behavior.

Violence prevention techniques can be organized in a three-part sequence—conflict avoidance, conflict management, and leaving the conflict—with the later stages becoming necessary only when the preceding stages were unsuccessful. Youth can avoid interpersonal problems by steering clear of unsafe places and people, inhibiting impulses to behave in a provocative manner, and when confronted with ambiguous behavior from other people, recognizing when they do not know the motive for a behavior, rather than jumping to an angry conclusion.

Conflict management strategies should be taught in a sequence that moves from the inside out, so the skills of emotional self-control, effective cognition, competent social behavior, and resisting peer pressure are developed in a progressive fashion. A four-step anger management technique can be used to reduce physiological arousal and remind the client of his best intentions for nonviolent self-control. With this accomplished, the client is in a position to analyze the problem and plan an appropriate response. Assertive behavior that is fair to both self and others provides a better chance for successful conflict management than either submissive or aggressive behavior. Effective communication involves attentive listening and speech that expresses perceptions, needs, and complaints in specific, behavioral terms. These skills are building blocks that can be combined in conflict resolution strategies, such as focusing on solutions, agreeing to disagree, compromise, apology, and restitution. When the other person in the conflict behaves less respectfully and reasonably than the client, leadership requires the ability to tolerate pain, resist the temptation to sink to the other person's level, and sustain behavior consistent with one's own values. Inner strengths like these make it possible to manage conflicts even with difficult, aggressive people.

Leaving a conflict is a difficult violence prevention strategy that is necessary only when the other person is impossible to work with and seems likely to go out of control. The inhibition of anger required by this strategy often leaves youth feeling extremely stressed; therapists should coach clients in coping strategies to help with this.

Psychodynamic therapy for violence addresses defense mechanisms and object relations that have contributed to the client's aggression. Parents can help by reducing or eliminating their use of corporal punishment. Therapists can help youth resist peer pressure to fight by pointing out that onlookers who urge violence are essentially looking for free entertainment at the youth's expense.

Case Study

Miguel learned the violence prevention techniques taught in therapy, and in situations calling for their use, he usually used them and occasionally did not. The frequency of his fights decreased a great deal, especially in school. The inhibition of anger necessary for accomplishing this often left him with tension headaches, which were somewhat ameliorated by stress management techniques.

Miguel expressed a positive view of violence prevention principles, and his ability to use self-control and conflict management strategies broadened his self-concept to include pride in his "inner strengths." However, he claimed that, on the streets, the influence of his peers sometimes made nonviolence impossible because he had to fight to maintain his reputation. Miguel achieved more progress in the school setting.

The therapist tried to add a social-ecological dimension to his work with Miguel by helping him find peers who were safer and more prosocial than the teens he hung out with. But despite encouragement from his parents, Miguel was uninterested in the supervised activities his counselor suggested, and he always returned to the playgrounds and corners where his friends were.

Miguel's learning of violence prevention strategies seemed to be an important addition to his behavioral repertoire that resulted in a substantial reduction in the frequency of his fights. Both his family's and his own motivation for treatment waned once the threat of expulsion from school receded, and therapy ended at this time. The therapist hoped Miguel's conflict management skills would continue to develop and that, with time and maturation, he would come to spend less of his time in social environments where violence prevention was difficult.

13

Anxiety

OBJECTIVES

This chapter explains:

- *The four dimensions of anxiety—emotion, physiology, cognition, and behavior.*
- *The behaviorist explanation of persistent, unrealistic anxiety: avoidance learning.*
- *Adaptive cognitions that acknowledge dangers without being overwhelmed by them.*
- *Why some anxious people need to overrule their gut feelings at times.*
- *How to help anxious children think about the probabilities of the events they fear.*
- *How to extinguish avoidance learning with the behavioral technique of exposure.*
- *Therapeutic techniques that make use of young children's unrealistic, magical thinking.*
- *How to help overprotective parents tolerate their child's anxiety.*

Case Study
Facing Fear

Jeffrey, a 12-year-old Caucasian boy, was brought to therapy by his parents because of his intense anxiety in a variety of social situations, which warranted a diagnosis of social anxiety disorder. Jeff was a good student, but school was a miserable experience for him because he was so uncomfortable interacting with peers. His parents reported that he had no real friends, and the therapist could see how socially awkward he was. His main activity outside of school was Little League baseball, but this was a problem, too, because Jeff was frightened of performing poorly and costing his team the game.

Jeff's middle-class parents described their marriage as close and affectionate, with little conflict. Jeff's 10-year-old sister, Alexandra, was the only age-mate with whom he felt comfortable.

Jeff's anxiety was strongest in the morning, when he anticipated all sorts of painful occurrences in the day ahead. In therapy, he gave a detailed picture of his experience as he boarded the school bus, and he felt his stomach tighten and his heart beat faster. His mind churned with thoughts about the various stupid and embarrassing things he might do during the day. He walked stiffly up the aisle with his head low, avoiding eye contact and hoping the other children would not see the fear on his face. As he passed the girl he secretly liked (but had never spoken to), she turned to her friend and made the L sign with her thumb and forefinger, signifying "Loser!"

Jeff seemed happy and grateful to meet his new therapist. He had heard therapists were nice people and said, "I hate being nervous all the time, so maybe this will help."

Diagnoses Treated in This Chapter

Specific Phobia

Specific phobia is defined by intense, unrealistic fears of a concrete object, situation, or event (e.g., dogs, heights, spiders). The resulting avoidance of the phobic object is extensive enough to impair everyday functioning. If avoidance is impossible, the child typically cries, clings, freezes, and tries to escape. The fear is not reduced by reality-oriented reassurances from caregivers.

Panic Disorder

A panic attack is a sudden onset of intense fear accompanied by physiological hyperarousal. Palpitations, sweating, shortness of breath, and a fear of dying often accompany these attacks. To warrant a diagnosis of panic disorder, the person must repeatedly experience unexpected panic attacks that are not elicited by any particular situation but happen "out of the blue." Also, there must be persistent worry about having panic attacks.

Agoraphobia

Agoraphobia is a fear of being out and about, in public spaces. The prototypical fear is of being away from one's home, and variations include fears of open spaces (e.g., parks), crowds, and public transportation. The feared event, in these settings, is of having an embarrassing experience, typically a panic attack, and of being unable to escape the situation.

Social Anxiety Disorder

Social anxiety disorder is defined by an intense fear of interacting with other people coupled with avoidance of social situations. These extremely shy individuals may feel comfortable with family members, but they are frightened of interacting with people they do not know well. Situations in which they believe they will be watched or evaluated by others prompt intense anxiety, because they fear doing something embarrassing and being humiliated or rejected.

Separation Anxiety Disorder

Separation anxiety is fear of being apart from parents or other attachment figures. These children attempt to cope with their anxiety by clinging to caregivers. Fears of terrible things happening to themselves or their parents are common. These youngsters are prone to homesickness. Their fear of separation often causes them to avoid school, sleepovers, and other age-appropriate ventures into independence.

Generalized Anxiety Disorder

The defining characteristic of generalized anxiety disorder (GAD) is diffuse, global worrying. Rather than having one particular fear, these individuals have numerous worries, which may be vague and changeable, and parents describe these children as worried about "anything and everything." Their anxieties may concern performance, rejection, health, and trivial matters. GAD is also associated with free-floating anxiety, in which there is no specific content at all. Restlessness, concentration difficulties, irritability, muscle tension, somatic complaints, and sleep disturbances are common symptoms of this disturbance.

Adjustment Disorder With Anxiety

In this disorder, the anxiety is a reaction to a specific, stressful event that occurred at most 3 months before the appearance of the disturbance.

Clinical Presentation and Etiology

The last three chapters of our book make up a section on internalizing problems. Following this chapter on anxiety, there are chapters on depression and on stress and trauma. These chapters address related client problems with related therapeutic techniques that are often combined in work with individual clients.

Most adults remember experiences of intense, unrealistic fear during childhood, especially at night, when awful imaginings of monsters and ghosts took hold, shadows on bedroom walls looked frightening, and ominous noises sounded like someone breaking into the house. People with anxiety disorders feel this way much of the time.

Anxiety has four dimensions, as shown in Table 13.1. The dimensions all influence each other, and causality flows in all directions. Cognitive interpretations of events influence emotional, physiological, and behavioral responses. Physiological states can be causes as well as effects: When people's hearts pound and their muscles tighten, thoughts of awful occurrences and feelings of fear are likely to follow. Behaviorally, when people repeatedly avoid the situations they fear, their anxiety about those situations grows and grows.

Table 13.1   The Four Dimensions of Anxiety

1. *Emotion:* Anxiety disorders involve fear, tension, nervousness, and panic.

2. *Physiology:* Anxiety is a physical as well as a mental state, and it includes stomach discomfort, muscle tension, rapid heartbeat and breathing, perspiration, and other manifestations of autonomic nervous system arousal.

3. *Cognition:* Anxious thoughts are inherently future-oriented, with overestimation of both the likelihood and the magnitude of possible negative events. Anxious children are plagued by fearful self-talk, and they underestimate their coping resources

4. *Behavior:* The behavioral hallmark of anxiety is *avoidance.* When the feared situation cannot be avoided, there may be agitation, clinging to parents, crying, disorganization, and aggression.

There is a substantial genetic component to the development of anxiety disorders, with estimates for different subgroups ranging from 39% to 64% (Gregory & Eley, 2007; Hallett, Ronald, Rijsdijk, & Eley, 2009). For both genetic and environmental reasons, a child's risk of having an anxiety disorder is 2.7 times higher when at least one parent has a history of anxiety and 4.7 times greater when at least one parent has a current anxiety disorder (van Gastel, Legerstee, & Ferdinand, 2009). Insecure parent-infant attachment predicts the future development of these disorders; a meta-analysis found a small/medium effect size of .30 for this link (Colonnesi et al., 2011).

Young children often have a variety of fears, but as they mature and develop more of an understanding of how the world works, their fears usually decline (Barrios & O'Dell, 1998). Youth tend to be afraid of different things at different ages. Fears of the dark, ghosts, and monsters commonly torment children below age 6, while the fears of school-aged children and adolescents more commonly focus on rejection, humiliation, and criticism from other people (Klein & Last, 1989). Thus, with development, there is movement from obviously unrealistic, magical fears of being physically hurt to more realistic anxieties about painful interpersonal experiences (Beidel & Alfano, 2011). Many fears lie in between the purely magical and the clearly realistic; these are fears of possible but rare events, such as earthquakes, fires, and kidnapping.

Neurobiological Etiologies

Neurobiological research has found differences between anxious individuals and normal controls in a number of brain structures, but the most important one seems to be the amygdala. This structure lies on the midline of the brain and has lobes on either side, so there is a left and a right amygdala, which do not always show the same relationships to anxiety. A study by De Bellis, Casey, et al. (2000) found that, compared to normal controls, youth with GAD had larger amygdalas, especially on the right side. Right amygdala activity correlates positively with self-reported anxiety (McClure et al., 2007; Monk et al., 2008). In laboratory experiments, people with anxiety disorders show more amygdala reactivity during exposure to frightening stimuli, such as fearful or angry faces, compared to normal controls (Nitschke et al., 2009).

Anxiety is associated with impaired functioning of the hypothalamic-pituitary-adrenal (HPA) axis, a brain/body system that regulates level of arousal, with the stress hormone cortisol playing an important role in this process (Belsky & Pleuss, 2009; Bremner, 2006; Del Giudice, Ellis, & Shirtcliff, 2011). In coordination with the autonomic nervous system, the HPA axis alters physiology throughout the body to prepare for a fight-or-flight response to a perceived threat. Arousal-related changes include elevated heart rate, blood pressure, and breathing rate, with increased blood flow to the muscles, along with down-regulation of routine physiological functions, such as digestion and immune system functioning. These changes are adaptive in emergency situations requiring intense physical exertion, but they are maladaptive in everyday problem situations that call for clear thinking and socially skilled responses. Thus, people with anxiety disorders experience a mismatch between their neurophysiological states and the challenging situations they face. Their bodies are pumped up as if they need to attack or run from a predator, while their minds must formulate a response to the very different types of stressors that people face in modern societies. Also, when the physiological changes elicited by (mis)perceived threats occur chronically, they increase risk for medical problems associated with the cardiovascular, digestive, and immune systems.

People with anxiety disorders experience a mismatch between their neurophysiological states and the challenging situations they face.

Research on temperament has illuminated the role of **behavioral inhibition** in the development of anxiety disorders. When infants as young as 4 months old are presented with a novel stimulus (e.g., a large, strange-looking toy), they show divergent responses: Some babies react with curiosity, and some react with fear and crying. Long-term longitudinal studies have found that infants who react with fear show high levels of inhibition, shyness, and avoidance, and they are frequently diagnosed with anxiety disorders, especially social anxiety disorder, in childhood and adolescence (Biederman et al., 2001; Kagan, Snidman, & Arcus, 1998; Moehler et al., 2008). Children with behavioral inhibition exhibit greater HPA axis and autonomic nervous system reactivity, elevated cortisol levels, heightened startle responses, and heightened amygdala activation in response to pictures of angry faces, compared to children without this behavior pattern (Perez-Edgar & Fox, 2005; Schwartz, Wright, Shin, Kagan, & Rauch, 2003). Adults who were identified as inhibited during infancy continue to show elevated amygdala activity (Schwartz et al., 2003). Approximately one third of these adults suffer from anxiety disorders decades after they were identified as inhibited infants in the laboratory (Kagan & Snidman, 2004; Kagan, Snidman, Arcus, & Reznick, 1994).

In several fundamental ways, the biological stress responses of youth with anxiety seem *opposite* to the responses of youth with conduct disorders, as described in Chapter 11. In other words, on a continuum of biological response to stress, anxiety disorders and conduct disorders are located at the two, opposite extremes, and adaptive functioning occurs in the midrange of this spectrum. Aristotle was right about neurobiology, too.

Underneath the technical details of research findings, the neuroscientific perspective means that sometimes anxiety begins as a neurobiological process. Sometimes brains and bodies just feel anxious. This physiological state might then produce misperceptions of threat, but these mental contents are not necessarily the cause of the physiological state, although they might feed back into it. Therapists can discuss this idea with clients and parents if the assessment suggests that neurobiological factors play a role in the anxiety disturbance.

Behavioral Etiologies

The behavioral explanation of the development of anxiety is based on a body of experimental research on **avoidance learning**. Many of these studies examined learning in animals. In the paradigmatic experiment, described by Spiegler and Guevremont (2010), a painful electric current is passed through one side of a chamber, and the animal can escape this shock only by moving to the other side. Animals learn this contingency quickly, and they replace escape with avoidance; in other words, they never set foot on the shock-associated side of the chamber again. The key point is this: If the electric shock is turned off, the animal will *never discover* that the contingency has changed, because he never ventures onto that side of the chamber again.

The two-factor explanation of avoidance learning combines classical and operant conditioning: Pavlovian conditioning causes anxiety to be associated with the shock-associated side of the chamber, and avoidance of that side is negatively reinforced by fear reduction (Mowrer, 1960). As a result, fears last a long time even when the original painful experience never happens again, because the avoidance of feared situations is reinforced by feelings of relief. For example, a child who once had a bad experience with swimming may feel anxious about this activity and may manage to avoid it for years. Each time she gets out of a swimming activity by means of some excuse, her feelings of relief reinforce her anxiety about swimming. Thus, avoidance prevents relearning.

The animal experiments also revealed the solution to the problem of avoidance-based fear: If the animal is pushed onto the previously shocking side of the chamber, he will show intense alarm, but if escape is prevented, anxiety will subside as the animal learns that the old contingency is no longer in force. The opposite of avoidance is **exposure** to the feared stimulus, which results in adaptive relearning. Therefore, the core change agent in behavioral treatment of anxiety is exposure, which means pushing the client into the situations she has been avoiding so she can learn that these situations are no longer dangerous.

In moderation, anxiety is an adaptive emotion that signals danger, and avoidance learning is an adaptive capability that protects us from harm. Three-year-old children who do not learn to be afraid of stimuli that signal an unpleasantly loud noise show elevated levels of aggression at 8 years old (Gao, Raine, Venables, Dawson, & Mednick, 2009) and high levels of both aggression and criminality at 23 years old (Gao, Raine, Venables, Dawson, & Mednick, 2010). In adulthood, extremely low levels of anxiety are associated with psychopathy and aggression, and psychopaths have *under*active amygdalas (Raine, 2013). It is sometimes useful to explain to parents and older clients that, in moderation, anxiety is not a bad thing and, in a sense, anxiety disorders involve too much of a good thing.

The core change agent in behavioral treatment of anxiety is exposure, which means pushing the client into the situations she has been avoiding so she can learn that these situations are no longer dangerous.

Although, historically, behaviorists discovered the anxiety-avoidance mechanism, other theories describe abstract versions of this process that occur in contexts more complex than laboratory experiments. Systems-oriented therapists often direct family members to engage in types of interaction they have avoided, so they can discover that these interactions are now safe and potentially positive. The dynamic technique of interpretation seems analogous to pulling an animal to the shock-associated side of the chamber because, by bringing previously unconscious issues into awareness and conversation, interpretation exposes clients to what they had feared and demonstrates that their fears are no longer necessary. Research on common factors in therapy has found that, across diverse types of counseling, successful clients often report that one of the keys to their progress was assistance in gradually facing issues they had avoided for a long time (Lambert & Ogles, 2004; Weinberger, 1995). The concept of exposure seems to describe a fundamental therapeutic change agent that, in different forms, crosscuts theoretical orientations.

Avoidance learning is not the only anxiety etiology described by behaviorists. Behavioral clinicians are also alert to the possibility that children might receive operant reinforcement for anxious behavior, typically from their caregivers (Burke & Silverman, 1987; Kearney, 2001). One common example occurs in school refusal: The child expresses anxiety about going to school, is allowed to stay home, and then spends the day playing and receiving attention. Parents' sympathy for their children sometimes causes them to reinforce precisely the behaviors they want to discourage.

Other behavioral explanations of anxiety emphasize skill deficits (Hudson & Rapee, 2004; Rapee, Wignall, Hudson, & Schniering, 2000). Anxiety can be viewed as the result of weak relaxation skills and, accordingly, treated with relaxation training. Also, many socially anxious clients have real problems in interpersonal situations—namely, a high likelihood of rejection due to weak social skills (Beidel & Alfano, 2011; Beidel et al., 2000). Jeffrey was a client of this type. The logical intervention for this etiology is social skills training, as described in Chapter 2 on behavior therapy.

Cognitive Etiologies

Cognitive analyses of the causes of anxiety emphasize fear-dominated attentional biases and misperceptions of threat. Even in laboratory situations, anxious children selectively attend to threatening stimuli (Bar-Haim, Lamy, Pergamin, Bakermans-Kranenburg, & van Ijzendoorn, 2007). These youth perceive more threat, perceive threat more quickly, and make more fearful interpretations and predictions when presented with ambiguous situations, so they perceive danger even in settings that nonanxious youth do not view as threatening (Cannon & Weems, 2010; Taghavi, Moradi, Neshat-Doost, Yule, & Dalgleish, 2000). Anxious individuals are pessimistic about both the likelihood and the magnitude of negative events, exaggerating both the probability and the catastrophic nature of the feared occurrences. Their self-talk is dominated by predictions of failure and painful events (Friedberg & McClure, 2002, 2014). In addition to overestimating external dangers, anxious individuals underestimate their ability to cope with negative events that do occur (Micco & Ehrenreich, 2008).

Anxious individuals sometimes become alarmed in response to their own physiological experiences of fear, especially when panicky feelings occur (Weems, Hammond-Laurence, Silverman, & Ginsburg, 1998; Higa-McMillan, Francis, & Chorpita, 2014; Weems, Hammond-Laurence, Silverman, & Ginsburg, 1998). These individuals sometimes misinterpret their uncomfortable physical sensations as signals that something terrible is about to happen, either externally (e.g., an assault or humiliating experience) or internally (e.g., a heart attack or going crazy). These misinterpretations cause **secondary anxiety**; the person is frightened of his fear, and the anxiety feeds off itself. While this dynamic can happen in any anxiety disorder, erroneous beliefs about physical sensations of fear are the main etiological mechanism in panic disorder.

Eckhart Tolle, in his aptly titled book, *The Power of Now* (2004), writes from an eastern spiritual perspective, but his thesis is a psychological one. Tolle asserts that we can always cope with the present, but we can never cope with the future. In other words, if a negative event happens and becomes an actual situation instead of a frightening possibility, there are always steps that can be taken to adapt. Research on **affective forecasting** supports Tolle's view. People's predictions about the impact of future events on their well-being are typically quite inaccurate, and in a systematic way: These predictions overestimate the impact of events, both negative and positive (Gilbert, Lieberman, Morewedge & Wilson, 2004; Wilson & Gilbert, 2003). People's happiness levels are generally fairly consistent, and fluctuations due to major events are usually followed by reversion to baseline. Predictions of the impact of negative events typically neglect the buffering effects of coping, as if people do not realize the degree to which their own efforts and ingenuity can help them recover from setbacks (Gilbert, Pinel, Wilson, Blumberg, & Wheatley, 1998; Hoerger, 2012). People with anxiety disorders underestimate the effects of coping even more than normal controls do (Micco & Ehrenreich, 2008).

According to Tolle (2004), it is impossible to cope with the future because we cannot take steps to address misfortunes that have not happened and might never happen, especially when anxious rumination posits so many different nightmare scenarios. He characterizes fears about possible future events as products of our "imagination" that reflect the vicissitudes of mental functioning more than solid reality. ACT shares this view (Eifert & Forsyth, 2005; Hayes et al. 2011; and see Chapter 4). Solid reality is to be found in full awareness of the present moment; this is the power of now.

Psychodynamic Etiologies

Psychodynamic theory describes several processes that result in anxiety, with the common theme being that the person is not consciously aware of the origin and nature of his fear (Compton, 1972; Fraiberg, 1959/1992; Freud, 1933, 1943). According to the theory, primitive, magical thinking—which is generally conscious in young children and unconscious in older children and adults—sometimes results in fears that are divorced from logic and external reality. Also, as discussed in Chapter 2, Behavior Therapy, people's anxieties are sometimes based on valid learning from past experiences that is misapplied to their current situation. Finally, anxiety is believed to occur in response to unacceptable impulses (e.g., anger, sexual desires, selfishness) that threaten to overcome internal controls and express themselves in action. The feared behaviors may be associated with punishment from the environment, but the punishment is seen as deserved, and the problem is located in the desire to do something morally wrong. In other theoretical scenarios, people are afraid of bad things happening to them, but in the psychodynamic scenario, people are also sometimes afraid of what they might *do*. In these etiological accounts, people are sometimes afraid of achieving the goals of their behavior, so that the fear *is* the wish—or, more precisely, the fear is that the wish might come true (A. Freud, 1946b; Hartmann, 1939/1958).

One example of this anxiety etiology is the child who experiences anger toward a loved one and feels frightened and guilty about the anger (Chethik, 2000; Parens, 1993). When primitive, magical thinking blurs the distinction between emotions and actions, children have the sense that intense feelings can somehow create effects in the world. For example, when young children feel jealous and angry toward new babies who suddenly absorb parental attention, they might become frightened that their "bad" feelings will somehow hurt the baby.

According to object relations theory, children who experience mistreatment, neglect, or rejection in the context of early caregiving often develop negative expectations of relationships that cause later movements toward closeness to be frightening, because dependency and love have been linked to pain (Baldwin, 1992; Greenberg & Mitchell, 1983; Jacobson, 1964). Such individuals might sabotage relationships that move toward affection in order to avoid the anxiety caused by closeness (Sullivan, 1953). Children who push their therapists away are often acting out this anxiety-based dynamic.

The irrational fears of fantasy figures—ghosts, monsters, and so forth—that are common in young children do not seem explicable by cognitive-behavioral theory. Learning-based explanations seem inadequate because there *are* no ghosts or witches and, if these things do not exist, how can children learn to be afraid of them? Parents and other adults with credibility insist that there are no monsters—but the child's anxiety is not reduced. Also, children sometimes say things like, "I know there's no such thing as ghosts—but I'm scared of them anyway." If these fears are not merely unrealistic but virtually unrelated to external reality, reason and evidence might not touch them. Instead, we seem to be in the land of unconscious, primitive, magical thinking. The fears of young children make sense (and do not make sense) in the same way that dreams, myths, and psychotic hallucinations and delusions do; these phenomena may make symbolic sense in that they represent emotional meanings in concrete forms (Fraiberg, 1959/1992; Gardner, 1993). Dynamic theory provides therapists with interpretive tools that can decode these meanings.

Systemic Etiologies

Parents influence the development of childhood anxiety disorders through several mechanisms. Studies of interactions between anxious children and their parents have found that parental messages can cause anxiety (Hudson & Rapee, 2004). Parental modeling of fear is usually followed by frightened, avoidant behavior in children (Gerull & Rapee, 2002). Fear can be passed from parents to children in a simple, straightforward way.

Overcontrolling, overprotective parenting is associated with anxiety disorders in children (Chorpita & Barlow, 1998; Hudson & Rapee, 2001). When overprotective parents shield their children from failure and rescue them from challenges, the parents unintentionally communicate that the child is incapable of handling stress, and they unintentionally reinforce the child's anxious behavior. Although these parents only want to help, these unneeded rescues send messages along the lines of "you can't do it on your own," and "anxiety is awful and must be ended immediately."

Temperament research reviewed earlier found that about one third of behaviorally inhibited infants grow up to be adults with anxiety disorders (Kagan et al., 1994; Kagan & Snidman, 2004). While this finding certainly demonstrates the importance of temperament, it also suggests the importance of environment, because two thirds of the inhibited infants did *not* have anxiety disorders as adults. What made the difference? One variable stood out in the research: The response of mothers to their infants' distress in novel, challenging, but safe situations. In both laboratory settings and everyday life, when mothers respond to their inhibited children's distress by rescuing and removing them from challenging situations, the children are likely to develop anxiety disorders. When parents respond to these situations with a combination of supportive soothing and encouragement to persevere in the stressful situation, most children with inhibited temperament do not develop anxiety disorders. Thus, parents who *gently push* their inhibited children to face challenges can overcome the risk factor of inhibited temperament and help their children grow up without anxiety disturbances.

Parents who gently push their inhibited children to face challenges can overcome the risk factor of temperament and help their children grow up without anxiety disturbances.

According to systems theory (see Chapter 7), anxiety also results from disruptions of family equilibria and from threats to the stability of these equilibria (Goldenberg & Goldenberg, 2012; Hoffman, 1981; Minuchin, 1974). Communication that is indirect, disguised, or self-contradictory may be anxiety-producing (Satir, 1972). The double bind is a particularly crazy-making form of communication that can cause people to feel anxious without knowing why, since problems are never acknowledged (Bateson, 1972).

Assessment

As is the case for psychopathology assessment in general, the level of agreement between children and parents in their descriptions of the child's anxiety symptoms is typically modest (Grills & Ollendick, 2003). Children tend to self-report fewer anxiety symptoms than their parents report for them. If a child seems guarded, clinicians should weigh the parent's reports more heavily in deciding on a diagnosis.

Behavioral observation often provides important information about a child's level of anxiety. Anxiety is typically manifested in behaviors such as a quavering or inaudible voice, trembling, fidgeting, avoiding eye contact, biting fingernails, and avoiding challenging tasks (Hudson, Hughes, & Kendall, 2004).

The well-established role of genetic and temperamental factors in the etiology of anxiety disorders (Biederman et al., 2001; Gregory & Eley, 2007; Hallett et al., 2009; Kagan & Snidman, 2004) means that clinicians should not insist on identifying life events, family processes, or internal mechanisms that account for the development of a client's anxiety. Some youth are nervous by their biological nature; they exhibit high baseline levels of arousal and neurophysiological overreactivity to stress (De Bellis, Casey, et al., 2000; Nitschke et al., 2009; Perez-Edgar & Fox, 2005; Schwartz et al., 2003). The likelihood of genetic and/or neurobiological etiology is increased by family histories of anxiety, onset of fearful behavior at very young ages, the occurrence of anxiety across situations, and an absence of problematic environmental factors or past traumatic events that would account for the anxiety. Also, some youth articulate a sequence in which, first, their bodies feel nervous, frightened, or uncomfortable, and then they begin to think about possible threats to their safety or well-being. It is as if the thoughts function merely to provide content or explanation for the anxious physiology that would occur regardless of whether environmental threats were perceived.

Here are some questions to ask children about their anxiety problems. Adaptations of these questions are appropriate for parents, as well:

- "What makes you scared?" "What makes you nervous?"

- "Do you have any worries?" "What do you worry about?"

- "What does your mind show you in its preview of what's going to happen?" (Assesses nonverbal imagery)

- "Are you scared of certain specific things, or is it more like you are just worried about everything?" (Diagnostic of GAD)

- "Does your body ever get nervous for no reason?" "When that happens, does your mind start looking for things to worry about?" (Assesses physiology)

- "What do you say to yourself when you're scared or worried?" "What are your nervous thoughts?" (Assesses cognition)

- "Who told you that _____ is so awful?" (Assesses systemic/cognitive processes)

- "Are you afraid of something you might do?" (Gets at possible unconscious impulses)

- "What happens when you show people or tell people that you are worried?" (Measures systemic and reinforcement processes)

- "Could there be anything good about _____?" (Assesses subtle reinforcement and possible role of unconscious wishes)

Treatment Planning

Outcome Research

Outcome research on anxiety disorders provides much more support for CBT than any other type of therapy. APA's Society of Clinical Psychology has given CBT a rating *of Strong Research Support* (the highest possible rating) as a treatment for generalized anxiety disorder, social anxiety disorder, and panic disorder. Exposure-based therapy has the same rating for specific phobia. APA's reviews focus on studies with adult clients, simply because most outcome research is with adults, but research on therapy for young clients tells the same story.

Outcome research on anxiety disorders provides much more support for CBT than any other type of therapy.

Reynolds et al. (2012) performed a meta-analysis of RCTs examining therapies for youth with anxiety disorders. They obtained a medium-sized overall effect of .65. The effect for comparisons with active, bona fide alternative treatments, such as TAU, was .35, which is small but still represents significant outperformance of alternative therapies. The 48 studies of CBT produced an overall effect size of .66. The seven studies of non-CBT therapies produced a considerably smaller effect size of .25. Effects were larger for adolescents than children. Individual therapy produced larger changes than group therapy. Longer-term therapy produced larger effects than brief therapy.

RCTs have consistently found that CBT is an effective treatment for children and adolescents with generalized, social, and separation anxiety disorders (e.g., Barrett, Dadds, et al., 1996; Kendall, 1994; Kendall et al., 2008; Nauta et al., 2003; Walkup et al., 2008). Collectively, these studies indicate that approximately 50%–70% of youth who receive CBT improve enough so that they no longer meet the criteria for an anxiety diagnosis, while about 10%–40% of youth who receive a pill placebo, wait-list assignment, or an alternative treatment exhibit this degree of improvement. In two follow-up studies conducted 3 and 7 years posttreatment, therapeutic gains were maintained, and 80%–90% of successfully treated children still did not meet criteria for an anxiety disorder (Kendall, Safford, Flannery-Schroeder, & Webb, 2004; Kendall & Southam-Gerow, 1996).

The Child/Adolescent Anxiety Multimodal Study was a large-scale RCT comparing CBT, a medication called sertraline, the combination of the two, and a pill placebo for youth aged 7–17 years. Immediately post-treatment, the combination treatment produced the highest rates of improvement and of remission (diagnostic criteria no longer met), while CBT and medication, by themselves, produced rates of improvement and remission that were similar to each other and higher than the placebo (Ginsburg et al., 2011). At 24- and 36-week follow-ups, there was some convergence between the combined treatment and its two components, but the combined treatment still produced the highest remission rates (Piacentini et al., 2014).

Social effectiveness training is an intervention for preadolescent children with social anxiety disorder that includes group as well as individual sessions. In a study by Beidel et al. (2000), this therapy enhanced social skills and reduced social anxiety, compared to a control intervention. At termination, 67% of the treated children no longer met criteria for social anxiety disorder, compared to just 5% of the control group. The gains were maintained at a 6-month follow-up. Three years post-termination, 72% of the treated youth did not meet criteria for social anxiety disorder, and they demonstrated maintenance of gains on a wide array of measures (Beidel, Turner, Young, & Paulson, 2005). Five years later, these gains were still maintained, and the overall functioning of youth who had responded positively to therapy was not different from a control group of adolescents who had never had a disorder (Beidel, Turner, & Young, 2006).

CBT for anxiety has demonstrated similar outcomes for youth from diverse cultures. Pina, Silverman, Fuentes, Kurtines, and Weems (2003) found that exposure-based CBT produced positive outcomes for both Latino/a and European American youth, and direct comparisons indicated no major differences between the gains achieved by the two groups. Treadwell, Flannery-Schroeder, and Kendall (1995) found similar outcomes in European American and African American youngsters who received CBT, and Walkup et al. (2008) found similar outcomes in White and Asian American young people. Yen et al. (2014) found that CBT was effective for children in Taiwan, and W. Lau, Chan, Li, and Au (2010) obtained positive results for children in Hong Kong; in both studies, the magnitude of effects was comparable to the results achieved in Western countries. Harmon, Langle, and Ginsburg (2006) provide further discussion of cultural factors in anxiety treatment for youth.

As discussed in Chapter 3, although use of cognitive techniques with young children has been controversial because of the thinking ability required for participation, developmentally appropriate modifications seem to make this work feasible and effective (Doherr et al., 2005; Grave & Blissett, 2004). Several outcome studies have demonstrated that CBT, with its cognitive components, provides benefits for young children with anxiety disturbances when it is modified in this way (Hirshfeld-Becker et al., 2010; Monga et al., 2009). Children as young as four years old can benefit from some CBT techniques.

Hogendoorn et al. (2014) performed a mediation analysis using short-term longitudinal data collected over the course of therapy with children and adolescents. They found that decreases in anxiety symptoms were preceded by client use of three coping strategies taught by therapists—problem solving, cognitive restructuring, and seeking distraction—as well as increases in two cognitive change processes linked to anxiety reduction—perceived control and positive thoughts. Changes in negative thoughts did not mediate treatment effects. Three studies have found that decreases in anxious self-statements mediated reductions in anxiety symptoms (Kendall & Treadwell, 2007; Lau et al., 2010; Treadwell & Kendall, 1996). Overall, these results suggest that CBT for anxiety works largely through the mechanisms of change hypothesized by the theory.

Researchers have examined whether including parents in therapy augments the efficacy of individual CBT for the child. In a very broad meta-analysis that included all types of psychotherapies and all disorders for which there were RCTs, Dowell and Ogles (2010) found that parent involvement generally increased the efficacy of child treatment, but its effects were smaller for CBT, compared to other therapies. Thulin, Svirsky, Serlachius, Andersson, and Ost (2014) performed a meta-analysis of 16 studies that examined the effects of augmenting individual child CBT with parent participation in therapy. They found no evidence of an augmentation effect. The meta-analysis by Reynolds et al. (2012), reviewed earlier, also found that parent involvement did not add to the effectiveness of CBT. A meta-analysis of eight RCTS comparing family CBT to individual or group child-only CBT produced a small but significant effect size of .26 (Brendel & Maynard, 2014).

Although the overall implication of the research is that the effects of parent involvement are weak, some careful studies have revealed subtle but important forms of added value for parent involvement in CBT. A meta-analysis by Manassis et al. (2014) found that, while parent involvement did not increase the effects of CBT measured immediately post-treatment, children whose parents were involved increased their gains between termi-nation and a 1-year follow-up, while children whose parents were not involved maintained but did not increase their gains. Manassis et al. suggested that parental use of contingency management to sustain and increase children's exposure to challenging situations, as well as reduction in anxiogenic behaviors by parents, would explain the post-treatment gains achieved by their children. Also, research on moderator effects suggests that adding a par-ent training component to individual child CBT does produce immediate benefits for *some* children—namely, those who are younger and female, and whose mothers exhibit high levels of anxiety (Barrett, Dadds, et al., 1996; Cobham, Dadds, & Spence, 1998; Dadds, Holland, Barrett, Laurens, & Spence, 1997).

Most outcome research has examined treatment packages that combine several CBT techniques. However, these techniques might not be equally necessary. Two dismantling studies found that, for most clients, exposure is the crucial component of therapy, and the other techniques are not necessary for achieving positive outcomes (Storch, 2014; Zalta & Foa, 2012).

Research on mindfulness-based cognitive therapy for children (Semple & Lee, 2011) has just begun to occur. Semple, Lee, Rosa, and Miller (2010) randomly assigned a small, nonclinical sample of 9–13-year-old children to a mindfulness intervention or a wait-list control. The intervention produced significant reductions in attention problems and over-all emotional problems. These gains were maintained at a 3-month follow-up.

I could locate no outcome studies of psychodynamic therapy for children with anx-iety disorders. Keefe, McCarthy, Dinger, Zilcha-Mano, and Barber (2014) conducted a meta-analysis of dynamic therapy for anxiety disorders in adults. They obtained a medium effect size of .64 in comparisons with no-treatment controls. Effect sizes were nonsignificant for comparisons between dynamic therapy and alternative interventions. A meta-analysis by Barber, Muran, McCarthy, and Keefe (2013) found no differences between CBT and dynamic therapy in outcomes for adults with anxiety disorders. These results suggest that dynamic therapy might be useful for some young people whose anxiety is not effectively treated by CBT.

Clinical Considerations

CBT includes a wide variety of techniques, and therapists can choose from among them by ascertaining which dimensions of anxiety seem most troublesome to the client and then selecting techniques that target those dimensions. Relaxation training treats the physiolog-ical aspect of anxiety. The behavioral aspect is treated by exposure to feared situations and by training in whatever psychosocial skills are needed for adaptation to those situations. The cognitive dimension of anxiety is addressed by treating self-talk, interpretations, and beliefs. As discussed earlier, dismantling studies suggest that, for most youth, exposure is the crucial ingredient of therapy, but clinical assessment might suggest whether a particular client would benefit from additional components of therapy.

Identification of the interventions needed by a client should be based on the content, settings, and causes of her symptoms. Anxiety about being rejected by peers might be due to a real deficit in social skills, in which case therapy should include social skills training, or social anxiety might be due to unrealistic thinking about rejection (such as the notion that only inadequate people are rejected), which would call for cognitive intervention. Panic attacks might be due to physiological over-reactivity to stress, in which case relax-ation training would probably help, or panic might occur because the client misinterprets the physical changes associated with anxiety as indicating real danger, in which case psychoeducation should be a component of therapy. If the assessment suggests that genetic and neurobiological factors play an important role in the disturbance, so that some anxious thoughts and feelings would probably persist following intervention, ACT provides clients with a way to achieve some independence from these mental contents and construct lives they value despite the occurrence of anxiety. Work with parents should probably be part of treatment when caregivers model anxiety, reinforce fearful behavior, and/or overprotect the child by rescuing him from stressors that he could learn to handle.

Some clinical situations suggest a need to venture outside the empirically supported realm of behavioral and cognitive intervention to select therapeutic strategies that seem capable of addressing etiologies that contribute to the client's anxiety. A fear of burglars breaking into one's house might be realistic in the child's neighborhood, in which case counseling would need to deal with this reality, or a fear of burglars might symbolize an abstract feeling of vulnerability or a fear of aggressive impulses that the child cannot verbalize, which suggests the need for a dynamic aspect of treatment. Separation anxiety might derive from an insecure attachment to the parents resulting from disruption in early caregiving, which suggests a need to address the client's unconscious object relations, or this disorder might reflect parental discomfort with the client's growing autonomy, which would call for systems-oriented therapy or parent counseling. When more than one etiological mechanism seems to contribute to the client's disturbance, multiple therapeutic strategies would be appropriate.

Cognitive-Behavioral Therapy

Most research on CBT for children's anxiety has examined Kendall and Hedtke's *Coping Cat* intervention, which is clearly the preeminent treatment package in this field. Implemented on the basis of a therapist's manual (Kendall & Hedtke, 2006a), a workbook for the child (Kendall & Hedtke, 2006b), and materials for parents (Kendall, Podell, & Gosch, 2010), this structured program for children aged 6–14 uses cartoons of a cat with excellent coping skills to present an intervention combining affective education, self-instruction, problem solving, external reinforcement, self-reinforcement, and skill practice through imaginal and live exposure. Other CBT interventions with empirical support include Beidel et al.'s (2000) social effectiveness therapy for socially anxious youth, and Wood, Piacentini, Southam-Gerow, Chu, and Sigman's (2006) family therapy version of CBT for anxiety.

CBT for anxiety generally divides into two treatment phases: **facilitative strategies** and **exposure**. Facilitative strategies come first, and exposure comes second. Family involvement and contingency management may occur throughout the sequence.

Exposure, the opposite of avoidance, means to enter, remain in, and survive the feared situation. Exposure is the clinical equivalent of the experimental procedure of pulling an animal to the part of the chamber in which, in the past, she was shocked; this is the only way to learn that what was frightening in the past no longer needs to be feared. Since avoidance is the behavioral hallmark of anxiety disorders, it makes sense that CBT for anxiety hinges on the concrete reversal of avoidance. In our case example, Jeff needed to practice coping with the social situations he had avoided.

If exposure results in a traumatic experience for the client, her anxiety might worsen. To prevent this possibility, therapists prepare clients for exposure and implement this

Table 13.2   When to Use Different Cognitive-Behavioral Techniques for Anxiety Disorders

Intervention	A Must	Applicable if Indicated	Indications
Psychoeducation	X		
Exposure	X		
Contingency management		X	Client needs external motivation for full engagement in treatment tasks, especially exposure.
Relaxation		X	High frequency or intensity of physical tension.
Imagery		X	Child reports anxiety-producing images and has the ability to create new mental images.
Problem solving		X	Problematic external situations are causing realistic anxiety.
Self-instruction		X	Self-critical, alarmist, pessimistic internal dialogue.
Rational analysis		X	Cognitive distortions and catastrophizing.
Social skills training		X	Social skills deficits contribute to anxiety.
Family involvement		X	Parents are highly anxious and/or overprotective; clients are young and/or female.

procedure in a gradual, step-by-step way. Often it is necessary to help clients strengthen the skills they need to succeed in situations where, in the past, they failed. For Jeff, social skills training, described in Chapter 2, Behavior Therapy, was an important component of treatment.

Therapy components should be chosen selectively, so treatment is efficient. Table 13.2 indicates which techniques are "musts," which are optional, and when the optional techniques should be used.

Education About Anxiety and Its Management

CBT begins by educating the child about anxiety and socializing her into the treatment model (Chow & Pincus, 2014; Kendall, 2011; Kendall & Hedtke, 2006a; O'Neil, Brodman, Cohen, Edmunds, & Kendall, 2012). We want clients to become experts on anxiety and its management, to an age-appropriate extent. In CBT, there is no mystery about how therapy works; the rationales for techniques are transparent. Many clients find this approach normalizing, demystifying, and empowering.

The first psychoeducational objective is for the client to recognize when he becomes anxious at an early point in the process, because these are the occasions that call for implementation of anxiety management strategies. Because knowing what to look for helps people identify experiences, it may be useful to teach clients the four dimensions of anxiety presented earlier in this chapter. Therapists should individualize the model by alternating between presentation of general information (e.g., "anxiety happens in our bodies, including … ") and questions to the client about how his experiences fit within the general framework (e.g., "What happens in your body when you get scared?"). To track progress, therapists can teach clients to rate the intensity of their anxiety using a 0–10 scale.

Once the counselor has identified the thoughts behind the client's anxiety, she can explain that fear is an understandable response to a catastrophic interpretation of a situation—for instance:

- "No wonder you are afraid of being in a crowd, if you think you might suffocate and faint."
- "No wonder you are afraid of trying to make friends, if you think you will say something stupid and make a fool of yourself."
- "It makes sense to me why you feel this way, but we can change it."

The more intellectually inclined the client, the more extensive affective education can be. Also, phobic clients can research many of the objects of their fears online or in books (e.g., animals they fear, fainting, and medical procedures). Such research is an intellectual version of approach behavior that demystifies the phobic object, indicates the boundaries of the threat, and begins the development of a sense of mastery.

As discussed in Chapter 8, grasping the idea of semiautonomous brain structures seems to provide some clients with an adaptive way of understanding their difficulties. When clients realize that automatic, gut reactions are a result of brain functioning as well as external situations, and that their own neurophysiology includes an anxiety-prone quirk, they sometimes become able to discount their reflexive reactions and place their behavior more under the control of reality-oriented (i.e., cortical) thinking. This understanding is compatible with the ACT approach, which relinquishes the goal of reducing unpleasant feelings and helps clients achieve the replacement goal of constructing a valued life despite these feelings (Eifert & Forsyth, 2005; Hayes et al., 2011). Counselors can say:

"The key to having a good life with an overactive amygdala is to be the master of it, rather than letting it be the master of you. It isn't easy but it's possible to decide when to believe what it says and when not to. You can decide when to obey your gut feelings of fear and when to say, 'Nope, I'm going ahead anyway.'"

Facilitative Strategies

Exposure is the critical component of CBT for anxiety, but it is usually difficult and even painful, so most clients need some preparation with softer, gentler techniques before they feel ready to begin exposure. Counselors can choose facilitative techniques that seem to address the anxiety etiologies most relevant to each client's disturbance. The main options are presented next.

Relaxation Training. Relaxation training (see Chapter 2, Behavior Therapy) seems to be especially appropriate for treatment of GAD, which does not have a specific phobic object or situation that can be the focus of exposure (Hayes-Skelton, Roemer, Orsillo (2013).

Relaxation training treats the somatic tension component of anxiety. The more prominent this dimension is for a client, the more important relaxation training would be to her therapy (Eisen & Silverman, 1993, 1998).

Relaxation procedures seem to be most effective when they are initiated at the first sign of an increase in anxiety (Beidel & Alfano, 2011). When clients cannot do a full progressive muscle relaxation exercise, taking a few deep, slow breaths while stretching or flexing and then relaxing their muscles may efficiently evoke much of the benefit of the full exercise, especially if they have developed this skill through repeated practice.

Social Skills Training. When social anxiety disorder is associated with weak interpersonal skills that really do make rejection likely, social skills training should be a component of therapy (Cummings, Kendall, & Mazza, 2014). Because Jeff felt nervous about pairing up with work partners in school, his therapist worked with him on strategies for meeting this challenge. The plan included deciding, in advance, which classmate seemed most likely to make a good partner and which peers should be viewed as fallback possibilities. Then, Jeff and his therapist rehearsed the specific behaviors involved in pairing up with a partner (making eye contact, gestures, smiling, etc.). The clinician often rejected Jeff's advances to give him practice in coping with negative outcomes.

Overt and Covert Modeling. Modeling procedures, introduced in Chapter 2 on behavior therapy, include both overt activities, such as watching others demonstrate skills, and covert procedures, such as storytelling. The key to effective modeling is to realistically acknowledge the feared threat before overcoming it, rather than depicting the problem as easily solved, so the modeling depicts coping rather than easy mastery (Meichenbaum, 1971).

Kendall and Hedtke (2006a) recommend that therapists use themselves as coping models, when possible, by disclosing experiences in which they faced and overcame anxiety-producing challenges similar to the client's. If the clinician does not have experiences like these in her past, or if the client seems more likely to relate to a child's experience than an adult's, counselors can offer accounts of other clients' anxiety treatment as a source of covert modeling. Fictional or nonfictional stories about youngsters facing difficulties like the client's provide another possibility. Finally, clients can always use themselves as covert models of success, as in the technique of envisioning, described in Chapter 1.

Self-Instruction. Self-instruction is a cognitive technique that helps children increase the realism and optimism of their internal dialogue (Meichenbaum, 1985; Velting et al., 2004). Therapists can use this technique to teach anxious youngsters how to talk themselves through the situations that scare them. Friedberg and McClure (2002, 2014) provide a number of self-instructional tasks and examples.

Most self-instructional approaches are divided into a sequence of preparation, application, and self-reward, which are used before, during, and after confronting the feared situation. Self-instructions for the preparation stage help clients anticipate the stressor in an adaptive way, for example, by thinking:

"Relax. I can stay in control by checking in with my fear level. I've trained for this; I'm ready to face my hurdles."

During the application phase, children confront the feared situation. Here is an example of a self-instruction for this phase:

"I'm handling this. If I just keep breathing and focus on what I need to do next, I'll tame the worry beast."

Finally, children enter the self-reward phase—for example:

"I did it; I ran the fear marathon. I didn't avoid anything. This is a win."

CBT for young children uses play activities to engage clients and provide skill practice (Knell, 1993; Knell & Meena, 2011; Pincus, Chase, Chow, Weiner, & Pian, 2011). The externalization metaphor from narrative therapy (Madigan, 2010; Payne, 2005; White, 2006) is often imported into this work. Clients can draw their anxiety as they picture it, and can depict its size in relation to a self-representation; hopefully these relative sizes will change as therapy progresses. The scoring system of the client's favorite sport can be used to track treatment ups and downs, with the goal being for "Team _____ (client's name)" to win against "Team Anxiety."

Talking Back to Fear (Friedberg & McClure, 2002) is a self-instructional protocol in which children construct a new script to counter their anxious self-talk. Young children enact their new internal dialogues through role-plays and puppet play. It is usually best for the therapist to play the role of fear and to articulate the anxious thoughts, while the client takes the role of coping and practices adaptive talk. Similarly, Knell (1993) suggests having the child take the role of a therapist with an anxious puppet who needs help with coping. Early in treatment, however, clients are sometimes unable to come up with coping self-statements, and then it is necessary to reverse these roles. The following example utilizes the preferable arrangement that facilitates internalization of adaptive self-instructions:

THERAPIST: Okay, let's pretend this ferocious tiger is your fear talking. You try to talk back to your fear with your mighty dinosaur puppet.

CHILD: Okay.

THERAPIST: I am your worries talking! That nervous feeling in your tummy means something really bad is going to happen. You won't be able to handle your feelings, and I will win.

CHILD: No you won't! That feeling in my stomach just means you are trying to make me *think* something bad will happen. I can handle anything that comes up because I'm stronger than you.

Mental imagery is a version of self-instruction in which the client envisions the behaviors he wants to perform in anxiety-producing situations. One client called this "changing the script of the movie." This technique was used to counter the distressing images that Jeff saw when he imagined himself coming up to bat in a Little League game. He saw himself flailing at each pitch and striking out. He imagined the disappointment of his teammates, while his own self-criticism echoed in his head. In the past, he usually did "choke," and imagination and reality reinforced each other in a vicious cycle. Therefore, the therapist and Jeff developed imagery that replaced the anxiety-ridden images with a calm focus on the task at hand:

> "It's just me and the pitcher out here. I will tune out the crowd noise and concentrate on doing my next step. I've done this in practice a thousand times. My feet are planted solidly. I see the ball coming toward me in slow motion. I get a jolt of energy, and I feel myself swing, shifting my weight forward as I connect and swing through the ball."

Cognitive Restructuring.   Cognitive restructuring or rational analysis is a useful technique for clients with sufficient cognitive maturity to reflect on their thoughts and evaluate how well their beliefs fit the evidence. **Decatastrophizing** means bringing the client's percep-tions or anticipations of a situation into line with what is realistic. Typically, the possibil-ities in question would be unpleasant but not disastrous, and it is this distinction between the unfortunate and the catastrophic that needs to be appreciated by clients (Beidel & Alfano, 2011; Cummings et al., 2014; Kendall, 2006a; O'Neil et al., 2012). The therapeu-tic message is, "It's bad, yes, but it's not *that* bad."

In the technique called **scaling the problem**, clients use a scale from zero to ten to rate the severity of difficulties they encounter or anticipate (Spirito & Esposito, 2008; Spirito, Esposito-Smythers, Wolff, & Uhl, 2011). Zero should be defined as no problem, with ten as a true catastrophe. Applying this scale to the events and situations of everyday life facil-itates decatastrophizing by activating the type of thinking involved in careful, calibrated judgement. By directing attention to gradations in problem seriousness, scaling the prob-lem seems to increase appreciation of the shades of gray that lie between black and white. Most youth come to see that most of their problems are of mild to moderate severity. Those clients who do face severe difficulties may benefit by more clearly perceiving the differences between their serious problems and their ordinary difficulties, so emotional reactions can be differentiated accordingly. Counselors can provide guided practice in scaling problems during sessions, and parents can prompt client use of the technique when stressors occur at home.

J. S. Beck (2011) suggests the following three questions for clients, asked in the order given, as tools in work on decatastrophization:

- What's the worst thing that could happen?
- What's the best thing that could happen?
- What's the most likely thing to happen?

When exploring the child's thinking, counselors should make sure to elicit the most catastrophic prediction, because this is usually the thought driving the anxiety response. If a client says, "the The worst thing that could happen is that I'd get really nervous," it is unlikely that the bottom layer of catastrophic anticipation has been reached. Therefore, such a response should be probed.

Therapists can help clients assess the accuracy of their anxious predictions by provid-ing a structure for comparing these predictions to what actually happens (Friedberg & McClure, 2002, 2014). In advance, the client identifies the event anticipated to be dis-tressing and predicts her degree of distress on a numerical scale. Sophisticated clients can make two ratings, one for the prediction of their emotions or "gut" (limbic system) and one for the prediction of their "head" (prefrontal cortex). Later, when the event occurs, the youngster rates how distressing (or how "bad") the experience turned out to be. In a retrospective version of this technique, clients think back to previous months and years, remember what they were worried about then, and assess how things turned out. For most anxious clients, predicted distress is usually greater than actual distress, sometimes much greater.

A simplified version of this technique for young children replaces numerical scales with a dichotomy of *real alarms* versus *false alarms* (Friedberg & McClure, 2002, 2014). Therapists can use the analogy of fire alarms eliciting a rush of sirens and trucks to help children understand the concept. Then, anticipated stress can be compared to experienced stress.

Self-Knowledge and Self-Correction. There are two possible reasons why a situation could look scary: One is that it really is dangerous, and one is that our minds make things look this way even when they are not. When the scaling exercise is repeated a number of times, most anxiety-prone clients notice a pattern: Their anticipations of the future are consistently more negative than what the future actually brings, so most of the disasters they predict never occur. This is an insight about the relationship between the self and the world. Clients who grasp the distinction between the way things feel and the way things really are learn to correct for their cognitive styles. Self-knowledge produces more accurate expectations of the external world.

Clients who grasp the distinction between the way things feel and the way things really are learn to correct for their cognitive styles.

This formulation applies to therapy for cognitive biases in general, but here the focus is on anxiety. Two metaphors can help clients understand the relationship between their cognitive style and external reality. Here is one:

> "Let's say you were target shooting with a rifle, looking through your scope, and you got the bulls-eye right in the cross-hairs, so you could shoot it perfectly in the middle. But, after shooting, when you go up to the target to see how you did, all your bullet-holes are about six inches to the left of the bulls-eye. What is the solution to this problem?"

Most clients will say the solution is to aim six inches to the right; if they do not, the counselor can make this point. Another metaphor is based on the eyeglasses that correct our vision. Opticians assess the lenses of our eyes to see exactly how they bend light in a distorted way, and then they design artificial lenses to bend light in exactly the opposite way, so the net effect (distortion + distortion) is accuracy. Our habitual biases are like the lenses of our eyes, and the rational part of our brain can become like eyeglasses that correct for these biases. Counselors can say:

> "You frequently feel like awful things are going to happen, but we've learned that usually they don't. So, to know what you can expect, start with your gut feeling and then figure things will probably turn out better than that."

Anxious youth are often glad to discover they have a pessimistic bias because, equipped with this self-knowledge, they can attribute some of their anxiety to pessimism, rather than to real dangers of terrible events. Some clients can be quantitative about their personal correction factors. If they have kept records of predictions and outcomes with a numerical scale, this is simply a matter of subtraction. The new cognitive move is to subtract their correction factor from their reflexive or habitual expectations of events. In other words, if the records indicate that feared events usually turn out to be about three scale-points less aversive than what is anticipated, and the client faces a challenge that feels like an eight, she can logically figure that it will probably turn out to be about a five. This cortical calculation might not convince her amygdala, so her stomach might still tighten up, but the client could base her decisions about what to do on her corrected estimate of how painful the situation will probably turn out to be.

Self-correction is made possible by self-discovery, in a process I call "creating a user's manual for your mind." This is a remarkable human capability in which our mental lens turns back on itself, and the mind assesses the mind. I invite clients to share in the wonder of this capability by saying, "It seems impossible—and yet it happens every day!" (The miracle is made possible by the modular nature of the brain, discussed in Chapters 5 and 8.)

Probability and Anxiety.   Nonpsychotic children above age 6 rarely fear events that are literally impossible. Instead, these children usually fear disasters that are extremely improbable but *could* happen, such as kidnapping, house fires, and tornadoes. The difficulty for parents and therapists trying to reassure these children is that we cannot provide absolute statements that the feared event will not happen. Life does include catastrophic events. Nevertheless, most people manage to live without daily anxiety about these possibilities, and it is the business of therapists to figure out how they do it and how our clients can do it, too.

Categorical thinking seems to be one factor. Because children's quantitative thinking ability is limited, they tend to recognize three categories of probability: (1) things that definitely will happen, (2) things that might happen, and (3) things that definitely will not happen. Cognitively, the source of anxiety about unlikely disasters is located in Category 2. Anxious children do not seem to appreciate the enormous range within the "might happen" category (i.e., between 0.01% and 99.99% probability of occurrence). As a result, their sense of the likelihood that, for example, they will get cancer or their house will burn down is that it "might happen"—quite a frightening thought, if left unqualified.

The concept missing from the cognitive repertoire of these youngsters is that of "extremely unlikely." This is the concept that counselors need to teach. The term I use for this idea is, "very, very, very, very … unlikely." I use the example of being struck by lightning. Comparing this example to clients' far-fetched but not impossible worries is often effective, because children understand that they *could* worry about being struck by lightning, since it has happened, but they do not need to worry about it, because this event is "very, very … " (Here, the experienced client will chime in.)

Anxious clients face the unavoidable challenge of reconciling themselves to the human condition, which does not include ironclad guarantees against the occurrence of catastrophe. Nonetheless, people seem to feel better when they replace the question, "Can I be 100% sure that nothing bad will happen?" with the question, "Is there any reason to believe that something bad will happen?"

Another useful message derives from the fact that anxiety, by definition, is *anticipatory* suffering (Tolle, 2004). Anxious clients are distinguished by their capacity for worrying about things that have not happened to them and probably never will. The message to these clients should include the following sequence: (a) They have suffered much anxiety about dangers that never materialized, (b) if negative events do occur, they will then know what they are and will be able to respond to them, therefore, (c) there is no reason to begin suffering in advance. As Tolle says, we can always cope with the present, but we can never cope with the future. Everyday language supplies two additional sayings:

- "So far, so good."
- "I'll cross that bridge if I come to it."

Exposure

Exposure is the core of CBT for anxiety (Chow & Pincus, 2014; Davis et al., 2012; Grills-Taquechel & Ollendick, 2013). For many clients, it is the only technique necessary to achieve remission of anxiety disorders (Storch, 2014; Zalta & Foa, 2012). Psychotherapy has no change process more reliable than exposure.

What do clients need to be exposed *to*? The answer is, the stimuli they fear. Most diagnoses indicate what the target of exposure should be. Children with specific phobias need to be exposed to their phobic object or situation; children with social anxiety need to be exposed to social situations; clients with separation anxiety need to experience separation from parents; and youth with GAD and panic disorder need to be exposed to their thoughts and feelings.

For most children, exposure is a counterintuitive form of help—it seems like a terrible idea, at first. Clients need age-appropriate explanations to understand the rationale for the procedure. The key point is the connection between anxiety and avoidance. Here is one way to explain it:

"It's like you and your fear are on a seesaw together, and only one of you will come out on top. (Hand motions can pantomime the inverse relationship.) Every time you avoid the thing that frightens you, your fear gets stronger and you get weaker. And every time you face the thing you're scared of, no matter how anxious you feel, you get stronger and your fear gets weaker. Being brave is hard, but it pays off big-time."

If the client is resistant, it might be useful to ask him to list the advantages and disadvantages of trying to overcome his fears (Fishbein & Izjen, 2009). Often, the disadvantages reflect irrational beliefs that underlie the avoidance. Once these beliefs are identified, cognitive restructuring can be used to modify the unrealistic assumptions and expectations. If this does not work, incentives for engaging in exposure can be provided (discussed later).

Therapists can sometimes increase client motivation to engage in exposure by explaining the meaning of this choice in a fashion that recruits self-concept aspirations to therapeutic work. Such explanations seek to extend the client's concepts of strength and courage so they incorporate participation in exposure. The explanations begin from the point that people do not choose their fears; these come to us without permission. Confronting fears requires tolerating distress and overcoming impulses to flee, but we can choose this action to build a better life for ourselves. Courage can be defined as doing the right thing even when this is difficult and painful. (People who do not have fears to overcome are not braver than the client, just luckier.) Therefore, clients who go through exposure procedures must be considered courageous.

Most anxious youngsters fear losing control. Counselors should reassure these children that they will have control over the exposure process, so they can stop it anytime they want. Therapists should ask for fear ratings frequently, so the client understands that her distress level is being carefully monitored.

In the Coping Cat program, increasingly frightening situations are depicted visually on a "Fear Ladder," which the client climbs as she progresses through therapy. Client reports of mild to moderate anxiety indicate that the pace of exposure is about right. It is useful to plan a systematic series of steps such as the following, which was used to treat a phobia of dogs. The client: (1) looked at pictures of dogs, (2) went into a pet store where there were dogs, (3) tolerated being in a home where there was a dog in another room, (4) tolerated being in the same room with a dog, and (5) petted a dog.

Exposure works best when the client achieves success in every trial. It is important for the client to understand that success, here, does not necessarily mean reduced anxiety; success means staying in the situation and surviving. Failure consists of avoidance or escape from the feared situation. This conception might be difficult for clients to understand because they believe success experiences should feel good. Anxiety reduction is the eventual goal, and in most exposure trials anxiety first peaks and then declines, but the best objective for the client to focus on is a behavioral, not an emotional, objective.

If the client cannot tolerate the exposure, the procedure should be terminated. Damage control is then necessary. Therapists should take a short break, do a facilitative technique such as relaxation or reframing, and then backtrack to an easier version of the feared situation. The objective is to end the session with a success experience.

Weisz (2004) provided some imaginative examples of exposure procedures for clients with social anxiety. In one example, the client was assigned the task of ordering food from a vendor and repeatedly changing her mind about the order, so she could discover that making mistakes and even being annoying would not result in terrible retaliation from other people. Another client who was anxious about humiliating himself in public was asked to bring a large pile of papers to the clinic lobby and, as he walked by the people there, to fall, sending the papers flying in all directions. While procedures like these are stressful, when clients face their worst fears and survive, the world is never quite so scary again.

In GAD and panic disorder, the targets of exposure are less concrete than in the other anxiety diagnoses (Grills-Taquechel & Ollendick, 2013; Hudson et al., 2004). Clients with panic disorder need to be exposed to their own physical sensations of anxiety. Clients with GAD need to be exposed to their own anxious thoughts. In both diagnoses, the client needs to habituate to stimuli that come from within, not from the environment. In these exposure procedures, clients purposefully evoke anxious physical sensations and/or cognitive worries, using their memory or imagination to bring on the anxious contents as vividly and in as much detail as possible.

The homework assignment of "worry time" should be regularly scheduled, preferably daily (Leahy, Holland, & McGinn, 2011). I present this "anti-anxiety exercise" as a way to practice managing anxiety in order to gain control, take charge, and eventually reduce the worrying. At times and places of the client's own choosing, he purposely invites the troublesome thoughts and feelings into his mind and accepts their activity there for a predetermined amount of time, usually about 5–10 minutes. The invitation can be embellished with challenges to the worries to "give me all you've got." The voluntary nature of the exercise seems to strengthen clients' control over their mental contents just as, in relaxation training, tensing our muscles helps us learn to relax them.

ACT includes innovative variations on the exposure technique (Hayes, Pankey, & Greg, 2002; Murrell, Coyne, & Wilson, 2004), such as the client imagining her fears expressed in absurd, caricatured forms (Harris, 2013). For example, the client could imagine her fears being sung by dancing cartoon characters, shouted at her by monsters, or rapped by hipsters with green hair. Jeff performed this exercise with thoughts such as, "I'm the worst baseball player ever," and, "I'm the biggest dork in the school."

Chapter 8's graph in which distress first increases and then markedly decreases as a situation is faced applies to the typical course of exposure-based anxiety treatment. Sketching this graph and tracking clients' progress on the curve as they go through progressive exposure help to reframe anxiety as an emotion that feels bad but may indicate something good—anxiety is the feeling of confronting and overcoming fears.

Reinforced Exposure. Because exposure is an aversive experience, clients need strong motivation to persevere until success is achieved. For many clients, explanations of what can be gained coupled with a desire to please the therapist and parents are sufficient to produce the necessary motivation. For other clients, especially young children who might not understand the rationale for exposure, tangible rewards provide the necessary external inducement (Davis et al., 2012; James, Cowdry & James, 2012).

Reinforced exposure is a contingency management procedure that does not directly treat anxious feelings but produces the behaviors that result in extinction of anxiety. Rewards are used, in a sense, to drag the child into the situation she fears so that, once there, she can discover it is not really dangerous.

Sometimes contingency management is surprisingly effective at vanquishing fears that seemed to have real emotional strength. One 5-year-old client repeatedly awoke in the middle of the night and, citing her fears of monsters, climbed into her parents' bed. The sleepy parents were never willing to deal with the hysteria that occurred when they tried to return her to her room. A straightforward behavioral intervention was tried. The goal of sleeping all night in her own room was established with the child; on the mornings after each successful night, the parents praised her and gave her a pretty sticker for her chart; and the parents said that when she reached the criterion of five consecutive nights in her own room, she would receive the pet hamster she had wanted for months. The intervention worked; the hamster turned out to be mightier than the monsters.

Psychodynamic Therapy

Client fears that are impervious to reality talk suggest the relevance of dynamic factors, because this theory describes internal processes that do not merely distort reality but are oblivious to it. Dynamic therapy is appropriate when the source of the client's anxiety is internal and unconscious, even when these dynamics manifest themselves as a fear of something external (which they often do). This seems to be most often the case with children below age 7 or so.

G. Silver, Shapiro, and Milrod (2013) provide a manual for dynamic treatment of children aged 8–16 years with generalized, social, and separation anxiety disorders. The therapist interprets conflicts, concerns, and defenses related to the client's anxiety, with particular attention to their manifestation in the transference, and suggests alternative, healthier possibilities for dealing with the issues that have funneled into anxiety symptoms. Although the manual does not emphasize exposure in the way that CBT treatments do, the counselor definitely encourages the child to face the situations that have made her anxious, and the clinician verbally reinforces these efforts to achieve mastery.

Anxious children present with a myriad of specific worries, but beneath them several basic sources of anxiety typically emerge (Compton, 1972; Fraiberg, 1959/1992; A. Freud, 1946b). Therapists should look for themes like these in the client's talk, play, drawings, fantasies, and behavior patterns:

- The child feels angry with people she loves and is afraid her anger might somehow, magically, harm them.
- The youth experiences impulses that are unacceptable to his conscience; in addition to feeling guilty for having these feelings, he is scared he might lose control of them.
- The child feels insecure about her relationship with caregivers even when there is nothing in the caregivers' current behavior that should cause such insecurity.
- The child's object relations involve a sense of the self as vulnerable and images of other people as aggressive and hurtful.

One useful question for clinicians to ask themselves is, what is the client *really* afraid of? The answer will not be the ghosts and witches that often populate the frightened fantasies of young children. Instead, clients' true fears usually concern emotions that feel unacceptable and/or relationships between the self and others. When the real-world anxieties underlying the client's fantasy fears are uncovered, they can usually be reassured, resolved, or, at minimum, coped with more effectively.

The chains of association linking specific anxieties and underlying dynamics may be complex and surprising. Dynamic theory offers no rules of thumb on the basis of which specific links can be made. It would be nice if there were algorithms along the lines of "elevator phobias are caused by conflicted anger toward fathers," but no such rules exist, and connections between symptoms and dynamics can be established only on the basis of individualized knowledge of clients. Nonetheless, some generalizations can be made about basic insights that many anxious clients need to achieve (Compton, 1972; Silver et al., 2013).

Some interpretations make connections between conscious fears and the emotional concerns that are their true, albeit unconscious, source—for example:

- "I wonder if this is really about camping and whether it's dangerous. I think this is more about you and your dad, and how scary he gets when he's mad."
- "You're worried about somebody being mad at you, and you're scared their anger might be so big and awful it could kill you, but I don't think it's a monster—I think it's a person you're really worried about."

Sometimes, as therapy unfolds, it becomes apparent that children who have been terrified of monsters actually, secretly, *like* them, and are excited and impressed by the monsters. Children sometimes identify with monsters because these fantasy figures epitomize the rage they feel and the power they wish they had; then they sometimes terrify themselves with these representations of their own vengeful cruelty. This is the process called **projection**. As internal mechanisms like these are brought out, it becomes possible to talk about the child's "monster feelings" and "the monster inside," and to identify connections between real-life issues and fantasy-based symptoms—for instance:

- "Sometimes you get so mad at your mom's new boyfriend—and your anger is so ugly and scary—that it feels like a monster."
- "Sometimes big brothers get very mad at babies for taking all the attention, and they wish a monster would come and eat them—but then they think, with mean thoughts like that, maybe the monster will eat *me*."

The transference behavior of anxious children often reveals the object relations driving their fears and suggests what types of help they need (Gardner, 1993; Glickauf-Hughes & Wells, 2006). When are they more afraid of you, and when less afraid? What are they scared you might do (e.g., hit, be disappointed, reject them)? Is their fear based on a belief about themselves (e.g., their needs are annoying), a belief about others (e.g., adults do not care about children), or some interaction between the two? For instance, a child who needs to be competent in all situations might live in constant anxiety that others will see through her veneer of perfection. An appropriate interpretation for such a child might be:

"You get so nervous whenever you make a mistake or mess something up, it's like you think you have to be perfect all the time or I won't like you."

For relatively mature and high-functioning clients, the achievement of insight usually leads to resolution of symptoms, with little additional input needed from the therapist. However, in child therapy, insight is frequently not enough, and therapists often need to help clients understand and cope with the life problems that underlie their symptoms.

Psychodynamic work with anxious children sometimes reveals that the client's fears of his own anger lie at the root of his anxiety symptoms (Chethik, 2000; Gardner, 1993). Children are sometimes afraid their anger will harm the person toward whom it is directed. Some children feel that being mad at someone they love means they are bad. Each of these fears can be treated by helping the client develop a more accurate view of this emotion—for instance:

"When your anger is boiling inside, it feels so strong that you think it might hurt your little sister. But that's not really true, because as long as you control what you do, your feelings stay inside you and don't touch anyone."

In dynamic therapy, the client-therapist relationship is the forum in which corrective emotional experiences take place. The objective is to make your relationship with the client a living, breathing refutation of his anxiety-laden misunderstandings of other people. This may require more than exhibiting generally therapeutic qualities, such as warmth, respect, and so forth. Your behavior should contain good news about possible human relationships, and this news should be *specific*; it should address each client's expectations and fears.

The objective is to make your relationship with the client a living, breathing refutation of his anxious misunderstandings and fears of other people.

Children who are anxious about expressing anger usually have difficulty expressing this emotion toward their therapist (Cashdan, 1988; Winnicott, 1971). These children may present as extremely compliant and eager to please. You will probably learn about their anger by indirect means, perhaps when it leaks out in their play behavior or when the parent reports it to you. When this occurs, it is often useful to bring the issue up, because if you wait for the child to do so you might wait a long time, and the occurrence of a situation the child fears is an opportunity for new learning.

To help clients learn to deal with anger in a relationship, therapists should model an empathic, constructive attitude about this emotion. We should make sure not to tiptoe around the issue and should bring it up in a forthright manner, softened by a warm, cheerful tone of voice—for example:

> "Your mom told me what you said driving home after our last session . . . . Eek [empathic facial expression] ... Look, you're not busted, because you're allowed to be mad at me. I just want to take a look at this, because maybe we'll learn something, and you'll end up feeling better. I'm sure there was a reason, so, what were you mad at me about?"

From an object relations perspective, this intervention would convey to the client that, even when she gets angry: (a) she is neither dangerous nor reprehensible, (b) other people are neither fragile nor vengeful, and (c) honest talk about anger can manage the problem. From a cognitive perspective, the intervention decatastrophizes the experience of anger. From a behavioral perspective, it is an exposure procedure.

Magical Solutions for Magical Problems

Although classic dynamic practice focuses on in-session activities, psychodynamic ideas can also be used to design interventions for parents to implement in the client's everyday environment. In work with young children, therapists can treat problems based on magical thinking with interventions that are also based on magical thinking. Such interventions might resolve symptoms in a symbolic fashion and, in so doing, might also address the life problems underlying the symptoms. I know of no EBPs for the early childhood fears discussed ahead, so we have no alternative to clinical reasoning as a source of guidance for battling these ghosts, witches, and monsters. In my experience, these interventions sometimes work like a charm and sometimes do not work at all.

In the magical thinking of young children, emotional forces and meanings travel, interact, and produce their effects in ways that are oblivious to the laws of logic and physics (Fraiberg, 1959/1992; A. Freud, 1946b; Gardner, 1993). As one category of example, young children often imbue inanimate objects with qualities such as comfort and power, and therapists can sometimes figure out ways to harness these potential sources of help. Counselors can sometimes engender a magically therapeutic thought process by asking the child how he could summon and direct the power of his action figures, stuffed animals, or equivalent talismans to defeat the awful forces he imagines are arrayed against him. One boy who had been frightened of his bathroom at night solved the problem by placing the right figures in the right positions on the floor to destroy any monsters that intruded. The tiny size of his toy soldiers was not a problem: "They'll shoot the monsters through their feet." Another boy turned his protective figures toward his bedroom window, so their power would repel any ghost that tried to come in.

Therapists cannot think of these strategies—the client must create the magic that makes sense to her. We can, however, galvanize a therapeutic collaboration by suspending our own logical thinking, reigniting the imaginative, dreamy thought process we all had as young children, asking the right questions, and rolling with the mysterious spirit of this type of problem solving. It is a mental shifting of gears. Questions with which to start include, "Who is really strong?" and then, "How could they help you with this?"

Artwork can sometimes be used in a symbolic fashion with magical power for young clients. In therapy for separation anxiety, for example, counselors can guide clients to find visual metaphors for staying emotionally connected to parents while being physically apart. One child drew a rainbow connecting herself and her mother. Children can draw words moving across bridges and loving feelings travelling through the air like telephone calls. As rational adults, we would say these metaphors symbolically *depict* solutions, but to young children, this type of artwork can magically *create* solutions.

Swearing at the monsters is a technique that may be appropriate when the child's fears involve a sense of herself as small and weak in relation to outside forces that are large and cruel. This technique transforms fear into anger, turns the aggression toward the fantasy figures that have intimidated the client, and empowers her by demonstrating that she can do this without suffering retaliation.

The therapist, the parent, or both can conduct the intervention. The adult tells the client, in a serious voice, that these ghosts/monsters/witches are horrible, because they have been terrifying the child for no good reason, so they deserve to receive the child's full anger in raw form, with no holds barred, including swearing. The adult then gives the child formal permission to call the monsters anything she wants. Some children also benefit from expressing their anger physically by hitting the imagined monster or drawing a picture of it and then tearing the picture up. (Some children gleefully put these pictures through the office paper shredder.) If the child expresses fear of retaliation, the adult can say that he is responsible for the swearing and/or destruction because it was his idea.

This is a funny intervention, for several reasons. The release of the usual inhibition against swearing in front of adults sometimes imparts a giddy quality to the procedure. The adult must make sure to keep a straight face as the child calls the monsters, for example, "doody-face," "toilet-head," and so forth. Finally, humor derives from the child's awareness that the adult is encouraging him to treat as real something that, on some level, he knows is not.

In some magical way, this intervention sometimes restores a healthy balance of power between the child and his troublesome emotions (symbolized by the monsters). When fear is transformed into anger, the result is sometimes a more confident sense of self. Although no child would articulate this, some seem to feel that by extravagantly dissing the monsters and getting away with it, they have achieved some dominance and control over the angry, ugly feelings that only the therapist knows are the real monster.

Monster spray is the basis of a simple intervention for young children whose fears have a definite physical location, such as their bedroom; this is typically the case for nighttime fears. The parent performs the intervention. "Monster spray" is water with some food coloring in a plastic spray bottle. The parent says to the child, in a grave, purposeful tone, that she has had it with the monsters, and she has obtained some magical spray that repels and/or kills them. The parent then asks the child to indicate the places where the monsters might come. Parents should embellish the activity of spraying by following the child's lead in expressing emotions—for instance, confidence in safety (e.g., "No ghost will come anywhere *near* here, now") or angry triumph (e.g., "Ha! This spray will kill any witch that tries to come in your room").

Making friends with the monsters (Chethik, 2000) is a counterintuitive approach that makes sense only in the realm of primitive, magical thinking but, for some clients, makes wonderful sense in this realm. The counselor introduces the strange idea that maybe the monsters are not so bad, and maybe they would even become nice if the child tried to make friends with them. It may be useful to flesh out this fantasy-based problem solving by enacting it in drawings or in scenes with dolls, puppets, or just an empty chair where the witch sits while the client offers her a cup of tea. The most important work might be done at home in the feared situation (typically in bed at night), as the child reaches out in fantasy friendliness to his fantasy fear and, in so doing, sometimes tames the monstrous emotions that have been terrorizing him. On a symbolic level, this technique might make peace between the child's angry impulses and her conscious sense of self (Chethik, 2000).

How should a therapist decide which of these magically oriented interventions to try? Client answers to the following question might provide a hint:

> "If you could say (or do) anything you wanted to the ghost, and he couldn't do anything back, what would you like to say (or do)?"

If the child's response hints at a need to tell the monsters off, a wish never to see them again, or a desire to reconcile with the monsters, then the appropriate treatment technique is apparent. Often, however, there is no way to know in advance what the client needs to accomplish, psychologically. Trial and error may produce useful results. It is not usually necessary to implement the entire technique to assess whether the child resonates with it. The child's initial response to suggestions to spray, swear at, or make friends with the monsters may provide a sense of whether these ideas make emotional sense to her.

Parent-Child Work

Counselors should help parents understand the negative effects of overprotecting anxiety-prone children (Barrett, Dadds, et al., 1996; Chorpita & Barlow, 1998; Hudson & Rapee, 2001; Kagan & Snidman, 2004). The quandary for parents is that they want to comfort their child when she is frightened but, from an operant learning perspective, soothing an anxious child is reinforcing her anxious behavior. The issue here is a version of the one facing parents of noncompliant children whose deficient self-regulation skills cause them to become overwhelmed with negative emotion when limits are set on their behavior, as discussed in Chapters 10 and 11. In both cases, parents and therapists need to ascertain the degree to which the child's problematic behavior is due to inadequate self-regulatory capabilities versus the degree to which the behavior is potentially under the child's control and so could respond to environmental cues and reinforcement. The objective is to push for a degree of self-management that is greater than the child's current level but within her capabilities, so the child stretches and tries but is not overwhelmed with anxiety. This determination cannot be made on the basis of a single discussion in the office. It is necessary to assess patterns in the child's responses to different parental actions and to conduct brief experiments to see how the child does.

Overprotection is not so much a bad thing as too much of a good thing; this is a two-sided issue that can be represented on a spectrum with maladaptive parenting at both extremes and optimal parenting in the mid-range of the continuum. Therapists can use the spectrum/moderation procedure to acknowledge the legitimacy of the parent's previous way of protecting the child, point out the advantages of the alternative, and help the parent conceptualize and develop protective behaviors that strike an adaptive balance.

In a combination of systemic and behavior therapy, counselors can have parents observe exposure trials and practice withholding rescue. This is a double exposure procedure: one for the child and one for the parent. The parent faces a frightening situation—seeing his child experience anxiety—and he has the task of resisting the behavior that has reliably brought relief before. The therapeutic message is that, painful though it might be, sometimes the most loving and helpful thing a parent can do is to leave his child in a stressful situation so she can learn to tolerate anxiety and deal with challenges on her own.

There is one additional note to make about a small proportion of cases of separation anxiety. Clinically, it seems there are some parents who are themselves uncomfortable with the child's growing independence, and who feel happiest and most needed when the child clings firmly to them. Such children may develop separation anxiety because their parent has conveyed to them that separation is a terrible thing. In such cases, it is crucial to address the parent's own distress about her child's growing autonomy.

The Hansel and Gretel Technique for Separation Anxiety

The technique described next is appropriate for children between 3 and 9 years of age whose separation anxiety is not fueled by parental discomfort with separation. The procedure consists of building a type of symbolic umbilical cord between the parent and child. The technique is peppered with humorous drama and exaggeration so that it becomes silly and fun. It can usually be completed in three sessions. A mini-manual follows.

Phase I: The Secret Password and the Trial Separation. Following an explanation to the parents, the intervention begins in the waiting room. Children with separation anxiety often glue themselves to their parents, so the therapist's first challenge is to get the client into the therapy room without the parent. The therapist's first statement to the child takes the following form:

> "Sally, I see that it is very, very important that you know where your mother is at all times. So, I have an idea: How about coming up with a *password* or signal that lets me know it is time to check on Mom. (If the child does not suggest one, the therapist will.) Let's say, 'ice cream.' When you say 'ice cream,' both of us will stop whatever we're doing and RUN, not walk, but RUN to check and see that Mom is still here and is okay."

The child is encouraged to practice by stepping inside the office for "only one second, no more" to test the password and make sure it works. The game is repeated several times, with encouragement to wait a little longer each time. After several trials, the therapist will usually sense that the child is secure about his ability to control reunions with his mother, and an invitation to explore the toys in the office is now possible.

Phase II: Long-Distance Separation and the Trail of Crumbs. Next, the therapist proposes a new game that involves making a literal trail between the child and mother. Using poker chips, pennies, or Lego pieces, the therapist invites the child to lay a trail beginning at the mother's feet and leading to the therapy room. The mother is instructed to find the therapist and the child using the trail, and then the roles are reversed, and the child tracks down the parent using the same procedure.

The distance between the child and parent is progressively lengthened, and the parent and child take turns laying the trail and finding each other. Eventually, you might have to explain to the neighbors in your building why there are trails of Legos leading through the halls and up the stairs. With each reunion, the therapist should echo the child's delight and relief.

Phase III: Tracking With Maps. By this time, the physical trail of items has been extended to the limits of the building. The therapist then initiates the next step:

> "I have another idea! How about making a *map* of the playroom and waiting room and halls, and we'll show Mom how to find us by looking at the map. Here, let's make a square for the office. Where would the door be?"

The therapist helps the child construct a simple map and indicate with an "X" where he and the therapist will wait for the parent to find them. Different floors can be shown as separate rectangles labeled with their numbers. Room numbers can be included. The child draws trails with arrows indicating the direction the mother should take. The parent is given the map, and the therapist and child run off to hide. Then, the game is extended to stores and other locations on the block. At this point, statements like the following summarize the child's therapeutic movement and help to solidify these changes:

> "When you first came to see me, you didn't know that you could figure stuff out so well and that your mom always knows where to find you, so there don't have to be worries. I used to see a scared, nervous Sally, but now I see a strong, happy Sally who is enjoying herself and learning that, no matter where she is or where Mom is, they always get back together."

At this point, the therapist should suggest that whenever the child goes to a friend's house or the mother goes somewhere on her own, they can exchange maps of where they are, with arrows showing how they would get from one place to the other. (These need not be precise.) One 7-year-old boy was able to tolerate his parents' vacation by tracking their whereabouts on a map with his babysitter. The parents called daily to update him on their itinerary, and he dutifully marked their location on the map, knowing that the trail would eventually lead back home.

Children do not need these physical aids for long, and the maps, like the previous passwords and trails, should be faded out as the client learns to do without them. This process may take a few months, and its endpoint sometimes comes after therapy has been terminated. In time, these concrete props are usually replaced by an internal sense of secure attachment.

The Hansel and Gretel technique seems to involve change processes from several theoretical orientations. From a behavioral perspective, the core of the technique is gradual exposure. The procedure involves meeting the child halfway by giving her some of what she wants before asking her to change, as suggested in Chapter 8. The technique has a psychodynamic quality, although there is no interpretation or insight, because it operates in magical terms that are meaningful to young children but divorced from adult rationality. From this perspective, the technique is a symbolic enactment of separation and attachment issues and their resolution.

Summary

In the paradigmatic experiment on avoidance learning, an animal receives an electric shock in one area of his chamber; he learns to spend all his time in the safe areas where shock does not occur; and, when the contingency changes and the current is turned off, the animal never returns to the shock-associated area of the chamber again. In the behavioral conceptualization of the etiology of anxiety disorders, the person has a painful experience in a particular type of situation; she learns to avoid all situations of this type, with immediate anxiety reduction as the reinforcer; and she remains afraid and avoidant indefinitely because the experiences that would show her the situation has changed cannot occur. Even if the initial experience was only mildly distressing, the avoidance learning mechanism can generate its own momentum and result in an anxiety problem grossly disproportionate to the distress that set the process in motion.

If the animal is dragged into the previously painful area of the chamber, he will exhibit a surge of distress, discover that the contingency has changed, and learn to relax in the area that, formerly, he had feared and avoided. If an anxious person faces the situation she fears, and she has enough courage and support to remain in this situation for a period of time, she will experience a surge of anxiety and then her fear will dissipate, as she achieves mastery over the previously frightening situation. The behavioral technique called exposure is the therapeutic analogue of dragging an animal into the area of the chamber that he fears. Exposure produces adaptive relearning and, therefore, is the key component of anxiety treatment for most clients.

A variety of facilitative strategies may be useful for preparing clients to face their fears. These techniques include relaxation training, modeling, self-instruction, cognitive restructuring, and social skills training.

In cognitive restructuring, clients tabulate personal data to assess the accuracy of their predictions. With these data, counselors can help clients discern consistent relationships between their fears and external reality. As clients learn about the lenses through which they perceive the world, they can develop personal correction factors to compensate for biases in these lenses. This type of self-knowledge might reduce feelings of anxiety and, if not, provide a basis for overriding gut impulses in choosing behaviors. The better we know ourselves, the more accurately we can perceive the world.

Therapy for anxiety, like treatment for externalizing problems, should include both soft and hard aspects, with their proportioning based on the client's needs. Parents should provide support and comfort to reduce the child's distress, but they should also gently push the youth to persist in anxiety-producing situations so more self-sufficiency can develop.

Therapy outcome studies on child and adolescent anxiety provide strong support only for cognitive-behavioral interventions. Psychodynamic therapy has received substantial support as a treatment for adults, so it warrants consideration for children who do not respond to CBT.

According to dynamic theory, the many different fears exhibited by anxious children typically trace back to a small number of unconscious issues, including the child's anxiety about her own impulses and object relations involving danger and insecurity. Dynamic therapists treat anxiety disturbances by attempting to uncover and resolve the real-life issues that underlie anxiety's various manifestations. It is also sometimes possible to address fantasy fears on their own magical terms by implementing interventions that, in some symbolic way, seem to resolve underlying emotional issues without ever bringing them to the client's conscious attention.

Case Study

Jeff's therapy consisted of straightforward application of cognitive-behavioral techniques. Initially, there was a good deal of reality to his fears of rejection by peers. The development of Jeff's social skills had been delayed by years of avoiding peer interaction, and he needed training in conversation and friendship initiation. The therapist suggested that Jeff find a social setting in addition to school where he could build peer relationships, and he found a church youth group that fulfilled this function.

When clients practice social skills in their natural environments, the outcomes are inconsistent because, no matter how ably they interact, peers sometimes respond negatively. Jeff's therapist managed this unpredictability by helping his client develop a constructive view of both types of outcomes. Positive peer responses were naturally reinforcing and so needed no reframing. For negative outcomes, the counselor provided an explanation of exposure, emphasized its necessity to the process of overcoming fears, and framed unfriendly peer responses as irreplaceable opportunities for Jeff to practice coping with rejection. Jeff disliked these experiences, of course, but he learned to cope with them by means of adaptive self-statements.

Jeff never became popular, but he made friends with a few boys who were on the shy, quiet side like he was, and these peer relationships provided some sense of belonging. The threat of rejection lost most of its sting, and by the conclusion of therapy, Jeff no longer experienced his social world as a hurtful, frightening place.

14

Depression

OBJECTIVES

This chapter explains:

- *How people's causal attributions for events influence their emotional reactions and self-esteem.*
- *How self-blame can be adaptive.*
- *Assessment and management of suicidal clients.*
- *The intervention of behavioral activation.*
- *How to help clients assess the evidence for and against their beliefs about themselves.*
- *How to reduce self-blame by increasing clients' awareness of the obstacles they have faced.*
- *The relationship between self-esteem and values.*
- *What to do if reason and evidence have no effect on client self-criticisms.*

Case Study
Secrets

Terriana, a 15-year-old European American girl, was brought to therapy by her mother and stepfather because "she's so unhappy." The parents said their daughter was "mopey" most of the time. She became frustrated easily and often, with temper outbursts when she was told to do something (e.g., homework) and, especially, when she was reprimanded. She spent a lot of time alone in her room watching TV, listening to music, and playing computer games. Terriana talked about hating herself and hating her life, saying things like "I'm a loser," and "I hate when people tell me to have a good day, because I never have a good day."

The parents described deterioration in Terriana's mood during the past several years, with no particular event seeming responsible for this. Her academic performance and peer relationships were unremarkable. The counselor made a diagnosis of persistent depressive disorder.

Terriana's parents divorced when she was 8 years old. The mother and stepfather said her relationship with her father was not close, and he was unreliable about spending time with her, but she seemed happy to see him when he came, and the relationship seemed to be positive for her. She got along "okay" with her stepfather and two younger half-brothers, who were offspring of the mother and stepfather.

The parents described a warm family life, with time spent together in enjoyable activities, such as picnics and board games. They could not understand where Terriana's self-derogating statements came from, because they considered her "a good kid," and they said they expressed this view of her frequently. The parents saw her misbehaviors as minor and typical of teenagers, and they viewed her distress about mild disciplinary consequences as over-reactions.

Terriana presented as a quiet, shy girl with an apologetic manner. Initially, it was difficult for the clinician to establish rapport with her and, while Terriana was cooperative, questions about her unhappiness received superficial answers that did not seem to explain anything. Terriana drew well, and she seemed better able to express herself in pictures than words.

Diagnoses Treated in This Chapter

Major Depressive Disorder

Major depressive disorder is the acute, severe form of depression. Its hallmark is depressed, sad mood that fills most of the day, nearly every day, for a 2-week period. In children, depression sometimes manifests itself as anger and irritability, so these emotions justify the diagnosis in children. The diagnosis requires **anhedonia**: a lack of enjoyment of activities that are usually considered pleasant. Associated symptoms include disturbed eating and sleeping, psychomotor agitation or retardation, lethargy, somatic complaints, poor self-concept, indecisiveness, difficulty concentrating, suicidal ideation, and suicide attempts.

Persistent Depressive Disorder

This diagnosis is distinguished by its duration, not its intensity. If major depressive disorder lasts for more than a year, this diagnosis should be added. (The client would then have two depression diagnoses.) The first criterion is the presence of depressed or angry/irritable mood for most of the day, during most days, for at least a year. The associated symptoms are mostly the same as those for major depressive disorder, except that anhedonia, suicidal ideation, and suicide attempts are not included, and fewer associated symptoms are required for the diagnosis. The diagnosis requires clinically significant distress and/or functional impairment in school, work, or social relationships.

Disruptive Mood Dysregulation Disorder

This diagnosis, which is new to DSM-5, represents full recognition that depression in children can manifest itself as anger and irritability; sadness is not part of the definition of this disorder. The diagnosis is defined by severe, recurrent temper outbursts that are manifested either verbally or physically and are grossly out of proportion to whatever frustrating event occurred. The child's mood between outbursts is usually angry and/or irritable, too. These criteria must be met in more than one setting. The symptoms must appear by age 10, although the diagnosis cannot be made before the child is 6 years old. The diagnosis cannot be made along with a diagnosis of ODD; if both sets of symptoms are present, only disruptive mood dysregulation disorder should be noted.

Adjustment Disorder With Depressed Mood

This diagnosis is not a true mood disorder like those just described, but it has enough features in common with them to justify inclusion in this chapter. The diagnosis requires only the presence of depressed mood and functional impairment; no associated features need be present.

Clinical Presentation and Etiology

This is the second chapter of this book's three-chapter sequence on internalizing dysfunction. These chapters describe related disorders and techniques that often apply across the three categories of disturbance.

The prototypical feeling of depression is sadness. This feeling is the hallmark of depression in adolescents and adults, but in children the emotional picture is more complicated, because children sometimes do not experience sadness in its mature form even when they feel dysphoric. In children, negative emotion frequently takes the forms of irritability and anger (and anxiety, but that has its own diagnostic category). Fifty years ago, the prevalent view was that depression was rare or nonexistent in children. Currently, the same set of observations has been reinterpreted to mean that depression manifests itself differently in children than in adolescents and adults.

The symptoms of depression, like anxiety, can be divided into the four dimensions of emotion, physiology, thoughts, and behavior, as shown in Table 14.1.

Research on emotion has found that that the presence of negative affect and the absence of positive affect are not two sides of the same coin but are separate, statistically independent emotional problems (Clark & Watson, 1991; Rothbart & Posner, 2006). Anhedonia—the absence of positive emotion—is a distinctive feature of depression that differentiates it from other emotional disturbances such as anxiety, in which both negative and positive emotions are present (Chorpita, Daleiden, Moffitt, Yim, & Umemoto, 2000; Lambert, McCreary, Joiner, Schmidt, & Ialongo, 2004). Depressed children do not show the same enthusiasm for play and activities that other children do. Although depression

---

Table 14.1   Four Dimensions of Depression

1. *Emotion:* Depression involves both the presence of negative feelings and the absence of positive feelings, with sadness common in adolescents, irritability common in younger children, and guilt, shame, and loneliness as frequent concomitants.

2. *Physiology:* Depression can involve either lethargy or agitation, insomnia or excessive sleeping, and overeating or loss of appetite.

3. *Cognition:* Depressive cognition is marked by pessimistic, self-blaming distortions of the self, world, and future, and by causal explanations for events that result in low self-esteem and hopelessness.

4. *Behavior:* Depressive behavior is usually marked by low energy, passivity, apathy, and withdrawal, although agitated behavior may also occur.

and anxiety are different emotional states, they frequently co-occur in the same people (Masi et al., 2003).

Depression is the disturbance most closely associated with low self-esteem (A. Beck & Alford, 2009; Kashani & Sherman, 1988). Depressed people often suffer from feelings of worthlessness and inferiority, guilt, shame, and even self-hatred.

Like most disorders, depression tends to run in families. Studies of adults report heritability estimates of around .4, with more variance accounted for by environmental factors than genetics (Lau & Eley, 2010). Genetic factors seem to play a somewhat less important role in unipolar depression than in many other disorders, and associations between parent and child depression are primarily attributable to shared family environment (Silberg, Maes, & Eaves, 2010).

Historically, depression has been considered much less common in childhood than adolescence and adulthood (American Academy of Child and Adolescent Psychiatry, 2007). The new diagnosis of disruptive mood regulation disorder will undoubtedly change the incidence statistics. Regardless, depression typically takes different forms at different ages (Avenevoli, Knight, Kessler, & Merikangas, 2008; Hammen, Rudolph, & Abaied, 2014). Childhood depression is often expressed as irritability, anger, and also vague somatic complaints (e.g., stomachache and headache) that do not have an identifiable medical cause. In adolescence, depression more frequently takes the form of sad feelings, self-derogating statements, and low energy, as it does in adulthood.

Until age 11, depression is equally common in boys and girls, but sex differences appear at early puberty, with girls' rates rising much faster than boys' rates, and adult females exhibiting twice the frequency of depressive disorders as adult males (Kessler et al., 2012; Merikangas et al., 2010). This pattern does not suggest a higher incidence of general psychopathology in females, because male rates of externalizing disorders are much higher than female rates.

Neurobiological Etiologies

Neuroscientific research on depression has focused on the functioning of neurotransmitters, especially serotonin and also dopamine. The most prominent neurobiological theory of depression states that this disturbance is caused by low levels of serotonin activity at the synapses of neurons that regulate mood, activity, motivation, and response to reward (Hasler, 2010; Maletic et al., 2007). This is not apparently due to low serotonin production but to inefficient functioning of serotonin receptors and abnormal transport of this neurotransmitter, especially in major depressive disorder. The most compelling evidence for this theory is that medicines that increase levels of serotonin at synapses reliably reduce depression (Preskorn, Ross, & Stanga, 2004). Selective serotonin reuptake inhibitors (SSRIs) block the reuptake of serotonin from the spaces between neurons, resulting in its accumulation at synapses. This accumulation results in more frequent firing of adjacent neurons.

Depressed individuals exhibit dysfunction of the hippocampus, a brain structure involved in the transfer of information from short-term to long-term memory and regulation of the hypothalamic-pituitary-adrenocortical (HPA) axis, which governs responses to stress. In depressed people, the hippocampus is reduced in volume (Hulvershorn, Cullen, & Anand, 2011). Small size of the hippocampus is also associated with high levels of early life adversity (Rao et al., 2010). Reduced hippocampal volume contributes to dysregulation of the HPA axis, resulting in chronically elevated cortisol levels, which, in turn, impair the functioning of a number of systems throughout the body (Guerry & Hastings, 2011; MacQueen & Frodl, 2011).

Below the technical details of research findings, the neuroscientific perspective, applied to depression, means that this disturbance sometimes begins as a biological condition. Sometimes brains and bodies just feel sad. There might be no other cause. This brain-state produces sad feelings and depressive thoughts, but these mental contents are not necessarily the cause of the brain-state, although they might feed back into it. Therapists can offer this idea to clients and parents if the assessment does not indicate other etiological factors and suggests that neurobiological factors play an important role in the depression.

Behavioral Etiologies

Depressed behavior is usually characterized by a low overall rate of activity (although the pendulum sometimes swings to the other extreme in agitated depression and bipolar disorder). Apathy, passivity, and lethargy are common features of depression. Depressed youth often spend much of their time in their rooms, and depression is associated with extensive television watching. From an operant perspective, this low activity level can be explained as the result of a low rate of positive reinforcement (Kanter, Busch, & Rusch, 2009; Stark, Ostrander, Kurowski, Swearer, & Bowen, 1995).

Depressed individuals' avoidance of social activities and challenging situations play an important role in their low rate of positive reinforcement, because one cannot receive rewards in situations one does not enter (Dimidjian, Barrera, Martell, Muñoz, & Lewinsohn, 2011; Manos, Kanter, & Busch, 2010). Longitudinal research has documented that avoidance plays a significant role in the maintenance of depression (Carvalho & Hopko, 2011). Avoidance is similar but not identical in anxiety and depression: Anxious individuals avoid situations they associate with threat, and depressed people avoid situations they associate with failure.

From an operant perspective, the low activity level characteristic of depression can be explained as the result of a low rate of positive reinforcement.

Depressed children have social skills deficits that result in unpopularity and loneliness (Lewinsohn, 1974; Prinstein et al., 2005; Shih et al., 2009). Depressed mood is itself a social liability, because it brings other people down. Depressed children's irritability, reassurance seeking, unassertiveness, dependency, and lack of friendship initiation skills cause other youngsters to perceive them as unappealing and to avoid them. When depressed children perceive themselves as socially incompetent and have pessimistic expectations for their peer relationships, this might be a matter of cognitive distortion, but it might also be a function of real skill deficits.

Cognitive Etiologies

Historically, cognitive therapy has been closely associated with treatment for depression. The "depressive triad" consists of negative views of the self, world, and future (A. Beck, 1967, 1976; A. Beck & Alford, 2009). Depressed people interpret the events that happen to them in self-critical, pessimistic, and, well, depressing ways. Their interpretations tend to distort the meaning of events in a negative direction, so they experience disappointment and a sense of failure in situations that other people would not find depressing (Maalouf &

Brent, 2012). Depressed youth selectively attend to negative stimuli and events (Maalouf et al., 2011). They underestimate their competence, compared to objective ratings (Brendgen, Vitaro, Turgeon, & Poulin, 2002). As a result, given identical performances, depressed youth typically believe they performed relatively poorly, while nondepressed youth believe they performed well.

Dysfunctional beliefs do not seem to produce depression on their own but by interacting with stressful events (Abela & Skitch, 2007; Hankin, Abramson, Miller, & Haeffel, 2004). In other words, if nothing bad happens, these beliefs do not show strong effects on mood. However, when negative events occur, dysfunctional beliefs result in more severe implications for self-concept and anticipations of the future (Abela, 2001, 2002). The relationship between depressive cognition and symptoms seems to be reciprocal: Dysphoric mood leads to depressive cognition, and cognition affects mood (LaGrange et al., 2011.)

Ginsburg et al. (2009) factor analyzed several self-report questionnaires assessing depression-relevant cognitions frequently employed in clinical research with adolescents. They identified four main factors: (1) Cognitive distortions and maladaptive beliefs, (2) cognitive avoidance, (3) (low) positive outlook, and (4) (low) solution-focused thinking. Thus, this study obtained evidence that etiological factors emphasized by cognitive therapy, ACT, and solution-focused therapy play roles in adolescent depression.

Attribution theory, an area of research in social-cognitive psychology, has produced important insights about how depressed people think about the events in their lives. To **attribute** means to explain or, more precisely, to assign a cause to an event. The causes we assign to events make a big difference to both emotional reactions and future expectations. For instance, if a student attributes her score of 90% on a test to good luck or an easy exam, she will not feel much pride in her performance, nor will she expect to do particularly well on tests in the future. If a student attributes the same score of 90% to his intelligence and the effort he put into studying, he will probably feel proud of himself and optimistic about his future performance.

When depressed people experience negative events, they tend to attribute these outcomes to internal, global, stable factors, while nondepressed people attribute their negative events to external, specific, unstable factors (Abela, 2001, 2002; Abramson, Seligman, & Teasdale, 1978; Nolen-Hoeksema, Girgus, & Seligman, 1992). The attributions made by depressed people result in self-derogation and pessimism. The attributions made by nondepressed people facilitate coping and optimism. Table 14.2 describes these three dimensions of attribution that play a role in depression.

Table 14.2   Depression and Three Dimensions of Attribution

1. Compared to nondepressives, depressed people attribute their failures more **internally** (to factors like low ability) and their successes more **externally** (to factors like luck and low task difficulty).

2. When negative events occur, nondepressed people make attributions to small, **specific** causes (e.g., being weak in algebra), while depressed individuals see their failures as caused by large, **global** causes (e.g., being unintelligent).

3. When negative events occur, nondepressed individuals make attributions to temporary, **unstable** factors (e.g., taking an unfair test), while depressed people attribute their failures to long-term, **stable** factors (e.g., being in a bad school).

Table 14.3   Differences Between Depressive and Coping Cognitions

Depressive Cognitions	Coping Cognitions
Stable attribution: "She turned me down because she doesn't like me."	*Unstable attribution:* "She turned me down because we just met and she doesn't know me yet."
Global attribution: "She said no because I'm unattractive, dumb, and boring."	*Specific attribution:* "She said no because I'm not good at being smooth with girls I don't know well."
Internal attribution: "She turned me down because I don't know how to talk to girls."	*External attribution:* "She turned me down because she's a snob."

Depressive attribution causes the normal ups and downs of life to produce low self-esteem and pessimistic expectations, even if the same set of outcomes would produce high self-esteem and optimistic expectations in someone with the opposite cognitive style. Consider the example of a 16-year-old boy who asks a girl out on a date, and she says no. Of course, this outcome would be disappointing to anyone, but whether it causes depression depends largely on attributions for the event, as illustrated in Table 14.3.

When depressed people experience negative events, they tend to attribute these outcomes to internal, global, stable factors, while nondepressed people attribute their negative events to external, specific, unstable factors.

Within the category of internal attribution for negative events, there is an important distinction between **characterological** self-blame—in which a negative event is attributed to a permanent trait of the self—and **behavioral** self-blame, in which a bad outcome is blamed on a specific behavior (Janoff-Bulman, 1979). This distinction mirrors the one between parental criticism of a child's personality and criticism of a child's behavior, as discussed in Chapter 1. Characterological self-blame causes guilt, low self-esteem, and depression, but behavioral self-blame can actually be adaptive. Attributing a negative outcome to a mistake or an ineffective strategy implies that there are ways to fix the problem and do better in the future, while attributing a negative event to a personal deficiency leads to helplessness, hopelessness, and self-derogation (Anderson & Arnoult, 1985; Tilghman-Osborne, Cole, Felton, & Ciesla, 2008).

Cognitive theory explains depressive self-criticism as the result of maladaptive cognitions learned from other people, either by observing models who derogate themselves or by internalizing negative messages about the self from others. Most learning is thought to occur in the context of relationships, and the media and society are thought to play a role as well (A. Beck, 1976; A. Beck & Alford, 2009; Ellis, 1962).

Psychodynamic Etiologies

Psychodynamic and cognitive theories emphasize some of the same processes in depression—namely, harsh standards of self-evaluation, bias against the self, and self-punishment. However, the two theories provide different explanations of why these processes occur.

Dynamic theory acknowledges that much depressive cognition results from the learning processes emphasized by cognitive theory but does not attribute all depressive cognition to these straightforward mechanisms. Clinically, there do seem to be children whose critical self-commentary cannot be traced to messages received from their social environment. For instance, Terriana's parents did not make global criticisms of their daughter and never called her anything like "a loser," but she frequently made this type of derogatory statement about herself.

Dynamic theory is concerned with the possibility that specific self-criticisms are the result of a deeper, nonspecific sense of guilt, inadequacy, or failure (Gray, 1994; Horowitz, 1998; Michels, 1982). When no external source of self-derogation is apparent, dynamic therapists explain negative thoughts about the self as the result of internal, unconscious dynamics. Because these dynamics involve developmentally primitive, emotion-dominated aspects of mind, they are capable of producing grossly unrealistic self-criticisms that have nothing to do with contemporary input from others. Adults, including therapists, might attempt to refute these self-criticisms with reason and evidence, and the youth might concede their points on any number of specific issues, but if her internalized sense of badness remains, she might generate self-criticisms faster than anyone can refute them. Experiences that damage a person's basic sense of self-worth might give rise to all sorts of self-criticisms, even if that experience is long past and/or irrelevant to the aspects of self currently subjected to derogation—unless that experience is consciously reexamined and reworked in a cognitively mature way.

Dynamic therapists are alert to the possibility that maladaptive defense mechanisms might lead to depressive symptoms. One example of this is called **anger turned inward** (Klein, 1932; Parens, 1993). In this process, the child feels enraged at her parent but is terribly uncomfortable with her anger because love and dependency are strongly present, too. The child is unable to stop feeling the emotion, but on an unconscious level the anger toward the parent is transformed into anger toward the self, as the lesser of two evils. This process could be verbalized as, "I feel so angry when I'm with my mother that I know one of us must be bad, and it can't be her, so it must be me." The key to understanding this mechanism is to realize that a positive image of a parental figure is sometimes more important to children than good self-esteem, because it might feel safer and better to be a bad child with a good parent than to be a good child with a bad parent.

Systemic Etiologies

The parents of depressed youth sometimes create family environments that result in depression. These parents provide their children with less social support (Stice, Ragan, & Randall, 2004), and their families engage in fewer recreational activities together (Stark, Humphrey, Crook, & Lewis, 1990), compared to the families of nondepressed youngsters.

Observational research has revealed more negative exchanges and fewer positive interactions between depressed children and their parents, compared to nondepressed children and theirs (Abaied & Rudolph, 2014). These interactions show patterns of reciprocal causality that cause progressive deterioration in the relationships over time. Depression in youth causes increased stress for parents and deterioration in family relationships (Lewinsohn, Rohde, Seeley, Klein, & Gotlib, 2003; Raposa, Hammen, & Brennan, 2011), while these youth perceive their parents to be less supportive and more harsh, hostile, and inconsistent over time (Kim, Conger, Elder, & Lorenz, 2003; Needham, 2007).

Stark's research on interactions between parents and their depressed children provides a bridge between the cognitive-behavioral and family systems approaches to depression (Stark, Banneyer, Wang, & Arora, 2012; Stark et al., 1995). Parents of depressed children often exhibit the same type of cognitive distortions as their children. These parents frequently have inappropriately high standards for performance that make it difficult for their children to perform at a level the parents consider successful, resulting in low frequencies of praise for performance. Thus, the cognitive factor of high performance standards in parents results in the behavioral process of low reinforcement rates for children.

Romantic breakups are frequent precipitants of depressive episodes in adolescents (Joyner & Udry, 2000). The relationship between depression and romantic disappointment is a reciprocal one: Depressed adolescents elicit high levels of partner dissatisfaction and stress in romantic relationships, and then, when rejection results, the depression worsens (Hankin, Mermelstein, & Roesch, 2007; Rao, Hammen, & Daley, 1999). However, families with low levels of conflict and high levels of support buffer young people against the depressogenic effects of romantic breakups (Steinberg & Davila, 2008).

Assessment

Behavioral observation provides important assessment information about depression. Depressed youth typically present with sad or flat affect, slow motor movement, and an air of weariness and unhappiness, without the animation and spontaneity associated with positive mood states. However, depressed children are not always visibly sad, and their depression is sometimes manifested in irritable, angry behavior that suggests a "bad mood."

DBT chain analysis (Linehan, 1993a, 1993b, 2014; Rathus & Miller, 2014), described in Chapter 4, is applicable to assessment of depression that is episodic, with marked increases and decreases. By tracking depressive episodes backward in time, precipitants can often be identified. The precipitants can then become targets of intervention. Solution-focused assessment inverts this inquiry by identifying variables that prevent, mitigate, or reverse the client's depression (de Shazer & Dolan, 2007; O'Hanlon & Weiner-Davis, 2003; Selekman, 2010). Chain analysis and solution-focused inquiry are less applicable to depression that is long-term and consistent over time, as in persistent depressive disorder.

Adolescents usually know the word "depressed," but young children might not, and even for teenagers this word might not be a natural way of referring to their dysphoric feelings. Clinicians should follow the client's lead in word choice. The everyday word for depressed is "sad". Because this word suggests a vulnerable quality, some youth, especially boys, feel more comfortable with words like "down," "bummed out," and "feeling crummy." The word "bored" is often used by depressed youngsters to describe their mood, particularly when the depression has an empty, apathetic quality. In the interview questions that follow, these synonyms can be substituted for the word "sad:"

- "What makes you sad?" "How much of the time do you feel sad?"
- "How sad do you feel?" (Older children can use scales from 0 to 10.) "Do you feel a little sad, pretty sad, or very sad?"
- "What goes through your mind when you're feeling down?" "What do you say to yourself when you're depressed?" (Assesses cognition)
- "What do you do when you're depressed?" (Measures symptom manifestations)
- "What do you do when you're sad to try to feel better?" (Assesses coping and defenses)
- "Would you feel less depressed if your life were different in some way?" (Assesses environmental factors and skill deficits)
- "Are you depressed more because of things you've done or more because of things that have happened to you?" (Examines guilt versus sense of misfortune)

- "What do people in your family do when you're depressed?" (Addresses systemic and reinforcement factors)
- "Do you know why you're depressed, or maybe you're not sure why you feel sad?" (Examines self-understanding and, possibly, dynamic and neurophysiological factors)
- "Do you like yourself?" "What do you like about yourself?" "What don't you like?" (Assesses self-esteem)

The interview should also include questions about activity level, eating, and sleeping. Versions of these questions can be asked of the child's parents.

Questions about attribution should be applied to the issues of concern to the youth. The basic questions of, "Why do you think that is?" and "Why did that happen?" should be applied to situations and events that seem involved in the client's depression. To differentiate within the category of internal attribution, ask: "What do you think it was *about* you that made that happen?" To differentiate between behavioral and characterological self-blame, ask: "Was it because of something you did, or was it just because of the way you are?"

Several types of evidence suggest a role for neurobiology in a client's depression. These include an early age of onset, a family history of depression suggesting a role for genetics, and prominent symptoms related to physiological functioning, including disturbances of activity level, sleeping, and eating. Also, an absence of environmental etiological factors suggests a role for neurobiology in the depression. Thus, if the child's depression emerged gradually without an apparent precipitating event, does not seem to wax and wane in response to events, occurs across situations, does not seem affected by changes in cognition or rate of positive reinforcement, and does not seem linked to family problems or unconscious dynamics, the possibility of neurobiological etiology is supported.

Treatment Planning

Outcome Research

A narrative review by David-Ferdon and Kaslow (2008) applied standard criteria for research evidence to the outcome literature on youth depression and concluded that CBT is the only well-established intervention for this population. Nevertheless, outcome research on CBT for depression is not as unequivocally supportive as outcome research on CBT for anxiety. Because research on depression has included many more studies of CBT than alternative therapies, there have been many more findings supporting CBT, but when direct comparisons were made, the results did not generally indicate that CBT was superior to other active, bona fide treatments.

Outcome research on CBT for depression is not as unequivocally supportive as outcome research on CBT for anxiety. Cuijpers et al. (2013) performed a meta-analysis of 75 studies comparing CBT to a control condition for adult, depressed clients. The analysis yielded an average effect size of .71, which is in the medium/large range. However, there was evidence that publication bias inflated the estimate. Also, studies with low methodological quality produced larger effect sizes than higher-quality investigations, although these effect sizes were still in the medium range. The analysis found no differences between outcomes produced by CBT and by alternative, active therapies.

J. Klein, Jacobs, and Reineke (2007) performed a meta-analysis of 11 RCTS investigating CBT for depressed adolescents. They obtained a medium-sized average effect of .53, which supports the efficacy of CBT. However, the results exhibited a historical trend in which effect sizes were larger in early studies and have declined since. This trend did not seem attributable to historical change in the effectiveness of CBT but to change in the methodological quality of the outcome studies. Effect sizes were smaller when methodology was more rigorous—that is, when CBT was compared to active, bona find treatments rather than placebo controls, when the studies were conducted in clinical settings, and when intent-to-treat analyses controlled for the effects of dropout. These findings suggest that the average effect size might overestimate the real effectiveness of CBT.

Weisz, McCarty, and Valeri (2006) conducted a meta-analysis of 35 studies of psychotherapy for depressed children and adolescents. They obtained an overall effect size of .34, which is of small/medium magnitude. There was no difference between CBT and alternative therapies in their effects. Treatment gains were maintained in the short term but not the long term.

In the prominent investigation by the Treatment for Adolescents with Depression Study Team (TADS; 2004), clients who received CBT alone did not show more improvement than youth who received a pill placebo. TADS is one of several studies finding that CBT adds an increment of effectiveness to antidepressant medication: The combination of an antidepressant + CBT produced more improvement for participants than medication alone. In Brent et al.'s (2008) study of depressed youth who did not respond to an SSRI, the combination of a new medication + CBT resulted in better outcomes than the new medicine alone. In a study by Asarnow et al. (2009), the larger the number of comorbid diagnoses, the greater was the advantage of combined treatments over medication alone. In a study of young people who had successfully completed a 12-week trial of an antidepressant, medication management + CBT resulted in a lower relapse rate than medication management alone (Kennard et al., 2008).

Weisz et al. (2009) compared CBT to usual care for depressed clients aged 8–15 in a community clinical setting. Clients were randomly assigned to CBT or TAU. Clients who received either type of therapy demonstrated significant reductions in depression, and by the end of treatment three quarters of both groups no longer had a depressive disorder. There was no difference between the outcomes produced by CBT and TAU. However, CBT did outperform TAU in some ways. CBT was briefer, less expensive, and, following termination, associated with fewer additional services, including medication.

In research with adults, **behavioral activation** (therapist-directed increases in activity level) has received more support than any other single component of CBT for depression. According to APA's Society of Clinical Psychology, behavioral activation has *Strong Research Support* for this population. A meta-analysis by Mazzucchelli, Kane, and Rees (2009) compared behavioral activation to a variety of control conditions; they obtained a medium/large effect size of .78 for all depressed clients and .74 for clients with major depressive disorder. There was no difference in the outcomes produced by behavioral activation alone and behavioral activation plus other CBT techniques. In a meta-analysis by Ekers, Richards, and Gilbody (2008), behavioral activation produced larger reductions in depression than several active comparison therapies, with effect sizes in the medium to large range. Again, there was no difference between behavioral activation alone and this strategy plus other CBT techniques.

Research on stand-alone behavioral activation therapy for children and adolescents is just beginning to occur. Small-sample pilot studies by Jacob, Keeley, Ritschel, and

Craighead (2013) and Ritschel, Ramirez, Jones, and Craighead (2011) have produced encouraging results, suggesting that behavioral activation has similar effects on depression in youth and adults.

There is some evidence that augmenting individual CBT with parent-child work improves outcomes for depressed children. Eckshtain and Gaynor (2012) added caregiver-child sessions to individual CBT for a small sample of 8- to 14-year-old youth. This study did not have a control group, but comparisons were made with benchmark data from the CBT literature. The augmented therapy produced more reduction of depression than no-treatment and placebo controls, and equaled individual child CBT on some indices of change while outperforming it on others. A long-term follow-up study by the same authors (2013) found that the gains were maintained for 2–3 years.

Research on moderator or interaction effects has produced information about which clients receive more and less benefit from CBT. This type of therapy produced less positive outcomes for clients of low SES (Asarnow et al., 2009), youth from families with a high level of conflict (Feeny et al., 2009), youth whose parents were depressed (Asarnow et al., 2009), and clients with a history of abuse (Lewis et al., 2010).

Several studies have conducted mediation analyses of behavioral and cognitive interventions for depressed youth. Two studies found that reductions in depression were mediated by improved parent-child interactions (Gaynor & Harris, 2008; Riley & Gaynor, 2014). Three studies found that decreases in depression were mediated by increases in pleasant activities (Gaynor & Harris, 2008; Riley & Gaynor, 2014; Stice et al., 2010), but one study found no association between these activities and reduced depression (Kaufman et al., 2005). Two studies found that reductions in depressive symptoms were associated with the adaptive changes in attribution patterns predicted by cognitive theory (Jaycox et al., 1994; Yu & Seligman, 2002). Studies of nonattributional negative cognitions as mediators of change in depression have obtained some predicted results but a number of inconsistent findings (Ackerson et al., 1998; Kaufman et al., 2005; Stice et al., 2010). A review by Weisz et al. (2013) noted that, overall, there is some evidence for attributional style as a mediator of therapeutic effects but only mixed evidence for negative cognitions and pleasant activities as mediators.

L. Hayes, Boyd, and Sewell (2011) randomly assigned a small sample of depressed adolescents to receive either ACT or TAU at a psychiatric outpatient service. ACT produced larger reductions in depression, with a small/medium effect size of .38. Fifty-eight percent of the ACT clients demonstrated a clinically reliable degree of change, which was 1.58 times the rate of the control group.

APA rated psychodynamic therapy for depression in adults as having *Modest Research Support*. Trowell et al. (2007) compared psychodynamic and family systems therapy for depressed children and adolescents in England, Greece, and Finland. Both types of intervention produced substantial reductions in depression and comorbid conditions, with approximately three quarters of the clients no longer clinically depressed at therapy's conclusion. There were no differences in the outcomes produced by dynamic and family therapy. At a 6-month follow-up, gains were maintained for both groups, and none of the clients who received dynamic therapy were in the clinical range for depression, suggesting a sleeper effect.

Outcome research on *attachment-based family therapy* (ABFT; Diamond, 2014; Diamond et al., 2003, 2014) was reviewed in Chapter 7. Several studies have produced encouraging results for ABFT as a treatment for adolescent depression, suicidal ideation, and disrupted attachment relationships with parents.

Interpersonal psychotherapy for adolescents (IPT-A; Mufson, Dorta, Moreau, & Weissman, 2004, 2011) is a multicomponent treatment that includes cognitive-behavioral procedures and techniques drawn from other approaches. Mufson, Weissman, Moreau, and Garfinkel (1999) found that this intervention reduced depression and improved social functioning and problem-solving skills in depressed adolescents. A study in Taiwan by Tang, Jou, Ko, Huang, and Yen (2009) found that IPT-A produced larger reductions in depression than TAU. Rossello and Bernal (1999) compared CBT, IPT, and a wait-list control condition in a sample of depressed Puerto Rican adolescents. Both therapies produced reductions in depression. Rossello and Bernal (2005) found stronger results for CBT than IPT with this population.

Clinical Considerations

Because CBT has more supportive evidence than any other type of therapy, treatment planning for depression should begin with CBT. However, sometimes cognitive restructuring convinces clients that their thoughts are irrational and unrealistic but they continue to experience them, nonetheless. In such cases, one of which was Terriana's, psychodynamic work might help to break the logjam.

ACT is another alternative. When clients are unable to stop intrusive self-talk, sometimes the best available option is to learn to live with this unwanted mental activity, and ACT provides an array of techniques for doing so (Harris, 2013; Hayes et al., 2011; Murrell et al., 2004). Also, in my experience, ACT methods are more acceptable to clients *after* they have applied cognitive techniques to the thoughts that trouble them, because logical examination seems to be a necessary precondition for the radical change in attitude toward thoughts on which ACT is based. When clients believe their thoughts are true, therapist recommendations to picture and repeat these thoughts in caricatured forms might seem nonsensical and invalidating to clients. However, when clients believe their thoughts are not true but they cannot get rid of them, placing these thoughts in forms that undercut their power seems like the best available option, and ACT provides the way to do this.

Terriana's therapy illustrates several issues that make treatment planning complicated and difficult, but not impossible, if the counselor can follow the twists and turns of the course of therapy. In her first few sessions, this client connected feelings of depression and low self-esteem to criticism and reprimands from her parents, especially her stepfather. She described him as extremely angry with her when she misbehaved, and she practically trembled as she gave these accounts. She drew a picture of a large, enraged man towering over a small child cowering on the floor. Terriana did not portray her parents as unfair for correcting her, but blamed herself for what she described as cursedly stupid mistakes. When she described her everyday misbehaviors, she became upset, seized her hair in her hands, and said things like, "Why did I *do* that? I'm such an idiot."

The therapist's first hypothesis was that the parents disciplined Terriana in harsh, demeaning ways, and these put-downs had damaged her self-esteem. The parents never exhibited these behaviors in the office, but parents are often on their best behavior in this setting. However, the emotional quality of Terriana's accounts was incongruent with the parental behavior she herself reported. She described no physical punishment, and the parental statements she recounted, although upsetting to her, seemed ordinary to the clinician. For instance, beneath pictures of terrifying parental rebuke, she wrote words like, "That's it, go to your room," and "I'm going to think of a punishment for that one."

Thus, it seemed that Terriana misperceived appropriate discipline as crushing disapproval. And while oversensitive to criticism, she seemed insensitive to praise. The parents spoke quite positively about her to the counselor, and they said they frequently complimented her at home, but these positive statements were missing from the client's picture of her interactions with her parents. It seemed that something was preventing her from knowing the truth about the way her parents viewed her.

The counselor proposed bringing the parents into sessions so Terriana's impression of their views could be tested against direct evidence. However, Terriana reacted with extreme distress to this suggestion and would not explain why. The therapist suspected that the most important issues were not on the table. Because direct questioning had not produced a clear picture, some sessions were spent in unstructured conversation and drawing.

Special Topic: Suicide Risk

Suicidal ideation and behavior are not uniquely associated with depression, but they are more closely associated with depression than any other type of psychopathology, especially in adolescents (Cha & Nock, 2014). To severely depressed clients, suicide sometimes seems like the best available response to the emotional pain, self-hatred, and hopelessness they feel.

Evaluating the youth's level of depression is the first step in assessing his risk of suicide. However, factors other than depression also affect risk. The discussion and recommendations ahead borrow from Pfeffer (2003), Joiner (2005), Berman, Jobes, and Silverman (2006), and Gutierrez and Osman (2008).

A brief screening for suicidal ideation can be accomplished with the question, "Have you ever felt so sad that you kinda wished you were dead?" If the answer is no, and the child seems to be answering honestly, the screening is over. If the answer is yes, there should be further investigation. An answer of yes, by itself, does not necessarily indicate significant risk of harm, because many adolescents occasionally experience a fleeting wish to be dead (Nock et al., 2008). Although such thoughts might not represent a real self-destructive intention, they always warrant inquiry.

Further assessment should inquire about why the suicidal impulses occur, with questions about associated events, interpersonal interactions, and thoughts. It is vital to find out whether any self-harming behavior has already happened, because past behavior is the best predictor of future self-harming behavior. All attempts should be taken seriously, even if they had no potential lethality and seem naïve (e.g., taking a bottle of aspirin). Such attempts might represent "a cry for help" rather than a true attempt to die, but such cries can injure or kill youngsters regardless of whether this is their intention.

Questions about the meanings involved in the client's suicidal impulses are useful both for assessing risk and for planning therapy. Because hopelessness is a stronger predictor of suicide than is depression (J. M. Smith, Alloy, & Abramson, 2006; Wenzel & Beck, 2008), the child should be asked about possibilities for future change in her life. The feeling of being a burden on others is an even stronger predictor of suicide than hopelessness (Joiner et al., 2009), so clinicians should inquire about this issue. Counselors should ask clients what reactions from other people they would expect if they committed suicide, because self-destructive behavior is sometimes motivated by a desperate desire to elicit such reactions (e.g., "Then they would know how horribly they hurt me").

Protective factors should also be evaluated. People are less likely to attempt suicide when there are some positive areas in their lives, particularly close relationships. Traditional religious beliefs can be powerful disincentives for suicide, because this act is prohibited by mainstream religions. Sense of purpose, goals, and feeling needed by another person (e.g., a younger sibling) are protective factors. One way to learn about these factors is to ask the client what has prevented him from hurting himself when this impulse occurred in the past. ("What stopped you?" "How did you know you didn't really want to die?")

Inquiring about plans for future suicidal behavior is a critical part of the assessment. This is not a yes/no question; a vague intention to attempt suicide is less alarming than a specific, detailed, potentially lethal plan of action. Clinicians should investigate the client's thoughts about methods of self-harm and should evaluate whether these thoughts represent depressed ruminations or real consideration of different options.

Suicide assessment should include an interview with the child's parents or guardians. It is important to assess practical factors, such as the safety of the youth's home, particularly her access to potentially lethal materials, such as guns and narcotics, and the supervision capabilities of the caregivers.

Management of Suicide Risk

There is no clinical situation more difficult for therapists than caring for a suicidal client. Worry about handling the situation effectively and fear of being responsible for the death of a client are common even in seasoned clinicians. If you find yourself feeling panicky, preoccupied, or avoidant, the best response is usually to consult with a colleague or seek supervision on the case.

The biggest single decision is whether to initiate psychiatric hospitalization. This option has the major advantage of providing safety. Hospitalization also offers clinicians the relief of passing on responsibility for the client, at least for the time being, and this may be reassuring from a liability perspective.

Hospitalization also entails costs and disadvantages. This intervention is extremely expensive. Suicide risk exists at various levels among a significant proportion of the population, and if every adolescent who said he wished he was dead were hospitalized, the mental health system would be overwhelmed. Also, hospitalization can be traumatic and humiliating for young people. It removes youth from their everyday environments, and learning to feel better in a hospital may not transfer to everyday settings. This strategy provides no long-term solution because insurance usually pays only for brief stays, so the practical question is whether you think a week or so in a hospital would do much to change the factors responsible for the youth's suicide risk.

The complexities boil down to this: Psychiatric hospitalization for suicide risk seems appropriate only when the youth is in imminent danger of harming herself and there is no other strategy (e.g., close parental supervision) that seems capable of ensuring safety. The best policy is to do everything possible to minimize risk and to use hospitalization as a last resort, when there is no other way of preventing self-harm.

There are practical strategies short of hospitalization that can increase client safety. The parents should empty the home of as many potentially lethal objects and substances as possible, including guns, sharp knives, razor blades, dangerous medications, and toxic cleaning agents. There should be close supervision of the youngster at all times. If the client has not had a psychiatric evaluation for possible medication, a referral should be made.

Suicidal ideation calls for an immediate therapeutic response. The counselor's statements should be strong and clear. If you believe the client would feel supported if she knew you were genuinely concerned about her, then this is a time to be emotionally sincere, even intense. The goal is to achieve quick, substantial input into the youth's experience by conveying that she is a valuable person who is feeling suicidal not because her life is worthless but because she is extremely depressed, and the solution is not death but amelioration of depression—for instance:

"I'm really worried about you, Bob, because of this feeling that you want to die. I see how depressed you are, how awful you feel, and I understand that (... summarize what the client has said about his distress), but killing yourself is not the solution for any of that. The solution is for you, me, and your parents to roll up our sleeves and get to work at helping you feel better. We won't be able to do that if you're dead.

I've talked to other kids who have been just as depressed as you, who have felt like they wanted to die, but thankfully they didn't, and when they look back they are *glad* they gave themselves the chance to see that things can get better. You're a good kid who doesn't deserve to die. And it may be a cliché, but it's true: You've got your whole life ahead of you, so let's make an appointment for next week, and we'll get to work on some of these problems so your future will be better than your past."

Spirito and Esposito (2008; Spirito, Esposito-Smythers, Wolff, & Uhl, 2011) describe therapeutic strategies for preventing suicide in adolescents. Their approach received preliminary support in a pilot study (Donaldson, Spirito, & Esposito-Smythers, 2005). These therapists recommend asking clients to compose a "personal reasons to live" list, which should include at least five reasons (e.g., to see a younger sibling grow up, to start a family). They also recommend that the counselor and teen write a list of coping strategies that can be used in stressful situations, along with phone numbers of people to contact in an emergency. These contingency plans should be summarized on a small card placed in the client's wallet so it is available at all times.

Therapists should make a written contract with suicidal clients in which the youth promises not to hurt herself (Figure 14.1). The contract should cover the longest period

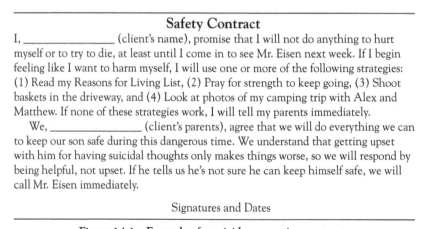

Safety Contract

I, _____ (client's name), promise that I will not do anything to hurt myself or to try to die, at least until I come in to see Mr. Eisen next week. If I begin feeling like I want to harm myself, I will use one or more of the following strategies: (1) Read my Reasons for Living List, (2) Pray for strength to keep going, (3) Shoot baskets in the driveway, and (4) Look at photos of my camping trip with Alex and Matthew. If none of these strategies work, I will tell my parents immediately.

We, _____ (client's parents), agree that we will do everything we can to keep our son safe during this dangerous time. We understand that getting upset with him for having suicidal thoughts only makes things worse, so we will respond by being helpful, not upset. If he tells us he's not sure he can keep himself safe, we will call Mr. Eisen immediately.

Signatures and Dates

Figure 14.1   Example of a suicide prevention contract.

of time that the youth can agree to in a sincere fashion. When suicidal ideation is strong, the first step is to get the client to agree not to hurt herself until the next session, at which time another contract should be made. The contract should specify what the client will do if she feels an urge to hurt or kill herself. The contingency plan should include calling the therapist, with an option of setting up an emergency appointment, and the plan should also include any other form of help available to the youngster, such as talking to family or friends. The contract should also specify what the parents will do in the event of a dangerous situation.

Spirito and Esposito (2008; Spirito et al., 2011) conceptualize suicide attempts as failures of problem solving. They offer this conceptualization to clients along with an offer to collaborate on more effective solutions to the problems that led to the suicidal ideation or attempts.

Cognitive-Behavioral Therapy

Because of the close affinity between cognitive therapy and depression, many of the techniques presented in Chapter 3 are potentially applicable to this disturbance. Thought diaries are useful with older children and adolescents. Depressive automatic thoughts should be treated with self-monitoring and self-instruction. Cognitive restructuring can ameliorate clients' negative views of the self, world, and future.

Because of the overlap between anxiety and depression, therapy for depression often includes many of the cognitive-behavioral techniques presented in the previous chapter, including affective education, testing pessimistic predictions, and helping the client learn to compensate for habitual cognitive biases. Many depressed clients also benefit from training in relaxation and social skills (Chapter 2), assertiveness (Chapter 12), and problem solving (Chapter 10).

Symptoms of depression often interfere with treatment for depression. Pessimistic clients may feel that counseling, like everything else they try, will fail. At the beginning of therapy, clients who feel hopeless need a statement of encouragement from their counselor. To be effective, these statements must show some understanding of the youth's specific, painful situation, or the counselor's words will sound like something she says to all her clients. Statements like the following should be made after the counselor has summarized the client's description of his difficulties (also note the narrative therapy element):

" … and I see how lousy, how depressed you feel about all this. When kids feel this depressed, sometimes they feel like giving up on everything, because nothing seems to work, and that includes what we're doing right now—you know, therapy. The depression tries to convince you that you've always been depressed, you always will be depressed, and nothing you do will make any difference. Do you feel like that sometimes? Right now?

But I'm here to tell you that it's not so. This kind of hopelessness isn't truth talking—it's depression talking. Therapy really can help if you give it an honest try. So let's meet next week, and we'll team up and get to work at finding ways to improve your life. What do you say? Will you give it a shot with me?"

Behavioral Activation

Behavioral activation is a direct therapeutic strategy that addresses an important etiological factor. Since depressed people experience a low rate of pleasant events, one way to increase this rate is by *scheduling* pleasant events to occur more frequently (Carvalho & Hopko, 2011; Kanter et al., 2010; Kanter & Puspitasari, 2012; Mendlowitz, 2014). These events can include any activity the youth might enjoy. Jacob et al. (2013) developed a manual for implementing behavioral activation with young people.

Pleasant event scheduling is a simple therapeutic technique (which is not a criticism). The counselor uses her credibility to give the youth and parent permission and motivation to find enjoyable things for the youth to do. If the depressed client and, perhaps, her parents have been in an inactive rut, this technique might increase their willingness to spend some time and money on recreation because it is "doctor's orders." Research on emotion suggests that positive feelings can undo or reverse negative emotions (Ehrenreich, Fairholme, Buzzella, Ellard, & Barlow, 2007; Fredrickson, 2001). At any one time, our consciousness contains only a limited capacity for experience, so if we bring positive emotions into our minds, negative feelings may be crowded out.

Behavioral activation overlaps with DBT stress tolerance techniques (Linehan, 1993a, 1993b, 2014; Rathus & Miller, 2014). Lists of these techniques, such as the one in Chapter 4, include small versions of pleasant activities, such as petting an animal, holding a door for someone, and taking a shower. Enjoyable micro-activities like these provide a place to start for clients who have been very inactive and anhedonic. After these clients have been eased from their state of inertia, the goal should be to initiate the larger activities making up behavioral activation.

Just as anxious clients' fear may be the largest obstacle to their participation in exposure, the biggest obstacle to pleasant event scheduling may be the client's depression itself. Pessimistic, anhedonic clients often wearily resist suggestions for pleasant event scheduling because they do not "feel like" doing the activities and do not think they would be fun. These clients need to understand that depression and inactivity often form a positive feedback loop (Rohde, Lewinsohn, Klein, Seeley, & Gau, 2013). Behavioral activation is based on the idea that if depressed clients wait to feel like doing enjoyable activities, they might wait forever, but if they purposefully initiate these activities anyway, eventually they will feel like doing them.

If depressed clients wait to feel like doing enjoyable activities, they might wait forever, but if they purposefully initiate these activities anyway, eventually they will feel like doing them. Identifying activities the youth would find enjoyable sometimes takes some work. A solution-focused approach would involve asking the youth to identify the bits of fun he occasionally experiences and then expanding these intimations into significant sources of enjoyment. It is useful to ask youngsters what they enjoyed before they became depressed and what they think they might enjoy, even if they have never done the activity. Sometimes this search includes inquiry into the youth's values and discussion of how these values could connect with practical, available activities (Lejuez, Hopko, Acierno, Daughters, & Pagoto, 2011). As discussed in Chapter 4's description of ACT, young people's values can be defined in a concrete manner as what they consider fun, cool, admirable, and worthwhile. Behavioral activation is about ordinary, available activities, although something more substantial and enlivening than watching TV or playing computer games is required.

Table 14.4 Terriana's Pleasant Activities Schedule

	Morning	*Afternoon*	*Evening*
Monday			Call a friend to chat
Tuesday		Browse in pet store	Card game with family
Wednesday		Go to mall w/friends	Work on scrapbook
Thursday		Go swimming at Y	Call a friend to chat
Friday			Curl up with a good book
Saturday	Breakfast out with Grandma or Aunt Nancy	Shop with Mom; go swimming at Y	Make plans with friend(s)
Sunday	Work on scrapbook	Visit a friend	

Therapists should be specific and concrete in implementing this behavioral strategy. For example, parent-child games of catch might be scheduled on Wednesday evenings and Sunday afternoons, weather permitting. This might seem contrived, but behaviorists made an important discovery when they found that positive activities alleviate depression even when they are done in a purposeful rather than spontaneous spirit. Other examples of pleasant events include play dates, hikes, water parks, shopping, arts activities, and so forth—whatever the client likes or might learn to like. Terriana's activities schedule is presented in Table 14.4.

Considerable work might be necessary to overcome the obstacles that have prevented the client from engaging in positive activities in the past. This usually includes CBT strategies, such as problem solving and social skills training (Rohde et al., 2005). ACT techniques (S. Hayes et al., 2011; Hayes, Luoma, Bond, Masuda, & Lillis, 2006; Murrell et al., 2004) seem well suited to facilitating behavioral activation because they directly address avoidance, a formidable obstacle to engagement in positive activities. Parents can encourage clients' engagement in new activities by using reinforcers that are already effective (e.g., money) to increase engagement with potential reinforcers that could become effective (Stark et al., 2006; Stark, Streusand, Arora, & Patel, 2011). Mood monitoring should occur throughout treatment so clients can note contingent relationships between different activities and their mood.

Testing Beliefs With Evidence

Tests of evidence, a component of cognitive restructuring (see Chapter 3), involve collecting observations and facts and then using this empirical information to evaluate beliefs (J. Beck, 2011; Brent, Poling, & Goldstein, 2011; Clark & Reynolds, 2013; Verduyn & Rogers, 2009). This therapeutic strategy has much in common with the scientific method and also with legal trials in that, in all three, observable evidence is the criterion of the validity of beliefs. Tests of evidence are often useful in treatment for clients whose depression involves unrealistic, self-derogating cognitions. The technique can be introduced to youth by saying something like, "I know you've got a lot of feelings and ideas about yourself, but let's take a look at some facts."

Counselors should begin by writing down the beliefs to be tested. For depressed youth, these will usually be depressing beliefs, such as "I'm a loser," "I will never be happy," "I will never have a boyfriend," and "It's my fault that my parents are miserable." Below these beliefs, the relevant facts are arrayed in two columns, with headings of: Facts That Support My Belief and Facts That Do Not Support My Belief.

Then, the therapist guides the child through the process of filling in the columns. The client provides the data, observations, and ideas, and makes the final decisions about what is placed where. The clinician's role is to ask questions, probe, organize the child's observations, cite evidence the client does not think of citing, and offer information and input when needed.

To start where the child is, begin with the first (depressive) column. Ask the youth what convinces her that the belief is true, and record the reasons she gives. Then, have the client rate her level of depression on a scale from 0 to 10.

Next, move to the antidepression column. To prompt for data inconsistent with the negative view, ask questions like:

- "Do you ever feel a little unsure about the belief being true? What makes you think twice about it?"
- "Has anything ever happened that made you think the belief might not be completely true?"
- "Would everyone who knows you think the belief is true?" "What would a friend say about whether this belief is true?"
- "What would be another way to look at this?"

This strategy involves searching for any crack in the wall of the client's depressive negativity and then inserting a lever into the crack; solution-focused therapists call this "searching for exceptions" (de Shazer, 1985; Kim, 2013; O'Hanlon & Weiner-Davis, 2003). For example, a counselor could ask, "Is there anything about you that doesn't fit the definition of a loser?," "Could there be some possibility that you might have a boyfriend someday?," or "Have you ever done anything that your parents liked?" The purpose of these questions is not only to get a yes/no answer but also to redirect the client's attention from depressing to nondepressing aspects of experience.

Then, with the child's observations on the table, the therapist can begin questioning the data. The clinician should scan the first column for any maladaptive thoughts and feelings disguised as facts. For example, if under the belief, "I am dumb in school," the child has written, "All the other kids are smarter than me," the clinician should ask for the evidence supporting this supposed fact. The clinician should question such entries and try to persuade the client to remove them from the column.

The therapist can also suggest alternative explanations of the observations and cite facts that are inconsistent with the depressing view. When possible, counselors and clients should be true to the empirical spirit of the endeavor by obtaining new data to test the client's beliefs. For instance, if the child believes her father thinks she is a failure when she gets poor grades in school, the therapist might suggest bringing the father into the session and asking directly whether this belief is true. Sometimes, counselors can assign clients the task of obtaining relevant data as a homework assignment.

When the therapist or client thinks of a plausible alternative explanation for an observation cited as supporting the negative belief, the observation should be removed from this column. Note that only one plausible alternative explanation is needed for this purpose. ("How can we know this fact supports the belief if there is another possible explanation for the fact?") When it is not clear in which column an observation belongs, the best option is to have it in neither, or you can add a column labeled "Unsure."

We are now coming down the home stretch of this rational analysis task. The counselor and client should review the facts that support the belief and those that do not. Then ask the child to develop a summary statement that considers all the data and possible explanations. Finally, ask the child to rate the depression level associated with this summary.

Therapists should be realistic about what they expect from client re-examination of beliefs. Night is not turned into day; the change is usually a matter of degree. Typically, the client comes to view the situation as less clear and more mixed than he initially realized, with both positive and negative facts and many unknowns. These cognitive changes do not transform depression into happiness, but they modulate debilitating feelings of inferiority into emotions such as disappointment and frustration, which might be realistic and, depending on what follows them, even adaptive.

Scripted techniques need to balance positive content and realism just like conceptual techniques do. Positive self-affirmations slightly improve the affect of people with high self-esteem but actually worsen the affect of people with low self-esteem (Wood et al., 2009). Preplanned self-talk is most likely to be effective if it is realistic and plausible, rather than extremely positive (Loades et al., 2014). For example, "I'm just as smart as any kid in my class" might backfire if it is not true, while, "If I work hard, my skills will grow" expresses a positive view that can survive encounters with reality (Dweck, 2007).

Reattribution

Reattribution means changing causal explanations for events in a realistic, self-enhancing, optimistic direction (S. Clark, Bowers, & Reynolds, 2014; Reivich, Gillham, Chaplin, & Seligman, 2013; Seligman, Reivich, Jaycox, & Gillham, 1995). Because complex cognitions are usually truer to reality than simple ones, reattribution tends to increase client awareness of the multiple factors that have contributed to the outcomes they experienced. And because intense self-blame in children is generally unfair and unrealistic, reasonable explanations of negative events usually decrease guilt and shame in depressed youth.

Since reattribution involves principles of formal logic, it should be noted that for an effect to be attributable to a single cause, the cause must be **necessary** and **sufficient** to produce the outcome; only one cause can produce the effect, and the cause always leads to that outcome. Few events in life work this way, because most outcomes are complex. In addition to the basic *why* questions asked repeatedly in attributional work, the following questions are useful:

- "Do you think what you did was the *only* reason why it happened?"
- "Do you think *any* time a kid did what you did, that would happen?"
- "Is this all there is to it?"

If the answer to any of those questions is no, you have begun the process of constructing a multifactor explanation of an outcome.

"Characterological and behavioral self-blame" are big words, but therapists can translate them into kid language. Behavioral self-blame equals "something you did." Characterological self-blame equals "something about the way you are."

Contrary to a common view, it is not always helpful for therapists to tell clients that the bad things that happened to them were not their fault, because the idea that events are uncontrollable may increase helplessness at the same time that it decreases guilt (Janoff-Bulman, 1979; Shapiro, 1995; and see Chapter 15's discussion of therapy for sexual abuse). Sometimes, depending on the specifics of the situation, it might be useful to help clients identify small, controllable aspects of their selves—behaviors, mistakes, and ineffective strategies—that caused the negative outcome they experienced (C. Anderson & Jennings, 1980; Romero, Master, Paunesku, Dweck, & Gross, 2014; Tilghman-Osborne et al., 2008). Changing characterological self-blame to behavioral self-blame may reduce depression and also lead naturally to training in the skills and strategies capable of making future outcomes better than past ones—for example:

> "If you think you did something wrong that caused this to happen, let's figure out what that was, so you can avoid similar mistakes in the future. But I don't think there's anything about you as a person that made this happen."

Reattribution involves changing clients' attributions for negative events from global, stable attributions to explanations that emphasize specific, unstable, changeable factors (Reivich et al., 2013; Seligman et al., 1995)—for example:

- "How do you know it was *everything* about you that he didn't like; maybe it was just one or two things."
- "You're making this so big; the truth is usually something smaller and more specific."
- "Okay, you messed up the game, but that doesn't make you a lousy player, because you've done better in other games. Was the problem in your shot selection? You've talked about that before."

Reattribution work can help clients interpret negative feedback from parents, teachers, and other authority figures in an accurately specific, delimited fashion. Depressed youth sometimes have excessively distressed reactions to reprimands because of their interpretation that the adult "hates" them, in a characterological way. Counselors can help clients pare down this global interpretation by citing occasions when the authority figure gave them positive feedback, which indicates that he does like the client as a person—he just did not like a specific behavior the client did.

Helping Clients With Guilt.   Guilt is not necessarily a mental health problem; this is a matter of degree and appropriateness. As discussed in Chapter 11, a pronounced lack of guilt is a symptom of conduct disturbance (Frick et al., 2014; Lahey & Waldman, 2003). In this respect, depression is the opposite of CD: Many depressed youth feel excessive and inappropriate guilt (O'Connor et al., 1999; Tilghman-Osborne et al., 2012). Aristotle was right about this, too.

When negative events occur, the attributional processes discussed earlier play an important role in determining whether the individual feels guilty or unfortunate. Most real-world outcomes have multiple causes, and clients sometimes need help to identify and organize the contributions of multiple factors to events and situations. The **responsibility pie** (J. Beck, 2011; Padesky & Greenberger, 1995) is a useful visual technique that depicts the relative contributions of several causes to an outcome.

The first step in constructing a responsibility pie is to write the event to be explained at the top of a piece of paper. Examples include an argument between family members, loss of a friendship, and, on the positive side, a victory for the client's team. Next, ask the youth to think of as many factors contributing to the event as she can (Figure 14.2).

In step two, the youth allocates a portion of the pie to each cause. This task requires clients to divide up the pie in a way that gives each factor its due. Adolescents can use percentages to do this task, with their assignment being to account for 100% of the causation of the event. Usually, it is realistic to allot some percentage to unknown factors.

Finally, ask the client to make a verbal statement summarizing the information about responsibility that he has depicted visually. It is important that the youngster account for others' responsibility as well as his own. The objective is for the client to replace simple, self-blaming statements with reasonably complex, balanced descriptions of how internal and external factors combined to produce the event under consideration.

Sometimes *any* internal attribution is unrealistic and unfair to the client. Depressed people often assume responsibility for negative outcomes over which they had little or no control (A. Beck, 1967; O'Connor et al., 1999; Tilghman-Osborne et al., 2012). Therapists

Why did Mom get in a car accident?

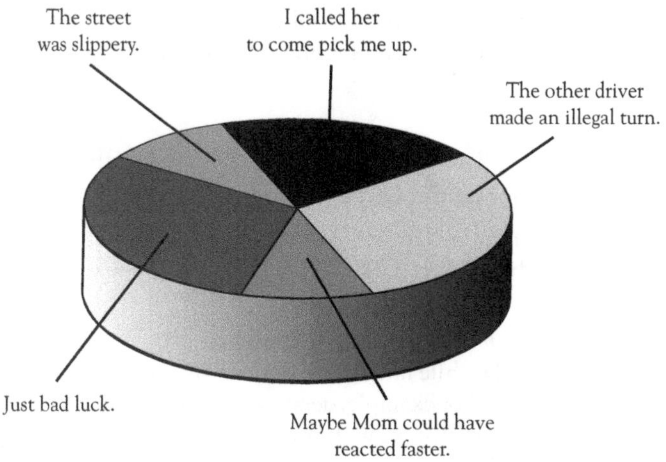

The street was slippery.

I called her to come pick me up.

The other driver made an illegal turn.

Just bad luck.

Maybe Mom could have reacted faster.

Figure 14.2   Example of a responsibility pie.

can help such clients by directing their attention to external factors in negative outcomes and portraying their pattern of self-blame as unfair—for example:

- "You wouldn't blame everything that goes wrong on a friend, so why do you do this to yourself?"
- "Maybe you shouldn't have said that, but couldn't she have handled it differently and, if she had, wouldn't things have worked out better?"
- "It doesn't really matter what you did or didn't do; parents get divorced because of problems in their relationship, not because of their kids."

When events occur and people try to explain them, internal and external attribution must add up to a constant; they must combine to explain the event. The more weight is assigned to one type of attribution, the less will be assigned to the other. When negative events happen, the depressive biases toward internal attribution and against external attribution are two sides of the same coin. As a result, one way for counselors to reduce guilt in depressed clients is by directing their attention to external causes of outcomes for which they blame themselves. With more of an appreciation for the part played by factors beyond their control, there is less attributional space for guilt.

Usually, explanations of these outcomes are complicated and ambiguous because some behavior of the client *was* involved in what happened: She might have misread a situation, made a mistake under pressure, reacted emotionally, and so forth. In these situations, it seems that typical depressed clients focus harshly on their own behavior and ignore the *context* of that behavior, which consisted of the situation as they perceived it. Even when their information was incomplete or misleading, the other person's behavior was distressing or disruptive, and their ability to influence events was minimal or nonexistent, typical depressed individuals seem to focus on the ineffective nature of their behavior in the midst of this swirl. When negative events occur, the decontextualized nature of depressive self-evaluation seems to be a major factor in their guilt, self-criticism, and low self-esteem. Therapists can intervene in this thought process by drawing the client's attention to the context of her behavior and asking why she did what she did, reminding her of what she knew and did not know at the time, and highlighting the obstacles to effective behavior she faced—for example:

- "Wait a minute: Were you 'stupid,' or were there reasons for what you did?"
- "How could you have problem-solved effectively with him yelling at you like that?"
- "Sure, if you knew then what you know now, you would have done things differently—but you didn't, so it doesn't seem fair to beat yourself up about this."

In a related type of unfair self-evaluation, depressed people castigate themselves for actions that worked out badly while failing to take into account that there were no better alternatives available to them. For example, depressed clients sometimes blame themselves for failing to develop good relationships with people who are either unwilling or unable to have a good relationship with them, no matter what the client does.

In these cases, the therapeutic objective is to increase the client's empathy for himself by reminding him of the situational constraints and experiences from which his behavior emerged. Many depressed youth have a "no excuses" attitude toward their behavior, but explanations are different from excuses, and it does not make sense to hold people (whether self or others) responsible for outcomes over which they had no control. When depressed youth give fair consideration to what they were up against in situations that went badly for them, their self-blame and guilt usually decrease—for instance:

> "But wait a minute: At the time, you just said you liked the ice skates—you didn't know paying for them would be a problem for your mom."

There is one more level of complexity. When one carefully considers issues of causality and control in human realities, the distinction between internal and external factors no longer seems sharp and dichotomous, and a grey area emerges. In an abstract but meaningful sense, the inner-most layer of "context" involves aspects of our minds that we cannot control and that envelop our core selves. We choose what we try to do, how much effort we exert, what we sacrifice in pursuit of our priorities, and how much pain we tolerate as the price of doing so, but our efforts occur in the context of unchosen layers of self that influence our ability to translate intentions into actions and outcomes. Motivational factors such as choice and effort seem close to the core of self; these factors seem integral to what we are. Aptitudes and capabilities (aside from their cultivation through effort) seem to be comparatively peripheral aspects of self; capabilities are something that we have. We do not choose and cannot control our aptitudes—in a sense, they are a matter of luck.

When depressed youth give fair consideration to what they were up against in situations that went badly for them, their self-blame and guilt usually decrease.

Some capability-related factors vary as a function of the immediate situation—for example, physiological states, emotions, information we have and do not have, and perceptions that may be accurate or inaccurate. Some of these factors are constant across time and situations—for example, genetic endowment, neurobiological characteristics, and intellectual aptitudes. In the midst of these powerful contextual forces, we make choices and exert efforts in attempts to influence our personal outcomes.

Just as family members become less angry when they attribute each other's troublesome behaviors to incapability rather than motivation (see Chapter 7), this type of reattribution can reduce anger toward the self. It seems neither valid nor fair to evaluate people without taking into account the effects of unchosen constraints on their behavior—and internal factors can be just as uncontrollable as external ones. Therapists can help by reminding clients of the reasons for their failures to make things go the way they wanted:

- "I'm sorry you freaked out, too. But calling it weakness ignores how your heart was pounding and what happened the last time you were in that situation. You didn't choose any of that—what you chose was to bring this up for us to work on, and I think that took strength."
- "The more you tell me about what you were going through, the more I understand why you did it. I want you to come along with me in this, so your self-understanding replaces your guilt."

Helping clients appreciate the obstacles they face increases the pride they feel when they succeed, just as it decreases the guilt they feel when they fail—for example:

- "Anyone can take a risk if they have no fear of the consequences. For you to step up and do that in the face of all your anxiety took real strength."

- "You had to overcome so much of your past to do that, but you did."
- "What could be more courageous than trying to overcome fear?"
- "What could be more unselfish than trying to overcome selfishness?"

The final step is to generalize the learning by identifying the relevant principle. When clients understand that their habitual way of thinking underemphasizes contextual sources of difficulty, they can recruit their most conscious, objective aspects of mind to compensate. Clients can learn to identify feelings of guilt or self-hatred as a cue and to respond with self-statements like, "I know I'm trying my best here, so if I'm having trouble there must be reasons for that; what is making this so hard for me?"

The philosophical issue here was broached in Chapter 8's section on fear of failure. Because we cannot control our talents or circumstances, no one who tries her best has anything to be ashamed of—in a way, everything else is luck. Nothing is more worthy of respect than effort.

Self-Esteem and Values

Low self-esteem is not merely associated with depression; it is a component of the disturbance (American Psychiatric Association, 2013). Longitudinal research suggests that low self-esteem is a vulnerability factor that leads to progressive worsening of depression over time (Orth & Robins, 2013). The cognitive strategies for treating depression discussed thus far in this chapter, as well as the techniques presented in Chapter 3, focus largely on self-esteem. In this section, I offer one additional strategy for addressing this aspect of depression.

Because people generally have a mixture of strengths and weaknesses, self-esteem is largely a function of which of our characteristics we focus on and weigh heavily and which we de-emphasize. The low self-esteem of depressed people results largely from overgeneralizations that focus on negative information about the self while ignoring positive information (A. T. Beck, 1967, 1976; A. T. Beck & Alford, 2009). If we emphasize the attributes in which we are weak, we will have low self-esteem, and if we focus on dimensions that are strengths, we will have positive self-concepts. Therapists can counter the selective focus of depressed clients by guiding them through a more complete, unbiased survey of the variety of human attributes.

The question is, what are the behaviors, characteristics, and qualities that are potentially valuable and admirable in human beings? A research-based guide for this survey is provided by Peterson and Seligman's (2004) classification of human strengths and virtues. Compiling a list of these attributes and inviting clients to rate themselves on each one may reduce their focus on the dimensions they consider weaknesses and prompt new recognition of strengths they had not previously considered or emphasized.

The psychological issue of self-esteem is related to the values issue of what makes human beings worthwhile and admirable. Some youth have low self-esteem because they lack the conventionally valued characteristics of academic intelligence, athletic ability, artistic talent, good looks, and social popularity. However, many of these young people are rich in strengths that are less shiny and obvious but probably do more to make the world a better place, such as kindness, loyalty, trustworthiness, humor, humility, sense of beauty, and authenticity.

As discussed in several previous chapters, therapists have traditionally viewed their role as value-neutral, but this stance may prevent us from offering input that could help clients with their difficulties. The quiet virtues are subtle—they receive little public attention—so most youth who possess them are unlikely to gain an appreciation of these virtues on their own. Counselors are in a position to guide a deeper thought process capable of illuminating meaningful strengths that often go unappreciated by the people who have them, especially if they also have low self-esteem. The same type of values discussion can also help parents expand their conception of admirable qualities to include the strengths their child has. (See Chapter 8's discussion of the extendincorp strategy.)

The psychological issue of self-esteem is related to the values issue of what makes human beings worthwhile and admirable.

Coping With Romantic Breakups

Romantic breakups are frequent precipitants of depressive episodes in adolescents (Joyner & Udry, 2000). One reason is overgeneralization or extrapolation from this painful event. Depressed teens sometimes believe their grief about the breakup will never end because the lost partner is the only person they could ever love, and some believe that since they were unable to keep this person's affection, no one desirable will ever want to be with them. Whether because of the first cognition or the second, rejection is most depressogenic when the individual does not believe in the possibility of romantic happiness with another person (J. S. Beck, 2011; Lazarus & Folkman, 1984).

When clients believe that the lost person is the only one who could make them happy, therapists should help them assess the uniqueness of the ex-boyfriend or ex-girlfriend. One useful question asks how it could be that the client happened to meet the only person in the world who could make her happy at such a young age. While the lost person might have impressive strengths, it is not plausible that he has a monopoly on those strengths. The relevant, accurate cliché is, "There are plenty of fish in the sea."

The thinking error of overgeneralization (A. T. Beck, 1967, 1976), applied to romance, means that if one person rejected the client, everyone else will, too. Compounding the problem, adolescents often have a simplistic conception of attractiveness in which desirability varies on a single, vertical dimension, and everyone tries to link up with the most appealing person they can. However, romantic tastes and preferences are actually varied, individual, and quirky. Especially when one gets beyond physical looks, romantic chemistry is mostly a horizontal matter of fit, compatibility, and finding the person who is right for you.

People often get rejected because of qualities that someone else would like (e.g., shyness, rebelliousness, studiousness). Therefore, rather than indicating an objective lack of attractiveness, rejection just means that compatibility with the other person was not there. Being rejected by one person is not very predictive of being rejected by someone else. And virtually everyone has been rejected—probably including the therapist, who could offer himself as a coping model.

Psychodynamic Therapy

Dynamic therapy and cognitive therapy have important elements in common. Both types of therapy target irrational thinking that is unfairly negative toward the self, and both seek to strengthen the logic and realism of the client's thinking. The main difference is that cognitive therapists focus exclusively on the client's conscious and preconscious thoughts, while psychodynamic clinicians also look below this level of cognition for hidden sources of irrationality. Dynamic therapists investigate the possibility that past experiences have imbued unconscious self-representations with qualities of guilt and shame that *then* give rise to conscious self-criticisms about whatever material is available at the moment (Horowitz, 1998; Kegerreis, 2010; Kernberg, 1993). The dynamic approach assumes that these underlying wellsprings of self-derogation must be addressed, or the client will generate new self-criticisms as fast as the cognitive therapist can refute them.

When clients voice self-criticisms that seem logically unfair and unrealistic, the first appropriate response is to evaluate these thoughts with reason and evidence. Often this will work, and the client's cognitive style and level of depression will change. Sometimes, however, this will not work. When cognitive intervention seems to come up against a brick wall, therapists should consider a change of strategy. A transition from cognitive to dynamic therapy can be initiated by a counselor statement like the following:

> "It seems like we keep going around in circles. There are so many things you don't like about yourself, and I keep telling you reasons why these things aren't so bad, but, as fast as I do, you think of something else you don't like.
>
> Now I have a bigger question. Beyond all this stuff about forgetting your line in the play, that thing you said to Noah, and dropping the fly ball, what I really want to know is this: What do you have *against* yourself? What did you do to deserve these put-downs all the time?"

Therapists can engender insight by pushing the client to think beyond her specific self-accusations and asking her to wonder about the larger issue of why she criticizes herself so much—for example:

- "Why are you so hard on yourself?"
- "Where did this come from?"
- "Why don't you ever give yourself a break?"
- "What's the crime you keep punishing yourself for?"
- "It's like there's a prosecuting attorney inside your head, but there's no defense lawyer."

Insight is an important step toward the resolution of guilt when clients replace a global sense of personal badness with an understanding of the reasons for their guilty feelings (Gardner, 1993; Glickauf-Hughes & Wells, 2006; Michels, 1982). Sometimes, guilt is based on a misunderstanding of something that happened in the past. Sometimes, the client's sense of badness developed as an internalization of derogating messages, mistreatment, or neglect from important figures. Sometimes (as in Terriana's case), these messages were not truly derogating, but the client's way of interpreting them resulted in her feeling guilty or ashamed. Whatever the proportions of reality and distortion, depressed clients need to become aware of their self-perceived crimes, sins, or failures so they can re-evaluate them. In other words, insight into unconscious dynamics must sometimes occur for cognitive work on the core depressogenic schemas to become possible.

Some cases of depression result from object relations consisting of the self as unlovable and/or other people as unloving (Blatt & Homann, 1992; Bowlby, 1980; Cashdan, 1988). Putting this awareness into words—moving it from an unexamined, gut sense of the way things are into conceptual, verbal terms—might initiate questioning of the schema. Conscious thinking and talking about this view of self and others might lead to the realization that the view is not a reflection of reality but a conclusion resulting from particular experiences, and this conclusion might not apply to life outside the boundaries of those experiences (see the discussion of misapplied learning in Chapter 2, Behavior Therapy)—for example:

Insight into unconscious dynamics must sometimes occur for cognitive work on the core depressogenic schemas to become possible.

"From what we know about your early years, your grandmother was angry about your mom being in jail, and she did not like the responsibility of taking care of you. This must have made you feel like a bother at times, and you might have been scared your grandma would get tired of the whole thing and throw you out. It must have been terribly hard—but that sure doesn't mean there was anything wrong with you, and it doesn't mean the parents who adopted you will ever feel this way."

When a client's feeling of being unlovable is the result of critical or rejecting behavior by caregivers, therapists need to interpret the connection between these messages and the child's sense of self. The metaphor of a tape recording in the mind can be useful:

"The reason you feel like you're no good and no one will love you isn't because it's *true*; the reason is that your dad treated you that way for such a long time. It's like those awful things he said got tape-recorded into your mind, so that now, even when he's not around, those messages keep playing over and over. But it's not the truth. The truth is simple, even though it's hard to believe: Your father was wrong."

For some clients, insight means learning about how their old, abandonment-oriented scripts have distorted their experiences with other people. This type of object relation becomes a self-fulfilling prophecy if the client's pessimism about relationships causes him to sabotage his chances for finding closeness (Glickauf-Hughes & Wells, 2006; Kernberg, 1980; Westen, 1991). This sometimes occurs when clients unconsciously push away closeness because they do not want to invest emotionally in a relationship they believe will eventually end, because the more one cares, the more this hurts. In another mechanism, clients do not desire rejection, but they repeatedly test the other person in an attempt to achieve a feeling of security, and these tests disrupt the relationship.

After several sessions of exploratory work, Terriana drew a picture in which she was separated from her parents, half-brothers, and the family dog by a large wall, which she entitled "The Wall of Secrets." She wouldn't tell the counselor the secrets, either—until one day, while discussing this, she drew a frightening picture of a person in outer space who flew into the sun and was annihilated. ("Her heart exploded and she burned up.") This explosion of anxiety signaled that something terrifying was about to emerge. Terriana's secret concerned her feelings about her place in her family. The mother and stepfather had always minimized her relationship with her biological father, insisting it made no difference that she was not the stepfather's offspring. Their intentions were loving, but to

Terriana biological parentage *did* make a difference. She loved her stepfather, but she never forgot whose biological daughter she was. Terriana believed that her mother and stepfather thought it was wrong to care about biological connections, and she thought they hated her father (which was somewhat true), so she believed her feelings for him would offend her mother and stepfather, if they knew. The therapist asked whether Terriana's constant sense of concealing something important about herself created an ongoing fear of being discovered—and contributed to her extreme distress in response to ordinary reprimands. She affirmed this interpretation.

When dynamic therapists working with young children seek to go beyond insight by providing psychoeducation, they need concrete, experiential ways to convey their lessons about life. For example, a 5-year-old playing with clay tried to make a dog, but she repeatedly pounded her attempts flat, saying they were no good. The therapist observed, "You are so hard on yourself. You smash the things you try, and then you have nothing." Following this interpretation, the therapist offered a suggestion: "Why don't we have this dog be dog #1 and, instead of smashing it, we'll put it over here. Then we'll see what dog #2 looks like. I bet dog #3 will be better yet." The therapist's interpretation, by itself, would probably have done little to help the girl develop a more optimistic attitude toward her endeavors. Therefore, the counselor concretely *modeled* a realistically positive attitude in hopes that the client would internalize it.

Client disclosures of guilt or shame are important opportunities for corrective emotional experiences. This is when you can violate their expectations of disapproval, show that your agenda is not to judge but to understand and help, and teach self-acceptance by demonstrating acceptance, even (especially) when you know the worst about them. At these times, it may be a *lack* of change in your response to the child that is most therapeutic, because this consistency demonstrates that the new disclosure, which the client feared might ruin your opinion of him, has resulted in no change at all.

Many children who feel severely criticized, rejected, or abandoned by their parents have a hard time believing they could be part of a positive caregiver-child relationship (Bowlby, 1980; Kegerreis, 2010). Our only chance of countering such deep-level learning is with cognitively fundamental, emotionally powerful messages. These messages need to convey that, contrary to the child's experience, she is a valuable, worthy person, and there are kind, nurturing people in the world. Because reason and evidence might not touch children at the deep levels of experiential learning most relevant to this issue, counselors need to communicate not so much what they think as how they *see* the child:

> "You're a good kid—I see it, I know it. I'm sorry your mother was so messed up she couldn't. And I believe that, even though you've been hurt, you still want to be close with people—if only you could figure out who.
>
> Let me tell you something: There are good people in the world. They can be hard to find, so you have to keep your eyes open and be patient. And I hope you'll be ready to be with good people, or you'll push them away without realizing who they are."

Nonverbal channels of communication are as important as verbal ones in this type of message. This is not a time to have a neutral, professional-sounding tone of voice but to be earnest and sincere, as befits the emotional intensity of this type of issue for clients. Hugs can occasionally be an appropriate part of therapeutic work with children, although it is vital to ensure that this does not create hopes for more of a real relationship than is possible.

Depressed children sometimes benefit from exchanging personal tokens with their counselors. Examples include photographs, cards, and any object that carries some essence of the other person. Such tokens can help children who have difficulty holding onto a sense of an enduring relationship during periods of separation. Exchanged tokens are a psychic analogue of mutual memories: They help the child picture the therapist when he is gone, and they reassure the child that the therapist remembers her during the time between sessions.

Systemic Intervention

Because children learn their cognitive styles largely from their parents, it is often useful for interventions targeting beliefs, attributions, and styles of evaluating outcomes to include both parties. Stark and his colleagues developed a structured, manualized program that integrates cognitive-behavioral parent work and child therapy for depression (Stark et al., 2006, 2012).

When parents evaluate their children's behavior with the same type of harsh, critical bias that characterizes depressed children's self-evaluation, it might help to do cognitive work with the parents as well as the children. Because parents might perceive this strategy as implying a criticism of them, the most tactful way to begin is with a meeting between the adults. The counselor can introduce the idea that the child's self-derogation might be fueled by parental messages and can assess whether the parent is willing to examine and modify this behavior.

If the answer is yes, the therapist can inquire into the background of the parent's critical stance. Sometimes parents respond by describing the harsh feedback they received from their parents while growing up. If so, counselors can invite them to step back, consider the intergenerational transmission of this parenting style in their family, and think about whether they want to maintain or modify this pattern. Some of these parents believe that harsh criticism is the most effective strategy for motivating people to improve (e.g., "In my family while I was growing up, we thought the way to get someone to do better was to tell them how bad they were"). Counselors can validate the parent's goal of motivating the child to improve and propose less hurtful, more effective routes to this goal.

The behavioral, cognitive, and dynamic factors discussed in this chapter may manifest themselves on the plane of family functioning, and treatment of these factors in individual youth is sometimes facilitated by helping parents and siblings move in the same direction. This type of intervention might help the family, as a whole, become more actively engaged with enjoyable activities and become more fair and positive in the way they assess each other. Pleasant event scheduling, cognitive restructuring, tests of beliefs, and reattribution can all be shared, family interventions as well as individual ones.

Terriana needed to gain some understanding of her conflicting feelings about family relationships through individual work before she was able to discuss these issues with her parents. She signaled her readiness to move from individual to family therapy in an eloquent manner. One day, she took out the picture of herself and her family separated by a barrier and asked, "Could I draw some cracks in the wall?" Then, expressing emotions of both anger and triumph, scribbling with her pen, she obliterated the wall, finally depicting it as a pile of rubble, and said, "That's my problem when it's all taken care of." Finally, she gave the therapist permission to bring her parents into the next session.

The meetings that followed were emotional for everyone involved. Terriana shared her "wall pictures" with her parents. They understood that the wall symbolized an emotional barrier, but initially they misunderstood Terriana's sense of separation as based on her lack of genetic relationship with the stepfather. The client explained that she felt cut off from the family not because of the facts of her origin but because the blood relationship with her father did matter to her, and she felt her mother and stepfather treated her investment in this relationship as mistaken and disloyal. She said she never talked about her father because she felt they did not want to hear about him. These feelings were the secrets that separated Terriana from her family.

Summary

Behavioral explanations of the etiology of depression attribute this disturbance to low rates of enjoyable activities and positive reinforcement. Cognitive formulations note that, as a result of their interpretive biases, depressed people experience less feeling of success and more sense of failure than nondepressed people do in response to the same outcomes. Part of the reason for this difference is that depressed people tend to attribute negative events to internal, stable, and global factors. Dynamic theory suggests that maladaptive thinking about immediate, specific outcomes sometimes derives from unconscious guilt, shame, and negative views of the self.

Suicidal ideation and behavior are associated with depression. Although fleeting wishes to die are occasionally experienced by many people, clinicians must respond carefully to indications of suicide potential because of the potential lethality of this danger. Therapists should provide an assessment of risk, strong statements designed to impart hope, referral to a psychiatrist for possible psychotropic medication, and work with parents on practical precautions. On the infrequent occasions when these steps cannot provide safety, therapists should make a referral for psychiatric hospitalization.

Outcome research on depression has produced more findings supporting CBT than any other approach, but this is because more outcome studies on CBT have been performed, not because this approach has outperformed other types of therapy. Meta-analyses have generally indicated smaller effect sizes for CBT interventions for depression, compared to CBT interventions for most other types of disturbance. Behavioral activation is the component of CBT that has received the strongest support. If this strategy does not ameliorate the child's depression, or if etiologies it does not address seem important, other therapeutic strategies warrant consideration.

Behavioral activation purports to increase the client's activity level and frequency of positive reinforcement in a direct manner by identifying activities the youth would enjoy and scheduling them to occur more frequently. Often it is necessary to assess and overcome the obstacles that have prevented the child's engagement in pleasant activities in the past. This work might include problem solving, ACT techniques to reduce avoidance, and social skills training.

Cognitive therapy for depression focuses on self-evaluation, attribution, and expectations for the future. The counselor and client collaborate on careful analyses of the events, situations, and outcomes of the youth's life, with the aim of testing whether the client's interpretations of these data are realistic and fair. Therapists show depressed clients how they have ignored positive information about themselves, overgeneralized from negative outcomes, made self-derogating, pessimistic attributions, and ignored plausible explanations of events. Then, counselors cite positive data the client has not considered, highlight the multiple causal factors involved in most outcomes, offer plausible re-interpretations of occurrences, and propose revisions of any reasoning that is unfairly negative toward the client. Increasing the youth's appreciation of the obstacles he has faced and expanding his view of admirable human qualities may improve his self-esteem. If the client's parents exhibit cognitive distortions that might contribute to his maladaptive thinking, cognitive work can be conducted in a parent counseling or family therapy modality.

Dynamic therapy views the verbalized particulars of the client's self-criticism as less important than her general sense of self, which exists on both conscious and unconscious levels. This approach treats negative self-evaluation due to unconscious guilt, magical thinking, anger turned inward, and maladaptive object relations by uncovering these dynamics, guiding the client to a more adaptive understanding of the life issues involved in them, and providing an interpersonal experience that corrects her distorted images of self and others.

The various options for treating depression can be organized in a pragmatic fashion as follows. Behavioral activation should be considered as the way to start, because it has the most supportive evidence and can be implemented quickly. If skills deficits block the potential benefits of pleasant event scheduling, skills training should be provided. If these behavioral interventions do not work, or cognitive distortions seem so prominent from the start that they cannot be ignored, cognitive intervention is appropriate. If CBT does not sufficiently reduce the depression, other approaches should be considered. The parents should be assessed for cognitive distortions that might affect their behavior toward the client, and if this etiology seems to occur, parent counseling should be provided. If the parent-child attachment relationship seems damaged, ABFT should be implemented. If none of the foregoing options works or seems likely to work, psychodynamic techniques can be used to facilitate the emergence of material that can then be addressed with interpretation, psychoeducation, and/or corrective emotional experiences. If this too proves ineffective, perhaps because neurobiological factors maintain the depression, ACT furnishes a final fallback plan. If the client's depressive mental activity cannot be crowded out by pleasant activities, reasoned away by evidence, or traced back to parental influences or unconscious processes that can be countered, then perhaps the mental activity will have to stay—but it can be defused and deprived of its power so the client can live a valued life, even if depressive contents continue to come and go in her mind.

Case Study

The final objective of Terriana's therapy was to help her feel comfortable in her relationships with her biological father and stepfather, without a sense of conflict or competition between the two. The counselor proposed that Terriana's valuation of biological connection should be viewed as a fact to be respected, not a problem to be solved. He also suggested that, if the family could accept this relationship, Terriana and her stepfather would have an opportunity to develop a close, affectionate relationship on their own terms.

Terriana's brothers participated in several family sessions. They had questions about her father they had never asked, and these questions were answered. At home, the client showed her brothers photographs of her father that they had not seen before.

With her sense of security in the family strengthened, Terriana no longer became unduly upset in response to reprimands. She told the therapist that it was actually easier to talk about her father with her stepfather than with her mother, because this woman still harbored angry feelings from the divorce, while the stepfather had given up on the idea of being her only important paternal figure, so he could help Terriana sort out her feelings without taking things personally. The parents' initial hope that therapy would enable her to embrace the stepfather as her main paternal figure was not fulfilled, but the family's set of relationships felt more clear, clean, and open, and the client's depression abated.

15

Stress and Trauma

OBJECTIVES

This chapter explains:

- *The effects of stressful and traumatic events, with a focus on sexual abuse, parental divorce, and bereavement.*
- *The Serenity Prayer as a summary of research on coping.*
- *The use of exposure in trauma therapy.*
- *The use of guided imagery in therapy for traumatized children and other clients.*
- *How to help clients deal with the reality of bad things happening to good people.*
- *The choice faced by acrimonious ex-spouses: prioritizing their love for their child or their anger toward each other.*
- *Resolving grief by internalizing the lost loved one as a part of the self.*
- *How to treat self-blame and helplessness in sexually abused children.*

Case Study
Memories

Robin, a 10-year-old European American girl, was brought to therapy by her parents because of anxiety symptoms linked to sexual abuse committed by a 15-year-old boy in her neighborhood. Robin reported this boy had fondled her genitals "once or twice" several months previously. The case was adjudicated in juvenile court, and the boy was ordered to receive therapy and to have no contact with Robin. According to parental report, the client complained of nervousness, nightmares, a "crawly feeling" in her body, and an inability to stop thinking about the abuse. She seemed tense and jumpy, withdrew from many activities, and wanted to stay home much of the time. The therapist made a diagnosis of posttraumatic stress disorder.

Robin's family, which included one younger sister, seemed close and supportive, with no significant dysfunction. The parents described Robin as a shy girl who had trouble asserting herself, but they described no mental health problems prior to the molestation.

Initially, Robin was resistant to therapy because she did not want to talk about the abuse. She said the problem was that she could not get it out of her mind, and talking about the memories only made her feel worse. Robin squirmed in her chair, covered her face with her hands, and said she wished everyone would leave her alone so she could forget about the awful thing that happened to her.

Diagnoses Treated in This Chapter

Posttraumatic Stress Disorder

The diagnostic criteria for posttraumatic stress disorder (PTSD) begin, not with a symptom, but with an external event: a traumatic occurrence. According to *DSM-5*, trauma involves actual, threatened, or witnessed physical injury, violation of physical integrity (including sexual assault), or the threat of death. Also, learning about the occurrence of a traumatic event to a loved one fulfills this diagnostic criterion. PTSD is an anxiety-related disorder involving vacillation between two opposite features: (1) overaroused flooding with intrusive memories that, in some clients, are so intense that it is like reexperiencing the trauma ("flashbacks"), and (2) avoidance, emotional numbing, and sometimes amnesia for aspects of the trauma. For children 6 years old or younger, the diagnostic criteria are slightly different, with less emphasis on subjective symptoms that the child might not be able to verbalize and more emphasis on observable behavior. PTSD takes both acute and chronic forms, and sometimes its emergence is delayed for months or even years after the traumatic event.

Acute Stress Disorder

Acute stress disorder is a variant of PTSD that is distinguished by its briefer time course and the smaller number of symptoms required to make the diagnosis. By definition, it lasts for up to 1 month following the occurrence of a stressor. If the disturbance persists past this time, the diagnosis should be changed to PTSD.

Clinical Presentation and Etiology

This chapter is about negative events and situations, their effects on youth, and therapeutic interventions capable of overcoming the harmful effects of stress and trauma. While the topics of the other chapters in this half of the book are defined by diagnosis, that is less true here. This chapter describes therapy for PTSD and related disturbances, and it also presents interventions for client needs that are defined, not by symptoms, but by the event the client has experienced. This chapter focuses on three important examples of stressful or traumatic occurrences: sexual abuse, parental divorce, and bereavement.

Posttraumatic Stress Disorder

Potentially traumatic events are common in the lives of American youth, with approximately two thirds experiencing an extreme stressor (e.g., abuse, crime, serious accident, natural disaster) prior to age 18 (Copeland, Keeler, Angold, & Costello, 2007; Finkelhor,

Ormrod, & Turner, 2007). Most youth exposed to such stressors do not develop the full diagnostic syndrome of PTSD, although the majority experiences some transient stress symptoms. Estimates across studies suggest that PTSD develops in approximately one third of youth who experience a traumatic event (Nader & Fletcher, 2014). Vulnerability factors include low SES, parental mental health problems, and insecure attachment to caregivers (Bakermans-Kranenburg & van Ijzendoorn, 2010; Nader, 2008).

Twin studies demonstrate that genetic factors play a significant role in PTSD, accounting for approximately one third of the variance in risk (Koenen, 2007). One particular gene—the short allele (variant) of 5-HTTLPR—has been linked to several mechanisms involved in response to stress. The short allele of this gene is associated with abnormal serotonin transportation at neuronal synapses, hyper-reactivity of the amygdala and hypothalamic-pituitary-adrenal (HPA) axis, and high levels of depression and suicidality in response to stress (Caspi, Hariri, Holmes, Uher, & Moffitt, 2010; Furman, Hamilton, Joormann, & Gotlib, 2011).

Trauma symptoms vary as a function of the child's developmental level (Berliner, 1997; De Young et al., 2013). In young children, re-experiencing symptoms often manifest themselves as repeated enactment of the trauma in play. For example, a child who was in an automobile accident might repeatedly crash toy cars together. Other common reactions in young children include nightmares, separation fears, crying, aggression, and regression to immature behaviors, such as thumb-sucking and bed-wetting. Older children are more likely to verbalize worries about recurrence of the trauma, concerns about death, preoccupation with gruesome details, and revenge fantasies.

Parental Divorce

Almost half of all American marriages end in divorce, and child therapists frequently find themselves dealing with this issue. Divorce is less a discrete event than a process that begins with marital conflict, moves to the legal event of divorce itself, and then changes the child's family relationships for the rest of her growing-up period. Both parental conflict and divorce are associated with maladjustment in children, and it is difficult to separate their effects (Ehrenberg, Regev, Lazinski, Behrman, & Zimmerman, 2014; Harvey & Fine, 2010).

Children of divorced parents are at heightened risk for a variety of mental health problems, including both internalizing and externalizing forms of dysfunction (Amato, 2001; Lansford et al., 2006). In a longitudinal study by Hetherington and Kelly (2003), children's disruptive behavior and conflict with their parents increased during the 2 months following divorce. Two years later, these problems had decreased but not disappeared. In adolescence and adulthood, children of divorced parents frequently experience anxiety in romantic relationships (Wallerstein, Lewis, & Blakeslee, 2000). In adulthood, they also have lower levels of educational achievement, more disagreements with their spouses, and poorer relationships with their parents, compared to adults whose parents remained married (Amato & Cheadle, 2005).

Bereavement

Unlike most other stressful events, bereavement is a universal, inescapable human experience. The severity of grief is usually a function of the relationship with the deceased person, with the loss of a parent generally most traumatic for children.

Grief is a normal reaction to the death of a loved one, not a mental health problem. Clinicians and researchers have distinguished normal grieving from prolonged, complicated grief, in which acute reactions do not subside but continue to interfere with functioning beyond the first 6 months of bereavement (Boelen & Van den Bout, 2008; Prigerson, 2004). In children, prolonged grief reactions can be distinguished from depression and anxiety disorders and from normal grieving (Dillen, Fontaine, & Verhofstadt-Deneve, 2008). Complicated grief is associated with impaired mental and physical health (Cohen & Mannarino, 2004).

Research on bereavement has found that death does not end the psychological reality of important relationships (Pearlman, Schwalbe, D'Angelo, & Cloitre, 2010; Worden, 2008). Children continue and even reformulate their relationships with deceased parents by talking to them, feeling the parent's presence as a caring observer, and imagining what the parent would say about situations and decisions they face. Generally, these experiences are normal and adaptive.

Sexual Abuse

Sexual abuse is generally defined as sexual activity with a child that involves either: (1) use of force, threat, or manipulation, or (2) an age difference of 5 or more years between the older person and the victim. The principle underlying this two-part definition is that sexual activity is abusive when there is no *consent*, and consent cannot be genuine unless the person is able to make a meaningful choice and to say no without fear of repercussions. Thus, sexual activity would generally be considered abusive if it involves a person who is very young, developmentally delayed, intoxicated, or dependent on the initiator of the activity. Victimizations range in severity from "hands off" offenses, such as exhibitionism and voyeurism, to fondling, to sexual intercourse.

Estimates of sexual victimization during childhood are generally in the range of 30% of females and 10% of males (Finkelhor, 2009). There seems to be a historical trend of declining rates in recent years (Jones & Finkelhor, 2003). The vast majority of perpetrators are male. Although people's fear often focuses on strangers, perpetrators and victims usually know each other. In most cases of intrafamilial abuse, the perpetrator is a sibling, but abuse by a parent or parent figure produces the most severe consequences for mental health.

Children who are victimized once are at increased risk of being victimized again (Finkelhor et al., 2007). This might be because victimization impairs the ability to recognize and respond to risky situations and untrustworthy people, possibly because dissociation screens out information that people need to detect danger (Gobin & Freyd, 2009; Zurbriggen, Gobin, & Freyd, 2010). Another possibility is that abuse increases children's feelings of vulnerability, and pedophiles have fine-tuned their ability to sense this vulnerability. Multiple victimizations are associated with increased rates of mental health problems, compared to single victimizations (Anda et al., 2006; Finkelhor et al., 2007).

Sexually abused children are at increased risk of developing psychological problems (Kendall-Tackett, 2012). These disturbances take a wide variety of forms, including both internalizing and externalizing problems, but abuse histories show their strongest associations with PTSD (Kolko et al., 2010) and sexual acting out (Tarren-Sweeney, 2008). Nevertheless, most abused children are able to get through this experience without showing lasting ill effects, as is the case with divorce, bereavement, and stressful experiences in general.

Neurobiological Etiologies

Childhood trauma may cause enduring brain dysfunction, which, in turn, affects development, health, and quality of life (Anda et al., 2006). Childhood trauma, especially when repeated, causes dysregulation of the autonomic nervous system and HPA axis (Heim, Plotsky, & Nemeroff, 2004; Hulme, 2011). Even with no threat present, the brains of PTSD victims are often hyper-aroused, with activity patterns associated with fight-or-flight responses to danger. In PTSD, an intense physical response was usually appropriate in the original traumatic situation, but once this situation has passed, repeated triggering of fight-or-flight responses impairs both mental and physical health (Belsky & Pleuss, 2009; Bremner, 2006).

Neurophysiological processes seem to explain the emotionally powerful and cognitively disorganized nature of traumatic memories (Brewin, 2001; Brewin & Holmes, 2003). Frightening, painful stimuli activate the amygdala, which plays an important role in the encoding of new memories. At the same time, extreme arousal interferes with the functioning of the hippocampus, a higher-level brain structure that organizes memories into meaningful sequences. Adults with abuse-related PTSD show reduced volume of the hippocampus, probably because stress inhibits neurogenesis there (Bremner, 2006). Extreme stress also disrupts the functioning of the anterior cingulate region and other structures of the prefrontal cortex (De Bellis, Keshavan, Spencer, & Hall, 2000). Thus, trauma both intensifies sensory memory acquisition by the amygdala and disrupts memory organization by the hippocampus and prefrontal cortex. This is apparently why traumatic events are burned into memory as chaotic surges of sensory and emotional experience, rather than coherent narratives, and why re-experiencing symptoms ("flashbacks") are often triggered by incidental stimuli that were conditioned to the traumatic experience but had no causal relationship to it. This formulation suggests that therapy should recruit high-level, conceptual functions to the task of reprocessing traumatic memories, so these memories can be organized and their implications can be delimited in a realistic fashion.

Trauma both intensifies sensory memory acquisition by the amygdala and disrupts memory organization by the hippocampus and prefrontal cortex.

When increased cortisol release is repeatedly triggered by perceptions of threat, sometimes there is an eventual rebound effect in which the body's capability to produce this hormone is depleted, and cortisol levels drop below normal concentrations (McCleery & Harvey, 2004; Miller, Chen, & Zhou, 2007). Thus, chronic PTSD can result in elevated cortisol levels, extremely low levels, and fluctuations between both. In all three cases, there is disruption of the normal cortisol biorhythm through the day, which we need to regulate cycles of high energy and rest. People with PTSD sometimes feel hyper-aroused and tense and sometimes feel burned out and exhausted.

Behavioral Etiologies

There seem to be two levels of etiology in trauma-related disturbance. First, on a basic level of limbic system functioning and conditioning, the problem is that the victim's brain continues to reverberate with the sensory and emotional experiences produced by the trauma. Second, on a more conceptual, cortical level of mental functioning, the problem is that comfortable assumptions about the self and world have been shattered by traumatic events. The conceptual level of trauma is addressed by cognitive, dynamic, and constructivist interventions. The conditioning level is addressed by behavior therapy, particularly exposure procedures.

Behavioral theory views PTSD as a continuation of the physiological reactions, emotions, and behaviors that were normal as immediate responses to the trauma but became dysfunctional when they persisted after the occurrence was over.

Behavioral theory views PTSD as a continuation of the physiological reactions, emotions, and behaviors that were normal as immediate responses to the trauma but became dysfunctional when they persisted after the occurrence was over (Perrin et al., 2004). It is as if the brain cannot turn off its fear response even though the danger has passed, so the person, lying safe in her bed at night, continues to experience the arousal and hypervigilance that were appropriate to the traumatic situation. PTSD is caused by overgeneralized, misapplied learning, as discussed in Chapter 2 on behavior therapy.

Learning theory formulations of PTSD involve both operant and classical conditioning (Fletcher, 2003; Zalta & Foa, 2012). Pavlovian conditioning explains the situationally inappropriate fear experienced by many traumatized children; the traumatic event was an unconditioned stimulus that transformed associated neutral stimuli into conditioned fear stimuli. This seems to be why painful memories and emotions are sometimes evoked by innocuous stimuli that just happened to be present in the traumatic situation. For example, some abuse victims experience anxiety in response to any smell that was present during their molestation (e.g., coffee that was brewing at the time). The avoidant behavior characteristic of PTSD is attributable to the combination of classical and operant conditioning called avoidance learning (Mowrer, 1960; Spiegler & Guevremont, 2010), as explained in Chapter 13, Anxiety.

Cognitive Etiologies

Traumatic experiences contradict people's assumptions about their lives, worlds, and selves.

Cognitively, traumatic experiences contradict people's assumptions about their lives, worlds, and selves (Janoff-Bulman, 1992; Landsman, 2002). Perhaps the most important of these assumptions is the belief in a **just world**, in which bad things do not happen to good people (Lerner, 1998; Lerner & Miller, 1978). The occurrence of trauma seems to imply either that the world or the self is bad.

When assumptions are shattered, people try to revise their understanding of life in order to recover their confidence that things make sense (Corr, 2002; Janoff-Bulman, 1992). Efforts to figure out the meaning of stressful events have an adaptive purpose, but the experience may be painful, at least until the person develops a new understanding that provides some resolution. Often, distress first increases and then decreases to below its initial level as victims move through the sequence (Silver, Boon, & Stones, 1983), in the pattern graphed in Chapter 8's Figure 8.3. However, if the person cannot construct an acceptable interpretation of the trauma, he may stay stuck at a high level of distress.

To adults, one of the most striking aspects of child sexual abuse is victim self-blame. Such self-blame is common (Daigneault, Hebert, & Tourigny, 2006; Steel, Sanna, Hammond, Whipple, & Cross, 2004). Abuse victims who blame themselves experience more depression and trauma symptoms than those who attribute their abuse to external factors (Brown, Albrecht, McQuaid, Munoz-Silva, & Silva, 2004; Canton-Cortes, Canton, & Cortes, 2012; Valle & Silovsky, 2002). Some children of divorce blame themselves for the breakup of their parents' marriage, especially if their misbehavior was a subject of contention between the parents (Ehrenberg et al., 2014; Harvey & Fine, 2010).

Victims of all sorts of misfortune sometimes engage in self-blame. When bad things happen, people ask, "Why me?" The need to believe in an orderly world makes it hard to believe that negative events, especially when they happen repeatedly, could be the result of factors that are random with respect to the self (Lerner, 1998; Lerner & Miller, 1978). Clients whose lives have gone poorly for a long time sometimes reject bad luck as an explanation and say things like, "I'm the common denominator here." They seem to believe that people somehow call forth from the universe the types of experiences that are naturally theirs.

Self-blame is not the only problem related to self-concept that results from abuse. Children sometimes understand that the abuse was not their fault while also believing that it has permanently damaged them in some way (Berliner, 1997; Cheung, 2012). These self-perceptions, which are often unrealistic, may concern physical damage from the molestation, such as sexually transmitted disease. Boys molested by men sometimes believe the abuse will cause them to become homosexual (Durham, 2003; Spiegel, 2003).

Trauma victims often have thoughts about their PTSD symptoms that increase their distress. When Robin experienced intrusive memories of her abuse, she had thoughts like, "I'm going crazy," and "I'll never get over this." PTSD, like panic disorder, often includes anxiety about anxiety, or secondary distress. Therapists can assist clients by helping them understand that trauma symptoms, while painful, do not signal anything terrible beyond themselves.

Coping With Stress

Research on coping has identified numerous coping strategies, but they can be organized into a few basic categories. Lazarus and Folkman (1984) distinguished between **problem-focused coping**, in which the person aims to change the situation causing stress, and **emotion-focused coping**, in which the person seeks to change her response to a stressful situation. A similar distinction was proposed by Rothbaum, Weisz, and Snyder (1982), who distinguished between attempts to achieve **primary control** over the stressful situation versus **secondary control** over one's reaction to the stressor. Both typologies emphasize the difference between internally and externally oriented coping efforts, or, in Rothbaum et al.'s words, attempts to change the world versus attempts to change the self.

Hundreds of studies of coping with dozens of stressors have produced an extremely complicated, mixed set of results that do not identify a manageable number of consistently effective coping strategies that can be recommended to clients. However, the research has yielded one large theme: It is important to *match* coping strategies to the realities of stressful situations. In other words, the key to coping is not to learn and consistently use inherently effective techniques, because different strategies are effective in different situations—instead, the key is knowing what to do when (Carver, 2011). G. Bonanno and Burton (2013) refer to this capability as **regulatory flexibility**. (See Chapter 8's discussion of connections between human evolution, adaptive versatility, and moderation.)

The most important dimension of fit concerns the distinction between problem-focused and emotion-focused coping in relation to the controllability of the stressor. If the stressful situation is potentially controllable, problem-focused coping leads to better outcomes, and if the situation is uncontrollable, emotion-focused strategies produce better outcomes (Aldridge & Roesch, 2007; Babb, Levine, & Arseneault, 2010).

One generalization that has been supported by meta-analysis is that avoidant coping strategies are often helpful in the short term but, in the long run, avoidant coping is usually maladaptive. Littleton, Horsley, John, and Nelson (2007), averaging across studies, obtained a small/medium-sized correlation of .37 between avoidant coping and distress, with no correlation between approach-oriented coping and distress. However, there are exceptions to this rule. When stressors are uncontrollable and/or severe, approach-oriented strategies that are usually adaptive become maladaptive, and avoidant coping becomes relatively helpful (Compas, Connor, Saltzman, Thomsen, & Wadsworth, 2001; Gonzales, Tein, Sandler, & Friedman, 2001). Studies with low-income, urban, African American youth have found positive effects of avoidant coping, perhaps because, in the largely uncontrollable environments in which they live, active attempts to solve unsolvable problems only exacerbate distress (Dempsey, 2002; Dempsey, Overstreet, & Moely, 2000).

Seeking social support is usually an effective coping strategy (Ben-Zur, 2009; Compas et al., 2001), but this generalization, too, has a limit. As mentioned in Chapter 14, depressed youth sometimes seek reassurance from others so frequently that the effects on their relationships are negative (Prinstein, Borelli, Cheah, Simon, & Aikins, 2005; Shih, Abela, & Starrs, 2009).

Assessment

Child self-report, reports by parents and other adults, and therapist observation all contribute to assessment of stress and trauma (Berliner, 1997; Cohen, Mannarino, & Deblinger, 2006). For example, avoidance might be indicated by a child's statement that he never thinks about his molestation, a parent's report that he resists going into the room where it occurred, and a therapist's observation that he switches topics quickly when the issue comes up.

Assessment should investigate the child's functioning before and after the stressor so that changes can be ascertained. The possibilities of preexisting and comorbid disturbance, as well as stressors less prominent than those at the focus of attention, should be investigated (Briere & Scott, 2014).

One question faced by clinicians assessing traumatized children, especially sexual abuse victims, is how directly to inquire into the details of the experience. Of course, it is important to find out what happened, but this does not necessarily mean that a detailed inquiry should be conducted right away. Clinicians should remember that their responsibility is treatment, not forensic investigation. If the child finds it extremely upsetting to describe her trauma, prolonged questioning might interfere with the development of a therapeutic relationship.

Sometimes it is effective to adopt a patient approach and give the client time to provide information in increments, as he becomes more comfortable and ready to disclose. Asking about trauma-related thoughts and feelings before investigating concrete details sends the respectful message that you care about the child's views and experiences more than the particulars of what happened. Robin needed to share her emotional reactions and efforts to understand the meaning of her abuse before she was able to disclose everything that occurred. As is often the case in sexual abuse, her first report was the tip of an iceberg. There had been numerous incidents of abuse by the 15-year-old over a 6-month period and, in addition to the fondling Robin initially reported, the boy had forced her to stroke his genitals to the point of orgasm.

Assessment of PTSD should, at some point, include direct questions about the details of the traumatic events (van Eys & Truss, 2012). Counselors need to know the specifics of what happened to understand cues for stress reactions and to plan therapy, particularly exposure procedures. Therapists should ask clients to walk us through the sequence of events slowly and carefully so we can understand exactly what they went through.

Here are some interview questions about core symptoms of PTSD:

- "Do you ever feel like _____ (the negative event) is going to happen again?" "How much do you feel that way?"

- "When you are reminded of _____, what goes through your mind?" "How does your body feel?" "Does your heart beat fast?" "Do you sweat?"

- "Are there things about _____ that you can't remember no matter how hard you try?"

- "Since _____, do you get surprised or startled more easily?"

Especially after they have disclosed painful material, clients may need some empathy and encouragement to continue with the assessment. You can say something like:

"I know this is hard, but you're doing great; you're telling me what I need to know to help you. We'll finish soon, but I have a few more questions."

Drawing and other artistic activities may facilitate self-disclosure in traumatized children who find it difficult to give verbal reports of what occurred (Case & Dalley, 2014; Malchiodi, 2006, 2011). Play with dolls and toys provides a source of information about the child's trauma-related thoughts and feelings (Briggs, Runyon, & Deblinger, 2011; Gil, 2012; Goodyear-Brown, 2012), although this play should not necessarily be viewed as a depiction of actual events.

There are two basic assessment questions about client interpretations of stressful events. The first, which is oriented toward the past, is what the client believes *caused* the event. The second, which concerns the present and future, is what the youth believes about the *consequences* of the event. The questions ahead focus on sexual abuse for the sake of consistency, but the questions can be adapted for other traumatic experiences as well.

Questions about causality and responsibility may be threatening to clients, and therapists should provide a gentle introduction—for example:

"Now I'm going to ask you a hard question, and you might not know the answer to it: Why do you think the abuse happened?"

Clinical experience suggests that some youth are intellectually aware that their abuse was the perpetrator's fault (perhaps because adults have told them so), but they harbor nagging feelings of self-blame, nonetheless. When clients deny self-blame, clinicians can follow up by saying:

"You're certainly right that it was his fault, but, still, have you ever worried that it might have been your fault in a way, too?"

To assess whether the youth feels the abuse damaged her in some permanent way, the counselor can ask:

> "Did the abuse change you? Do you think you might be different now, in some way, because of what happened?"

It is important to investigate the nature of victims' relationships with their perpetrators, especially in cases of intrafamilial abuse (Gannon, Gilchrist, & Wade, 2008; Trickett, Noll, Reiffman, & Putnam, 2001). In order to assess ambivalence, clinicians should give clients opportunities to describe positive as well as negative aspects of the perpetrator (e.g., "Did he ever do good things, too?"). Another question with which to investigate these feelings is:

> "If you were a judge, and it was up to you to decide what to do with _____ (the perpetrator), what would you do?"

Finally, it is useful to ask clients whether they have any questions about sexual abuse, either their own or the problem in general. Asking whether there is anything the client finds herself wondering about or trying to understand often reveals areas of confusion and misunderstanding.

Assessing the effects of parental divorce should include asking the child why he thinks the divorce occurred and what he thinks the effects of the divorce have been and might be, both for himself and other family members (Ehrlich, 2014; Harvey & Fine, 2010). Clinicians should ask about the acrimony between partners that usually precedes divorce, as well as the separation process itself. The client's feelings about practical issues, such as custody and visitation arrangements, should be examined. Another question is whether the child has accepted the finality of the divorce, or whether there is a wish that, somehow, the parents will reunite someday. Counselors should investigate whether the client worries about the possibility of further family changes or relationship losses.

Assessment of grief should inquire about the client's understanding of the reasons for the death and her thoughts about possible effects of this loss on her future (Ayers et al., 2014; Goldman, 2012). The loss of one parent sometimes leads to anxiety about losing the other because death no longer seems like an unlikely event. Spiritual beliefs about an afterlife influence the child's understanding of the deceased person's existence.

Treatment Planning

Outcome Research

Outcome research on PTSD provides its strongest support for cognitive-behavioral therapy.

Outcome research on PTSD provides its strongest support for cognitive-behavioral therapy. The APA Society of Clinical Psychology has given a rating of *Strong Research Support* to a cognitive-behavioral intervention for adults similar to Cohen et al.'s (2006) intervention for youth called *trauma-focused cognitive behaviour therapy* (TF-CBT).

De Arellano et al. (2014) performed a systematic assessment of the evidence base for TF-CBT by considering the quality of study methodologies as well as the results they produced. They rated the level of evidence for TF-CBT as High (the best possible designation) on the basis of 10 RCTs. They noted that this intervention reliably reduces PTSD symptoms and has weaker evidence for its efficacy at decreasing depression and behavior problems.

Cary and McMillen (2012) conducted three related meta-analyses of PTSD outcome studies: One examined research on Cohen et al.'s (2006) TF-CBT, one examined similar but not identical interventions, and one examined cognitive-behavioral therapies that included four of five fundamental TF-CBT strategies. The results produced by the three analyses were very similar, suggesting that Cohen et al.'s specific manual and general exposure-based CBT for PTSD are equivalent in effectiveness. Compared to a variety of control conditions, cognitive-behavioral therapies demonstrated a medium/large effect size of .67 for PTSD symptoms and achieved small effects on depression and behavior problems. These effects were generally maintained at follow-up assessments.

Deblinger, Mannarino, Cohen, Runyon, and Steer (2011) performed a dismantling study in which they compared TF-CBT with and without the trauma narrative component as a treatment for sexually abused children with PTSD. The two interventions produced similar improvements on most of the study's measures, but inclusion of the trauma narrative did seem to increase the effectiveness of therapy for children whose predominant symptom was anxiety, compared to children exhibiting pronounced externalizing problems. Also, many of the clients cited their work on a trauma narrative as an especially important and helpful aspect of therapy.

Effectiveness research has investigated the outcomes produced by TF-CBT in "real-world" community settings, which differ from the more controlled conditions of university-affiliated clinics, where most past efficacy studies were performed. Webb, Hayes, Grasso, Laurenceau, and Deblinger (2014) performed a study at a multisite community mental health agency. This research did not include a control group but compared change on the outcome measures to the effects demonstrated in past efficacy studies. The intervention produced significant reductions in PTSD symptoms and internalizing and externalizing problems during the 6 months following intake, and these gains were maintained over the next 6 months. The magnitudes of these improvements were similar to those of past efficacy trials.

In a Norwegian effectiveness study by T. Jensen et al. (2014), clients with a mean age of 15 years were randomly assigned to receive either TF-CBT or TAU. Youth who received TF-CBT showed greater reductions in PTSD symptoms, depression, general mental health symptoms, and functional impairment, with a nonsignificant trend for anxiety reduction. Post-treatment, fewer youth in the TF-CBT group met criteria for a PTSD diagnosis, compared to youth receiving TAU.

Gilboa-Schechtman et al. (2010) conducted an RCT examining the efficacy of exposure therapy versus psychodynamic therapy for adolescents with PTSD who had experienced single-event traumas. Both interventions resulted in decreased PTSD symptoms and improved functioning across a range of measures, but the beneficial effects of exposure therapy were larger in magnitude. At termination, 68% of the clients who received exposure treatment no longer met criteria for PTSD, compared to 37% who received dynamic therapy. Both groups maintained their treatment gains at 6- and 17-month follow-ups.

Sánchez-Meca, Rosa-Alcázar, and López-Soler (2011) performed a meta-analysis of 33 studies (only some of which were RCTs) of therapy for sexually abused children. Almost all the interventions were based on CBT, but some of them also included components of supportive therapy and psychodynamic play therapy. Overall, the results indicated significant effect sizes, mostly in the medium to large range, across a number of outcome measures. The most notable finding was that effects for CBT plus supportive and/or dynamic components were larger than effects for unadulterated CBT. "Supportive" therapy is difficult to define, but apparently this term referred to interventions, like dynamic therapy, in which significant time was spent expressing and discussing emotions.

In their review of mediating variables in child therapy research, Weisz, Ng, Rutt, Lau, and Masland, (2013) noted that they could find no studies examining mediation effects in TF-CBT or any other therapy for trauma. Future research is needed to provide empirical information about how these therapies work.

There has been little research on individual therapy for children of divorced parents. In a study by Burroughs, Wagner, and Johnson (1997), one group of clients received a cognitive-behavioral intervention that provided information about divorce and training in coping skills, while the other group received nondirective therapy. Clients in both groups showed decreases in depression and anxiety, and there were no differences in the effects of the two interventions.

Almost all research on interventions for children of divorce has examined group programs, delivered in schools, which purported to prevent the development of mental health problems. Stathakos and Roehrle (2003) performed a meta-analysis of 23 outcome studies of these preventive interventions and obtained a small/medium-sized effect of .43. Pedro-Carroll (2005; Pedro-Carroll, Sutton, & Wyman, 1999) found that a preventive group intervention reduced children's adjustment problems both immediately postintervention and at a 2-year follow-up.

There has also been little research on therapy for bereavement in youth, and most of the few existing studies have examined group therapies (Pearlman et al., 2010). Research on therapy for bereaved adults may provide suggestive information. Currier et al. (2010) performed a meta-analysis of 11 studies of CBT interventions. When researcher allegiance was taken into account, there were no differences between CBT treatments and other therapies. CBT outperformed a no-treatment control condition immediately postintervention, with a small effect size of .38, but the benefits dissipated at follow-up.

In their meta-analysis of 14 RCTs, Wittouck et al. (2011) drew a distinction between *preventive* interventions—which occurred soon after the loved one's death, before symptoms of complicated grief had time to materialize—and *treatment* inventions, which were administered to individuals showing symptoms of prolonged, complicated grief some time after the loved one's death. The preventive interventions showed nonsignificant standardized mean differences (similar to effect sizes) between participants and controls, while the treatment interventions demonstrated a medium-sized mean difference of .53 immediately postintervention and a large mean difference of 1.38 at follow-up. This set of results suggests that, at least for adults, bereavement therapy has little to offer individuals in the immediate aftermath of bereavement but has much to offer people who, some time later, continue to suffer from prolonged, complicated grief.

The Family Bereavement Program (Ayers et al., 2014; Sandler et al., 2003) is a cognitive-behavioral intervention for families in which a parent has died. The program targets possible mediators of resilience with CBT for youth and training for parents. Sandler et al. (2003) found that, compared to a bibliotherapy control group, the intervention improved caregiver-child relationships and caregiver mental health, and enhanced children's coping, accuracy of beliefs about control, and emotional expression. Effects on measures of child mental health were few and inconsistent. However, at a 6-year follow-up, program participation was associated with reduced externalizing problems and intrusive thoughts about the loss and with increased self-esteem (Sandler et al., 2010).

Clinical Considerations

Currently, outcome research on PTSD provides strong support only for cognitive-behavioral therapy, so it seems clear that CBT should be the first approach considered for most children and adolescents. Sánchez-Meca et al.'s (2011) meta-analysis of outcome studies on sexually abused children supported the central importance of CBT but also suggested that adding a psychodynamic or supportive component creates a more effective intervention than CBT alone.

Deblinger et al.'s (2011) dismantling study of therapy for sexually abused children produced results with implications for treatment planning. They found that if externalizing problems are the main symptoms, narrative work does not improve outcomes for clients, but if anxiety symptoms are prominent, work on a trauma narrative produces important therapeutic benefits. The presence of internalizing symptoms might suggest an important etiological role for client attributions, beliefs, and interpretations of meanings related to the abuse. Thus, conceptual forms of intervention such as cognitive restructuring, narrative, and dynamic therapy may be important components of treatment for clients with prominent symptoms of anxiety or depression, while these components may be unnecessary for youth whose symptoms consist primarily of externalizing problems.

Gil (2012) and Bonner, Walker, and Berliner (1999) describe psychodynamic play therapy for sexually abused children. This approach provides children with a wide degree of latitude for expressing the fears, conflicts, and misunderstandings that, in addition to straightforward traumatization, contribute to maladjustment in the aftermath of molestation. Especially for young children, the opportunity to express concerns and struggle with meanings in symbolic form might enable deeper and more extensive communication between therapist and client than would be possible by discussing the abuse in the more direct fashion characteristic of CBT.

Intrafamilial sexual abuse calls for a family therapy component of treatment because this type of victimization is generally a function not only of perpetrator psychopathology but also of family dysfunction (De Young et al., 2013; Engel, 2000; Gannon et al., 2008). The relationship between the child and nonoffending parent(s) is particularly important and sometimes problematic because abuse involves a breakdown of the protective function of this relationship, either because the parent did not respond adequately to the child's disclosure or because the channel of communication was not sufficiently clear for a disclosure to take place (Berliner, 1997; Bratton, Ceballos, Landreth, & Costas, 2012). Therapeutic work on this parent-child relationship is often an important part of treatment for incest. When abusive behavior by a parent or sibling is revealed, family relationships are usually severely stressed, and systems-oriented counseling is needed to address the disruption.

Cognitive-Behavioral Therapy

In their review of CBT interventions for trauma in children, Cary and McMillen (2012) noted that TF-CBT (Cohen et al., 2006) is currently the predominant cognitive-behavioral intervention for this population, although there are other, similar versions of this approach. TF-CBT was originally developed as a treatment for child sexual abuse, and this remains a major application of the treatment package (Cohen, Mannarino, & Knudsen, 2005; Deblinger, Mannarino, Cohen, & Steer, 2006), but it has also been applied to other stressful events, such as domestic violence and traumatic loss (Cohen, Mannarino, & Iyengar, 2011; Cohen, Mannarino, Perel, & Staron, 2007). Although based primarily on cognitive-behavioral principles, TF-CBT includes other components drawn from family systems theory and narrative therapy. These components of the intervention are described in the systems-oriented and constructivist sections of this chapter.

TF-CBT consists of a sequence of eight components, which are implemented in order at a pace determined by the child's and parent's readiness to move to the next step. The first letters of the components form the acronym PRACTICE. These components are: (P) psychoeducation and parenting skills, (R) relaxation, (A) affective expression and regulation, (C) cognitive coping, (T) trauma narrative development and processing, (I) in vivo gradual exposure, (C) conjoint parent-child sessions, and (E) enhance safety and future development. Throughout the intervention, parents are taught how to review and rehearse the knowledge and skills their child is learning in therapy.

To organize the components of CBT into larger chunks, there are three main types of intervention. As in therapy for other anxiety-related disorders, the key procedure is exposure. Training in coping skills is used to reduce the pain of exposure to trauma-related stimuli and to reduce distress in the child's everyday life. Cognitive therapy addresses the upsetting misunderstandings, especially self-blame, that frequently accompany abuse and trauma, and helps clients develop realistic, adaptive understandings of what happened.

Exposure

In therapy for PTSD, clients are not usually exposed to external situations but to the contents of their own minds—namely, their memories of trauma (Cohen, Murray, & Mannarino, 2013; Foa et al., 2007; Ford & Cloitre, 2009). Sometimes there are also external stimuli, objects, or places that were associated with the events and that became anxiety-producing for the youth. If this is the case, exposure procedures should target these stimuli, objects, and settings as well as the client's trauma-associated memories.

Of course, clients do not become desensitized to trauma itself, but they can become desensitized to trauma-related memories, thoughts, and stimuli. Exposure-based treatment enables clients to remember their negative experiences without being flooded by them. This strategy makes sense because the proximal cause of PTSD is not a past event but a memory that occurs in the present.

Discussions of exposure in Chapters 2 and 13 provide a framework for using this technique; the present chapter focuses on specific applications of exposure to trauma symptoms. The counselor's first step is to obtain a detailed description of the stressful experience from the client. Then the therapist leads the client through the painful memories in a gradual fashion.

Initially, this procedure might seem threatening, and it might not make sense to the client as a way to feel better. Therefore, it is important to explain why the technique can be helpful—for example:

"You've been trying to cope with these memories by avoiding them in your mind, but that hasn't worked for you, so we need to try something else. In fact, we need to try the opposite: turning around and facing the fears. The way to do this is for you to tell me exactly what happened, and to go over it again and again, until you don't have trouble talking about it anymore. We don't have to be afraid of these words; we can just say them. You might feel like this will be impossibly hard, but we'll start slow, work on it gradually, and it will get easier and easier with practice. We will wear those memories out. Once you can talk about them and think about them whenever you want, you'll be able to drop them when that's what you want, and they won't have power over you, because you'll have taken control of them."

Counselors should begin by exposing clients to relatively mild memories and then move up the hierarchy as mastery is achieved. Deblinger and Heflin's (1996) outline of an anxiety hierarchy for sexually abused children includes, in ascending order: general information about abuse; memories of nonabusive interactions with the perpetrator; memories of disclosing the abuse; and, finally, memories of the molestations themselves, beginning with the least and ascending to the most upsetting incidents. Therapists should let the client begin with abstract, vague descriptions and add emotional and sensory detail as he progresses. In the final stage of exposure work, the client should verbalize explicit, detailed descriptions of the sexually abusive acts so he becomes desensitized even to his most painful memories.

TF-CBT includes a component of narrative therapy, as described in Chapter 6. Children compose a narrative of their trauma. This work begins as a verbal account delivered to the counselor, who may ask questions to clarify the account. As this material coheres into an organized story, the child puts it into writing. These narratives are often revised in successive drafts as the client becomes clearer about what she wants to say, recalls more details, and reorganizes her understanding of what happened. From a neurobiological perspective, transforming a swirl of horrible sensations and emotions into a sequence of cause and effect means that raw, amygdala-based memories are organized by higher hippocampal and cortical processes into a more coherent, manageable history.

In TF-CBT for young children, clients reenact traumatic experiences in the form of pretend play (Briggs et al., 2011). Many traumatized children seem to do these exposure activities on their own. This type of play often begins as an intense, disorganized discharge of intense emotions. While this can be useful at first, therapists can then help the child organize his narrative by asking what happened when, establishing sequences, and inquiring about the reasons for things. If the play seems repetitive and "stuck," counselors can suggest different endings to try.

Clients can also read books with trauma-related themes and draw pictures of traumatic events. Sequences of events can be depicted in a comic strip format. Resick and Calhoun's (2001) *cognitive processing therapy* uses journal writing and reading as formats for controlled exposure to traumatic material. Nonclinical research with adults by Pennebaker and colleagues (Baddeley & Pennebaker, 2011; Pennebaker & Seagal, 1999) has found that expressive journal writing, by itself, produces a wide range of benefits, including reduced stress and depression, enhanced immune system functioning, improved physical health, closer relationships, and better college grades. Writing activities must have certain characteristics to achieve these effects. The writing must focus on a painful event or situation, express emotions openly and extensively, and identify connections between events, meanings, and emotions. This type of journal writing can be helpful to a variety of clients besides those with PTSD.

Self-Instruction and Guided Imagery

Training in self-instruction (Friedberg & McClure, 2002, 2014; Kendall & Hedtke, 2006a, 2006b), described in Chapters 3 and 13, can help clients cope with intrusive memories and reexperiencing symptoms of PTSD. Therapists and clients can collaborate to compose self-instructions like the following:

- "Here is a memory coming up again … ow, it hurts. But, the fear will go up a little bit—and I'll keep on breathing, slow and deep—and then I'll watch the fear go down."
- "I might not be able to stop this memory from coming, but I can do something about how I react to it. I didn't have power then, but I do have power now."

Self-instruction can help clients manage the pain that typically accompanies exposure exercises. However, therapists should take care to ensure that the client uses self-instruction and relaxation only to help him *tolerate* exposure, not to *distract him from* trauma-related memories, because attention is necessary for exposure to work. (Distraction is often a helpful coping technique, but not during exposure procedures.)

Guided imagery can reduce distress and strengthen coping in trauma victims (Lueger, 2002; Taal & Krop, 2002). Post-traumatic images often reflect memories of the self as helpless, terrorized, and suffering in a dangerous world. Counselors and clients can collaborate on the development of competing images of the self as secure and calm, in a safe world—or, perhaps more realistically, in a stormy world that they are able to manage.

Guided imagery is often conducted in conjunction with relaxation. In this combination of techniques, the client sits comfortably in a chair, closes his eyes, and pictures the images in his mind as he engages in deep breathing, possibly following progressive muscle relaxation. The discussion ahead focuses on trauma but also applies to imagery work for anxiety and depression.

Therapists and clients can construct pleasant imagery by brainstorming together (Friedberg & McClure, 2002, 2014; Loades et al., 2014). One way to begin is to ask the youth what she likes—what sorts of places, objects, and activities. Clients may respond by talking about beaches, meadows, cozy rooms, floating on clouds, playing sports, and so forth. Therapeutic visualization evolves as the child experiments with the imagination process and finds images that work for her. As the client pictures her scenes, the therapist should ask for details about what she sees and how things work in her imagined place. Then, the therapist and child weave these good things into a coherent, happy scene that makes emotional sense to the client. For example, here is some of Robin's imagery:

"I am sailing over the ocean in a safe, sturdy boat that has everything in it I need. All my favorite things are there: American Girl dolls, the best books and music, arts and crafts, a computer, two cats to keep me company, everything. We sail around the world, to tropical islands and beautiful places, with blue water, gentle breezes, and dolphins coming up to say hi. Usually I live in the real world with my family, but when things there get too tense, I take off in my boat until I'm ready to come back."

Two types of guided imagery can be helpful to clients. The first type, just illustrated, is purely positive in content; its purpose is to help the child distract and escape from his painful memories. The second type of imagery, based on the extendincorp strategy (Chapter 8), acknowledges the existence of stress and pain but incorporates those elements into an overarching image of containment and mastery of the challenge. The purpose of this type of imagery is to help the youth cope with and build upon the reality of stress and trauma by encompassing its pain with resilience.

Three metaphors are often useful in guided imagery of this type. The first takes off from the boat metaphor presented earlier. In this variation, the seas are not calm—the boat is traveling through a violent storm with thunder, lightning, driving rain, and crashing waves. The boat is tossed about by the sea, and the child is assailed by stress and fear. However, the little boat in the big storm is sturdy, strong, and watertight, with all openings sealed. The engine continues to run. The good things in the boat are still there for the child.

Here, the counselor can add an element to encourage the client to persist with the difficult work of exposure and cognitive reprocessing of the trauma. We can say that the client has a choice about which way to steer the boat, but only one of the options will really work. If the boat is turned around to flee, the storm will overtake it; the boat cannot outrun the storm. If the boat is steered right into the storm, it can power through and eventually emerge into peaceful seas. The only way out is through—and the child and his boat are capable of the journey.

A related metaphor consists of journeying down a road, with the portion already traversed as the past, the person's current position as the present, and the road ahead as the future; time is represented as space. Painful experiences are symbolized as rough portions of the road that were difficult and hurtful to get through, with mud, debris, and obstacles; good times are symbolized in the opposite way. Progress on the road requires working through challenges and obstacles, which sometimes occurs in a straight-ahead fashion, sometimes involves twists and turns, and sometimes involves the road bending backwards. The trauma is located on a part of the road that has already been traversed.

The third metaphor involves physical enclosure of painful experiences inside some type of container. In this visualization, painful memories and associated emotions are placed inside some type of locked box, closet, or building—you can even offer to keep the memories in your desk drawer, perhaps in the client's chart, as long as he is assured that you can store this material without being hurt. In the imagery, clients take the memories out of their box to review them and then return the memories to their containers, with solid walls separating the client from his pain.

Distraction

Distraction can be an effective coping mechanism because it is harder to stop thinking about something than to start thinking about something *else*. Distraction reduces distress by replacing painful mental content with more positive material. For example, Robin was usually unsuccessful when she tried to stop thinking about the abuse, but she was more successful when she tried to picture her favorite dolls in as much detail as possible. There are maladaptive versions of distraction (e.g., drug use), but effective versions enhance adjustment. Distraction is especially useful for countering the intrusive thoughts and re-experiencing symptoms associated with PTSD (Ford & Cloitre, 2009).

Distraction can involve any activity capable of absorbing the client's attention. Counselors and youth should brainstorm options, and clients should select the ones most likely to work for them. As discussed in Chapter 4, DBT provides extensive guidance about therapeutic use of distraction (Linehan, 1993a, 1993b, 2014; Rathus & Miller, 2014). Table 4.1 lists a variety of distress tolerance techniques. Also, mindfulness exercises can help clients with PTSD by diverting their attention away from trauma-related memories of the past and fears of the future toward the present moment, in which we are generally safe and okay.

Distraction can involve activities ranging from the tiny to the large. Dolan (1998) observed that, for many clients dealing with trauma or grief, the most helpful strategy is neither delving into negative emotions nor trying to galvanize positive ones but focusing on concrete, constructive *actions*, no matter how small. People dealing with wrenching change often find that maintaining elements of their routine and attending to practical tasks help them feel that normal life is continuing. Putting one foot in front of the other does not solve problems or undo traumas, but coping by means of a narrowed, pragmatic focus of attention often helps people get through hard times. Alcoholics Anonymous's advice to people struggling with difficulties, no matter how large or small, is to "do the next right thing." In the immediate aftermath of trauma, children sometimes need a reduction of demands, but once some time has gone by, coping is usually facilitated by refocusing on schoolwork, chores, hobbies, and so forth.

At each moment, people can attend to any aspect of their lives. Even in the midst of painful situations, focusing on one good thing, no matter how small, can enhance adjustment, because there is a big difference between having a little bit of goodness in one's life and having none at all.

One way to help clients become aware of their opportunities for attentional redirection is to ask them to list the domains of their life—activities, values, goals, relationships, and so forth—and to say which were damaged or destroyed by the negative event and which are still intact and available to them. Going through the list usually demonstrates to clients that, while much was lost, much remains.

Some forms of distraction are valuable not only for what they remove attention *from* but also for what they direct attention *to*. Any and all worthwhile activities can facilitate redirection of attention. Robin was good at arts and crafts, and her counselor encouraged her to make use of this strength in coping with reexperiencing symptoms. During the bad times, she painted intricate designs on clay pottery, and her awful memories of the abuse were somewhat replaced by anticipation of the happy expressions on her relatives' faces when she gave them these gifts. The word *distraction* does not do justice to this type of coping that, in its broadest definition, encompasses all efforts to live well—and constructing a good life is the ultimate coping mechanism.

Cognitive Restructuring

Victims can recover from trauma when they revise their view of the world enough to incorporate the reality of what happened without sacrificing their sense that life is fundamentally good.

Victims can recover from trauma when they revise their view of the world enough to incorporate the reality of what happened without sacrificing their sense that life is fundamentally good (De Young et al., 2013; Goldman, 2002). For example, sexual abuse imposes the lesson that some people cannot be trusted, but children might still be able to believe that authority figures will come to their aid and that they themselves are strong enough to survive these occurrences. Resilience requires a balance of optimism and realism.

Although many people express belief in a just world (Lerner, 1998; Lerner & Miller, 1978), neither systematic nor everyday observation indicates that life is reliably fair. Belief in a just world might reassure people when they see others suffer misfortune, but this cognition boomerangs on victims. Therapists should intervene with clients who interpret their misfortune as evidence of their badness. One way to do this is by invoking our experience and authority:

> "I have worked with lots of people on lots of things, and I can tell you this: Bad things happen to good people *all the time*."

Another way is to invoke clients' sympathy for others:

> "If we went to the pediatric cancer unit of the hospital, walked around, and met the kids, there's no way you would say to me, 'Well, they must have done something to deserve having cancer.' The same thing is true of _____ (the client's misfortune)."

For many clients, the underlying issue is religious. Of course, therapists should never try to change clients' beliefs, but sometimes it is therapeutically useful to encourage an accurate understanding of the religion to which they adhere. In mainstream interpretations of the Judeo-Christian tradition, God grants justice in an afterlife, but there is no justice on earth other than what mankind can cobble together for ourselves. Both the prophets of the Old Testament and Jesus in the New Testament responded to the unfortunate with kindness and compassion, not with a sense that they must have gotten what they deserved. Clients can respond to their own misfortune in the same way.

Coaching Clients in Coping

Therapists have opportunities to coach clients in coping with all sorts of stressors, including but not limited to those discussed in this chapter. Research reviewed earlier provides a framework: The key to effective coping is matching strategy to situation, so problem-focused coping is used in response to controllable stressors and emotion-focused coping is used in response to uncontrollable stressors (Aldridge & Roesch, 2007; Carver, 2011).

Many clients and parents have heard of the **Serenity Prayer**, which was composed by the theologian Reinhold Neibuhr and is the credo of Alcoholics Anonymous:

> God grant me the serenity to accept the things I cannot change, courage to change the things I can, and wisdom to know the difference.

Whether understood religiously or psychologically, this prayer is a poetic, evocative summary of coping research, because it clarifies the uses of problem-focused and emotion-focused coping and the types of situations that call for each. The elegant simplicity of this prayer provides an effective launch for the planning of coping strategies. Then therapists need to become analytical to help clients understand and plan for the complexities of the challenges they face.

The first complexity is that, in many situations, the question of whether to use action-oriented or emotion-oriented coping is not an either/or choice. Many situations include some aspects that are potentially controllable and some that are not, and counselors can help young people disentangle the two. For example, children cannot control whether their parents get divorced, but they might be able to influence how much their parents draw them into the conflict. In complex situations, effective adaptation often requires the flexibility to shift back and forth between problem- and emotion-focused coping. The counselor might first help the child develop the serenity to accept his parents' divorce and then bolster his courage to resist being drawn into their conflict.

There is a saying that describes how uncontrollable and controllable factors combine to produce outcomes: "You can't control the cards you are dealt, but you can control how you play those cards." As discussed in Chapter 3 on cognitive therapy, life is a lot like poker in this way. This saying helps clients distinguish between controllable and uncontrollable factors, so they can accept one and try to influence the other.

Thompson, Nanni, and Levine (1994) distinguish between **central control**—which is control over the occurrence of events—and **consequential control**—which is control over the effects of events. There are many stressful situations— including bereavement, sexual abuse, and parental divorce—in which central control is not possible but consequential control is. Therapists can help clients adapt to uncontrollable events by encouraging them to identify elements of their current situations, including consequences of the uncontrollable event, which they can control. For instance, a child of divorce could devote some energy to setting up her bedroom in the noncustodial parent's home in just the way she wants it. Even if our biggest wishes cannot come true, people adjust more effectively when they focus their attention on goals that are achievable, even if small. Even in terrible circumstances, options exist, and the question for youth to ask themselves is: "What is the best available thing to do in this situation?" For example, during his internment in a concentration camp during World War II, with people dying all around him, the psychiatrist Victor Frankl wrote notes on scraps of paper, which he hid, for his future book about the experience, called *Man's Search for Meaning* (1959/1992).

Determining what is and is not controllable is often difficult and sometimes impossible to do in advance; sometimes, there is no way to know until you try. Attempting to control a stressor and failing is a disappointment, but it brings positive by-products: reliable information about controllability and a clearer way forward to acceptance. I sometimes say to clients that the Serenity Prayer was written in the wrong order: First we should try to change the things we can, and only then should we accept the things we now know we cannot change. Exhausting the problem-focused option may help people switch to the emotion-focused one without nagging doubts, because doing everything possible means there is nothing more to do—so acceptance is justified. There is a religious saying that portrays this mental gear-switch from striving to acceptance: "Let go and let God." Depending on the client's spiritual beliefs, it might be useful to offer this saying.

Acceptance seems to include two components: realizing that what happened cannot be changed and believing that, despite this, life is okay— acceptable.

What does it mean to "accept" something? Acceptance seems to include two components: realizing that what happened cannot be changed and believing that, despite this, life is okay—acceptable. If a situation is unchangeable, hope equals denial, which prevents acceptance. In these situations, the adaptive response is giving up. Once acceptance has been accomplished, the mind is not repeatedly shocked by reminders of the trauma or loss. Our energies are freed and can be redirected toward aspects of our lives that can be changed, repaired, and enhanced. Therapists can help clients combine these components of realism and optimism by, in Thompson et al.'s (1994) terms, acknowledging their lack of central control while highlighting the possibility of consequential control:

> "So I guess there's good news and bad news. The bad news is that your parents are never going to get back together; it isn't going to happen. And it's possible that they'll keep sniping and bad-mouthing each other forever. But the good news is that this doesn't have to ruin your life. It doesn't even have to ruin your life with your parents. It's going to be harder than it would be if their marriage were good, but it's still possible for you to get along with your mom and get along with your dad and have good times when you're with them, separately."

The concept of acceptance applies to a wide variety of negative events that extends beyond the specific stressors and traumas we focus on in this chapter. The dual process of giving up on one goal while investing in others helps young people recover from disappointments as diverse as romantic rejection, unwanted geographical relocation, physical disability, and failure to be accepted by a desired school, sports, or arts program.

Many people who experience painful events are left with a need to *do* something about what happened. Often, the problem is that the direct actions they want to take are impossible: Abuse victims cannot shoot their perpetrators, children of divorce cannot reunify their parents, and grieving youth cannot bring their loved ones back to life. In such situations, the challenge is to think of actions that are both feasible and sufficiently related to the client's core desire to bring some resolution. For example, abuse victims can write letters to perpetrators in which they express anger, reject offender rationalizations, and confront abusers with the truth about what they did. Bereaved children can gather mementoes of deceased loved ones to create a physical collection of memories. Finally, when people take action to protect others from a type of harm they suffered themselves, their pain is transformed into energy for doing good in the world. The imprint of this high-level coping process is evident in organizations like Mothers Against Drunk Driving and in the custom of mourners donating money to organizations working on treatments for the disease that took their loved one's life.

One important question for people dealing with stress is how much to focus on the upsetting situation and how much to distract themselves by focusing on something else. Numerous studies have addressed this question for different stressors and produced complex, inconsistent results. The underlying difficulty might be that this is a two-sided issue: There can be value in focusing on what happened, and there can be value in redirecting attention to other aspects of life. Perhaps the compromise most capable of maximizing the benefits of both would be to:

- Occasionally think about the trauma in a focused, intense way, perhaps by talking about it with someone or writing about it in a journal.
- Most of the time, avoid preoccupation with the trauma and focus on other aspects of life.

Post-traumatic growth is a remarkable but common phenomenon in which people report that terrible events are followed by unexpected, positive by-products, such as increased strength, spirituality, understanding and appreciation of life, and closer relationships with others (Tedeschi & Calhoun, 2004). Post-traumatic growth has been documented in adolescents following serious car accidents (Salter & Stallard, 2004), the death of a family member (Ickovics et al., 2006), diagnosis of cancer (Barakat, Alderfer, & Kazak, 2006), and natural disasters (Cryder, Kilmer, Tedeschi, & Calhoun, 2006). This phenomenon demonstrates that effective coping not only mitigates harm but also sometimes produces benefits.

Psychodynamic Therapy

According to dynamic theory, the effects of trauma are largely a function of the person's preexisting development, wishes, fears, and object relations (Lieberman, Ippen, & Marans, 2009; Moss, 2009; Schottenbauer, Glass, Arnkoff, & Gray, 2008). In this view, the impact of traumatic events is likely to be influenced by what the person brought into the stressful situation as well as what occurred there. For example, a youth who had been troubled by sexual concerns and then was molested might, consciously or unconsciously, interpret the abuse as a deserved punishment, a disturbing form of wish fulfillment, or both. The immature ego does not recognize randomness; co-occurrences are interpreted as causal connections, even if the mechanism is magical (Dewald, 1971). One objective of therapy with such a client would be to help her sever any perceived causal relationship between her preexisting sexual issues and her victimization.

Children who rely on primitive defenses to deal with stress are likely to experience more disturbance than those who use mature coping strategies. For example, when their parents divorce, children sometimes try to simplify the emotionally complicated situation by viewing one parent as all good and the other as all bad. This simplification comes at too high a price—namely, damage to the child's relationship with one of his parents.

In PTSD, the extreme emotional distress associated with re-experiencing symptoms can disrupt reality-oriented thinking. When this happens, counselors can help by stating very obvious truths in a heartfelt manner, because there is an immature, emotion-dominated level of client functioning that has lost awareness of these truths and needs to hear them again. For example, when clients are overwhelmed by intense re-experiencing symptoms in sessions, counselors can insistently remind them that what happened is *over* now, is *done*, finished, in the past, history—and so is not happening anymore. Statements like these can help clients develop a sense of separation from their past traumatic experiences, so they do not feel like these experiences are bleeding into their present lives.

Robin was troubled by nagging feelings that other people could tell by looking at her that she had been molested, and she imagined others viewing her as prematurely sexualized ("slutty"). She was intellectually aware that this was not possible, so evaluating the evidence was not a useful technique. The therapist interpreted Robin's feeling as a result of projection. This interpretation helped her face the real issue—namely, her own fear that the abuse had "rubbed off" on her in some awful, sexual, permanent way.

Constructivist Therapy

From a constructivist perspective, the purpose of therapy for PTSD is to help clients reconstruct their problem-saturated stories of victimization, shame, and fear into solution-focused narratives of endurance and survival (Duvall & Béres, 2007; White, 2005). To be effective, personal narratives must acknowledge the reality of painful events but affirm the value of the self in new ways. Traumatic events disconfirm people's images of themselves as safe and fortunate, but these events can be incorporated into an expanded image of the self as a strong, resilient person. No one wants to experience pain, but the struggle to overcome adversity has dignity and can be the basis of pride. There is a type of trade-off here: The person cannot consider himself lucky, but he has an (unasked for) opportunity to demonstrate the admirable qualities of courage and hardiness.

Traumatic events disconfirm people's images of themselves as safe and fortunate, but these events can be incorporated into an expanded image of the self as a strong, resilient person.

A solution-focused approach to trauma therapy would begin by asking the client how he has coped with the painful event and continued to function during the time between its occurrence and the beginning of therapy (Bertolino & O'Hanlon, 2002). The clinician would ask how he has dealt with past stressors and difficulties in his life. The client's strengths and coping mechanisms that worked in the past would be used as a foundation on which to build new ways of coping.

Narrative therapists help clients develop personal stories in which they overcome bad experiences to move from a traumatic past into a safer and, perhaps, more vital future. Work on a trauma narrative is a component of the primarily cognitive-behavioral intervention, TF-CBT. Timelines provide a visual way of conveying this message. The traumatic event can be placed in a biographical context by summarizing the client's life before, during, and after the traumatic event(s), using words and/or pictures. Then expected events can be placed on a dotted line representing the future.

In a proactive version of this technique, the timeline is drawn *before* the occurrence of a stressful event (e.g., a parental divorce or painful medical procedure). The child narrates this event and her recovery from it before either actually happens. Repetition of this sequence of images helps the child incorporate the stressor into a story with a positive ending.

Systems-Oriented Intervention

Trauma therapy should generally include work with caregivers because their reactions influence children's adjustment to negative events (Berliner, 1997; Bratton et al., 2012; De Young et al., 2013). Parents often experience vicarious traumatization when their child is hurt, and they may need to work through their own distress before they can focus on the child's needs. Exploration of the parent's interpretation of the trauma, with psychoeducational input as needed, may address the source of the child's misunderstandings and maladaptive attributions.

Effective caregiver support for traumatized children takes two main forms. The most important one, sometimes called TLC (tender loving care), includes overt expressions of caring, physical affection, reassurances of safety, and efforts to comfort the child by providing soothing and enjoyable experiences. Parents can offer favorite foods, backrubs, a game of cards, a new toy, and, most importantly, the message that "we will get through this together."

Caregiver support can also include talking about the distressing experience. Therapists should generally recommend that parents give the child a great deal of control over these conversations, so she receives the amount and type of talk she needs. Caregivers should make it clear both that they are willing to talk about the trauma if the child so desires and that they will not push the child to talk. If the youngster wants to discuss what happened, parents should listen carefully, express empathy, and provide assurances of safety. If the youth's distress seems partly attributable to misinformation or misunderstanding, parents can help by offering realistic thinking and information about the situation.

Therapy for Parental Divorce

This final part of our book departs from the previous chapter structures: Rather than organizing the material by diagnosis or theory, the next sections describe therapy for three types of stressful events. Regardless of their diagnosis, children dealing with parental divorce, bereavement, or sexual abuse confront certain characteristic issues, and these themes provide the basis of organization for the rest of the chapter.

Individual Therapy With the Child

Children generally experience the divorce of their parents as a breaking apart of their family. The goal of therapy is to help clients construct an emotionally acceptable understanding of their new family arrangements that includes the divorce and maintains their attachment to both parents. Children dealing with divorce often struggle with issues of divided loyalty, insecurity about relationships with their parents, disrupted routines and living arrangements, and concerns about the stability of romantic relationships in general. Discussions by Ehrlich (2014), J. Harvey and Fine (2010), Pedro-Carroll (2005; Pedro-Carroll & Jones, 2004), Wallerstein et al. (2000), and Ehrenberg et al. (2014) address these issues and form the basis of the recommendations ahead.

Parents should provide their child with an accurate, age-appropriate explanation of the reasons for the divorce and its likely consequences for the youngster. Children sometimes fill information voids with unrealistic, upsetting speculations, and clear explanations provide the best antidote for cognitive distortions. Whenever possible, parents should talk to the child together, so that separate explanations do not result in conflicting messages.

The core of an appropriate explanation is usually that the parents cannot get along and no longer love each other, so they need to live separately. Parents should make it clear that they are divorcing each other, not the child. The idea that people can stop loving each other might have frightening implications for the client, so the parents should explain that, while this sometimes happens between spouses, they would never stop loving their children.

The youth should be told what changes will occur in her living arrangements and contact with the parents. As is generally the case when sharing bad news with children, parents should allow themselves some open expression of emotion while also conveying that they are not overwhelmed and they remain capable of taking good care of the child. The youngster should be invited to ask any questions that occur to him at any time.

Children of divorce are frequently troubled by *conflicts between relationships*. They may find it difficult to understand why two people whom they love, both of whom are good, have rejected each other. Youth often feel that the acrimony between their parents creates a conflict between their relationship with their mother and their relationship with their father. The question for the youngster is, "How can I love and be loyal to both my parents, without hurting or angering the other?" One task of therapy is to help clients orchestrate these relationships.

Systems-oriented explanations of divorce blame neither parent but, instead, attribute the breakup to problems in the relationship. Such explanations include no heroes or villains but offer a narrative of two good people who are wrong for each other.

Loyalty conflicts are likely to occur when divorced parents fail to respect the difference between their feelings about the ex-spouse and the child's feelings about that parent. Such parents may implicitly or explicitly demand that the child share their emotions, resulting in messages along the lines of, "If you are not mad at Dad for what he has done, I am disappointed in you." When children ally with one parent and take on her grievances, their relationship with the other parent is damaged. Therapists can help with statements like the following:

> "You're not a clone of your mom; you should be allowed to have your own ideas and feelings about this divorce, and they might not be the same as hers—or your dad's, either."

In their need for someone to lean on, divorced parents sometimes implicitly or explicitly ask their children to perform age-inappropriate functions, such as listening to intimate feelings, providing emotional support, giving advice, mediating, and problem solving. The resulting sense of responsibility places excessive pressure on the youngster, and therapists should help him relinquish this sense of responsibility. Helping young people distinguish between aspects of their family situation that they can and cannot control is an important goal of therapy for children of divorce (Ehrlich, 2014; Pedro-Carroll, 2005; Pedro-Carroll & Jones, 2004).

Sometimes the reason that children feel they must choose between their parents is that the parents really do convey this message. One therapeutic option is to coach the child in ways to articulate her needs to her parents. It may be useful to help the child write out a list of requests, such as, "Please don't ask for my opinion about what Mom did in court." These requests can be delivered either at home, when the problems arise or, proactively, in parent-child sessions. Training the client in assertive communication, including I-statements (see Chapter 12, Aggression), might be useful here (e.g., "I don't want to listen to you bad-mouth Dad anymore—it just upsets me").

Sometimes it is unrealistic to expect children to influence these parental behaviors. In such cases, parent counseling is needed to change the child's external reality to one that supports healthy adaptation.

Parent Counseling

Divorced parents, like their children, face conflicts between the relationships in their lives. They face the challenge of separating their feelings about the ex-spouse from their commitment to the child's needs, so they can support the child's relationship with a person toward whom they may be angry (Ehrlich, 2014; Harvey & Fine, 2010; Pedro-Carroll, 2010). Given the hurtful things that people sometimes do to each other in the context of divorce, this may be a difficult task. Therapists should try to help parents develop this self-mastery.

The first step is to hear the parent out and empathize with the hurt and anger he feels, because your input will have little credibility until the parent feels you understand the reasons for his view of the ex-spouse. The next step is psychoeducational. The principle to be conveyed is that, unless a parent's behavior is clearly abusive or harmful, children need close relationships with both their parents. Therefore, when a parent tells you about the terrible things her ex-spouse has done, the most appropriate response is usually to say that, nevertheless, this is the only father her child has, and true commitment to the child's well-being requires her to support this relationship.

Divorced parents face a choice: They must decide what is more important to them, their anger at the ex-spouse or their love for the child.

Divorced parents face a choice: They must decide what is more important to them, their anger at the ex-spouse or their love for the child. Of course, if asked, parents will say the child is more important, but in acrimonious divorce situations, some parents battle each other in ways that hurt their son or daughter. This often occurs in disputes about scheduling time with the child. For instance, if the child has a special opportunity that would require her to be away for a period of time, both parents might say they want the child to enjoy this opportunity—but only if she does so during time scheduled with the other parent. If neither one is willing to give up some scheduled time, the result will be a disappointed youngster and two parents blaming each other for this disappointment.

There is a story in the Bible that illuminates this type of choice for parents (I Kings, 3:14). Two women came to King Solomon with a dispute: Each claimed the same baby as her own. King Solomon proposed a compromise: Split the baby in two, and let each woman have half. One woman agreed to this, and one did not; she preferred losing the baby to seeing him harmed. King Solomon then identified this woman as the true mother. This story is about the *other*-directedness of parental love; devotion means valuing the child's welfare more than the gratification of possessing the child. Winning a power struggle with an ex-spouse is a hollow victory if it comes at the expense of a child's well-being.

Therapists should help parents view the family's situation from their children's perspective. Children want peace between their caregivers. Divorced parents who understand this will make it their goal to encourage the best possible parenting behavior in each other. Any action that interferes with this purpose should be rejected.

Custody and visitation disputes often exacerbate conflict between parents (Ehrlich, 2014; Wallerstein et al., 2000). While parents certainly have a legal right to pursue their aims in court, attorneys and therapists often approach conflict in different ways. Attorneys typically view divorce as a battle to be won, with the goal being the best possible outcome for their client, while child therapists view divorce as a problem to be managed, with the goal being the best possible adjustment for the child. Attorneys often support and even fuel their clients' sense that they are right, their spouse is wrong, and justice requires them to fight and win. Therapists usually encourage parents to work toward conciliation and compromise, even at the expense of a possible victory in court.

Therapy for Bereavement

Through effective mourning, bereaved individuals relinquish the deceased person as a physical, living presence but preserve this relationship as an internalized part of their lives and selves.

Bereavement therapy is often described as an effort to facilitate the natural process of grieving. While this process does not involve an orderly sequence of stages as was once thought, there is an overall movement from acute grief, in which the loss feels like an intolerable wound, to a sense of acceptance, in which the loss is incorporated into a revised view of an acceptable world. Through effective mourning, bereaved individuals relinquish the deceased person as a physical, living presence but preserve this relationship as an internalized, and therefore permanent, part of their lives and selves. My suggestions for helping clients achieve this type of resolution are based largely on work by Neimeyer and Wogrin (2008), Pearlman et al. (2010), Worden (2008), Goldman (2012), and Ayers et al. (2014).

Bereavement therapy does not have the simple goal of helping clients feel better. Grief is a valid response to death. Mourning is a necessary way of honoring deceased loved ones and an inescapable part of the good-bye that needs to be said. Because funerals and related rituals contribute to this process, parents should encourage (although not push) their children to attend.

In the immediate aftermath of a loved one's death, most children have three main needs: empathic validation, accurate information, and security regarding their future. Parents and therapists should give children permission to feel whatever emotions they have, without preconceptions about what "should" be felt.

Second, children need age-appropriate explanations of the mystery of death, the most important element of which is death's finality; the loved one is no longer anywhere on earth and will not reappear or come back. The family's religious beliefs generally determine what the child believes about an afterlife, and therapists should support these beliefs.

Third, most children (like most adults) respond to death with a mixture of grief about the deceased person and concern about what the loss will mean for their own life. This issue is especially serious if the youth lost a caregiver. Therapists and parents should give children permission to be concerned about themselves without feeling selfish for doing so. Once fears are expressed, they can usually be reassured, and adults should help children feel they will be safe and well cared for even though one caregiver is gone.

The psychodynamic perspective, with its cognizance of the type of primitive, magical thinking that occurs when emotions are intense, may be helpful for making sense of client experiences that, otherwise, would be difficult to understand. This perspective prepares counselors to respond to grief reactions such as anger at the loved one for dying and guilt about anger toward this person. In such cases, therapeutic messages include the ideas that people do not choose their feelings; there are immature, emotion-dominated parts of our mind in which irrational feelings are natural; and feelings do not affect other people unless they are translated into behavior.

In some clients, debilitating grief is due to a conscious or unconscious belief that suffering demonstrates love for the deceased and that recovery would indicate a lack of caring. Thus, one client who was locked in depression for a year following his father's death said, "It's how I show that I love my dad." Therapists can sometimes help these clients by asking what their loved one would want them to do in the process of grieving. Most clients reply that the deceased would want them to recover and live a good, happy life. This intervention encourages the client to preserve his goal—demonstrating loyalty to the departed—but suggests a different route to that goal (see Chapter 8). With this reframing, the child's love for the deceased can become a force for recovery. The way to demonstrate enduring love is with enduring love, not enduring grief.

Finding positive meaning in the death of a loved one is a terribly difficult task because none of the obvious meanings is positive. Nevertheless, research on bereaved adolescents (Ickovics et al., 2006) and adults (Folkman, 2001) indicates that many people do identify benefits that occur as by-products of their tragedies. In a study by Nolen-Hoeksema and Larson (1999), most partners of AIDS patients identified something positive that came from the illness and death of their loved one. The partners said the experience resulted in a deepening of their values and spirituality, increased their compassion for other people, made them aware of strengths they did not know they had, and reduced their fear of death.

Religious beliefs and rituals are often important to people in times of grief because religion provides overarching narratives with positive meanings into which death can be incorporated. Nolen-Hoeksema and Larson (1999) found that bereaved individuals with strong religious beliefs were more able to find meaning in the deaths of loved ones than bereaved people without such beliefs. Therapists should encourage clients to turn to their spiritual traditions for aid in coping with trauma and loss.

Internalizing the Loved One

Later stages of mourning involve reviewing, organizing, and completing the relationship with the deceased person (Neimeyer & Wogrin, 2008; Worden, 2008). Adults should hear and validate all of the child's feelings to help her construct a mental image of the deceased that acknowledges any disappointing elements of the relationship, cherishes positive aspects, and integrates both in a totality that is positive and psychologically realistic. There should be attention to unanswered questions and unfinished business, with efforts to lay unresolved issues to rest.

Memory is a central issue in bereavement (Goldman, 2012; Smith, 2012). The function of rumination about the loved one, painful as it often is, may be to facilitate the transfer of recollections into long-term memory. Young children who know that people their age usually do not bring many memories into adulthood sometimes fear that they will forget their loved one. Therapists can help by offering memory-enhancement techniques, such as reviewing recollections until they become well established, recording memories in writing and drawing, collecting photographs and mementos of the deceased, and, perhaps, compiling these materials in a memory book.

Death does not necessarily mean the complete loss of a loved one. In effective mourning, a living relationship with a physical person is transformed into an internalized relationship with someone who, physically, is gone. This type of relationship is purely psychological, but that does not mean it is unreal. Neimeyer (2012) describes how writing letters to deceased loved ones can contribute to the mourning process. It is not uncommon for children and adults to have mental conversations with people who have died, even years after the death. Internalized relationships exist in the sense that, as a result of knowing the loved one, the client is a different person than he would otherwise be, with memories that guide and enrich his life. Achieving a solid internalization of a departed loved one makes it possible to accept the physical loss of this person. Counselors can say:

- "Your dad is gone from the world, but he is not gone from your heart. You can remember him, think about him, and talk to him in your mind. You can let his memory talk to you, comfort you, and guide you."

- "If now it's like your sister never existed, then you have nothing left. But if she has become a part of you, then you still have her, and you can never lose her."

The wisdom of departed loved ones is an important part of their legacy. Perhaps the most substantive way to honor someone is to be influenced by her example and to do things differently because of what she believed, said, and did—for example:

"When you're in a tough situation, deciding what to do, you can think about your grandmother. You can think about what she would say if she were there and what you could do that would make her proud of you."

Bereavement is usually a family tragedy and a family transition (Ayers et al., 2014; Nadeau, 2001). Each family member's grieving affects the mourning of the others. In shared reminiscing, family members offer their recollections of the departed, with some of their observations reinforcing the child's own memories and some coming from times before he was born. By sharing memories in this way, families cross boundaries of time and space and provide children with the heritage of stories, laughter, eccentricities, and accomplishments bound up in their memories of departed loved ones.

Therapy for Sexual Abuse

Psychotherapy for sexually abused children and adolescents is largely based on therapy for PTSD. This is because abuse is usually traumatic in the sense of causing distress and shattering assumptions, although many victims do not have PTSD. The material ahead focuses on special issues related to sexual abuse and describes therapeutic strategies that could add to general treatment of trauma.

Many of these strategies are cognitive and informational, so they require some cognitive maturity from the client. To complement this style, Springer and Misurell (2014) translated CBT techniques into a variety of game-like activities that provide a lively way of engaging children in therapy for abuse.

Perhaps more than any other common type of trauma, sexual abuse is a shockingly strange and confusing experience for young people. Children know that people die and parents sometimes get divorced, but in sexual abuse many undergo an experience that they did not even know existed. Furthermore, the only adult present in the situation, who can convey to the child what it all means, is the perpetrator. As a result, sexual abuse is usually a profoundly invalidating experience. As one important example, perpetrators often behave as if the sexual activity feels good, while to most children the sexual activity feels terribly bad. This jarring contrast, especially if repeated, sometimes teaches children that their emotions are unreliable, incorrect, and should not be felt (Wagner & Linehan, 1997, 2006). Therapists need to provide empathic validation so their clients can relearn the truth that their emotions do make sense, once understood (see Chapter 4's section on DBT).

Treating Damage to Self-Concept

Sexually abused children often have unrealistic, maladaptive beliefs about the causes, consequences, and meanings of their victimizations (Berliner, 1997; Cheung, 2012; Cohen et al., 2006). The secrecy with which abuse is surrounded cuts the child off from valid information, leaving the perpetrator as the only source of input about the meaning of the sex acts. Therefore, countering misconceptions with psychoeducation is an important aspect of therapy for abuse. Perhaps the most common misunderstanding expressed by victims is that the abuse was their fault (Brown et al., 2004; Daigneault et al., 2006; Steel et al., 2004).

Self-blame is not a unitary phenomenon, and to treat it therapists need to understand distinctions within this category of cognition. The discussions of different types of self-blame and attribution in Chapter 14, Depression, are relevant to therapy for victims of trauma.

When adults encounter victim self-blame, they are usually quick to provide reassurances that "it's not your fault." Generic reassurances are certainly valid and possibly helpful, but therapist reassurances are more likely to be credible when the client believes the clinician understands the specifics of her situation, which in this case means the reasons why she feels responsible for the abuse. Children blame themselves for a variety of reasons, such as that they did not call for help, the perpetrator said they seduced him, they did not tell someone after the first incident, and they experienced physical stimulation from the touching. The content of the client's self-blame should determine the therapist's response.

Perhaps the first thing for victims to understand about sexual abuse is that it is a known, common phenomenon that, unfortunately, has happened to many young people beside themselves. Even with increased public awareness, many victims suffer from the feeling that they are "the only one." According to attribution theory (Kelley, 1973), believing that one's negative outcomes are highly infrequent increases self-blame and feelings of deviancy. Group therapy is the most direct, concrete way to show victims that they are not alone. Individual therapists can convey this information by stating it and by talking about other victims.

Talking about abuse issues with third-person pronouns normalizes the experience (e.g., "Kids who have been abused often feel …"). Many victims are harder on themselves than they would be on other people, and counselors can make use of this tendency. In Deblinger and Heflin's (1996) "Best Friends Role Play" exercise, the therapist plays a friend with self-blaming cognitions, and the client tries to convince his peer that these self-punishing thoughts are not true. As a more elaborate format for perspective switching, these authors suggest a game about a radio call-in program on the topic of sexual abuse; the client plays the therapist host of the program, and the (real) therapist plays people calling in with maladaptive thoughts about their victimizations. Once the client's realistic thinking about other victims has been verbalized, the therapist can ask why he considers blame of other victims to be unfair while directing the same type of criticism toward himself.

There is an important difference between self-blame for *causing* a victimization and self-blame for *failing to prevent* one (Miller & Porter, 1983). Children who blame themselves for causing their abuse need to learn that there is no behavior or quality of a child that can cause an older person to molest her. While this truth might sound too obvious to need saying, it is not: I have heard many victims say, "There must have been something about me" that made the perpetrator want to molest them. One common source of this misinformation is the perpetrator himself; they sometimes claim their victims were seductive and wanted to engage in the sexual activity (Terry, 2012).

Failures of self-protection are a more complex issue, because it is possible that there was something the client could have done to prevent the abuse. Or, rather, there might have been something *physically* possible to do. When Robin looked back on her abuse, she was troubled by the fact that the perpetrator had not used physical force to secure her compliance. Instead, he threatened to tell all the kids in the neighborhood about their sexual activities, in detail, if she did not come with him when he intercepted her on the way home from school. This threat was effective because it made Robin feel that she was the one with something to be ashamed of and to hide. Paralyzed by this manipulation, she was psychologically incapable of preventing the abuse—and yet she felt guilty about not protecting herself. In therapy, the more Robin understood about the coercion to which she had been subjected, the less she blamed herself for the victimization.

However, external attribution for abuse is a double-edged sword: It reduces guilt, but it might increase feelings of fear and helplessness about the danger of future abuse because, if there was no way to prevent molestation in the past, how can it be prevented in the future? This inverse relationship between self-blame and helplessness initially seemed to confront therapists with a dilemma (Lamb, 1986). Fortunately, there is a way out. The resolution hinges on the distinction between control in the past and control in the future, which might seem like two sides of the same coin but in fact are separate issues (Brickman et al., 1982). For example, people with diabetes are not responsible for causing their disease, but they are responsible for managing it through self-monitoring and diet. Counselors can treat self-blame by emphasizing the victim's lack of control over past occurrences of abuse, and they can treat feelings of helplessness by emphasizing the client's ability to exercise greater control in the future (Shapiro, 1995). (This distinction between past and future control provides therapists with a tool for helping clients who are caught between self-blame and helplessness in regard to many issues besides abuse.)

Counselors can treat self-blame by emphasizing the victim's lack of control over past occurrences of abuse, and they can treat feelings of helplessness by emphasizing the client's ability to exercise greater control in the future.

The difference between past and future control is not primarily a matter of interpretation; therapy needs to provide clients with knowledge and skills that increase their real self-protection abilities. The necessary type of instruction is abuse prevention training (Shapiro, 1998). There are many published materials of this type (see Wurtele, 2009, for a review). In prevention training, children learn how to recognize unsafe people and situations, distinguish appropriate and inappropriate touching, resist unwanted advances as assertively as possible, and, most important, tell a parent or other adult about any abuse that occurs. Prevention training should teach youth how to see through perpetrator manipulations designed to enforce secrecy and cut them off from help by convincing them that if they report the abuse, no one will believe them, and if they are believed, they will be blamed. Children equipped with prevention knowledge are not literally invulnerable, but neither are they helpless, because the skills of recognition, resistance, and disclosure provide significant self-protection capability.

When molesters use subtle methods of coercion and lace the abuse with elements of gratification for the victim, the mix may be especially toxic, because it manipulates the child into feeling like a voluntary participant in her own molestation (Berliner, 1997; Cheung, 2012; Shapiro, 1995). Flattery, attention, affection, gifts, and sexual stimulation inject a disturbing element of confusion into victimization experiences. Therapists should respond by providing a valid understanding of the pleasurable elements of some sexual abuse. The provision of affection or gifts by perpetrators is an aspect of their manipulation strategy. Children's desire for attention and affection is healthy and positive; the problem is that perpetrators sometimes use good things about children for their own perverse ends. Sexual arousal is an automatic response of the body to certain types of touching, which in no way indicates that people want or choose to be abused. Clients need to understand that elements of gratification, far from indicating complicity in abuse, represent one more way that offenders harm children:

"Perpetrators have different ways of making kids do things. One way is to use force or threats. Another way is to confuse the kid by putting something nice into the abuse to make it seem okay. It's a clever way to trick someone, but it sure doesn't mean the kid wanted to be abused. It's actually a very mean thing to do, because it makes the abuse worse for the kid."

According to object relations theory, the most important factor in the development of self-esteem is children's internalization of the way they are viewed and treated by other people (Cashdan, 1988; Kernberg, 1980; Westen, 1991). Applied to sexual abuse, this theory implies that the youth's self-concept will be affected by his relationship with the perpetrator and the messages about himself he received from this person. Perpetrators sometimes treat victims as if they are sexual and seductive, and they sometimes treat children as if they are unimportant, without value, and appropriate for exploitation, so their preferences and distress do not matter. If the client has come to view herself in the way the perpetrator viewed her, corrective emotional experiences in the context of a strong therapeutic relationship would be a vital aspect of therapy.

Helping Victims With Sexual Issues

Initially, talking about sex abuse is embarrassing for most victims. The embarrassment is due partly to the client's expectations of other people's reactions. Counselors can modify these expectations by reacting to disclosures with empathy for the client's experience and with nothing else, thus conveying that the problem is what happened, not talking about what happened. Robin feared reactions along the lines of, "Listening to this is disgusting," but she received responses like, "I am so sorry you had to go through that." When internalized, such therapeutic responses can change the child's self-directed feelings from shame and disgust to self-compassion.

Victims often anticipate that people will perceive the abusive sexual acts as weird and disgusting, and they fear others will view them as weird and disgusting because they were part of those acts. Therapists should respond by portraying the sexual activities as authored, owned, and reflecting on the perpetrator only; these activities were inflicted on the child but did not come from the child, so they were unwanted, temporary experiences that say nothing about her—for example:

> "The abuse doesn't say any more about you than some mud you fell into—he's the one who did it, so he's the one who's disgusting. You might be afraid some of that disgustingness has rubbed off on you, but it hasn't—not in any way that sticks. You can wash the mud off and leave it behind."

The objective is to help the client sequester or limit the application of her learning to those situations to which the learning truly applies.

Many abuse victims develop a fear of males and/or anxiety and distress about sexual activity in general (Berliner, 1997; Briere & Scott, 2014; Friedrich, 2007). These abuse effects seem to be straightforward instances of overgeneralized learning. As discussed in Chapter 2, Behavior Therapy, counseling in such cases is a matter of discrimination learning: The objective is to help the client *sequester* or limit the application of her learning to those situations to which the learning truly applies (Dollard & Miller, 1950; Wachtel, 1977). Therapy cannot undo the pain of terrible experiences, but it can prevent the effects of those occurrences from spreading through the client's life and poisoning her experience of situations that are not fundamentally similar to the traumatic ones, although they might share some features. Sexually abused children face the challenge of figuring out what the molestation means and does not mean about men, sexuality, trust, the self, and so forth.

For Robin, sequestration of learning required thinking and talking about the differences between the boy who abused her and other boys, and it also required controlled exposure to adolescent males (cousins and neighbors), so she could relearn this difference experientially. Robin's therapist was a man, and, while this made the first session or two more difficult for her, the therapist's gender probably created an exposure process that helped countercondition Robin's fear of males.

Abused children have been subjected to a distorted version of human sexuality (Berliner, 1997; Briere & Scott, 2014; Friedrich, 2007). If victims internalize this conception, their future sexual lives may be damaged. If they try to cope by changing their role within the script, as in the defense of turning passive into active, they may become sexually aggressive themselves. Counselors should address this form of harm with age-appropriate education about the biological, emotional, and interpersonal aspects of human sexuality (Shapiro, 1998).

Some abused children act out sexually, with behaviors including compulsive or public masturbation, depicting sex acts with toy figures, seductive behavior toward others, and sexual aggression (Kendall-Tackett, 2012; Silovsky, Swisher, Widmeld, & Burris, 2012). Such acting out may be due to the continuing effects of physical stimulation from the abuse. Therapists and parents need to help these children develop appropriate sexual boundaries by talking about where, when, and with whom sexual activity is appropriate and inappropriate and by explaining the importance of privacy in sexual behavior.

Sexually abused males face some distinctive issues (Durham, 2003; Spiegel, 2003). Boys molested by males are often troubled by concerns related to homosexuality: Some believe they were targeted because the offender perceived something homosexual about them, and some fear that the molestation, no matter what its cause, will result in their becoming homosexual in the future. Once again, the provision of valid information is an important element of therapy. Boys abused by males need to understand that pedophiles are attracted to children, not gay people, and that being molested does not cause children to become homosexual.

Intrafamilial Abuse

Intrafamilial abuse, or incest, is significantly different from extrafamilial abuse in both causes and consequences (Gannon et al., 2008; Trickett et al., 2001). If the perpetrator is a father or paternal figure, then family dysfunction, including a disturbed marital relationship, is usually a factor in the abuse, although offender pathology is still the main factor. Mother-child relationships are often impaired, and victims may feel as much anger toward their mothers for failing to protect them as they feel toward the offenders (Bratton et al., 2012; Engel, 2000).

In work with any form of maltreatment, the first and most important priority is not therapy but child safety. If the perpetrator is an adult, he should be removed from the home until he has acknowledged responsibility for the abuse, completed a treatment program, and there is clear evidence that the victim would be safe with him back at home (Doren, 2006; Terry, 2012). If the abuser is a sibling, removal might still warrant consideration. If the disadvantages seem to outweigh the advantages, strong supervisory measures should be taken to ensure the victim's safety and sense of security.

Perpetrators should not be included in family sessions until they have made enough progress in their own treatment to acknowledge and take full responsibility for the abuse. Once this prerequisite has been achieved, family therapy usually aims to rectify blurred or inappropriate boundaries between the marital and parent-child subsystems, correct cognitive distortions related to the abuse, develop valid attributions of responsibility, and provide explicit apologies to the victim from the offender and any other family members who were complicit in the abuse or the failure to stop it.

Summary

Traumatic experiences can damage children's sense of security and self-concept. PTSD involves sensory and emotional reverberations on a neurophysiological level, as the person continues to experience the trauma long after the event is over. When victims misapply or overgeneralize learning derived from traumatic experiences, the harmful effects invade sectors of their lives that are not genuinely related to the traumatic event.

Outcome research on PTSD provides extensive support for cognitive-behavioral therapy. For sexually abused children, the combination of CBT and psychodynamic or supportive therapy produces better outcomes than CBT alone. Conceptual forms of intervention such as narrative and dynamic therapy might be more important for clients with internalizing problems than for those with externalizing dysfunction.

The Serenity Prayer provides a poetic and accurate summary of research on coping. Problem-focused responses are most effective when stressors are controllable, and emotion-focused coping is most effective when they are not. Many stressful situations involve both controllable and uncontrollable elements, so a combination of both types of coping is usually most adaptive. The key to effective coping is not reliance on certain techniques but flexible matching of strategy to situation.

CBT for PTSD, as for anxiety, is based on exposure. The difference is that, in PTSD treatment, the primary targets of exposure are the client's trauma-related memories and thoughts, although some clients also need desensitization to external stimuli associated with the trauma. CBT can also include psychoeducation, self-instruction, guided imagery, cognitive restructuring, and distraction techniques.

Narrative therapy helps children construct personal stories that include their painful experiences but add accounts of effective coping, leave the trauma in the past, and conclude with a positive vision of the future. Dynamic therapy emphasizes the effects of clients' preexisting development and psychological issues on their reactions to stressful or traumatic events. Systems-oriented work addresses the effects of these events on the network of relationships in the family, with an emphasis on parental support for the youth's recovery.

Many children of divorce must cope with conflict and acrimony between the two people they love most. Therapy for these clients often includes psychoeducational work on what children can and cannot control, encouraging the parents to put their anger aside so they can cooperate on the child's behalf, and helping the child build positive, separate relationships with his parents.

Grief counseling is structured around the goal of acceptance, which includes a relinquishing and a reinvesting. Bereaved children need to accept the finality of their loss and to give up on their relationship with the loved one as a living person. However, the necessary goodbye becomes more bearable and possible when the client's memories of the loved one are organized into an internal representation solid enough to be a permanent aspect of the youth's self. In this way, the relationship continues to be a part of the client's life.

Sexual abuse subjects children to false, malignant messages about human sexuality, the trustworthiness of other people, and their own value. Counseling should address the maladaptive lessons that victims often derive from these experiences. Therapists can counter the perpetrator's distorted version of sexuality by providing age-appropriate sex education.

Counselors can ameliorate self-blame by offering valid information and realistic thinking about the dynamics of power, control, and responsibility that operated during the abuse. Finally, therapists can address feelings of helplessness with prevention skills training that strengthens clients' ability to protect themselves in the future.

Case Study

Robin's therapy involved both imaginal exposure during sessions and in vivo exposure in her environment. The counselor led her through memories of the abuse again and again, until her ability to cope with even the most difficult recollections demonstrated to Robin that she had nothing more to fear from her own memories and thoughts. Robin's parents accompanied her to places in the neighborhood where the molestations occurred—places that, before therapy, Robin had avoided—and they coached her in use of the coping techniques she had learned in therapy. These techniques significantly reduced the anxiety, intrusive memories, and re-experiencing symptoms that had troubled her.

Robin's counseling included abuse prevention training. There were role-plays in which she practiced resisting and refusing attempts to manipulate her into potentially unsafe situations. Because Robin's behavior style was initially somewhat passive, her therapist also provided assertiveness training, as described in Chapter 12, on aggression.

There was still one important element of the abuse to which Robin had not been exposed. The boy who molested her still lived in the neighborhood, and when Robin occasionally saw him, she experienced the pounding heart and rapid breathing characteristic of PTSD. Therefore, the therapist carefully engineered exposure to the perpetrator, who was in counseling, too. There was a meeting with both therapists present. Robin confronted the boy with a clear, extremely angry description of her experience of the abuse. The boy responded with an apology that seemed sincere. By the end, Robin felt that she no longer had anything to be afraid of walking around in her neighborhood, because he was the one with something to be ashamed of, and if anyone should slink out of the other person's way, it was the offender, not the survivor.

Afterword

The Therapist's Experience

This book would not be complete without mention of an element of the therapeutic equation that is often overlooked: the experience of the professionals who do this work. The therapist's job involves more than the utilization of technical skills. Therapy is a direct and deeply personal encounter with our fellow human beings. This work engages us on a wide range of intellectual and emotional levels, calling on our hearts as well as our minds. Counseling is not simply a job; it should also be a vocation, a calling.

The deep levels of engagement usually involved in this work can bring important benefits in terms of job satisfaction and personal development. However, this type of engagement sometimes entails costs. The word *burnout* has become part of everyday language, but this term was originally coined by Freudenberger (1975) to describe the experiences of human service professionals. While any job can be stressful, working with people on emotional and behavioral problems seems to involve particularly high levels of stress (Coster & Schwebel, 1997; Jankoski, 2012). Therapists come into direct contact with human suffering on a daily basis. The distress of children, who are often helpless in the face of their circumstances, seems to be especially disturbing to clinicians. Because of the complexity of our field, it is hard to know exactly what to do, and therapists might be troubled by doubts about whether their services are as helpful as they could be. Because of limitations on the effectiveness of existing interventions, and especially because of the impact on clients of factors beyond therapists' control, there are significant numbers of youth whose disturbances persist despite their counselor's best efforts.

The *Maslach Burnout Inventory* (Maslach & Jackson, 1981; Maslach, Jackson, & Leiter, 1997), a widely used measure for human service professionals, assesses three factors of burnout: lack of a sense of accomplishment, emotional exhaustion, and depersonalization of clients. Research with this instrument indicates that burned-out professionals believe they have been unable to accomplish much with their clients and, as a result, they lack energy for work and an appreciation of their clients as individuals. The term *compassion fatigue* also describes this phenomenon. Burnout is associated with decreased work effectiveness, absenteeism, and job turnover (Freudenberg, 1975; Koeske, Kirk, Koeske, & Rauktis, 1994; Maslach et al., 1997). Thus, in addition to being a personal issue for therapists, burnout is a client care issue for the mental health field.

In their exploration of work-related cognitions, Shapiro, Dorman, Burkey, and Welker (1999) found that, perhaps surprisingly, job satisfaction was unrelated to measures of optimism and pessimism about work with clients. However, highly satisfied professionals expressed a distinctive combination of hope and realism; to a greater extent than burned-out respondents, they agreed with questionnaire items that both acknowledged limits to clients' potential for change and expressed appreciation of changes that, within these constraints, were possible (e.g., "While some clients may never be able to function really well, effective services can be of some benefit to even the most impaired clients," and, "I do not expect myself to resolve all of my clients' difficulties, and I am content if I have a significant positive impact, even if many problems remain"). Thus, satisfied and burned-out counselors differed not in their expectations for client progress but in the amount of satisfaction they derived from modest, limited amounts of progress.

These results suggest that therapists can cope with the emotional challenges of their work and maintain positive job experiences by calibrating their expectations for client progress in a realistic manner and valuing the changes their clients achieve, even if those improvements are considerably less than complete (Dorman & Shapiro, 2004). Realistic expectancies probably help clinicians set achievable goals and evaluate treatment progress in relation to the client's own starting point, not in relation to an abstract standard of how well people should be able to function. It may be adaptive for therapists to accept the reality that serious problems are not uncommon in the lives of youth, so our encounters with these problems do not cause shock. Counselors seem to cope most effectively when they do not take responsibility for the many factors beyond their control and they focus on what they can achieve—namely, the provision of high-quality mental health services. (The Serenity Prayer, discussed in the previous chapter, encapsulates this view.) Clinicians who maintain this stance seem most able to meet clients where they are and focus on helping them move forward from this point.

Although the emotional range and intensity involved in therapy might contribute to burnout, this aspect of our vocation also makes it unique in a potentially positive way. Most occupations involve concentrated attention to one specialized, narrow slice of the world—plumbers keep water flowing through pipes, accountants track money and goods, an engineer might devote years to the manufacture of a single product, and so forth. Other occupations are not necessarily less important or valuable than counseling—society would collapse much more quickly without farmers than without therapists—but I can think of no occupation in which professionals deal with issues as central to human existence as the issues that therapists address every day. Our jobs are about happiness and sadness, discipline and fun, misfortune and strength, and the way the mind works—the stuff of life.

Because counseling involves such broadly important issues, therapists have oppor-tunities to bring more aspects of self into their work than do most other professionals. Many aspects of the human mind and heart resonate to the work of counseling, and many capabilities—intellectual, intuitive, interpersonal, and emotional—are called on in these jobs. Perhaps someday a neuroscientist will document that conducting therapy activates more areas of the brain than any other occupation.

Therapy is the application of scientific, professional, and, perhaps, personal knowledge to the task of helping people with mental health problems by talking with them. Many areas of knowledge beyond the study of therapy, per se, are potentially relevant to our work. Nonclinical areas of psychology, all of the social sciences, and even philosophy, religion, and literature contain knowledge and ideas that, sometimes, are relevant to clients' issues. Observations and insights gleaned from family members, friends, and our own personal experiences also occasionally emerge as useful in clinical work. With so many aspects of life germane to our jobs, the world becomes our laboratory, and our everyday experiences are filled with opportunities to learn something useful for our work.

Conversely, the knowledge and skills gained in the process of becoming and working as therapists can enhance our lives outside of work (Kottler, 2003). Our training and clinical experience can strengthen our ability to understand ourselves and other people, cope with stress, manage interpersonal conflicts, and solve problems. It is inadvisable to go through our days analyzing everything, and talking like a therapist to one's family and friends is a bad idea. But although the application of therapy-related knowledge can be overdone (as anything can be), if this body of theory and research is valid, it must apply to our own lives as well as to our clients. Because the subject matter of therapy overlaps so much with the content of life, what we learn about one is usually applicable to the other, and this two-way street makes a cross-fertilization process possible. Personal growth can contribute to professional effectiveness, and professional development can contribute to personal growth. We have a great job.

Writing this book was a remarkable experience for me, requiring excursions far and wide through the field of psychotherapy and also personal travel backward in time through my own training, supervision, clinical, and individual experiences. I tried to cull the best I have read, heard, seen, thought, and done.

Authors are like funnels: We take in large quantities of reading, training, observation, and experience, and we try to summarize this learning in books that, however long they might seem to our readers, are much briefer than the years of education and experience they distill. Now you have an opportunity to play this role for your clients. The streams of learning I have funneled to you from the literature and my experiences will join and mix with the many other streams of learning made up of all you have read, heard, seen, thought, and done. The next time you see a client, and you look to your store of theory, research, techniques, and good things to say, your memories of this book will be there, and I hope its contribution to your repertoire proves valuable to your clients.

References

Abaied, J. L., & Rudolph, K. D. (2014). Family relationships, emotional processes, and adolescent depression. In S. Richards & M. O'Hara (Eds.), *The Oxford handbook of depression and comorbidity* (pp. 460–475). Oxford, UK: Oxford University Press.

Abbass, A. A., Rabung, S., Leichsenring, F., Refseth, J. S., & Midgley, N. (2013). Psychodynamic psychotherapy for children and adolescents: A meta-analysis of short-term psychodynamic models. *Journal of the American Academy of Child & Adolescent Psychiatry, 52*(8), 863–875.

Abela, J. R. Z. (2001). The hopelessness theory of depression: A test of the diathesis-stress and causal mediation components in third and seventh grade children. *Journal of Abnormal Child Psychology, 29,* 241–254.

Abela, J. R. Z. (2002). Depressive mood reactions to failure in the achievement domain: A test of the integration of the hopelessness and self-esteem theories of depression. *Cognitive Therapy and Research, 26,* 531–552.

Abela, J. R. Z., & Skitch, S. A. (2007). Dysfunctional attitudes, self-esteem, and hassles: Cognitive vulnerability to depression in children of affectively ill parents. *Behaviour Research and Therapy, 45,* 1127–1140.

Ablon, J. S., & Jones, E. E. (1998). How expert clinicians' prototypes of an ideal treatment correlate with outcome in psychodynamic and cognitive-behavior therapy. *Psychotherapy Research, 8,* 71–83.

Ablon, J. S., Levy, R. A., & Katzenstein, T. (2006). Beyond brand names of psychotherapy: Identifying empirically supported change processes. *Psychotherapy: Theory, Research, Practice, Training, 43,* 216–231.

Abramson, L. Y., Seligman, M. E. P., & Teasdale, J. D. (1978). Learned helplessness in humans: Critique and reformulation. *Journal of Abnormal Psychology, 87,* 49–74.

Achenbach, T. M., & Rescorla, L. A. (2000). *Manual for the ASEBA preschool forms and profiles.* Burlington: University of Vermont Department of Psychiatry.

Achenbach, T. M., & Rescorla, L. A. (2001). *Manual for the ASEBA school-age forms and profiles.* Burlington: University of Vermont, Research Center for Children, Youth, and Families.

Achenbach, T. M., & Rescorla, L. A. (2007). *Multicultural supplement to the manual for the ASEBA school-age forms & profiles.* Burlington: University of Vermont, Research Center for Children, Youth, & Families.

Achenbach, T. M., & Rescorla, L. A. (2010). *Multicultural supplement to the manual for the ASEBA preschool forms & profiles.* Burlington: University of Vermont, Research Center for Children, Youth, & Families.

Ackerman, N. W. (1966). *Treating the troubled family.* New York: Basic Books.

Ackerson, J., Scogin, F., McKendree-Smith, N., & Lyman, R. D. (1998). Cognitive bibliotherapy for mild and moderate adolescent depressive symptomatology. *Journal of Consulting and Clinical Psychology, 66,* 685–690.

Adams, H. E., Wright, L. W., & Lohr, B. A. (1996). Is homophobia associated with homosexual arousal? *Journal of Abnormal Psychology, 105,* 440–445.

Aguilera, A., Garza, M. J., & Munoz, R. F. (2010). Group cognitive-behavioral therapy for depression in Spanish: Culture-sensitive manualized treatment in practice. *Journal of Clinical Psychology: In Session, 66,* 857–867.

Aknin, L. B., Dunn, E. W., & Norton, M. I. (2012). Happiness runs in a circular motion: Evidence for a positive feedback loop between prosocial spending and happiness. *Journal of Happiness Studies, 13,* 347–355.

Aldao, A., Nolen-Hoeksema, S., & Schweizer, S. (2010). Emotion-regulation strategies across psychopathology: A meta-analytic review. *Clinical Psychology Review, 30,* 217–237.

Aldridge, A. A., & Roesch, S. C. (2007). Coping and adjustment in children with cancer: A meta-analytic study. *Journal of Behavioral Medicine, 30,* 115–129.

Alexander, J., & Parsons, B. V. (1982). *Functional family therapy.* Pacific Grove, CA: Brooks/Cole.

Alexander, J. F., Waldron, H. B., Robbins, M. S., & Neeb, A. A. (2013). *Functional family therapy for adolescent behavior problems.* Washington, DC: American Psychological Association.

Allen-Eckert, H., Fong, E., Nichols, M. P., Watson, N., & Liddle, H. A. (2001). Development of the Family Therapy Enactment Rating Scale. *Family Process, 40,* 469–478.

Alvidrez, J., & Arean, P. A. (2002). Psychosocial treatment research with ethnic minority populations: Ethical considerations in conducting clinical trials. *Ethics and Behavior, 12,* 103–116.

Amato, P. R. (2001). Children of divorce in the 1990s: An update of the Amato and Keith (1991) meta-analysis. *Journal of Family Psychology, 15,* 355–370.

Amato, P. R., & Cheadle, J. (2005). The long reach of divorce: Divorce and child well-being across three generations. *Journal of Marriage and Family, 67,* 191–206.

American Academy of Child and Adolescent Psychiatry. (2007). Practice parameters for the assessment and treatment of children and adolescents with depressive disorders. *Journal of the American Academy of Child and Adolescent Psychiatry, 46,* 1503–1526.

American Psychiatric Association. (2013). *Diagnostic and statistical manual of mental disorders* (5th ed.). Washington, DC: Author.

American Psychological Association. (2007). Guidelines for psychological practice with girls and women. *American Psychologist, 62,* 949–979.

American Psychological Association, Council of National Psychological Associations for the Advancement of Ethnic Minority Interests. (2003). *Psychological treatment of ethnic minority populations.* Washington, DC: Association of Black Psychologists.

American Psychological Association, Division 44 Task Force on Guidelines for Psychotherapy with Lesbian, Gay, and Bisexual Clients. (2012). Guidelines for psychotherapy with lesbian, gay, and bisexual clients. *American Psychologist, 67,* 10–42.

American Psychological Association Presidential Task Force on Evidence-Based Practice. (2006). Evidence-based practice in psychology. *American Psychologist, 61,* 271–285.

American Psychological Association, Task Force on Resilience and Strength in Black Children and Adolescents. (2008). *Resilience in African American children and adolescents: A vision for optimal development.* Washington, DC: Author.

American Psychological Association, Task Force on Socioeconomic Status. (2007). *Report of the APA Task Force on Socioeconomic Status.* Washington, DC: American Psychological Association.

Anastopoulos, A. D., Shelton, T. L., DuPaul, G. J., & Guevremont, D. C. (1993). Parent training for attention-deficit hyperactivity disorder: Its impact on parent functioning. *Journal of Abnormal Child Psychology, 21,* 581–596.

Anda, R. F., Felitti, V. J., Bremner, J. D., Walker, J. D., Whitfield, C., Perry, B. D., ... Giles, W. H. (2006). The enduring effects of abuse and related adverse experiences in childhood: A convergence of evidence from neurobiology and epidemiology. *European Archives of Psychiatry and Clinical Neuroscience, 256*, 174–186.

Anderson, C. A., & Arnoult, L. H. (1985). Attributional style and everyday problems in living: Depression, loneliness and shyness. *Social Cognition, 3*, 16–35.

Anderson, C. A., & Jennings, D. L. (1980). When experiences of failure promote expectations of success: The impact of attributing failure to ineffective strategies. *Journal of Personality, 48*, 393–407.

Anderson, C. A., Shibuya, A., Ihori, N., Swing, E. L., Bushman, B. J., Sakamoto, A., ... Saleem, M. (2010). Violent video game effects on aggression, empathy, and prosocial behavior in Eastern and Western countries. *Psychological Bulletin, 136*, 151–173.

Anderson, H. (1997). *Conversation, language and possibilities: A postmodern approach to therapy.* New York, NY: Basic Books.

Anderson, S. H., & Middleton, V. A. (2011). *Explorations in diversity.* Belmont, CA: Cengage.

Angold, A., Costello, E. J., & Erkanli, A. (1999). Comorbidity. *Journal of Child Psychology and Psychiatry, 40*, 57–87.

Antony, M. M., & Roemer, L. (2011). *Behavior therapy.* Washington, DC: APA Books.

Antshel, K. M., & Remer, R. (2003). Social skills training in children with attention deficit hyperacticity disorder: A randomized-controlled clinical trial. *Journal of Clinical Child and Adolescent Psychology, 32*, 153–165.

Aponte, H. J., & DiCesare, E. J. (2000). Structural theory. In F. M. Dattilio & L. J. Bevilacqua (Eds.), *Comparative treatments for relationship dysfunction* (pp. 45–57). New York, NY: Springer.

Arch, J. J., Eifert, G. H., Davies, C., Vilardaga, J. C. P., Rose, R. D., & Craske, M. G. (2012). Randomized clinical trial of cognitive behavioral therapy (CBT) versus Acceptance and Commitment Therapy (ACT) for mixed anxiety disorders. *Journal of Consulting and Clinical Psychology, 80*, 750–765.

Aristotle . (2002). *Nicomachean ethics* (J. Sachs, Trans.). Newburyport, MA: Focus.

Arnett, J. J. (2009). The neglected 95%: Why American psychology needs to become less American. *American Psychologist, 63*, 602–614.

Arseneault, L., Bowes, L., & Shakoor, S. (2010). Bullying victimization in youths and mental health problems: "Much ado about nothing"? *Psychological Medicine, 40*, 717–729.

Arseneault, L., Walsh, E., Trzesniewski, K., Newcombe, R., Caspi, A., & Moffitt, T. E. (2006). Bullying victimization uniquely contributes to adjustment problems in young children: A nationally representative cohort study. *Pediatrics, 118*, 130–138.

Asarnow, J. R., Emslie, G., Clarke, G., Wagner, K. D., Spirito, A., Vitiello, B., ... Keller, M. (2009). Treatment of selective serotonin reuptake inhibitor-resistant depression in adolescents: Predictors and moderators of treatment response. *Journal of the American Academy of Child and Adolescent Psychiatry, 48*, 330–339.

Ascherman, L. I., & Rubin, S. (2008). Current ethical issues in child and adolescent psychotherapy. *Child and Adolescent Psychiatric Clinics of North America, 17*, 21–35.

Asendorpf, J. B., Warkentin, V., & Baudonniere, P. (1996). Self-awareness and other-awareness II: Mirror self-recognition, social contingency awareness, and synchronic imitation. *Developmental Psychology, 32*, 313–321.

Atkinson, J. W., & Raynor, J. O. (1974). *Motivation and achievement*. Washington, DC: Winston.

Avenevoli, S., Knight, E., Kessler, R. C., & Merikangas, K. R. (2008). Epidemiology of depression in children and adolescents. In J. R. Z. Abela & B. L. Hankin (Eds.), *Handbook of depression in children and adolescents* (pp. 6–34). New York, NY: Guilford Press.

Axline, V. M. (1947). *Play therapy*. Boston, MA: Houghton Mifflin.

Ayers, T. S., Wolchik, S. A., Sandler, I. N., Twohey, J. L., Weyer, J. L., Padgett-Jones, S., … Kriege, G. (2014). The family bereavement program: Description of a theory-based prevention program for parentally-bereaved children and adolescents. *Omega: Journal of Death and Dying, 68*, 293–314.

Babb, K., Levine, L., & Arseneault, J. (2010). Shifting gears: Coping flexibility in children with and without ADHD. *International Journal of Behavioral Development, 34*, 10–23.

Bach, P. A., & Moran, D. J. (2008). *ACT in practice: Case conceptualization in Acceptance and Commitment Therapy*. Oakland, CA: New Harbinger.

Baddeley, J. L., & Pennebaker, J. W. (2011). The expressive writing method. In L. L'Abate & L. G. Sweeney (Eds.), *Research on writing approaches in mental health* (pp. 85–92). Bingley, UK: Emerald Group.

Baer, R. A. (2003). Mindfulness training as a clinical intervention: A conceptual and empirical review. *Clinical Psychology: Science & Practice, 10*, 125–143.

Baer, R. A., & Krietemeyer, J. (2006). Overview of mindfulness- and acceptance-based treatment approaches. In R. A. Baer (Ed.), *Mindfulness-based treatment approaches: A clinician's guide* (pp. 3–27). San Diego, CA: Elsevier.

Baglivio, M. T., Jackowski, K., Greenwald, M. A., & Wolff, K. T. (2014). Comparison of multisystemic therapy and functional family therapy effectiveness: A multiyear statewide propensity score matching analysis of juvenile offenders. *Criminal Justice and Behavior, 41*, 1033–1056.

Baker, L., Raine, A., Liu, J., & Jacobsen, K. C. (2008). Genetic and environmental influences on reactive and proactive aggression in children. *Journal of Abnormal Child Psychology, 36*, 1265–1278.

Bakermans-Kranenburg, M., & van IJzendoorn, M. (2010). Review article: Parenting matters: Family science in the genomic era. *Family Science, 1*, 26–36.

Balch, W. R., Myers, D. M., & Papotto, C. (1999). Dimensions of mood in mood-dependent memory. *Journal of Experimental Psychology: Learning, Memory, and Cognition, 25*, 70–83.

Baldwin, M. W. (1992). Relational schemas and the processing of social information. *Psychological Bulletin, 112*, 461–484.

Baldwin, S. A., Christian, S., Berkeljon, A., Shadish, W. R., & Bean, R. (2012). The effects of family therapies for adolescent delinquency and substance abuse: A meta-analysis. *Journal of Marital and Family Therapy, 38*, 281–304.

Bale, T. L., Baram, T. Z., Brown, A. S., Goldstein, J. M., Insel, T. R., McCarthy, M. M., … Nestler, E. J. (2010). Early life programming and neurodevelopmental disorders. *Biological Psychiatry, 68*, 314–319.

Balk, D. E., & Hogan, N. S. (1995). Religion, spirituality, and bereaved adolescents. In D. W. Adams & E. J. Deveau (Eds.), *Beyond the innocence: Helping children and adolescents cope with death and bereavement* (Vol. 3, pp. 61–88). Amityville, NY: Baywood.

Ballou, M., & Brown, L. S. (2002). *Rethinking mental health and disorder: Feminist perspectives*. New York, NY: Guilford Press.

Balsam, K. F., & Mohr, J. J. (2007). Adaptation to sexual orientation stigma: A comparison of bisexual and lesbian/gay adults. *Journal of Counseling Psychology, 54,* 306–319.

Bandura, A. (1977). *Social learning theory*. Englewood Cliffs, NJ: Prentice-Hall.

Bandura, A. (1986). *Social foundations of thought and action: A social-cognitive theory*. Englewood Cliffs, NJ: Prentice-Hall.

Barakat, L. P., Alderfer, M. A., & Kazak, A. E. (2006). Posttraumatic growth in adolescent survivors of cancer and their mothers and fathers. *Journal of Pediatric Psychology, 31,* 413–419.

Barber, J. P., Muran, J. C., McCarthy, K. S., & Keefe J. R. (2013). Research on dynamic therapies. In M. J. Lambert (Ed.), *Bergin and Garfield's handbook of psychotherapy and behavior change* (6th ed., pp. 443–494). Hoboken, NJ: Wiley.

Bar-Haim, Y., Lamy, D., Pergamin, L., Bakermans-Kranenburg, M. J., & van IJzendoorn, M. H. (2007). Threat-related attentional bias in anxious and nonanxious individuals: A meta-analytic study. *Psychological Bulletin, 133,* 1–24.

Barkley, R. A. (2006). A theory of ADHD. In R. A. Barkley (Ed.), *Attention-deficit hyperactivity disorder: A handbook for diagnosis and treatment* (3rd ed., pp. 297–335). New York, NY: Guilford Press.

Barkley, R. A. (2013). *Defiant children: A clinician's manual for assessment and parent training* (3rd ed.). New York, NY: Guilford Press.

Barkley, R. A., Edwards, G., Laneri, M., Fletcher, K., & Metevia, L. (2001). The efficacy of problem-solving communication training alone, behavior management training alone, and their combination for parent-adolescent conflict in teenagers with ADHD and ODD. *Journal of Consulting and Clinical Psychology, 69,* 926–941.

Barkley, R. A., & Robin, A. L. (2014). *Defiant teens: A clinician's manual for assessment and family intervention* (2nd ed.). New York, NY: Guilford Press.

Barnett, A., Sussman, S., Smith, C., Rohrbach, L. A., & Spruijt-Metz, D. (2012). Motivational interviewing for adolescent substance use: A review of the literature. *Addictive Behaviors, 37,* 1325–1334.

Barrett, H. C., Cosmides, L., & Tooby, J. (2007). The hominid entry into the cognitive niche. In S. W. Gangestad & J. A. Simpson (Eds.), *The evolution of mind: Fundamental questions and controversies* (pp. 241–248). New York, NY: Guilford Press.

Barrett, M. S., & Berman, J. S. (2001). Is psychotherapy more effective when therapists disclose information about themselves? *Journal of Consulting and Clinical Psychology, 69,* 597–603.

Barrett, P. M., Dadds, M. R., & Rapee, R. M. (1996). Family treatment of childhood anxiety: A controlled study. *Journal of Consulting and Clinical Psychology, 64,* 333–342.

Barrett, P. M., Sonderegger, R., & Xenos, S. (2003). Using FRIENDS to combat anxiety and adjustment problems among young migrants to Australia: A national trial. *Clinical Child Psychology and Psychiatry, 8,* 241–260.

Barrios, B. A., & O'Dell, S. L. (1998). Fears and anxieties. In E. J. Mash & R. A. Barkley (Eds.), *Treatment of childhood disorders* (pp. 249–337). New York: Guilford.

Barton, C., Alexander, J. F., Waldron, H., Turner, C. W., & Warburton, J. (1985). Generalizing treatment effects of functional family therapy: Three replications. *American Journal of Family Therapy, 13*, 16–26.

Baskin, T. W., Tierney, S. C., Minami, T., & Wampold, B. E. (2003). Establishing specificity in psychotherapy: A meta-analysis of structural equivalence of placebo controls. *Journal of Consulting and Clinical Psychology, 71*, 973–979.

Bateson, G. (1972). *Steps to an ecology of mind.* New York, NY: Dutton.

Bateson, G. (1979). *Mind and nature: A necessary unity.* New York, NY: Dutton.

Baumeister, R. F., Campbell, J. D., Krueger, J. I., & Vohs, K. D. (2005). Exploding the self-esteem myth. *Scientific American Mind, 16*, 50–57.

Baumeister, R. F., Smart, L., & Boden, J. M. (1996). Relation of threatened egotism to violent, oppressive, and aggressive behavior: The dark side of high self-esteem. *Psychological Review, 103*, 5–33.

Baumeister, R. F., & Tierney, J. (2011). *Willpower: Rediscovering the greatest human strength.* New York, NY: Penguin.

Beauchaine, T. P., Hinshaw, S. P., & Pang, K. L. (2010). Comorbidity of attention-deficit/hyperactivity disorder and early-onset conduct disorder: Biological, environmental, and developmental mechanisms. *Clinical Psychology: Science and Practice, 17*, 327–336.

Beauchaine, T. P., Webster-Stratton, C., & Reid, M. J. (2005). Mediators, moderators, and predictors of 1-year outcomes among children treated for early-onset conduct problems: A latent growth curve analysis. *Journal of Consulting and Clinical Psychology, 73*, 371–388.

Beaudoin, M.-N., & Zimmerman, J. (2011). Narrative therapy and interpersonal neurobiology: Revisiting classic practices, developing new emphases. *Journal of Systemic Therapies, 30*, 1–13.

Beck, A. T. (1967). *Depression: Clinical, experimental, and theoretical aspects.* New York, NY: Harper & Row.

Beck, A. T. (1976). *Cognitive therapy and the emotional disorders.* New York, NY: International Universities Press.

Beck, A. T. (2008). The evolution of the cognitive model of depression and its neural correlates. *American Journal of Psychiatry, 165*, 969–977. Retrieved from http://ajp.psychiatryonline.org

Beck, A. T., & Alford, B. A. (2009). *Depression: Causes and treatment* (2nd ed.). Philadelphia: University of Pennsylvania Press.

Beck, A. T., & Emery, G. (2005). *Anxiety disorders and phobias: A cognitive perspective.* New York, NY: Basic Books.

Beck, A. T., & Haigh, E. A. P. (2014). Advances in cognitive theory and therapy: The generic cognitive model. *Annual Review of Clinical Psychology, 10*, 1–24.

Beck, J. S. (2011). *Cognitive behavior therapy: Basics and beyond* (2nd ed.). New York, NY: Guilford Press.

Beck, J. S., Beck, A. T., & Jolly, J. (2001). *Beck Youth Inventories of emotional and social impairment.* San Antonio, TX: Harcourt Assessment.

Becvar, D. S., & Becvar, R. J. (2012). *Family therapy: A systemic integration* (8th ed.). New York, NY: Pearson.

Bednar, R. L., Burlingame, G. M., & Masters, K. S. (1988). Systems of family treatment: Substance or semantics? *Annual Review of Psychology, 39*, 401–434.

Beelmann, A., Pfingston, U., & Losel, F. (1994). Effects of training social competence in children: A meta-analysis of recent evaluation studies. *Journal of Clinical Child Psychology, 23*, 260–271.

Beidel, D. C., & Alfano, C. A. (2011). *Child anxiety disorders: A guide to research and treatment* (2nd ed.). New York, NY: Routledge/Taylor & Francis.

Beidel, D. C., Turner, S. M., & Morris, T. L. (2000). Behavioral treatment of childhood social phobia. *Journal of Consulting and Clinical Psychology, 68*, 1072–1080.

Beidel, D. C., Turner, S. M., & Young, B. J. (2006). Social effectiveness therapy for children: Five years later. *Behavior Therapy, 37*, 416–425.

Beidel, D. C., Turner, S. M., Young, B. J., & Paulson, A. (2005). Social effectiveness therapy for children: Three-year follow-up. *Journal of Consulting and Clinical Psychology, 17*, 721–725.

Beitel, M., Ferrer, E., & Cecero, J. J. (2005). Psychological mindedness and awareness of self and others. *Journal of Clinical Psychology, 61*, 739–750.

Bell, M. C., & McDevitt M. A. (2014). Conditioned reinforcement. In F. K. McSweeney & E. S. Murphy (Eds.), *The Wiley Blackwell handbook of operant and classical conditioning* (pp. 221–248). Oxford, UK: Wiley-Blackwell.

Belsky, J., & Pleuss, M. (2009). Beyond diathesis stress: Differential susceptibility to environmental influences. *Psychological Bulletin, 135*, 885–908.

Benish, S. G., Quintana, S., & Wampold, B. E. (2011). Culturally adapted psychotherapy and the legitimacy of myth: A direct-comparison meta-analysis. *Journal of Counseling Psychology, 58*, 279–289.

Ben-Zur, H. (2009). Coping styles and affect. *International Journal of Stress Management, 16*, 87–101.

Berg, I. K., & Steiner, T. (2003). *Children's solution work*. New York, NY: Norton.

Berkowitz, L. (1993). *Aggression: Its causes, consequences and control*. New York, NY: Academic Press.

Berliner, L. (1997). Intervention with children who experience trauma. In D. Cicchetti & S. Toth (Eds.), *The effects of trauma and the developmental process* (pp. 491–514). New York, NY: Wiley.

Berman, A. L., Jobes, D. A., & Silverman, M. M. (2006). *Adolescent suicide: Assessment and intervention* (2nd ed.). Washington, DC: American Psychological Association.

Bernal, G., & Saez-Santiago, E. (2006). Culturally centered psychosocial interventions. *Journal of Community Psychology, 34*, 121–132.

Bernal, G., & Scharron-del-Rio, M. R. (2001). Are empirically supported treatments valid for ethnic minorities? Toward an alternative approach for treatment research. *Cultural Diversity and Ethnic Minority Psychology, 7*, 328–342.

Bernard, M. E., & Joyce, M. R. (1984). *Rational-emotive therapy with children and adolescents*. New York, NY: Wiley.

Bernstein, D. A., & Carlson, C. R. (1993). Progressive relaxation: Abbreviated methods. In P. M. Lehrer & R. L. Woolfolk (Eds.), *Principles and practice of stress management* (2nd ed., pp. 53–87). New York, NY: Guilford Press.

Bernstein, D. A., Carlson, C. R., & Schmidt, J. E. (2007). Progressive relaxation: Abbreviated methods. In P. M. Lehrer, R. L. Woolfolk, & W. E. Sime (Eds.), *Principles and practice of stress management* (3rd ed., pp. 88–122). New York, NY: Guilford Press.

Bertalanffy, L. V. (1968). *General systems theory: Foundation, development, applications*. New York, NY: Braziller.

Bertolino, B., & O'Hanlon, B. (2002). *Even from a broken web: Brief, respectful solution-oriented therapy for sexual abuse and trauma.* New York, NY: Norton.

Biederman, J., Hirshfeld-Becker, D. R., Rosenbaum, J. F., Herot, C., Friedman, D., Snidman, N., ... Faraone, S. V. (2001). Further evidence of association between behavioral inhibition and social anxiety in children. *American Journal of Psychiatry, 158,* 1673–1679.

Biegel, G. M., Brown, K. W., Shapiro, S. L., & Schubert, C. M. (2009). Mindfulness-based stress reduction for the treatment of adolescent psychiatric outpatients: A randomized clinical trial. *Journal of Consulting and Clinical Psychology, 77,* 855–866.

BigFoot, D. S., & Schmidt, S. R. (2010). Honoring children, mending the circle: Cultural adaptation of trauma-focused cognitive-behavioral therapy for American Indian and Alaska Native children. *Journal of Clinical Psychology: In Session, 66,* 847–856.

Biglan, A., Hayes, S. C., & Pistorello, J. (2008). Acceptance and commitment: Implications for prevention science. *Prevention Science, 9,* 139–152.

Blackledge, J. T. (2003). An introduction to relational frame theory: Basics and applications. *Behavior Analyst Today, 3,* 421–34

Blatt, S. J., & Homann, E. (1992). Parent-child interaction in the etiology of dependent and self-critical depression. *Clinical Psychology Review, 12,* 47–91.

Blatt, S. J., Stayner, D. A., Auerbach, J. S., & Behrends, R. S. (1996). Change in object and self-representations in long-term, intensive, inpatient treatment of seriously disturbed adolescents and young adults. *Psychiatry, 59,* 82–107.

Bleiberg, E. (2001). *Treating personality disorders in children and adolescents: A relational approach.* New York, NY: Guilford Press.

Bodine, R. J., & Crawford, D. K. (1997). *The handbook of conflict resolution education.* San Francisco, CA: Jossey-Bass.

Boelen, P. A., & van den Bout, J. (2008). Complicated grief and uncomplicated grief are distinguishable constructs. *Psychiatry Research, 157,* 311–314.

Bohart, A. C., Elliott, R., Greenberg, L. S., & Watson, J. C. (2002). Empathy. In J. C. Norcross (Ed.), *Psychotherapy relationships that work: Therapist contributions and responsiveness to patients* (pp. 89–108). New York, NY: Oxford University Press.

Bohart, A. C., & Wade, A. G. (2013). The client in psychotherapy. In M. J. Lambert (Ed.), *Bergin and Garfield's handbook of psychotherapy and behavior change* (6th ed., pp. 219–257). Hoboken, NJ: Wiley.

Bonanno, G. A., & Burton, C. L. (2013). Regulatory flexibility: An individual differences perspective on coping and emotion regulation. *Perspectives on Psychological Science, 8,* 591–612.

Bonanno, R., & Hymel, S. (2013). Cyber bullying and internalizing difficulties: Above and beyond the impact of traditional forms of bullying. *Journal of Youth and Adolescence, 42,* 685–697.

Bond, M., & Perry, J. C. (2004). Long-term changes in defense styles with psychodynamic psychotherapy for depressive, anxiety, and personality disorders. *American Journal of Psychiatry, 161,* 1665–1671.

Bond, C., Woods, K., Humphrey, N., Symes, W., & Green, L. (2013). Practitioner review: The effectiveness of solution focused brief therapy with children and families: A systematic and critical evaluation of the literature from 1990–2010. *Journal of Child Psychology and Psychiatry, 54,* 707–723.

Bongers, I. L., Koot, H. M., der Ende, J., & Verhulst, F. C. (2004). Developmental trajectories of externalizing behaviors in childhood and adolescence. *Child Development, 75,* 1523–1537.

Bonner, B., Walker, C. E., & Berliner, L. (1999). *Treatment manual for dynamic group play therapy for children with sexual behavior problems and their parents/caregivers.* Washington, DC: National Clearinghouse on Child Abuse and Neglect.

Borgonovi, F. (2008). Doing well by doing good. *The relationship between formal volunteering and self-reported health and happiness. Social Science & Medicine, 66,* 2321–2334.

Bornovalova, M. A., Hicks, B. M., Iacono, W. G., & McGue, M. (2010). Familial transmission and heritability of childhood disruptive disorders. *American Journal of Psychiatry, 167,* 1066–1074.

Boulanger, J. L., Hayes, S. C., & Pistorello, J. (2010). Experiential avoidance as a functional contextual concept. In A. M. Kring, D. M. Sloan, A. M. Kring, D. M. Sloan (Eds.), *Emotion regulation and psychopathology: A transdiagnostic approach to etiology and treatment* (pp. 107–136). New York, NY: Guilford Press

Bowen, M. (1978). *Family therapy in clinical practice.* New York, NY: Aronson.

Bowlby, J. (1969). *Attachment and loss: Vol. 1. Attachment.* London, UK: Hogarth Press.

Bowlby, J. (1980). *Attachment and loss. Vol. 3. Loss: Sadness and depression.* New York, NY: Basic Books.

Boylan, K., Vaillancourt, T., Boyle, M., & Szatmari, P. (2007). Comorbidity of internalizing disorders in children with oppositional defiant disorder. *European Child & Adolescent Psychiatry, 16,* 484–494.

Boysen, G. A., & Vogel, D. L. (2008). The relationship between level of training, implicit bias, and multicultural competency among counselor trainees. *Training and Education in Professional Psychology, 2,* 103–110.

Brammer, R. (2012). *Diversity in counseling.* Belmont, CA: Cengage.

Brach, T. (2012). Mindful presence: A foundation for compassion and wisdom. In C. K. Germer, R. D. Siegel, C. K. Germer, R. D. Siegel (Eds.), *Wisdom and compassion in psychotherapy: Deepening mindfulness in clinical practice* (pp. 35–47). New York, NY: Guilford Press.

Bratton, S. C., Ceballos, P. S., Landreth, G. L., & Costas, M. B. (2012). Child-parent relationship therapy with nonoffending parents of sexually abused children. In P. Goodyear-Brown (Ed.), *Handbook of child sexual abuse: Identification, assessment, and treatment* (pp. 321–339). Hoboken, NJ: Wiley.

Brehm, J. W. (1993). Control, its loss, and psychological reactance. In G. Weary, F. Gleicher, & K. L. Marsh (Eds.), *Control motivation and social cognition* (pp. 3–30). New York, NY: Springer-Verlag.

Bremner, J. D. (2006). Stress and brain atrophy. *CNS and Neurological Disorders—Drug Targets, 5,* 503–512.

Brendel, K. E., & Maynard, B. R. (2014). Child-parent interventions for childhood anxiety disorders: A systemic review and meta-analysis. *Research on Social Work Practice, 24,* 287–295.

Brendgen, M., Vitaro, F., Turgeon, L., & Poulin, F. (2002). Assessing aggressive and depressed children's social relations with classmates and friends: A matter of perspective. *Journal of Abnormal Child Psychology, 30,* 609–624.

Brent, D., Emslie, G., Clarke, G., Wagner, K. D., Asarnow, J. R., Keller, M., … Zelazny, J. (2008). Switching to another SSRI or to venlafaxine with or without cognitive behavioral therapy for adolescents with SSRI-resistant depression: The TORDIA randomized controlled trial. *Journal of the American Medical Association, 299,* 901–913.

Brent, D. A., Poling, K. D., & Goldstein, T. R. (2011). *Treating depressed and suicidal adolescents: A clinician's guide.* New York, NY: Guilford Press.

Brestan, E. V., & Eyberg, S. M. (1998). Effective psychosocial treatments of conduct-disordered children and adolescents: 29 years, 82 studies, and 5272 kids. *Journal of Clinical Child Psychology, 27,* 179–188.

Brestan, E. V., Eyberg, S. M., Boggs, S., & Algina, J. (1997). Parent-child interaction therapy prescriptions of untreated siblings. *Child and Family Behavior Therapy, 19,* 13–28.

Brewer, M. B. (1996). When contact is not enough: Social identity and intergroup cooperation. *International Journal of Intercultural Relations, 20,* 291–303.

Brewin, C. R. (2001). A cognitive neuroscience account of posttraumatic stress disorder and its treatment. *Behaviour Research and Therapy, 39,* 373–393.

Brewin, C. R., & Holmes, E. A. (2003). Psychological theories of post-traumatic stress disorder. *Clinical Psychological Review, 23,* 339–376.

Brickman, P., Rabinowitz, V. C., Karuza, J., Coates, D., Cohen, E., & Kidder, L. (1982). Models of helping and coping. *American Psychologist, 37,* 368–384.

Briere, J. N., & Scott, C. (2014). *Principles of trauma therapy: A guide to symptoms, evaluation, and treatment* (2nd ed.). Thousand Oaks, CA: SAGE.

Briggs, K., Runyon, M., & Deblinger, E. (2011). The use of play in trauma-focused cognitive-behavioral therapy. In S. Russ & L. Niec (Eds.), *Play in clinical practice* (pp. 168–200). New York, NY: Guilford Press.

Brinkmeyer, M., & Eyberg, S. M. (2003). Parent–child interaction therapy for oppositional children. In A. E. Kazdin & J. R. Weisz (Eds.), *Evidence based psychotherapies for children and adolescents* (pp. 204–223). New York, NY: Guilford Press.

Broadbent, D. E. (1977). The hidden preattentive processes. *American Psychologist, 32,* 109–118.

Brofenbrenner, U. (1977). Toward an experimental ecology of human development. *American Psychologist, 52,* 513–531.

Brown, E. J., Albrecht, A., McQuaid, J., Munoz-Silva, D. M., & Silva, R. R. (2004). Treatment of children exposed to trauma. In R. R. Silva (Ed.), *Posttraumatic stress disorders in children and adolescents handbook* (pp. 257–286). New York, NY: Norton.

Brown, K. W., West, A. M., Loverich, T. M., & Biegel, G. M. (2011). Assessing adolescent mindfulness: Validation of an Adapted Mindful Attention Awareness Scale in adolescent normative and psychiatric populations. *Psychological Assessment, 23,* 1023–1033.

Bruner, J. (1987). Life as narrative. *Social Research, 54,* 11–32.

Buchalter, S. I. (2009). *Art therapy techniques and applications.* London, UK: Jessica Kingsley.

Buchmann, A., Hohmann, S., Brandeis, D., Banaschewski, T., & Poustka, L. (2014). Aggression in children and adolescents. In K. A. Miczek & A. Meyer-Lindenberg (Eds.), *Neuroscience of aggression* (pp. 421–442). New York, NY: Springer.

Buckley, W. (1967). *Sociology and modern systems theory.* Englewood Cliffs, NJ: Prentice-Hall.

Budhani, S., & Blair, R. J. R. (2005). Response reversal and children with psychopathic tendencies: Success is a function of salience of contingency change. *Journal of Child Psychology and Psychiatry, 46,* 972–981.

Burke, A. E., & Silverman, W. K. (1987). The prescriptive treatment of school refusal. *Clinical Psychology Review, 7,* 353–362.

Burke, J. D., Waldman, I., & Lahey, B. B. (2010). Predictive validity of childhood oppositional defiant disorder and conduct disorder: Implications for DSM-V. *Journal of Abnormal Psychology, 119,* 739–751.

Burns, D. D., & Beck, A. T. (1980). *Feeling good: The new mood therapy.* New York, NY: Morrow.

Burroughs, M. S., Wagner, W. W., & Johnson, J. T. (1997). Treatment with children of divorce: A comparison of two types of therapy. *Journal of Divorce and Remarriage, 27,* 83–99.

Burton, D., & Naylor, S. (2002). The Jekyll/Hyde nature of goals: Revisiting and updating goal setting in sport. In T. S. Horn (Ed.), *Advances in sport psychology* (2nd ed., pp. 459–499). Champaign, IL: Human Kinetics.

Burton, D., & Weiss, C. (2008). The fundamental goal concept: The path to process and performance success. In T. Horn (Ed.), *Advances in sport psychology* (3rd ed., pp. 339–375). Champaign, IL: Human Kinetics.

Bushman, B. B., & Peacock, G. G. (2010). Does teaching problem-solving skills matter? An evaluation of problem-solving skills training for the treatment of social and behavioral problems in children. *Child and Family Behavior Therapy, 32,* 103–124.

Bushman, B. J., Baumeister, R. F., Thomaes, S., Ryu, E., Begeer, S., & West, S. G. (2009). Looking again, and harder, for a link between low self-esteem and aggression. *Journal of Personality, 77,* 427–446.

Butler, S., Guterman, J. T., & Rudes, J. (2009, July 1). Using puppets with children in narrative therapy to externalize the problem. *Journal of Mental Health Counseling,* The Free Library. Retrieved from http://www.thefreelibrary.com/Using puppets with children in narrative therapy to externalize the ... -a0204682044

Cabaniss, D. L., Cherry, S., Douglas, C. J., Graver, R., & Schwartz, A. R. (2013). *Psychodynamic formulation.* Hoboken, NJ: Wiley.

Cabaniss, D. L., Cherry, S., Douglas, C. J., & Schwartz, A. R. (2011). *Psychodynamic psychotherapy: A clinical manual.* Hoboken, NJ: Wiley.

Cabe, N. (2001). Relaxation training: Bubble breaths. In H. G. Kaduson & C. E. Schaefer (Eds.), *101 more favorite play therapy techniques* (pp. 346–349). Lanham, MD: Jason Aronson.

Cain, S. (2012). *Quiet: The power of introverts in a world that can't stop talking.* New York, NY: Crown.

Callahan, C. (2008). *Dialectical Behavior Therapy: Children and adolescents.* Boca Raton, FL: Premier.

Camodeca, M., & Goossens, F. A. (2005). Aggression, social cognitions, anger and sadness in bullies and victims. *Journal of Child Psychology and Psychiatry, 46,* 186–197.

Canada, G. (2010). *Fist stick knife gun: A personal history of violence* (Rev. ed.). Boston, MA: Beacon Press.

Canino, I. A., & Spurlock, J. (2000). *Culturally diverse children and adolescents: Assessment, diagnosis, and treatment* (2nd ed.). New York, NY: Guilford Press.

Cannon, M. F., & Weems, C. F. (2010). Cognitive biases in childhood anxiety disorders: Do interpretive and judgment biases distinguish anxious youth from their non-anxious peers? *Journal of Anxiety Disorders, 24,* 751–758.

Canter, L. (1993). *Homework without tears.* New York, NY: William Morrow.

Canton-Cortes, D., Canton, J., & Cortes, M. R. (2012). The interactive effect of blame attribution with characteristics of child sexual abuse on posttraumatic stress disorder. *Journal of Nervous and Mental Disease, 200,* 329–335.

Capaldi, D. M., Conger, R. D., Hops, H., & Thornberry, T. P. (2003). Introduction to special section on three-generation studies. *Journal of Abnormal Child Psychology, 31,* 123–125.

Cappadocia, M. C., Desrocher, M., Pepler, D., & Schroeder, J. H. (2009). Contextualizing the neurobiology of conduct disorder in an emotion dysregulation framework. *Clinical Psychology Review, 29,* 506–518.

Card, N. A., & Little, T. D. (2006). Proactive and reactive aggression in childhood and adolescence: A meta-analysis of differential relations with psychosocial adjustment. *International Journal of Behavioral Development, 30,* 466–480.

Card, N. A., & Little, T. D. (2007). Differential relations of instrumental and reactive aggression with maladjustment: Does adaptivity depend on function? In P. H. Hawley, T. D. Little, & P. C. Rodkin (Eds.), *Aggression and adaptation: The bright side to bad behavior* (pp. 107–134). Mahwah, NJ: Erlbaum.

Card, N. A., Stucky, B. D., Sawalani, G. M., & Little, T. D. (2008). Direct and indirect aggression during childhood and adolescence: A meta-analytic review of gender differences, intercorrelations, and relations to maladjustment. *Child Development, 79,* 1185–1229.

Cardemil, E. V., & Battle, C. (2003). Guess who's coming to therapy? Getting comfortable with conversations about race and ethnicity in psychotherapy. *Professional Psychology: Research & Practice, 34,* 278–286.

Carey, B. (2011). Expert on mental illness reveals her own fight. *New York Times,* June 23, 2011. Retrieved March 22, 2015, from http://www.nytimes.com/2011/06/23/health/23lives.html?pagewanted=all&_r=0.

Carey, M., Walther, S., & Russell, S. (2009). The absent but implicit: A map to support therapeutic enquiry. *Family Process, 48,* 319–331.

Cary, C. E., & McMillen, J. C. (2012). The data behind the dissemination: A systematic review of trauma–focused cognitive behavioral therapy for use with children and youth. *Children and Youth Services Review, 34,* 748-757.

Carlson, E. A. (1998). A prospective longitudinal study of attachment disorganization/ disorientation. *Child Development, 69,* 1107–1128.

Carlson, C. R., & Hoyle, R. H. (1993). Efficacy of abbreviated progressive muscle relaxation training: A quantitative review of behavioral medicine research. *Journal of Consulting and Clinical Psychology, 61,* 1059–1067.

Carlsson, R., & Björklund, F. (2010). Implicit stereotype content: Mixed stereotypes can be measured with the Implicit Association Test. *Social Psychology, 41,* 213–222.

Carney, D., Cuddy, A. J. C., & Yap, A. (2010). Power posing: Brief nonverbal displays affect neuroendocrine levels and risk tolerance. *Psychological Science, 21,* 1363–1368.

Cartledge, G., & Milburn, J. F. (1996). *Cultural diversity and social skills instruction: Understanding ethnic and gender differences.* Champaign, IL: Research Press.

Carvalho, J. P., & Hopko, D. R. (2011). Behavioral theory of depression: Reinforcement as a mediating variable between avoidance and depression. *Journal of Behavior Therapy and Experimental Psychiatry, 42,* 154–162.

Carver, C. S. (2011). Coping. In R. J. Contrada & A. Baum (Eds.), *The handbook of stress science: Biology, psychology, and health.* (pp. 220–229). New York, NY: Springer.

Cary, C. E., & McMillen, J. C. (2012). The data behind the dissemination: A systematic review of trauma-focused cognitive behavioral therapy for use with children and youth. *Children and Youth Services Review, 34*, 748–757.

Case, C., & Dalley, T. (2014). *The handbook of art therapy* (3rd ed.). New York, NY: Routledge.

Cashdan, S. (1988). *Object relations therapy: Using the relationship.* New York, NY: Norton.

Cashin, A., Browne, G., Bradbury, J., & Mulder, A. M. (2013). The effectiveness of narrative therapy with young people with autism. *Journal of Child and Adolescent Mental Health Nursing, 26*, 32–41.

Caspi, A., Hariri, A., Holmes, A., Uher, R., & Moffitt, T. (2010). Genetic sensitivity to the environment: The case of the serotonin transporter gene and its implications for studying complex diseases and traits. *American Journal of Psychiatry, 167*, 509–527.

Cepukiene, V., & Pakrosnis, R. (2011). The outcome of Solution-Focused Brief Therapy among foster care adolescents: The changes of behavior and perceived somatic and cognitive difficulties. *Children and Youth Services Review, 33*(6), 791–797.

Cha, C. B., & Nock, M. K. (2014). Suicidal and nonsuicidal self-injurious thoughts and behaviors. In E. J. Mash & R. A. Barkley (Eds.), *Child psychopathology* (3rd ed., pp. 317–342). New York, NY: Guilford Press.

Chacko, A., Wymbs, B. T., Wymbs, F. A., Pelham, W. E., Jr., Swanger-Gagne, M. S., Girio, E., … O'Connor, B. (2009). Enhancing traditional parent training for single mothers of children with ADHD. *Journal of Clinical Child and Adolescent Psychology, 38*, 206–213.

Chambers, J. R., & Davis, M. H. (2012). The role of the self in perspective-taking and empathy: Ease of self-simulation as a heuristic for inferring empathic feelings. *Social Cognition, 30*, 153–180.

Chartrand, T. L., & van Baaren, R. D. (2009). Human mimicry. In M. P. Zanna (Ed.), *Advances in experimental social psychology* (Vol. 41, pp. 219–274). San Diego, CA: Academic Press.

Chase, R. M., & Eyberg, S. M. (2008). Clinical presentation and treatment outcome for children with comorbid externalizing and internalizing symptoms. *Journal of Anxiety Disorders, 22*, 273–282.

Chen, E., Matthews, K. A., & Boyce, W. T. (2002). Socioeconomic differences in children's health: How and why do these relationships change with age? *Psychological Bulletin, 128*, 295–329.

Chen, E. W. (2009). *Encyclopedia of Asian American issues today* (Vol. 1, pp. 222–223). Santa Barbara, CA: Greenwood.

Chethik, M. (2000). *Techniques of child therapy: Psychodynamic strategies* (2nd ed.). New York, NY: Guilford Press.

Cheung, M. (2012). *Child sexual abuse: Best practices for interviewing and treatment.* Chicago, IL: Lyceum Books.

Child Trends. (2010). Family structure. Retrieved from www.childtrendsdatabank.org/?q=node/231.

Chorpita, B. F., & Barlow, D. H. (1998). The development of anxiety: The role of control in the early environment. *Psychological Bulletin, 124*, 3–21.

Chorpita, B. F., Daleiden, E. L., Moffitt, C., Yim, L., & Umemoto, L. A. (2000). Assessment of tripartite factors of emotion in children and adolescents: I. *Structural validity and* normative data of an affect and arousal scale. *Journal of Psychopathology and Behavioral Assessment, 22,* 141–160.

Choudhuri, D. D., Santiago-Rivera, A. L., & Garrett, M. T. (2012). *Counseling and diversity.* Belmont, CA: Cengage.

Chow, C., & Pincus, D. B. (2014). Anxiety disorders in children and adolescents. In S. G. Hofmann, D. J. A. Dozois, W. Rief, & J. A. J. Smits (Eds.), *The Wiley handbook of cognitive behavioral therapy* (Vols. *1–3,* pp. 849–873). Hoboken, NJ: Wiley-Blackwell.

Ciarrochi, J., & Bailey, A. (2008). *A CBT practitioner's guide to ACT: How to bridge the gap between cognitive behavioral therapy and Acceptance and Commitment Therapy.* Oakland, CA: New Harbinger.

Cicchetti, D., & Walker, E. (Eds.). (2003). *Neurodevelopmental mechanisms in psychopathology.* New York, NY: Cambridge University Press.

Ciucci, E., & Baroncelli, A. (2014). The emotional core of bullying: Further evidences of the role of callous–unemotional traits and empathy. *Personality and Individual Differences, 67,* 69–74.

Clark, D. M., Ball, S., & Pape, D. (1991). An experimental investigation of thought suppression. *Behaviour Research and Therapy, 29,* 253–257.

Clark, D. M., Salkovskis, P. M., Hackmann, A., Middleton, H., Anastasiades, P., & Gelder, M. (1994). A comparison of cognitive therapy, applied relaxation and imipramine in the treatment of panic disorder. *British Journal of Psychiatry, 164,* 759–769.

Clark, L. A., & Watson, D. (1991). Tripartite model of anxiety and depression: Psychometric evidence and taxonomic implications. *Journal of Abnormal Psychology, 100,* 316–336.

Clark, S., Bowers, G., & Reynolds, S. (2014). Managing negative thoughts, Part I: Cognitive restructuring and behavioral experiments. In E. S. Sburlati, H. J. Lyneham, C. A. Schniering, & R. M. Rapee (Eds.), *Evidence-based CBT for anxiety and depression in children and adolescents: A competencies based approach* (pp. 159–175). Hoboken, NJ: Wiley-Blackwell.

Clark, S., & Reynolds, S. (2013). Depressive disorders. In P. Graham & S. Reynolds (Eds.), *Cognitive behaviour therapy for children and families* (pp. 292–309). Cambridge, UK: Cambridge University Press.

Clarke, G. N., DeBar, L. L., & Lewinsohn, P. M. (2003). Cognitive-behavioral group treatment for adolescent depression. In A. E. Kazdin & J. R. Weisz (Eds.), *Evidence-based psychotherapies for children and adolescents* (pp. 120–134). New York, NY: Guilford Press.

Clarkin, J. F., & Levy, K. N. (2004). The influence of client variables on psychotherapy. In M. J. Lambert (Ed.), *Bergin and Garfield's Handbook of Psychotherapy and Behavior Change* (5th ed., pp. 194–226). New York, NY: Wiley.

Clarkin, J. F., Levy, K. N., Lenzenweger, M. F., & Kernberg, O. F. (2007). Evaluating three treatments for borderline personality disorder: A multiwave study. *The American Journal of Psychiatry, 164,* 922–928.

Coatsworth, J. D., Duncan, L. G., Greenberg, M. T., & Nix, R. L. (2010). Changing parent's mindfulness, child management skills and relationship quality with their youth: Results from a randomized pilot intervention trial. *Journal of Child and Family Studies, 19,* 203–217.

Coatsworth, J. D., Santisteban, D. A., McBride, C. K., & Szapocznik, J. (2001). Brief strategic family therapy versus community control: Engagement, retention, and an exploration of the moderating role of adolescent symptom severity. *Family Process, 40,* 313–332.

Cobham, V. E., Dadds, M. R., & Spence, S. H. (1998). The role of parental anxiety in the treatment of childhood anxiety. *Journal of Consulting and Clinical Psychology, 66,* 893–905.

Cohen, J. (1988). *Statistical power analyses for the behavioral sciences* (2nd ed.). Hillsdale, NJ: Erlbaum.

Cohen, J. A., & Mannarino, A. P. (2004). Treatment of childhood traumatic grief. *Journal of Clinical Child and Adolescent Psychology, 33,* 819–831.

Cohen, J. A., Mannarino, A. P., & Deblinger, E. (2006). *Treating trauma and traumatic grief in children and adolescents.* New York, NY: Guilford Press.

Cohen, J. A., Mannarino, A. P., & Iyengar, S. (2011). Community treatment for post-traumatic stress disorder for children exposed to intimate partner violence. *Archives of Pediatrics and Adolescent Medicine, 165,* 16–21.

Cohen, J. A., Mannarino, A. P., & Knudsen, K. (2005). Treating sexually abused children: One year follow-up of a randomized controlled trial. *Child Abuse & Neglect, 29,* 135–145.

Cohen, J. A., Mannarino, A. P., Perel, J. M., & Staron, V. (2007). A pilot randomized controlled trial of combined trauma-focused CBT and sertraline for childhood PTSD symptoms. *Journal of the American Academy of Child and Adolescent Psychiatry, 46,* 811–819.

Cohen, J. A., Murray, L. K., & Mannarino, A. P. (2013). Trauma-focused cognitive behaviour therapy for child sexual abuse. In P. Graham & S. Reynolds (Eds.), *Cognitive behaviour therapy for children and families* (3rd ed., pp. 145–158). New York, NY: Cambridge University Press.

Colapinto, J. (1991). Structural family therapy. In A. S. Gurman & D. P. Kniskern (Eds.), *Handbook of family therapy* (Vol. 2, pp. 417–434). New York, NY: Brunner/ Mazel.

Cole, P. M., Bruschi, C. J., & Tamang, B. L. (2002). Cultural differences in children's emotional reactions to difficult situations. *Child Development, 73,* 983–996.

Colonnesi, C., Draijer, E. M., Stams, G. J. J. M., Van der Bruggen, C. O., Bogels, S. M., & Noom, M. J. (2011). The relation between insecure attachment and child anxiety: A meta-analytic review. *Journal of Clinical Child and Adolescent Psychology, 40,* 630–645.

Committee for Children. (2002). *Second step: A violence prevention curriculum* (3rd ed.). Seattle, WA: Author.

Compas, B. E., Connor-Smith, J. K., Saltzman, H., Thomsen, A. H., & Wadsworth, M. E. (2001). Coping with stress during childhood and adolescence: Problems, progress, and potential in theory and research. *Psychological Bulletin, 127,* 87–127.

Compton, A. (1972). A study of the psychoanalytic theory of anxiety: II: Developments in the theory of anxiety since 1926. *Journal of the American Psychoanalytic Association, 20,* 341–394.

Conduct Problems Prevention Research Group. (2002). Evaluation of the first three years of the Fast Track prevention trial with children at high risk of adolescent conduct problems. *Journal of Abnormal Child Psychology, 14,* 927–945.

Connolly Gibbons, M. B., Crits-Christoph, P., Barber, J. P., Wiltsey-Stirman, S., Gallop, R., Goldstein, L. A., ... Ring-Kurtz, S. (2009). Unique and common mechanisms of change across cognitive and dynamic psychotherapies. *Journal of Consulting and Clinical Psychology, 77*, 801–813.

Connor, D. F. (2002). *Aggression and antisocial behavior in children and adolescents: Research and treatment.* New York, NY: Guilford Press.

Connor, D. F. (2006). Stimulants. In R. A. Barkley (Ed.), *Attention-deficit hyperactivity disorder: A handbook for diagnosis and treatment* (3rd ed., pp. 608–647). New York, NY: Guilford Press.

Conroy, D. E. (2004). The unique meaning of multidimensional fears of failing. *Journal of Sport and Exercise Psychology, 26*, 484–491.

Cooper, M., O'Hara, M., Schmid, P., & Bohard, A. (2013). *The handbook of person-centered psychotherapy and counseling* (2nd ed.). London, UK: Palgrave MacMillan.

Cooper, S. H. (1992). The empirical study of defensive processes: A review. In J. W. Barron, M. N. Eagle, & D. L. Wolitzky (Eds.), *Interface of psychoanalysis and psychology* (pp. 327–346). Washington, DC: American Psychological Association.

Copeland, W., Keeler, G., Angold, A., & Costello, E. (2007). Traumatic events and posttraumatic stress in childhood. *Archives of General Psychiatry, 64*, 577–584.

Corcoran, J. (2006). A comparison group study of solution-focused therapy versus "treatment-as-usual" for behavior problems in children. *Journal of Social Service Research, 33*, 69–81.

Corcoran, K. M., Farb, N., Anderson, A., & Segal, Z. V. (2010). Mindfulness and emotion regulation: Outcomes and possible mediating mechanisms. In A. M. Kring, D. M. Sloan, A. M. Kring, D. M. Sloan (Eds.), *Emotion regulation and psychopathology: A transdiagnostic approach to etiology and treatment* (pp. 339–355). New York, NY: Guilford Press.

Corr, C. A. (2002). Coping with challenges to assumptive worlds. In J. Kauffman (Ed.), *Loss of the assumptive world: A theory of traumatic loss* (pp. 127–138). New York, NY: Brunner-Routledge.

Cosmides, L., & Tooby, J. (1994). Origins of domain specificity: The evolution of functional organization. In L. A. Hirschfeld & S. A. Gelman (Eds.), *Mapping the mind: Domain specificity in cognition and culture* (pp. 85–116). New York, NY: Cambridge University Press.

Costantino, G., Malgady, R. G., & Cardalda, E. (2005). TEMAS narrative treatment: An evidence-based, culturally competent therapy modality. In E. D. Hibbs & P. S. Jensen (Eds.), *Psychosocial treatments for child and adolescent disorders: Empirically based strategies for clinical practice* (2nd. ed., pp. 717–742). Washington, DC: American Psychological Association.

Coster, J. S., & Schwebel, M. (1997). Well-functioning in professional psychologists. *Professional Psychology: Research and Practice, 28*, 5–13.

Covington, M. V. (2000). Goal theory, motivation, and school achievement: An integrative review. *Annual Review of Psychology, 51*, 171–200.

Cozolino, L. (2006). *The neuroscience of human relationships: Attachment and the developing social brain.* New York, NY: Norton.

Cramer, P. (2006). *Protecting the self: Defense mechanisms in action.* New York, NY: Guilford Press.

Crick, N. R., & Werner, N. E. (1998). Response decision processes in relational and overt aggression. *Child Development, 69*, 1630–1639.

Crits-Christoph, P., Connolly Gibbons, M. B., & Mukherjee, D. (2013). Psychotherapy process-outcome research. In M. J. Lambert (Ed.), *Bergin and Garfield's handbook of psychotherapy and behavior change* (6th ed., pp. 298–340). Hoboken, NJ: Wiley.

Crowell, S. E., Beauchaine, T. P., & Linehan, M. (2009). A biosocial developmental model of BPD: Elaborating and extending Linehan's theory. *Psychological Bulletin, 135,* 495–510.

Cryder, C. H., Kilmer, R. P., Tedeschi, R. G., & Calhoun, L. G. (2006). An exploratory study of posttraumatic growth in children following a natural disaster. *American Journal of Orthopsychiatry, 76,* 65–69.

Cuijpers, P., Berking, M., Andersson, G., Quigley, L., Kleiboer, A., & Dobson, K. S. (2013). A meta-analysis of cognitive-behavioural therapy for adult depression, alone and in comparison with other treatments. *The Canadian Journal of Psychiatry, 58,* 376–385.

Cuijpers, P., van Straten, A., Andersson, G., & van Oppen, P. (2008). Psychotherapy for depression in adults: A meta-analysis of comparative outcome studies. *Journal of Consulting and Clinical Psychology, 76,* 909–922.

Cummings, C. M., Kendall, P. C., & Mazza, A. B. (2014). Anxiety disorders in children. In L. Grossman & S. Walfish (Eds.), *Translating psychological research into practice* (pp. 17–24). New York, NY: Springer.

Cunningham, P. B., Foster, S. L., & Warner, S. E. (2010). Culturally relevant family-based treatment for adolescent delinquency and substance abuse: Understanding within-session processes. *Journal of Clinical Psychology: In Session, 66,* 830–846.

Currier, J. M., Holland, J. M., & Neimeyer, R. A. (2010). Do CBT-based interventions alleviate distress following bereavement? A review of the current evidence. *International Journal of Cognitive Therapy, 3,* 77–93.

Curry, J. F., Wells, K. C., Brent, D. A., Clarke, G. N., Rohde, P., Albano, A. M., … March, J. S. (2003). *Treatment for Adolescents with Depression Study (TADS) cognitive behavior therapy manual: Introduction, rationale, and adolescent sessions.* Durham, NC: Duke University Medical Center, The TADS Team.

Curtis, D. F. (2010). ADHD symptom severity following participation in a pilot, 10-week, manualized family based behavioral intervention. *Child and Family Behavior Therapy, 32,* 231–241.

Dadds, M. R., Holland, D. E., Barrett, P. M., Laurens, K. R., & Spence, S. H. (1997). Prevention and early intervention for anxiety disorders: A controlled trial. *Journal of Consulting and Clinical Psychology, 65,* 627–635.

Daigneault, I, Hebert, M., & Tourigny, M. (2006). Attributions and coping sexually abused adolescents referred for group treatment. *Journal of Child Sexual Abuse, 15,* 35–59.

Damasio, A. (2010). *Self comes to mind: Constructing the conscious brain.* New York, NY: Vintage.

Damasio, A. R. (1994). *Descartes' error: Emotion, reason, and the human brain.* New York, NY: Picador.

Dandreaux, D. M., & Frick, P. J. (2009). Developmental pathways to conduct problems: A further test of the childhood and adolescent-onset distinction. *Journal of Abnormal Child Psychology, 37,* 375–385.

David-Ferdon, C., & Kaslow, N. J. (2008). Evidence-based psychosocial treatments for child and adolescent depression. *Journal of Clinical Child & Adolescent Psychology, 37,* 62–104.

Davidson, R. J., Kabat-Zinn, J., Schumacher, J., Rosenkranz, M., Muller, D., ... Sheridan, J. F. (2003). Alterations in brain and immune function produced by mindfulness meditation. *Psychosomatic Medicine, 65,* 564–570.

Davis III, T. E., Whiting, S. E., & May, A. C. (2012). Exposure therapy for anxiety disorders in children. In P. Neudeck & H.-U. Wittchen (Eds.), *Exposure therapy: Rethinking the model—Refining the method* (pp. 111–125). New York, NY: Springer.

Deakin, E. K., & Nunes, M. T. (2009). Effectiveness of child psychoanalytic psychotherapy in a clinical outpatient setting. *Journal of Child Psychotherapy, 35,* 290–301

de Arellano, M. A. R., Lyman, R. D., Jobe-Shields, L., Preethy, G., Dougherty, R. H., Daniels, A. S., ... Delphin-Rittmon, M. E. (2014). Trauma-focused cognitive-behavioral therapy for children and adolescents: Assessing the evidence. *Psychiatric Services, 65,* 591–602.

Deault, L. C. (2010). A systematic review of parenting in relation to the development of comorbidities and functional impairments in children with attention-deficit/hyperactivity disorder (ADHD). *Child Psychiatry and Human Development, 41,* 168–192.

De Bellis, M. D., Casey, B. J., Dahl, R. E., Birmaher, B., Williamson, D. E., Thomas, K. M., & Ryan, N. D. (2000). A pilot study of amygdala volumes in pediatric generalized anxiety disorder. *Biological Psychiatry, 48,* 51–57.

De Bellis, M. D., Keshavan, M. S., Spencer, S., & Hall, J. (2000). N-acetylaspartate concentration in the anterior cingulate of maltreated children and adolescents with PTSD. *The American Journal of Psychiatry, 157,* 1175–1177.

Deblinger, E., & Heflin, A. H. (1996). *Treating sexually abused children and their non-offending parents: A cognitive-behavioral approach.* Thousand Oaks, CA: SAGE.

Deblinger, E., Mannarino, A. P., Cohen, J. A., Runyon, M. K., & Steer, R. A. (2011). Trauma-focused cognitive behavioral therapy for children: Impact of trauma narrative and treatment length. *Depression and Anxiety, 28,* 67–75.

Deblinger, E., Mannarino, A. P., Cohen, J. A., & Steer, R. A. (2006). A follow-up study of a multi-site, randomized, controlled trial for children with sexual abuse-related PTSD symptoms. *Journal of the American Academy of Child and Adolescent Psychiatry, 45,* 1474–1484.

de Castro, B. O., Brendgen, M., van Boxtel, H., Vitaro, F., & Schaepers, L. (2007). Accept me or else: Disputed overestimation of social competence predicts increases in proactive aggression. *Journal of Abnormal Child Psychology, 35,* 1573–2835.

de Castro, B. O., Merk, W., Koops, W., Veerman, J. W., & Bosch, J. D. (2005). Emotions in social information processing and their relations with reactive and proactive aggression in referred aggressive boys. *Journal of Clinical Child and Adolescent Psychology, 34,* 105–116.

de Castro, B. O., Veerman, J. W., Koops, W., Bosch, J. D., & Monshouwer, H. J. (2002). Hostile attribution of intent and aggressive behavior: A meta-analysis. *Child Development, 73,* 916–934.

Decety, J. (2011). The neuroevolution of empathy. *Annals of the New York Academy of Sciences, 1231,* 35–45.

De Jong, P., & Berg, I. K. (2012). *Interviewing for solutions* (4th ed.). Stamford, CT: Cengage Learning.

DeLeon, I. G., Bullock, C. E., & Catania, A. C. (2013). Arranging reinforcement contingencies in applied settings: Fundamentals and implications of recent basic and applied research. In G. J. Madden, W. V. Dube, T. D. Hackenberg, G. P. Hanley, & K. A.

Lattal (Eds.), *APA handbook of behavior analysis: Vol. 2. Translating principles into practice* (pp. 47–75). Washington, DC: American Psychological Association.

De Los Reyes, A., & Kazdin, A. E. (2005). Informant discrepancies in the assessment of childhood psychopathology: A critical review, theoretical framework, and recommendations for further study. *Psychological Bulletin, 131*, 483–509.

de Maat, S., de Jonghe, F., de Kraker, R., Leichsenring, F., Abbass, A., Luyten, P., … Dekker, J. (2013). The current state of the empirical evidence for psychoanalysis: A meta-analytic approach. *Harvard Review of Psychiatry, 21*, 107–137.

de Maat, S., de Jonghe, F., Schoevers, R., & Dekker, J. (2009). The effectiveness of long–term psychoanalytic therapy: A systematic review of empirical studies. *Harvard Review of Psychiatry, 17*, 1–23.

Dempsey, M. (2002). Negative coping as mediator in the relation between violence and outcomes: Inner-city African American youth. *American Journal of Orthopsychiatry, 72*, 102–109.

Dempsey, M., Overstreet, S., & Moely, B. (2000). Approach and avoidance coping and PTSD symptoms in inner-city youth. *Current Psychology, 19*, 28–46.

Denborough, D. (2014). *Retelling the stories of our lives: Everyday narrative therapy to draw inspiration and transform experience.* New York, NY: Norton.

DeRosier, M. E. (2004). Building relationships and combating bullying: Effectiveness of a school-based social skills group intervention. *Journal of Clinical Child and Adolescent Psychology, 33*, 196–201.

Derrida, J. (1992). *Derrida: A critical reader (D. Wood, Ed.).* Oxford, UK: Blackwell.

de Shazer, S. (1985). *Keys to solution in brief therapy.* New York, NY: Norton.

de Shazer, S. (1993). Creative misunderstanding: There is no escape from language. In S. Gilligan & R. Price (Eds.), *Therapeutic conversations* (pp. 81–90). New York, NY: Norton.

de Shazer, S., & Dolan, Y. (2007). More than miracles: The state of the art of solution-focused brief therapy *(Haworth Brief Therapy series).* New York, NY: Routledge.

Dewald, P. A. (1971). *Psychotherapy: A dynamic approach* (2nd ed.). New York, NY: Basic Books.

Dewald, P. A. (1982). Psychoanalytic perspectives on resistance. In P. Wachtel (Ed.), *Resistance: Psychodynamic and behavioral approaches* (pp. 45–88). New York: Plenum Press.

Dewald, P. A. (1994). Principles of supportive psychotherapy. *American Journal of Psychiatry, 48*, 505–518.

De Young, A. C., Kenardy, J. S., & van Eys, P. (2013). Post-Traumatic Stress Disorder in children. In L. Grossman & S. Walfish (Eds.), *Translating psychological research into practice* (pp. 73–82). New York, NY: Springer.

Diamond, G. M. (2014). Attachment-based family therapy interventions. *Psychotherapy, 51*, 15–19.

Diamond, G. S., Diamond, G. M., & Levy, S. A. (2014). *Attachment-based family therapy for depressed adolescents.* Washington, DC, US: American Psychological Association.

Diamond, G. S., & Liddle, H. A. (1996). Resolving a therapeutic impasse between parents and adolescents in multidimensional family therapy. *Journal of Consulting and Clinical Psychology, 64*, 481–488.

Diamond, G. S., & Siqueland, L. (1998). Emotions, attachment and the relational reframe: The first session. *Journal of Systemic Therapies, 17*, 36–50.

Diamond, G. S., Siqueland, L., & Diamond, G. M. (2003). Attachment-based family therapy for depressed adolescents: Programmatic treatment development. *Clinical Child and Family Psychology Review*, 6, 107–127.

Diamond, G. S., Wintersteen, M. B., Brown, G. K., Diamond, G. M., Gallop, R., Shelef, K., & Levy, S. (2010). Attachment-based family therapy for adolescents with suicidal ideation: A randomized controlled trial. *Journal of the American Academy of Child & Adolescent Psychiatry*, 49, 122–131.

Diaz-Martinez, A. M., Interian, A., & Waters, D. M. (2010). The integration of CBT, multicultural and feminist psychotherapies with Latinas. *Journal of Psychotherapy Integration*, 20, 312–326.

DiGiuseppe, R. A. (1999). Rational Emotive Behavior Therapy. In H. T. Prout & D. T. Brown (Eds.), *Counseling and psychotherapy with children and adolescents: Theory and practice for school and clinical settings* (pp. 252–301). New York, NY: Wiley.

DiGiuseppe, R. A., Doyle, K. A., Dryden, W., & Backx, W. (2014). *A practitioner's guide to Rational Emotive Behavior Therapy* (3rd ed.). New York, NY: Oxford University Press.

Dijk, S. V. (2013). *DBT made simple: A step-by-step guide to Dialectical Behavior Therapy.* Oakland, CA: New Harbinger.

Dillen, L., Fontaine, J. R. J., & Verhofstadt-Deneve, L. (2008). Are normal and complicated grief different constructs? A confirmatory factor analytic test. *Clinical Psychology and Psychotherapy*, 15, 386–395.

Dimeff, L. A., & Koerner, K. (2007). *Dialectical behavior therapy in clinical practice: Applications across disorders and settings.* New York, NY: Guilford Press.

Dimidjian, S., Barrera, Jr., M., Martell, C., Muñoz, R. F., & Lewinsohn, P. (2011). The origins and current status of behavioral activation treatments for depression. *Annual Review of Clinical Psychology*, 7, 1–38.

Dishion, T. J., Bullock, B. M., & Granic, I. (2002). Pragmatism in modeling peer influence: Dynamics, outcomes and change processes. *Development and Psychopathology*, 14, 969–981.

Dishion, T. J., McCord, J., & Poulin, F. (1999). When interventions harm: Peer groups and problem behavior. *American Psychologist*, 54, 755–764.

Dishion, T. J., & Patterson, G. R. (1992). Age effects in parent training outcome. *Behavior Therapy*, 23, 719–729.

Dixhoorn, J. V. (2007). Whole-body breathing: A systems perspective on respiratory retraining. In P. M. Lehrer, R. L. Woolfolk, & W. E. Sime (Eds.), *Principles and practice of stress management* (3rd ed., pp. 291–332). New York, NY: Guilford Press.

Dobson, D., & Dobson, K. S. (2009). *Evidence-based practice of cognitive-behavioral therapy.* New York: Guilford Press.

Dobson, K. S. (2014). Cognitive therapy process. In G. R. VandenBos, E. Meidenbauer, & J. Frank-McNeil (Eds.), *Psychotherapy theories and techniques: A reader* (pp. 67–78). Washington, DC: American Psychological Association.

Dodge, K. A., & Coie, J. D. (1987). Social information processing factors in reactive and proactive aggression in children's peer groups. *Journal of Personality and Social Psychology*, 53, 1146–1158.

Dodge, K. A., Laird, R., Lochman, J. E., Zelli, A., & Conduct Problems Prevention Research Group. (2002). Multi-dimensional latent construct analysis of children's social information processing patterns: Correlations with aggressive behavior problems. *Psychological Assessment*, 14, 60–73.

Doherr, L., Reynolds, S., Wetherly, J., & Evans, E. H. (2005). Young children's ability to engage in cognitive therapy tasks: Associations with age and educational experience. *Behavioural and Cognitive Psychotherapy, 33,* 201–215.

Dolan, Y. M. (1998). *One small step: Moving beyond trauma and therapy to a life of joy.* Kingston, RI: Papier-Mache Press.

Dollard, J., & Miller, N. E. (1950). *Personality and psychotherapy: An analysis in terms of learning, thinking, and culture.* New York, NY: McGraw-Hill.

Donaldson, D., Spirito, A., & Esposito-Smythers, C. (2005). Treatment for adolescents following a suicide attempt: Results of a pilot trial. *Journal of the American Academy of Child and Adolescent Psychiatry, 44,* 113–120.

Doren, D. (2006). Recidivism risk assessments: Making sense of controversies. In W. Marshall, Y. Fernandez, L. Marshall, & G. Serran (Eds.), *Sexual offender treatment: Controversial issues* (pp. 3–15). Chichester, UK: Wiley.

Dorman, R. L., & Shapiro, J. P. (2004). *Preventing burnout in your staff and yourself: A survival guide for human services supervisors.* Washington, DC: Child Welfare League of America Press.

Dowd, E. T. (2003). Cultural differences in cognitive therapy. *Behavior Therapist, 26,* 247–249.

Dowell, K. A., & Ogles, B. M. (2010). The effects of parent participation on child psychotherapy outcome: A meta-analytic review. *Journal of Clinical Child and Adolescent Psychology, 39,* 151–162.

Drewes, A. A., & Bratton, S. C. (2014). Play therapy. In E. J. Green & A. A. Drewes (Eds.), *Integrating expressive arts and play therapy with children and adolescents* (pp. 17–40). Hoboken, NJ: Wiley.

Drugli, M. B., Larsson, B., Fossum, S., & Morch, W. T. (2010). Five- to six-year outcome and its prediction for children with ODD/CD treated with parent training. *Journal of Child Psychology and Psychiatry, 51,* 559–566.

Duarte-Velez, Y., Guillermo, B., & Bonilla, K. (2010). Culturally adapted cognitive-behavioral therapy: Integrating sexual, spiritual, and family identities in an evidence-based treatment of a depressed Latino adolescent. *Journal of Clinical Psychology: In Session, 66,* 895–906.

Dumas, J. E. (1984). Interactional correlates of treatment outcome in behavioral parent training. *Journal of Consulting and Clinical Psychology, 52,* 946–954.

Duncan, B. L., & Miller, S. D. (2000). *The heroic client.* New York, NY: Jossey-Bass.

Dupree, D., Spencer, M. B., & Bell, S. (1997). African American children. In G. Johnson-Powell, J. Yamamoto, G. E. Wyatt, & W. Arroyo (Eds.), *Transcultural child development: Psychological assessment and treatment* (pp. 237–268). New York, NY: Wiley.

Durham, A. (2003). *Young men surviving child sexual abuse: Research stories and therapeutic practice.* Hoboken, NJ: Wiley.

Duvall, J., & Béres, L. (2007). Movement of identities: A conversational map for working with sexual abuse and trauma. In C. Brown & T. Augusta-Scott (Eds.), *Narrative therapy: Making meaning, making lives* (pp. 229–250). Thousand Oaks, CA: SAGE.

Dweck, C. (2007). *Mindsets: The new psychology of success.* New York, NY: Ballantine.

Eargle, A. E., Guerra, N. G., & Tolan, P. H. (1994). Preventing aggression in inner-city children: Small group training to change cognitions, social skills, and behavior. *Journal of Child and Adolescent Group Therapy, 4,* 229–242.

Eckshtain, D., & Gaynor, S. T. (2012). Combining individual cognitive behavior therapy and caregiver-child sessions for childhood depression: An open trial. *Clinical Child Psychology and Psychiatry, 17*, 266–283.

Eckshtain, D., & Gaynor, S. T. (2013). Combined individual cognitive behavior therapy and parent training for childhood depression: 2- to 3-year follow-up. *Child & Family Behavior Therapy, 35*, 132–143.

Ecton, R. B., & Feindler, E. L. (1990). Anger control training for temper control disorders. In E. L. Feindler & G. R. Kalfus (Eds.), *Adolescent behavior therapy handbook* (pp. 351–371). New York, NY: Springer.

Egan, S. J., Piek, J. P., Dyck, M. J., & Rees, C. S. (2007). The role of dichotomous thinking and rigidity in perfectionism. *Behaviour Research and Therapy, 45*, 1813–1822.

Ehrenberg, M., Regev, R., Lazinski, M., Behrman, L. J., & Zimmerman, S. (2014). Adjustment to divorce for children. In L. Grossman & S. Walfish (Eds.), *Translating psychological research into practice* (pp. 1–8). New York, NY: Springer.

Ehrenreich, J. T., Fairholme, C. P., Buzzella, B. A., Ellard, K. K., & Barlow, D. H. (2007). The role of emotion in psychological therapy. *Clinical Psychology: Science and Practice, 14*, 422–428.

Ehrlich, J. (2014). *Divorce and loss: Helping adults and children mourn when a marriage comes apart*. Lanham, MD: Rowman & Littlefield.

Eifert, G. H., & Forsyth, J. P. (2005). *Acceptance and commitment therapy for anxiety disorders: A practitioner's treatment guide to using mindfulness, acceptance, and values-based behavior change strategies*. Oakland, CA: New Harbinger Publications.

Eisen, A. R., & Silverman, W. K. (1993). Should I relax or change my thoughts? A preliminary examination of cognitive therapy, relaxation, and their combination with overanxious children. *Journal of Cognitive Psychotherapy, 1*, 265–279.

Eisen, A. R., & Silverman, W. K. (1998). Prescriptive treatment for generalized anxiety disorder in children. *Behaviour Therapy, 29*, 105–121.

Eisenberg, N. (2000). Emotion, regulation, and moral development. *Annual Review of Psychology, 51*, 665–697.

Ekers, D., Richards, D., & Gilbody, S. (2008). A meta-analysis of randomized trials of behavioural treatments of depression. *Psychological Medicine, 38*, 611–623.

Ellis, A. (1962). *Reason and emotion in psychotherapy*. New York, NY: Lyle Stuart.

Ellis, A. (1973). *Humanistic psychotherapy: The rational-emotive approach*. New York, NY: Julian.

Ellis, A. (2001). *Overcoming destructive beliefs, feelings, and behaviors: New directions for Rational Emotive Behavior Therapy*. Amherst, NY: Prometheus Books.

Ellis, A., & MacLaren, C. (2005). *Rational Emotive Behavior Therapy: A therapist's guide* (2nd ed.). Atascadero, CA: Impact.

Engel, B. (2000). *Families in recovery: Healing the damage of childhood sexual abuse*. New York, NY: McGraw-Hill.

Epston, D., Freeman, J., & Lobovits, D. (1997). *Playful approaches to serious problems: Narrative therapy with children and their families*. New York, NY: Norton.

Epston, D., & White, M. (1992). *Experience, contradictions, narrative and imagination*. Adelaide, Australia: Dulwich Centre.

Erikson, E. (1963). *Childhood and society*. New York, NY: Norton.

Eyberg, S. M., Funderburk, B. W., Hembree-Kigin, T., McNeil, C. B., Querido, J., & Hood, K. K. (2001). Parent-child interaction therapy with behavior problem children: One and two year maintenance of treatment effects in the family. *Child and Family Behavior Therapy, 23,* 1–20.

Fabiano, G. A., Vujnovic, R. K., Pelham, W. E., Waschbusch, D. A., Massetti, G. M., Pariseau, M. E., ... Volker, M. (2010). Enhancing the effectiveness of special education programming for children with attention deficit hyperactivity disorder using a daily report card. *School Psychology Review, 39,* 219–239.

Falicov, C. J. (2009). Commentary: On the wisdom and challenges of culturally attuned treatments for Latinos. *Family Process, 48,* 292–309.

Fan, X., Xu, M., & Hess, E. J. (2010). D2 dopamine receptor subtype-mediated hyperactivity and amphetamine responses in a model of ADHD. *Neurobiology of Disease, 37,* 228–236.

Farb, N. A., Segal, Z. V., Mayberg, H., Bean, J., McKeon, D., ... Anderson, A. K. (2007). Attending to the present: Mindfulness meditation reveals distinct neural modes of self-reference. *Social Cognitive and Affective Neuroscience, 2,* 313–322.

Farber, B. A., & Lane, J. S. (2002). Positive regard. In J. C. Norcross (Ed.), *Psychotherapy relationships that work: Therapist contributions and responsiveness to patients* (pp. 175–194). New York, NY: Oxford University Press.

Feeny, N. C., Silva, S. G., Reinecke, M. A., McNulty, S., Findling, R. L., Rohde, P., ... March, J. S. (2009). An exploratory analysis of the impact of family functioning on treatment for depression in adolescents. *Journal of Clinical Child and Adolescent Psychology, 38,* 814–825.

Feindler E. L., & Engel, E. C. (2011). Assessment and intervention for adolescents with anger and aggression difficulties in school settings. *Psychology in the Schools, 48,* 243–253.

Fenichel, O. (1945). *The psychoanalytic theory of neurosis.* New York, NY: Norton.

Fernandez, M. A., & Eyberg, S. M. (2009). Predicting treatment and follow-up attrition in parent-child interaction therapy. *Journal of Abnormal Child Psychology, 37,* 431–441.

Finger, E. C., Marsh, A. A., Mitchell, D. G., Reid, M. E., Sims, C., Budhani, S., ... Blair, J. R. (2008). Abnormal ventromedial prefrontal cortex function in children with psychopathic traits during reversal learning. *Archives of General Psychiatry, 65,* 586–594.

Finkelhor, D. (2009). The prevention of childhood sexual abuse. *The Future of Children, 19,* 169–194.

Finkelhor, D., Ormrod, R., & Turner, H. (2007). Re-victimization patterns in a national longitudinal sample of children and youth. *Child Abuse and Neglect, 31,* 479–502.

Fishbein, H. D. (2002). *Peer prejudice and discrimination: The origins of prejudice* (2nd ed.). Mahwah, NJ: Erlbaum.

Fishbein, M., & Izjen, I. (2009). *Predicting and changing behavior: The reasoned action approach.* New York, NY: Psychology Press.

Fisher, C. B., Hoagwood, K., Boyce, C., Duster, T., Frank, D. A., Grisso, T., ... Zayas, L. H. (2002). Research ethics for mental health science involving ethnic minority children and youths. *American Psychologist, 57,* 1024–1040.

Fisher, L., & Blair, R. J. R. (1998). Cognitive impairment and its relationship to psychopathic tendencies in children with emotional and behavioral difficulties. *Journal of Abnormal Child Psychology, 26,* 511–519.

Fite, P. J., Colder, C. R., Lochman, J. E., & Wells, K. C. (2006). The mutual influence of parenting and boys' externalizing behavior problems. *Journal of Applied Developmental Psychology, 27,* 151–164.

Fletcher, K. E. (2003). Posttraumatic stress disorder. In E. J. Mash & R. A. Barkley (Eds.), *Childhood psychopathology* (2nd ed., pp. 330–371). New York: Guilford.

Foa, E. B., Hembree, E. A., & Rothbaum, B. O. (2007). *Prolonged exposure therapy for PTSD: Emotional processing of traumatic experiences, therapist guide.* New York, NY: Oxford University Press.

Folkman, S. (2001). Revised coping theory and the process of bereavement. In M. S. Stroebe, R. O. Hansson, W. Stroebe, & H. Schut (Eds.), *Handbook of bereavement research* (pp. 563–584). Washington, DC: American Psychological Association.

Follette, W. C., & Darrow, S. M. (2014). Clinical behavior analysis. In F. K. McSweeney & E. S. Murphy (Eds.), *The Wiley Blackwell handbook of operant and classical conditioning* (pp. 669–693). Oxford, UK: Wiley-Blackwell.

Fonagy, P., & Target, M. (1996). Predictors of outcome in child psychoanalysis: A retrospective study of 763 cases at the Anna Freud Centre. *Journal of the American Psychoanalytic Association, 44,* 27–77.

Fonagy, P., & Target, M. (1998). Mentalization and the changing aims of child psycho-analysis. *Psychoanalytic Dialogues, 8,* 87–115.

Fontana, D., & Slack, I. (1997). *Teaching meditation to children: A practical guide to the use and benefits of meditation techniques.* Boston, MA: Element.

Ford, J. D., & Cloitre, M. (2009). Best practices in psychotherapy for children and adolescents. In C. A. Courtois & J. D. Ford (Eds.), *Treating complex traumatic stress disorders* (pp. 59–81). New York, NY: Guilford Press.

Forer, B. R. (1949). The fallacy of personal validation: a classroom demonstration of gullibility. *The Journal of Abnormal and Social Psychology, 44,* 118–123.

Forgatch, M. S., & Patterson, G. R. (2010). Parent management training—Oregon model: An intervention for antisocial behavior in children and adolescents. In J. R. Weisz & A. E. Kazdin (Eds.), *Evidence-based psychotherapies for children and adolescents* (2nd ed., p. 159–177). New York, NY: Guilford Press.

Fortuna, L. R., Alegria, M., & Gao, S. (2010). Retention in depression treatment among ethnic and racial minority groups in the United States. *Depression and Anxiety, 27,* 485–494.

Foster, J. A., & MacQueen, G. (2008). Neurobiological factors linking personality traits and major depression. *La Revue Canadienne de Psychiatrie, 53,* 6–13.

Foucault, M. (1973). *The birth of the clinic.* London, UK: Routledge (Original work published 1963).

Foucault, M. (1984). *The Foucault reader* (P. Rabinow, Ed.). London, UK: Penguin.

Fraiberg, S. (1992). *The magic years.* New York, NY: Simon & Schuster. (Original work published 1959)

Frankl, V. E. (1959/1992). *Man's search for meaning: An introduction to Logotherapy.* Boston, MA: Beacon Press. (Original work published 1959)

Franklin, A. J., Boyd-Franklin, N., & Draper, C. V. (2002). A psychological and educational perspective on Black parenting. In H. P. McAdoo (Ed.), *Black children: Social, educational, and parental environments* (2nd ed., pp. 119–140). Thousand Oaks, CA: SAGE.

Franklin, C., Moore, K., & Hopson, L. (2008). Effectiveness of solution-focused brief therapy in a school setting. *Children & Schools, 30,* 15–26.

Franzoi, S. L. (1996). *Social psychology.* Madison, WI: Brown & Benchmark.

Fredrickson, B. L. (2001). The role of positive emotions in positive psychology: The broaden-and-build theory of positive emotions. *American Psychologist, 56,* 218–226.

Freedheim, D. K., & Shapiro, J. P. (1999). *The clinical child documentation sourcebook.* New York, NY: Wiley.

Freud, A. (1946a). *The ego and the mechanisms of defense.* New York, NY: International Universities Press. (Original work published 1936)

Freud, A. (1946b). *The psychoanalytic treatment of children.* London, UK: Imago.

Freud, A. (1968). Indications and contradictions for child analysis. *Psychoanalytic Study of the Child, 26,* 79–80.

Freud, S. (1923). The ego and the id. In J. Strachey (Ed.), *The standard edition of the complete psychological works of Sigmund Freud* (Vol. 19, pp. 1–59). London, UK: Hogarth Press.

Freud, S. (1933). New introductory lectures on psychoanalysis. In J. Strachey (Ed.), *The standard edition of the complete psychological works of Sigmund Freud* (Vol. 22, pp. 1–182). London, UK: Hogarth Press.

Freud, S. (1935). *Autobiography.* New York, NY: Norton.

Freud, S. (1943). *A general introduction to psychoanalysis.* New York, NY: Garden City.

Freud, S. (1957). The unconscious. In J. Strachey (Ed. & Trans.), *The standard edition of the complete psychological works of Sigmund Freud* (Vol. 14, pp. 159–215). London, UK: Hogarth Press. (Original work published 1915)

Freud, S. (1958). The dynamics of transference. In J. Strachey (Ed. & Trans.), *The standard edition of the complete psychological works of Sigmund Freud* (Vol. 12, pp. 99–108). London, UK: Hogarth Press. (Original work published 1912)

Freud, S. (1962). *Civilization and its discontents.* New York, NY: Norton. (Original work published 1930)

Freudenberger, H. J. (1975). The staff burnout syndrome in alternative institutions. *Psychotherapy: Theory, Research, and Practice, 12,* 73–82.

Frewen, P. A., Dozois, D. J. A., & Lanius, R. A. (2008). Neuroimaging studies of psychological interventions for mood and anxiety disorders: Empirical and methodological review. *Clinical Psychology Review, 28,* 229–247.

Frick, P. J., Cornell, A. H, Barry, C. T., Bodin, S. D., & Dane, H. A. (2003). Callous-unemotional problems in the prediction of conduct problem severity, aggression, and self-report of delinquency. *Journal of Abnormal Child Psychology, 31,* 457–470.

Frick, P. J., Cornell, A. H., Bodin, S. D., Dane, H. E., Barry, C. T., & Loney, B. R. (2003). Callous-unemotional traits and developmental pathways to severe conduct problems. *Developmental Psychology, 39,* 246–260.

Frick, P. J., Lilienfeld, S. O., Ellis, M., Loney, B., & Silverthorn, P. (1999). The association between anxiety and psychopathy dimensions in children. *Journal of Abnormal Child Psychology, 27,* 383–392.

Frick, P. J., & Nigg, J. T. (2012). Current issues in the diagnosis of attention deficit hyperactivity disorder, oppositional defiant disorder, and conduct disorder. *Annual Review of Clinical Psychology, 8,* 77–107.

Frick, P. J., Ray, J. V., Thornton, L. C., & Kahn, R. E. (2014). Can callous-unemotional traits enhance the understanding, diagnosis, and treatment of serious conduct problems in children and adolescents?: A comprehensive review. *Psychological Bulletin, 140,* 1–57.

Frick, P. J., & Viding, E. M. (2009). Antisocial behavior from a developmental psychopathology perspective. *Development and Psychopathology, 21,* 1111–1131.

Friedberg, R. D., & McClure, J. M. (2002). *Clinical practice of cognitive therapy with children and adolescents: The nuts and bolts.* New York, NY: Guilford Press.

Friedberg, R. D., & McClure, J. M. (2014). *Cognitive therapy techniques for children and adolescents: Tools for enhancing practice.* New York, NY: Guilford Press.

Friedrich, W. N. (2007). *Children with sexual behavior problems*. New York, NY: Norton.

Fruzzetti, A. R., & Fruzzetti, A. E. (2008). Dialectics in cognitive and behavior therapy. In W. T. O'Donohue, J. E. Fisher, W. T. O'Donohue, & J. E. Fisher (Eds.), *Cognitive behavior therapy: Applying empirically supported techniques in your practice* (2nd ed.; pp. 132–141). Hoboken, NJ: Wiley.

Fruzzetti, A. E., Santisteban, D. A., & Hoffman, P. D. (2007). Dialectical Behavior Therapy with families. In L. A. Dimeff & K. Koerner (Eds.), *Dialectical Behavior Therapy in clinical practice: Applications across disorders and settings* (pp. 222–244). New York, NY: Guilford Press.

Fry, R. (2010). *Hispanics, high school dropouts and the GED*. Retrieved from http://pewhispanic.org/reports/report.php?ReportID=122

Funderburk, B., & Eyberg, S. M. (2011). Parent-child interaction therapy. In J. C. Norcross, G. R. VandenBos, & D. K. Freedheim (Eds.), *History of psychotherapy: Continuity and change* (2nd ed., pp. 415–420). Washington, DC: American Psychological Association.

Furman, B., & Ahola, T. (1992). *Solution talk: Hosting therapeutic conversations*. New York, NY: Norton.

Furman, D., Hamilton, P., Joormann, J., & Gotlib, I. (2011). Altered timing of amygdala activation during sad mood elaboration as a function of 5-HTTLPR. *Biological Psychiatry, 6,* 270–276.

Gabel, S., Oster, G., Pfeffer, C., & Marlier, R. (1988). *Difficult moments in child psychotherapy*. Northvale, NJ: Aronson.

Gallo, L. C., & Matthews, K. A. (2003). Understanding the association between socioeconomic status and physical health: Do negative emotions play a role? *Psychological Bulletin, 129,* 10–51.

Gannon, T. A., Gilchrist, E., & Wade, K. A. (2008). Intrafamilial child and adolescent sexual abuse. In C. Hilarski, J. S. Wodarski, & M. D. Feit (Eds.), *Handbook of social work in child and adolescent sexual abuse* (pp. 71–101). New York, NY: Haworth Press/Taylor & Francis.

Gao, Y., Raine, A., Venables, P. H., Dawson, M. E., & Mednick, S. A. (2009). Association of poor childhood fear conditioning and adult crime. *American Journal of Psychiatry, 167,* 56–60.

Gao, Y., Raine, A., Venables, P. H., Dawson, M. E., & Mednick, S. A. (2010). Reduced electrodermal fear conditioning from ages 3 to 8 years is associated with aggressive behavior at age 8 years. *Journal of Child Psychology and Psychiatry, 51,* 550–558.

Gardner, R. A. (1993). *Psychotherapy with children*. Northvale, NJ: Jason Aronson.

Garrity, C., Jens, K., Porter, W., Sager, N., & Short-Camilli, C. (2000). *Bullyproofing your school: A comprehensive approach for elementary schools*. Longmont, CO: Sopris West.

Gartner, J., Harmatz, M., Hohmann, A., Larson, D., & Gartner, A. F. (1990). The effect of patient and clinician ideology on clinical judgment: A study of ideological countertransference. *Psychotherapy, 27,* 98–106.

Gates, G. J. (2011). *How many people are lesbian, gay, bisexual, and transgender?* Retrieved from http://wiwp.law.ucla.edu/research/census-lgbt-demographics-studies/how-many-people-are-lesbian-gay-bisexual-and-transgender/

Gaylin, N. L. (1999). Client-centered child and family therapy. In S. W. Russ & T. H. Ollendick (Eds.), *Handbook of psychotherapies with children and families* (pp. 107–120). New York, NY: Kluwer Academic/Plenum Press.

Gaynor, S. T., & Harris, A. (2008). Single-participant assessment of treatment mediators: Strategy description and examples from a behavior activation intervention for depressed adolescents. *Behavior Modification, 32,* 372–402.

Geller, S. M., Greenberg, L. S., & Watson, J. C. (2011). Therapist and client perceptions of therapeutic presence: The development of a measure. *Psychotherapy Research, 20,* 599–610.

Gerber, A. J., Kocsis, J. H., Milrod, B. L., Roose, S. P., Barber, J. P., Thase, M. E., … Leon, A. C. (2011). A quality-based review of randomized controlled trials of psychodynamic psychotherapy. *The American Journal of Psychiatry, 168,* 19–28.

Gerdes, A. C., Haack, L. M., & Schneider, B. W. (2012). Parental functioning in families of children with ADHD: Evidence for behavioral parent training and importance of clinically meaningful change. *Journal of Attention Disorders, 16,* 147–156.

Gergen, K. (2009). *An invitation to social constructivism* (2nd ed.). Thousand Oaks, CA: SAGE.

Gerull, F. C., & Rapee, R. M. (2002). Mother knows best: Effects of maternal modeling on the acquisition of fear and avoidance behaviour in toddlers. *Behaviour Research and Therapy, 40,* 279–287.

Gibbs, J. C. (2003). *Moral development and reality: Beyond the theories of Kohlberg and Hoffman.* Thousand Oaks, CA: SAGE.

Gil, E. (2012). Trauma-focused integrated play therapy (TF-IPT). In P. Goodyear-Brown (Ed.), *Handbook of child sexual abuse: Identification, assessment, and treatment* (pp. 251–278). Hoboken, NJ: Wiley.

Gil, E., & Drewes, A. A. (2005). *Cultural issues in play therapy.* New York, NY: Guilford Press.

Gilbert, D. T. (2007). *Stumbling on happiness.* New York, NY: Vintage.

Gilbert, D. T., Lieberman, M. D., Morewedge, C. K., & Wilson, T. D. (2004). The peculiar longevity of things not so bad. *Psychological Science, 15,* 14–19.

Gilbert, D. T., Pinel, E. C., Wilson, T. D., Blumberg, S. J., & Wheatley T. P. (1998). Immune neglect: A source of durability bias in affective forecasting. *Journal of Personality and Social Psychology, 75,* 617–638.

Gilboa-Schechtman, E., Foa, E. B., Shafran, N., Aderka, I. M., Powers, M. B., Rachman, L., … Apter, A. (2010). Prolonged exposure versus dynamic therapy for adolescent PTSD: A pilot randomized controlled trial. *Journal of the American Academy of Child and Adolescent Psychiatry, 49,* 908–989.

Gill, M. M. (1982). *Analysis of transference: Vol. 1. Theory and technique.* New York, NY: International Universities Press.

Gilmore, K. J., & Meersand, P. (2013). *Normal child and adolescent development: A psychodynamic primer.* Arlington, VA: American Psychiatric.

Gingerich, W. J., & Peterson, L. T. (2013). Effectiveness of solution-focused brief therapy: A systematic qualitative review of controlled outcome studies. *Research on Social Work Practice, 23,* 266–283.

Gini, G., Pozzoli, T., & Hauser, M. (2011). Bullies have enhanced moral competence to judge relative to victims, but lack moral compassion. *Personality and Individual Differences, 50,* 603–608.

Ginsburg, G. S., Kendall, P. C., Sakolsky, D., Compton, S. N., Piacentini, J., Albano, A. M., … March, J. (2011). Remission after acute treatment in children and adolescents with anxiety disorders: Findings from the CAMS. *Journal of Consulting and Clinical Psychology, 79,* 806–813.

Ginsburg, G. S., Silva, S. G., Jacobs, R. H., Tonev, S., Hoyle, R. H., Kingery, J. N., ... March, J. S. (2009). Cognitive measures of adolescent depression: Unique or unitary constructs? *Journal of Clinical Child and Adolescent Psychology, 38*, 790–802.

Ginsburg, G. S., & Silverman, W. K. (1996). Phobic and anxiety disorders in Hispanic and Caucasian youth. *Journal of Anxiety Disorders, 10*, 517–528.

Gladding, S. T. (2014). *Family therapy: History, theory, and practice* (6th ed.). New York, NY: Pearson.

Glick, B., & Gibbs, J. C. (2010). *Aggression replacement training: A comprehensive intervention for aggressive youth* (3rd ed.). Champaign, IL: Research Press.

Glickauf-Hughes, C., & Wells, M. (2006). *Object relations psychotherapy: An individualized and interactive approach to diagnosis and treatment.* New York, NY: Jason Aronson.

Gobin, R., & Freyd, J. (2009). Betrayal and revictimization: Preliminary findings. *Psychological Trauma: Theory, Research, Practice, and Policy, 1*, 242–257.

Gold, D. B., & Wegner, D. M. (1995). Origins of ruminative thought: Trauma, incompleteness, nondisclosure, and suppression. *Journal of Applied Social Psychology, 25*, 1245–1261

Goldbeck, L., & Schmid, K. (2003). Effectiveness of autogenic relaxation training on children and adolescents with behavioral and emotional problems. *Journal of the American Academy of Child and Adolescent Psychiatry, 42*, 1046–1054.

Goldenberg, H., & Goldenberg, I. (2012). *Family therapy: An overview* (8th ed.). Stamford, CT: Cengage.

Goldfried, M. R., Burckell, L. A., & Eubanks-Carter, C. (2003). Therapist self-disclosure in cognitive-behavior therapy. *Journal of Clinical Psychology, 59*, 555–568.

Goldman, L. (2002). The assumptive world of children. In J. Kauffman (Ed.), *Loss of the assumptive world: A theory of traumatic loss* (pp. 193–203). New York, NY: Brunner-Routledge.

Goldman, L. (2012). Memory work with children. In R. A. Neimeyer (Ed.), *Techniques of grief therapy: Creative practices for counseling the bereaved* (pp. 240–243). New York, NY: Routledge.

Gollwitzer, P. M. (1999). Implementation intentions: Strong effects of simple plans. *American Psychologist, 54*, 493–503.

Gollwitzer, P. M., & Brandstaetter, V. (1997). Implementation intentions and effective goal pursuit. *Journal of Personality and Social Psychology, 73*, 186–199.

Gonzales, N. A., Tein, J. Y., Sandler, I. N., & Friedman, R. J. (2001). On the limits of coping: Interaction between stress and coping for inner-city adolescents. *Journal of Adolescent Research, 16*, 372–395.

Goodman, T., Greenland, S. K., & Siegel, D. J. (2012). Mindful parenting as a path to wisdom and compassion. In C. K. Germer, R. D. Siegel, C. K. Germer, R. D. Siegel (Eds.), *Wisdom and compassion in psychotherapy: Deepening mindfulness in clinical practice* (pp. 295–310). New York, NY: Guilford Press.

Goodyear-Brown, P. (2012). Flexibly sequential play therapy (FSPT) with sexually victimized children. In P. Goodyear-Brown (Ed.), *Handbook of child sexual abuse: Identification, assessment, and treatment* (pp. 297–319). Hoboken, NJ: Wiley.

Gordon, D. A., Arbuthnot, J., Gustafson, K. E., & McGreen, P. (1988). Home-based behavioral-systems family therapy with disadvantaged juvenile delinquents. *American Journal of Family Therapy, 16*, 243–255.

Gordon, D. A., Graves, K., & Arbuthnot, J. (1995). The effect of functional family therapy for delinquents on adult criminal behavior. *Criminal Justice and Behavior, 22*, 60–73.

Gordon, M. (2009). *Roots of empathy: Changing the world child by child*. New York, NY: The Experiment.

Gottlieb, D. A., & Begej, E. L. (2014). Principles of Pavlovian conditioning: Description, content, function. In F. K. McSweeney & E. S. Murphy (Eds.), *The Wiley Blackwell handbook of operant and classical conditioning* (pp. 3–25). Oxford, UK: Wiley-Blackwell.

Gould, D., Voelker, D. K., Damarjian, N., & Greenleaf, C. (2014). Imagery training for peak performance. In J. L. Van Raalte & B. W. Brewer (Eds.), *Exploring sport and exercise psychology*. Washington, DC: American Psychological Association.

Gouldner, A. (1960). The norm of reciprocity: A preliminary statement. *American Sociological Review, 25*, 161–178.

Grabovac, A. D., Lau, M. A., & Willett, B. R. (2011). Mechanisms of mindfulness: A Buddhist psychological model. *Mindfulness, 2*, 154–166.

Grace, R. C., & Hucks, A. D. (2013). The allocation of operant behavior. In G. J. Madden, W. V. Dube, T. D. Hackenberg, G. P. Hanley, & K. A. Lattal (Eds.), *APA handbook of behavior analysis: Vol. 1. Methods and principles* (pp. 307–337). Washington, DC: American Psychological Association.

Granic, I., & Dishion, T. J. (2003). Deviant talk in adolescent friendships: A step toward measuring a pathogenic attractor process. *Social Development, 12*, 314–334.

Grave, J., & Blissett, J. (2004). Is cognitive behavior therapy developmentally appropriate for young children? A critical review of the evidence. *Clinical Psychology Review, 24*, 399–420.

Graves-Alcorn, S. L., & Green, E. J. (2013). The expressive arts therapy continuum: History and theory. In E. J. Green & A. A. Drewes (Eds.), *Integrating expressive arts and play therapy with children and adolescents* (pp. 1–16). Hoboken, NJ: Wiley.

Gray, P. (1994). *The ego and analysis of defense*. Northvale, NJ: Jason Aronson.

Greco, L. A., & Hayes, S. C. (Eds.). (2008). *Acceptance and mindfulness treatments for children and adolescents: A practitioner's guide*. Oakland, CA: New Harbinger.

Greco, L. A., & Morris, T. L. (2005). Factors influencing the link between social anxiety and peer acceptance: Contributions of social skills and close friendships during middle childhood. *Behavior Therapy, 36*, 197–205.

Greenberg, J. R., & Mitchell, S. (1983). *Object relations in psychoanalytic theory*. Cambridge, MA: Harvard University Press.

Greenberg, L. S. (2002). *Emotion-focused therapy: Coaching clients to work through their feelings*. Washington, DC: American Psychological Association.

Greenberg, L. S., & Malcolm, W. (2002). Resolving unfinished business: Relating process to outcome. *Journal of Consulting and Clinical Psychology, 70*, 406–416.

Greenberg, L. S., & Pascual-Leone, A. (2006). Emotion-focused therapy: A practice-friendly research review. *Journal of Clinical Psychology: In Session, 62*, 611–630.

Greenberg, M. T., DeKlyen, M., Speltz, M. L., & Endriga, M. C. (1997). The role of attachment processes in externalizing psychopathology in young children. In L. Atkinson & K. J. Zucker (Eds.), *Attachment and psychopathology* (pp. 196–222). New York, NY: Guilford Press.

Greene, R. W. (2001). *The explosive child: Understanding and parenting easily frustrated, "chronically inflexible" children*. New York, NY: HarperCollins.

Greene, R. W. (2010). Collaborative problem solving. In R. C. Murrihy, A. D. Kidman, & T. H. Ollendick (Eds.), *Clinical handbook of assessing and treating conduct problems in youth* (pp. 193–220). New York, NY: Springer.

Greene, R. W., & Ablon, J. S. (2006). *Treating explosive kids: The collaborative problem-solving approach.* New York, NY: Guilford Press.

Greene, R. W., Ablon, J. S., & Goring, J. C. (2003). A transactional model of oppositional behavior: Underpinnings of the collaborative problem solving approach. *Journal of Psychosomatic Research, 55,* 67–75.

Greene, R. W., Ablon, J. S., Goring, J. C., Fazio, V., & Morse, L. R. (2004). Treatment of oppositional defiant disorder in children and adolescents. In P. M. Barrett & T. H. Ollendick (Eds.), *Handbook of interventions that work with children and adolescents: Prevention and treatment* (pp. 369–394). Chichester, UK: Wiley.

Greene, R. W., Ablon, J. S., Goring, J, C., Raezer-Blakely, L., Markey, J., Monuteaux, M. C., ... Rabbitt, S. (2004). Effectiveness of collaborative problem solving in affectively dysregulated children with oppositional-defiant disorder: Initial findings. *Journal of Consulting and Clinical Psychology, 72,* 1157–1164.

Gregory, A. M., & Eley, T. C. (2007). Genetic influences on anxiety in children: What we've learned and where we're heading. *Clinical Child and Family Psychology Review, 10,* 199–212.

Gregory, B. (2011). *Cognitive-behavioral therapy skills workbook.* Eau Claire, WI: Premier.

Grills, A. E., & Ollendick, T. H. (2003). Multiple informant agreement and the Anxiety Disorders Interview Schedule for Parents and Children. *Journal of the American Academy of Child and Adolescent Psychiatry, 42,* 30–40.

Grills-Taquechel, A. E., & Ollendick, T. H. (2013). *Phobic and anxiety disorders in children and adolescents.* Cambridge, MA: Hogrefe.

Guerra, N. G., Nucci, L., & Huesmann, L. R. (1994). Moral cognition and childhood aggression. In L. R. Huesmann (Ed.), *Aggressive behavior: Current perspectives* (pp. 13–33). New York, NY: Plenum Press.

Guerra, N. G., & Slaby, R. G. (1990). Cognitive mediators of aggression in adolescent offenders: II. Intervention. *Developmental Psychology, 26,* 269–277.

Guerry, J. D., & Hastings, P. D. (2011). In search of HPA axis dysregulation in child and adolescent depression. *Clinical Child and Family Psychology Review, 14,* 135–160.

Guilford, J. P. (1984). Varieties of divergent production. *Journal of Creative Behavior, 18,* 1–10.

Guinther, P. M., & Dougher, M. J. (2013). From behavioral research to clinical therapy. In G. J. Madden, W. V. Dube, T. D. Hackenberg, G. P. Hanley, & K. A. Lattal (Eds.), *APA handbook of behavior analysis: Vol. 2. Translating principles into practice* (pp. 3–32). Washington, DC: American Psychological Association.

Gunderson, E. A., Gripshover, S. J., Romero, C., Dweck, C. S., Goldin-Meadow, S., & Levine, S. C. (2013). Parent praise to 1- to 3-year-olds predicts children's motivational frameworks 5 years later. *Child Development, 84,* 1526–1541.

Guterman, J. T. (2013). *Mastering the art of solution-focused counseling* (2nd ed.). Alexandria, VA: American Counseling Association.

Guterman, J. T., & Rudes, J. (2005). A narrative approach to strategic eclecticism. *Journal of Mental Health Counseling, 27,* 1–12.

Gutierrez, P. M., & Osman, A. (2008). *Adolescent suicide: An integrated approach to the assessment of risk and protective factors.* DeKalb: Northern Illinois University Press.

Guzman, M. R., & Carrasco, N. (2011). *Counseling Latino/a Americans.* Belmont, CA: Cengage.

Haghbin, M., McCaffrey, A., & Pychyl, T. A. (2012). The complexity of the relation between fear of failure and procrastination. *Journal of Rational-Emotive and Cognitive-Behavior Therapy, 30,* 249–263.

Haimovitz, K. C., & Henderlong, J. (2011). Effects of person versus process praise on student motivation: Stability and change in emerging adulthood. *Educational Psychology, 31,* 595–609.

Haley, J. (1963). *Strategies of psychotherapy.* New York, NY: Grune & Stratton.

Haley, J. (1996). *Learning and teaching therapy.* New York, NY: Guilford Press.

Hallett, V., Ronald, A., Rijsdijk, F., & Eley, T. C. (2009). Phenotypic and genetic differentiation of anxiety-related behaviors in middle childhood. *Depression and Anxiety, 26,* 316–324.

Hammen, C. L., Rudolph, K. D., & Abaied, J. L. (2014). Child and adolescent depression. In E. J. Mash & R. A. Barkley (Eds.), *Child psychopathology* (3rd ed., pp. 225–263). New York, NY: Guildford Press.

Hanh, T. N. (1991). *Peace is every step: The path of mindfulness in everyday life.* New York, NY: Bantam.

Hanh, T. N. (1999). *The Miracle of mindfulness: An introduction to the practice of meditation.* Boston, MA: Beacon Press.

Hankin, B. L., Abramson, L. Y., Miller, N., & Haeffel, G. J. (2004). Cognitive vulnerability-stress theories of depression: Examining affective specificity in the prediction of depression versus anxiety in three prospective studies. *Cognitive Therapy and Research, 28,* 309–345.

Hankin, B. L., Mermelstein, R., & Roesch, L. (2007). Sex differences in adolescent depression: Stress exposure and reactivity models in interpersonal and achievement contextual domains. *Child Development, 78,* 279–295.

Hann, D. L., & Borek, N. B. (2002). *Taking stock of risk factors for child/youth externalizing behavior problems.* National Institutes of Mental Health. Retrieved from http://www.nimh.nih.gov/childhp/takingstock.pdf

Hanson, M., & Gutheil, I. A. (2004). Motivational strategies with alcohol-involved older adults: Implications for social work practice. *Social Work, 49,* 364–372.

Hariri, A. R., Bookheimer, S. Y., & Mazziotta, J. C. (2000). Modulating emotional responses: Effects of a neocortical network on the limbic system. *Neuroreport: For Rapid Communication of Neuroscience Research, 11*(1), 43–48.

Harmon, H., Langle, A., & Ginsburg, G. (2006). The role of gender and culture in treating youth with anxiety disorders. *Journal of Cognitive Psychotherapy: An International Quarterly, 20,* 301–310.

Harpaz-Rotem, I., Leslie, D., & Rosenheck, R. A. (2004). Treatment retention among children entering a new episode of mental health care. *Psychiatric Services, 55,* 1022–1028.

Harris, J. R. (2009). *The nurture assumption: Why children turn out the way they do* (2nd rev. ed.). New York, NY: Free Press.

Harris, P. (2000). *The work of the imagination.* Oxford, UK: Blackwell.

Harris, R. (2009). *ACT made simple: An easy-to-read primer on Acceptance and Commitment Therapy.* Oakland, CA: New Harbinger.

Harris, R. (2013). *Getting unstuck in ACT: A clinician's guide to overcoming common obstacles in Acceptance and Commitment Therapy.* Oakland, CA: New Harbinger.

Hartmann, H. (1958). *Ego psychology and the problem of adaptation.* New York, NY: International Universities Press. (Original work published 1939)

Harvey, E. A., & Metcalf, L. A. (2012). The interplay among preschool child and family factors and the development of ODD symptoms. *Journal of Clinical Child and Adolescent Psychology, 41*, 458–470.

Harvey, J. H., & Fine, M. A. (2010). *Children of divorce: Stories of loss and growth* (2nd ed.). New York, NY: Routledge.

Harvey, P., & Penzo, J. A. (2009). *Parenting a child who has intense emotions: Dialectical Behavior Therapy skills to help your child regulate emotional outbursts and aggressive behaviors.* Oakland, CA: New Harbinger.

Harvey, P., & Rathbone, B. H. (2014). *Dialectical Behavior Therapy for at-risk adolescents: A practitioner's guide to treating challenging behavior.* Oakland, CA: New Harbinger.

Hasler, G. (2010). Pathophysiology of depression: Do we have any solid evidence of interest to clinicians? *World Psychiatry, 9*, 155–161.

Hastings, P. D., Zahn-Waxler, C., Robinson, J., Usher, B., & Bridges, D. (2000). The development of concern for others in children with behavior problems. *Developmental Psychology, 36*, 531–546.

Hatzenbeuhler, M. L. (2011). The social environment and suicide attempts in lesbian, gay, and bisexual youth. *Pediatrics, 127*, 896–903.

Hayes, S. C. (2004). Acceptance and Commitment Therapy and the new behavior therapies. In S. C. Hayes, V. M. Follette, & M. M. Linehan (Eds.), *Mindfulness and acceptance: Expanding the cognitive behavioral tradition* (pp. 1–29). New York, NY: Guilford Press.

Hayes, S. C., Barnes-Holmes, D., & Roche, B. (Eds.). (2001). *Relational frame theory: A post-Skinnerian account of human language and cognition.* New York, NY: Plenum Press.

Hayes, S. C., Luoma, J. B., Bond, F. W., Masuda, A., & Lillis, J. (2006). Acceptance and Commitment Therapy: Model, processes and outcomes. *Behaviour Research and Therapy, 44*, 1–25.

Hayes, S. C., Pankey, J., & Gregg, J. (2002). Acceptance and commitment therapy. In R. A. DiTomasso, E. A. Gosch, R. A. DiTomasso, E. A. Gosch (Eds.), *Comparative treatments for anxiety disorders* (pp. 110–136). New York, NY: Springer Publishing Co.

Hayes, S. C., Pistorello, J., & Levin, M. E. (2012). Acceptance and Commitment Therapy as a unified model of behavior change. *The Counseling Psychologist, 40*, 976–1002.

Hayes, S. C., Strosahl, K. D., & Wilson, K. G. (2011). *Acceptance and Commitment Therapy: The process and practice of mindful change* (2nd ed.). New York, NY: Guilford Press.

Hayes-Skelton, S. A., Roemer, L., & Orsillo, S. M. (2013). A randomized clinical trial comparing an acceptance-based behavior therapy to applied relaxation for generalized anxiety disorder. *Journal of Consulting and Clinical Psychology, 81*, 761–773.

Hays, P. A. (2008). *Addressing cultural complexities in practice: Assessment, diagnosis, and therapy* (2nd ed.). Washington, DC: American Psychological Association.

Hazlett-Stevens, H., & Bernstein, D. A. (2012). Relaxation. In W. T. O'Donohue & J. E. Fisher (Eds.), *Cognitive behavior therapy: Core principles for practice* (pp. 105–132). Hoboken, NJ: Wiley.

Hazlett-Stevens, H., & Craske, M. G. (2009). Breathing retraining and diaphragmatic breathing techniques. In W. T. O'Donohue & J. E. Fisher (Eds.), *General principles and empirically supported techniques of cognitive behavior therapy* (pp. 167–172). Hoboken, NJ: Wiley.

Head, L. S., & Gross, A. M. (2009). Systematic desensitization. In W. T. O'Donohue & J. E. Fisher (Eds.), *General principles and empirically supported techniques of cognitive behavior therapy* (pp. 640–647). Hoboken, NJ: Wiley.

Heim, C., Plotsky, P., & Nemeroff, C. (2004). Importance of studying the contribution of early adverse experiences to neurobiological findings in depression. *Neuropsychopharmacology, 29*, 641–648.

Held, B. S. (1995). *Back to reality: A critique of postmodern theory in psychotherapy.* New York, NY: Norton.

Hendren, R. L., De Backer, I., & Pandina, G. J. (2000). Review of neuroimaging studies of child and adolescent psychiatric disorders from the past 10 years. *Journal of the American Academy of Child and Adolescent Psychiatry, 39*, 815–828.

Henggeler, S. W., & Borduin, C. M. (1990). *Family therapy and beyond: A multisystemic approach to treating the behavior problems of children and adolescents.* Pacific Grove, CA: Brooks/Cole.

Henggeler, S. W., Letourneau, E. J., Chapman, J. E., Borduin, C. M., Schewe, P. A., & McCart, M. R. (2009). Mediators of change for multisystemic therapy with juvenile sexual offenders. *Journal of Consulting and Clinical Psychology, 77*, 451–462.

Henggeler, S. W., Cunningham, P. B., Schoenwald, S. K., Borduin, C. M., & Rowland, M. D. (2009). *Multisystemic therapy for antisocial behavior in children and adolescents* (2nd ed.). New York, NY: Guilford Press.

Henggeler, S. W., & Santos, A. B. (1997). *Innovative approaches for difficult-to-treat populations.* Washington, DC: American Psychiatric Association.

Henggeler, S. W., Schoenwald, S. K., Rowland, M. D., & Cunningham, P. B. (2002). *Serious emotional disturbance in children and adolescents: Multisystemic therapy.* New York, NY: Guilford Press.

Hernandez, B., Garcia, J. I. R., & Flynn, M. (2010). The role of familism in the relation between parent-child discord and psychological distress among emerging adults of Mexican descent. *Journal of Family Psychology, 24*, 105–114.

Hetherington, E. M., & Kelly, J. (2003). *For better or worse: Divorce reconsidered.* New York, NY: Norton.

Hetherington, E. M., & Stanley-Hagan, M. (1999). The adjustment of children with divorced parents: A risk and resiliency perspective. *Journal of Child Psychology and Psychiatry, 40*, 129–140.

Higa-McMillan, C. K., Francis, S. E., & Chorpita, B. F. (2014). Anxiety disorders. In E. J. Mash & R. A. Barkley (Eds.), *Child psychopathology* (3rd ed., pp. 345–428). New York, NY: Guilford Press.

Hill, C. E., & Knox, S. (2002). Therapist self-disclosure. In J. C. Norcross (Ed.), *Psychotherapy relationships that work: Therapist contributions and responsiveness to patients* (pp. 255–265). Oxford, UK: Oxford University Press.

Himelstein, S. (2013). *A mindfulness-based approach to working with high-risk adolescents.* New York, NY: Taylor & Francis.

Hinshaw, S. P., & Lee, S. S. (2003). Conduct and oppositional defiant disorders. In E. J. Mash, R. A. Barkley, E. J. Mash, R. A. Barkley (Eds.), *Child psychopathology* (2nd ed., pp. 144–198). New York, NY: Guilford Press.

Hirshfeld-Becker, D. R., Masek, B., Henin, A., Blakely, L. R., Pollock-Wurman, R. A., McQuade, J., ... Biederman, J. (2010). Cognitive behavioral therapy for 4- to 7-year-old children with anxiety disorders: A randomized clinical trial. *Journal of Consulting and Clinical Psychology, 78*, 498–510.

Hoerger, M. (2012). Coping strategies and immune neglect in affective forecasting: Direct evidence and key moderators. *Judgment and Decision Making, 7*, 86–96.

Hoffman, L. (1981). *Foundations of family therapy.* New York, NY: Basic Books.

Hoffman, M. L. (1983). Affective and cognitive processes in moral internalization. In E. T. Higgins, D. Ruble, & W. Hartup (Eds.), *Social cognition and social development: A sociocultural perspective* (pp. 236–274). Cambridge, UK: Cambridge University Press.

Hoffman, M. L. (2001). Toward a comprehensive empathy-based theory of prosocial moral development. In A. C. Bohart & D. J. Stipek (Eds.), *Constructive and destructive behavior: Implications for family, school, and society* (pp. 61–86). Washington, DC: American Psychological Association.

Hofmann, S. G. (2011). *An introduction to modern CT: Psychological solutions to mental health problems*. Oxford, UK: Wiley.

Hofmann, S. G., Asmundson, G. J. G., & Beck, A. T. (2013). The science of cognitive therapy. *Behavior Therapy, 44,* 199–212.

Hofmann, S. G., Ellard, K. K., Siegle, G. J. (2012). Neurobiological correlates of cognitions in fear and anxiety: A cognitive–neurobiological information-processing model. *Cognition and Emotion, 26,* 282–299.

Hofmann, S. G., Meuret, A. E., Rosenfield, D., Suvak, M. K., Barlow, D. H., Gorman, J. M., ... Woods, S. W. (2007). Preliminary evidence for cognitive mediation during cognitive-behavioral therapy of panic disorder. *Journal of Consulting and Clinical Psychology, 75,* 374–379.

Hofmann, S. G., Sawyer, A. T., Witt, A. A., & Oh, D. (2010). The effect of mindfulness-based therapy on anxiety and depression: A meta-analytic review. *Journal of Consulting and Clinical Psychology, 78,* 169–183.

Hofstra, M. B., van der Ende, J., & Verhulst, F. C. (2000). Continuity and change of psychopathology from childhood into adulthood: A 14-year follow-up study. *Journal of the American Academy of Child and Adolescent Psychiatry, 39,* 850–858.

Hogan, A. E. (1999). Cognitive functioning in children with oppositional defiant disorder. In H. C. Quay, A. E. Hogan, H. C. Quay, A. E. Hogan (Eds.), *Handbook of disruptive behavior disorders* (pp. 317–335). Dordrecht, Netherlands: Kluwer Academic Publishers.

Hogendoorn, S. M., Prins, P. J. M., Boer, F., Vervoort, L. Wolters, L. H., Moorlag, H., ... de Haan, E. (2014). Mediators of cognitive behavioral therapy for anxiety-disordered children and adolescents: Cognition, perceived control, and coping. *Journal of Clinical Child and Adolescent Psychology, 43,* 486–500.

Holmes, P., Georgescu, S., & Liles, W. (2005). Further delineating the applicability of acceptance and change to private responses: The example of Dialectical Behavior Therapy. *The Behavior Analyst Today, 7,* 301–311.

Hölzel, B. K., Lazar, S. W., Gard, T., Schuman-Olivier, Z., Vago, D. R., & Ott, U. (2011). How does mindfulness meditation work? Proposing mechanisms of action from a conceptual and neural perspective. *Perspectives on Psychological Science, 6,* 537–559.

Hooker, K. E., & Fodor, I. E. (2008). Teaching mindfulness to children. *Gestalt Review, 12,* 75–91.

Horowitz, M. J. (1998). *Cognitive psychodynamics: From conflict to character*. Hoboken, NJ: Wiley.

Horvath, A. O., Del Re, A. C., Fluckiger, C., & Symonds, D. (2011). Alliance in individual psychotherapy. In J. C. Norcross (Ed.), *Psychotherapy relationships that work: Evidence-based responsiveness* (pp. 25–69). New York, NY: Oxford University Press.

Howe-Martin, L. S., Murrell, A. R., & Guarnaccia, C. A. (2012). Repetitive nonsuicidal self-injury as experiential avoidance among a community sample of adolescents. *Journal of Clinical Psychology, 68,* 809–829.

Hudson, J. L., Hughes, A. A., & Kendall, P. C. (2004). Treatment of Generalized Anxiety Disorder in children and adolescents. In P. M. Barrett & T. O. Ollendick (Eds.), *Handbook of interventions that work with children and adolescents* (pp. 115–144). Hoboken, NJ: Wiley.

Hudson, J. L., & Rapee, R. M. (2001). Parent-child interactions and anxiety disorders: An observational study. *Behaviour Research and Therapy, 39,* 1411–1427.

Hudson, J. L., & Rapee, R. M. (2004). From anxious temperament to disorder: An etiological model. In R. G. Heimberg, C. L. Turk, & D. S. Mennin (Eds.), *Generalized anxiety disorder: Advances in research and practice* (pp. 51–74). New York, NY: Guilford Press.

Huey, S. J., Henggeler, S. W., Brondino, M. J., & Pickrel, S. G. (2000). Mechanisms of change in multisystemic therapy: Reducing delinquent behavior through therapist adherence and improved family and peer functioning. *Journal of Consulting and Clinical Psychology, 68,* 451–467.

Huey, S. J., Jr., & Polo, A. J. (2008). Evidence-based psychosocial treatments for ethnic minority youth. *Journal of Clinical Child and Adolescent Psychology, 37,* 262–301.

Huey, W. C., & Rank., R. C. (1984). Effects of counselor and peer-led group assertiveness training on black adolescent aggression. *Journal of Counseling Psychology, 31,* 95–98.

Hulme, P. (2011). Childhood sexual abuse, HPA axis regulation, and mental health: An integrative review. *Western Journal of Nursing Research, 33,* 1069–1097.

Hulvershorn, L., Cullen, K., & Anand, A. (2011). Toward dysfunctional connectivity: A review of neuroimaging findings in pediatric major depressive disorder. *Brain Imagining and Behavior, 5,* 307–328.

Hwang, W.-C., & Goto, S. (2009). The impact of perceived racial discrimination on the mental health of Asian American and Latino college students. *Asian American Journal of Psychology, 1,* 15–28.

Iacoboni, M. (2009). Imitation, empathy, and mirror neurons. *Annual Review of Psychology, 60,* 653–670.

Ickovics, J. R., Meade, C. S., Kershaw, T. S., Milan, S., Lewis, J. B., & Ethier, K. A. (2006). Urban teens: Trauma, posttraumatic growth, and emotional distress among adolescent females. *Journal of Consulting and Clinical Psychology, 74,* 841–850.

Imel, Z., & Wampold, B. (2008). The importance of treatment and the science of common factors in psychotherapy. In S. D. Brown & R. W. Lent (Eds.), *Handbook of counseling psychology* (4th ed., pp. 249–262). Hoboken, NJ: Wiley.

Inbar, Y., & Lammers, J. (2012). Political diversity in social and personality psychology. *Perspectives on Psychological Science, 7,* 496–503.

Ivey, A. E., D'Andrea, M. J., & Ivey, M. B. (2011). *Theories of counseling and psychotherapy: A multicultural perspective.* Boston, MA: Allyn & Bacon.

Jackson, D. D. (1965). The study of the family. *Family Process, 4,* 1–20.

Jacob, M., Keeley, M. L., Ritschel, L., & Craighead, W. E. (2013). Behavioural activation for the treatment of low-income, African American adolescents with major depressive disorder: A case series. *Clinical Psychology & Psychotherapy, 20,* 87–96.

Jacobs, W. J., & Blackburn, J. R. (1995). A model of Pavlovian conditioning: Variations in representations of the unconditional stimulus. *Integrative Physiological and Behavioral Science, 30,* 12–33.

Jacobson, E. (1964). *The self and the object world.* New York: International Universities Press.

Jaffee, W. B., & D'Zurilla, T. J. (2003). Adolescent problem solving, parent problem solving, and externalizing behavior in adolescents. *Behavior Therapy, 34,* 295–311.

James, A., Cowdrey, F., & James, C. (2012). Anxiety disorders in children and adolescents. In P. Sturmey & M. Hersen (Eds.), *Handbook of evidence-based practice in clinical psychology: Vol. 1. Child and adolescent disorders* (pp. 545–557). Hoboken, NJ: Wiley.

Jankoski, J. A. (2012). Vicarious traumatization. In L. Lopez-Levers (Ed.), *Trauma counseling: Theories and interventions* (pp. 540–553). New York, NY: Springer.

Janoff-Bulman, R. (1979). Characterological versus behavioral self-blame: Inquiries into depression and rape. *Journal of Personality and Social Psychology, 37,* 1798–1809.

Janoff-Bulman, R. (1992). *Shattered assumptions: Towards a new psychology of trauma.* New York, NY: Free Press.

Jansz, J. (2000). Masculine identity and restrictive emotionality. In A. H. Fischer (Ed.), *Gender and emotion: Social psychological perspectives* (pp. 166–187). Cambridge, UK: Cambridge University Press.

Jarrett, M., Siddiqui, S., Lochman, J., & Qu, L. (2014). Internalizing problems as a predictor of change in externalizing problems in at-risk youth. *Journal of Clinical Child and Adolescent Psychology, 43,* 27–35.

Jaycox, L., Reivich, K., Gillham, J. E., & Seligman, M. E. P. (1994). Prevention of depressive symptoms in school children. *Behavioral Research and Therapy, 32,* 801–816.

Jenkins, A. H. (1982). *The psychology of the Afro-American.* New York, NY: Pergamon Press.

Jensen, C. D., Cushing, C. C., Aylward, B. S., Craig, J. T., Sorell, D. M., & Steele, R. G. (2011). Effectiveness of motivational interviewing interventions for adolescent substance use behavior change: A meta-analytic review. *Journal of Consulting and Clinical Psychology, 79,* 433–440.

Jensen, T. K., Holt, T., Ormhaug, S. M., Egeland, K., Granly, L., Hoass, L. C., … Wentzel-Larsen, T. (2014). A randomized effectiveness study comparing trauma-focused cognitive behavioral therapy with therapy as usual for youth. *Journal of Clinical Child Psychology, 43,* 356–369.

Jetha, M. K., & Segalowitz, S. (2008). *Adolescent brain development: Implications for behavior.* Salt Lake City, UT: Academic Press.

Jha, A. P., Stanley, E. A., Kiyonaga, A., Wong, L., & Gelfand, L. (2010). Examining the protective effects of mindfulness training on working memory capacity and affective experience. *Emotion, 10,* 54–64.

Johansen, P. O., Krebs, T. S., Svartberg, M., Stiles, T. C., & Holen, A. (2011). Change in defense mechanisms during short-term dynamic and cognitive therapy in patients with cluster C personality disorders. *Journal of Nervous and Mental Disease, 199,* 712–715.

Joiner, T. E. (2005). *Why people die by suicide.* Cambridge, MA: Harvard University Press.

Joiner, T. E., Van Oden, K. A., Witte, T. K., Selby, E. A., Ribeiro, J. D., Lewis, R., … Rudd, M. D. (2009). Main predictions of the interpersonal-psychological theory of suicidal behavior: Empirical tests in two samples of young adults. *Journal of Abnormal Psychology, 118,* 634–646.

Jones, A. P., Laurens, K. L., Herba, C., Barker, G., & Viding, E. (2009). Amygdala hypoactivity to fearful faces in boys with conduct problems and callous-unemotional traits. *American Journal of Psychiatry, 166,* 95–102.

Jones, E. E., & Pulos, S. M. (1993). Comparing the process in psychodynamic and cognitive-behavioral therapies. *Journal of Consulting and Clinical Psychology, 61,* 306–316.

Jones, L. M., & Finkelhor, D. (2003). Putting together evidence on declining trends in sexual abuse: A complex puzzle. *Child Abuse & Neglect, 27*, 133–135.

Jose, P. E., Kljakovic, M., Scheib, E., & Notter, O. (2012). The joint development of traditional bullying and victimization with cyber bullying and victimization in adolescence. *Journal of Research on Adolescence, 22*, 301–309.

Joyce, A. S., & Piper, W. E. (1998). Expectancy, the therapeutic alliance, and treatment outcome in short-term individual psychotherapy. *Journal of Psychotherapy Practice and Research, 7*, 236–248.

Joyner, K., & Udry, J. R. (2000). You don't bring me anything but down: Adolescent romance and depression. *Journal of Health and Social Behavior, 41*, 369–391.

Jurbergs, N., Palcic, J. L., & Kelley, M. L. (2010). Daily behavior report cards with and without home-based consequences: Improving classroom behavior in low income, African American children with ADHD. *Child and Family Behavior Therapy, 32*, 177–195.

Kabat-Zinn, J. (1994). *Wherever you go, there you are: Mindfulness meditation in everyday life*. New York, NY: Hyperion.

Kabat-Zinn, J. (2012). *Mindfulness for beginners: Reclaiming the present moment—and your life*. Louisville, CO: Sounds True.

Kabat-Zinn, J. (2013). *Full catastrophe living: Using the wisdom of your body and mind to face stress, pain, and illness* (Rev. ed.). New York, NY: Bantam.

Kagan, J., & Snidman, N. (2004). *The long shadow of temperament*. Cambridge, MA: Belknap Press/Harvard University Press.

Kagan, J., Snidman, N., & Arcus, D. (1998). Childhood derivatives of high and low reactivity in infancy. *Child Development, 69*, 1483–1493.

Kagan, J., Snidman, N., Arcus, D., & Reznick, J. S. (1994). *Galen's prophecy: Temperament in human nature*. New York, NY: Basic Books.

Kahn, J. S., Kehle, T. J., Jenson, W. R., & Clark, E. (1990). Comparison of cognitive-behavioral, relaxation, and self-modeling interventions for depression among middle-school students. *School Psychology Review, 19*, 196–211.

Kallestad, H., Valen, J., McCullough, L., Svartberg, M., Hoglend, P., & Stiles, T. C. (2010). The relationship between insight gained during therapy and long-term outcome in short-term dynamic psychotherapy and cognitive therapy for cluster C personality disorders. *Psychotherapy Research, 20*, 526–534.

Kaminski, J. W., Valle, L. A., Filene, J. H., & Boyle, C. L. (2008). A meta-analytic review of components associated with parent training effectiveness. *Journal of Abnormal Child Psychology, 36*, 567–589.

Kanter, J. W., Busch, A. M., & Rusch, L. C. (2009). *Behavioral activation: Distinctive features*. London, UK: Routledge Press.

Kanter, J. W., Manos, R. C., Bowe, W. M., Baruch, D. E., Busch, A. M., & Rusch, L. C. (2010). What is behavioral activation? A review of the empirical literature. *Clinical Psychology Review, 30*, 608–620.

Kanter, J. W., & Puspitasari, A. J. (2012). Behavioral activation. In W. T. O'Donohue & J. E. Fisher (Eds.), *Cognitive behavior therapy: Core principles for practice* (pp. 215–250). Hoboken, NJ: Wiley.

Kashani, J. H., & Sherman, D. D. (1988). Childhood depression: Epidemiology, etiological models, and treatment implications. *Integrative Psychiatry, 6*, 1–21.

Kasser, T. (2002). *The high price of materialism*. Cambridge, MA: MIT Press.

Kassinove, H., & Tafrate, R. C. (2002). *Anger management: The complete treatment guidebook for practitioners.* Atascadero, CA: Impact.

Kaufman, N. K., Rohde, P., Seeley, J. R., Clarke, G. N., & Stice, E. (2005). Potential mediators of cognitive-behavioral therapy for adolescents with co-morbid major depression and conduct disorder. *Journal of Consulting and Clinical Psychology, 73,* 38–46.

Kavale, K. A., & Forness, S. R. (1996). Social skills deficits and learning disabilities: A meta-analysis. *Journal of Learning Disabilities, 29,* 226–237.

Kazantzis, N., Whittington, C., & Dattilio, F. (2010). Meta-analysis of homework effects in cognitive and behavioral therapy: A replication and extension. *Clinical Psychology: Science and Practice, 17,* 144–156.

Kazdin, A. E. (2003). Problem-solving skills training and parent management training for conduct disorder. In A. E. Kazdin & J. R. Weisz (Eds.), *Evidence-based psychotherapies for children and adolescents* (pp. 241–262). New York, NY: Guilford Press.

Kazdin, A. E. (2005). *Parent management training: Treatment for oppositional, aggressive, and antisocial behavior in children and adolescents.* New York, NY: Oxford University Press.

Kazdin, A. E. (2010). Problem-solving skills training and parent management training for oppositional defiant disorder and conduct disorder. In J. R. Weisz & A. E. Kazdin (Eds.), *Evidence-based psychotherapies for children and adolescents* (2nd ed., pp. 211–226). New York, NY: Guilford Press.

Kazdin, A. E. (2012). *Behavior modification in applied settings.* Long Grove, IL: Waveland Press.

Kazdin, A. E., Bass, D., Siegel, T., & Thomas, C. (1989). Cognitive-behavioral therapy and relationship therapy in the treatment of children referred for antisocial behavior. *Journal of Consulting and Clinical Psychology, 57,* 522–535.

Kazdin, A. E., Siegel, T. C., & Bass, D. (1992). Cognitive problem-solving skills training and parent management training in the treatment of antisocial behavior in children. *Journal of Consulting and Clinical Psychology, 60,* 733–747.

Kazdin, A. E., & Wassell, G. (2000). Therapeutic changes in children, parents, and families resulting from treatment of children with conduct problems. *Journal of the American Academy of Child and Adolescent Psychiatry, 39,* 414–420.

Kearney, C. A. (2001). *School refusal behaviour in youth: A functional approach to assessment and treatment.* Washington, DC: American Psychological Association.

Keefe, J. R., McCarthy, K. S., Dinger, U., Zilcha-Mano, S., & Barber, J. P. (2014). A meta-analytic review of psychodynamic therapies for anxiety disorders. *Clinical Psychology Review, 34,* 309–323.

Kegerreis, S. (2010). *Psychodynamic counselling with children and young people.* New York, NY: Palgrave MacMillan.

Kehyayan, A., Best, K., Schmeing, J. B., Axmacher, N., & Kessler, H. (2013). Neural activity during free association to conflict–related sentences. *Frontiers in Human Neuroscience, 7*(705). doi:10.3389/fnhum.2013.00705

Kelley, H. H. (1973). The processes of causal attribution. *American Psychologist, 28,* 107–128.

Kelly, S. (2006). Cognitive-behavioral therapy with African Americans. In P. A. Hays & G. Y. Iwamasa (Eds.), *Culturally responsive cognitive-behavioral therapy: Assessment, practice, and supervision* (pp. 97–116). Washington, DC: American Psychological Association.

Kendall, P. C. (1993). Cognitive-behavioral therapies with youth: Guiding theory, current status, and emerging developments. *Journal of Consulting and Clinical Psychology, 61,* 235–247.

Kendall, P. C. (1994). Treating anxiety disorders in children: Results of a randomized clinical trial. *Journal of Consulting and Clinical Psychology, 62,* 100–110.

Kendall, P. C. (2011). Anxiety disorders in youth. In P. C. Kendall (Ed.), *Child and adolescent therapy: Cognitive-behavioral procedures* (4th ed., pp. 143–189). New York, NY: Guilford Press.

Kendall, P. C., & Hedtke, K. (2006a). *Cognitive-behavioral therapy for anxious children: Therapist manual* (3rd ed.). Ardmore, PA: Workbook.

Kendall, P. C., & Hedtke, K. (2006b). *The Coping Cat workbook* (2nd ed.). Ardmore, PA: Workbook.

Kendall, P. C., Hudson, J. L., Gosch, E., Flannery-Schroeder, E., & Suveg, C. (2008). Cognitive-behavioral therapy for anxiety disordered youth: A randomized clinical trial evaluating child and family modalities. *Journal of Consulting and Clinical Psychology, 76,* 282–297.

Kendall, P. C., Podell, J. L., & Gosch, E. A. (2010). *The Coping Cat parent companion.* Ardmore, PA: Workbook.

Kendall, P. C., Safford, S., Flannery-Schroeder, E., & Webb, A. (2004). Child anxiety treatment: Outcomes in adolescence and impact on substance use and depression at 7.4-year follow-up. *Journal of Consulting and Clinical Psychology, 72,* 276–287.

Kendall, P. C., & Southam-Gerow, M. A. (1996). Long-term follow-up of a cognitive-behavioral therapy for anxiety-disordered youth. *Journal of Consulting and Clinical Psychology, 64,* 724–730.

Kendall, P. C., & Treadwell, K. H. (2007). The role of self-statements as a mediator in treatment for youth with anxiety disorders. *Journal of Consulting and Clinical Psychology, 75,* 380–389.

Kendall-Tackett, K. (2012). The long-term health effects of child sexual abuse. In P. Goodyear-Brown (Ed.), *Handbook of child sexual abuse: Identification, assessment, and treatment* (pp. 49–67). Hoboken, NJ: Wiley.

Kennard, B., Emslie, G., Mayes, T., Nightingale-Teresi, J., Nakonezny, P. A., Hughes, J. L., …Jarrett, R. B. (2008). Cognitive-behavioral therapy to prevent relapse in pediatric responders to pharmacotherapy for major depressive disorder. *Journal of the American Academy of Child and Adolescent Psychiatry, 47,* 1395–1404.

Kensinger, E. (2007). Negative emotion enhances memory accuracy: Behavioral and neuroimaging evidence. *Current Directions in Psychological Science, 16,* 213–221.

Kernberg, O. F. (1980). *Internal world and external reality: Object relations therapy applied.* New York, NY: Aronson.

Kernberg, O. F. (1993). *Object relations theory and clinical psychoanalysis.* New York, NY: Jason Aronson.

Kernberg, O. F., Yeomans, F. E., Clarkin, J. F., & Levy, K. N. (2008). Transference focused psychotherapy: Overview and update. *International Journal of Psychoanalysis, 89,* 601–620.

Kernberg, P. F., & Chazan, S. E. (1991). *Children with conduct disorders: A psychotherapy manual.* New York, NY: Basic Books.

Kernberg, P. F., Weiner, A. S., & Bardenstein, K. K. (2000). *Personality disorders in children and adolescents*. New York, NY: Basic Books.

Kerr, C. E., Sacchet, M. D., Lazar, S. W., Moore, C. I., & Jones, S. R. (2013). Mindfulness starts with the body: Somatosensory attention and top-down modulation of cortical alpha rhythms in mindfulness meditation. *Frontiers in Human Neuroscience, 7*. doi:10.3389/fnhum.2013.00012.

Kerr, M. E., & Bowen, M. (1988). *Family evaluation*. New York, NY: Norton.

Kessler, R. C., Avenevoli, S., Costello, E. J., Georgiades, K., Green, J. G., Gruber, M. J., ... Merikangas, K. R. (2012). Prevalence, persistence, and socio-demographic correlates of DSM-IV disorders in the National Comorbidity Survey-Replication Adolescent Supplement. *Archives of General Psychiatry, 69*, 372–380.

Khoury, B., Lecomte, T., Fortin, G., Masse, M., Therien, P., Bouchard, V., ... Hofmann, S. G. (2013). Mindfulness-based therapy: A comprehensive meta-analysis. *Clinical Psychology Review, 33*, 763–771.

Kim, B. S. K. (2007). Adherence to Asian and European American cultural values and attitudes toward seeking professional psychological help among Asian American college students. *Journal of Counseling Psychology, 54*, 474–480.

Kim, B. S. K. (2011). *Counseling Asian Americans*. Belmont, CA: Cengage.

Kim, J. (2013). *Solution-focused brief therapy: A multicultural approach*. Thousand Oaks, CA: SAGE.

Kim, J. S. (2008). Examining the effectiveness of solution-focused brief therapy: A meta-analysis. *Research On Social Work Practice, 18*, 107–116.

Kim, J. K., Conger, R. D., Elder, G. H., Jr., & Lorenz, F. O. (2003). Reciprocal influences between stressful life-events and adolescent internalizing and externalizing problems. *Child Development, 74*, 127–143.

Kimonis, E. R., Frick, P. J., Fazekas, H., & Loney, B. R. (2006). Psychopathy, aggression, and the processing of emotional stimuli in non-referred girls and boys. *Behavioral Sciences and the Law, 24*, 21–37.

Kimonis, E. R., Frick, P. J., & McMahon, R. J. (2014). Conduct and oppositional defiant disorders. In E. J. Mash & R. A. Barkley (Eds.), *Child psychopathology* (3rd ed., pp. 145–179). New York, NY: Guilford Press.

Kinnaman, J. E. S., & Bellack, A. S. (2012). Social skills. In W. T. O'Donohue & J. E. Fisher (Eds.), *Cognitive behavior therapy: Core principles for practice* (pp. 251–272). Hoboken, NJ: Wiley.

Kivlighan, D., M. Jr., Multon, K. D., & Patton, M. J. (2000). Insight and symptom reduction in time-limited psychoanalytic counseling. *Journal of Counseling Psychology, 47*, 50–58.

Klein, J. B., Jacobs, R. H., & Reinecke, M. A. (2007). Cognitive behavioral therapy for adolescent depression: A meta-analytic investigation of changes in effect-size estimates. *Journal of the American Academy of Child and Adolescent Psychiatry, 46*, 1403–1413.

Klein, M. (1932). *The psycho-analysis of children*. London, UK: Hogarth Press.

Klein, M., Golden, G. G., Michels, J. L., & Chisholm-Stockard, S. (2002). Congruence. In J. C. Norcross (Ed.), *Psychotherapy relationships that work: Therapist contributions and responsiveness to patients* (pp. 195–215). New York: Oxford University Press.

Klein, R. G., & Last, C. G. (1989). *Anxiety disorders in children*. Newbury Park, CA: Sage.

Kliem, S., Kröger, C., & Kosfelder, J. (2010). Dialectical behavior therapy for borderline personality disorder: A meta-analysis using mixed-effects modeling. *Journal of Consulting and Clinical Psychology, 78*, 936–951.

Knafo, A., Jaffee, S. R., Matthys, W., Vanderschuren, L. J., & Schutter, D. J. (2013). The neurobiology of oppositional defiant disorder and conduct disorder: Altered functioning in three mental domains. *Development and Psychopathology, 25,* 193–207.

Knell, S. M. (1993). *Cognitive-behavioral play therapy.* Northvale, NJ: Jason Aronson.

Knell, S. M., & Meena, D. (2011). Cognitive-behavioral play therapy. In S. W. Russ & L. N. Niec (Eds.), *Play in clinical practice: Evidence-based approaches* (pp. 236–263). New York, NY: Guilford Press.

Knox, M., King, C., Hanna, G. L., Logan, D., & Ghaziuddin, N. (2000). Aggressive behavior in clinically depressed adolescents. *Journal of the American Academy of Child and Adolescent Psychiatry, 39,* 611–618.

Kodak, T., Lerman, D. C., Volkert, V., & Trosclair, N. (2007). Further examination of factors that influence preference for positive versus negative reinforcement. *Journal of Applied Behavior Analysis, 40,* 25–44.

Koenen, K. (2007). Genetics of posttraumatic stress disorder: Review and recommendations for future studies. *Journal of Traumatic Stress, 20,* 737–750.

Koerner, K. (2007). Case formulation in Dialectical Behavior Therapy for borderline personality disorder. In T. E. Eehls (Ed.), *Handbook of case formulation in psychotherapy* (2nd ed., pp. 317–348). New York, NY: Guilford Press.

Koerner, K. (2012). *Doing Dialectical Behavior Therapy: A practical guide.* New York: Guilford.

Koeske, G. F., Kirk, S. A., Koeske, R. D., & Rauktis, M. B. (1994). Measuring the Monday blues: Validation of a job satisfaction scale for the human services. *Social Work Research, 18,* 27–35.

Kohatsu, E. L., Concepcion, W. R., & Perez, P. (2009). Incorporating levels of acculturation in counseling practice. In J. G. Ponterotto, J. M. Casas, L. A. Suzuki, & C. M. Alexander (Eds.), *Handbook of multicultural counseling* (3rd ed., pp. 343–356). Thousand Oaks, CA: SAGE.

Kolko, D. J., Hurlburt, M. S., Zhang, J., Barth, R. P., Leslie, L. K., & Burns, B. J. (2010). Posttraumatic stress symptoms in children and adolescents referred for child welfare investigation: A national sample of in-home and out-of-home care. *Child Maltreatment, 15,* 48–63.

Kolko, D. J., & Pardini, D. A. (2010). ODD dimensions, ADHD, and callous-unemotional traits as predictors of treatment response in children with disruptive behavior disorders. *Journal of Abnormal Psychology, 119,* 713–725.

Koocher, G. P. (2003). Ethical issues in psychotherapy with adolescents. *Journal of Clinical Psychology, 59,* 1247–1256.

Kottler, J. A. (2003). *On being a therapist.* San Francisco, CA: Jossey-Bass.

Kramer, U., Despland, J.-N., Michel, L., Drapeau, M., & de Roten, Y. (2010). Change in defense mechanisms and coping over the course of short-term dynamic psychotherapy for adjustment disorder. *Journal of Clinical Psychology, 66,* 1232–1241.

Kreidler, W. J. (1997). *Conflict resolution in the middle school.* Cambridge, MA: Educators for Social Responsibility.

Kring, A. M., & Gordon, A. H. (1998). Sex differences in emotion: Expression, experience, and physiology. *Journal of Personality and Social Psychology, 74,* 686–703.

Krumholz, L. S., Ugueto, A. M., Santucci, L. C., & Weisz, J. R. (2014). Social skills training. In E. S. Sburlati, H. J. Lyneham, C. A. Schniering, & R. M. Rapee (Eds.), *Evidence-based CBT for anxiety and depression in children and adolescents: A competencies based approach* (pp. 260–274). Hoboken, NJ: Wiley-Blackwell.

Kvarme, L. G., Helseth, S., Sørum, R., Luth-Hansen, V., Haugland, S., & Natvig, G. K. (2010). The effect of a solution-focused approach to improve self-efficacy in socially withdrawn school children: A non-randomized controlled trial. *International Journal of Nursing Studies, 47,* 1389–1396.

Kuhlberg, J. A., Pena, J. B., & Zayas, L. H. (2010). Familism, parent-adolescent conflict, self-esteem, internalizing behaviors and suicide attempts among adolescent Latinas. *Child Psychiatry and Human Development, 41,* 425–440.

Kuyken, W., Padesky, C. A., & Dudley, R. (2009). *Collaborative case conceptualization: Working effectively with clients in cognitive behavioral therapy.* New York, NY: Guilford Press.

LaGrange, B., Cole, D. A., Jacquez, F., Ciesla, J., Dallaire, D., Pineda, A., … Felton, J. (2011). Disentangling the prospective relations between maladaptive cognitions and depressive symptoms. *Journal of Abnormal Psychology, 120,* 511–527.

Lahey, B. B., & Waldman, I. D. (2003). A developmental propensity model of the origins of conduct problems during childhood and adolescence. In B. B. Lahey, T. E. Moffitt, A. Caspi, B. B. Lahey, T. E. Moffitt, A. Caspi (Eds.), *Causes of conduct disorder and juvenile delinquency* (pp. 76–117). New York, NY, US: Guilford Press.

Laird, J. (1993). Lesbian and gay families. In F. Walsh, F. Walsh (Eds.), *Normal family processes* (2nd ed., pp. 282–328). New York, NY: Guilford Press.

Lakes, K. D., & Hoyt, W. T. (2004). Promoting self-regulation through school-based martial arts training. *Journal of Applied Developmental Psychology, 25,* 283–302.

Lamarre, B. W., & Nosanchuk, T. A. (1999). Judo—The gentle way: A replication of studies on martial arts and aggression. *Perceptual and Motor Skills, 88,* 992–996.

Lamb, S. (1986). Treating sexually abused children: Issue of blame and responsibility. *American Journal of Orthopsychiatry, 56,* 303–307.

Lambert, S. F., McCreary, B. T., Joiner, T. E., Schmidt, N. B., & Ialongo, N. S. (2004). Structure of anxiety and depression in urban youth: An examination of the tripartite model. *Journal of Consulting and Clinical Psychology, 72,* 904–908.

Lambert, M. J., & Ogles, B. M. (2004). The efficacy and effectiveness of psychotherapy. In M. J. Lambert (Ed.), *Bergin and Garfield's Handbook of Psychotherapy and Behavior Change* (5th ed., pp. 139–193). New York: Wiley.

Lamberton, A., & Oei, T. P. S. (2008). A test of the cognitive content specificity hypothesis in depression and anxiety. *Journal of Behavior Therapy and Experimental Psychiatry, 39,* 23–31.

Landreth, G. L. (2012). *Play therapy: The art of the relationship* (3rd ed.). New York, NY: Routledge.

Landsman, I. S. (2002). Crises of meaning in trauma and loss. In J. Kauffman (Ed.), *Loss of the assumptive world: A theory of traumatic loss* (pp. 13–30). New York, NY: Brunner-Routledge.

Lang, R., O'Reilly, M., Rispoli, M., Shogren, K., Machalicek, W., Sigafoos, J., & Regester, A. (2009). Review of interventions to increase functional and symbolic play in children with autism. *Education and Training in Developmental Disabilities, 44,* 481–492.

Lansford, J. E., Malone, P. S., Castellino, D. R., Dodge, K. A., Pettit, G. S., & Bates, J. E. (2006). Trajectories of internalizing, externalizing, and grades for children who have and have not experienced their parents' divorce or separation. *Journal of Family Psychology, 20,* 292–301.

Lansford, J. E., Sharma, C., Malone, P. S., Woodlief, D., Dodge, K. A., & Oburu, P. (2014). Corporal punishment, maternal warmth, and child adjustment: A longitudinal study in eight countries. *Journal of Clinical Child and Adolescent Psychology, 43*, 670–685.

Lantieri, L., Miller, C., Lieber, C. M., & Roderick, T. (1998). *Conflict resolution in the high school: 36 lessons*. Cambridge, MA: Educators for Social Responsibility.

Larson, J. (2005). *Think first: Addressing aggressive behavior in secondary schools*. New York, NY: Guilford Press.

Larson, K. A., & Gerber, M. M. (1987). Effects of social metacognitive training for enhancing overt behavior in learning disabled and low achieving delinquents. *Exceptional Children, 54*, 201–211.

Larson, J., & Lochman, J. E. (2011). *Helping schoolchildren cope with anger: A cognitive-behavioral intervention* (2nd ed.). New York, NY: Guilford Press.

Larson, K. A., & Gerber, M. M. (1987). Effects of social metacognitive training for enhancing overt behavior in learning disabled and low achieving delinquents. *Exceptional Children, 54*, 201–211.

Latham, G., & Locke, E. A. (2002). Building a practically useful theory of goal setting and task motivation. *American Psychologist, 57*, 705–17

Lather, P. (1991). *Getting smart: Feminist research and pedagogy within/in the postmodern*. New York, NY: Routledge.

Lattal, K. M. (2013). Pavlovian conditioning. In G. J. Madden, W. V. Dube, T. D. Hackenberg, G. P. Hanley, & K. A. Lattal (Eds.), *APA handbook of behavior analysis: Vol. 1. Methods and principles* (pp. 283–306). Washington, DC: American Psychological Association.

Lau, A. S., Fung, J. J., & Yung, V. (2010). Group parent training with immigrant Chinese families: Enhancing engagement and augmenting skills development. *Journal of Clinical Psychology: In Session, 66*, 880–894.

Lau, J. Y., & Eley, T. C. (2010). The genetics of mood disorders. *Annual Review of Clinical Psychology, 6*, 313–337.

Lau, W.-Y., Chan, C. K.-Y., Li, J. C.-H., & Au, T. K.-F. (2010). Effectiveness of group cognitive-behavioral treatment for childhood anxiety in community clinics. *Behaviour Research and Therapy, 48*, 1067–1077.

Laungani, P. (2004). Counseling and therapy in a multi-cultural setting. *Counselling Psychology Quarterly, 17*, 195–207.

Lavigne, J. V., Gouze, K. R., Hopkins, J., Bryant, F. B., & LeBailly, S. A. (2012). A multi-domain model of risk factors for ODD symptoms in a community sample of 4-year-olds. *Journal of Abnormal Child Psychology, 40*, 741–757.

Layous, K., Nelson, S. K., Oberle, E., Schonert-Reichl, K. A., & Lyubomirsky, S. (2012). Kindness counts: Prompting prosocial behavior in preadolescents boosts peer acceptance and well-being. *PLoS ONE 7*(12), e51380. doi:10.1371/journal.pone.0051380

Lazarus, R. S., & Folkman, S. (1984). *Stress, appraisal and coping*. New York, NY: Springer.

Leahy, R., Holland, S. J. F., & McGinn, L. K. (2011). *Treatment plans and interventions for depression and anxiety disorders* (2nd ed.). New York, NY: Guilford Press.

LeDoux, J. (1998). *The emotional brain: The mysterious underpinnings of emotional life*. New York, NY: Simon & Schuster.

LeDoux, J. E. (2002). *Synaptic self: How our brains become who we are*. New York, NY: Viking Penguin.

Lee, C. C. (2006). Ethical issues in multicultural counseling. In B. Herlihy & G. Corey (Eds.), *ACA ethical standards casebook* (6th ed., pp. 159–168). Alexandria, VA: American Counseling Association.

Lefkowitz, E. S., Romo, L. F. L., Corona, R., Au, T. K.-F., & Sigman, M. (2000). How Latino American and European American adolescents discuss conflicts, sexuality, and AIDS with their mothers. *Developmental Psychology, 36,* 315–325.

Leichsenring, F. (2001). Comparative effects of short-term psychodynamic psychotherapy and cognitive-behavioral therapy in depression: A meta-analytic approach. *Clinical Psychology Review, 21,* 401–419.

Lejuez, C. W., Hopko, D. R., Acierno, R., Daughters, S. B., & Pagoto, S. (2011). Ten-year revision of the behavioral activation treatment for depression (BATD-R): Revised treatment manual. *Behavior Modification, 35,* 111–161.

Lerner, M. J. (1998). The two forms of belief in a just world: Some thoughts on why and how people care about justice. In L. Montada & M. J. Lerner (Eds.), *Responses to victimizations and belief in a just world* (pp. 247–269, 278). New York, NY: Plenum Press.

Lerner, M. J., & Miller, D. T. (1978). Just world research and the attribution process: Looking back and ahead. *Psychological Bulletin, 85,* 1030–1051.

Lester, K., Resick, P. A., Young-Xu, Y., & Artz, C. (2010). Impact of race on early treatment termination and outcomes in posttraumatic stress disorder treatment. *Journal of Consulting and Clinical Psychology, 78,* 480–489.

Lewinsohn, P. M. (1974). Clinical and theoretical aspects of depression. In K. S. Calhoun, H. E. Adams, & K. M. Mitchell (Eds.), *Innovative treatment methods of psychopathology* (pp. 63–120). New York: Wiley.

Lewinsohn, P. M., Rohde, P., Seeley, J. R., Klein, D. N., & Gotlib, I. H. (2003). Psychosocial functioning of young adults who have experienced and recovered from major depressive disorder during adolescence. *Journal of Abnormal Psychology, 112,* 353–363.

Lewis, C. C., Simons, A. D., Nguyen, L. J., Murakami, J. L., Reid, M. W., Silva, S. G., & March, J. S. (2010). Impact of childhood trauma on treatment outcome in the Treatment for Adolescents with Depression Study (TADS). *Journal of the American Academy of Child and Adolescent Psychiatry, 49,* 132–140.

Lewis, P. A., & Critchley, H. D. (2003). Mood-dependent memory. *Trends in Cognitive Science, 7,* 431–433.

Lieberman, A. F., Ippen, C. G., & Marans, S. (2009). Psychodynamic therapy for child trauma. In E. B. Foa, T. M. Keane, M. J. Friedman, & J. A. Cohen. *Effective treatments for PTSD: Practice guidelines from the International Society for Traumatic Stress Studies* (2nd ed., pp. 370–387). New York, NY: Guilford Press.

Lindblad-Goldberg, M., & Northey Jr., W. F. (2013). Ecosystemic structural family therapy: Theoretical and clinical foundations. *Contemporary Family Therapy: An International Journal, 35,* 147–160.

Linehan, M. M. (1987). Dialectical Behavior Therapy for borderline personality disorder: Theory and method. *Bulletin of the Menninger Clinic, 51,* 261–276.

Linehan, M. M. (1993a). *Cognitive behavioral treatment for borderline personality disorder.* New York, NY: Guilford Press.

Linehan, M. M. (1993b). *Skills training manual for treating borderline personality disorder.* New York, NY: Guilford Press.

Linehan, M. M. (1997). Validation and psychotherapy. In A. Bohart & L. Greenberg (Eds.), *Empathy reconsidered: New directions in psychotherapy* (pp. 353–392). Washington, DC: American Psychological Association.

Linehan, M. M. (2014). *DBT skills training manual* (2nd ed.). New York, NY: Guilford Press.

Lipchik, E., Derks, J., LaCourt, M., & Nunnally, E. (2012). The evolution of solution-focused brief therapy. In C. Franklin, T. S. Trepper, W. J. Gingerich, E. E. McCollum, C. Franklin, T. S. Trepper, ... E. E. McCollum (Eds.), *Solution-focused brief therapy: A handbook of evidence-based practice* (pp. 3–19). New York, NY: Oxford University Press.

Lipsey, M. W. (1995). What do we learn from 400 studies on the effectiveness of treatment with juvenile delinquents? In J. McGuire (Ed.), *What works: Reducing reoffending: Guidelines from research and practice* (pp. 63–78). New York: Wiley.

Little, L. M., & Pisterman, M. L. (1989). The efficacy of response cost procedures for reducing children's noncompliance to parental instructions. *Behavior Therapy, 20,* 515–534.

Littleton, H., Horsley, S., John, S., & Nelson, D. V. (2007). Trauma coping strategies and psychological distress: A meta-analysis. *Journal of Traumatic Stress, 20,* 977–988.

Liu, W. M., Ali, S. R., Soleck, G., Hopps, J., Dunston, K., & Pickett, T. (2004). Using social class in counseling psychology research. *Journal of Counseling Psychology, 51,* 3–18.

Liu, W. M., & Clay, D. L. (2002). Multicultural counseling competencies: Guidelines in working with children and adolescents. *Journal of Mental Health Counseling, 24,* 177–187.

Liu, W. M., Pickett, T., & Ivey, A. E. (2007). White middle-class privilege: Social class bias and implications for training and practice. *Journal of Multicultural Counseling and Development, 35,* 194–206.

Loades, M., Clark, S., & Reynolds, S. (2014). Managing negative thoughts, Part II: Positive imagery, self-talk, thought stopping, and thought acceptance. In E. S. Sburlati, H. J. Lyneham, C. A. Schniering, & R. M. Rapee (Eds.), *Evidence-based CBT for anxiety and depression in children and adolescents: A competencies based approach* (pp. 176–193). Hoboken, NJ: Wiley-Blackwell.

Lochman, J. E. (2004). Contextual factors in risk and prevention research. *Merrill-Palmer Quarterly, 50,* 311–325.

Lochman, J. E., Boxmeyer, C. L., Powell, N. P., Barry, T. D., & Pardini, D. A. (2010). Anger control training for aggressive youths. In J. R. Weisz & A. E. Kazdin (Eds.), *Evidence-based psychotherapies for children and adolescents* (2nd ed., pp. 227–242). New York, NY: Guilford Press.

Lochman, J. E., Powell, N. P., Boxmeyer, C. L., & Baden, R. E. (2012). Disruptive behavior disorders. In E. Szigethy, J. R. Weisz, & R. L. Findling (Eds.), *Cognitive-behavior therapy for children and adolescents* (pp. 435–465). Arlington, VA: American Psychiatric Association.

Lochman, J. E., Powell, N. P., Boxmeyer, C. L., Kelly, M., Dillon, C., & Bradshaw, C. (2013). Anger management in schools: The Coping Power program for children and early adolescents. In E. Fernandez (Ed.), *Treatments for anger in specific populations: Theory, application, and outcome* (pp. 176–196). New York, NY: Oxford University Press.

Lochman, J. E., & Wells, K. C. (2002). Contextual social cognitive mediators and child outcome: A test of the theoretical model in the Coping Power Program. *Development and Psychopathology, 14,* 971–993.

Lochman, J. E., & Wells, K. C. (2004). The coping power program for preadolescent aggressive boys and their parents: Outcome effects at the 1-year follow-up. *Journal of Consulting and Clinical Psychology, 72,* 571–578.

Lochman, J. E., Wells, K. C., & Lenhart, L. (2008). *Coping power child group program: Facilitator guide.* New York, NY: Oxford University Press.

Locke, E., & Latham, G. (2006). New directions in goal-setting theory. *Association for Psychological Science, 15,* 265–268.

Loeber, R., & Hay, D. F. (1997). Key issues in the development of aggression and violence from childhood to early adulthood. *Annual Review of Psychology, 48,* 371–410.

Lohaus, A., & Klein-Hessling, J. (2003). Relaxation in children: Effects of extended and intensified training. *Psychology and Health, 18,* 237–249.

Lombardi, R. (2013). Art therapy. In E. J. Green & A. A. Drewes (Eds.), *Integrating expressive arts and play therapy with children and adolescents* (pp. 41–49). Hoboken, NJ: Wiley.

Loney, B. R., Frick, P. J., Clements, C. B., Ellis, M. L., & Kerlin, K. (2003). Callous-unemotional traits, impulsivity, and emotional processing in antisocial adolescents. *Journal of Clinical Child and Adolescent Psychology, 32,* 139–152.

Longmore, R. J., & Worrell, M. (2007). Do we need to challenge thoughts in cognitive behavior therapy? *Clinical Psychology Review, 27,* 173–187.

Loo, S., & Makieg, S. (2012). Clinical utility of EEG in attention-deficit/hyperactivity disorder: A research update. *Neurotherapeutics, 9,* 569–587.

Looyeh, M. Y., Kamali, K., & Shafieian, R. (2012). An exploratory study of the effectiveness of group narrative therapy on the school behavior of girls with attention-deficit/hyperactivity symptoms. *Archives of Psychiatric Nursing, 26,* 404–410.

Lopez-Baez, S. I. (2006). Counseling Latinas: Culturally responsive interventions. In C. C. Lee (Ed.), *Multicultural issues in counseling* (3rd ed., pp. 187–194). Alexandria, VA: American Counseling Association.

Lorant, V., Deliege, D., Eaton, W., Robert, A., Philippot, P., & Ansseau, M. (2003). Socioeconomic inequalities in depression: A meta-analysis. *American Journal of Epidemiology, 157,* 98–112

Lourie, I. S., & Hernandez, M. (2003). A historical perspective on national child mental health policy. *Journal of Emotional and Behavioral Disorders, 11,* 4–8.

Lueger, R. J. (2002). Imagery techniques in cognitive behavior treatments of anxiety and trauma. In A. A. Sheikh (Ed.), *Healing images: The role of imagination in health* (pp. 75–84). Amityville, NY: Baywood.

Lum, D. (2011). *Culturally competent practice.* Belmont, CA: Cengage.

Lundahl, B., Moleni, T., Burke, B. L., Butters, R., Tollefson, D., Butler, C., & Rollnick, S. (2013). Motivational interviewing in medical care settings: A systematic review and meta-analysis of randomized controlled trials. *Patient Education and Counseling, 93,* 157–168.

Lundahl, B. W., Kunz, C., Brownell, C., Tollefson, D., & Burke, B. L. (2010). A meta-analysis of motivational interviewing: Twenty-five years of empirical studies. *Research on Social Work Practice, 20,* 137–160.

Lundgren, T., Dahl, J., & Hayes, S. C. (2008). Evaluation of mediators of change in the treatment of epilepsy with Acceptance and Commitment Therapy. *Journal of Behavioral Medicine, 31,* 225–235.

Luoma, J., Hayes, S. C., & Walser, R. (2007). *Learning ACT: An Acceptance and Commitment Therapy skills-training manual for therapists*. Oakland, CA: New Harbinger.

Lynam, D. R., & Henry, B. (2001). The role of neuropsychological deficits in conduct disorders. In J. Hill & B. Maughan (Eds.), *Conduct disorders in childhood and adolescence* (pp. 235–263). Cambridge, UK: Cambridge University Press.

Lynch, T. R., Chapman, A. L., Rosenthal, M. Z., Kuo, J. R., & Linehan, M. M. (2006). Mechanisms of change in Dialectical Behavior Therapy: Theoretical and empirical observations. *Journal of Clinical Psychology, 62*, 459–480.

Lynch, T. R., Trost, W. T., Salsman, N., & Linehan, M. M. (2006). Dialectical Behavior Therapy for borderline personality disorder. *Annual Review of Clinical Psychology, 3*, 181–205.

Lyubomirsky, S. (2008). *The how of happiness: A new approach to getting the life you want*. New York: Penguin.

Maalouf, F. T., & Brent, D. A. (2012). Depression and suicidal behavior. In E. Szigethy, J. R. Weisz, & R. L. Findling (Eds.), *Cognitive-behavior therapy for children and adolescents* (pp. 163–184). Arlington, VA: American Psychiatric Association.

Maalouf, F. T., Brent, D., Clark, L., Tavitian, L., McHugh, R. M., Sahakian, B. J., & Phillips, M. L. (2011). Neurocognitive impairment in adolescent major depressive disorder: State vs. Trait illness markers. *Journal of Affective Disorders, 133*, 625–632.

MacPherson, H. A., Cheavens, J. S., & Fristad, M. A. (2013). Dialectical behavior therapy for adolescents: Theory, treatment adaptations, and empirical outcomes. *Clinical Child and Family Psychology Review, 16*, 59–80.

MacQueen, G., & Frodl, T. (2011). The hippocampus in major depression: Evidence for the convergence of the bench and bedside in psychiatric research? *Molecular Psychiatry, 16*, 252–264.

Madanes, C. (1991). Strategic family therapy. In A. S. Gurman & D. P. Kniskern (Eds.), *Handbook of family therapy* (Vol. 2, pp. 396–416). New York, NY: Brunner/ Mazel.

Madigan, S. (2010). *Narrative therapy*. Washington, DC: American Psychological Association.

Malchiodi, C. A. (2006). *Art therapy sourcebook* (2nd ed.). New York, NY: McGraw-Hill.

Malchiodi, C. A. (2011). *Handbook of art therapy* (2nd ed.). New York, NY: Guilford Press.

Maletic, V., Robinson, M., Oakes, T., Iyengar, S., Ball, S. G., & Russell, J. (2007). Neurobiology of depression: An integrated view of key findings. *International Journal of Clinical Practice, 61*, 2030–2040.

Malgady, R. G. (2010). Treating Hispanic children and adolescents using narrative therapy. In J. R. Weisz & A. E. (Eds.), *Evidence-based psychotherapies for children and adolescents* (2nd ed., pp. 391–400). New York, NY: Guilford Press.

Malgady, R. G., & Costantino, G. (2003). Narrative therapy for Hispanic children and adolescents. In A. E. Kazdin & J. R. Weisz (Eds.), *Evidence-based psychotherapies for children and adolescents* (pp. 425–438). New York, NY: Guilford Press.

Mallinckrodt, B. (2010). The psychotherapy relationship as attachment: Evidence and implications. *Journal of Social and Personal Relationships, 27*, 262–270.

Manassis, K., Lee, T. G., Bennett, K., Zhao, X. Y., Mendlowitz, S., Duda, S., ... Wood, J. J. (2014). Types of parental involvement in CBT with anxious youth: A preliminary meta-analysis. *Journal of Consulting and Clinical Psychology, 82*, 1163–1172.

Manos, R. C., Kanter, J. W., & Busch, A. M. (2010). A critical review of assessment strategies to measure the behavioral activation model of depression. *Clinical Psychology Review, 30*, 547–561.

Mar, R. A., Tackett, J. L., & Moore, C. (2010). Exposure to media and theory-of-mind development in preschoolers. *Cognitive Development, 25*, 69–78.

Marci, C. D., Ham, J., Moran, E., & Orr, S. P. (2007). Physiologic correlates of perceived therapist empathy and social-emotional process during psychotherapy. *Journal of Nervous & Mental Disease, 195*, 103–111.

Marcus, D. K., Kashy, D. A., & Baldwin, S. A. (2009). Studying psychotherapy using the one-with-many design: The therapeutic alliance as an exemplar. *Journal of Counseling Psychology, 56*, 537–548.

Markey, P. M., & Markey, C. N. (2010). Vulnerability to violent video games: A review and integration of personality research. *Review of General Psychology, 14*, 82–91.

Marsh, A. A., Finger, E. C., Mitchell, D. G., Reid, M. E., Sims, C., Kosson, D. S., … Blair, R. J. (2008). Reduced amygdala response to fearful expressions in children and adolescents with callous-unemotional traits and disruptive behavior disorders. *American Journal of Psychiatry, 165*, 712–720.

Martel, M. M., Gremillion, M. L., & Roberts, B. (2012). Temperament and common disruptive behavior problems in preschool. *Personality and Individual Differences, 53*, 874–879.

Martin, A., Krieg, H., Esposito, F., Stubbe, D., & Cardona, L. (2008). Reduction of restraint and seclusion through collaborative problem solving: A five-year prospective inpatient study. *Psychiatric Services, 59*, 1406–1412.

Martin, G., & Pear, J. (2014). *Behavior modification* (10th ed.). New York, NY: Pearson.

Martin, K. A., Moritz, S. E., & Hall, C. R. (1999). Imagery use in sport: A literature review and applied model. *Sport Psychologist, 13*, 245–268.

Masi, G., Millepiedi, S., Mucci, M., Pascale, R. P., Perugi, G., & Akiskal, H. S. (2003). Phenomenology and comorbidity of dysthymic disorder in 100 consecutively referred children and adolescents: Beyond DSM-IV. *Canadian Journal of Psychiatry, 48*, 99–105.

Maslach, C., & Jackson, S. E. (1981). The measurement of experienced burnout. *Journal of Occupational Behavior, 2*, 99–113.

Maslach, C., Jackson, S. E., & Leiter, M. P. (1997). Maslach Burnout Inventory (3rd ed.). In C. P. Zalaquett & R. J. Wood (Eds.), *Evaluating stress: A book of resources* (pp. 191–218). Lanham, MD: Scarecrow Education.

Matthys, W., Cuperus, J. M., & Van Egeland, H. (1999). Deficient social problem-solving in boys with ODD/CD, with ADHD, and with both disorders. *Journal of the American Academy of Child and Adolescent Psychiatry, 38*, 311–321.

Matthys, W., & Lochman, J. E. (2010). *Oppositional defiant disorder and conduct disorder in childhood*. Oxford, UK: Wiley-Blackwell.

Mazzucchelli, T., Kane, R., & Rees, C. (2009). Behavioral activation treatments for adults: A meta-analysis and review. *Clinical Psychology: Science and Practice, 16*, 383–411.

McCabe, K. M., Hough, R., Wood, P. A., & Yeh, M. (2001). Childhood and adolescent onset conduct disorder: A test of the developmental taxonomy. *Journal of Abnormal Child Psychology, 29*, 305–316.

McCart, M. R., Priester, P. E., Davies, W. H., & Azen, R. (2006). Differential effectiveness of behavioral parent-training and cognitive-behavioral therapy for antisocial youth: A meta-analysis. *Journal of Abnormal Child Psychology, 34*, 527–543.

McCleery, J. M., & Harvey, A. G. (2004). Integration of psychological and biological approaches to trauma memory: Implications for pharmacological prevention of PTSD. *Journal of Traumatic Stress, 17*, 485–496.

McClelland, D. C., Atkinson, J. W., Clark, R. A., & Lowell, E. L. (1953). *The achievement motive.* New York: Appleton-Century-Crofts.

McClure, E. B., Monk, C. S., Nelson, E. E., Parrish, J. M., Adler, A., Blair, R. J. R., ... Pine, D. S. (2007). Abnormal attention modulations of fear circuit function in pediatric generalized anxiety disorder. *Archives of General Psychiatry, 64,* 97–106.

McGoldrick, M., Gerson, R., & Petry, S. (2008). *Genograms: Assessment and intervention* (3rd ed.). New York, NY: Norton.

McGuigan, F. J., & Lehrer, P. M. (2007). Progressive relaxation: Origins, principles, and clinical applications. In P. M. Lehrer, R. L. Woolfolk, & W. E. Sime (Eds.), *Principles and practice of stress management* (3rd ed., pp. 57–87). New York, NY: Guilford Press.

McHugh, L., & Stewart, I. (2012). *The self and perspective-taking: Contributions and applications from modern behavioral science.* Oakland, CA: New Harbinger.

McIlvane, W. J. (2013). Simple and complex discrimination learning. In G. J. Madden, W. V. Dube, T. D. Hackenberg, G. P. Hanley, & K. A. Lattal (Eds.), *APA handbook of behavior analysis: Vol. 2. Translating principles into practice* (pp. 129–163). Washington, DC: American Psychological Association.

McKenzie, I. K. (2004). The Stockholm Syndrome revisited: Hostages, relationships, prediction, control and psychological science. *Journal of Police Crisis Negotiations, 4,* 5–21.

McLeod, B. D. (2011). Relation of the alliance with outcomes in youth psychotherapy: A meta-analysis. *Clinical Psychology Review, 31,* 603–616.

McMahon, R. J., & Forehand, R. L. (2005). *Helping the noncompliant child: Family-based treatment for oppositional behavior* (2nd ed.). New York, NY: Guilford Press.

McNeil, C., & Hembree-Kigin, T. (2011). *Parent-child interaction therapy* (2nd ed.). New York, NY: Springer.

McNerney, N. (2011). *Homework: A parent's guide to helping out without freaking out!* Skokie, IL: Integrated Press.

McNulty, J. K., & Fincham, F. D. (2012). Beyond positive psychology? Toward a contextual view of psychological processes and well-being. *American Psychologist, 67,* 101–110.

McWilliams, N. (2011). *Psychoanalytic diagnosis: Understanding personality structure in the clinical process* (2nd ed.). New York, NY: Guilford Press.

Medini, G., & Rosenberg, E. H. (1976). Gossip and psychotherapy. *American Journal of Psychotherapy, 30,* 452–462

Mehlum, L., Tormoen, A. J., Ramberg, M., Haga, E., Diep, L. M., Laberg, S., & Grøholt, B. (2014). Dialectical Behavior Therapy for adolescents with repeated suicidal and self-harming behavior: A randomized trial. *Journal of the American Academy of Child & Adolescent Psychiatry, 53,* 1082–1091.

Meichenbaum, D. H. (1971). Examination of model characteristics in reducing avoidance behavior. *Journal of Personality and Social Psychology, 17,* 298–307.

Meichenbaum, D. H. (1985). *Stress inoculation training.* New York, NY: Pergamon Press.

Meier, A., & Musick, K. (2014). Variation in associations between family dinners and adolescent well-being. *Journal of Marriage and Family, 76,* 13–23.

Mendlowitz, S. L. (2014). Changing maladaptive behaviors, Part II: The use of behavioral activation and pleasant events scheduling with depressed children and adolescents. In E. S. Sburlati, H. J. Lyneham, C. A. Schniering, & R. M. Rapee (Eds.), *Evidence-based CBT for anxiety and depression in children and adolescents: A competencies based approach* (pp. 208–224). Hoboken, NJ: Wiley-Blackwell.

Menting, A. T. A., de Castro, B. O., & Matthys, W. (2013). Effectiveness of the Incredible Years parent training to modify disruptive and prosocial child behavior: A meta-analytic review. *Clinical Psychology Review, 33,* 901–913.

Merikangas, K. R., He, J., Burstein, M., Swanson, S. A., Avenevoli, S., Cui, L., … Swendsen, J. (2010). Lifetime prevalence of mental disorders in U.S. adolescents: Results from the National Comorbidity Survey Replication-Adolescent Supplement (NCS-A). *Journal of the American Academy of Child and Adolescent Psychiatry, 49,* 980–989.

Metcalf, L. (2008). *Counseling toward solutions: A practical solution-focused program for working with students, teachers, and parents.* New York, NY: Jossey-Bass.

Meyer-Lindenberg, A., Buckholtz, J. W., Kolachana, B., Hariri, A. R., Pezawas, L., Blasi, G., … Weinberger, D. R. (2006). Neural mechanisms of genetic risk for impulsivity and violence in humans. *Proceedings of the National Academy of Sciences, USA, 103,* 6269–6274.

Micco, J. A., & Ehrenreich, J. T. (2008). Children's interpretation and avoidant response biases in response to non-salient and salient situations: Relationships with mothers' threat perception and coping expectations. *Journal of Anxiety Disorders, 22,* 371–385.

Michels, R. (1982). The basic propositions of psychoanalytic theory. In S. Gilman (Ed.), *Introducing psychoanalytic theory* (pp. 5–15). New York, NY: Brunner/Mazel.

Micucci, J. S. (2009). *The adolescent in family therapy: Harnessing the power of relationships* (2nd ed.). New York, NY: Guilford Press.

Miller, A. L., Rathus, J. H., & Linehan, M. M. (2007). *Dialectical Behavior Therapy with suicidal adolescents.* New York, NY: Guilford Press.

Miller, D. T., & Porter, C. A. (1983). Self-blame in victims of violence. *Journal of Social Issues, 39,* 139–152.

Miller, G., Chen, E., & Zhou, E. (2007). If it goes up, must it come down?: Chronic stress and the hypothalamic-pituitary-adrenocortical axis in humans. *Psychology Bulletin, 133,* 24–25.

Miller, W. R., & Rollnick, S. (2012). *Motivational interviewing: Helping people change* (3rd ed.). New York, NY: Guilford Press.

Miller, W. R., & Rose, G. S. (2009). Toward a theory of motivational interviewing. *American Psychologist, 64,* 527–537.

Milner, J., & Bateman, J. (2011). *Working with children and teenagers using solution focused approaches: Enabling children to overcome challenges and achieve their potential.* London, UK: Jessica Kingsley.

Miltenberger, R. G. (2015). *Behavior modification: Principles and procedures* (6th ed.). Belmont, CA: Cengage.

Minuchin, S. (1974). *Families and family therapy.* Cambridge, MA: Harvard University Press.

Minuchin, S., & Fishman, H. C. (1981). *Family therapy techniques.* Cambridge, MA: Harvard University Press.

Minuchin, S., Lee, W.-Y., & Simon, G. M. (1996). *Mastering family therapy: Journeys of growth and transformation.* New York, NY: Wiley.

Minuchin, S., Reiter, M. D., Borda, C., Walker, S. A., Pascale, R., & Reynolds, H. T. M. (2014). *The craft of family therapy: Challenging certainties.* New York, NY: Routledge/Taylor & Francis Group.

Mitchell, P. (2011). Acquiring a theory of mind. In A. Slater & G. Bremner (Eds.), *An introduction to developmental psychology* (2nd ed., pp. 357–384). Chichester, UK: Wiley-Blackwell.

Miville, M. (2009). Latino/a identity development: Updates on theory, measurement, and counseling implications. In J. G. Ponterotto, J. M. Casas, L. A. Suzuki, & C. M. Alexander (Eds.), *Handbook of multicultural counseling* (3rd ed., pp. 241–252). Thousand Oaks, CA: SAGE.

Modecki, K. L., Minchin, J., Harbaugh, A. G., Guerra, N. G., & Runions, K. C. (2014). Bullying prevalence across contexts: A meta-analysis measuring cyber and traditional bullying. *Journal of Adolescent Health, 55*, 602–611.

Moehler, E., Kagan, J., Oelkers-Ax, R., Brunner, R., Poustka, L., Haffner, J., & Resch, F. (2008). Infant predictors of behavioural inhibition. *British Journal of Developmental Psychology, 26*, 145–150.

Moeller, T. G. (2001). *Youth aggression and violence: A psychological approach.* Mahwah, NJ: Erlbaum.

Moffitt, T. E. (2003). Life-course persistent and adolescence-limited antisocial behavior: A 10-year research review and research agenda. In B. B. Lahey, T. E. Moffitt, & A. Caspi (Eds.), *Causes of conduct disorder and juvenile delinquency* (pp. 49–75). New York, NY: Guilford Press.

Moffitt, T. E., Arseneault, L., Jaffee, S. R., Kim-Cohen, J., Koenen, K. C., Odgers, C. L., ... Viding, E. (2008). DSM-V conduct disorder: Research needs for an evidence base. *Journal of Child Psychology and Psychiatry, 49*, 3–33.

Moffitt, T. E., Ross, S., & Raine, A. (2011). Crime and biology. In J. Q. Wilson & J. Petersilia (Eds.), *Crime and public policy* (2nd ed., pp. 53–87). Oxford, UK: Oxford University Press.

Monastra, V. J., Lubar, J. F., & Linden, M. (2001). The development of a quantitative electroencephalographic scanning process for attention deficit-hyperactivity disorder: Reliability and validity studies. *Neuropsychology, 15*, 136–144.

Monga, S., Young, A., & Owens, M. (2009). Evaluating a cognitive behavioral therapy group program for anxious five to seven year old children: A pilot study. *Depression and Anxiety, 26*, 243–250.

Monk, C. S., Telzer, E. H., Mogg, K., Bradley, B. P., Mai, X., Louro, H., ... Pine, D. S. (2008). Amygdala and ventrolateral prefrontal cortex activation to masked angry faces in children and adolescents with generalized anxiety disorder. *Archives of General Psychiatry, 65*, 568–576.

Moonshine, C. (2008). *Dialectical Behavior Therapy: Vol. 1. The clinician's guidebook.* Boca Raton, FL: Premier.

Moore, M., & Russ, S. (2008). Follow-up of a pretend play intervention: Effects on play, creativity and emotional processes in children. *Creativity Research Journal, 20*, 427–436.

Morales, E., & Norcross, J. C. (2010). Evidence-based practice with ethnic minorities: Strange bedfellows no more. *Journal of Clinical Psychology: In Session, 66*, 821–829.

Moran, G., & Diamond, G. M. (2008). Generating nonnegative attitudes among parents of depressed adolescents: The power of empathy, concern, and positive regard. *Psychotherapy Research, 18*, 97–107.

Moran, G., Diamond, G. M., & Diamond, S. (2005). The relational reframe and parents' problem constructions in Attachment-Based Family Therapy. *Psychotherapy Research, 15*, 226–235.

Morgan, W. D., Morgan, S. T., & Germer, C. K. (2013). Cultivating attention and compassion. In C. K. Germer, R. D. Siegel, P. R. Fulton, C. K. Germer, R. D. Siegel, P. R. Fulton (Eds.), *Mindfulness and psychotherapy* (2nd ed., pp. 76–93). New York, NY: Guilford Press.

Morokoff, P. J. (1985). Effects of sex guilt, repression, sexual "arousability," and sexual experience on female sexual arousal during erotica and fantasy. *Journal of Personality and Social Psychology, 49*, 177–187.

Moss, E. (2009). The place of psychodynamic psychotherapy in the integrated treatment of posttraumatic stress disorder and trauma recovery. *Psychotherapy: Theory, Research, Practice, Training, 46*, 171–179.

Mowrer, O. H. (1960). *Learning theory and behavior.* Oxford, UK: Wiley.

Mueller, C. M., & Dweck, C. S. (1998). Praise for intelligence can undermine children's motivation and performance. *Journal of Personality and Social Psychology, 75*, 33–52.

Mufson, L., Dorta, K. P., Moreau, D., & Weissman, M. M. (2004). Interpersonal psychotherapy for depressed adolescents. *Archives of General Psychiatry, 61*, 577–584.

Mufson, L., Dorta, K. P., Moreau, D., & Weissman, M. M. (2011). *Interpersonal psychotherapy for depressed adolescents* (2nd ed.). New York, NY: Guilford Press.

Mufson, L., Weissman, M., Moreau, D., & Garfinkel, R. (1999). Efficacy of interpersonal psychotherapy for depressed adolescents. *Archives of General Psychiatry, 56*, 573–579.

Muñoz, L. C., Qualter, P., & Padgett, G. (2011). Empathy and bullying: Exploring the influence of callous-unemotional traits. *Child Psychiatry and Human Development, 42*, 183–196.

Muratori, F., Picchi, L., Bruni, G., Patarnello, M., & Romagnoli, G. (2003). A two-year follow-up of psychodynamic psychotherapy for internalizing disorders in children. *Journal of the American Academy of Child and Adolescent Psychiatry, 42*, 331–339.

Muratori, F., Picchi, L., Casella, C., Tancredi, R., Milone, A., & Patarnello, M. G. (2002). Efficacy of brief dynamic psychotherapy for children with emotional disorders. *Psychotherapy and Psychosomatics, 71*, 28–38.

Murphy, E. S., & Lupfer, G. J. (2014). Basic principles of operant conditioning. In F. K. McSweeney & E. S. Murphy (Eds.), *The Wiley Blackwell handbook of operant and classical conditioning* (pp. 167–194). Oxford, UK: Wiley-Blackwell.

Murphy, J. J. (2008). *Solution-focused counseling in schools* (2nd ed.). Alexandria, VA: American Counseling Association.

Murray, J., & Farrington, D. P. (2010). Risk factors for conduct disorder and delinquency: Key findings from longitudinal studies. *Canadian Journal of Psychiatry, 55*, 633–642.

Murrell, A. R., Coyne, L. W., & Wilson, K. G. (2004). ACT with children, adolescents, and their parents. In S. C. Hayes & K. D. Strosahl (Eds.), *A practical guide to Acceptance and Commitment Therapy* (pp. 249–273). New York, NY: Springer.

Murrell, A. R., & Scherbarth, A. J. (2011). State of the research & literature address: ACT with children, adolescents and parents. *International Journal of Behavioral Consultation and Therapy, 7*, 15–22.

Musick, K., & Meier, A. (2012). Assessing causality and persistence in associations between family dinners and adolescent well-being. *Journal of Marriage and Family, 74*, 476–493.

Nadeau, J. (2001). Meaning making in family bereavement: A family systems approach. In M. S. Stroebe, R. O. Hansson, W. Stroebe, & H. Schut (Eds.), *Handbook of bereavement research* (pp. 329–348). Washington, DC: American Psychological Association.

Nader, K. (2008). *Understanding and assessing trauma in children and adolescents: Measures, methods, and youth in context.* New York, NY: Routledge.

Nader, K., & Fletcher, K. E. (2014). Childhood posttraumatic stress disorder. In E. J. Mash & R. A. Barkley (Eds.), *Child psychopathology* (3rd ed., pp. 476–528). New York, NY: Guilford Press.

Najavits, L. M., & Strupp, H. H. (1994). Differences in the effectiveness of psychodynamic therapists: A process-outcome study. *Psychotherapy: Theory, Research, Practice, Training, 31,* 114–123.

National Association of Social Workers National Committee, Committee on Racial and Ethnic Diversity. (2001). NASW standards for cultural competence in social work practice. Retrieved from http://www.naswdc.org/sections/credentials/cultural_comp.asp

Nauta, M., Scholing, A., Emmelkamp, P., & Minderaa, R. B. (2003). Cognitive-behavioral therapy for children with anxiety disorders in a clinical setting: No additional effect of cognitive parent training. *Journal of the American Academy of Child and Adolescent Psychiatry, 42,* 1270–1278.

Neacsiu, A. D., Bohus, M., & Linehan, M. M. (2014). Dialectical Behavior Therapy: An intervention for emotion dysregulation. In J. J. Gross (Ed.), *Handbook of emotion regulation* (2nd ed., pp. 491–507). New York, NY: Guilford Press.

Neacsiu, A. D., Rizvi, S. L., & Linehan, M. M. (2010). Dialectical behavior therapy skills use as a mediator and outcome of treatment for borderline personality disorder. *Behaviour Research and Therapy, 48,* 832–839.

Needham, B. L. (2007). Reciprocal relationships between symptoms of depression and parental support during the transition from adolescence to young adulthood. *Journal of Youth and Adolescence, 37,* 893–905.

Neimeyer, R. A. (2012). Correspondence with the deceased. In R. A. Neimeyer (Ed.), *Techniques of grief therapy: Creative practices for counseling the bereaved* (pp. 259–262). New York, NY: Routledge.

Neimeyer, R. A., & Wogrin, C. (2008). Psychotherapy for complicated bereavement: A meaning-oriented approach. *Illness, Crisis, & Loss, 16,* 1–20.

Newcombe, M. J., & Ashkanasy, N. M. (2002). The code of affect and affective congruence in perceptions of leaders: An experimental study. *Leadership Quarterly, 13,* 601–604.

Newman, L. S., Duff, K., & Baumeister, R. F. (1997). A new look at defensive projection: Thought suppression, accessibility, and biased person perception. *Journal of Personality and Social Psychology, 72,* 980–1001.

Newport, F. (2011). For first time, majority of Americans favor legal gay marriage. Retrieved from http://gallup.com/poll/147662/First-Time-Majority-Americans-Favor-Legal-Gay-Marriage.asp

Nichols, M. P. (1999). *Inside family therapy.* Boston, MA: Allyn & Bacon.

Nichols, M. P. (2012). *Family therapy: Concepts and methods* (10th ed.). New York, NY: Pearson.

Nichols, M. P., & Fellenberg, S. (2000). The effective use of enactments in family therapy: A discovery-oriented process study. *Journal of Marital and Family Therapy, 26,* 143–152.

Nickel, C., Lahmann, C., Tritt, K., Loew, T. H., Rother, W. K., & Nickel, M. K. (2005). Short communication: Stressed aggressive adolescents benefit from progressive muscle relaxation: A random, prospective, controlled trial. *Stress and Health: Journal of the International Society for the Investigation of Stress, 26,* 169–175.

Nickel, M., Luley, J., Krawczyk, J., Nickel, C., Widermann, C., Lahmann, C., … Loew, T. (2006). Bullying girls—Changes after Brief Strategic Family Therapy: A randomized, prospective, controlled trial with one-year follow-up. *Psychotherapy and Psychosomatics, 75*, 47–55.

Nicolas, G., Arntz, D. L., Hirsch, B., & Schmiedigen, A. (2011). Cultural adaptation of a group treatment for Haitian American adolescents. *Professional Psychology: Research and Practice, 40*, 378–384.

Nigg, J. T. (2006). *What causes ADHD?* New York, NY: Guilford Press.

Nitschke, J. B., Sarinopoulos, I., Oathes, D. J., Johnstone, T., Whalen, P. J., Davidson, R. J., & Kalin, N. H. (2009). Anticipatory activation in the amygdala and anterior cingulate in generalized anxiety disorder and prediction of treatment response. *American Journal of Psychiatry, 166*, 302–310.

Nixon, R. D. V., Sweeney, L., Erickson, D. B., & Touyz, S. W. (2004). Parent-child interaction therapy: One-and two-year follow-up of standard and abbreviated treatments for oppositional preschoolers. *Journal of Abnormal Child Psychology, 32*, 263–271.

Nock, M. K., Borges, G., Bromet, E. J., Cha, C. B., Kessler, R. C., & Lee, S. (2008). Suicide and suicidal behavior. *Epidemiologic Reviews, 30*, 133–154.

Nock, M. K., & Ferriter, C. (2005). Parent management of attendance and adherence in child and adolescent therapy: A conceptual and empirical review. *Clinical Child and Family Psychology Review, 8*, 149–166.

Nolen-Hoeksema, S., Girgus, J. S., & Seligman, M. E. (1992). Predictors and consequences of childhood depressive symptoms: A 5-year longitudinal study. *Journal of Abnormal Psychology, 101*, 405–422.

Nolen-Hoeksema, S., & Larson, J. (1999). *Coping with loss.* Mahwah, NJ: Erlbaum.

Norcross, J. C. (2010). The therapeutic relationship. In M. A. Hubble, B. L. Duncan, & S. D. Miller (Eds.), *The heart and soul of change: What works in therapy* (pp. 113–142). Washington, DC: American Psychological Association.

Northoff, G., Heinzel, A., de Greck, M., Bermpohl, F., Dobrowolny, H., & Panksepp, J. (2006). Self-referential processing in our brain: Meta-analysis of imaging studies on the self. *Neuroimage, 31*, 440–457.

Novaco, R. W. (1975). *Anger control: The development and evaluation of an experimental treatment.* Lexington, MA: Heath.

Oaten, M., & Cheng, K. (2006). Improved self-control: The benefits of a regular program of academic study. *Basic and Applied Social Psychology, 28*, 1–16.

Oaten, M., & Cheng, K. (2007). Improvements in self-control from financial monitoring. *Journal of Economic Psychology, 28*, 487–501.

Oatley, K. (2011). *Such stuff as dreams: The psychology of fiction.* Hoboken, NJ: Wiley.

Ochsner, K. N., & Gross, J. J. (2005). The cognitive control of emotion. *Trends in Cognitive Sciences, 9*, 242–249.

Ochsner, K. N., & Gross, J. J. (2008). Cognitive emotion regulation: Insights from social cognitive and affective neuroscience. *Current Directions in Psychological Science, 17*, 153–158.

O'Connell, B. (2012). *Solution-focused therapy.* Thousand Oaks, CA: SAGE.

O'Connor, L. E., Berry, J. W., & Weiss, J. (1999). Interpersonal guilt, shame, and psychological problems. *Journal of Social and Clinical Psychology, 18*, 181–203.

O'Hanlon, B. (2000). *Do one thing different: And other uncommonly sensible solutions to life's persistent problems.* New York, NY: HarperCollins.

O'Hanlon, B., & Beadle, S. (1997). *A guide to possibility land: Fifty-one methods for doing brief, respectful therapy*. New York, NY: Norton.

O'Hanlon, B., & Weiner-Davis, M. (2003). *In search of solutions: A new direction in psychotherapy* (Rev. ed.). New York, NY: Norton.

Olson, S. L., Lopez-Duran, N., Lunkenheimer, E. S., Chang, H., & Sameroff, A. J. (2011). Individual differences in the development of early peer aggression: Integrating contributions of self-regulation, theory of mind, and parenting. *Development and Psychopathology, 23*, 253–266.

Olweus, D. (1993). *Bullying at school: What we know and what we can do*. Cambridge, MA: Blackwell.

Olweus, D., & Limber, S. P. (2010). The Olweus Bullying Prevention Program: Implementation and evaluation over two decades. In S. R. Jimerson, S. M. Swearer, & D. L. Espelage (Eds.), *New handbook of bullying in schools: An international perspective* (pp. 377–401). York, NY: Routledge/Taylor & Francis.

O'Neil, K. A., Brodman, D. M., Cohen, J. S., Edmunds, J. M., & Kendall, P. C. (2012). Childhood anxiety disorders: The Coping Cat Program. In E. Szigethy, J. R. Weisz, & R. L. Findling (Eds.), *Cognitive-behavior therapy for children and adolescents* (pp. 227–261). Arlington, VA: American Psychiatric Association.

Opree, S. J., Buijzen, M., & Valkenburg, P. M. (2012). Lower life satisfaction related to materialism in children frequently exposed to advertising. *Pediatrics, 130*, 486–491.

Organista, K. C. (2006). Cognitive-behavioral therapy with Latinos and Latinas. In P. A. Hays & G. Y. Iwamasa (Eds.), *Culturally responsive cognitive-behavioral therapy: Assessment, practice, and supervision* (pp. 73–96). Washington, DC: American Psychological Association.

Orlinsky, D. E., Grave, K., & Parks, B. K. (1994). Process and outcome in psychotherapy – Noch einmal. In A. E. Bergin & S. L. Garfield (Eds.), *Handbook of psychotherapy and behavior change* (pp. 257–310). New York, NY: Wiley.

Orth, U., & Robins, R. W. (2013). Understanding the link between low self-esteem and depression. *Current Directions in Psychological Science, 22*, 455–460.

Oshio, A. (2009). Development and validation of the Dichotomous Thinking Inventory. *Social Behavior and Personality: An International Journal, 37*, 729–741.

Overholser, J. C. (1993). Elements of the Socratic method: I. *Systematic questioning. Psychotherapy, 30*, 67–74.

Overholser, J. C. (2010). Psychotherapy according to the Socratic method: Integrating ancient philosophy with contemporary cognitive therapy. *Journal of Cognitive Psychotherapy, 24*, 354–363.

Overholser, J. C. (2013). Guided discovery: Problem-solving therapy integrated within the Socratic method. *Journal of Contemporary Psychotherapy, 43*, 73–82.

Owen, J. J., Tao, K., Leach, M. M., & Rodolfa, E. (2011). Clients' perceptions of their psychotherapists' multicultural orientation. *Psychotherapy, 48*, 274–282.

Padesky, C. A. (1994). Schema change processes in cognitive therapy. *Clinical Psychology and Psychotherapy, 1*, 267–278.

Padesky, C. A., & Greenberger, D. (1995). *Clinician's guide to mind over mood*. New York, NY: Guilford Press.

Pantalone, D. W., Iwamasa, G. Y., & Martell, C. R. (2010). Cognitive-behavioral therapy with diverse populations. In K. S. Dobson (Ed.), *Handbook of cognitive-behavioral therapies* (3rd ed., pp. 445–464). New York, NY: Guilford Press.

Pardini, D. A., Fite, P. J., & Burke, J. D. (2008). Bidirectional associations between parenting practices and conduct problems in boys from childhood to adolescence: The moderating effect of age and African-American ethnicity. *Journal of Abnormal Child Psychology, 36,* 647–662.

Pardini, D. A., Lochman, J. E., & Powell, N. (2007). The development of callous-unemotional traits and antisocial behavior in children: Are there shared and/or unique predictors? *Journal of Clinical Child and Adolescent Psychology, 36,* 319–333.

Parens, H. (1993). Rage toward self and others in early childhood. In R. A. Glick, & S. P. Roose (Eds.), *Rage, power, and aggression* (pp. 123–147). New Haven, CT: Yale University Press.

Pargament, K. I. (1997). *The psychology of religion and coping: Theory, research, practice.* New York, NY: Guilford Press.

Parham, T. A., Ajamu, A., & White, J. L. (2011). *The psychology of Blacks: Centering our perspectives in the African consciousness.* Boston, MA: Prentice Hall.

Park-Taylor, J., Ventura, A. B., & Ng, V. (2009). Multicultural counseling and assessment with children. In J. G. Ponterotto, J. M. Casas, L. A. Suzuki, & C. M. Alexander (Eds.), *Handbook of multicultural counseling* (3rd ed., pp. 621–636). Thousand Oaks, CA: SAGE.

Parsons, B. V., & Alexander, J. F. (1973). Short-term family intervention: A therapy outcome study. *Journal of Consulting and Clinical Psychology, 41,* 195–201.

Passamonti, L., Fairchild, G., Goodyer, I., Hurford, G., Hagan, C., Rowe, J., & Calder, A. (2010). Neural abnormalities in early-onset and adolescence-onset conduct disorder. *Archives of General Psychiatry, 67,* 729–738.

Passer, M. W. (1983). Fear of failure, fear of evaluation, perceived competence, and self-esteem in competitive-trait-anxious children. *Journal of Sport Psychology, 5,* 172–188.

Patterson, G. R. (1982). *Coercive family process.* Eugene, OR: Castalia.

Patterson, G. R., & Chamberlain, P. (1994). A functional analysis of resistance during parent-training therapy. *Clinical Psychology: Science and Practice, 1,* 53–70.

Patterson, G. R., Dishion, T. J., & Chamberlain, P. (1993). Outcomes and methodological issues relating to treatment of antisocial children. In T. R. Giles (Ed.), *Handbook of effective psychotherapy* (pp. 43–88). New York, NY: Plenum Press.

Patterson, G. R., Reid, J. B., & Dishion, T. J. (1992). *Antisocial boys.* Eugene, OR: Castalia.

Patterson, J., Williams, L., Edwards, T. M., Chamow, L., & Grauf-Grounds, C. (2009). *Essential skills in family therapy: From the first interview to termination* (2nd ed.). New York, NY: Guilford Press.

Pavlov, I. P. (1927). *Conditioned reflexes: An investigation of the physiological activity of the cerebral cortex* (G. V. Annep, Ed. & Trans.). London, UK: Oxford University Press.

Payne, M. (2005). *Narrative therapy* (2nd ed.). London, UK: SAGE.

Pearlman, M. Y., Schwalbe, K. D., & Cloitre, M. (2010). *Grief in childhood: Fundamentals of treatment in clinical practice.* Washington, DC: American Psychological Association.

Pedersen, P. B., & Pope, M. (2010). Inclusive cultural empathy for successful global leadership. *American Psychologist, 65,* 841–854.

Pedro-Carroll, J. L. (2005). Fostering resilience in the aftermath of divorce: The role of evidence-based programs for children. *Family Court Review, 43,* 52–64.

Pedro-Carroll, J. L. (2010). *Putting children first: Proven parenting strategies for helping children thrive through divorce.* New York, NY: Avery/Penguin.

Pedro-Carroll, J. L., & Jones, S. (2004). A play-based intervention to foster resilience in the aftermath of divorce. In L. Reddy, C. E. Schaefer, & T. Hall (Eds.), *Empirically-based play interventions for children* (pp. 51–75). Washington, DC: American Psychological Association.

Pedro-Carroll, J. L., Sutton, S. E., & Wyman, P. A. (1999). A two-year follow-up evaluation of a preventive intervention for young children of divorce. *School Psychology Review, 28,* 467–476.

Pelham, W. E., & Fabiano, G. A. (2008). Evidence-based psychosocial treatments for attention-deficit/hyperactivity disorder. *Journal of Clinical Child and Adolescent Psychology, 37,* 184–214.

Pelham, W. E., & Waschbusch, D. A. (1999). Behavioural intervention in attention-deficit/hyperactivity disorder. In H. C. Quay & A. E. Hogan (Eds.), *Handbook of disruptive behavior disorders* (pp. 255–278). New York, NY: Kluwer Academic.

Pennebaker, J. W., & Seagal, J. D. (1999). Forming a story: The health benefits of narrative. *Journal of Clinical Psychology, 55,* 1243–1254.

Perez-Edgar, K., & Fox, N. A. (2005). Temperament and anxiety disorders. *Child and Adolescent Psychiatric Clinics of North America, 14,* 681–706.

Persons, J. B. (2008). *The case formulation approach to cognitive-behavior therapy.* New York, NY: Guilford Press.

Peterson, C., & Seligman, M. E. P. (2004). *Character strengths and virtues: A handbook and classification.* New York, NY: Oxford University Press.

Pfeffer, C. R. (2003). Assessing suicidal behavior in children and adolescents. In R. J. King & A. Apter (Eds.), *Suicide in children and adolescents* (pp. 294–312). New York, NY: Cambridge University Press.

Pfiffner, L. J., & McBurnett, K. (1997). Social skills training with parent generalization: Treatment effects for children with attention deficit disorder. *Journal of Consulting and Clinical Psychology, 65,* 749–757.

Phelan, T. W. (2014). *1-2-3 magic: Effective discipline for children 2–12* (5th ed.). Glen Ellyn, IL: Parent Magic.

Piacentini, J., Bennett, S., Compton, S. N., Kendall, P. C., Birmaher, B., Albano, A. M., … Walkup, J. (2014). 24- and 36-week outcomes for the Child/Adolescent Anxiety Multimodal Study (CAMS). *Journal of the American Academy of Child and Adolescent Psychiatry, 53,* 297–310.

Pierre, M. R., & Mahilik, J. R. (2005). Examining African self-consciousness and Black racial identity as predictors of Black men's psychological well-being. *Cultural Diversity andn Ethnic Minority Psychology, 11,* 28–40.

Pina, A. A., Silverman, W. K., Fuentes, R. M., Kurtines, W. M., & Weems, C. F. (2003). Exposure-based cognitive-behavioral treatment for phobic and anxiety disorders: Treatment effects and maintenance for Hispanic/Latino relative to European-American youths. *Journal of the American Academy of Child & Adolescent Psychiatry, 42,* 1179–1187.

Pincus, D. B., Chase, R. M., Chow, C., Weiner, C. L., & Pian, J. (2011). Integrating play into cognitive-behavioral therapy for child anxiety disorders. In S. W. Russ & L. N. Niec (Eds.), *Play in clinical practice: Evidence-based approaches* (pp. 218–235). New York, NY: Guilford Press.

Pinker, S. (2002). *The blank slate: The modern denial of human nature.* New York, NY: Penguin.

Pinker, S. (2009). *How the mind works.* New York, NY: Norton.

Pisterman, S., McGrath, P., Firestone, P., Goodman, J. T., Webster, I., & Mallory, R. (1989). Outcome of parent-mssssiated treatment of preschoolers with attention deficit disorder with hyperactivity. *Journal of Consulting and Clinical Psychology, 57,* 628–635.

Plomin, R., DeFries, J. C., Knopik, V. S., Jenae M., & Neiderhiser, J. M. (2012). *Behavioral genetics.* Duffield, UK: Worth.

Polman, H., de Castro, B. O., Koops, W., van Boxtel, H. W., & Merk, W. W. (2007). A meta-analysis of the distinction between reactive and proactive aggression in children and adolescence. *Journal of Abnormal Child Psychology, 35,* 522–535.

Pomerantz, E. M., & Kempner, S. G. (2013). Mothers' daily person and process praise: Implications for children's theory of intelligence and motivation. *Developmental Psychology, 49,* 2040–2046.

Pope, S. T., & Jones, R. S. P. (1996). The therapeutic effect of reactive self-monitoring on the reduction of inappropriate social and stereotypic behaviors. *British Journal of Clinical Psychology, 35,* 585–594.

Post, B. C., & Wade, N. G. (2009). Religion and spirituality in psychotherapy: A practice-friendly review of research. *Journal of Clinical Psychology, 65,*131–146.

Powell, N. P., Boxmeyer, C. L., Baden, R., Stromeyer, S., Minney, J. A., Mushtaq, A., & Lochman, J. E. (2011). Assessing and treating aggression and conduct problems in schools: Implications from the Coping Power program. *Psychology in the Schools, 48,* 233–242.

Preskorn, S. H., Ross, R., & Stanga, C. Y. (2004). Selective serotonin reuptake inhibitors. In S. H. Preskorn, H. P. Feighner, C. Y. Stanga, & R. Ross (Eds.), *Antidepressants: Past, present and future* (pp. 241–262). Berlin: Springer.

Preston, S. D., & Hofelich, A. J. (2012). The many faces of empathy: Parsing empathic phenomena through a proximate, dynamic-systems view of representing the other in the self. *Emotion Review, 4,* 24–33.

Prigerson, H. G. (2004). Complicated grief: When the path of adjustment leads to a dead-end. *Bereavement Care, 23,* 38–40.

Prinstein, M. J., Borelli, J. C., Cheah, C. S. L., Simon, V. A., & Aikins, J. W. (2005). Adolescent girls' interpersonal vulnerability to depressive symptoms: A longitudinal examination of reassurance-seeking and peer relationships. *Journal of Abnormal Psychology, 114,* 676–688.

Prochaska, J. O., DiClemente, C. C., & Norcross, J. C. (1992). In search of how people change: Applications to addictive behaviors. *American Psychologist, 47,* 1102–1114.

Prochaska, J. O., & Norcross, J. C. (2010). *Systems of psychotherapy: A transtheoretical analysis* (7th ed.). Belmont, CA: Brooks/Cole.

Prothrow-Stith, D. (1987). *Violence prevention curriculum for adolescents.* Newton, MA: Education Development Center.

Prouty, G. (1994). *Theoretical evolutions in person-centered/experiential therapy.* Westport, CT: Praeger.

Putallaz, M., & Wasserman, A. (1990). Children's entry behavior. In S. R. Asher & J. D. Coie (Eds.), *Peer rejection in childhood* (pp. 60–89). New York, NY: Cambridge University Press.

Quinn, M. M., Kavale, K. A., Mathur, S. R., Rutherford, R. B., Jr., & Forness, S. R. (1999). A meta-analysis of social skill interventions for students with emotional or behavioral disorders. *Journal of Emotional and Behavioral Disorders, 7,* 54–65.

Raine, A. (2011). An amygdala structural abnormality common to two subtypes of conduct disorder: A neurodevelopmental conundrum. *American Journal of Psychiatry, 168,* 569–571.

Raine, A. (2013). *The anatomy of violence: The biological roots of crime.* New York, NY: Random House.

Raine, A., Buchsbaum, M. S., & LaCasse, L. (1997). Brain abnormalities in murderers indicated by positron emission tomography. *Biological Psychiatry, 42,* 495–508.

Raine, A., Dodge, K. A., Loeber, R., Gatzke-Kopp, L., Lynam, D., Reynolds, C., ... Liu, J. (2006). The reactive-proactive aggression questionnaire: Differential correlates of reactive and proactive aggression in adolescent boys. *Aggressive Behavior, 32,* 159–171.

Rao, U., Chen, L., Bidesi, A., Shad, M., Thomas, M., & Hammen, C. (2010). Hippocampal changes associated with early-life adversity and vulnerability to depression. *Biological Psychiatry, 67,* 357–364.

Rao, U., Hammen, C., & Daley, S. (1999). Continuity of depression during the transition to adulthood: A 5-year longitudinal study of young women. *Journal of the American Academy of Child and Adolescent Psychiatry, 38,* 908–915.

Rapee, R. M., Lyneham, H. J., Schniering, C. A., Wuthrich, V., Abbott, M., Hudson, J., & Wignall, A. (2006). *Cool Kids Child and Adolescent Anxiety Program therapist manual.* Sydney: Centre for Emotional Health, Macquarie University.

Rapee, R. M., Wignall, A., Hudson, J. L., & Schniering, C. A. (2000). *Evidence-based treatment of child and adolescent anxiety disorders.* Oakland, CA: New Harbinger.

Raposa, E. B., Hammen, C. K., & Brennan, P. A. (2011). Effects of child psychopathology on maternal depression: The mediating role of child-related acute and chronic stressors. *Journal of Abnormal Child Psychology, 39,* 1177–1186.

Rathus, J. H., & Miller, A. L. (2000). DBT for adolescents: Dialectical dilemmas and secondary treatment targets. *Cognitive and Behavioral Practice, 7,* 425–434.

Rathus, J. H., & Miller, A. L. (2002). Dialectical Behavior Therapy adapted for suicidal adolescents. *Suicide and Life-Threatening Behavior, 32,* 146–157.

Rathus, J. H., & Miller, A. L. (2014). *DBT skills manual for adolescents.* New York, NY: Guilford Press.

Redding, R. E. (2001). Sociopolitical diversity in psychology: The case for pluralism. *American Psychologist, 56,* 205–215.

Reid, J. B., Patterson, G. R., & Snyder, J. (2002). *Antisocial behavior in children and adolescents: A developmental analysis and model for intervention.* Washington, DC, US: American Psychological Association.

Reivich, K., Gillham, J. E., Chaplin, T. M., & Seligman, M. E. P. (2013). From helplessness to optimism: The role of resilience in treating and preventing depression in youth. In S. Goldstein & R. B. Brooks (Eds.), *Handbook of resilience in children* (2nd ed., pp. 201–214). New York, NY: Springer Science.

Rejani, T. G., Oommen, A., Srinath, S., & Kapur, M. (2012). Efficacy of multimodal intervention for children with attention deficit hyperactivity disorder (ADHD): An Indian study. *Journal of Behavioral and Brain Sciences, 2,* 117–127.

Resick, P. A., & Calhoun, K. S. (2001). Postraumatic stress disorder. In D. H. Barlow (Ed.), *Clinical handbook of psychological disorders: A step-by-step treatment manual* (pp. 60–113). New York, NY: Guilford Press.

Reyno, S. M., & McGrath, P. J. (2006). Predictors of parent training efficacy for child externalizing behavior problem--a meta-analytic review. *Journal of Child Psychology and Psychiatry, 47*, 99–111.

Reynolds, S., Wilson, C., Austin, J., & Hooper, L. (2012). Effects of psychotherapy for anxiety in children and adolescents: A meta-analytic review. *Clinical Psychology Review, 32*, 251–262.

Reynolds, W. M., & Coats, K. I. (1986). A comparison of cognitive-behavioral therapy and relaxation training for the treatment of depression in adolescents. *Journal of Consulting and Clinical Psychology, 54*, 653–660.

Ricci, M. C. (2013). *Mindsets in the classroom: Building a culture of success and student achievement in school.* Waco, TX: Prufrock.

Rice, K. G., Ashby, J. S., & Gilman, R. (2011). Classifying adolescent perfectionists. *Psychological Assessment, 23*, 563–577.

Rice, N., & O'Donohue, W. (2002). Cultural sensitivity: A critical examination. *New Ideas in Psychology, 20*, 35–48.

Richardson, T. Q., Bethea, A. R., Hayling, C. C., & Williamson-Taylor, C. (2009). African and Afro-Caribbean American identity development: Implications for theory and practice. In J. G. Ponterotto, J. M. Casas, L. A. Suzuki, & C. M. Alexander (Eds.), *Handbook of multicultural counseling* (3rd ed., pp. 227–240). Thousand Oaks, CA: SAGE.

Rickel, A. U., & Brown, R. T. (2007). *Attention-deficit/hyperactivity disorder in children and adults.* Ashland, OH, US: Hogrefe & Huber Publishers.

Ridley, C. R., Mollen, D., & Kelly, S. M. (2011). Beyond microskills: Toward a model of counseling competence. *Counseling Psychologist, 39*, 825–864.

Rienzo, B. A., Button, J. W., Sheu, J-J., & Li, Y. (2006). The politics of sexual orientation issues in American schools. *Journal of School Health, 76*, 93–97.

Rigazio-DiGilio, S. A., & McDowell, T. (2013). Family therapy. In J. Frew & M. D. Spiegler (Eds.), *Contemporary psychotherapies for a diverse world* (pp. 415–458). New York, NY: Routledge/Taylor & Francis.

Riley, A. R., & Gaynor, S. T. (2014). Identifying mechanisms of change: Utilizing single-participant methodology to better understand behavior therapy for child depression. *Behavior Modification, 38*, 636–664.

Rinsley, D. (1980). *Treatment of the severely disturbed adolescent.* New York, NY: Aronson.

Ritschel, L. A., Ramirez, C. L., Jones, M., & Craighead, W. E. (2011). Behavioral activation for depressed teens: A pilot study. *Cognitive and Behavioral Practice, 18*, 281–299.

Rizvi, S. L., Steffel, L. M., & Carson-Wong, A. (2013). An overview of dialectical behavior therapy for professional psychologists. *Professional Psychology: Research and Practice, 44*, 73–80.

Robin, A. L. (1981). A controlled evaluation of problem-solving communication training with parent-adolescent conflict. *Behavior Therapy, 12*, 593–609.

Robin, A. L., & Foster, S. L. (1989). *Negotiating parent-adolescent conflict: A behavioral-family systems approach.* New York, NY: Guilford Press.

Robbins, M. S., Alexander, J. F., Newell, R. M., & Turner, C. W. (1996). The immediate effect of reframing on client attitude in family therapy. *Journal of Family Psychology, 10*, 28–34.

Robbins, M. S., Alexander, J. F., & Turner, C. W. (2000). Disrupting defensive family interactions in family therapy with delinquent adolescents. *Journal of Family Psychology, 14*, 688–701.

Robbins, M. S., Horigian, V., Szapocznik, J., & Ucha, J. (2010). Treating Hispanic youths using brief strategic family therapy. In J. R. Weisz & A. E. Kazdin (Eds.), *Evidence-based psychotherapies for children and adolescents* (2nd ed., pp. 375–390). New York, NY: Guilford Press.

Rogers, C. R. (1951). *Client-centered therapy*. Boston, MA: Houghton Mifflin.

Rogers, C. R. (1957). The necessary and sufficient conditions for psychotherapeutic personality change. *Journal of Consulting Psychology, 21*, 95–103.

Rohde, P., Lewinsohn, P. M., Clarke, G. N., Hops, H., & Seeley, J. R. (2005). The adolescent coping with depression course: A cognitive-behavioral approach to the treatment of adolescent depression. In E. D. Hibbs & P. S. Jensen (Eds.), *Psychosocial treatments for child and adolescent disorders: Empirically based strategies for clinical practice* (2nd ed., pp. 219–237). Washington, DC: American Psychological Association.

Rohde, P., Lewinsohn, P. M., Klein, D. N., Seeley, J. R., & Gau, J. M. (2013). Key characteristics of major depressive disorder in childhood, adolescence, emerging adulthood, and adulthood. *Clinical Psychological Science, 1*, 41–53.

Romero, C., Master, A., Paunesku, D., Dweck, C. S., & Gross, J. J. (2014). Academic and emotional functioning in middle school: The role of implicit theories. *Emotion, 14*, 227–234.

Rosengren, D. B. (2009). *Building motivational interviewing skills*. New York, NY: Guilford Press.

Rossello, J., & Bernal, G. (1999). The efficacy of cognitive-behavioral and interpersonal treatments for depression in Puerto Rican adolescents. *Journal of Consulting and Clinical Psychology, 67*, 734–745.

Rossello, J., & Bernal, G. (2005). New developments in cognitive-behavioral and interpersonal treatments for depressed Puerto Rican adolescents. In E. D. Hibbs & P. S. Jensen (Eds.), *Psychosocial treatments for child and adolescent disorders: Empirically based strategies for clinical practice* (2nd ed., pp. 187–217). Washington, DC: American Psychological Association.

Rothbart, M. K., & Posner, M. I. (2006). Temperament, attention, and developmental psychopathology. In D. Cicchetti & D. J. Cohen (Eds.), *Developmental psychopathology: Vol. 2. Developmental neuroscience* (2nd ed., pp. 465–501). Hoboken, NJ: Wiley.

Rothbaum, F., Weisz, J., & Snyder, S. (1982). Changing the world and changing the self: A two-process model of perceived control. *Journal of Personality and Social Psychology, 42*, 5–37.

Rowland, M. R., Halliday-Boykins, C. A., Henggeler, S. W., Cunningham, P. B., Lee, T. G., Kruesi, M. J. P., & Shapiro, S. B. (2005). A randomized trial of multisystemic therapy with Hawaii's Felix Class youths. *Journal of Emotional and Behavioral Disorders, 13*, 13–23.

Russ, S. W. (2004). *Play in child development and psychotherapy: Toward empirically supported practice*. Mahwah, NJ: Erlbaum.

Russ, S. W., Fiorelli, J., & Spannagel, S. C. (2011). Cognitive and affective processes in play. In S. W. Russ & L. N. Niec (Eds.), *Play in clinical practice: Evidence-based approaches* (pp. 3–22). New York, NY: Guilford Press.

Rutherford, R. B., Quinn, M. M., & Mathur, S. R. (1996). *Effective strategies for teaching appropriate behaviors to children with emotional and behavioral disorders*. Reston, VA: Council for Children with Behavioral Disorders.

Rutter, J. G., & Friedberg, R. D. (1999). Guidelines for the effective use of Socratic dialogue in cognitive therapy. In L. VandeCreek, S. Knapp, & T. L. Jackson (Eds.),

Innovations in clinical practice: A sourcebook (Vol. 17, pp. 481–490). Sarasota, FL: Professional Resource Press.

Saez-Santiago, E., & Bernal, G. (2003). Depression in ethnic minorities: Latinos and Latinas, African Americans, and Native Americans. In G. Bernal, J. E. Trimble, & F. T. L. Leong (Eds.), *Handbook of racial and ethnic minority psychology* (vol. 4, pp. 401–428). Thousand Oaks, CA: SAGE.

Salmivalli, C., & Peets, K. (2009). Bullies, victims, and bully-victim relationships in middle childhood and early adolescence. In K. H. Rubin, W. M. Bukowski, & B. Laursen (Eds.), *Handbook of peer interactions, relationships and groups* (pp. 322–335). New York, NY: Guilford Press.

Salter, E., & Stallard, P. (2004). Posttraumatic growth in child survivors of a road traffic accident. *Journal of Traumatic Stress, 17*, 335–340.

Sánchez-Meca, J., Rosa-Alcázar, A. I., & López-Soler, C. (2011). The psychological treatment of sexual abuse in children and adolescents: A meta-analysis. *International Journal of Clinical and Health Psychology, 11*, 67–93.

Sandler, I. N., Ayers, T. S., Wolchik, S. A., Tein, J.-Y., Kwok, O.-M., Haine, R. A., ... Griffin, W. A. (2003). The family bereavement program: Efficacy evaluation of a theory-based prevention program for parentally bereaved children and adolescents. *Journal of Consulting and Clinical Psychology, 71*, 587–600.

Sandler, I. N., Ma, Y., Tein, J.-Y., Ayers, T. S., Wolchik, S., Kennedy, C., & Millsap, R. (2010). Long-term effects of the family bereavement program on multiple indicators of grief in parentally bereaved children and adolescents. *Journal of Consulting and Clinical Psychology, 78*, 131–143.

Santisteban, D. A., Coatsworth, J. D., Perez-Vidal, A., Kurtines, W. M., Schwartz, S. J., LaPerriere, A., & Szapocznik, J. (2003). The efficacy of Brief Strategic Family Therapy in modifying Hispanic adolescent behavior problems and substance use. *Journal of Family Psychology, 17*, 121–133.

Santisteban, D. A., Mena, M. P., & Abalo, C. (2013). Bridging diversity and family systems: Culturally informed and flexible family-based treatment for Hispanic adolescents. *Couple and Family Psychology: Research and Practice, 2*, 246–263.

Santisteban, D. A., Muir, J. A., Mena, M. P., & Mitrani, V. B. (2003). Integrative borderline adolescent family therapy: Meeting the challenges of treating adolescents with borderline personality disorder. *Psychotherapy: Theory, Research, Practice, Training, 40*, 251–264.

Santisteban, D. A., Perez-Vidal, A. Coatsworth, J. D., Kurtines, W. M., Schwartz, S. J., Arthur LaPerriere, A., & Szapocznik, J. (2003). Efficacy of brief strategic family therapy in modifying Hispanic adolescent behavior problems and substance use. *Journal of Family Psychology, 17*, 121–133.

Satir, V. M. (1967). *Conjoint family therapy.* Palo Alto, CA: Science and Behavior Books.

Satir, V. M. (1972). *Peoplemaking.* Palo Alto, CA: Science and Behavior Books.

Schaeffer, C. M., & Borduin, C. M. (2005). Long-term follow-up to a randomized clinical trial of multisystemic therapy with serious and violent juvenile offenders. *Journal of Consulting and Clinical Psychology, 73*, 445–453.

Schafer, R. (1983). *The analytic attitude.* New York, NY: Basic Books.

Scharff, D. E., & Scharff, J. S. (1987). *Object relations family therapy.* Northvale, NJ: Aronson.

Schniering, C. A., & Rapee, R. M. (2004). The relationship between automatic thoughts and negative emotions in children and adolescents: A test of the cognitive content-specificity hypothesis. *Journal of Abnormal Psychology, 113*, 464–470.

Schofield, W. (1964). *Psychotherapy: The purchase of friendship*. Englewood Cliffs, NJ: Prentice Hall.

Schonert-Reichl, K. A., Smith, V., Zaidman-Zait, A., & Hertzman, C. (2012). Promoting children's prosocial behaviors in school: Impact of the 'Roots of Empathy' program on the social and emotional competence of school-aged children. *School Mental Health, 4*, 1–21.

Schor, J. B. (2005). *Born to buy: The commercialized child and the new consumer culture*. New York: Scribner.

Schottenbauer, M. A., Glass, C. R., Arnkoff, D. B., & Gray, S. H. (2008). Contributions of psychodynamic approaches to treatment of PTSD and trauma: A review of the empirical treatment and psychopathology literature. *Psychiatry: Interpersonal and Biological Processes, 71*, 13–34.

Schwartz, C. E., Wright, C. I., Shin, L. M., Kagan, J., & Rauch, S. L. (2003). Inhibited and uninhibited infants "grown up": Adult amygdalar response to novelty. *Science, 300*, 1952–1953.

Scott, D. (2011). Coming out: Intrapersonal loss in the acquisition of a stigmatized identity. Retrieved from www.yourtherapist.org/www/wp-contentuploads/coming_out .pdf

Seaton, E. K., Caldwell, C. H., Sellers, R. M., & Jackson, J. S. (2011). An intersectional approach for understanding perceived discrimination and psychological well-being among African American and Caribbean Black youth. *Developmental Psychology, 46*, 1372–1379.

Sekaquaptewa, D., Espinoza, P., Thompson, M., Vargas, P., & von Hippel, W. (2003). Stereotypic explanatory bias: Implicit stereotyping as a predictor of discrimination. *Journal of Experimental Social Psychology, 39*, 75–82.

Selekman, M. D. (2010). *Collaborative brief therapy with children*. New York, NY: Guilford Press.

Seligman, M. E. P., Reivich, K., Jaycox, L., & Gillham, J. (1995). *The optimistic child*. Boston, MA: Houghton Mifflin.

Sells, S. (2009). Parenting with love and limits. In A. R. Roberts (Ed.), *Social workers' desk reference* (2nd ed., pp. 457–467). New York, NY: Oxford University Press.

Sells, S. P. (2004). *Treating the tough adolescent: A family-based, step-by-step guide*. New York, NY: Guilford Press.

Sells, S. P., Winokur-Early, K., & Smith, T. E. (2011). Reducing adolescent oppositional and conduct disorders: An experimental design using parenting with love and limits. *Professional Issues in Criminal Justice, 6*, 9–30.

Semple, R., & Lee, J. (2011). *Mindfulness-based cognitive therapy for anxious children: A manual for treating childhood anxiety*. Oakland, CA: New Harbinger.

Semple, R., Lee, J., Rosa, D., & Miller, L. F. (2010). A randomized trial of mindfulness-based cognitive therapy for children: Promoting mindful attention to enhance social-emotional resiliency in children. *Journal of Child and Family Studies, 19*, 218–229.

Sexton, T. (2011). *Functional family therapy in clinical practice: An evidence-based treatment model for working with troubled adolescents*. New York, NY: Routledge/ Taylor.

Sexton, T., & Turner, C. W. (2010). The effectiveness of functional family therapy for youth with behavioral problems in a community practice setting. *Journal of Family Psychology, 24,* 339–348.

Sexton, T., & Turner, C. W. (2011). The effectiveness of functional family therapy for youth with behavioral problems in a community practice setting. *Couple and Family Psychology: Research and Practice, 1,* 3–15.

Shadish, W. R., & Baldwin, S. A. (2003). Meta-analysis of MFT interventions. *Journal of Marital and Family Therapy, 29,* 547–570.

Shafranske, E. P. (2013). Addressing religiousness and spirituality in psychotherapy: Advancing evidence-based practice. In R. F. Paloutzian & C. L. Park (Eds.), *Handbook of the psychology of religion and spirituality* (2nd ed., pp. 595–616). New York, NY: Guilford Press.

Shamsie, J. (1981). Antisocial adolescents: Our treatments do not work—Where do we go from here? *Canadian Journal of Psychiatry, 26,* 357–364.

Shapiro, J. P. (1995). Attribution-based treatment of self-blame and helplessness in sexually abused children. *Psychotherapy: Theory, Research, Practice, Training, 32,* 581–591.

Shapiro, J. P. (1998). Psychotherapeutic utilization of prevention education in treatment for sexually abused children. *Journal of Child Sexual Abuse, 7,* 105–122.

Shapiro, J. P. (2003). *Peacemakers: A violence prevention program.* Bloomington, IN: National Educational Service.

Shapiro, J. P. (2009). Integrating outcome research and clinical reasoning in psychotherapy planning. *Professional Psychology: Research and Practice, 40,* 46–53.

Shapiro, J. P. (2011, September 23). Class warfare. War on business. War on teachers. War in America? *Christian Science Monitor.* Retrieved from http://www.csmonitor.com/Commentary/Opinion/2011/0923/Class-warfare.-War-on-teachers.-War-on-business.-War-in-America

Shapiro, J. P., Burgoon, J. D., Welker, C. J., & Clough, J. B. (2002). Evaluation of the Peacemakers Program: School-based violence prevention for students in grades four through eight. *Psychology in the Schools, 39,* 87–100.

Shapiro, J. P., Dorman, R. L., Burkey, W. M., & Welker, C. J. (1999). Predictors of job satisfaction and burnout in child abuse professionals: Coping, cognition, and victimization history. *Journal of Child Sexual Abuse, 7,* 23–42.

Shapiro, J. P., Dorman, R. L., Burkey, W. M., Welker, C. J., & Clough, J. B. (1997). Development and factor analysis of a measure of youth attitudes toward guns and violence. *Journal of Clinical Child Psychology, 26,* 311–320.

Shapiro, J. P., Welker, C. J., & Jacobson, B. J. (1997). A naturalistic study of psychotherapeutic methods and client in-therapy functioning in a child community setting. *Journal of Clinical Child Psychology, 26,* 385–396.

Shapiro, L. (2008). *Learning to listen, learning to care: A workbook to help kids learn self-control and empathy.* Oakland, CA: Instant Help.

Shedler, J. (2010). The efficacy of psychodynamic psychotherapy. *American Psychologist, 65,* 98–109.

Shedler, J. (2011). Science or ideology? *American Psychologist, 66,* 152–154.

Shenk, C., & Fruzzetti, A. E. (2011). The impact of validating and invalidating responses on emotional reactivity. *Journal of Social and Clinical Psychology, 30,* 163–183.

Sherif, M. (1966). *In common predicament.* Boston, MA: Houghton Mifflin.

Sherry, J. L. (2007). Violent video games and aggression: Why can't we find effects? In R. W. Preiss, B. M. Gayle, N. Burrell, M. Allen, & J. Bryant (Eds.), *Mass media effects research: Advances through meta-analysis* (pp. 245–262). Mahwah, NJ: Erlbaum.

Shih, J. H., Abela, J. R. Z., & Starrs, C. (2009). Cognitive and interpersonal predictors of stress generation in children of affectively ill parents. *Journal of Abnormal Child Psychology, 37,* 195–208.

Shuman, A. L., & Shapiro, J. P. (2002). The effects of preparing parents for child psychotherapy on accuracy of expectations and treatment attendance. *Community Mental Health Journal, 38,* 3–16.

Shure, M. B. (1996). *Raising a thinking child: Help your young child to resolve everyday conflicts and get along with others.* New York, NY: Pocket Books.

Silberg, J. L., Maes, H., & Eaves, L. J. (2010). Genetic and environmental influences on the transmission of parental depression to children's depression and conduct disturbance: An extended Children of Twins study. *Journal of Child Psychology and Psychiatry, 51,* 734–744.

Silovsky, J. F., Swisher, L. M., Widdmeld, J., & Burris, L. (2012). Clinical considerations when children have problematic sexual behavior. In P. Goodyear-Brown (Ed.), *Handbook of child sexual abuse: Identification, assessment, and treatment* (pp. 401–428). Hoboken, NJ: Wiley.

Silver, E., Williams, A., Worthington, F., & Phillips, N. (1998). Family therapy and soiling: An audit of externalizing and other approaches. *Journal of Family Therapy, 20,* 413–422.

Silver, G., Shapiro, T., & Milrod, B. (2013). Treatment of anxiety in children and adolescents: Using child and adolescent anxiety psychodynamic psychotherapy. *Child and Adolescent Psychiatric Clinics of North America, 22,* 83–96.

Silver, R. L., Boon, C., & Stones, M. H. (1983). Searching for meaning in misfortune: Making sense of incest. *Journal of Social Issues, 39,* 81–102.

Skinner, B. F. (1938). *Behavior of organisms.* New York, NY: Appleton-Century-Crofts.

Skinner, B. F. (1953). *Science and human behavior.* New York, NY: Free Press.

Skinner, B. F. (1974). *About behaviorism.* Oxford, UK: Knopf.

Slaby, R. G., & Guerra, N. G. (1988). Cognitive mediators of aggression in adolescent offenders: I. Assessment. *Developmental Psychology, 24,* 580–588.

Smeets, K. C., Leeijen, A. A. M., Molen, M. J., Scheepers, F. E., Buitelaar, J. K., & Rommelse, N. N. J. (2014). Treatment moderators of cognitive behavior therapy to reduce aggressive behavior: A meta-analysis. *European Child & Adolescent Psychiatry, 24*(3), 255–264. doi:10.1007/s00787-014-0592-1

Smith, D., Wright, C., Allsopp, A., & Westhead, H. (2007). It's all in the mind: PETTLEP-based imagery in sports performance. *Journal of Applied Sport Psychology, 19,* 80–92.

Smith, H. A. (2012). En-training memoir slices. In R. A. Neimeyer (Ed.), *Techniques of grief therapy: Creative practices for counseling the bereaved* (pp. 237–240). New York, NY: Routledge.

Smith, J. C. (2007). The psychology of relaxation. In P. M. Lehrer, R. L. Woolfolk, & W. E. Sime (Eds.), *Principles and practice of stress management* (3rd ed., pp. 38–52). New York, NY: Guilford Press.

Smith, J. M., Alloy, J. B., & Abramson, L. Y. (2006). Cognitive vulnerability to depression, rumination, hopelessness, and suicidal ideation: Multiple pathways to self-injurious thinking. *Suicide and Life-Threatening Behavior, 36,* 443–454.

Smith, L. (2010). *Psychology, poverty, and the end of social exclusion.* New York, NY: Teachers College Press.

Smith, T. B., Bartz, J., & Richards, P. S. (2007). Outcomes of religious and spiritual adaptations to psychotherapy: A meta-analytic review. *Psychotherapy Research, 17,* 643–655.

Smith, T. B., Rodriguez, M. D., & Bernal, G. (2011). Culture. *Journal of Clinical Psychology: In Session, 67,* 166–175.

Smith, T. E., Sells, S. P., Rodman, J., & Reynolds, L. R. (2006). Reducing adolescent substance abuse and delinquency: Pilot research of a family-oriented psychoeducation curriculum. *Journal of Child and Adolescent Substance Abuse, 15,* 105–115.

Smith-Acuna, S. (2010). *Systems theory in action: Applications to individual, couple, and family therapy.* Hoboken, NJ: Wiley.

Smithmyer, C. M., Hubbard, J. A., & Simons, R. F. (2000). Proactive and reactive aggression in delinquent adolescents: Relations to aggression outcome expectancies. *Journal of Clinical Child Psychology, 29,* 86–93.

Snyder, C. R., Michael, S. T., & Cheavens, J. S. (1999). *Hope as a psychotherapeutic foundation of common factors, placebos, and expectancies.* In M. A. Hubble, B. L. Duncan, & S. D. Miller. *The heart and soul of change: What works in therapy.* Washington, DC: American Psychological Association.

Sonderegger, R., & Barrett, P. M. (2004). Assessment and treatment of ethnically diverse children and adolescents. In P. M. Barrett & T. H. Ollendick (Eds.), *Handbook of interventions that work with children and adolescents: Prevention and treatment* (pp. 89–112). Chichester, UK: Wiley.

Spear, L. (2009). *The behavioral neuroscience of adolescence.* New York, NY: Norton.

Speltz, M. L., DeKlyen, M., & Greenberg, M. T. (1999). Attachment in boys with early onset conduct problems. *Development and Psychopathology, 11,* 269–285.

Spence, S., Donovan, C., & Brechman-Toussaint, M. (1999). Social skills, social outcomes, and cognitive features of childhood social phobia. *Journal of Abnormal Child Psychology, 108,* 211–221.

Spence, S. H. (2003). Social skills training with children and young people: Theory, evidence and practice. *Child and Adolescent Mental Health, 8,* 84–96.

Spiegel, J. (2003). *Sexual abuse of males: The SAM model of theory and practice.* New York, NY: Brunner-Routledge.

Spiegler, M. D. (2013). Behavior therapy I: Traditional behavior therapy. In J. Frew & M. D. Spiegler (Eds.), *Contemporary psychotherapies for a diverse world* (pp. 259–300). New York, NY: Routledge/Taylor & Francis.

Spiegler, M. D., & Guevremont, D. C. (2010). *Contemporary behavior therapy* (5th ed.). Stamford, CT: Cengage.

Spirito, A., & Esposito, C. (2008). Evidence-based therapies for adolescent suicidal behavior. In R. Steele, D. Elkin, & M. Roberts (Eds.), *Handbook of evidence-based therapies for children and adolescents* (pp. 177–196). New York, NY: Springer.

Spirito, A., Esposito-Smythers, C., Wolff, J., & Uhl, K. (2011). Cognitive-behavioral therapy for adolescent depression and suicidality. *Child and Adolescent Psychiatric Clinics of North America, 20,* 191–204.

Spivack, G., & Shure, M. B. (1982). The cognition of social adjustment: Interpersonal cognitive problem solving thinking. In B. B. Lahey & A. E. Kadzin (Eds.), *Advances in clinical child psychology* (Vol. 5, pp. 323–372). New York, NY: Plenum Press.

Springer, C., & Misurell, J. (2014). *Game-based cognitive-behavioral therapy for child sexual abuse: An innovative treatment approach.* New York, NY: Springer.

Spritz, B. L., & Sandberg, E. H. (2010). The case for children's cognitive development: A clinical-developmental perspective. In E. H. Sandberg & B. L. Spritz (Eds.), *A clinician's guide to normal cognitive development in childhood* (pp. 3–19). New York, NY: Taylor & Francis.

Sroufe, L. A. (2005). Attachment and development: A prospective, longitudinal study from birth to adulthood. *Attachment and Human Development, 7*, 349–367.

Stadler, C., Kroeger, A., Weyers, P., Grasmann, D., Horschinek, M., Freitag, C., ... Clement, H. W. (2011). Cortisol reactivity in boys with attention-deficit/hyperactivity disorder and disruptive behavior problems: The impact of callous unemotional traits. *Psychiatry Research, 187*, 204–209.

Stallard, P. (2002). Cognitive behaviour therapy with children and young people: A selective review of key issues. *Behavioural and Cognitive Psychotherapy, 30*, 297–309.

Stambaugh, L. F., Mustillo, S. A., Burns, B. J., Stephens, R. L., Baxter, B., Edwards, D., & Dekraai, M. (2007). Outcomes from wraparound and multisystemic therapy in a center for mental health services system-of-care demonstration site. *Journal of Emotional and Behavioral Disorders, 15*, 143–155.

Stark, K. D., Banneyer, K. N., Wang, L. A., & Arora, P. (2012). Child and adolescent depression in the family. *Couple and Family Psychology: Research and Practice, 1*, 161–184.

Stark, K. D., Humphrey, L. L., Crook, K., & Lewis, L. (1990). Perceived family environments of depressed and anxious children: Child's and maternal figure's perspectives. *Journal of Abnormal Child Psychology, 18*, 527–547.

Stark, K. D., Ostrander, R., Kurowski, C. A., Swearer, S., & Bowen, B. (1995). Affective and mood disorders. In M. Hersen & R. T. Ammerman (Eds.), *Advanced abnormal child psychology* (pp. 253–282). Hillsdale, NJ: Erlbaum.

Stark, K. D., Simpson, J., Schnoebelen, S., Hargrave, J., Glenn, R., & Molnar, J. (2006). *Therapist's manual for ACTION.* Broadmore, PA: Workbook.

Stark, K. D., Streusand, W., Arora, P., & Patel, P. (2011). Childhood depression: The ACTION treatment program. In P. C. Kendall (Ed.), *Child and adolescent therapy: Cognitive-behavioral procedures* (4th ed., pp. 190–233). New York, NY: Guilford Press.

Stathakos, P., & Roehrle, B. (2003). The effectiveness of intervention programmes for children of divorce—A meta-analysis. *International Journal of Mental Health Promotion, 5*, 31–37.

Steel, J., Sanna, L., Hammond, B., Whipple, J., & Cross, H. (2004). Psychological sequelae of childhood sexual abuse: Abuse-related characteristics, coping strategies, and attributional style. *Child Abuse and Neglect, 28*, 785–801.

Steinberg, S. J., & Davila, J. (2008). Romantic functioning and depressive symptoms among early adolescent girls: The moderating role of parental emotional availability. *Journal of Clinical Child and Adolescent Psychology, 37*, 350–362.

Stice, E., Ragan, J., & Randall, P. (2004). Prospective relations between social support and depression: Differential direction of effects for parent and peer support? *Journal of Abnormal Psychology, 113*, 155–159.

Stice, E., Rohde, P., Seeley, J. R., & Gau, J. M. (2010). Testing mediators of intervention effects in randomized controlled trials: An evaluation of three depression prevention programs. *Journal of Consulting and Clinical Psychology, 78*, 273–280.

Stifter, C. A., Spinrad, T. L., & Braungart-Rieker, J. M. (1999). Toward a developmental model of child compliance: The role of emotion regulation in infancy. *Child Development, 70*, 21–32.

Stingaris, A., & Goodman, R. (2009). Longitudinal outcome of youth oppositionality: Irritable, headstrong, and hurtful behaviors have distinctive predictions. *Journal of the American Academy of Child and Adolescent Psychiatry, 48*, 404–412.

Stoeber, J., & Childs, J. H. (2010). The assessment of self-oriented and socially pre-scribed perfectionism: Subscales make a difference. *Journal of Personality Assessment*, 92, 577–585.

Stoltz, S., van Londen, M., Dekovic, M., de Castro, B. O., Prinzie, P., & Lochman, J. E. (2013). Effectiveness of an individual school-based intervention for children with aggressive behavior: A randomized controlled trial. *Behavioral and Cognitive Psychotherapy*, 41, 525–548.

Storch, E. A. (2014). Can we improve psychosocial treatments for child anxiety? *Depression and Anxiety*, 31, 539–541.

Strait, G. G., McQuillin, S., Smith, B., & Englund, J. A. (2012). Using motivational interviewing with children and adolescents: A cognitive and neurodevelopmental perspective. *Advances in School Mental Health Promotion*, 5, 290–304.

Strayhorn, J. M. (2002). Self-control: Theory and research. *Journal of the American Academy of Child and Adolescent Psychiatry*, 41, 7–16.

Strong, M. (1999). *A bright red scream: Self-mutilation and the language of pain*. New York, NY: Penguin.

Strosahl, K., Hayes, S. C., & Wilson, K. G. (2004). An Acceptance and Commitment Therapy primer: Core therapy process, intervention strategies, and therapist com-petencies. In S. C. Hayes & K. Strosahl (Eds.), *A practical guide to Acceptance and Commitment Therapy* (pp. 31–58). New York, NY: Springer.

Stroul, E., Blau, G., Broderick, S., & Lourie, I. (2008). *The system of care handbook: Transforming mental health services for children, youth, and families*. Baltimore, MD: Brooks.

Strunk, D. R., DeRubeis, R. J., Chiu, A. W., & Alvarez, J. (2007). Patients' competence in and performance of cognitive therapy skills: Relation to the reduction of relapse risk following treatment for depression. *Journal of Consulting and Clinical Psychology*, 75, 523–530.

Sue, D. W., Bucceri, J., Lin, A. I., Nadal, K. L., & Torino, G. C. (2007). Racial microag-gressions and the Asian American experience. *Cultural Diversity and Ethnic Minority Psychology*, 13, 72–81.

Sue, D. W., & Sue, D. (2013). *Counseling the culturally diverse: Theory and practice* (6th ed.). Hoboken, NJ: Wiley.

Sue, S. (1999). Science, ethnicity, and bias: Where have we gone wrong? *American Psychologist*, 54, 1070–1077.

Sue, S., Zane, N., Nagayama Hall, G. C., & Berger, L. K. (2009). The case for cul-tural competency in psychotherapeutic interventions. *Annual Review of Psychology*, 60, 525–548.

Sugarman, A. (2003). Dimensions of the child analyst's role as a developmental object: Affect regulation and limit setting. *Psychoanalytic Study of the Child*, 58, 189–213.

Sukhodolsky, D. G., Kassinove, H., & Gorman, B. S. (2004). Cognitive-behavioral therapy for anger in children and adolescents: A meta-analysis. *Aggression and Violent Behavior*, 9, 247–269.

Sukhodolsky, D. G., & Scahill, L. (2012). *Cognitive-behavioral therapy for anger and aggression in children*. New York, NY: Guilford Press.

Sullivan, H. S. (1953). *The interpersonal theory of psychiatry*. New York, NY: Norton.

Summers, R. F., & Barber, J. P. (2012). *Psychodynamic therapy: A guide to evidence-based practice*. New York, NY: Guilford Press.

Sundberg, N. D. (1981). Cross-cultural counseling and psychotherapy: A research overview. In A. J. Mansella & P. B. Pedersen (Eds.), *Cross-cultural counseling and psychotherapy* (pp. 29–38). New York, NY: Pergamon Press.

Surrey, J. L., & Kramer, G. (2013). Relational mindfulness. In C. K. Germer, R. D. Siegel, P. R. Fulton, C. K. Germer, R. D. Siegel, P. R. Fulton (Eds.), *Mindfulness and psychotherapy* (2nd ed., pp. 94–111). New York, NY: Guilford Press.

Swanson, J. M., Baler, R. D., & Volkow, N. D. (2011). Understanding the effects of stimulant medications on cognition in individuals with attention-deficit hyperactivity disorder: A decade of progress. *Neuropsychopharmacology, 36,* 207–226.

Sweeney, M., Robins, M., Ruberu, M., & Jones, J. (2005). African-American and Latino families in TADS: Recruitment and treatment considerations. *Cognitive and Behavioral Practice, 12,* 221–229.

Szapocznik, J., Hervis, O. E., & Schwartz, S. (2003). *Brief strategic family therapy for adolescent drug abuse.* Rockville, MD: National Institute on Drug Abuse.

Szapocznik, J., & Kurtines, W. M. (1989). *Breakthroughs in family therapy with drug abusing and problem youth.* New York, NY: Springer.

Szapocznik, J., Rio, A., Murray, E., Cohen, R., Scopetta, M. A., Rivas-Vasquez, A., … Kurtines, W. (1989). Structural family versus psychodynamic child therapy for problematic Hispanic boys. *Journal of Consulting and Clinical Psychology, 57,* 571–579.

Taal, J., & Krop, J. (2002). Imagery in the treatment of trauma. In A. A. Sheikh (Ed.), *Healing images: The role of imagination in health* (pp. 396–407). Amityville, NY: Baywood.

Tabery, J. (2014). *Beyond versus: The struggle to understand the interaction of nature and nurture.* Cambridge, MA: MIT Press.

Taghavi, M. R., Moradi, A. R., Neshat-Doost, H. T., Yule, W., & Dalgleish, T. (2000). Interpretation of ambiguous emotional information in clinically anxious children and adolescents. *Cognition and Emotion, 14,* 809–822.

Tang, T. C., Jou, S. H., Ko, C. H., Huang, S. Y., & Yen, C. F. (2009). Randomized study of school-based intensive interpersonal psychotherapy for depressed adolescents with suicidal risk and parasuicide behaviors. *Psychiatry and Clinical Neurosciences, 63,* 463–470.

Tang, T. Z., & DeRubeis, R. J. (1999). Sudden gains and critical sessions in cognitive-behavioral therapy for depression. *Journal of Consulting and Clinical Psychology, 67,* 894–904.

Tannock, R. (1998). Attention deficit hyperactivity disorder: Advances in cognitive, neurobiological, and genetic research. *Journal of Child Psychology and Psychiatry, 39,* 65–100.

Tarren-Sweeney, T. (2008). Predictors of problematic sexual behavior among children with complex maltreatment histories. *Child Maltreatment, 13,* 182–198.

Taylor, C. A., Manganello, J. A., Lee, S. J., & Rice, J. C. (2010). Mothers' spanking of 3-year-old children and subsequent risk of children's aggressive behavior. *Pediatrics, 125,* 1057–65.

Teasdale, J. D., Moore, R. G., Hayhurst, H., Pope, M., Williams, S., & Segal, Z. V. (2002). Metacognitive awareness and prevention of relapse in depression: Empirical evidence. *Journal of Consulting and Clinical Psychology, 70,* 275–287.

Tedeschi, R. G., & Calhoun, L. G. (2004). *Posttraumatic growth: Conceptual foundation and empirical evidence.* Philadelphia, PA: Erlbaum.

Terry, K. J. (2012). *Sexual offenses and offenders: Theory, practice, and policy.* Stamford, CT: Cengage.

Thomas, R., & Zimmer-Gembeck, M. J. (2007). Behavioral outcomes of parent-child interaction therapy and Triple P-Positive Parenting Program: A review and meta-analysis. *Journal of Abnormal Child Psychology, 35,* 475–495.

Thompson, S. C., Nanni, C., & Levine, A. (1994). Primary versus secondary disease versus consequence-related control in HIV-positive men. *Journal of Personality and Social Psychology, 67,* 540–547.

Thulin, U., Svirsky, L., Serlachius, E., Andersson, G., & Ost, L. (2014). The effect of parent involvement in the treatment of anxiety disorders in children: A meta-analysis. *Cognitive Behaviour Therapy, 43,* 185–200.

Thurston, I. B., & Phares, V. (2008). Mental health utilization among African American and Caucasian mothers and fathers. *Journal of Consulting and Clinical Psychology, 76,* 1058–1067.

Tilghman-Osborne, C., Cole, D. A., & Felton, J. W. (2012). Inappropriate and excessive guilt: Instrument validation and developmental differences in relation to depression. *Journal of Abnormal Child Psychology, 40,* 607–620.

Tilghman-Osborne, C., Cole, D. A., Felton, J. W., & Ciesla, J. A. (2008). Relation of guilt, shame, behavioral and characterological self-blame to depressive symptoms in adolescents over time. *Journal of Social and Clinical Psychology, 27,* 809–842.

Tolle, E. (2004). *The power of now: A guide to spiritual enlightenment.* Novato, CA: New World Library.

Tonge, B. J., Pullen, J. M., Hughes, G. C., & Beaufoy, J. (2009). Effectiveness of psychoanalytic psychotherapy for adolescents with serious mental illness: 12 month naturalistic follow-up study. *Australian and New Zealand Journal of Psychiatry, 43*(5), 467–475

Torneke, N. (2010). *Learning RFT: An introduction to Relational Frame Theory and its clinical applications.* Oakland, CA: Context Press.

Treadwell, K. R. H., Flannery-Schroeder, E. C., & Kendall, P. C. (1995). Ethnicity and gender inrelation to adaptive functioning, diagnostic status, and treatment outcome in children from an anxiety clinic. *Journal of Anxiety Disorders, 9,* 373–384.

Treadwell, K. H., & Kendall, P. C. (1996). Self-talk in youth with anxiety disorders: States of mind, content specificity. *Journal of Consulting and Clinical Psychology, 64,* 941–950.

The Treatment for Adolescents with Depression Study Team. (2004). Fluoxetine, cognitive-behavioral therapy, and their combination for adolescents with depression. *Journal of the American Medical Association, 292,* 807–820.

Tremblay, R. E. (2014). Early development of physical aggression and early risk factors for chronic physical aggression in humans. In K. A. Miczek & A. Meyer-Lindenberg (Eds.), *Neuroscience of aggression* (pp. 315–328). New York, NY: Springer.

Trickett, P. K., Noll, J. G., Reiffman, A., & Putnam, F. W. (2001). Variants of intrafamilial sexual abuse experience: Implications for short- and long-term development. *Development and Psychopathology, 13,* 1001–1019.

Trowell, J., Joffe, I., Campbell, J., Clemente, C., Almqvist, F., Soininen, M.,... Tsiantis, J. (2007). Childhood depression: A place for psychotherapy. An outcome study comparing individual psychodynamic psychotherapy and family therapy. *European Child & Adolescent Psychiatry, 16,* 157–167.

Tsai, M., Kohlenberg, R. J., Kanter, J., Kohlenberg, B., Follette, W., & Callaghan, G. (2009). *A guide to functional analytic psychotherapy: Awareness, courage, love and behaviorism.* New York, NY: Springer.

Tucker, C. M., Daly, K. D., & Herman, K. C. (2010). Customized multicultural health counseling: Bridging the gap between mental and physical health for racial and ethnic minorities. In J. G. Ponterotto, J. M. Casas, L. A. Suzuki, & C. M. Alexander (Eds.), *Handbook of multicultural counseling* (3rd ed., pp. 505–516). Thousand Oaks, CA: SAGE.

Tucker, C. M., & Herman, K. C. (2002). Using racially sensitive theories and research to meet the academic needs of low-income African American children. *American Psychologist, 57,* 762–773.

Tucker, C. M., Nghiem, K. N., Marsiske, M., & Robinson, A. C. (2013). Validation of a patient-centered culturally sensitive health care provider inventory using a national sample of adult patients. *Patient Education and Counseling, 91,* 344–349.

U.S. Census Bureau (2012). *The statistical abstract: Income, expenditures, poverty and wealth.* Retrieved from http://www.census.gov/compendia/statab/cats/income_ expenditures_poverty_wealth.html

Valle, L. A., & Silovsky, J. F. (2002). Attributions and adjustment following child sexual and physical abuse. *Child Maltreatment, 7,* 9–24.

Van der Stouwe, T., Asscher, J. J., Stams, G. J., Deković, M., & van der Laan, P. H. (2014). The effectiveness of multisystemic therapy (MST): A meta-analysis. *Clinical Psychology Review, 34,* 468–481.

Van Eys, P., & Truss, L. (2012). Comprehensive and therapeutic assessment of child sexual abuse: A bridge to treatment. In P. Goodyear-Brown (Ed.), *Handbook of child sexual abuse: Identification, assessment, and treatment* (pp. 143–170). Hoboken, NJ: Wiley.

Van Gastel, W., Legerstee, J. S., & Ferdinand, R. F. (2009). The role of perceived parenting in familial aggregation of anxiety disorders in children. *Journal of Anxiety Disorders, 23,* 46–53.

Van Harreveld, F., van der Pligt, J., & de Liver, Y. (2009). The agony of ambivalence and ways to resolve it: Introducing the MAID model. *Personality and Social Psychology Review, 13,* 45–61.

Vedder, P., & Phinney, J. S. (2014). Identity formation in bicultural youth: A developmental perspective. In V. Benet-Martinez & Y.-Y. Hong (Eds.), *The Oxford handbook of multicultural identity* (pp. 335–354). New York, NY: Oxford University Press.

Velting, O. N., Setzer, N. J., & Albano, A. M. (2004). Update on and advances in assessment and cognitive-behavioral treatment of anxiety disorders in children and adolescents. *Professional Psychology: Research and Practice, 35,* 42–54.

Verduyn, C., & Rogers, J. (2009). *Depression: Cognitive behaviour therapy with children and young people.* New York, NY: Routledge.

Vermote, R., Lowyck, B., Luyten, P., Vertommen, H., Corveleyn, J., Verhaest, Y., & Peuskens, J. (2010). Process and outcome in psychodynamic hospitalization-based treatment for patients with a personality disorder. *Journal of Nervous & Mental Disease, 198,* 110–115.

Vitaro, F., Brendgen, M., & Barker, E. D. (2006). Subtypes of aggressive behaviors: A developmental perspective. *International Journal of Behavioral Development, 30,* 12–19.

Vitaro, F., Brendgen, M., & Tremblay, R. E. (2000). Influence of deviant friends on delinquency: Searching for moderator variables. *Journal of Abnormal Child Psychology, 28*, 313–325.

Volkow, N. D., Wang, G.-J., Kollins, S. H., Wigal, T. L., Newcorn, J. H., Telang, F., ... Swanson, J. M. (2009). Evaluating dopamine reward pathway in ADHD: Clinical implications. *Journal of the American Medical Association, 302*, 1084–1091.

Vromans, L. P., & Schweitzer, R. D. (2011). Narrative therapy for adults with major depressive disorder: Improved symptom and interpersonal outcomes. *Psychotherapy Research, 21*, 4–15.

Vurbic, D., & Bouton, M. E. (2014). A contemporary behavioral perspective on extinction. In F. K. McSweeney & E. S. Murphy (Eds.), *The Wiley Blackwell handbook of operant and classical conditioning* (pp. 53–76). Oxford, UK: Wiley-Blackwell.

Wachtel, E. (1994). *Treating troubled children and their families.* New York, NY: Guilford Press.

Wachtel, P. L. (1977). *Psychoanalysis and behavior therapy: Toward an integration.* New York, NY: Basic Books.

Wade, N. G., Worthington Jr., E. L., & Vogel, D. L. (2007). Effectiveness of religiously tailored interventions in Christian therapy. *Psychotherapy Research, 17*, 91–105.

Wagner, A. W., & Linehan, M. M. (1997). Biosocial perspective on the relationship of childhood sexual abuse, suicidal behavior, and borderline personality disorder. In M. Zanarini (Ed.), *The role of sexual abuse in the etiology of borderline personality disorder* (pp. 203–223). Washington, DC: American Psychiatric Association.

Wagner, A. W., & Linehan, M. M. (2006). Applications of Dialectical Behavior Therapy to PTSD and related problems. In V. Follette & J. Ruzek (Eds.), *Cognitive-behavioral therapies for trauma* (2nd ed., pp. 117–145). New York, NY: Guilford Press.

Waldhauser, G. T., Johansson, M., & Hanslmayr, S. (2012). Alpha/Beta oscillations indicate inhibition of interfering visual memories. *Journal of Neuroscience. 32*, 1953–1961.

Walker, D. F., Reese, J. B., Hughes, J. P., & Troskie, M. J. (2010). Addressing religious and spiritual issues in trauma-focused cognitive behavior therapy for children and adolescents. *Professional Psychology, Research and Practice, 41*, 174–180.

Walkup, J. T., Albano, A. M., Piacentini, J., Birmaher, B., Compton, S. N., Sherrill, J. T., ... Kendall, P. C. (2008). Cognitive behavioral therapy, sertraline, or a combination in childhood anxiety. *New England Journal of Medicine, 359*, 2753–2766.

Wallerstein, J., Lewis, J. and Blakeslee, S. (2000). *The unexpected legacy of divorce: A 25 year landmark study.* New York: Hyperion.

Wampold, B. E. (2010). The research evidence for common factors models: A historically situated perspective. In B. L. Dunca, S. D. Miller, B. E. Wampold, & M. A. Hubble (Eds.), *The heart and soul of change: Delivering what works* (2nd ed., pp. 49–82). Washington, DC: American Psychological Association.

Wampold, B. E., & Imel, Z. E. (2015). *The great psychotherapy debate: The evidence for what makes psychotherapy work* (2nd ed.). New York, NY: Routledge.

Watson, J. B. (1924). *Behaviorism.* Chicago, IL: University of Chicago Press.

Watzlawick, P. (1978). *The language of change.* New York, NY: Basic Books.

Watzlawick, P., Weakland, J., & Fisch, R. (1974). *Change: Principles of problem formation and problem resolution.* New York, NY: Norton.

Weakland, J., & Fisch, R. (1992). Brief therapy—MRI style. In S. H. Budman, N. F. Hoyt, & S. Friedman (Eds.), *The first session in brief therapy* (pp. 306–323). New York, NY: Guilford Press.

Webb, C., Hayes, A. M., Grasso, D., Laurenceau, J.-P., & Deblinger, E. (2014). Trauma-focused cognitive behavioral therapy for youth: Effectiveness in a community setting. *Psychological Trauma: Theory, Research, Practice, and Policy, 6*, 555–562.

Webster-Stratton, C., & Reid, M. J. (2003). The Incredible Years parents, teachers, and children's training: A multifaceted treatment approach for young children with conduct problems. In A. E. Kazdin & J. R. Weisz (Eds.), *Evidence-based psychotherapies for children and adolescents* (pp. 224–241). New York, NY: Guilford Press.

Weems, C. F., Hammond-Laurence, K., Silverman, W. K., & Ginsburg, G. S. (1998). Testing the utility of the anxiety sensitivity construct in children and adolescents referred for anxiety disorders. *Journal of Clinical Child Psychology, 27*, 69–77.

Wegner, D. M., Schneider, D. J., Carter, S., & White, T. (1987). Paradoxical effects of thought suppression. *Journal of Personality and Social Psychology, 53*, 5–13.

Wegner, D. M., & Zanakos, S. (1994). Chronic thought suppression. *Journal of Personality, 62*, 615–640.

Weinberg, R. S. (2014). Goal setting in sport and exercise: Research to practice. In J. L. Van Raalte & B. W. Brewer (Eds.), *Exploring sport and exercise psychology* (3rd ed., pp. 33–54). Washington, DC: American Psychological Association.

Weinberger, D. R., Elvevåg, B., & Giedd, J. N. (2005). *The adolescent brain: A work in progress*. Washington, DC: The National Campaign to Prevent Teen Pregnancy.

Weinberger, J. (1995). Common factors aren't so common: The common factors dilemma. *Clinical Psychology: Science and Practice, 2*, 45–69.

Weiner, I. B., & Bornstein, R. F. (2009). *Principles of psychotherapy: Promoting evidence-based psychodynamic practice* (3rd ed.). Hoboken, NJ: Wiley.

Weiss, B., Han, S., Harris, V., Catron, T., Ngo, V. K., Caron, A., … Guth, C. (2013). An independent randomized clinical trial of multisystemic therapy with non-court-referred adolescents with serious conduct problems. *Journal of Consulting and Clinical Psychology, 81*, 1027–1039.

Weisz, J. R. (2004). *Psychotherapy for children and adolescents: Evidence-based treatments and case examples*. New York, NY: Cambridge University Press.

Weisz, J. R., & Jensen, P. S. (1999). Efficacy and effectiveness of child and adolescent psychotherapy and pharmacotherapy. *Mental Health Services Research, 1*, 125–157.

Weisz, J. R., McCarty, C. A., & Valeri, S. M. (2006). Effects of psychotherapy for depression in children and adolescents: A meta-analysis. *Psychological Bulletin, 132*, 132–149.

Weisz, J. R., Ng, M. Y., Rutt, C., Lau, N., & Masland, N. (2013). Psychotherapy for children and adolescents. In M. J. Lambert (Ed.), *Bergin and Garfield's handbook of psychotherapy and behavior change* (6th ed., pp. 541–586). Hoboken, NJ: Wiley.

Weisz, J. R., Southam-Gerow, M. A., Gordis, E. B., Connor-Smith, J. K., Chu, B. C., Langer, D. A., … Weiss, B. (2009). Cognitive-behavioral therapy versus usual clinical care for youth depression: An initial test of transportability to community clinics and clinicians. *Journal of Consulting and Clinical Psychology, 77*, 383–396.

Weisz, J. R., Thurber, C. A., Sweeney, L., Proffitt, V. D., & LeGagnoux, G. L. (1997). Brief treatment of mild-to-moderate child depression using primary and secondary control enhancement training. *Journal of Consulting and Clinical Psychology, 65*, 703–707.

Wells, K. C. (2004). Treatment of ADHD in children and adolescents. In P. M. Barrett & T. H. Ollendick (Eds.), *Handbook of interventions that work with children and adolescents: Prevention and treatment* (pp. 343–368). Chichester, UK: Wiley.

Wenzel, A., & Beck, A. T. (2008). A cognitive model of suicidal behavior: Theory and treatment. *Applied and Preventive Psychology, 12,* 189–201.

West-Olatunji, C. A., & Conwill, W. (2011). *Counseling African Americans.* Belmont, CA: Cengage.

Westen, D. (1988). Transference and information processing. *Clinical Psychology Review, 8,* 161–179.

Westen, D. (1991). Social cognition and object relations. *Psychological Bulletin, 109,* 429–455.

Westen, D. (2005). Implications of research in cognitive neuroscience for psychodynamic psychotherapy. In G. O. Gabbard, J. S. Beck, & J. Holmes (Eds.), *The Oxford textbook of psychotherapy* (pp. 443–448). Oxford, UK: Oxford University Press.

Westen, D., & Gabbard, G. (2002). Developments in cognitive neuroscience, 1: Conflict, compromise, and connectionism. *Journal of the American Psychoanalytic Association, 50,* 54–98.

White, M. (1989). *Selected papers.* Adelaide, Australia: Dulwich Centre.

White, M. (1995). *Re-authoring lives: Interviews and essays.* Adelaide, Australia: Dulwich Centre.

White, M. (2005). Children, trauma and subordinate storyline development. *International Journal of Narrative Therapy and Community Work, 3&4,* 10–23.

White, M. (2006). Narrative practice with families with children: Externalising conversations revisited. In M. White (Ed.), *Narrative therapy with children and their families* (pp. 1–56). Adelaide, Australia: Dulwich Centre.

White, M. (2007). *Maps of narrative practice.* New York, NY: Norton.

White, M. (2011). *Narrative practice: Continuing the conversations.* New York, NY: Norton.

White, M., & Epston, D. (1990). *Narrative means to therapeutic ends.* New York, NY: Norton.

White, M., & Morgan, A. (2006). *Narrative therapy with children and their families.* Adelaide, Australia: Dulwich Centre.

Wicksell, R. K., Melin, L., Lekander, M., & Olsson, G. L. (2009). Evaluating the effectiveness of exposure and acceptance strategies to improve functioning and quality of life in longstanding pediatric pain—A randomized controlled trial. *Pain, 141,* 248–257.

Williams, S. C., Lochman, J. E., Phillips, N. C., & Barry, T. D. (2003). Aggressive and non-aggressive boys' physiological and cognitive processes in response to peer provocations. *Journal of Clinical Child and Adolescent Psychology, 32,* 568–576.

Wilson, K. G., & DuFrene, R. (2009). *Mindfulness for two: An Acceptance and Commitment Therapy Approach to mindfulness in psychotherapy.* Oakland, CA: New Harbinger.

Wilson, K. G., & Murrell, A. R. (2004). Values work in Acceptance and Commitment Therapy: Setting a course for behavioral treatment. In S. C. Hayes, V. M. Follette, & M. Linehan (Eds.), *Mindfulness and acceptance: Expanding the cognitive-behavioral tradition* (pp. 120–151). New York, NY: Guilford Press.

Wilson, P. (1999). Delinquency. In M. Lanyado & A. Horne (Eds.), *The handbook of child and adolescent psychotherapy: Psychoanalytic approaches* (pp. 311–327). Florence, KY, US: Taylor & Frances/Routledge.

Wilson, S. J., & Lipsey, M. W. (2006). *The effects of school-based social information process-ing interventions on aggressive behavior. Part II: Selected or indicated pull-out programs.* Retrieved from CampbellCollaboration.org

Wilson, S. J., Lipsey, M. W., & Derzon, J. H. (2003). The effects of school-based interven-tion programs on aggressive behavior. *Journal of Consulting and Clinical Psychology, 71,* 136–149.

Wilson, T. D., & Gilbert, D. T. (2003). Affective forecasting. *Advances in Experimental Social Psychology, 35,* 345–411.

Wilton, L. (2009). Where do we go from here? Raising the bar of what constitutes multicul-tural competence in working with lesbian, gay, bisexual, and transgender communities. In J. G. Ponterotto, J. M. Casas, L. A. Suzuki, & C. M. Alexander (Eds.), *Handbook of multicultural counseling* (3rd ed., pp. 313–328). Thousand Oaks, CA: SAGE.

Winnicott, D. W. (1971). *Playing and reality.* Oxford, UK: Penguin.

Winokur-Early, K., Chapman, S., & Hand, G. (2013). Family-focused juvenile reentry services: A quasi-experimental design evaluation of recidivism outcomes. *Journal of Juvenile Justice, 2,* 1–22.

Winslade, J. M., & Monk, G. D. (2006). *Narrative counseling in schools: Powerful and brief* (2nd ed.). Thousand Oaks, CA: Corwin Press.

Wittouck, C., Van Autreve, S., Da Jaegere, E., Portzky, G., & van Heeringen, K. (2011). The prevention and treatment of complicated grief: A meta-analysis. *Clinical Psychology Review, 31,* 69–78.

Wood, J. J., Piacentini, J. C., Southam-Gerow, M., Chu, B. C., & Sigman M. (2006). Family cognitive behavioral therapy for child anxiety disorders. *Journal of the American Academy of Child and Adolescent Psychiatry, 45,* 314–321.

Wood, J. V., Perunovic, W. Q. E., & Lee, J. W. (2009). Positive self-statements: Power for some, peril for others. *Psychological Science, 20,* 860–866.

Worden, J. W. (2008). *Grief counseling and grief therapy: A handbook for the mental health practitioner* (4th ed.). New York, NY: Springer.

Wurtele, S. K. (2009). Preventing sexual abuse of children in the twenty-first century: Preparing for challenges and opportunities. *Journal of Child Sexual Abuse, 18,* 1–18.

Yang, Y. L., & Raine, A. (2009). Prefrontal structural and functional brain imaging find-ings in antisocial, violent, and psychopathic individuals: A meta-analysis. *Psychiatric Research: Neuroimaging, 174,* 81–88.

Yeager, D. S., Miu, A. S., Powers, J., & Dweck, C. S. (2013). Implicit theories of personality and attributions of hostile intent: A meta-analysis, an experiment, and a longitudinal intervention. *Child Development, 84,* 1651–1667.

Yeager, D. S., Trzesniewski, K. H., Tirri, K., Nokelainen, P., & Dweck, C. S. (2011). Adolescents' implicit theories predict desire for vengeance after peer conflicts: Correlational and experimental evidence. *Developmental Psychology, 47,* 1090–1107.

Yeh, C. B., Huang, W. S., Lo, M. C., Chang, C. J., Ma, K. H., & Shyu, J. F. (2012). The rCBF brain mapping in adolescent ADHD comorbid with developmental coordi-nation disorder and its changes after MPH challenging. *European Journal of Paediatric Neurology, 16,* 613–618.

Yeh, C. J., & Kwong-Liem, K. K. (2009). Advances in multicultural assessment and coun-seling with adolescents: An ecological perspective. In J. G. Ponterotto, J. M. Casas, L. A. Suzuki, & C. M. Alexander (Eds.), *Handbook of multicultural counseling* (3rd ed., pp. 637–648). Thousand Oaks, CA: SAGE.

Yen, C., Chen, Y., Cheng, J., Liu, T., Huang, T., Wang, P., ... Chou, W. (2014). Effects of cognitive-behavioral therapy on improving anxiety symptoms, behavioral problems and parenting stress in Taiwanese children with anxiety disorders and their mothers. *Child Psychiatry and Human Development*, 45, 338–347.

Young, J. E., Klosko, J. S., & Weishaar, M. E. (2003). *Schema therapy: A practitioner's guide*. New York, NY: Guilford Press.

Yu, D. L., & Seligman, M. E. P. (2002, May 8). Preventing depressive symptoms in Chinese children. *Prevention and Treatment*, 5(1). Article 9.

Zafar, N. (2011, August 4). The five secrets of Silicon Valley. *Atlantic*. Retrieved from http://www.theatlantic.com/business/archive/2011/08/the-5-secrets-of-silicon-valley/242958/

Zalta, A. K., & Foa, E. B. (2012). Exposure therapy: Promoting emotional processing of pathological anxiety. In W. T. O'Donohue & J. E. Fisher (Eds.), *Cognitive behavior therapy: Core principles for practice* (pp. 75–104). Hoboken, NJ: Wiley.

Zillmann, D. (1993). Mental control of angry aggression. In D. M. Wegner, J. W. Pennebaker, D. M. Wegner, J. W. Pennebaker (Eds.), *Handbook of mental control* (pp. 370–392). Englewood Cliffs, NJ: Prentice-Hall.

Zurbriggen, E., Gobin, R., & Freyd, J. (2010). Childhood emotional abuse predicts late adolescent sexual aggression perpetration and victimization. *Journal of Aggression, Maltreatment and Trauma*, 19, 204–223.

Author Index

Subject Index